Also by Arthur Rubinstein

MY YOUNG YEARS

This is a Borzoi Book, published in New York by Alfred A. Knopf.

MY MANY YEARS

ARTHUR RUBINSTEIN

MY MANY YEARS

Alfred A. Knopf, New York, 1980

THIS IS A BORZOI BOOK
PUBLISHED BY ALFRED A. KNOPF, INC.

LIBRARY OF CONGRESS CATALOGING IN PUBLICATION DATA
Rubinstein, Arthur, 1886-   My many years.
Includes index.
1. Rubinstein, Arthur, 1886-   2. Pianists—
Biography. I. Title.
ML417.R79A28   786.1'092'4 [B]   79-2231
ISBN 0-394-42253-8

Manufactured in the United States of America

Published January 31, 1980
Second Printing, March 1980

*To Annabelle, my devoted
friend and companion, with
my love and gratitude.*

Contents

	Preface	ix
One	THE PROMISED LAND—LATIN AMERICA AND THE END OF WORLD WAR I	1
Two	A SECOND ATTEMPT IN THE UNITED STATES AND MEXICAN ADVENTURES	43
Three	EUROPE AFTER THE WAR AND THE GAY TWENTIES	71
Four	MARRIAGE AND FAMILY	301
Five	A GREAT ORIENTAL TOUR	361
Six	1937: MY LONGEST TOUR AND A TRIUMPHANT RETURN TO THE USA	401
Seven	WORLD WAR II, ESCAPE TO HOLLYWOOD AND MY AMERICAN CITIZENSHIP	461
Eight	HOME AGAIN IN PARIS, MORE CONCERT TOURS AND RECORDINGS	549
	Epilogue	605
	Index	607
	Photograph Credits	627

Photographs will be found following pages *212* and *436*

Preface

This second book about my life has been a strange adventure. I have not written it by my own hand but was forced to dictate it. It would have been impossible to accomplish it without the invaluable help of Tony Madigan, who took down patiently my dictation for a large part of the beginning, and later on until the bitter end, of Annabelle Whitestone, who not only wrote down but helped me considerably with her fluent English style which encouraged me for two long years to continue this difficult task which tested my memory to the extreme. This work was done out of sheer memory without the help of documentation or exterior help. I would like to express here my deep gratitude to my two co-creators of this voluminous autobiography. Whatever the literary value of it is, the accomplishment of this book gave me a new lease of life and made me love life more than ever at the ripe age of ninety-two.

One

The Promised Land—
Latin America and the
End of World War I

1

The First World War changed everything in my life. Born in Poland, still under the Tsarist rule, I was forced to become an expatriate when Russia became Communist.

I happened to be in London when the war broke out, and I went immediately to Paris to join a Polish Legion there, but after the Tsar withdrew his permission for the Legion I had to return to London. There, thanks to a series of lucky circumstances, I was asked to play in San Sebastián instead of a French pianist who had enlisted in the war. It was this summer concert in the Spanish sea resort that opened up my whole career. The Spanish audiences, the press, and indeed the royal family took me to their hearts and even considered me the only authentic performer of Spanish music. I spent the first two years of the war in Spain playing to full houses in most of the cities there, yet feeling a deep pang of guilt that I owed the success in part to a war that prohibited other pianists from appearing in this country.

In 1917, at the age of thirty, the good name I had earned in Spain reached the Latin Americas. I was offered a contract for a substantial sum—and thus began a career of really making money. I crossed on the Spanish steamer *Infanta Isabel* in the company of my concert agent, Ernesto de Quesada, who had agreed to be my secretary for the duration of these engagements.

My first contact with what was to be for me the promised land was hardly promising. We docked in Buenos Aires late in the evening. Faustino da Rosa, the great impresario of the Teatro Colón and the Odeon, sent his secretary to meet us and take us to the best hotel in town, the Plaza.

Regina Badet, who had been my charming and hospitable neighbor on the boat, where I had succeeded in persuading our steward—with the help of a good tip—to open the connecting doors of our cabins, insisted on spending her last night with me; she had to leave the next day with her company for Chile. So that night this lovely French actress played a real-life farce with me as partner. The Plaza management had provided a comfortable room for me with a couch beside the bed. Regina came to my room and we prepared to spend our last night. At one point, the telephone unexpectedly rang. "The lady must leave your room right away." It was the manager. "The hotel does not allow unmarried couples to stay in the same room."

I dressed in a hurry and rushed down to explain that my friend would be leaving in the morning. That did not convince the stubborn manager. After a fruitless discussion we left Regina in my room and he escorted me to one of the rooms provided by the hotel for private valets of guests. After a tearful good-night I spent a sleepless and thoroughly uncomfortable night in the tiny room which had neither air nor running water. Fortunately the ordeal did not last too long—I had to get up early to take Regina to the railway station and see her off for Chile.

Once settled in my own room again, I tried to go to sleep when a sharp telephone ring woke me—it was Quesada, who was staying at another hotel. "You have to get ready," he said. "Two gentlemen from the da Rosa office are on their way to make plans for the concerts." In less than an hour, two young men accompanied by Ernesto de Quesada entered the room. "Are your programs ready?" they asked. "We need three of them right away for a subscription series of six concerts." I promised to have them ready by that afternoon. "No," said one of them, "this afternoon must be devoted to visiting the Buenos Aires newspapers." Noticing my astonishment, he added, "There are only five of them." I retorted incredulously, "What for? You can deliver the programs by yourselves!"

"Oh no, this is a highly important matter. The editors always expect a visit from performers when they arrive in this country."

"You mean I have to beg them to be kind to me?" I asked impatiently. "I have never done that before and do not intend to do so now."

"Even Caruso had to pay a visit to our newspapers!" they shouted.

"I am a modest pianist but I still have some pride left and I refuse to genuflect before the potentates of the press!"

The scene turned into a row; the four of us screamed and Ernesto, to my dismay, took their side. But when they saw me getting into a real rage they lowered their tone and asked, "Don Arturo, if you would agree to but one single visit to *La Nación*, our most important morning paper, its owner, Don Luis Mitre, a real music lover, will certainly be glad to meet you."

The name Mitre startled me. "Mitre, Mitre," I said. "This name seems somehow familiar to me." I suddenly remembered. During the last days in Madrid I had seen Manuel de Falla and the famous gypsy dancer and singer Pastora Imperio almost every day. She was then dancing *El Amor brujo* by de Falla and after her midnight performance the composer and I used to take her to the Mallorquina, a famous place for hot chocolate. She usually arrived accompanied by hungry relations of hers, cousins, nieces, nephews, and the like, and I was host.

Pastora was always convinced that no man in her immediate presence could fail to fall violently in love with her, and so she would look at me, her eyes filled with pity, and say, "Tsk, tsk, pobrecito de mi alma."* At our farewell party she had made me accept a tiny chain with a medal of St. Christopher and handed me a letter, saying, "Deliver this to a great friend of mine. It can help you very much in your career." I refused at first, being stubbornly opposed to this kind of letter, but she forced it on me, so I took it with no intention of delivering it. It was addressed to a Don Luis Mitre and its phonetic spelling made me blush at the thought of somebody reading it.

So, at the mention of the name Don Luis Mitre, I stammered, "Gentlemen, you will laugh but I have a letter in my suitcase addressed to a man of the same name."

They smiled and asked, "From whom?"

"Oh," I laughed, "a Spanish flamenco dancer assured me that it would help me in my career."

The two men did not laugh. "What is her name?"

"Um, Pastora Imperio," I said. They were thunderstruck.

"What!" they all cried together. "What a miracle. This is the very Luis Mitre we've been talking about. He is crazy about Pastora Imperio and there is not a thing he wouldn't do to please her. Give us the letter immediately and we will take it to him!" I was flabbergasted; the same deus ex machina at work which had so shaped my young years.

Pastora's childlike missive, introducing her *pobrecito* in glowing terms, produced immediate dynamic results. Mitre called the principal music critic of *La Nación* and ordered him to write a magnificent story for the front page about Rubinstein, about his success in Spain, and how eagerly his arrival was anticipated. Mr. José Ojeda, the music critic, obeyed without batting an eye and I may confess meekly that without this marvelous introduction I would have had a much harder time with the critics.

My first concert was on the second of July, 1917, in the Teatro Odeon. As the sales of my subscriptions for the six announced concerts had been rather poor, I was astonished to see the elegant theater well filled. Most surprising of all, the boxes, usually hard to sell according to the da Rosa office, were filled with the best families of Buenos Aires. For my debut I chose an eclectic program; there was a Bach toccata, a Beethoven sonata,

---

* My poor little darling.

Chopin of course, and some of my most successful Spanish pieces, such as the *Navarra* of Albéniz. One was a first performance in Buenos Aires of "Ondine" from *Gaspard de la nuit* by Ravel, and I finished with the surefire Twelfth Rhapsody of Liszt.

The classical numbers were received with reserve, either because the audience was not sure that my approach to these works was the right one or because they were unfamiliar with them. "Ondine" was greeted with silence, as no one was quite sure when it was over. However, *Navarra* did its duty and there was such applause after the Rhapsody that I was obliged to give four encores. The loudest and heartiest ovation came from the members of the Madrid company of the Teatro Lara who were in the wings; they considered themselves my faithful supporters and defenders, as it was in Spain that I had my first real success. Both Faustino da Rosa and the box office were well satisfied with my debut although we were apprehensive about the press notices. The next morning at breakfast I received the four morning papers, which I started to read with a beating heart.

"Long live Pastora Imperio!" I cried when I read Ojeda's ecstatic account in *La Nación*. But my face fell when I read the other papers. Mr. Laguardia of *La Prensa*, the rival of *La Nación*, was noted for his intransigence toward foreign artists. He was the one who made Paderewski leave the country before he had completed his tour. My Bach and Beethoven struck him as being immature, my Chopin put him in a better mood, but he found the end of my program to be nothing but showpieces for the gallery. The rest of the press was less aggressive but far from enthusiastic. Accustomed as I was to facing hostile criticism, as usual I was not particularly affected. *La Razón*, an afternoon paper, carried a review by a Mr. Miguel Mastrogianni, who bluntly attacked the management of my concerts for charging so much to hear such a young and immature pianist. My managers gathered for a consultation and tried to reassure me with *La Nación*. "We told you it was necessary to visit the press."

I smiled proudly. "I'm still glad I didn't do it." We feared, of course, that attendance would drop for my next concert, which was five days later.

But just before, to my surprise, I received a warmly worded invitation from the widow of a well-loved president of Argentina, Manuel Quintana, as well as one from the composer Maestro Alberto Williams for a dinner at his house, where, he wrote, I would meet most of the important musicians of Buenos Aires. Both invitations impressed my manager. I assumed that they had come thanks to Luis Mitre, but this was not the case.

Señora Quintana lived in a vast house with two married daughters and four grownup grandchildren. Her guests were the cream of a society which was even more exclusive than the Faubourg St. Germain in Paris. The houses of Alvear, Unzue, Gainza-Paz, Miguel Martínez de Hoz, Anchorena Sánchez-Elia were impenetrable to anybody who did not "belong." A few moments after I arrived at her tea party, it became clear why I had been asked. The husband of Señora Quintana's youngest daughter, Mr. Moreno, was at that time the minister of Argentina in Madrid (there being no ambassadors then) and had been one of my most enthusiastic listeners, never missing a concert. So he couldn't resist the temptation to write to his somewhat estranged wife about his enthusiasm for me, telling her to do everything in her power to hear me and meet me. At the same party I was introduced to the Marquesa Salamanca, the daughter of the president of the Jockey Club, Miguel Martínez de Hoz. The readers of my first book will readily understand what the name Salamanca meant to me. I could call them quite frankly my best friends in Spain and they remain so at this moment as I write. The Marques Luís Salamanca had written a long letter to his wife asking her to have the door of her parents' house wide open for me. Again the old miracle happened: The stiff Buenos Aires society, rather well known for its absence at other concerts, had filled the boxes at my first concert and continued to monopolize my appearances at the Odeon. It was a sacred duty to have a subscription for the opera season, which more often than not ruined their finances for the rest of the year. Nonetheless, they never failed me at the Odeon.

At the Quintana reception I offered to play for the guests, something I have rarely done in my whole life. When I took my leave, my hostess said to me, "Venez diner ou déjeuner quand vous voulez, votre couvert est toujours mis."* In this old lady of nearly eighty, I found a most devoted, motherly friend whose memory fills my heart.

The composer Alberto Williams was a pupil of César Franck. He started what became a strange phenomenon in Argentina when he founded the first conservatory in Buenos Aires, which he named after himself. It had an extraordinary success, with hundreds of young music students flocking there. As well, it developed that he was a commercial genius not unlike the great North American moneymakers. Selecting the best of his pupils, he would send them out to the larger provincial towns such as Rosario, Córdoba, Mendoza, and others to open "Alberto Williams Conservatories" and, once established, they would provide him with a good percentage of the receipts. I found, on my arrival, a veritable conservatory empire. Pianists, violinists, and other instrumentalists, as well as singers, attracted by the fortune of the Alberto Williams institutions, soon followed suit and opened conservatories on just about every street corner, called Conserva-

* Come to lunch or dinner whenever you like; your place is always set.

torio Verdi, Mozart, Bach, and even Caruso. Pablo Casals and Harold Bauer, who visited Buenos Aires a few years before me, called it a "conservatropolis." A few years later, I even had the supreme honor of having a conservatory named Arturo Rubinstein in Belgrano, a suburb of Buenos Aires.

When I was entertained by Williams in his sumptuous house in the midst of a vast beautiful garden, I was immediately warmly received by the elderly gray-haired gentleman himself. His face had good features and he spoke in a gentle way about my concert. He introduced me to his guests, among whom I found Mr. Mastrogianni of *La Razón* and another critic, Mr. José Frías, who had not written favorably about me either. The rest of the company consisted of the professors of his conservatory, teachers, performers, mostly musicians, and some well-known amateurs. At one point, an ugly man of about forty-five rushed up to me and shouted with an ugly German accent, "Welcome, my dear colleague. I too was a pupil of Barth." His name was Ernesto Drangosh. "I have my own conservatory" (of course) "and you must come and visit us."

I was not particularly gratified by this invitation, but I soon fell into the clutches of this importunate musical comrade. The rest of the people were nice and surrounded me with evident goodwill. A fine dinner was served at several tables and I was toasted by the host. While we were having coffee, the violin professor of the Williams Conservatory asked me if I would care to play something. I suggested, "Why don't we play a violin and piano sonata?" He accepted my offer enthusiastically.

"Which sonata shall we play?"

"What about the *Kreutzer?*" I asked. At that, Don Alberto said regretfully, "I have no music for violin and piano in my house. I keep everything at the Conservatory."

"Could you play it by heart?" I asked the violinist. At this he was a bit taken aback.

"Well, I can try . . ." He fetched his instrument, having evidently planned on playing that evening. The guests, including the two critics, gathered around expectantly and a little skeptically. My vast and long experience of playing violin sonatas with my dear friend Paul Kochanski served me well. Also I was lucky; the violinist was good and we played the whole *Kreutzer* with care and mutual understanding. Our unusual feat drew thunderous applause from our audience, which emboldened me to ask my partner if he would risk playing the Brahms D minor, my favorite sonata. Yes, he knew and loved it too. And so we played it with great élan as if it were a real concert. This time I won a smashing victory over my two antagonistic critics, Mastrogianni and Frías. They limply apologized for taking me for a shallow virtuoso and henceforth became my warmest supporters. My dear colleague Mr. Drangosh approached me with a greenish look of envy. "I'm sure you must play . . ." he said, mentioning a sonata of Schubert. My negative answer restored his normal color.

This evening was of great importance to me because from then on I had the critics and the "connoisseurs" on my side. However, a young man who worked for an unimportant weekly published a venomous attack accusing the management of charging an outrageous price to listen to a talentless pianist who dared to play after the divine Paderewski. Nobody paid much attention to this silly outburst except my dear Spanish companions from the Teatro Lara, who went into a frenzy of rage and swore they would kill the poor fellow. At the next concert he realized his mistake and came to my dressing room during an intermission. Smiling broadly, he shouted from the door, "Hoy sí!" (Today yes!), upon which three or four strong members of the Lara company beat him up with proverbial Spanish vehemence and threw him out into the gutter screaming, "Hoy sí for you, you rascal!" among other insults, some of them unprintable.

2

Ernesto de Quesada assured me happily that the battle of Buenos Aires had been won. The next concerts were well filled and one of them was sold out. I played rather daring programs for that time consisting of works by Karol Szymanowski, Prokofiev, Scriabin, Medtner, Ravel, and last but not least, the *Iberia* of Albéniz. All these pieces were unfamiliar to this extremely piano-minded city.

The house of the Quintanas became like a home for me. I had lunch there almost every day and the Marquesa Nena Salamanca had me often for dinner.

After the sixth recital my original contract with the chocolate manufacturer was completed. I still owed him four recitals in Montevideo at the Teatro Solis. There was only one way to reach the Uruguayan capital from Buenos Aires. Every day a large steamer with narrow one-person cabins left at 10 p.m. from Buenos Aires while another left from Montevideo, each arriving the following morning at seven. Quesada and I were seasick on my first trip across the wide Río de la Plata, which reminded me of the famous Dover–Calais ordeals, only worse. When we arrived at that early hour, I spotted at the dock the familiar face of Wilhelm Kolischer, a Polish pianist who had studied with my Professor Heinrich Barth and with whom I used to spend whole days in Cracow or Berlin or wherever we met. Now he was accompanied by some friends of his, all young musicians, among them Eduardo Fabini, a composer, and Joaquín Mora, a violinist, who turned out to have been Paul Kochanski's roommate in Brussels, where they both had studied. Kolischer and his friends became my constant companions and remained so whenever I returned to Montevideo.

The atmosphere of Montevideo was quite different from that of Buenos Aires. In those days Uruguay boasted of being the most democratic and free country in the world. There were no class distinctions and the peso had doubled its value during the war. Montevideo had few conservatories but the people there were more devoted to good music than those in Buenos Aires. The manager of the Teatro Solis made the most of the publicity from Spain provided by Quesada and, thanks to my new friends who were the city's most important musicians, my first concert was completely sold out. The program was the same as my first concert at the Odeon but this time the thunderous applause, the shouting for more, and other demonstrations of enthusiasm were so wild that I became suspicious that my new friends had prepared it all. After an unusual number of encores I was allowed to leave the theater. But in the square outside, something unexpected and rather frightening happened; my friends and several young music students hoisted me up into the air as if I were a stuffed puppet and raced me across the square—and not until we reached my hotel was I allowed to get on my own feet again. Later at dinner, my suspicious nature led me to ask Kolischer if the whole thing had been a show prepared by my manager or by some very efficient publicity man. He laughed. "My dear, a Uruguayan would rather go to jail than agree to do something of that kind." Only then did I begin to enjoy this extraordinary success. I gave many concerts in Montevideo in the years to come and always found the same enthusiasm— except that as I became heavier and the young men grew older I began having to walk back to my hotel.

I finished my four concerts in less than two weeks and went back to Buenos Aires. "From now on you are a free lance," said Ernesto de Quesada one morning. "What shall we do? Do you intend to go back to Spain? If not, I believe there is much more money to be made if you continue to play here. Renato Salvati, the director of the opera in Santiago de Chile, wrote me that he hoped you might play there." Before I made a decision I consulted Don Luis Mitre and Señora Susana Quintana as well as my friends the Martínez de Hozes, who all assured me that my real success had only just begun. "You can make much more money, my dear," said Señor Martínez de Hoz. "I myself propose a concert at the Jockey Club for the sum of twenty thousand pesos" (then equal to $10,000). As Quesada and I began to make plans, the managerial talent of Ernesto came to life. While before he had seemed rather indifferent, he now became overnight a feverish impresario. He signed up for three concerts in Santiago and two in Valparaiso, Chile, and made arrangements with the owners of the Teatro Odeon for another four concerts, this time with a percentage of the receipts, which was of course much more to my advantage. As to Montevideo, he baldly announced three more concerts. After the first of these in this city I had a lovely surprise. I was still in bed when someone knocked on the door. "Adelante!" I shouted, thinking it was breakfast. When the door opened the whole Diaghilev ballet burst into the room; I love to exaggerate; not all of it, only the best of it. My dearest friends and companions from the unforgettable San Sebastián season had landed that morning. It was a joyous reunion. Lydia Lopoukhova, my old pal from San Sebastián, who later became the wife of the economist Maynard Keynes, told me all the gossip of the troupe and about the curious contract which brought them to South America. The Colón Opera House had wanted the Diaghilev ballet; they desperately needed great attractions as the war made many famous singers and conductors wary of risking the voyage. Diaghilev, on the other hand, desperately needed the money to hold his company together. But there was a hitch: The Colón would not hear of any leading dancer other than Nijinsky, and after Diaghilev's complete break with his former star it was a terribly difficult matter. It meant not only getting Nijinsky to agree but finding a way to get him out of enemy territory—that is, Hungary, his wife's homeland. But the way was found. The intricate diplomatic maneuvers of Diaghilev's friends were successful and the very willing Nijinsky was brought, by some obscure means, to Argentina. Diaghilev and Massine, his new star, decided to remain in Europe, but my old friend Ernest Ansermet was again the conductor. I was thrilled to hear all this exciting news. I had known Nijinsky well in London and had seen him again in Madrid quite often before I sailed for Buenos Aires. It had been my pleasure to take him to the famous Basque jai alai games, where the violent leaping and running of the players excited him so much that once he actually fell off his chair. "They are the most perfect dancers," he screamed. "I would like to jump down there and dance with them right away."

"You better not," I warned. "One touch of that little ball would kill you on the spot." I also took him to a bullfight but at the entrance gate he stopped suddenly, became ashen pale, and whispered, "Let's go back. I couldn't stand that." It was the first time I saw in his eyes a sign of madness.

Back in Buenos Aires for my next concerts, I reveled in the ballet evenings at the opera house. They gave all my favorite ballets: *Schéhérazade, Petrushka, L'Après-midi d'un faune, Les Sylphides, Le Spectre de la rose*—without my beloved Karsavina—and the dances of *Prince Igor*. In the daytime I saw much of Ansermet, a man of great personal charm and vast erudition. I introduced him to some important people who became beneficial to him in the future. He became a great friend of Victoria Ocampo, who to her death was considered the intellectual leader of her country.

One night a dreadful thing happened at the Colón. The evening began with *L'Après-midi d'un faune*, in which, after a few bars from the orchestra, the curtain is supposed to go up on a Greek landscape with Nijinsky in the scant costume of a faun. Ansermet conducted the beginning better than ever, but when the curtain rose, no Nijinsky. The orchestra continued to play, unaware of any mishap. But some violent voices were soon heard backstage and the curtain was rushed down. In the wings an alarming drama was taking place; Nijinsky had suddenly decided not to dance, probably in a moment like the one outside the bull ring in Madrid. Neither the stage manager nor his fellow dancers, not even his wife, could induce him. So someone called the police. In Spanish-speaking countries there is a law which compels a scheduled performer to go on stage, even if he has not been paid. They consider that the public is entitled to get what they paid their money for. At the sight of the two policemen, the terrified Nijinsky ran onto the stage. Soon the performance resumed. And he danced better than ever.

When the ballet season was over, I bade farewell to my old companions with kisses and hugs. To my astonishment Nijinsky and his wife stayed behind. A few days later Madame Nijinska begged to see me on an important matter. "I have to ask of you a great favor," she began. "Vaslav and I have a serious problem. We entered this country with Hungarian papers which are not acceptable in the Western countries now at war. But we have been encouraged to stay in Uruguay by the British minister, who will provide us with British passports if Vaslav dances in a concert in Montevideo for the Red Cross. Although this arrangement is quite acceptable, it is difficult because my husband has no solo repertoire. All he could do would be to dance with piano accompaniment the three dances from *Sylphides*. So," she added hesitantly with an imploring look in her eyes, "would you be generous enough to play in such a concert and so enable us to get back to Europe?"

This request came at an inconvenient moment. Quesada had opened the subscription for my new recitals in Montevideo and my appearing there at high prices in a gala night could keep the wealthy box holders away from my concerts. When I spoke to Quesada about this he practically had a stroke. "This is crazy! It could ruin us!"

I hate to mention in print my good heart, but somehow I felt that I couldn't refuse a great artist and a compatriot, nor could I face being haunted by that pathetic expression in his eyes which I had already seen twice, and so I promised to play, but only three pieces: two Spanish items and a waltz of Chopin.

The night before the gala concert, I took the boat to Montevideo. At the hotel I had just a cup of coffee and went to my room to recover from a dreadful crossing. On my way from the boat I had seen masses of posters with a large red cross in the center and above and below: RUBINSTEIN— NIJINSKY and NIJINSKY—RUBINSTEIN. I had never seen such a display of advertising. At nine o'clock I was awakened by a tap at the door. A young man entered the room, excused himself for disturbing me so early, and gave me the program of the evening to make sure the items were printed correctly. The program looked rather like a small book, containing scores of pages of paid advertisements. I had a hard time finding the page with the program. When I saw it I gave a shout of dismay. "Is this all the program you have?" I asked.

"Of course," he answered. "The committee did not want anybody else except the two big names Nijinsky and Rubinstein."

"But this is nonsense!" I jumped out of the bed, put on my dressing gown, and pointing at the page, shouted, "This program will last exactly twenty minutes! What do you think a gala is?" The young man was completely at a loss; he had no idea what I was talking about. "Go straightaway to the committee and tell them they must find other people to take part in this concert or else they will have a great scandal on their hands."

When he left, I dressed in a hurry and went down to the lobby to wait for news. Half an hour later, three ladies appeared. "We are in charge of this gala but we had nothing to do with the program. We sent it to the printer without looking at it." I told them coldly that I refused to take part in this kind of gala. The ladies were panic-stricken. "This is impossible!" they cried. "The President of Uruguay is coming, all the embassies have taken boxes, the house is sold out, and there is tremendous excitement building up in the city. Can't you find some way to help us?"

I knew from the beginning that I was going to be the victim of the whole affair. "Yes, dammit, I'll help you. Instead of my three wretched pieces, I shall play the first part of a usual piano recital. After a lengthy intermission Nijinsky can produce his three Chopin dances. After another

lengthy intermission I will have to finish with the rest of a recital program."
And I scribbled wretchedly the pieces I was prepared to play which
wouldn't interfere too much with my own subscription programs. The ladies
left after trying to kiss my hand. I returned to my room to rest from this
new disaster. Ten minutes later the same young man reappeared. "The
ladies sent me to ask you if you would allow the Municipal Band to play the
national anthems of the Allies before the concert and during the intermissions." I had nothing against this. He rushed away with the good news. Not
half an hour had passed before two of the ladies entered my room. "We
have a brilliant idea," they announced. "As Nijinsky's pieces are short, a
young poet will read an essay he has written called 'The Dance.' He would
be happy to read it before Nijinsky's numbers." This idea disquieted me
slightly, as I have always been allergic to public recitations. But I did not
want to disappoint the by now over-anxious ladies.

In the evening, with all this settled and the program printed, I dressed
and left for the theater. My dressing room was next door to Nijinsky's and I
heard him exercising with great jumps which made my room tremble. Punctually at nine-thirty the President and dignitaries settled in their boxes, the
Municipal Band blared out the Uruguayan national anthem followed by the
French and English ones. Then I started my recital, which began with a
Beethoven sonata followed by two shorter pieces, all of which took half an
hour. I was greatly applauded, had to bow several times, and retired to my
room. Somebody tapped at my door; an elegant elderly gentleman introduced himself as the French ambassador. "Monsieur," he said, "I have
something difficult to tell you: poor Nijinsky complains of something on his
foot. It is wet or sore or something, but he insists on you playing the other
part of your program now, after the intermission, to give him time to
recover." This one I took very badly; I became rather indignant and replied,
"I made a great sacrifice in expanding my program at all and I have no
intention of disappointing the audience by appearing instead of Nijinsky!"
The ambassador began to implore, insist, and would not give up. "Le
pauvre Nijinsky est dans un état terrible. Il est si nerveux que je crains qu'il
ne puisse décider de ne pas danser du tout."*

Again I gave in, but I made one condition: "Somebody has to go out
on stage and tell the public that I have kindly consented to play now instead
of at the end because of Nijinsky's wet feet or whatever it is." The ambassador shook my hand warmly and went to find the right man to give the
message.

The stage was crowded with agitated young busybodies all wearing the

* Poor Nijinsky is in a terrible state. He is so nervous that I am afraid he might
decide not to dance at all.

insignia of the gala committee and selling the expensive program. But when the French ambassador attempted to find a volunteer to address the public, they all disappeared like rats in less than a minute. Spanish-speaking people would rather die than go on a stage unexpectedly. The ambassador shrugged his shoulders: "You see? Impossible." This time I was adamant and the situation became untenable. The French diplomat went to consult with his British colleague, a curious fellow who looked exactly like Don Quixote. Smiling amenably, he said, "No trouble, I can tell them myself." He walked out, obtained the silence of the audience, and laughing uproariously between each short sentence, spoke more or less the following:

"Nijinsky"—he laughed—"con los feet, something, ho, ho"—clapping the sole of his shoe in the air. "Nada nada"—he waved his hand consolingly —"ballet go on, but ahora"—laughing again and playing an imaginary piano in the air. "Rubinstein, ho, ho!" I don't know if anyone in the audience made sense of this, but the charming man told us triumphantly, "You see, very simple; they understood perfectly." My usual sense of humor got the better of me and I laughed uproariously too.

The bell rang for the beginning of the second part. The band played some more Allied anthems—I couldn't say which, perhaps Belgian, Japanese, or Italian—in any case, they played three or more, the audience standing respectfully. I was about to go on to play when I suddenly heard the sound of a violin and piano. Completely taken aback, I peered onto the stage and saw a violinist reading from the score of a piece of Spanish café music, accompanied by a pianist of the same caliber. I asked someone near the stage what all this meant. The answer was: "As you were so nervous about the shortness of the program, they asked this charming violinist from the café on the corner to play something."

I lost my temper; I had had enough. I played my next numbers in a showy way to attract easy applause in order to punish Nijinsky, who I suspected simply wanted to have the last ovation of the concert like so many ambitious virtuosos. I did not know that this farcical evening was in fact the last tragic appearance of one of the greatest artists I have known. The public gave me a huge ovation and with their clapping and shouting insisted on three encores. By then it was past midnight. Again, a lengthy intermission; I was invited to join the committee in their box for Nijinsky's appearance. The Municipal Band played a few more anthems to the standing audience, who were by now somewhat tired. The last anthem was longer than any of the others. I whispered, "What country's anthem is that?" Nobody could give me a satisfactory answer, but we stood while it went on and on; then suddenly the rhythm changed and the march swung into a lively waltz. The people in the audience looked at each other open-mouthed, not knowing what to do, and eventually sat down. We found out later that the band had run out of anthems and decided that it would make a nice finale if they played a selection from an operetta which nobody recognized.

When this comic interlude ended, instead of Nijinsky a young man with a little book in his hand appeared and addressed the public with uncommonly feminine gestures. In a sweet voice he pronounced, "La Danza . . ." and went on to declaim a long essay on his conception of the dance in an irritating way. This was too much; the gallery, which had been so well-behaved during the long evening, suddenly lost all control. "Basta de danza!" someone screamed. "Mariconazo! Fuera!" The much alarmed poet left the stage precipitately. While calm was being restored, the curtain went down so that the stagehands could move the piano to one side of the stage. But they forgot to sprinkle the floor with water. Then Nijinsky appeared in the tights he wore in *Les Sylphides*. The piano stool was occupied by a stout lady who played the three dances of Chopin. I felt sorry for this lady; I could well imagine that she would have preferred to play some Spanish paso dobles and not Chopin pieces after my long recital. Nijinsky gave a few of his incomparable jumps, which raised such dust from the stage that the people in the first rows were choking. One felt it was dangerous for him to dance on that dry and dusty floor. To me, he looked even sadder than when he danced the death of Petrushka. I must confess unashamedly that I burst into tears. The horrible mixture of a seemingly endless farce with one of the most heartbreaking tragedies was more than one could bear. We gave him an endless ovation. I suddenly knew that everyone in the audience was aware of the drama on the stage. This was the last appearance of Vaslav Nijinsky, the greatest dancer of my time, who still after so many years remains unforgotten.

3

Quesada persuaded me to go to Chile and give more concerts in Buenos Aires and Montevideo on my return. "It will give a rest to your public and they will consider your next concerts an unexpected gift from heaven." I laughed at this shameless exuberance but I knew he was right.

To take the train to Chile was at that time a heroic venture entailing twenty-four hours in a stuffy English railway car (the railway belonged to a company which even monopolized the newsstands, where only English papers were sold). All the way, the dust of the Pampas invaded the cars and we arrived in Mendoza utterly exhausted. It took us a whole day to recover our senses before facing a worse ordeal: the train which left Mendoza at midnight and pushed its way through the Andes. At any moment there was the risk of an avalanche descending on us, but we were lucky—no avalanche this time. We were also spared the snow ever ready to bury you. Next morning we reached the beautiful city of Santiago, situated at the foot of the majestic cordillera of the Andes with is eternal snow shimmering in the sun. The beautiful capital of Chile laid out a red carpet for me; I received an ovation before I had struck a note on the keyboard. Once again it was Juanita Gandarillas who was my fairy godmother, as she had been in London, writing letters to her family and relatives, who owned practically everything in Chile. Besides having sold-out houses in both Santiago and Valparaiso, I was lionized by all the best families and was forced to accept the hospitality of the sister-in-law of Eugenia Errazuriz, who gave reception after reception for me. Believe it or not, but I was glad to return to Buenos Aires.

Here my second season of concerts changed my fortunes. After so many years of financial difficulties I suddenly felt rich. I was the one who could send flowers to lovely ladies; I could offer a costly present to some particularly nice one and even indulge, as ever before and after, in spending much of it on myself. I bought a thin platinum watch at the best jeweler's in Buenos Aires which had my initials on the back in white enamel. I was proud to know that nobody in this rich city had one like it.

Ernesto de Quesada had to leave for Spain when his wife suddenly called him back. But I remained for more than a month playing in both neighboring capitals, where I was engaged for good fees by musical societies which ran subscription concerts. There was one, which still exists as far as I know, proudly called Sociedad Wagneriana, which offered performances of solo instrumentalists, often chamber music, but never any orchestral concerts, and never a trace of a Wagnerian leitmotiv. I played there twice for a probably anti-Wagnerian audience. There was also a Sociedad Hebraïca so that Jews, the great lovers of music, wouldn't be deprived of it even in exile. They ran better series than the Wagneriana—their bitter rival. For my highly remunerative concert at the Jockey Club, my audience consisted of members who usually spent evenings playing cards or sleeping in comfortable leather seats with their newspapers slipping onto their laps. I had a hard time waking them up except when I would play certain chords fortissimo. With the champagne after the concert they became livelier.

During my lengthy stay I learned a good deal about the musical life in these countries. Unfortunately there were no composers writing music of serious original content. Alberto Williams would produce score after score of watered-down César Franck with some unexpected spots of Schumann here and there and occasionally a daring Debussy six-note scale. Other composers of Spanish or Italian descent picked up some folklore from their countries and tried to turn it into more serious shapes but without real inspiration. But quite unexpectedly, after dinner one night at the home of my recent adversary turned supporter, the critic Frías, a young man with unassuming manners went to the piano and asked Frías' eldest daughter, Brigidita, to sing some of his songs. This was a revelation. Some of the songs were clearly inspired by the style of Fauré, Duparc, and even Debussy, but the clear genuine talent of this young man, Carlos López Buchardo, made them original creations, full of the enchanting rhythms of the songs and dances of his country with a Schubertian quality in his use of brusque modulation. He had another incomparable asset: Brigidita had the most divine voice of velvet of all lieder singers I have ever heard. She sang his songs with a facility, a natural diction, and a wealth of emotion which brought tears to my eyes. Whenever I visited Buenos Aires I found great joy in hearing this couple again. Unfortunately López Buchardo was a member of the Argentinian "society" and what his education had taught him was, principally, laziness. So he was not easily induced to let loose his wonderful inspiration. Some two or three orchestral pieces exist but they were written without enough care for detail and have been forgotten. However, his songs still remain.

Since then music in Argentina has made great progress. Men like Alberto Ginastera have made international names for themselves, and serious music, not just opera, has become vitally important to the Argentinians. Even on my first trip, audiences showed a remarkable respect for the many pieces of then ultra-modern music which I played, often asking me to repeat such and such a piece by Prokofiev, Szymanowski, Ravel, Medtner, Scriabin, or Debussy, which was most encouraging. Albéniz became so popular that my concerts provided good royalties for the composer's family; there was also a feverish demand for other compositions of de Falla, who became so famous that he went to live in Córdoba, Argentina, during the Spanish Civil War. He died there in 1946. I have noticed, incidentally, with amazement how many composers became universally well known thanks to works which they themselves rather despised: for example, de Falla's *Fire Dance*, Ravel's *Bolero*, and Rachmaninoff's C-sharp minor Prelude.

One would have thought that the vast number of conservatories would have swamped the country with fine performers, but in 1917 there was not a conductor, pianist, violinist, cellist, or singer worthy of mention, whereas at present several Argentinian performers are universally acclaimed. The same process took place in Chile.

Before I returned to Spain, Faustino da Rosa and I signed a contract for the 1918 season which involved Brazil, Uruguay, Argentina, Chile, Peru, and Havana via Panama. The management was responsible for traveling expenses for me and providing a secretary as well as publicity and I was to receive 55 percent of the gross receipts. With my name now well established I accepted the terms of this contract with no little satisfaction. Doña Susana Quintana, whom I consulted, approved this agreement wholeheartedly. This remarkable lady behaved like a mother to me, inviting me almost daily for meals with her family, presiding proudly at my concerts, and even coming surreptitiously in the early morning to my hotel to see if my laundry and clothes were being well cared for. She recommended the finest Italian tailor in town, who dressed me in the best concert clothes of my life. She made me put the bulk of the money I had earned into the excellent bonds of the Credito Argentino, which was state-guaranteed and yielded 6 percent. "Arturito," she said, "I notice you are a spendthrift and I want to save this money for you." At our farewell she gave me a pearl with the most beautiful iris which had belonged to her husband as well as a silver box filled with the best cigars. I have worn her pearl in my tie every day up to this moment as I write.

4

Spain had by now become a second homeland to me. I gave a lengthy tour using my new Steinway, which I had purchased through their agents at Buenos Aires and had sent in the midst of the war from New York to Madrid. Playing now the proud role of the parvenu, I spent night after night with my young aristocratic friends, footing the bill more often than not. I even commissioned my friend de Falla to write an important piano piece and paid a good sum of money for the right to play it for a year from the manuscript. Meanwhile I included in my programs his *Andaluza* from the printed score. When the time approached to embark again for South America, I learned to my great disappointment that Ernesto

de Quesada would not sail with me. Without my knowledge he had established his own firm, Conciertos Daniel, in all the countries we had visited
together and now had to attend to his own affairs.

My aristocratic companions were not very musical; at my concerts
they would sit around backstage waiting impatiently for me to finish. "How
much longer will you be? Those silly people are still yelling! Can't you do
something to shut them up?" One night at our late supper, probably at four
in the morning, I expressed my misgivings about facing the huge tour all by
myself just when I needed desperately someone I could trust to watch the
receipts. The usual bunch was there as well as a new friend, a bright and
witty young man named Juan Avila.

"What do you pay a secretary?" he asked.

"A straight fee per month and of course all the expenses."

When I mentioned the sum he said, "If you could double the fee, I'll
take the job."

"Don't pull my leg. I know you are a married man and have children,
but if you really mean what you say"—I winked at the others—"then I'll
sign you up right now."

"I can sign the contract immediately!" We drafted a paper and signed
it carefully amidst general laughter. But as unbelievable as it seemed to me,
he was prepared to go. I found out he came from an old family and maybe
there was some family drama behind it, but I didn't care to inquire.

One evening at the Teatro Real, the Madrid opera house, I saw and
heard a sensational Carmen, Gabriella Besanzoni. She remains in my memory as the greatest Carmen I ever heard, a contralto whose lowest notes
sounded like those of a baritone although she could reach with perfect ease
the highest notes. There was something of a wild sensuous animal in her.
For once, Don José's tragedy was convincing. Though not exactly beautiful,
she was the perfect incarnation of Mérimée's gypsy. The thunderstruck
audience gave her the greatest ovation I have ever witnessed in Madrid.

Faustino da Rosa had come to Madrid to engage her for the Colón in
Buenos Aires and to make the final arrangements for my own tour. I saw
him every day in the round hall of the Palace Hotel sitting with the great
singer and another lady having coffee after their meals. Whenever I passed
by them hoping to meet her, da Rosa would jump up from his seat to talk to
me, clearly showing no intention of introducing me. So all I could do was
look at her to show her my admiration, which she acknowledged with a
faint smile. One night, after da Rosa had left, I saw her coming toward me
in a lonely corridor. I blushed with excitement. She suddenly stopped and I
approached to introduce myself when without a word she clutched my head
with both hands and kissed me so violently that she drew blood from my

lip. When we both recovered, I suggested that she take a drive with me along the Castellana in my open carriage the next day, which was to be the first day of the Madrid Carnival. She accepted, clapping her hands with delight.

In my hired carriage adorned with ribbons and flowers we drove along this majestic avenue thronged with people laughing and shouting and throwing flowers at each other and at us. We reciprocated, shaking hands heartily with those who recognized us, joking, laughing, playing the game, and kissing furtively whenever it was possible. When we returned to the hotel, Gabriella took my hand, led me to her room, and said, "Caro, let us lie down and rest." Three hours later, I left her room, tired but exuberantly happy. Proud of this lovely adventure, of having had Carmen in my arms, I thought of it as the passing whim of a passionate woman.

I was wrong. It rapidly turned into something serious. Gabriella behaved like a woman in love. She confessed, unasked, that she was having an affair with da Rosa and swore that it was only for her career's sake. "Povere donne!" she cried. I was not much impressed, having guessed it already, but I began to be disquieted about things to come. In any case, she had to leave in a few days for Buenos Aires and I still had concerts in Valencia and Barcelona, after which I had to leave my new Steinway in the care of my Barcelona manager, Joaquín Peña. Peña was the music critic of *La Vanguardia* and I gave him the right to sell the piano should he find a buyer at my price. Avila was to join me there to embark for Argentina. I took leave of the tearful Gabriella. "You will sing for me and I will play for you soon in Buenos Aires," I said to console her.

Two days later in Valencia, the director of the Teatro Principal told me, "The famous singer Gabriella Besanzoni is in the theater to hear you play." I was frightened. She was supposed to have sailed from Cadiz. After the concert she came to me and cried, "Arturo mio, I had to hear you play and now I am happy. I shall hear you also in Barcelona."

"But what about your boat?"

"I postponed my departure. I would love to make the journey with you." This I couldn't accept.

"No, no!" I cried. "It's impossible. If da Rosa sees us arriving together he might break off his contract with both of us."

Fortunately there was an Italian steamer from Genoa that stopped in Barcelona on the way to Buenos Aires. I forced her to take it. There was another tearful farewell, to the great disgust of Avila, who disliked operas and enjoyed only nasty stories about singers.

We sailed on the same boat I had taken the year before, the dear old *Infanta Isabel;* and a boisterous voyage it was. After two or three days,

Juan took over the ship. In his mid-twenties, of short stature, excellently well dressed, his dark hair always perfectly groomed, he had penetrating eyes of a strange greenish color. One couldn't call him handsome but he had a personality of magnetic appeal. His most characteristic feature was his mouth; it seemed to move in constant voluptuous greed, and he made everybody around him conscious of it. The few attractive women on board were soon falling under his spell. A lovely young French demimondaine who was returning to her *ami sérieux* in Brazil became Avila's slave. He handed her to me like a good dish; "Charlottavotte," he called her in French slang. I would enjoy her charms in the niches between the lifeboats on the upper deck when there was nobody around.

Avila himself had a keen eye for all the others. Our fellow travelers surrounded him at the bar, laughing uproariously at his jokes and admiring his wit. He extended his domain even into the kitchen. "What are we having today?" he would ask as he entered this temple of food. "Again the paella!" he cried, studying carefully the menu of the day. "Haven't you ever heard of a good French dish called *entrecôte minute?* Must it be rice all the time?" The terrified cooks did what they could to satisfy his difficult palate and during meals you heard the smacking of lips as the enchanted passengers looked thankfully at Juan, their benefactor.

Upon arrival, safely and comfortably lodged at the Plaza, it did not take five minutes to feel at home. A message was waiting for me from Nena Salamanca, whose husband was still in Madrid, inviting me the next night for dinner. I gladly accepted by telephone and mentioned that my secretary this time was a distinguished Spaniard named Juan Avila.

"*The* Juan Avila?" she cried with astonishment. "Isn't he the one I've heard so many stories about? Bring him along by all means! My parents will be thrilled to meet him." At dinner, even before the fish had been served, Avila was on intimate terms with everyone. He kept them in stitches with his gossip about Madrid society. When we took our leave they gave him a standing invitation for all the meals he cared to accept.

During that day, the da Rosa men had come to get the programs for the first concerts and to give me an outline of the tour; they were somewhat taken aback to find Avila at my side instead of Quesada. After my introduction of Juan, as my secretary, they decided to use him as their secretary as well and began giving him orders about this and that. Juan's response fell like a bombshell. "I'm not here to work for you," he said sternly, "but to keep a sharp eye on your dealings with my friend Arturo. We will both see to it that everything goes smoothly." I do not need to describe the change in expression and manners of the two gentlemen; they were scared out of their wits. I learned then that my tour would begin in Brazil and continue with Argentina and Uruguay, following up with the countries on the Pacific— Chile and Peru—and finish in Havana.

5

Gabriella arrived in Buenos Aires two or three days after me. I saw her but once. She had taken an apartment in a private home with her traveling companion. She told me nervously that da Rosa had been rather cool at her arrival and had postponed her debut. He made her rehearse from morning to night, try on costumes, visit the press, and give interviews. "But," she said, "I love you more than ever." But I too was a little apprehensive.

Because of the war, maritime communications between neutral Argentina and Brazil, which had declared war, were difficult. We were obliged to take a train which took four days to reach São Paulo.

My farewell with Gabriella was somewhat less than warm; the hostile behavior of da Rosa had much to do with it. Juan and I left for Montevideo to take the train to São Paulo. My Uruguayan friends warned me of the great discomfort we would suffer but I took it lightly and looked forward to seeing a new country, especially the fabulous Rio de Janeiro. The train turned out to be a miserable imitation of the North American system with lower and upper berths for the night, a car you could only derisively call a Pullman, and a dining car that was always dirty and served abominable meals.

The travelers made up a funny crowd; a black Jesuit priest, some Brazilian businessmen who chattered loudly and uninterruptedly, a few women, servile and submissive to their male companions, but no ladies. There was also a dangerous-looking man whose towering bulk filled the car. Baldish, with an untrimmed pepper-and-salt beard, a big red nose, and bloodshot eyes, he was called Don Salvador by some fellow travelers who knew him. The rest of us kept respectfully aloof.

The first day passed peacefully as we drove through the uncultivated plains and forests of Argentina and Uruguay. The air became warmer as we progressed and we all dozed as the train rocked along on the uneven rails. The only diversion came from Don Salvador. He disdained the dining car but frightened us by taking out of his pocket a huge, shiny jackknife. In his left hand he held a tin can which he slashed open with a couple of adroit strokes. Once he had the tin open, he put its contents serenely into his mouth with the point of his knife. Sated by one or two tins, he then gave us an unusual spectacle; he began to pick his teeth with the long knife with elegant and precise movements. We were treated to this show for the rest of the trip and experienced the same frightened shock every time we saw the jackknife come out, because Don Salvador, armed with his knife, always scrutinized us with ferocious glances.

On the second day, which was considerably hotter, we endured a fierce unexpected aggression: a billion locusts swarmed through the open windows of the train, hitting our heads and then settling on the floor up to our knees. The train stopped. The engineer, the conductor, and all the passengers took a hand in shoveling out these uninvited guests. It took us a few hours to be able to settle down again.

On the third day there was disastrous news; at a station early in the morning, our dining car was taken away. No explanation was given. The conductor, assailed with questions, shrugged his shoulders and said that the car showed some defect, adding with a smile, "There was no food left anyway." We went hungry the whole long day. I must say that our fellow travelers were not unkind; they offered to share whatever they had, a few pieces of hard bread and some cheese, and we accepted gratefully. At night, as we were getting ready to go to bed, our train stopped at some larger station. It was where we crossed the train coming from São Paulo. The Jesuit priest gave a shout: "They have a dining car!" These words aroused the dozing Avila, who changed suddenly into Napoleon Bonaparte. Shouting "Adelante!" he and the Jesuit priest as his aide-de-camp, with a few meek travelers, including me, behind them, assaulted the dining car of the other train. The Jesuit pushed the attendant aside with a punch in the stomach and he and Avila began emptying the contents of the larder. Most of us helped—nobody dared to interfere with Avila's commands, and so we returned victoriously with our booty. Don Salvador remained happy with his tin cans. We ate our first meal in twenty-four hours and went happily to bed. The next day we arrived at São Paulo.

This huge metropolis of many millions looked in those days like a small provincial town. The main street with its banks and shops reminded me of Lodz. There was, however, a residential quarter full of immense villas built by rich Italian immigrants. The dynamic potential for development which turned the city into one of the largest and wealthiest in the world was already there. Mr. Walter Mocchi, da Rosa's partner and director of the Teatro Municipal in Rio de Janeiro as well as the opera in São Paulo, sent his agent to meet us at the station. He took us to a modest-looking hotel of three floors, with simple but clean rooms and, best of all, *bathrooms*, into which we plunged and splashed about in utter bliss. Even the food was not bad; we ate with pleasure some wholesome and tasty Brazilian specialties. I remember a rice soup called *canja* which we ate daily throughout our stay in Brazil.

Juan announced gleefully, "There is a gambling casino in the hotel!" We didn't lose any time. In less than two minutes we were sitting around the roulette table, where my neighbor, a lady dressed all in black, turned out to be Anna Pavlova. She was on tour with her company and had three days still to go in São Paulo. After a short gambling bout during which I won a little (Avila lost, and had to borrow from me) we invited Pavlova to have a bite with us in the adjoining bar. When I told that great artist about all the hardships of Diaghilev and his superhuman efforts to keep his company alive and the sad story of Nijinsky, she burst into loud sobs and became almost hysterical. "Yes! It was all my fault," she cried. "I should have stayed with him. I am a terrible egoist, I wanted everything for myself!" Not a little alarmed and annoyed by her presumption, I calmed her down.

"Diaghilev is a sorcerer. He will always find a way. He proved it." She left us haughtily, like a Byzantine empress.

The next morning I was awakened by the telephone. "A car is waiting for you." I was surprised, as I was not expecting Mocchi's secretary until noon. But, thinking it might be urgent, I dressed in a hurry and went downstairs, where a chauffeur gave me a card which said: "Chéri, la voiture est à toi pour la journée—Charlottavotte."* I blushed and wrote quickly: "Utterly impossible to accept kind offer. Call me this evening," and sent the chauffeur away with my letter. That night we left for Rio by train.

It was wartime in Brazil. The few good hotels were closed. Our rooms were reserved in a small but engaging house which had been turned into a hostel for stranded tourists up in Tijuca, one of the famous promontories of this golden city. Our windows allowed us to get acquainted at once with the Sugarloaf Mountain that stood like a fairy-tale guard of the port. In 1918 one could not have called Rio de Janeiro a city that had been built and developed by its citizens; nature itself had created it. I would call it simply one of the masterpieces of nature. The inhabitants tried to spoil it later by building skyscrapers in imitation of New York but even the highest of them were dwarfed by the immense majesty of the surrounding mountains. Because it was divided up into several valleys and two or three disconnected beaches, it was impossible for the city to grow in this bay of paradise and so

* Darling, the car is yours for the whole day.

its fantastic beauty was preserved. I fell in love with the city and even that cynical gourmet of life, Avila, was speechless.

Mr. Walter Mocchi, unlike his partner in Buenos Aires, was a man of the world. He had a nice reception for me in the lobby of the Municipal Theater, where he introduced me to his co-workers, some musicians, and other prominent people. The publicity he gave me became the talk of the town. For example, in front of the theater there was a long wooden wall to protect it from an esplanade with trees and flowers which was then being built; along the whole length of this wall, my name had been painted in huge letters. To go from one letter to the next I had to take several steps. No wonder my six concerts were practically covered by subscription.

My debut took place five or six days after my arrival. I found a Steinway concert grand in good shape and was delighted with the acoustics of this opera house which was neither too large nor too small. It had the charm of the Italian opera houses. The program I chose was well tried out and surefire. I don't remember all of it but I am certain to have played the *Carnaval* of Schumann and three or four of my best Chopin topped by the Polonaise in A flat and *Navarra* among the encores. It was a hit. The public in the gallery clapped and yelled for half an hour after the last piece. I was overwhelmed with joy. On the way home it was good for my morale to hear the unmusical Avila say drily, "Aquí vas a ganar mucho dinero."* My performance meant nothing to him.

The press the next morning was enthusiastic except for one dissenter. A young man found this and that to criticize in my playing, showing off his knowledge of the pieces by using, like many others, good German dictionaries of music. Juan Avila got hold of him and, with a pistol in his hand or over a few glasses of wine or by some other means, persuaded him as if by a miracle to become my most fervent supporter.

6

The director of the National Conservatory, Maestro Oswaldo, a charming gentleman in his sixties, invited me for dinner and to spend an evening among the prominent musicians in town. This was a good chance to

* You will earn a lot of money here.

learn about musical life in Brazil. The host, hostess, and a score of guests occupied a long table; I was seated in the center between two important composers, professors of harmony and counterpoint, Francisco Braga and Alberto Nepomuceno. As usual with musicians, the conversation became quite lively after the first glass of wine, with many amusing stories, mostly anecdotes about opera singers along with good imitations of them. I reciprocated by telling a few of my own best ones with great success. At this our good humor began to turn into slight pandemonium with everyone trying to tell a better one and all shouting at the same time.

At the other side of the table sat a man who so far had hardly smiled. The expression on his face fascinated me—he looked more Brazilian than the others, who were mostly of Portuguese or Italian descent. But this quiet man had a round, clean-shaven, full face, a darker complexion than the others, and sad, intelligent eyes. What struck me most about him was his fluent French. During a quieter moment I addressed him: "Allow me to compliment you on your French; I have never heard a foreigner with such a command of this beautiful and difficult language."

He smiled. "I am a Frenchman," he said quietly, "and am the private secretary of the French minister. My name is Darius Milhaud and I am a violinist and composer." I had never heard of him.

"I was found unfit for military service," he went on, "and was brought here by our minister, M. Paul Claudel, as his secretary but mainly as a collaborator."

Claudel, Claudel . . . I thought. A few years before, Karol Szymanowski, while we were spending the summer at his family's estate in the Ukraine, had given me two small books to read; their author was a Paul Claudel. Both were dramas and I remember their titles: *L'Otage* and *L'Annonce faite à Marie*. After reading them with great interest I was convinced that the author had lived during the Napoleonic era. His style had something of a Chateaubriand or a Stendhal. I knew no more than that about him.

"Is the minister M. Claudel a descendant of the famous dramatist?" I asked Darius Milhaud. He was puzzled. "I don't know of any other dramatist of that name but our minister."

"This is fantastic," I said excitedly. "I loved those two dramas and was sure that the author had written them at the beginning of the nineteenth century." Darius Milhaud gave out his first hearty laugh. "This is the best story of the evening. I must call the minister and tell it to him." While we all had our coffee, he came back and said excitedly, "Claudel was so enchanted with your story that he is coming right away to join us."

A half hour later, the minister plenipotentiary of France entered the room. "Please excuse me for coming uninvited but I couldn't resist Milhaud's description of the party and want to meet your guest of honor, Mr. Rubinstein," he said in a precise and clipped voice. Then he whispered to Milhaud and me, "Allons-nous-en; on va souper."*

Paul Claudel looked rather more like a provincial squire than a diplomat. Tallish with square shoulders and an embonpoint, he frightened me a little. I felt that he would not tolerate contradiction, but his round peasant-like face with its large brow was illuminated by a noble temperament. We took leave of our charming hosts in haste, went out to the street, and entered the official car of the ministry. "Go to the restaurant on the roof where we went the other night," he said to his driver. A few minutes later we stopped at a house where an elevator took us all the way up to the roof. We entered a restaurant under the open sky; some people at two or three tables were finishing their meal. Seated at a table lit by one candle, Claudel took charge. He recommended a Brazilian dish, *vatapá*, which is so hot that it can be swallowed only when accompanied by a soft side dish, and with it you must drink a strong white wine. Hot and strong are understatements; when I swallowed the first big spoonful of *vatapá*, I jumped out of my chair with tears in my eyes and had to get rid of it in some corner of the roof. Claudel enjoyed this as a personal triumph. "I told you it was pretty hot!" I learned my lesson and continued to eat this volcano more cautiously. Three glasses of the strong beverage did their work. By then, we were the only occupants of the roof with one or two waiters in attendance. Taking advantage of this, M. Claudel began to recite poems of Arthur Rimbaud in his sharp penetrating voice and Milhaud and I were carried away by his fine performance. Fired by the wine, he then gave us a brilliant recitation of a passage from his latest book, for which Milhaud was to compose the music. This impressed me even more than the Rimbaud. The great writer felt elated; we had fruit on the table. He picked a small bunch of grapes, went to the border of the roof, and took aim at a passerby in the street. Missing him, he rushed for another bunch and this time hit a woman on the head. She started to scream and wave her fist at her invisible assailant, who was thoroughly enjoying his prank on the roof. A few people gathered and one of them called a policeman. The woman demanded the arrest of the grape thrower. After a while our waiter showed in a stern, dark policeman who came straight to our table and demanded in a threatening voice: "Who is the one who threw grapes on a lady who was passing by peacefully?" Claudel rose majestically to his feet and said in French, "My friend, I don't understand a word of Portuguese, so if you have something to ask me, get

* Let's go and have supper.

an interpreter." He added more loudly, "Eu ministro da Francia." Milhaud, who knew some Portuguese, explained quickly that one of us wanted to grab a bunch of grapes from another and it flew over the side. "So do not annoy the ambassador of France." The policeman retired with great obeisance.

"Milhaud, vous êtes un bon diplomate,"* said Claudel graciously. We left on insecure legs. The driver drove the two Frenchmen home and was told to take me to my hotel at Tijuca.

During an absence of Walter Mocchi, two of his representatives made the accounts with Avila after my concerts. I was present one night when these gentlemen, one of them a strong-looking native and the other a sly Italian named Pellas, showed Juan an unsatisfactory balance. Quick as a wildcat my small friend slammed his fist on the table. "You nasty thieves—hand over the right amount!" The two large men immediately produced the rest of the money with trembling hands.

Avila and I became almost daily guests at the French Embassy, where we met another remarkable man, Henri Hoppenot, the counselor of the embassy, and his charming wife. Claudel and Milhaud came to all six concerts and spent the intermissions with me chatting, criticizing, and discussing. Once during an intermission the most important critic, Mr. Oscar Guanabarino, and other friends came to the artists' room. A beautiful bouquet of flowers had been brought to me with a card attached. The ever nosy Mr. Guanabarino opened this card to find out who had sent it. A strong slap on his hand stopped him dead. "How dare you be so indiscreet?" Claudel shouted at him, his hand still threateningly raised. Mr. Guanabarino hastily dropped the card.

After the concerts we usually had jolly suppers at the embassy or in some restaurant. I remember one evening when Claudel, seeing me apprehensive as to the outcome of the war after the new great German offensive, laughed off my fears saying, "Après l'entrée des Américains, il n'y a rien à craindre. Nous tenons bon."† Milhaud introduced me to an extremely musical family with whom we used to play *Le Sacre du printemps* and other music four-hand. The daughter of the house was a fine pianist and she and Darius gave us beautiful performances of piano and violin sonatas, including one very fine one composed by Milhaud himself.

One day, Claudel "ordered" me to sit for him to be photographed. It was the time when he had developed a little mania for photography. I say "ordered" because in his imperative way the slightest demand sounded like an order and had better be obeyed. He arrived at my hotel accompanied by

* Milhaud, you're a good diplomat.
† After the Americans entered the war, there was nothing to fear. We stand firm.

Milhaud and Hoppenot, armed with a huge professional camera. I received him in my best suit in his honor. "C'est dégoutant de poser comme ça,"* he said. "Take off your jacket and open your collar. Then you will look like a decent human being." No photographer I can recall tortured me as he did. "Milhaud, close the curtain!" he screamed. "Hoppenot, open that window, the light comes in better from there," and to me, who was sitting quietly, "Ne faites pas des grimaces!" Then he covered his head with a black cloth and began staring at me through the lens. "You sit like a dead body!" he screamed. "Milhaud, move the curtain a bit!" This ordeal lasted for three hours. The only man looking happy and satisfied was Claudel. He did succeed in making a fine photo and he honored me by asking me to sign it. A few years ago his granddaughter made me a present of this photo, which she had inherited.

One night we were invited for a diplomatic dinner at the French Embassy. The wife of the Brazilian foreign minister, who was sitting at Claudel's right, tried to please him by uttering sharp criticisms of certain much read French writers. "Taisez-vous, vous dites des bêtises,"† Claudel snapped. To my amazement all the others pretended not to have heard him.

"M. Avila me plaît," the great writer said one day. "Son tour d'esprit est osé mais original et pas ennuyeux."** Juan was very flattered. "Arturo," he said, "we ought to give a dinner party for Claudel, Milhaud, and the Hoppenots. I think I can arrange it in a nice way." I gave him carte blanche. The dinner turned out to be a most luxurious banquet. Juan commandeered the entire hotel staff to surround the table. The decoration of the table was in itself a masterpiece with huge dark blue bunches of grapes lying on the pink silk and lace tablecloth. The handwritten menu read like a gala dinner at a royal court. Juan had emptied whole shops of the best wines including French champagne, difficult to find then, and all the other tidbits he could put his hands on. The main dish, I remember, was a duck prepared by a cook he had hired for the occasion. My guests were flabbergasted and even Claudel was amazed. It took two of my concerts to pay the bill but Avila enjoyed his personal triumph.

* It is horrible to pose like that.
† Shut up. You are talking nonsense.
** I like M. Avila. He is cheeky but original and not boring at all.

7

The programs of the first six concerts were more or less the same as those in Buenos Aires, but to my great satisfaction the modern pieces of Prokofiev, Szymanowski, and Ravel found much more receptive ears. I have often expressed the opinion that the two most musical nations on the American continent are Brazil and Mexico. Even then, in Brazil I met a few young promising composers and two brilliant pianists, Antonietta Rudge and Guiomar Novaës; Miss Novaës later made a name for herself in Paris and New York. In all I gave fifteen concerts at the Municipal Opera House followed by six in São Paulo that were no less successful—an unforgettable memory. The public of São Paulo made me think of Germany while the public of Rio were more like Italians; they listened to music as if it ran in their veins while in São Paulo they had the sophisticated approach of those who know music quite well. Luigi Schiafarelli, a great piano teacher whose fame attracted even pupils from abroad, was considered the equal of Isidor Philippe or Busoni. Both Novaës and Rudge were his pupils. Already in his sixties, he was a man of great intelligence, spoke four languages fluently, was well read, and had a vast understanding of human problems and world affairs. His most striking trait was a superb sense of humor. We became friends on my first visit to his house and remained so for years to come. I enjoyed the evenings at his home, playing works for two pianos or trying out my programs, and there were always endless lively comments at supper. These were good days in São Paulo!

I came back to Rio for a few more concerts; the last one, the fifteenth, took place on a Sunday afternoon. After a standing ovation the crowd in the street surrounded me as in Montevideo and some young men lifted me onto their shoulders. Avila, seeing this, screamed, "Arturo! Be careful! Don't let them steal your pearl!" We left for Buenos Aires, this time by steamer, thank God, and happy to find no Don Salvadors on board.

The welcome we received back in Buenos Aires was heartwarming. The concerts were sold out and there was no opposition from the critics. Only my old enemy, Mr. Laguardia of *La Prensa*, stuck to his guns. As to Avila, he became the pet of the upper class, which called themselves *la sociedad.* The attitude of these people has irritated me ever since my youngest years; in Poland it was the *arystokracja;* in Paris they were known modestly as *le monde*—"the world"! In the United States they liked to call their country clubs, golf or tennis clubs, or even hotels and restaurants "exclusive," a term which does not describe them but describes the ones not allowed in. Coming back to my story. I can say that all the doors opened for my friend Avila. Yet he did not neglect his duties—the box office was terrified of him.

I had tried out in Spain many new pieces to bring fresh blood to my programs. Most of them, like Ravel's *Gaspard de la nuit,* turned out to be first performances in Argentina. The new pieces were received with mixed reactions but always with great interest. I even dared to give a recital devoted entirely to Debussy in homage to the composer, who had recently died. My performances of Chopin, Albéniz, and the few dances of de Falla invariably got great ovations. It was still wartime, so there were no other concerts to speak of except for the series of the Sociedad Hebraïca and the Sociedad Wagneriana, where I spent some uninteresting evenings. There was, however, an Italian pianist of talent, Maria Carreras, who had married an Argentine named Carreras. I saw quite a lot of them and one day her husband, who was also her manager, brought me an interesting letter from New York.

A well-known American concert agent had proposed a tour of fifteen concerts in the United States at the fee of $400 per concert with all travel expenses and publicity to be paid by the management. In spite of the rather small sum offered me, I was thrilled to have the chance for a new shot at the formidable United States. I was happy to find out that it was not my South American success but Eugène Ysaye's warm recommendation that was responsible for this offer. But Mr. Carreras had a warning: "This manager's name is R. E. Johnson and he does not have the best reputation for honesty in his dealings with artists, so I strongly advise you to ask him to pay you in advance for your four last concerts before signing the contract." Carreras communicated my acceptance to R. E. Johnson along with this additional clause. I thanked him warmly for his intervention in this matter and waited for Johnson's answer.

The season at the Colón Opera House was brilliant. I heard *Carmen* there, of course, twice. The triumph was Besanzoni's, who was also an admirable Amneris and Azucena. Ansermet conducted a wonderful *Pelléas et Mélisande* with Ninon Vallin, a great singer and a musician too. I hardly saw Gabriella in private; we were both shy of the ogre da Rosa.

I must mention here an unexpected aspect of Juan's character. One night when each of us had gone out to a different place I was astonished not to find him back in his room. As a rule we liked to have lively discussions on the events of the evening. It became very late and still he didn't return. Knowing Juan, I began to worry. He entered his room at four in the morning to my relief. "What happened!" I shouted. "You gave me a sleepless night!" He came into my room, sat on my bed, and told me the following extraordinary story: "I read this morning in *La Nación* that a couple with a mother and five children were turned out of their house and have been sleeping for the past three days in an open building site. I was convinced that they had found help by now but I wanted to find out. And there they still were. Well, I found some cheap quarters for them for the night and tomorrow I shall speak about it with my rich friends. A great city like this should be ashamed of such things!" he exclaimed. That night I discovered another side of Juan.

One morning a few days before we left Chile, Juan startled me with some most unexpected advice: "Arturo, you need a personal valet. It is impossible for a man in your position to travel about the world without one. The valet of our floor in the hotel is just perfect for the job—you know, the little Gallego Enrique. I already talked to him and he's ready to come with us. His monthly pay is not much but of course you will have to be responsible for all his expenses." Like many others, I couldn't resist his arguments although I was not blind to the fact that Juan needed him much more than I did, as he had always had a valet and did not like to be without one. And so Enrique was hired there and then.

After some farewell dinners at Señora Susana's and at the Martínez de Hozes' the three of us left for Chile. On the train to Mendoza the dust almost choked Enrique and Avila to death but I was protected this time by a veil Señora Quintana had given me, saying, "Arturito, I always used it." The next morning, resembling three grenadiers back from a battle, we reached Santiago, where after a prolonged stay in our bathrooms we looked elegant again. I shall not dwell on Chile; there is nothing new to say. The hundreds of relatives of Eugenia Errazuriz gave us a royal welcome again and Juan, as always, shared my success.

After a few concerts at which my new pieces were received with finer understanding than in Buenos Aires, we sailed for Lima, Peru, where we arrived at the beginning of November. My Spanish successes were well known here and this accounted for a brilliant debut. The local musicians were astounded to see *la sociedad* of Peru attending my concerts. Four recitals were announced. Suddenly in the middle of the second one, pandemonium broke out in the theater. "Armisticio! Armisticio!" shouted the crowd, running into the streets. They forgot the concert; so did we. In less than a minute, throngs of people filled the large square, screaming, shouting, crying, singing, and I must admit I began to cry. Those four horrible years, the invasion of Belgium and France, the holocaust of Verdun and the Dardanelles and the last German offensive in the spring, passed through my mind in an instant. The sudden end of all this was too much to take in at once. We cried, screamed, and shouted a long time before returning to our senses.

Then came the natural reaction; we had to feast the victory. Juan and I invaded the nearest restaurant, roused the staff and clientele to their feet, and led them in the "Marseillaise." This was done in a fervent and noble way. We marched out of the restaurant followed by an ecstatic group who remained with us until the early hours of the morning. The quality of our noble enthusiasm deteriorated badly; at each nightclub, café, or anywhere we entered we forced anybody we found, however tired or unwilling, to roar out the unfortunate "Marseillaise," sometimes to my banged-out accompaniment on the nearest broken-down piano. I do not know how we finally reached the hotel and our beds but on November 12, I had the biggest hangover of my life. Juan, however, was his wide-awake self and at that point he gave me some bad news: "Arturo, don't be angry with me but I am going to leave you. At a time like this I want to be where things are happening, like Madrid or Paris. I know that you are obliged to finish your contract but frankly you don't need me any more." This was true to a certain extent, as we had been accompanied since Chile by a representative of da Rosa called Biancamano. But Avila's decision was a great blow to me. Our combined vitality gave me a curious feeling of power. After I had paid his fee he borrowed a larger sum from me and set off for Chile, leaving me in the hands of Biancamano, which were not as white as his name promised.

8

Instead of continuing my scheduled concerts I decided to give a gala for the combined Red Crosses of France, England, and the United States. The concert yielded a large sum of money which was delivered to the ambassadors of these countries. A Chilean boat took us to Panama, a long, tiring journey, stopping at various ports which were in the equatorial heat.

We left Callao and reached Colón with our shirts soaked. No concerts were planned here; we had simply to find a boat for Cuba. Colón was a huge American camp; we saw nothing but groups of marching soldiers, barracks, and blocks of houses evidently built during the war. In the lobby of our hotel we found two American Army men examining our passports. I had to give a lengthy explanation of my unusual Spanish passport, which stated that I was a free citizen of Poland, a country not yet free. The men were not quick in understanding this complicated document; how I missed Juan! I reached my room in an unbelievable sweat and felt an urge to jump right then into the shower with clothes and shoes on and all.

Enrique proved to be an excellent valet. He unpacked and arranged my things in no time and went down to bring me some food. That evening Mr. Biancamano brought me a letter and a wire, both of which had been sent from Rio de Janeiro by Gabriella Besanzoni. I opened the wire and was so puzzled by its contents that I reached for the letter hoping to find an explanation. Gabriella wrote that after a few appearances she had been stricken with Spanish influenza, a then much publicized epidemic. She felt lonely and was waiting for the moment to return to her Italy and to her mother. She expressed also very kindly an eternal love for me and finished the letter with "un grande baccio carissimo Tutullo,"* her detestable pet name for me. After this, the wire puzzled me more than ever. I shall try to quote it in English: "Completely recovered, have decided to join you in Panama. Arriving such and such a day in Santiago. Please have some friend take me to Valparaiso and put me on a boat for Panama. Can't wait to see you again." I fell on my bed to gather my wits in the face of this sudden and disquieting change in my life. Since Pola, I had never had a constant female companion. There is no denying that my masculine vanity was highly flattered but at the same time I was rather cowardly before new and complicated responsibilities. I had no intention of marrying Gabriella and I was terribly afraid that that was her goal. Anyway, I had no means of stopping her, as she was already on her way to Santiago. I sent a long telegram to my good friend Raúl von Shröder, a Chilean friend of the Allies in spite of his alarming name, gave him all the necessary instructions, and begged him to provide her with money if she needed any. He answered immediately, offering to help in any way. Two days later he wired me that she had arrived alone, in good health, and he named the boat which would bring her to Panama. I awaited her arrival in agony, having found out that all available ships in Panama had been taken over by the Army to bring the troops back from Europe. In my darkest hours I saw Gabriella and myself condemned to spend many months in this hellish hole of Panama.

* A big kiss, darling Tutullo.

And here she was, fresh as a daisy, kissing me and shouting, "Tutu, Tutullo, Tutullino!" We entered the hotel in a euphoric mood. I took her to a clean and comfortable room. She had closed the door behind us carefully when a sharp rap startled us. "The gentleman must leave immediately and go to his own room!" Opening the door, I saw one of the military men from downstairs. Gabriella was terrified; she thought I had committed some crime and that they had come for my execution. When I told her what the man wanted she was open-mouthed. "Ma come?" she screamed. "Dio mio, they are crazy! Since when do they stop a man and a woman from being happy?" But there was no way of convincing this sort of man and so we were condemned to seeing each other at meals or in the corridors but never in a room. When I told her that we were in for a long stay because of the lack of ships, she collapsed and became slightly hysterical. I had to do something about the situation and decided to visit the civil governor of the place. It took three days to convince his aides to allow me to see him in person. Finally a kindly-looking old man received me, and took my Spanish passport with its visa for Panama obtained in Chile. He heard my tale about the reasons for this Spanish passport and then asked me what my profession was. When I said concert pianist he looked at me for a long while, got up from his seat, and disappeared into another room. After a while he came back carrying a small booklet in his hand. "Have you ever played in Dresden, in Saxony?"

"Yes." I nodded. "But only once; I was then thirteen years old." At that he leafed through his little book and showed me a page where I saw my signature under a dedication. He said, "You told me in a train from Berlin that you were going to play in Dresden. I asked you in that train for your autograph and here it is." Again, the unexpected miracle. "What can I do for you?" said this charming gentleman, now evidently disposed to help me in every way. I told him in delicate terms that a famous Italian singer who was a great friend of mine, my valet, my agent Biancamano, and I were bound for Havana, she for the opera and I for my concerts, and that we were stranded here. Would he be good enough to advise us what to do?

"Let me keep your passport and the others as well. I shall give all of you a visa for the United States, which will allow you to leave Panama without difficulty. But," he added with a smile, "you must do something for me. It would be so nice if your great singer and you could give a concert for our boys in the Army. There is a huge camp for entertainment and I can provide a good piano for you. What do you say to that?" Under such circumstances I said nothing but "Yes, sir."

Well, we were in for it. Gabriella exclaimed her usual "Dio mio! Dio mio!" but she was ready to sing. The concert took place in an open field.

About ten thousand troops attended but could hardly hear a thing, although, led by their commanding officer, they applauded in the right places. My new friend the governor, who was sitting quite near us and so could enjoy our music, was delighted.

A few days later the governor himself came to our hotel to tell me that there was a Grace Fruit Company ship bound for Havana with stops at Santa Marta, Colombia, and New Orleans. He had talked to the captain, who was willing to take us without pay.

I jumped at this offer. Anything was better than sitting in this goddamned heat, chained to our lonely rooms. And then Biancamano decided to leave us.

The passage through the famous Panama Canal was a great experience. The raising and lowering of our big ship in the locks of Gatun and Culebra was fascinating to watch. It took us most of the day to reach Balboa on the Atlantic side, where, in the morning, released from the customs and military police, we boarded a steamship that had anything but accommodation for passengers. On the top deck we saw three or four cabins, evidently occupied by the officers. The rest were bunks for the sailors. The first mate showed us two of the bunks. "You can have one of these with your valet and we can give you another single one for the lady." I shivered at the idea of Gabriella condemned for days to such uncomfortable quarters. I tried to see the captain but he was unavailable. A kindly-looking gentleman, the ship's doctor, showed sympathy. "I shall be glad to offer my cabin to the lady, as I can easily share the cabin of another officer." We accepted with gratitude. After many hours of comings and goings, of sailors loading and unloading, a lugubrious, loud, and prolonged siren announced our departure. After a bite of the food we had brought with us Gabriella retired to her more or less comfortable cabin until the next morning. Enrique succeeded in finding a place for himself nearby and left the double bunk to me.

So far, so good. I slept, dreaming of a charming arrival in Havana, but I was awakened by loud talk and shouting at 6 a.m. My bunk was protected by a dirty sort of curtain. Peeping through it, I saw to my horror a bunch of men who looked more like cutthroats on a pirate ship than sailors. All I needed was to see one with a black patch over one eye and a wooden left leg to make the picture complete. They had the most colorful attire; some wore nothing but dirty trousers, others had vests obviously unwashed in weeks. Some of them had beards and all were unshaven. I had a crazy wish for us to spend the entire voyage without being seen and this applied mainly to Gabriella. As an expert connoisseur of American movies, I knew all about pirate ships swarming the Caribbean looting, shooting, and killing people. But this time I felt that I was unfortunately not just a horrified spectator. I waited carefully until all the men were busy with chores and stole quickly to the doctor's cabin, where Gabriella sat in frank terror, unable to utter a word. "Darling," I said in the trembling soprano voice of a chicken, "don't worry. I am here, I shall protect you." I did not see much trust come into her eyes. Still, there was no way out; we had to face the situation. For my part, I decided not to undress during the whole voyage in order to be ready for any emergency and I asked Enrique, who by now looked like a cowardly Sancho Panza, to keep a sharp and constant eye on the doctor's cabin and alert me in case of danger. Fortunately we took our meals with the officers, the only relief from the tension; we tried to prolong these meals for hours but were left miserably to ourselves with the waiters in white jackets. The minute we left the table we saw nothing but the hungry eyes of hyenas disguised as sailors looking up and down at the body of the only female on board, the great contralto Gabriella Besanzoni. I felt that they would jump on her at any moment and rape her one by one in no time. We spent three miserable days under these conditions until reaching Santa Marta, the port in Colombia where we had to take on a load of bananas.

Santa Marta managed to be hotter than Panama and for two days we were deprived of even the smallest zephyr on board. The bananas were loaded by singing Colombians in a chain. This time the lugubrious siren sounded like the beginning of a Mozart aria, so glad were we to leave this hell.

But the real hell had yet to come. The green unripe bunches of bananas were accompanied by their great lovers who could not live without them, worms and insects of all sorts. They became our constant uninvited visitors. We arrived in New Orleans on a clear morning. The air was humid but comfortably cool. Gabriella and I looked at each other with the same idea in our minds: To leave this boat! I decided to take the train from New Orleans to Florida and sail from there to Havana on the daily steamer. We thanked the doctor and with the help of Enrique removed our luggage and stood it in front of the passport control.

With the visas from Panama, Gabriella and Enrique passed without trouble. I passed the civil control but then had to show my passport to the military one, which, as during the war, was still in charge. The officer looked over my passport very attentively. "You are not a Spaniard, so how come you got a Spanish passport?" I explained it to him colorfully, mentioning the guarantee of my person by King Alfonso. At that the man threw my passport on the floor. "I don't care for that guy, and from what I see on that passport, what you really are is a Russian." He shouted to the other man, pointing a nasty finger at me, "This feller is a Russian!" He was sure he had put his hands on the arch-spy of the century. I was boiling with rage; I felt like killing both of them.

"The U.S. governor in Colón gave me a visa for safe entrance to this country. You must have overlooked it."

"No visa is good enough for us. Don't you forget that we are at war."

No argument was possible with a man like that. Then I remembered a letter which I had in one of my bags; a letter which Joseph E. Willard, the American ambassador in Madrid and a great lover of music, had given me for his colleague in Buenos Aires. I had never delivered it and had even forgotten about it. I thought it might be useful now to show to this obstinate fool. "Could I open one of my bags? I think I have there a document which might interest you." He smirked at that but showed me to my luggage. I found the letter all right and handed it to him.

He read it with growing amazement. "Why didn't you show me this letter right away?" he said.

"I had no reason to show you any private papers of mine. My official document was good enough and should have been honored by you." Enjoying this moment of triumph, I added, "Please give me your name and the place where one can reach you, for I intend to make a complaint about your behavior and the deep offense you have caused to the king of a friendly state."

I have never seen a more servile expression on anybody's face as he then stammered a few excuses about the war and his responsibilities, but I was not impressed. I made him write down his particulars carefully, found the panic-stricken Gabriella and Enrique, got a porter to take us to a taxi, which took us to the Charles Hotel. The officer followed us, entered the lobby, and began again to ask for mercy. He even tried to win Gabriella's goodwill with a gift of flowers. But she gave him the look she reserved for Don José in the last act. We couldn't stop him, however, from carrying our luggage to the station, where I bought tickets and reserved sleeping berths for Miami.

These difficult American sleeping accommodations and the not too good food in the diner seemed to us pure heaven. Nonetheless, we arrived exhausted in Miami, where we had to change trains for Key West. Another night's journey. Finally an eight-hour crossing on the daily steamer brought us to Havana. We found accommodations at the very pleasant Plaza Hotel, where we had two adjoining rooms overlooking the big square and the Opera House. Enrique was soon unpacking. It became too late to lunch out, so we ordered some cold snacks; Gabriella said, "Arturo mio, I am dead, I am going to sleep," and she disappeared into her room. As to myself, I was

planning to see the director of the Opera about my concerts, which had
been arranged by the Buenos Aires management. Instead of this I lay down
for a short rest and slept for a solid sixteen hours.

9

Next morning, Gabriella, elegantly dressed, woke me up, ordered
my breakfast, and waited patiently until I was ready too. I telephoned the
Opera House and asked to speak to Mr. Antonio Braccale, the director,
who was famous for his great opera seasons. After a moment he came to
the phone. I explained to him that Biancamano had deserted me. "I'm on
my own here and I would like to know if you have any dates for me."

"As I had no news from Buenos Aires, I did not announce any concerts. But do come and see me here in my office and we shall discuss dates
and programs."

One hour later I sat in Braccale's private rooms in the Opera House.
He certainly was a man of action. A small Italian, clean-shaven, he had
vivid eyes which never looked straight at you. We fixed four concerts to be
played over ten days. I had brought copies of my programs from Buenos
Aires and we picked four from the lot. Before I left he took me backstage,
where a Steinway concert grand stood well protected in a wooden box. "I'll
have it ready for you on the stage tomorrow morning. It is not new but I
think you will like it." When he asked me to have lunch with him I declined
and said a little shyly, "I'm traveling with a great friend of mine, an Italian
singer, and she is expecting me."

"An opera singer?" he asked. "What is her name?"

"She is a quite famous contralto, Gabriella Besanzoni." At that Braccale jumped in the air. "The great Besanzoni!" he cried. "This is miraculous! I have been trying to get her for two years. Can I come with you and
meet her?" I could not refuse although I felt a little nervous about Gabriella's reaction.

When we found her in the lobby, he rushed up to her without waiting
to be introduced, kissed both her hands, and exclaimed, "Grande diva! I am
the luckiest man in the world to see you here! You must sing for us." She
responded rather coolly but had to smile at his exuberance, and she ac-

cepted his invitation to lunch. During a lengthy meal he persuaded her to sing Amneris with Caruso and, later on, Carmen, which would be revived specially for her. When she mentioned her fee his enthusiasm subsided somewhat but he agreed to it nevertheless. From that moment on, we were caught up again in constant talks with interviewers, with never enough sleep, late luncheons, and late suppers instead of dinner. This was our life in Havana. I tried out the piano, which turned out to be better than I had expected. Gabriella had her rehearsals, first with the pianist and then with the orchestra led by the excellent conductor from Chicago Giorgio Polacco.

My coming concerts worried me as never before. My fingers did not obey me in many difficult passages. I realized what it meant not to have played for weeks. For once I practiced for almost full days in a back room of the Steinway agency, to the great disgust of Gabriella. On the pleasant side there were the divine cigars. No lover of cigars can imagine the voluptuous pleasure of sitting in a café sipping slowly a strong magnificent coffee and smoking rhythmically these divine leaves of Cuba.

Havana had a good conservatory, founded and run successfully by a Dutch musician, Mr. de Blanck. After a dinner at his house he took me to a popular ball attended mostly by the black population. "You will be amazed by their music and dancing." He was right. The Cuban samba has a different rhythm and is even more exciting than the Brazilian one. The band had a most colorful percussion ensemble which sometimes played alone. The dancers had the inimitable sense of rhythm which only the black race possesses. But they used it with almost invisible steps, the men and women clinging together as if glued and dancing faster and faster until the climax.

Both Gabriella and I had a big success. At my first recital I played mainly Chopin, including the Polonaise in A flat, and *Triana* and *Navarra*, which were irresistible to Spanish ears. For the final encore the *Fire Dance* of de Falla won the day. Braccale had visions of money flowing in for both of us and made plans for at least six concerts in the capital and a few others in the provinces. As to Besanzoni, her debut as Amneris in *Aida* was a complete triumph. The press declared unanimously that they had never heard a contralto with a voice of such volume and beauty. Unfortunately her debut was slightly marred by a comical incident. The great Caruso, who sang Radames, had received much publicity for obtaining ten thousand dollars for each performance. There were voices of discontent. The standard of living was very low in Cuba and such a sum represented years of work for an average inhabitant. It was no wonder you could feel a certain hostility in the audience.

And then it happened; in the middle of the famous march in which Radames is acclaimed for his victory, someone threw a stink bomb into the center of the stalls, where it exploded with a tremendous noise and the most dreadful odor. Caruso alias Radames picked up the skirts of his gorgeous white robe, hopped out of the theater and into the street, and galloped across the square to his hotel, pursued by newspaper reporters. One can easily imagine the consternation in the Opera House. I must quickly add that Gabriella behaved like a pharaoh's daughter. Of course, Mr. Braccale and the stage manager ran to the hotel, where they calmed the hero of the Ethiopian wars, and brought him back to his triumph. The evening ended with ovations, flowers, and so on. Both Aida and Amneris shared the success of the incomparable tenor. There was no sequel to the stink-bomb incident.

After my second concert, at which Maria Barrientos was present, this great Catalan coloratura came backstage to see me. I kissed her hand and invited her to lunch with me the next day. During our conversation she asked me, "When are you leaving for New York?" I replied that I had no intention of going at all. She opened her mouth in astonishment. "Why, I saw you announced as soloist with the Boston Symphony Orchestra for six concerts in New York, Philadelphia, Baltimore, Washington, and Boston and as far as I can remember your first performance takes place in a week!" She also admitted that R. E. Johnson was sometimes untrustworthy.

This alarming news hit me like a thunderbolt. I imagined that Johnson's contract and the money I had demanded had been sent but hadn't reached me. I got busy immediately. There was so much to do; concerts in Cuba to cancel, a telegram to be sent to R. E. Johnson announcing my arrival, a room to reserve at the Ritz-Carlton, recommended to me by Barrientos, and, most difficult of all, I had to tell Gabriella. Braccale was disconsolate but understanding. He tried to induce me to come back to Cuba quickly.

I sent a long cable to R. E. Johnson and only then did I find the courage to announce my plans to Gabriella. Her reaction was worse than I had feared; she decided immediately to come with me. "I want to stay with you. I will not remain alone with that devil Braccale in this opera." It took me some time to persuade her to carry out her contract and then join me.

Next morning the following telegram arrived from New York: "Made reservations for you at Biltmore Hotel. Expect to see you in my office upon arrival." Not a very satisfying message. But I didn't care too much, as the Boston Symphony engagement was the real reason for my departure. Before I left I asked a kind member of the company who sang the basso roles to watch over Gabriella and to help her. That same night Gabriella and Braccale saw me off.

Two

A Second Attempt in the United States and Mexican Adventures

10

After a long, tiring journey, Enrique and I arrived late at night in New York City. No one was expecting me; there were no taxis or anything. At the Biltmore, I found a note from Johnson saying that it was too late at night to fetch me and asking me to come and see him at noon in his office. There was another letter. Dagmar Godowsky, whom I hadn't seen since the Vienna days, wrote an enthusiastic welcome and asked me to take her to lunch the next day. My room was pleasant and I found a smaller one for Enrique. Hotels in America did not provide valet's rooms.

This was a sleepless night; there were too many things on my mind. But one thought, a very imperious one, prevailed. I dreaded seeing Muriel Draper again. Since she left London I had heard nothing from her and I always felt that there was something unfinished between us. Searching for the truth, I had to admit that I loved Gabriella but was not in love with her, while with Muriel Draper I felt exactly the contrary; I did not like her but was in love with her. And I was terribly afraid of falling again under her spell. As to Pola, I was convinced that she had found her children again and made peace with her family. That night I was acutely conscious of my complete loss of contact since the beginning of the war with my family and Pola, with Paul Kochanski and Szymanowski and all my friends in Poland. I was too cowardly even to want to think about whether they were alive or dead. Toward morning, after dozing a little while, I had Enrique attend to my things and help me to dress. I had breakfast in my room and telephoned Dagmar, who lived in my hotel. After a warm exchange of greetings I invited her to have lunch with me at the Ritz-Carlton. Then I went to meet R. E. Johnson at his office on Broadway and Thirty-ninth Street, opposite the old Metropolitan Opera House. I found him sitting in a swivel chair. He was broad-shouldered and had the face of an alcoholic: big teary eyes, a large nose of indeterminate color, clean-shaven, with a shock of blond and gray hair. He must have been in his sixties.

"Fine thing!" he shouted. "No sign, no nothing, and here you are. I sold you for the Boston concerts and now they went and took Rachmaninoff instead, couldn't wait." This made me furious.

I shouted back at him, "There I was waiting for your contract and the money in vain. I never received them. I would never have come at all if it hadn't been for Maria Barrientos. I have a mind to go right back to Cuba where I abandoned a tour and was making good money, and I can pick it up again." He stood up and I saw that he was lame. "But you didn't even bother to send me the money I demanded."

Hopping alertly on one leg, he yelled, "I'd sooner drop dead than pay advance money. That guy Carreras must be nuts!" I don't remember exactly how it continued but suddenly he shouted, "Lulu!" A buxom tall woman in her late forties came in. "Lulu," he repeated. "this boy here's got poisonality. I like 'im." Turning toward me, he smiled. "I got some good concerts for you. You don't need to go back to that goddam Cuba. Ysaye has you booked for two concerts in Cincinnata and Frederick Stock's got you with the Chicago Symphony, and I'll get Carnegie Hall for a recital." We parted good friends.

I rushed to the Ritz-Carlton just in time to meet Dagmar. She was late. I sat down to wait for her in the big lounge leading to the restaurant. And the first person who entered the lounge was Muriel Draper.

I jumped to my feet. She hadn't changed. I stammered, "Muriel!" She came toward me with an expression on her face as if she had expected to see me there. When I kissed her hand the strangest phenomenon occurred. I felt free. Free. As if I had never known her. All my apprehensions of the night before vanished. We had a short conversation, exchanging the usual news.

"I divorced Paul—what about you? I heard about your great success in South America."

"Yes," I told her, not without a display of vanity. "The bad times are over."

"I hope to see you sometime." Some friends arrived who took her to lunch. A few minutes later Dagmar came in. She had become a rather good-looking woman of a pronounced Jewish type, no longer the Persian miniature. But she had kept her vitality. Her strong German accent irritated me so soon after the war. But it brought back all the old days in Vienna. During our lunch she managed to relate to me all the gossip past and present. She had made movies, twice as an extra and once with a bit part, but nothing had come of it. I learned all one could learn about the artistic life in New York, which made me feel as if I had lived there for the past two years. But the extraordinary phenomenon prevailed; I simply forgot that Muriel was there in the same room.

Back in my room I was overwhelmed by one telephone call after another. I remember only two important ones. A Mr. Ernst Urchs, the man in charge of concert pianos at Steinway, offered to let me choose an instrument for my concert and to send a baby grand to my hotel room; a good deed of R. E. Johnson. The second call came from my good friend Adolf Bolm, the Diaghilev dancer who led the savage archers in *Prince Igor*. He had heard of my arrival from Dagmar, reminded me of the good days in San Sebastián, and invited me that night for supper. I pretended to be tired but he insisted. "A great friend of yours, Richard Ordynski, will be here and a Russian composer as well, Serge Prokofiev." I jumped out of my chair and screamed, "I'll be there!"

Pierre Monteux had told me just before the war that after their performance together of Prokofiev's first and second piano concertos, he considered Prokofiev the coming great composer. I had played for myself three of his published short pieces.

This supper party was a great event for me. After Szymanowski, Stravinsky, and Ravel, I met here another authentically great composer. Prokofiev looked younger than his years thanks to the boyish expression on his face which he kept all his life. Rather tall, strongly built, a little shy and gauche, he had the features of a white Negro, a flat nose and large red lips. He had white, almost invisible eyebrows and light hair. His complexion was so delicate that he blushed at the slightest provocation. Bolm embraced me and so did Ordynski, whom I knew from the time when he was assistant to Max Reinhardt in Berlin. Prokofiev gave me a vigorous handshake, as they do in Russia, but blushed slightly with discontent when I told him of Monteux's praise and of my joy in meeting him. After a gay session at table with vodka, pressed caviar, and other delicacies, Bolm drew me to the piano, where I played my beloved *Barcarolle* of Chopin and then, on their insistent demand, some of my best Spanish pieces. Prokofiev liked my playing and I felt happier about that than about the success of my whole tour in South America. Again the wonderful thing happened; we became friends that evening and remained so until his premature death in Russia. We were often together, sometimes just the two of us, sometimes with a Greco-Brazilian singer, Vera Janacopoulos, who sang Prokofiev's songs to his liking (she had a dreadful husband, however, a bearded Russian who drank vodka in great quantities).

Prokofiev played me his works in progress; he laughingly admitted that he had picked up two sonatas written for his exams in the conservatory and was now modernizing them. He gave me the proofs of the second sonata as a gift. He was also busy composing his third concerto and some short pieces he called *Visions fugitives*; he played a few of them for me. They sounded strange but had a refreshing novel quality which attracted me right away. Over the long years of my life I came to consider Prokofiev the most important Russian composer. Stravinsky became a cosmopolitan and this is expressed in his music. As to the other composers, one misses in them the authenticity of the Russian musical idiom that is in the works Prokofiev left us.

R. E. Johnson gave me the date of my debut in Carnegie Hall; it was to be on a Sunday afternoon some ten days after my arrival. I made up a program of my most successful pieces, starting with the *Waldstein* Sonata of Beethoven, followed by short pieces of Chopin, three or four by Debussy, *Triana* of Albéniz, and ending with the Schubert-Tausig *Marche militaire*. I spent many hours in the mornings at the piano, trying to give the music a new, careful look after too many routine performances. This debut meant very much to my career and I was painfully conscious of it. R.E. held daily conferences with me about publicity, interviews, and such things, usually in the huge bar of the Biltmore, which looked all through the day like what I imagine the stock market to be. You heard constant shouting, laughing, loud conversations conducted at a distance, complete pandemonium drowned in alcohol. My modest weak martini was not sufficient to allow me to participate in the general euphoria. R.E., good and drunk, had to be helped to his apartment more frequently than not, but the worst part of it was his passion for introducing me to other drunkards, shouting at the top of his voice, "This is Joe Smith, great feller, he can bring a lot of people to the concert. You like music, don't you, Joe?" he would shout at the stupefied face of the man, and then: "This boy's got poisonality, I tell ya. He's gonna knock 'em out."

One day there was a strange letter from Gabriella, sent from Cienfuegos, which I shall never forget: "The Peruvian basso," she wrote, "whom you asked to keep an eye on me and help me if I was in need, began to make the most shameless advances to me immediately. When I repulsed him and refused to speak to him he became violent. He has tried to break into my room using loud obscene language and one day threatening with a knife. I am frightened to death, Arturo. Nobody here has the courage to stop him. You must help me. Please, please ask the Cuban Embassy to do something—I am afraid the man is insane and should be locked up." I was terribly alarmed and felt guilty for having asked that madman to watch over her. I dashed to the Cuban consulate and was immediately received by the consul, to whom I read the letter. He got in touch with the police in Cienfuegos and later in the day gave me the news: the man was indeed dangerous; he had tried to attack the policeman and threatened to kill

Besanzoni. He was under arrest and believed to be not of sound mind. Gabriella sent me tearful thanks and I was pretty happy that the nightmare was over.

New York had become a military camp. The streets swarmed with homecoming soldiers. I saw two huge parades of local regiments which were allowed to pass through the Arch of Triumph on Washington Square. Thousands and thousands of people acclaimed them all along Fifth Avenue. Women threw flowers or rushed up to the boys to kiss them. There were many touching scenes, and a comical incident as well. At a very late hour one night I was awakened by screaming and shouting on my floor. When I opened the door to see what was happening, I saw a man in pajamas exchanging blows with three hotel men who finally forced him into an elevator and, as I heard the next day, threw him into the street. The story was that the man had arrived at the hotel and gone straight to a room occupied by a lady. The house detective had ordered him to leave at once but the man said angrily that the lady was his wife, that he was an officer just back from Europe and had left his luggage and all his papers and belongings on the ship. The puritanical house detective refused to believe him, which infuriated the man, and the battle followed with its nasty result. To the great satisfaction of all the hotel guests, the Biltmore Hotel was sued for $100,000 in damages and had to settle privately for a considerable sum. The man proved to be a war hero and was indeed the husband of the lady. The hypocritical puritanism of the American hotel system received a good slap which I specially enjoyed.

When Gabriella announced that she would join me after her last performance in Cuba, I became worried, remembering our fate at the Panama hotel. Some good friends reassured me. "If the lady has an apartment with a drawing room and an open door to the bedroom, she has the right to receive men guests at any hour of the day or night." Pretty cynical, I thought.

The victory brought the inhabitants of New York to a pitch of euphoria such as I have never witnessed. People were out in the street night and day, laughing, crying, talking to strangers, filling the bars, restaurants, and dancing places to the brim. It was almost dangerous not to respond. Dagmar's friends, and she had many, tried to draw me into the whirlpool, but in vain. I stuck during those days to my piano and to Prokofiev, who ignored the general hysteria. R.E., who was drinking more than ever, mostly in the company of Lulu, slurred, "Lulu, tell 'im about the box office."

"Tickets are selling good," said Lulu, half asleep.

Gabriella announced her arrival by telegram. Her boat was due early in the morning on the day before my concert. I met her at the dock and took her to the Biltmore, where I put her up in the spacious "apartment" on the first floor. My room was on the twelfth. It took a lot of explaining why I couldn't stay in her apartment. When she understood the reason she said, "America non mi piace."*

She recounted at length her recent troubles, using great gestures for dramatic impact. But in doing so she mentioned far too often the name of a good-looking baritone of the company who had been constantly at her side. When I questioned her ironically if he had been of any help in other ways too, she became over-indignant. A nasty quarrel ensued; I even showed some violence. But peace was restored with many tears and kisses. Her arrival and all the rest happening only one day before my first appearance in New York since 1906 had a bad effect on my nerves. I arrived at Carnegie Hall in poor condition, but the well-filled hall and the presence of Prokofiev, Josef Hofmann, and my old friends Joseph Lhévinne and Jacques Thibaud gave me courage and restored my self-confidence.

While bowing to the audience my eyes fell on Paul and Muriel Draper sitting peacefully together. My concert had brought about their reunion for the day at least.

I remember having played quite well, especially the shorter pieces. In the Beethoven my nerves still had the upper hand. R.E., astonishingly sober, was delighted with my success. "I took another date for you—*that* will knock 'em out!" My friends came backstage full of encouraging words and the usual friendly advice for the next program. Hofmann did not show up but I was told that he liked this and that and criticized that and this. Backstage everyone was impressed by the presence of Besanzoni, especially R.E. and Lulu, and Jacques Thibaud accepted an invitation to dine with me in Gabriella's apartment.

All the important critics were present. James Huneker, the most respected critic of the time, wrote a most friendly account but called me a brilliant miniaturist, a qualification not much to my liking. "My old friend" Henry Edward Krehbiel showed his German heavy hand by copying his review on my concert in 1906. In my anger I wished he would drop dead. (He did, a few years later. This is the only murder I've committed in my life.) The other papers were enthusiastic.

* I don't like America.

11

Overnight Besanzoni's presence in New York became the talk of the operatic and managerial circles. My telephone started to ring. The famous director of the Metropolitan Opera House, Giulio Gatti-Casazza, wanted to meet me urgently. The most active concert agency, Wolfson's, was keen on proposing a concert tour for her, and last but not least, the Victor Recording Company, which had Caruso, Destinn, and Paderewski among others, expressed the wish to talk to me about a contract for her. Perplexed by all these calls, I saw my status begin to change from that of a mere pianist to an agent of worldwide importance. For her part, Gabriella took all this as her due; singers, I observed, have no limit to their conceit. This also goes for most conductors.

Gatti-Casazza proved to be not only one of the most successful opera directors but a devilishly hard bargainer to boot. I discovered that I was talented in this way too. It took us two hours to work out a satisfactory contract for Gabriella. However, I could not get her an appearance as Carmen, a part "owned" by the beautiful Geraldine Farrar, who would have let herself be shot before yielding it. So poor Besanzoni was limited to the usual mezzo-soprano and contralto roles which were not always endowed with the importance of Bizet's heroine. At first Gabriella refused to sign the contract without Carmen, but realized after much persuasion on my part the importance of a debut at the famous Met.

Wolfson's offered on the spot ten concerts at three thousand dollars each. This was a magnificent offer but I was worried; my friend, as far as I knew, had no concert repertoire worth speaking about. I had never heard her mention any songs; it was all opera with her. She took my qualms lightheartedly: "Tutullo, you will help me learn a few songs," she announced. This was just what I dreaded.

She urged me with feverish impatience to see the boss of the powerful Victor Company as soon as possible. To be on the same list with Caruso and the other great ones was her dream. Calvin Childs, the president of this new and great industry, made me wait for half an hour before receiving me. He allowed me to sit down and began speaking of the business at hand with a condescension which I only found later in the moguls of Hollywood.

"Does she know anything about recording?" he asked.

"No, I don't think so."

"Well, we'll have to teach her."

"What is your offer?" I asked impatiently.

"What do you mean 'offer'? We'll give her ten percent of the sales like everybody else." I stood up and said, "I'm sorry but I don't think Madame Besanzoni will accept such an offer." At that he chuckled.

"You can bet your life she'll grab it." He didn't convince me. I was ready to leave but he stopped me at the door. "Don't be so rash. If you get her for us I could find you a spot for one or two little pieces for yourself. It'll help your career." I was pale with rage.

"This sounds like a bribe," I said indignantly. "You will have to deal with Besanzoni directly. Anyway, on your machines the piano sounds like a banjo." And I left.

When I got home my story did not appeal to Gabriella. She was so keyed up about making records that she reproached me for not accepting the ten percent and even for not agreeing to the "spots" for myself. A few days later she made the deal with the fellow by herself and signed the three contracts for the following autumn. Thus ended my managerial career.

Aside from all this, I went to a few concerts of great interest. The eighteen-year-old Jascha Heifetz had a sensational success. He amazed me with his beautiful big tone, his perfect intonation and fantastic virtuosity, and all of it produced with a superior air as if it were impossible for him to do otherwise. His bearing lent his performance a certain coldness which made his public for all the years to come applaud him enthusiastically but never warm up to him.

Dagmar Godowsky brought us together one day. She must have given him a colorful picture of me but he observed me searchingly to find out for himself. My playing did not impress him particularly but he was wildly interested in the shops where I bought my ties and shoes and in the golden chain which held my keys safely in my pocket, not to speak of my valet and Besanzoni herself. As the success of my New York debut could not be compared with his sensational one, he treated me as he did all other performers, whether pianists, violinists or cellists, as his satellite. Yet in his strange way he was fond of me.

There were two major orchestras in New York at that time: the old Symphony Orchestra with the veteran Walter Damrosch at its head and a newer one, the New York Philharmonic, which chose as its conductor an Austrian-American, Joseph Stransky. To describe his talents I have a story. At a party with many fun-loving performers present, Godowsky played the cello, Heifetz played the piano, Kreisler played the flute; Stransky conducted.

One day the newspapers announced a third orchestra, to be formed by a young, little-known French musician by the name of Varèse. Nobody really knew him personally but the gossip-hungry New Yorkers hated to admit their ignorance, so they invented little stories. In this case, it became known that the wife of one of the richest bankers in the States had offered Varèse the orchestra as one would offer a birthday cake. This was made plausible by the fact that he was known to be a very good-looking young man. New Yorkers flocked to the much advertised debut of this orchestra and its conductor, who had expressed publicly that musical life in the city was stagnant and that he promised to clean up the musical Augean stable.

The program contained nothing but first performances. There was an unpublished gigue by Debussy, two new works by Bartók, a larger piece by an American modernist, and the concert was to end with one of the never played symphonic poems of Liszt. Carnegie Hall was full, everyone chattering excitedly. Silence fell as the members of the orchestra trickled onto the stage. The appearance of the exceptionally good-looking conductor had a great effect on the female part of the audience but less on the rest, who gave him a tepid reception. It was one of the strangest concerts I have ever witnessed. As had been customary since the war, it began with "The Star-Spangled Banner" while the audience stood at attention. Varèse's beat came down—but it suddenly became evident that he did not know the anthem or perhaps was trying to convey that he didn't. Whatever it was, a muddle ensued: the orchestra stopped and there was loud booing in the hall and a few of the still war-minded shouted some insults. Unperturbed by this prelude, Varèse conducted the announced program without showing the slightest gift for conducting. Everything was shaky—the players looked to their young conductor for help which did not come; the public stopped listening and began commenting loudly on the proceedings. Three quarters of the audience left before the end. The next day the banker's wife dismissed the orchestra—and Mr. Varèse.

One didn't hear of Varèse for years and then after the last war his compositions began appearing on the programs of the post-Schönberg modernists. The leaders of the new movement, Boulez, Stockhausen, Nono, paid high tribute to his genius and proclaimed him as one of their courageous forerunners.

12

At that time a musical epidemic was taking place: the pianola. I had heard here and there in Europe of an invention by a certain Welte-Mignon which made it possible for pianists to hear their own performances played by another piano. All you had to do was insert a perforated roll into these novel instruments they called pianolas. Suddenly in New York musicians spoke of nothing else. The most interested ones were, of course, pianists; there was a lot of money to be earned.

In Europe, Busoni and even Ravel and Debussy were induced to try out this novel means of reproduction. Two big companies came to life in New York: the Aeolian Duo-Art and the Ampico Pianolas, run by the Knabe Company. The former offered me a five-year contract for a fee which, I found out, was lower than normal. I let them wait for my decision and then another offer came up, this time from Ampico, where my old friend George Hochman was now an official. When I mentioned this casually to the Aeolian people, they suddenly became feverishly interested in getting me, this time for a much higher fee. I was not slow in discovering a general attitude among Americans in their commercial dealings; they acted as if they were doing you a favor by offering you a contract, but should a rival company approach you your potential value rose considerably. And so I obtained from Aeolian a five-year contract at $6,000 a year to make three rolls a year. In addition I was reluctantly allowed to make three rolls for Ampico for a round sum. Among these first three was *Triana* of Albéniz.

And now I must tell of a shameful episode in which I shared with three colleagues. Leopold Godowsky, Mischa Levitzki, Leo Ornstein, and I agreed to appear in six cities (not including New York or Boston) playing one piece each on a pianola, then treating the public to a repetition of the piece by the machine, over which we were forced to preside feeling not very proud of ourselves.

I remember another story of these times. R.E. gave me the address of a concert hall in Brooklyn and the hour of my appearance there. On a cold snowy evening, accompanied by Enrique, I traveled by taxi to Brooklyn and when it stopped I sent Enrique to find out where the stage entrance was, as I was all dressed for the concert. After a few minutes Enrique came back all excited and told me that this couldn't be the right place as they were having a costume ball. This meant trouble. Our driver did not know of any other concert place. I decided to find out if there was another hall in this same building. The man I questioned said, "Are you Rubinstein? Good! We are looking forward to your concert." Seeing my very astonished expression, he added, "This is our annual Masonic feast. We picked you for the entertainment." Poor me. I had to play my lovely music to a public dressed up in funny hats and a kind of Oriental garb with chains, most of whom seemed a bit drunk. They were more disposed to joking than listening quietly to my music. Their applause always came too early and both my audience and I were relieved when it was all finished. When I told this story to my American friends, they saw nothing ridiculous in it. They felt respect for any honest work, no matter what, as long as it was for money.

Before my second recital at Carnegie Hall, I had two dates in Cincinnati, one with Eugène Ysaye conducting and the other a violin and piano recital with him. Gabriella insisted on accompanying me. She had heard a record of Wagner's "Preislied" played by the master which had made her weep. "I want to kiss his hands," she cried. "I will beg him on my knees to play it for me."

R.E. told me before my departure, "I made reservations for you in a hotel where the manager is a pal of mine—he's an Irishman," and he added with a twinkle in his eye, "He'll give you two rooms with a door open between them, ha, ha!" He did, too.

Ysaye had us both for dinner the first night. He kissed Besanzoni's hand and she tried to reciprocate but received instead a kiss on each cheek. The two of us exchanged memories of London and spoke of our joy at the victory. He toasted me with a glass of champagne: "A notre prochain concert à Bruxelles!" After dinner in his cozy living room Gabriella begged him with a quivering voice to play the "Preislied" for her. I offered to accompany him by heart. Ysaye became impatient. "I haven't played it in years. You will hear me at our concert." She wouldn't give in. She was ready to cry.

"I came especially to Cincinnati with this hope; please, please, please play it for me." And she actually covered his hand with kisses. The master gave up his resistance. He took out his Guarnerius, tuned it, and gave me the sign to begin.

A dreadful thing happened: With the first notes the hand holding the bow began to tremble. He stopped and tried again but to no avail. It was one of the saddest moments of my life. Ysaye sat down and whispered, "I am tired . . ." Gabriella cried gently and we took our leave in a hurry. Out in the street we couldn't talk for a long while.

The next morning we rehearsed the Beethoven Concerto in G major.

Ysaye was a conductor of the old school; he gave the beat to the orchestra but expected the musicians themselves to make the music sound as it should. The G major has been my favorite Beethoven concerto ever since I heard it played by D'Albert. It is difficult to find the right tempo for the first movement. The piano begins with the theme. A long tutti follows until the piano re-enters. I used to take the theme at a slower tempo in order to give it all the weight and lay a solid foundation for the whole movement. I asked Ysaye at the rehearsal to take up my pace at the beginning of the tutti and reach poco a poco the right tempo. He did not do it, however, and the movement sounded dull in the rehearsal as well as in the concert. I was very upset about it, as I had wanted to do honor to this great artist and wonderful man.

The second movement went beautifully. The stern utterances of the orchestra and the piano's imploring answers were very moving and we held out my last sigh as long as we could before starting the brilliant allegro. The musical public of Cincinnati received our performance with great applause in spite of that first movement. But as we were taking our bows for the third time the golden-hearted Ysaye did something which was to hurt me for years to come in Cincinnati: He made the orchestra stand up, not in their honor but in mine, and made them play a fanfare. The audience was visibly taken aback by this exaggerated expression of a triumph which was not in accord with the actual reception and it took me quite a few concerts to erase the bad impression it made. Poor Ysaye did not notice; he was too happy to have done this for me. The press, although they liked my performance, criticized the fanfare unanimously. "Ces idiots ne reconnaissent pas un vrai grand artiste," said Ysaye. "Mais ils se tuent pour acclamer un as de baseball."*

Our sonata recital was a genuine success. The old master showed his true mettle. The *Kreutzer* Sonata was played by a lion, the D Minor Brahms with the superb pride that lives in the music, and all his Gallic charm came out in the early Fauré sonata. We were really acclaimed and this time without a fanfare. For poor Besanzoni the sonatas did not match the beauty of the "Preislied" on the gramophone record but she knew she had heard a great artist.

Back in New York again I started to work seriously on my second recital. This time it was a Bach toccata, the B minor Chopin sonata and four of the largest pieces from *Iberia*, two early études by Szymanowski, and the *Mephisto Waltz* of Liszt. The audience was smaller at this concert

---

* Those fools don't recognize a really great artist, but they kill themselves over a baseball champion.

than at the first one, to the great disappointment of R.E. But he repeated grimly, "We'll knock 'em out yet!"

He was a full-blooded Irishman. The Irish in America were a sort of benevolent Mafia and were quickly recognizable by a certain twinkle of the eye, their drinking, and their ever-ready fists. Most policemen in New York City were Irish and their commissioner could never be anything else. I found out that the general manager of the Biltmore was Irish too and this accounted for a not small reduction in the price of my room, thanks to R.E. With the help of the manager, Bowman, R.E. ran a series called "The Biltmore Musicales" and would engage for these concerts two or three artists who had nothing in common; there would be a light operetta singer, a clavecinist who played Scarlatti, and a violinist of not the first order. As you may have guessed, he made me play. I did not boast to my friends about it.

These "musicales" were very fashionable thanks to an enterprising man named Bagby, who began them, using this French denomination, at the Waldorf-Astoria. The series was extremely chic, the subscribers being mostly the wives of Vanderbilts, Rockefellers, Goulds, and the like who would drop in for part of the program while shopping. The tickets were expensive and the house was usually sold out. Mr. Bagby's hobby was the luncheons after the concert, to which all available titled Europeans were invited. You would meet at his table such and such ex-archduke of Austria, the Princess Marina of Greece, who later became Duchess of Kent, Prince Obolensky, and some great names of New York society. At these luncheons he would introduce "his" artists as if he were showing prize cattle at a fair. If a performer canceled a concert, he took it easily but never pardoned an absence at a luncheon.

Mr. Bowman was then appointed general manager of the new Commodore Hotel, which was to be a deluxe skyscraper connected to Grand Central Station. For its opening R.E. suggested a super concert to inaugurate the super musicales of the Commodore. It is hard to believe but these two men succeeded in getting for this concert Caruso, Mischa Elman, Mary Garden, and me. For a whole year all the menus of the Biltmore restaurants bore our four names printed below the cheeses with the announcement: "Next year at the Commodore."

Far be it from me to make fun of New York's musical life. As a matter of fact, it had made giant strides since my last visit in 1906. The finest conductors, best instrumentalists, and greatest singers flocked to America. A real enthusiast of music, Mrs. Charles Lanier, founded the Friends of Music, which, after a modest beginning, soon became highly active. Artur Bodanzky, one of the young conductors at the Metropolitan, became its

musical adviser and led its orchestra. He gave brilliant performances of the
then much neglected Schumann and Schubert symphonies and successful
concert versions of the finest pieces of the Wagner operas. There was also a
choir called Schola Cantorum, conducted by an old friend of mine from
Berlin, Kurt Schindler. He was an excellent choirmaster and gave a yearly
series of concerts at which the best music was sung.

The trio of "untouchable" pianists was still Paderewski, Rachmaninoff, and Hofmann. Paderewski gave two victory concerts before becoming
Premier of Poland, and Rachmaninoff, who had arrived during the war by
way of Sweden, was an immediate hit as a pianist as well as composer. I
admired particularly his beautiful singing tone, so rare among pianists.
Hofmann was still the old wizard of dynamics but his playing never gave me
much pleasure. There was Godowsky with his fabulous technique, as well as
my old friend Ossip Gabrilówitsch, very refined, the husband of Mark
Twain's daughter and creator of the Detroit Symphony Orchestra. Harold
Bauer, an erstwhile violinist turned pianist of the very first rank, was an
especially fine player of chamber music. Among the younger generation I
had two successful rivals: Benno Moiseiwitsch and Mischa Levitzki. Joseph
and Rosina Lhévinne were both teaching at the Juilliard School, which
became one of the great conservatories of the world. The king of violinists
was still Fritz Kreisler, who in spite of fighting on the other side during the
war, was received with open arms in the States. Among the quite young
ones, Heifetz had won out against Zimbalist and Elman. The few American
composers were mostly replicas of well-known Europeans. MacDowell tried
to follow in the footsteps of Grieg, and Griffes tried to put some Debussy
flavor into his compositions, and there were a few others, mostly insignificant. The Metropolitan Opera House, the best without doubt in the world,
could afford all the famous singers and it flourished under Gatti-Casazza.

The only satisfaction I derived from my second recital at Carnegie
Hall was the review of James Huneker, in which he referred to me as "Pan
Artur," the polite Polish form of address, and apologized for calling me a
miniaturist. He fully recognized my talent and even showed a rare bit of
enthusiasm. Mr. Krehbiel did not attend the concert. The result of both
concerts was nothing to write home about; engagements did not flow in.
R.E. did succeed in getting me a few important engagements such as a
concert with the Detroit Symphony and Gabrilówitsch, a Brahms concerto
in New York under Damrosch, but several of the others were on the order
of the Biltmore musicales. Anyway, he offered me a solid tour of fifteen
concerts for the following season beginning in January 1920.

13

My social life was very active and Mrs. Lanier became a great and useful friend. She invited me to luncheon parties where I met interesting people of all sorts. There was Bob Chanler, my wild friend, and Adolph Ochs, the publisher of *The New York Times*. After one of these luncheons, sipping coffee, Mr. Ochs involved me in a political discussion about postwar matters in Europe and suddenly exclaimed, "Why don't you write a series of articles for my paper?" I blushed at such an incredible proposition. I said, "My ideas about the events might be useful but I can't see myself putting anything down on paper." And so I missed a profession as political commentator.

I must say more about Mrs. Lanier. She was small and dainty, always extremely elegant, with gray hair on a small head, a thin-lipped mouth, cold gray eyes, and a high-pitched metallic voice which frightened a lot of people away from her. Her husband, a wealthy banker, was so shy that at cocktail parties at their house people took him for a butler (he did look a little like one) and would order their drinks from him. A little characteristic trait of his wife: she liked to take me driving in Central Park in her open car to "talk music," as she put it. Thanks to her intervention, the Friends of Music had me as soloist.

I still had no news and no means of getting any from my family or my friends in Poland. Rumor had it that many people had fled from Poland to Russia during the German invasion. I was sure that the Kochanskis and Szymanowskis had done so. My sister Jadwiga and her family had been in Moscow until the Bolshevik Revolution, but since then there was no means of knowing anything. I planned, of course, to go back to Europe to be nearer to them all. My next tour in Spain was due in late autumn.

One day I received bad news from Stravinsky, who since before the war had been living in Vevey in Switzerland. He wrote that he was penniless—Diaghilev and ballet had no means of helping him. Could I do something about it in America?

I did not lose a moment. I turned to Mrs. Lanier and it was a good choice. She asked her husband to open a list for contributions to save the greatest composer of the time from the worst. The Laniers opened with $5,000. I proudly pitched in with $500. A few more contributions came in and soon the good sum of $10,000 was sent to Stravinsky. I received an exuberant letter of thanks with the announcement that he was composing his first piece for piano for me. "I wrote a few piano pieces at the conservatory but nothing else since then and this is the first piece for the real piano as I conceive it. I will send you my manuscript as soon as it is finished." One can imagine my joy; the first piece for the piano by Stravinsky dedicated to me.

Gabriella and I had a wonderful time in New York. She found some friends from Italy singing at the Met and I saw a lot of my fellow musicians. We also went often to the movies. We both adored Charlie Chaplin, Douglas Fairbanks, and Mary Pickford. The Polish beauty Pola Negri had become a big star in Hollywood. It was fascinating to watch the growing hold of the cinema on the public. We saw a musical comedy in which the young Fred and Adele Astaire had a sensational success. The theaters, dominated by the powerful Barrymores, were closed to us because Besanzoni knew nothing but Italian along with a sprinkling of Spanish which we used at random. When I went to the Laniers it was without Gabriella, as our relationship and the language problem made it difficult. My contacts with my musician colleagues never resulted in warm friendships. They constantly "talked shop," as one says—managers, fees, travel expenses, gossip about each other, but hardly ever a serious word about music. All through my life I suffered because of this sad characteristic. The only exceptions were the great composers Stravinsky, Prokofiev, Szymanowski, who honored me with their friendship, and of course my alter ego, Paul Kochanski. I preferred the company of men of letters, and in many countries up to this day they are my frequent companions and some of them are my closest friends.

Paul Draper came often to see me at my hotel, mostly in the early mornings, when we chatted about the glorious days in London. He was his same charming self. He and Muriel had divorced when she arrived in America and he lived now with his brother George, who was a doctor and, together with his wife and his sister Ruth, kept a sharp watch over his unfortunate addiction. He liked Besanzoni and we were often invited for dinner. The linguistic difficulties were largely compensated for by her singing. Paul was especially amazed by the range of her voice. He himself sang in several oratorios with the Boston Symphony but did not risk a solo recital as his voice had weakened considerably.

Gabriella planned to go back to Rome after the American season was over and I was burning to get to London, where I had a better chance of getting news from Poland. But fate in the person of a Mexican impresario disrupted our plans. Señor José Rivera came specially to New York to engage Gabriella to sing in *Carmen* and other operas. He had opened a season in Mexico City, where Titta Ruffo was the main star at the moment. The offer was generous. The acutely professional Besanzoni hated to refuse a chance to sing in a season of such importance; even Caruso had promised to join the company. "But I shall not go without Arturo!" she screamed. This was an outburst not only of love but of fear of the civil war raging in that country. I refused to go. I was set on going back to Europe. And then Señor Rivera started to work on me, dangling before me an offer of three concerts at a good price in gold. All this, however, did not shake my resolution until Gabriella began to remind me, with great pathos and dramatic gestures, of her immense sacrifice in not returning to Rome and her mother after the war, and crossing the continent instead, with terrible hardships, to join me. I yielded unhappily. I could not do otherwise. We signed our contracts but had to leave separately because Besanzoni's first performance was quite soon and I had still some pianola business to finish in New York.

One night at the Biltmore, after Gabriella's departure, Efrem Zimbalist proposed to take me to a private room for a little gambling. There I found Fritz Kreisler, Franz Kneisel of the famous quartet, Andrés de Segurola, a Catalan singer with a large monocle in his eye, a few other less known musicians, and the editor of the *Musical Courier*, Leonard Liebling. I felt safe in such company and we sat down to a little game of chemin de fer. Gambling even in private was prohibited in the United States. We each bought one hundred dollars' worth of chips and started to play in a friendly atmosphere. I played rather recklessly, shouting "Banco" constantly and often keeping my hand after three "coups." Playing that way you can be an easy loser but that night I was lucky. I won the nice sum of six or seven hundred, mainly from de Segurola, who reminded me of it for the rest of my life. We played again the next night and I won again—more than just a few dollars.

My long journey to Mexico was to start on a Sunday morning at eight o'clock. Enrique was so pleased at the prospect of living again in a Spanish-speaking country he packed my things on Saturday humming Galician folk tunes. The telephone rang. Mr. Leonard Liebling invited me for dinner at his house and added, "We'll have a little game after dinner."

"Thank you, but it is impossible. I have to be up at seven for my train to Mexico."

"But you have to dine," he insisted, "and you can leave whenever you want."

I made a condition: "I can stay until one o'clock and no later."

"O.K., O.K.," he replied.

At dinner there were some friends of his, most of whom I did not know except for two or three I had met only casually somewhere. They were all wealthy businessmen, Liebling told me. After a short meal, which his wife served in order to keep the whole thing secret, we sat down to play. I had my checkbook in my pocket and felt the hungry eyes of those men after my money. Liebling must have informed them that I was an easy victim.

It turned out to be my night of triumph. I had nothing but eights or nines throughout the whole evening and before midnight I was ahead by $7,500. Everybody was losing to me, including the host, who was out for a thousand dollars. I sold chips constantly, getting IOU's in exchange. When one o'clock came I felt that it was impossible to leave; my winnings were too high.

I tried hard to lose most of this money. I played not only recklessly but foolishly; I held my hands till they broke down. But my luck never faltered even though I did succeed in getting down to $3,500 by four in the morning, at which point I had to leave. "We are going on playing," they said.

"What shall I do with my IOU's?" Liebling, our host, gathered up the IOU's lying on the table in front of me and said, "Don't worry. Give me the name of your bank. I'll collect the money and put it into your account."

Back at my hotel I couldn't sleep for a while but then fell asleep so soundly that Enrique had a hard time waking me. I struggled into my clothes, had some breakfast, and off we went for the long journey south.

All the way to Laredo, Texas, the frontier with Mexico, I read books, newspapers, whatever I could get my hands on, interrupted only by the uninteresting food in the diner. From the Mexican side of Laredo it took us long hours to reach the capital.

The train stopped at unexpected places; passengers spoke of bandits, of trains being attacked, of rails being torn up. What a relief when we finally arrived!

14

At the Hotel Victoria, where I was to stay, they told me that Madame Besanzoni was at rehearsal. Mr. Rivera had not been gracious enough to meet me at the station.

I settled down in our apartment. We had a double bedroom and a charming living room, which had a not too bad piano in it.

When she returned, Besanzoni gave me bad news: "Rivera has gone bankrupt after the season with Titta Ruffo, who did not draw. I was on the verge of going back to New York, but a consortium of bankers and other people guaranteed the season. Rivera didn't even have the money to advertise your concerts, but the Teatro Arbeu, which is opposite the hotel, has a poster up and your concert is in three days."

In the afternoon, Mr. Rivera appeared and tried to calm my fears about the concert. "What Titta Ruffo did to me is disgraceful. But don't worry about your debut."

I saw my program printed on the poster. It was the usual one I played for a debut. I found an astonishingly good Steinway on the stage and spent the two days either at my piano in the hotel or in the theater. My audience, because of the lack of advertisement, did not reach a hundred. I know many artists who get frightfully discouraged by an empty hall. But I always used to make a point on such occasions to play better than ever, because the few people in the hall are the elite of a full house. The ones to blame are those walking up and down in the street who didn't come into the hall. And so I played with all my heart; and this meager audience responded. Mr. Rivera did not show up. Neither did my fee. Gabriella came backstage in a fury. "Questo mascalzone!" she said, meaning Rivera. Behind her, however, was a gentleman who, in perfect English, introduced himself as Mr. Rafael Sánchez, a lawyer, and seemed extremely enthusiastic. "I am ashamed for Mexico because of what that man did to you. The whole city should flock to your concerts. If you allow me, I shall take this case into my hands. We can annul the contract with Rivera even if he pays your fee tomorrow." (Fees are usually paid during the intermission.) "The Teatro Arbeu has no company playing at the moment because of the Civil War, so I can have it at your complete disposal. Please allow me to attend to all these matters and I shall try to bring you some news tomorrow." This man inspired confidence; I allowed him to take over.

Gabriella had her own troubles; she was not happy with the company. "But I have found a dear friend of mine from Rome, Ada Paggi, who sings small soprano roles. She arrived here from Chicago."

Mr. Rafael Sánchez came the following morning with good news. "This man Rivera," he said, "has no idea how to run concerts. He was a promoter of bullfights and was ill-advised to go into opera. I spoke to the owner of the Teatro Arbeu and he is willing to let you give concerts in his theater for two months at eighty-five percent for you and fifteen percent for himself. In addition, he agreed to be responsible for publicity." I, who had never heard of such an offer before, was perplexed for a moment. "This is a very generous offer," I said, "but what the devil shall I do in this theater for two months? I am not a show." He smiled. "I know the people of my city; when they like an artist they go all out for him." He insisted on announcing six concerts on subscription, which I accepted with misgivings. "The best way of doing it," he continued, "is to play Tuesday, Thursday, Saturday nights, and a Sunday matinee." "Good heavens," I cried, "remember what a poor house I had the other night! Wouldn't it be better to give another try with one single concert?" He brushed this away with colossal assurance. "Wait and see . . . Those hundred persons of yesterday will bring thousands more to your concerts."

And by Jove, he was right. I played twenty-six concerts in succession, four a week, as we planned, to full houses. Twenty-three of them in the Arbeu and an additional three at popular prices in a huge cinema shack on the outskirts of Mexico City. It was an overwhelming task making the programs for this avalanche of concerts. The first six were not difficult. I had played them all recently; but after the second of these concerts it became clear that I would have to continue. The only thing to do was to work thinking of the future. I hardly touched the programs of the first six but worked on four new programs and I adopted this system the entire seven weeks. To be truthful, I did find some stratagems for facilitating my task. An all-Chopin recital would contain pieces which I had played before, "repeated on public demand." I did the same with the *Iberia* of Albéniz. With time I became reckless, playing free arrangements of orchestral or operatic or ballet pieces I particularly liked—the dance of *Salome*, my arrangement of *Oiseau de feu* of Stravinsky, a fantasy I made up from the *Coq d'or* of Rimsky-Korsakov, of course the Wagner-Liszt *Tristan*, my own arrangement of "The Ride of the Valkyries," and I even learned a dreadful arrangement of the overlong Mexican anthem by Manuel Ponce, which I had to repeat at each concert. For a base I gathered all the Beethoven sonatas that I had studied since the early age of ten, much neglected Schumann and Mendelssohn, not so much Brahms, for whom the public showed a marked antagonism, and all the moderns whose music I had in my bag. Mexico City had a first-class music store, German of course, where I found all the sheet music I needed. My free evenings I spent, naturally, at the Teatro Esperanza Iris, where the opera season was going full blast. Most of the singers stayed at the Victoria, where we began to feel like a family. Gabriella's Carmen was, as everywhere, a triumph. The Mexicans went wild with enthusiasm over her, showered flowers on the stage, followed her in the streets, and besieged her for autographs. As for myself, my Sunday matinees gave my young enthusiasts the happy occasion to carry me on their shoulders across the street to the hotel; after which exploit they insisted on our appearance on our balcony and shouted, "Viva Polonia! Viva Italia!"

And all this happened in the midst of a terrible civil war. The President, Venustiano Carranza, who had dictatorial powers and who was not trusted by the people, was suspected of having banks attacked by his policemen disguised as bandits. Men in their mid-twenties were promoted to generals and visited bars and restaurants with big revolvers in both hip pockets. We were present once in an elegant bar when one of those "generals" started shooting at the bulbs in the chandelier to show off his marksmanship. Sometimes it was impossible to leave the theater for an hour or two after the concert because there was shooting in the streets. We read horrible tales of things happening in other cities. Trains were assaulted and bandits roamed the country. But nothing could dampen the incredible vitality of these people. At the Victoria, which was more a conservatory than a hotel, one heard singing and playing the whole day. There was the tenor Pergile, a great soprano, Rosa Raisa, and her husband, Giacomo Rimini. Pergile was a great cook and treated us to luscious minestrone and spaghetti. Gabriella couldn't cook but ate enough for two. The general euphoria had something to do with the fact that after every show our fees were paid in beautiful twenty-peso gold pieces. We used to amuse ourselves building piles of gold on the table and looking at them with wonder. Thanks to Carranza, paper money did not exist anymore.

One day will always remain in my memory. Gabriella had to sing *Carmen* that night. I was practicing in the living room when she shouted from the other room, "I won't sing tonight!" When I asked the reason for this outburst she shrieked bloody murder: "They took Frasquita away from Ada Paggi."

I soon found out what really happened. Her friend Ada Paggi sang the role of Frasquita at Gabriella's performances but some "demonic intrigue," as she called it, at the theater was trying to poison her existence by giving that small role to another singer whom Besanzoni didn't like. I tried to calm her, but that only made her more hysterical. "Everybody is against me," she shouted, "even you." The thing became intolerable. She sent word to the opera that she refused to sing that night. Back came a stern warning answer: "You know our laws. You will have to sing whether you want to or not." Gabriella stamped her feet. "I'll show them; my public will defend me and if anyone tries to do something to me, they might get killed." As the day went on, things became worse. Gabriella went to bed and declared in her strong voice, "I am ill."

In the late afternoon, an official doctor arrived. She tried to keep him out, but helped by two strong men from the management, he forced his way in, looked her over, and declared in writing that she was perfectly well. When the time came to dress, Gabriella wouldn't move. My soothing advice was met with hateful accusations of treason. At zero hour, two policemen appeared and ordered her to dress and leave with them for the theater; if not, they would arrest her. In silence, Gabriella dressed, put on her makeup, flung on a fur coat and hat, and was ready to go. At the door she turned to me. "Arturo, if they try to kill me, you must protect me." She left flanked by the two policemen and I followed meekly to the Esperanza Iris. The policemen led her backstage; I took my usual seat on the aisle of the stalls. The bullfight music of the overture resounded; I was pretty glad that things at last seemed to be going normally. The duet of the brave Micaela (I was on her side) and Don José soothed my nerves. The orchestra played the signal for Carmen's appearance and then . . . a horrible surprise. Besanzoni ran down the steps dressed in her street clothes, minus the fur coat but with hat and all. After a moment of stupor, loud protests broke out in the hall. She sang her first bars more perfectly than ever. But when she approached Don José for the famous Habanera, she stopped dead, raised her hands to silence the public, and in her mixed Spanish and Italian shouted ugly accusations against the injustice of Spanish laws and the sadistic cruelty of the management. Her voice was soon drowned out by insulting and threatening shouts from the gallery. The two brave policemen appeared on the stage and dragged her away. I sat in a sweat, feeling not enough of a hero to fight infuriated men armed with knives and pistols. So I rushed quickly backstage both to find out what had happened and to be able to hide somewhere. I found Gabriella in a state of complete collapse. Then automatically she began to put on her costume and returned to the stage. The conductor started the accompaniment of the Habanera and Gabriella became again the great Besanzoni. The Mexican public, like the Spanish, had been brought up at bullfights, and they would threaten and insult the torero for the smallest show of cowardice, but a moment later, after one or two glorious *pases*, they would applaud him in ecstasy. The same thing happened that night. The performance finished in triumph. Happy as a lark, I went to fetch her for supper. Two friends of ours had invited us to the only restaurant open at that hour. I was ravenously hungry, having spent the day practically without food. Gabriella said in a tone that admitted no discussion: "We must go immediately to all the newspapers to give them the real story." A big blow to my empty stomach. It took the four of us, in a miserable taxi, three hours to make the rounds of the important papers, where she found a lukewarm response to her incriminations.

At 3 a.m. we reached the restaurant. The supper was excellent—our friends saw to that. Gabriella enjoyed the food wholeheartedly, especially a salad of which she had three helpings. "What is it made of?" she asked. "I would like to know the recipe, my mother is a good cook." The chef gave her the information: "We have in our country some very tasty worms called *gusanos* which give a wonderful flavor to our salads." For a moment she was stunned, then came an inhuman shriek: "Assassini!" and Gabriella ran out of the room and down the street. We caught her only at the second block, still shouting, "Assassini!" Throughout the early hours of the morning I had to hold her head while she vomited incessantly.

Paggi sang Frasquita again and it turned out that the other singer, who was in the chorus, had a clause in her contract for two appearances as Frasquita. It was not easy to work on my programs in such circumstances. Even so, I found time to work with Gabriella on her concert repertoire for the United States. I played for her some of the finest Schubert, the best Schumann, and some easier French songs—no Brahms of course. She listened with great attention, seemed to be moved by Schumann's "Ich grolle nicht," and then she asked, "Conosci 'La Mattinata' de Leoncavallo?" When I shook my head she continued: "E la più bella canzone del mondo."* That settled it. I advised her to rely mainly on her operatic arias and on "Mattinata."

The Spanish Club in Mexico honored me with a banquet at which they presented me with a ring with a large emerald cabochon flanked by two diamonds. A regal present. Unfortunately the setting was not in good taste. The beautiful stones were set in three different shades of gold. Later in Paris I learned that the pilots during the war had rings made of black wood in order to touch it for good luck. I went to Cartier to have my stones set in black wood. "It is impossible," I was told. "Wood wouldn't hold the stones securely, but we can make it in gold covered by black enamel." This ring was much admired. When I wanted to present it to my wife, she refused to take it. "This is your good-luck ring, Arthur." I think she was right. As I write now it is still on my finger.

Due to the Civil War, musical life suffered. Talented Mexicans had left for other countries. There was no symphony orchestra and the foundations of a Palacio de Bellas Artes, which later became the temple of music, were abandoned for lack of funds.

The composer Manuel Ponce, a genuine talent, became a friend and dedicated to me a few piano pieces. His music was pleasant but not important. Still, he left a good violin concerto and a concerto for guitar, often played by Segovia. He came to all my concerts indefatigably with his charm-

---

* Do you know "La Mattinata" by Leoncavallo? It is the most beautiful song in the world.

ing wife and later in Paris we continued our friendly relations. He wrote casually a little song that he gave away for nothing. Later it was printed in the United States and sung on the radio by a crooner, becoming a smash hit all over the country. Heifetz arranged it for the violin and played it constantly on public demand. Ponce never received a penny for it. When I told him what he was missing by not putting in a claim, he smiled philosophically. "Let them have it."

My marathon of concerts came to an end. Rafael Sánchez was exultant. All through my series I followed his advice. We had "Three Last Concerts," then another three "Ultimos Recitales," and finally four rounds of "Goodbye to Mexico." The last concert was rather touching. I received a shower of flowers and a few lovely presents of Mexican craftsmanship, a sarape and the famous Mexican hat. At my hotel, under the bed I had a small case filled with gold twenty-peso coins; Gabriella had another one. We sometimes piled them up to see who had more.

The day of my farewell concert, a small bearded Jew from Cracow entered my room. "My name is Granat and I own a great movie theater in a suburb. Would you like to give three additional concerts in my theater? It holds more than three thousand people, so we could charge lower prices." I laughed out loud. "You are out of your head. If I played again after twenty-three concerts, they would chase me out of the city."

"I can bet you that we would have three sellouts," he said, with a quiet assurance that I found later in my famous manager Sol Hurok. To lure me, he brought out a sack of gold and said, "I can give you a fixed fee of five thousand pesos." I readily accepted. He was right. The three concerts were packed and to my great astonishment most of my followers of the Teatro Arbeu were present. Of course, the programs were made out of practically nothing but encore pieces, which the popular audience thoroughly enjoyed, grateful for the absence of the Beethovens.

One day in Mexico late in June the papers announced that a treaty had been signed at Versailles in the same hall where Bismarck had dictated his conditions to France in 1871.

By now the provincial capitals were clamoring for concerts. I gave a few in Guadalajara, and later on my way to Europe via New York, Gabriella and I appeared together in San Luis Potosí and the important city of Monterrey, where I was obliged to exchange my lovely golden pesos for American dollar bills; however, I did succeed in hiding a thousand pesos in gold. Gabriella had to go back to Mexico for her appearances with Caruso. We parted without shedding tears, as she was anxious to sing with the great tenor and I couldn't wait to get back to the old country.

15

In New York the season was over, the Army home. Life was not so feverish and the city seemed to be taking a rest. R. E. Johnson was much impressed by my tales of Mexico. "Lulu, did ya hear that?" he cried from his swivel chair. "He says he gave twenty-six concerts in that goddamn city—I think thirteen would sound good enough." He turned to me. "I guess you got a lotta dough." When he heard that they paid in gold: "God Almighty, if I could get my hands on *that*." Getting back to our business, he was optimistic about my next tour in January: "We got Boston with Monteux for you, and that guy Stokowski will give you a spot. Of course, Ysaye has you again; I might even talk him into a fiddle and piano recital here in New York." I lent to all this a half-believing ear, but still it sounded encouraging.

The Draper family, including Paul, left for somewhere on Long Island. Dagmar returned to California and all the musicians of my acquaintance had disappeared. I was lucky in securing a cabin on an English steamer bound for Liverpool. It was little short of a miracle. Everybody I knew craved to go to Europe. I sent a long telegram to Mrs. Bergheim to announce my arrival. She always understood my allergy to letter writing. She was the only one I could count on to be in London, as I had no idea what had happened to other friends.

At the Ritz-Carlton grill a Pole from Chicago came up to my table and said excitedly, "There is a Polish consulate in New York!" This was a bombshell. He accompanied me to a small office on the West Side where a plaque said "Consulate of the Republic of Poland" and gave the floor number. In the office were two men who knew who I was; one of them informed me that the consul hadn't arrived yet from Poland, that he was the vice-consul and in charge of the consulate. I asked him timidly, "Are you entitled to give me a Polish passport?"

"It depends on what document you can present." At that I produced my Spanish passport, where he found the item about my being recognized by King Alfonso as a citizen of independent Poland in the year 1917. He was beyond himself with amazement. "You can be proud," he exclaimed, "to be the first person to be recognized by another nation as a citizen of free Poland. I shall give you a temporary document right away but I must keep your precious passport." The vice-consul, Pan Kwapiczewski, who was later transferred to Washington, is still alive and still my friend.

Before sailing, I inquired at my bank to see if the deposit had been made by Mr. Liebling. The answer was negative. I took a chance and called on him at his office at the *Musical Courier*. I knocked at the door. "Come in," he said, but as I entered, I noticed on his face an expression of disagreeable surprise. After the exchange of greetings, I said, "You must have lost the address of my bank, because I didn't find the deposit." He answered quickly and nervously: "Ah, Rubinstein, I should have written to you. There was a fellow with us whom we found cheating. There was a little scandal and we returned the IOU's to the owners, we called the whole thing off." This easy lie infuriated me. "Look here," I said, "I came on invitation to your house with my checkbook in my pocket, ready to pay at any moment any eventual debt; what would have happened if I had lost?" He said, "I am sure they would have given you your money back." I laughed at that. "You are fortunate that I don't remember the names of the players and can't find out the truth, but whatever happened, I hold you responsible, as you were the host, and I came on your invitation; so I exact from you the full amount of thirty-five hundred dollars."

"You must be crazy. Why should I pay up for other people?"

"Then pay the thousand dollars of your own IOU, which you stole from me." Now he became cynical. "After you left"—he smirked—"I started winning and I haven't been paid either." I stood up and said to him sternly, "In Europe, debts of cards are debts of honor. As you don't seem to have any, if I ever find you in a friend's house I shall make you leave immediately." And I left, the loser of this nice sum of $3,500.

Three

Europe After the War
and the Gay Twenties

16

The crossing to England was pleasant in spite of the over-crowded ship and excited passengers. Enrique was put into a lower deck—I could get nothing better for him—and so I had to look after myself. I was already spoiled for the rest of my life. After the lengthy and tiresome customs and unloading of luggage in Liverpool, and the crowded train to London, I arrived exhausted but happy at Euston Station. Good old Mrs. Bergheim was there to meet me. "You must come and stay with me, Arthur dear, it is your home." Her generous English heart was still there, intact through all the war and its hardships. I accepted her invitation gratefully. The poor lady was taken aback a little bit seeing my two big trunks and other bags and almost fainted when I presented Enrique. To hear me say, "This is my valet," left her open-mouthed after knowing me during my penniless years. She took me to her car with my hand baggage and Enrique followed in a taxi with all the rest. Nothing had changed at Belsize Park. Wiggins was still there and stared in bewilderment at Enrique. Enrique somehow succeeded in making himself understood by clownish gesticula-tion. During and after dinner, the tales of my travels and adventures took hours. The old lady was exultant about my success. With her one-track English mind she was indifferent to all the countries I mentioned but Mex-ico. "Johnny [her husband] found fine orchids in Mexico in Yucatán; it must have been lovely for you to see them." I blushed with shame to have to admit that Yucatán was the one province I did not visit. When I asked her about wartime in England she reduced the conflagration to a domestic difficulty. "It was hard to get tea and sugar and other things I can't think of. It was becoming difficult to heat the hothouses."

Early next day I started telephoning and found to my joy that the Gandarillas were in town. I rushed that same afternoon to see them. It was a great reunion. Juanita had news from Chile of course and she and José Antonio listened to my stories with breathless interest. They had seen Sylvia Sparrow and Lionel Tertis. The only one missing was Eugenia Errazuriz, who had left for France.

It was good to see London itself again and the brave English people recovering from their four-year-long nightmare. They were proud of their victory but did not boast of it, and as befitted their proverbial fairness, they had praise for the bravery and the fighting spirit of the enemy. My close friends reflected this happy atmosphere. I responded to all this with a great display of personal vanity which exploded in a shopping tour in Bond Street. At Aspreys, the great place for expensive luxuries, I bought the best lady's handbag in the finest black crocodile for Mrs. Bergheim, French perfume for Sylvia, and a shower of flowers for everybody. I enjoyed to the full the effect these presents would make after my ever-miserable, penniless past in London, and I was not disappointed. Mrs. Bergheim was all flushed with excitement and exclaimed, "My Johnny never gave me such a beautiful handbag, but I always knew you were generous." Overnight I became "the rich friend."

A London concert manager, Mr. Mitchell, from a well-established agency proposed six concerts in England and Scotland for the coming season. "I've booked already the famous Emma Calvé and Jacques Thibaud and they would both love to have you as the third artist for this tour." A strange combination, I thought, but I accepted, hoping for much fun with Jacques Thibaud, who was a lover of practical jokes, and I looked forward to meeting Emma Calvé, who was, as far as I knew, the first Carmen. She must have been pretty old, I assumed. I observed that the English feel a predilection for their favorite artists when they reach a biblical age, but do not show enough appreciation for the talented young ones. We had a lovely chamber music session at Sylvia's studio with Albert Sammons, Lionel Tertis, and Warwick Evans.

It was a thrill to hear that there was now a Polish Embassy in London and I went to pay my respects to the Prince and Princess Sapieha—I had known the Princess in Warsaw. It was only then in London that I perceived clearly what had happened to our old world after the war. I knew now that the days of the Belle Epoque were over. After learning all the facts, my greatest admiration went to that man of great insight and integrity, President Woodrow Wilson. To begin with, the war could not have been won without his decision to enter the conflagration with all the might of the United States; and this Princeton professor hated war. His Fourteen Points and the plan for a League of Nations were monuments of statesmanship. Besides my admiration for this man, there was also a deep gratitude for what he did for the country of my birth. Paderewski emerged as a national hero. His fiery speeches roused the millions of Poles in Chicago, Buffalo, and Detroit to fight for the freedom of Poland. It was he who induced his great friend Colonel House, Wilson's right-hand counselor, to convince the

President of the need to restore the freedom and unity of Poland. Wilson did even better than that: he obtained for the city of Danzig and its ominous corridor an outlet to the sea with stronger frontiers on all sides. Paderewski, who had lived in voluntary exile in Switzerland, was brought back to Poland in triumph and was offered the first premiership by the grateful citizens. As such, he was the Polish envoy at the Versailles Treaty in June. Later in Paris they told me about his official visit to Clemenceau, who received him with great exclamations: "And who do I see here but the great Paderewski! I can hardly believe it is the great pianist before me, the great Paderewski! And now you are the Premier of Poland." Paderewski nodded. "What a comedown . . ." said the old tiger.

At the Sapiehas', I met my friend Richard Ordynski, who was on his way to Warsaw. As I had neither sent nor received news from my family, I begged him to try to find my sisters in Warsaw and give them fifty Mexican gold pieces for my parents and a cashmere shawl for my mother. Richard told me that there was practically a famine in Poland, so I gave him also an assortment of the most useful foods, such as powdered milk, nicely packed by Fortnum and Masons, which I asked him to deliver.

The joyful London days came to an end and it was time to return to Spain. On my way, I spent a few days in Paris, where I found my brother Ignacy at his room in the rue Campagne Première. He hadn't changed during the four years but had definitely abandoned his violin. He lived in close friendship with a French family, a couple with a grownup daughter. The husband was a reporter for the leftist paper *Dépêche de Toulouse*, and he employed my brother as astrologer for the paper, a work which Ignacy took up with great conviction. Again, as before, there was no warmth between us. He almost forced me to accept a lunch with this family in their modest quarters. They treated me to a lobster. It was evident that Ignacy was trying to impress me. He did have some news from home: The family was in Lodz; my sister Hela with her children were in Warsaw, but Jadwiga and her family had not come back yet from Russia and there was no news from them. He could give me no information about the Kochanskis and Szymanowskis and he confirmed that there was a famine in Poland. It was Herbert Hoover who brought relief to the starving Poles and a monument to him stands now in the city of Posen in gratitude. I hoped only for a quick delivery by Ordynski of my precious packages.

17

The tour in Spain was as successful as the previous ones. I sent Joaquín Peña a wire with the request to send my concert grand to Madrid. His answer came as a bad surprise. "I sold your piano to Mr. Mata for 10,000 pesetas [$2,000] and will give you this sum upon your arrival in Barcelona."

Ernesto de Quesada had established himself as the only concert agent in Spain. He organized the Asociación Musical in many cities, "helping them out" by selling to them on credit "concert pianos" which he had picked up here and there. He gathered a collection of old Erards, Pleyels, Blüthners, Sheedmiers, and restored them with new hammers and strings. For Madrid I found a Bechstein in not too bad shape but in places where there was an Asociación Musical I had a hard time with those old pianos. A few new cities invited me with great insistence—among them faraway places like Almería, Murcia, and Cartagena. I like new places and I was always an inveterate traveler, so I accepted with pleasure and with the condition that they put the Madrid Bechstein at my disposal.

Cartagena, a port situated on the extreme southern tip of the peninsula, had apparently never had a piano recital before. When I asked the manager of the Teatro Circo, where I had to play, if this was true, he answered with pride, "No, Maestro, I had one quite recently in a small hall where my public enjoyed enormously my brand-new pianola." The Teatro Circo was a round theater (hence its name) and was filled to the brim. A wide box facing the piano was occupied by the very tall mayor of the city. With him sat his wife and two daughters; all three of them one could call obese. This box built for at least ten persons could hardly hold them. The mayor, who must have been at a concert or two somewhere, took over the proceedings. The minute I appeared on the stage, he stood up, looked sternly at the audience, and gave a loud clap as the sign for applause; the public obeyed cowardly. He repeated this after every part of my sonata. But soon the audience began to behave just like any other public and stopped paying attention to the mayor's directions. He was furious, feeling his authority slipping away; he stood up after one of my four Chopin numbers

and addressed me in a loud voice: "Maestro, por favor, toque 'Las Golon-
drinas.'*" This caused general consternation. Instead of answering I quietly continued my Chopin. During intermission, while people were
congratulating me and asking for autographs, the mayor appeared. "Mr.
Mayor," I said, "excuse me please for not complying with your request, but
as far as I know the piece you asked me to play is an operetta and there is
no piano part in it." At that he gave me an encouraging pat on my back and
said, "Don't get upset. You will learn it"—"ya lo aprenderá."

I recall another amusing story from that tour. In the beautiful city of
Granada, Manuel de Falla, who was then living there, asked me to give two
concerts for the benefit of an orphanage in the city. The authorities made a
week-long fiesta of it. There were daily interviews, and large pictures of the
mayor, of de Falla, of me with the head of the orphanage were to be seen in
all the papers. The mayor gave a banquet and on the last day the curator of
the Alhambra gave us a feast at night in the Patio de los Leones, where we
were served plenty of *jamón serrano* and delicious dry *jerez*. From a balcony a quartet of guitarists played some lovely Spanish folk music. It was
really delightful. This feast lasted the whole night and there was no time for
sleep. The morning train for Madrid left at a very early hour, so I took a
seat on the aisle in a first-class compartment in order to be able to sleep as
much as possible. The two seats next to me were occupied by a large-
shouldered, big-faced *madrileño*, as I learned from his accent, and by his
tiny wife. The middle seat opposite was taken by a nice fat Andalusian lady
flanked on both sides by her young daughters. These three ladies had the
dreadful habit of opening and closing their wooden fans with a loud noise.
But that was not all; my sleep was shattered by the loud, deep alcoholic
voice of my neighbor. He was obviously an addict of political discussions in
cafés, very typical of the *madrileños*. "The French have a strong army on
the Spanish frontier," he rumbled. It was the start of a series of inanities
which he had picked up in some horrible partisan papers. Before entering
the compartment, I had been questioned by two English tourists about some
buildings they had observed through the window. I informed them: "No,
this is not the cathedral, it is the bullfight arena." After a good half hour of
the wooden fans and this nasty voice, I could stand it no longer. There was
no question of sleep. I addressed the man irritably in Spanish: "Señor, I
overheard what you said. I can assure you there is not one word of truth in
what you say." I saw a glint of triumph in his eyes. He had found a real café
adversary. "You are an Englishman?" he attacked. "No," I said.

"But I heard you speak English!"

* Maestro, please play "The Swallows."

"I know a few languages," I answered.

"Aha!" he said triumphantly. "You are a Frenchman!"

"No," I said quietly, "I am a Pole."

He stopped for a moment, thinking hard, then he turned toward me with full authority and said, "A Pole . . . a Pole . . . I have a good friend, a Pole: the pianist Arthur Rubinstein." I opened my mouth, but was too tired to enjoy to the full this situation. Instead of leading him on, I said with a tired dying voice, "But *I am* Arthur Rubinstein." A bombshell. The fat lady burst into the most Homeric laughter I ever heard. I don't think she stopped till Madrid. The man didn't say a word, stood up, and spent the rest of the journey in the corridor pretending to admire the landscape.

18

Ernesto informed me that he had established agencies of Conciertos Daniel in all the more important countries of South America. He said he could assure me of better earnings under his management. "After your American tour I suggest you come first to Brazil. I could prepare your concerts there in person and then you could go to Argentina and Uruguay, where my agency can secure the Teatro Odeon for your season. I am sure you would be more satisfied with me than with Mocchi and da Rosa." He had no difficulty in persuading me after the many ample proofs of his managerial abilities.

I hoped to see Juan again but was told that he hadn't returned yet from abroad. In Barcelona a letter from Mr. Peña awaited me at the Ritz. He excused himself for not meeting me, saying that he had to leave town for a few days, then declared that he had kept the money for the piano for the time being because he needed it badly and promised to pay me in small installments. I never received the first installment, not to speak of the rest. Pablo Casals hired him later as manager of his orchestra in Barcelona in spite of my warning that he was not to be trusted.

This time, at the end of the tour, I left straight for London to join my two companions for our short tour. We began with the Spring Sonata of Beethoven with Thibaud, followed by a classical aria by Madame Calvé. Then Jacques and I played our solo pieces and Madame Calvé finished the recital. She sang with a well-schooled voice but at her age there was little of it left. But she was a charming, always smiling old lady. As Jacques and I had lots of fun being together, she joined in, chuckling flirtatiously. This gave us a cue; we played the jealous lovers to perfection: "I saw you; you've looked at Jacques too often," I would say accusingly. "Ah, ce petit, ce petit!" she would laugh delightedly. Jacques was more enterprising. He would try to grab her around the waist, which tickled her to death, but she shook an admonishing finger at him. Our suppers after the concerts were long and gay and the Gallic spirit prevailed.

In London this time, I stayed at the Ritz. I unexpectedly found myself caught up in a social turmoil. José Antonio Gandarillas took me one day to visit the beautiful Diana Cooper, who had broken her leg at the Victory Ball. She received her friends lying in bed, dressed up beautifully and looking more lovely than ever. She seemed to be constantly surrounded by friends, and she was happily driven in her wheelchair by her husband. She introduced me to many people who began inviting me to lunches, dinners, and parties. Gandarillas made me a member of the Embassy, the most elegant nightclub on Bond Street. At the house of a well-known solicitor, Sir George Lewis, I met a young couple who fascinated me. He was a barrister with the stature and face of a future prime minister. His wife, Lesley, was a Scottish beauty. His name was William Jowitt and he became, after the Second World War, the Lord Chancellor of England. Both became my lifelong friends. Lesley showed me a page of her diary where she had written beautiful things about my playing at a concert which she had attended with a young protégée, Guiomar Novaës. In an instant I was at the center of London society. My photo was often seen in the fashionable illustrateds. The *Tatler* would show me with the Duchess of Rutland with the caption: "The Duchess of Rutland and a friend."

My Spanish pieces were in great demand whenever I played for these society people, especially *Navarra*, which became the greatest rival of the *Fire Dance*. One night at a party an American-born duchess in a state of inebriation mumbled tirelessly, "Please play Ramon Novarro."

Mr. Mitchell was an English gentleman elegantly casual in his dress and speech. Unfortunately, as I found out, his financial position was shaky. His young, good-looking wife went to Hamburg to take singing lessons, to no avail. Poor Mr. Mitchell, saddened by her absence and the expense involved, took heavily to drink, but never lost his poise and excellent manners. After a short exchange of plans about future concerts, he would propose in his charming way, "I say, Rubinstein, what about half a dozen oysters? I shall take you to an excellent place." There I discovered quickly that it was not so much the oysters as two or three straight Scotches that attracted him. But we all liked him.

A strange phenomenon puzzled me; my concerts in the provinces went very well. They were, of course, mostly subscription concerts, but in London I didn't seem to succeed. I could not fill even the small Bechstein Hall, now rebaptized Wigmore Hall, as the firm of Bechstein had gone bankrupt after the war. I was being lionized by society and my name was constantly in the best weekly illustrateds, so I could not understand why my public appearances did not meet with more success. After some time I found the reason and learned a good lesson: my popularity in the finest drawing rooms of London and my being "the friend" of duchesses in the *Sketch* or the *Tatler* did me the greatest harm in my career. The conceited London critics dismissed me with an easy "Rubinstein plays Spanish music well," and didn't care for the rest. As similar opinions were voiced by fellow pianists envious of my social success, London remained a difficult place to conquer and I had to wait until the end of the Second World War before I was accepted and loved there, perhaps more than in any other place.

19

Mrs. Bergheim had married again! This lonely woman who longed for a companion found an English widower from Mexico and shared with him her lovely house, hothouses and all. She was keen on showing him her high standing in the artistic world, so she telephoned: "Arthur dear, I would love to give a big party in your honor. Could you persuade your chamber music companions to play at this party—professionally, of course —and invite on my behalf all your society friends whom you care to name?" It was an amusing proposition and I accepted; Thibaud was in London and so he, Sammons, Tertis, the fine cellist Felix Salmond, and I would play quartets and quintets. Many of my titled friends accepted my invitation with pleasure; it was a novelty. Lady Diana Cooper was heartbroken that she couldn't go because of her wheelchair. "My dear," she said sadly, "the wheelchair doesn't fit into any car and Hampstead is too far to be pushed."

"Dear Diana," I said, "I promise to find a way to get you there." It proved to be difficult, as she had said. But I was set on having her. I found a way. I hired a hearse. The wheelchair entered easily—this was fun! Her wheelchair with her in it and a few friends motored to Hampstead in this splendid funeral vehicle and it became the topic of the evening. Mrs. Bergheim (I forget her new name) gave us a brilliant buffet supper and our concert was a great success.

On New Year's Eve, I gave a dinner at the Ritz with Lesley Jowitt, Juanita and José Antonio, and the lovely Cristabel McClaren, the famous London hostess. I wrote out the menu of the dinner and suspended it from a bright-colored balloon with just enough gas in it to keep it hovering above the table. We finished the night at the annual ball at Albert Hall.

During my stay in London, the Sitwell brothers spoke to me of a young composer whose music they wanted me to hear. They brought a slim fair-haired young man by the name of William Walton. He played for me a kind of concertino for piano and orchestra and I was very impressed. His music was refreshing and original and I promised him to play it. In time, Walton and Benjamin Britten became the most important English composers.

The Jowitts acquainted me with the family of Lord Asquith, the English Prime Minister during the war. Lord Asquith, who was Mr. Asquith then, and his wife, Margot, famous for her wit and repartee, and their very musical son, Anthony, took a liking to me. I spent two weekends at their estate near Oxford, where I played a lot for Anthony, whose nickname was Puffin because of his fuzzy hair. I played bridge with Mrs. Asquith and listened stolidly to stories which the host liked to tell me repeatedly. I heard his favorite story about half a dozen times. It was about the famous chess champion Johannes Zukertort, who used to drink tea while playing at the international championships. The minute it was served he would spit it out with rage, screaming, "This is not tea, this is urine!" This habit became well known. One day in Manchester, where he won all the games, he showed a particular dislike for the tea. A tall Englishman, gray-haired, wearing elegant and equally gray mustachios, approached Zukertort after the game was over. "Would you like to accept a job for two months of work for the sum of five thousand pounds, all expenses paid?" The champion opened his eyes wide. He had never had such a sum before. The chess prizes were not high. "Have I to murder somebody?" he asked. "No," smiled the man, "the only condition is that you can't smoke or drink."

"I never smoke or drink—only tea."

"That's just it. You see, my name is Thomas Lipton. I love chess and assisting at many of your tournaments I became aware that you are one of the greatest tea tasters I ever met. All you have to do is to go to Ceylon for two months and select my teas." It was a good story but not worth hearing six times.

Margot, who grew fond of me, once sat in the second row at an afternoon concert I gave at Wigmore Hall. That day I was in particularly good form. The Prelude, Chorale, and Fugue of Franck was a hit. The rest of the program, especially the Chopin and Albéniz, was much applauded and a Prokofiev march was cheered. After my success, in the best of moods, I remained offstage waiting for the usual bows and encores. I was prepared to give them three or four when I heard dead silence. Astonished, I asked the attendant, "Is somebody delivering a speech in the hall?" He peeked through the door and said, "No, sir, the audience has left."

"This is impossible!"

"Well, sir, the hall is empty. Have I permission to leave too?" I was flabbergasted. Such a thing had never happened before. I feared some sabotage, such as somebody calling "Fire!" A friend told me what had happened. After I left the stage at the end of the concert, Margot Asquith stood up, turned to the audience, raised both hands to stop the applause, and said in a very loud voice, "Didn't you get enough for your money? Do you want to kill the man? Go home and let him rest!" The good old English audience, in awe of the Prime Minister's wife, left quietly and sheepishly. I could have killed the woman if it hadn't been for the fact that Margot Asquith was a wonderful friend and meant well.

I remember well what happened later at a Semana Santa Feria in Seville. Margot and Puffin, the Jowitts, and the Baroness d'Erlanger were all there. I was the ideal guide, of course, having been known in Seville during previous *ferias* as an eager participant. I had a hard time making them appreciate the colorful processions, the passionate *saetas*, and the barefoot *cofradías*, which their Anglo-Saxon natures shied away from. "Is there never an end to this stuff?" asked Margot. "Or does it go on forever?" It was a Saturday. "Tonight," I answered, "there is a riot of festivities all over Spain. The restaurants and dancings are all open. We can enjoy ourselves to our hearts' delight." Margot insisted on seeing flamenco dancing and singing. My friend Juan Lafita helped me to get a box in a place where some sensational debuts had taken place. Mrs. Asquith, nobody knows why, arrived in a dress with a deep décolletage, quite unnecessarily because there was nothing to show, and sat in the front of the box with Lesley and Madame d'Erlanger. Lafita and I sat behind them, but Puffin, in order to see better, sat on the floor with his arms on his mother's lap. All this was visible to the crowd below, who were mostly from Triana and occupied all the tables. Margot's décolleté made them stare at her open-mouthed. When she became aware of it she lit a cigarette to a hum of horror from below. "Arthur," she said, "they recognize you, I think. They stare at you all the time!" And then she made an unfortunate gesture with her hand at the crowd which they took for an insult. Those who saw it gave a roar. They stood up and were ready to rush up to our box in the balcony. I felt the danger. Lafita screamed, "Follow me!" We got up in a hurry and ran.

We found our way through a passage backstage out into the street, where, by now panic-stricken, we raced down to the car. I think Juan Lafita saved the life of the widow of the English Prime Minister that night.

Mr. Mitchell offered some pleasant concerts for the autumn: a small tour with Elisabeth Schumann, an appearance at Queen's Hall with Sir Henry Wood, and three or four engagements, curiously enough, not in the big centers, but at sea resorts like Brighton, Bournemouth, Eastbourne, and Hastings. It was not the best way to become very well known in England.

20

I arrived in New York after heavy seas during the crossing. As soon as I entered my room at the Biltmore the telephone rang. It was the man who had worked with me on my pianola records for the Aeolian Company. This call made me impatient. I felt he could have given me a couple of days before starting to plan my programs, but I let him come up. "I see you are very tired," he said. "Why don't you buy a nice house on Long Island and have a good rest before your tour?" I answered politely, "I'm too busy. I've no time for such a thing."

"Well, why don't you take a nice apartment in New York? People wouldn't bother you and you could work in peace." I became a little annoyed. "Look here, let's get to our business. What do you suggest for my next recordings?" At this he smiled. "I don't work for Aeolian anymore; I'm now a real estate agent." I dismissed him in a hurry.

I then called Gabriella, who had sent her address and telephone number to London after bitter exchanges between Rome and London about my long silence. She answered the phone herself. Some soothing words calmed her resentment and she agreed to dine with me that evening at the Ritz-Carlton grill. I sent her some roses and waited for her in the lobby of the Ritz. She was half an hour late and when she entered her face was flushed. After embracing me warmly she excused herself for being late and informed me that her mother was with her in New York and that she had had to prepare her dinner. During dinner, Gabriella told me the whole sad story of her debut in New York. At the Met, even before rehearsals began she had felt a hostile atmosphere, a veritable cabal against her. "They have a German contralto, the Matzenauer, the most venomous creature I ever met. She knew that my arrival might be dangerous for her career and so she told strange tales about my artistic incapacity. She insinuated to critics, who regard her as the best mezzo-soprano in the world, that my success in South America and in Spain was faked, that my Carmen pleased not for my singing but for my indecent gestures which excited the men in the audience. Farrar, who sings Carmen here, helped her spread these lies. Caruso was the only friend I had and he tried to calm my nerves before my debut in *Aida*. He came several times to my dressing room to cheer me, and it is only thanks to him that I sang my best that evening. Matzenauer, whose best role is Amneris, paid a claque to boo me. Caruso was indignant. He told me later that many things of that kind had happened at the Met. Gatti-Casazza was kind, said that the audience liked me, that I should be patient, and that with the run of the season I would win out. But my contract expires at the end of January and he hasn't renewed it." Poor Gabriella. I found out later that all she said was true. Anyway, she was a real trooper and continued singing her two or three roles bravely in spite of this great injustice.

I took her home, stayed with her for hours, and tried to restore her courage and vitality. We saw each other almost daily whenever I was in New York. Her mother was not much help to her. Instead of soothing her daughter's resentment she encouraged her, screaming for revenge. Later on, I heard that her concert tour was canceled by mutual agreement with Mr. Wolfson. Gabriella herself felt that her lack of repertoire and the unkind press would allow her little chance of success. Wolfson gave her a handsome indemnity. Even the Victor Company let her down; they declared her first record faulty and made only vague promises for the future. Gabriella returned to Rome, where her star shone again, and also to South America for a new triumph.

R.E. let me see the calendar for my season, which was nothing to be proud of. "There are too many goddamn pianists in this city and the managers are clamoring for Hofmann and Rachmaninoff. Here only the box office talks." He engaged me for ten concerts; it was a second-rate tour. Small cities, no Carnegie Hall recital, one concert with Ysaye, and the promise of two or three orchestral engagements. The Commodore opening concert appeared to be the only real event of my season; and an event it was. The Irish friends of Mr. Bowman had had too many drinks at dinner to behave quietly at a concert. There was loud talk while we performed and they never failed to clap before the pieces ended. Caruso was almost mobbed and they kept yelling for him to join them in a bottle of champagne. At the appearance of Mary Garden some appreciative wolf whistles were heard. Elman and I had neither wolf whistles nor champagne.

I did play again in Cincinnati, this time the Saint-Saëns concerto. But Ysaye's fanfare of the year before had put the public on their guard.

On my return to New York, at the desk of the Biltmore, a small, carefully packed item which had arrived from Europe awaited me. My heart was beating as I opened it carefully. I knew what it was: the composition Stravinsky had promised me. The title of it was *Piano Rag Music*, dedicated to Arthur Rubinstein. It was a meticulously and beautifully written autographed manuscript. He had even drawn some flowers around my name. With awe I put this precious sheet on the desk of my piano and began to read it. It took me four or five readings to understand the meaning of this music. It bore out Stravinsky's indication that it was going to be "the first real piano piece." In his sense, it was just that; but to me it sounded like an exercise for percussion and had nothing to do with any rag music, or with any other music in my sense. I must admit I was bitterly, bitterly disappointed. Good musicians to whom I showed it shared my opinion.

After Gabriella's departure, I recovered my full freedom and concerned myself more with my career. Mrs. Lanier made me play again for the Friends of Music. Some friends of Willem Mengelberg, who liked my playing, persuaded him to engage me as soloist for the Brahms D minor Concerto. Mengelberg liked my performance, which encouraged me, especially as he pretended to have heard Brahms himself play this work. My success at this concert helped to get me some more important engagements. Stokowski invited me to play the B flat Brahms and was pleased. Another conductor who had conducted Wagner at the Met, Alfred Hertz, invited me to be his soloist at two concerts with his orchestra in San Francisco. To make the long journey more profitable, he assured me of two or three solo concerts. To my satisfaction I felt I was becoming less dependent on R.E. and could take my career in my own hands.

New York seemed to be living through a joyful bacchanal. The United States was becoming conscious of being the wealthiest and strongest nation in the world. The victory and the magnificent performance of its army made the country legitimately proud. All of this the people wanted to enjoy to the utmost, but a great shock was in store for them. The American government proposed a law prohibiting the consumption of alcohol in the whole country. At first, people laughed it off, but were stupefied when both houses passed this law. I was present at the wildest orgy anybody could imagine. It was the last day before prohibition. I wouldn't be surprised if the alcohol consumed that night could fill a river like the Mississippi. The Drapers invited me to this last feast, where I was horrified to see Paul drinking again.

It was dangerous to walk in the streets that night. One saw drunken people lying unconscious on the pavement, cars zigzagging along, men threatening to embrace you or to punch you, others who incoherently mumbled invitations to one last drink.

The next day, New Yorkers could proudly announce: "We had the greatest hangover in history." In the days that followed I felt a new kind of life in this great city. Everything seemed the same, but the behavior of the people had changed. There was a terrific air of conspiracy. From early morning on, you could be accosted by someone who had met you casually who would whisper, "Come to my place. I can get one for you." In the better restaurants, a serious wink of the eye by an important customer was the signal for a cup of tea which contained, instead of this nectar of the English, a good dose of alcohol of a questionable quality. Papers told stories of homemade brews which sometimes caused death by poisoning. One small consolation came from the Department of Health. Doctors declared that whiskey was a tonic for the heart. Nobody was astonished after that to see queues five blocks long outside pharmacies, everyone with prescriptions for a pint of whiskey.

The Commissioner of Police, an Irishman, Thomas Enright, asked his pal R.E. if I would take part in a concert for the benefit of the police force. "They'll give you a police badge afterward, so you'll be able to give hell to anybody just like a real cop," R.E. assured me. After the concert, at which I was frightened by the mass of policemen in the audience, Mr. Enright invited me to a party at police headquarters, where he was to present me with a badge. Escorted by R.E. and Lulu, I climbed the wide steps leading to the reception rooms of this ominous building. I was told that some poor Italians, caught with small glasses of Chianti in their hands, were occupying a few cells. Mr. Enright awarded me the badge in a short ceremony, after which an important officer invited me kindly to another room. "To the buffet . . ." he said. There I was offered drinks galore: champagne, rum, gin, and whiskey were served lavishly to the guests of the commissioner. I remember one elegant lady falling down the steps completely drunk and many others who could hardly walk.

I had still a month to go before leaving for South America. So at last I had the time to go to concerts of artists I was interested to hear. I heard Hofmann and Rachmaninoff give recitals. I heard the poetic Gabrilówitsch. Young Heifetz played to a packed Carnegie Hall but Kreisler still held his own. Most of these artists I had known and heard previously. I had also a chance to hear my direct rivals Benno Moiseiwitsch and Mischa Levitzki. I went with a strong resolution to listen to all they played as if it were for the first time. And God knows, most of their pieces I played myself.

To hear these great artists in quick succession gave me much to think about and learn. It confirmed my disdain for the then universally accepted "methods." Many young talented pianists fell for the "Leschetizky method" or the "Breithaupt method" and there were many others. These methods were shamelessly advertised by less gifted pupils of these masters who made a living from them. I was always of the opinion that a teacher, like a medical doctor, should treat each individual case in an attempt to detect the particular musical or technical gifts and shortcomings. Teachers ought to pay close attention to the physical differences among their pupils. A pianist of short stature has a different approach to the instrument than a person six feet tall. There are small hands and there are hands which are too large. There are too short fifth fingers; there is the question of stretches. Teachers ought to observe carefully all these different characteristics in their choice of pieces during the educational period. I observed that the best teachers are the professionals who are dedicated pedagogues. To be taught by famous pianists is often a great danger because unknowingly they impose their great personalities and more often than not turn their pupils into weak imitators. There are those who become so attached to the talents in their charge that they postpone for years their willingness to let them fly with their own wings. I give here my earnest advice, out of my heart and my long experience, to all promising talents to stop studying with their professors when they acquire a firm hold on the keyboard and have a technique well-developed enough to take on any piece of music—*and learn by themselves to make music*. Most young pianists are perfectly equipped for their career at the age of seventeen or eighteen and it is then that they should begin their personal dialogue with the composers. We interpreters have something in common with painters. If you have your portrait done by ten different painters you will look different in each one. But each artist will swear that that is the way he sees you. The same applies perfectly to our interpretation of music. Each of us brings to a work of music his own talents and tools, making the best of it through his own understanding and developing his interpretation of it according to his own unique personality. Another piece of advice: Beware of playing to an audience a work you do not love or understand but which seems to be useful for a program. You will not do service to the composer or to yourself.

All these thoughts were going through my mind during those days as I listened to these famous pianists. Rachmaninoff was a pianist after my heart. He was superlative when he played his own music. A performance of his concertos could make you believe that they were the greatest masterpieces ever written, while when played by other pianists, even at their best, they became clearly what they were: brilliantly written pieces with their Oriental languor which have retained a great hold on the public. But when he played the music of other composers, he impressed me by the novelty and the originality of his conceptions. When he played a Schumann or a Chopin, even if it was contrary to my own feelings, he could convince me by the sheer impact of his personality. He was the most fascinating pianist of them all since Busoni. He had the secret of the golden, living tone which comes from the heart and which is inimitable. In my strong opinion he was a greater pianist than a composer. I fall, I have to admit, under the charm of his compositions when I hear them but return home with a slight distaste for their too brazenly expressed sweetness.

Hofmann, two days later, upset me. Here was a man who was considered by prewar Russia and by the United States to be a giant, the heir of Anton Rubinstein. I had known him since my young years when he disillusioned me with his admitted indifference to music. With his famous gifts for mechanical matters, his main interest in the piano lay in possible changes in its construction, in the height of the keys, in different dispositions of the strings and of the acoustic holes in the frame. His magnificent grasp of the keyboard must have been inborn. Even in his playing of the masters, his chief interest lay in dynamics, in a slowly prepared crescendo ending in a volcanic outburst at the climax, and he felt great satisfaction in frightening the audience by using the violent contrast of a pianissimo followed by a sudden fortissimo smash. He had another irritating habit: He liked to bring out accompanying voices which you never heard in the performances of others. And yet, he was a pianist of great stature because, in spite of all I have said, a musical personality emerged at every concert which I cannot lightly dismiss.

During Gabrilówitsch's seraphic playing of romantic music one felt one saw a halo over his head. His devotion and integrity to the works performed were such that you felt as if you were sitting at a service in church. Everything sounded right with his pleasant tone and fine pedaling. All the right dynamics were there. I left the hall feeling that one couldn't play better, that everything was perfect, and yet I was not happy. The one thing worth living for, the *inspiration*, was not there. When I read these lines I begin to ponder. Here were three world-famous pianists who played much of the music of the same masters, occasionally even the same pieces, and at every one of these recitals they each made me live in a different world of music. A musical talent, whether that of a composer or an interpreter, is a germ that is born with the person and demands its natural development. You cannot learn music, you can only develop your own individual talent.

In the case of Moiseiwitsch and Levitzki, there's no denying that both were equipped with all the necessary ingredients for success. They had the technique, temperament, and memory and the solid musicality. Nothing was missing, but strangely enough, after their concerts you forgot you had heard them and if you closed your eyes you could easily take Levitzki for Moiseiwitsch and vice versa.

The time came to leave for South America to make some real money again. With my meager fees in the States and my expensive way of living, with a valet and all, things had become too costly. The Drapers, when they saw me off, brought foodstuffs to the ship. Ruth said, "Keep it all on ice. It will save you on the journey from being poisoned by the dreadful food they have on board." Munching their delicious goods, I felt sorry for my fellow passengers.

21

On my return to Rio after the glorious fifteen concerts of my first visit, I was full of great expectations. Upon arrival I found Ernesto de Quesada at the dock. He had come to Rio with his family, and with him in charge of my tour I was confident that this time I had found the right man. But a terrible shock awaited me. On the way to the hotel, Quesada told me blandly that he had opened a subscription for eight concerts, four by me and four by George Boskoff. Individual tickets would be sold after the subscription was closed. I was speechless; I knew Boskoff from Paris. Georges Enesco had brought him there from Rumania; he was a good pianist, had a certain charm, but his success was limited to a few Parisian salons—it never reached the public. The whole thing was quite clear. Quesada had engaged Boskoff for a few pennies and thought he would make a great profit by linking him with me after my exceptionally successful debut. And he had put his business before our friendship as well. I resented it bitterly. He lowered my grand reappearance to the level of a simple competition with another pianist.

After seeing some good friends of mine, I found right away that I was right. "How is that pianist Boskoff?" they asked with great interest, and I had to bite my lip and declare that he was very good indeed.

The subscription filled most of the theater. And there were, of course, high expectations for the new man, George Boskoff. So no wonder that in this as yet musically unsophisticated city the public as well as the critics enjoyed the chance to make comparisons between us. I was the winner with my Spanish pieces, including *Navarra*, and Boskoff insinuated himself into the favor of his listeners with his ultra-delicate Debussy.

George Boskoff was a refined little man with long black hair to his shoulders and sad poetic eyes, who always dressed in black in that very hot country and would carry a book of French poetry to the restaurant where we met. He would interrupt my meal to quote this or that passage from Verlaine or Mallarmé. He was cultured, polite, and modest, all qualities to my liking.

After the subscription I gave three more concerts to good houses, but to my surprise, the receipts represented a poor attendance. When I complained, the cashier showed me the remaining tickets to prove that there had been no mistake. But I became suspicious; I asked Enrique, who was a shrewd little fellow, to investigate in secret and see if there had been any conspiracy. And he came back with scandalous news: "I took the cashier to a bar, made good friends with him, and after two glasses of rum he confided that there were two ticket sheets and that he showed you the wrong one." I had a terrible scene with Ernesto, who seemed to know nothing about it. But in my great anger about the whole Brazilian affair I decided to continue my tour in Uruguay and Argentina with his partner alone.

My stay in Brazil was not all unpleasant and I have great moments to remember. Two young musicians, students of the conservatory and my great followers, told me wonders about a composer. "A genius," they said. "He was expelled twice from the conservatory for rejecting any intervention or criticism from the teachers. He didn't believe in any regular musical curriculum. We think that he is a man who relies entirely on his own creative genius and is completely independent." An introduction of that sort aroused my curiosity. "Where can one meet this man or hear his music?" I asked.

"We are ashamed to tell you this but he must make his living playing the cello with some colleagues in a movie on the Avenida Rio Branco."

"What do they play there?"

"They just have to accompany the proceedings on the screen, a quick galop when the Keystone Kops are running after a culprit or a sad ballad when the mother sits at the bed of her sick child." This didn't sound very encouraging. "Well, let's go and hear these galops and ballads."

We entered a dark cinema, empty at that hour of the day. On the screen was an American melodrama. Every scene had its appropriate music. There was an intermission; the lights went on and the five or six musicians waved to their friends and seemed to recognize me. After a short while they began to play again, but this time it was music, real music! It was made up of Brazilian rhythms which I easily identified but they were treated in a completely original way. It sounded confused, formless, but very attractive. My companions whispered, "He calls it 'The Amazon.' It is a choro for orchestra." I could make little of it but after the music stopped I asked them to introduce me to this Heitor Villa-Lobos. He was a short man of dark complexion, clean-shaven, with dark, disorderly hair and large sad eyes, but his hands were his most attractive feature with their lovely shape, sensitive and alive. I addressed him in my broken Portuguese and he answered in his broken French. I expressed my great interest in the work I had just heard and asked him politely if he had written anything for the piano. All of a sudden he became rude. "Pianists have no use for composers. All they want is success and money." This offended me and I turned my back, walking away. My two young friends ran after me. "Don't be angry," they beseeched me, "he is bitter about having had to play this silly movie music in your presence."

At a dinner at the Oswaldos' I heard upon my inquiry nothing but bad things about Villa-Lobos, about his insolence at the conservatory and about his conceit. Professor Nepomuceno said derisively, "He believes he is the greatest Brazilian composer." I didn't tell them of his rudeness toward me. "The Amazon" had impressed me.

A few days later, early in the morning, I was asleep under my mosquito net when somebody rapped at the door. It must be a telegram, I thought, and scrambled out from under the net to open the door. I saw to my surprise ten or twelve men carrying different musical instruments. One of them was Villa-Lobos, who tried to convey to me in his mixed French and Portuguese that he was here to comply with my wish to hear his compositions. "My friends are occupied during the day. This is the only time they are free to play." (It was only eight o'clock.) I was afraid of disturbing my neighbors, so I telephoned the desk and was told that I could go ahead with this early-morning concert as by that hour everybody was up and most people would be delighted to hear some music. There was another difficulty, however: how to place the musicians. I had a small bedroom leading to a little drawing room. We had to remove furniture and borrow chairs from the management before they could begin. They played a string quartet in which I heard a curious treatment of the instruments which lent the music an original and refreshing sound. After this I was simply enchanted by a little piece which he called "Choros," written for flute and clarinet. It was not an improvisation; it had a perfect form. I heard one or two more compositions for different combinations. Their form was not easy to grasp.

By then I was convinced that I was facing a great composer who had something important to say. I did not need to tell him so. He understood what I felt. When his friends had left, Villa-Lobos stayed behind and spent the whole day with me. He decided to miss his work at the cinema. At luncheon at my hotel he told me in a very colorful way much about his life. He had a wife, Lucille, who played the piano very well and for whom he had written a series of short pieces called *O Prole do Bebe*—meaning "the cradle of the baby"—in which he used nursery tunes. More and more animated, he began to tell me stories of his youth which sounded more like Jules Verne than anything believable. He pretended to be the first to have discovered the secret soul of Brazil. "I listened to the voices of the savages of the Amazon. I was living for weeks in the jungles of the Matto Grosso to catch the tunes of the *caboclos*. I was often in grave danger, but I didn't care." All this, he related with absolute conviction in a high-pitched voice in his difficult French, helped by gymnastic gesticulation. I found out that he did actually travel all over Brazil and gathered much folkloric material. During coffee, smoking large cigars, we became friends. He sent me, the next day, much of his piano music, which was printed by the publishing house of Arturo Napoleão, a onetime famous pianist who at the ripe age of ninety-eight played for me, with astonishing precision, a piece by Gottschalk. At my last concert in Rio, I played the first suite of *O Prole do Bebe* and was booed; later I received angry letters reproaching me for not playing some real Brazilian music like the lovely pieces by the professors of the conservatory. Villa-Lobos himself was philosophical about it: "I am still too good for them."

22

Montevideo and Buenos Aires received me like an old friend coming home. My concerts were sold out—fortunately for me, because Quesada's partner, Grassi, tried to get out of my earnings more than was his due. Then and there I hired a nice man named Francisco Ruiz, who accompanied me to provincial cities and proved to be helpful in every way.

My dear friends Nena Salamanca and the Quintana family greeted me with a sensational tale about Avila. They were bubbling with excitement. From what I gathered, Avila had brought off one of his amusing pranks. With his gift for observation he had noticed on his first visit that the city of Buenos Aires had no elegant shops with the kind of bric-a-brac you see in Italy or France—old snuffboxes, imitation jewelry, antiques, brocades from Florence, Venetian glass, and things of that kind. Nobody knows where he got the money to buy all of this stuff but he got it all safely through customs to Buenos Aires. The Plaza Hotel received him as a privileged guest and opened for him a large salon used for private receptions on the second floor, where Juan with his splendid taste displayed his goods on large tables with lovely flower decorations. He arranged special lights to illuminate some special objects and showed a genius for salesmanship. He sent out hundreds of delicately engraved invitations to all the members of society who had lionized him. At the opening the room was jammed; the novelty-hungry *porteños** were blinded with enchantment by the glittering display. They hadn't traveled enough to recognize it for the cheap stuff it was. And so, the sale on the first day surpassed all Juan's hopes. But there was a divine sequel to this. A well-known matron, one of the richest ladies of the country, picked up her lorgnette, examined the rug on the floor, and said, "What a beautiful carpet. I have never seen anything like it. What is the price of this carpet?" Juan put on a very serious expression. "This is a rare specimen of Bukhara. I did not mean to sell it, but as you are so fond of it, I will make a concession. The price is fifty thousand pesos [$25,000]." Before he had finished saying this she took out her checkbook, wrote out the check, and handed it to him.

That evening when everybody had gone, Avila asked the hotel director to come up and asked him, "What is the price of this carpet? I need it badly." The man looked astonished but on Avila's insistence he went to look it up in his books; he had paid a thousand pesos for it. "But as it is well worn, we'll sell it to you for five hundred." The story became the favorite topic in the city.

My programs that season had more Chopin than before. I played both sonatas, in which I discovered new things to say. The first movement of the B-flat Opus 35 was always taken fast by every pianist I had ever heard, including myself. On reading it carefully I became aware that this was wrong. Chopin knew very well the form of a sonata and wouldn't give the first allegro (in this case, the doppio movimento of the opening largo) a tempo which is more suitable for a last movement than it is a basis for a structure of a sonata. The eerie finale also gained by being played more slowly to make the short motive in major heard more clearly. Many new

* People of Buenos Aires.

ideas came to me by restudying pieces I had often played. We pianists are always in danger of falling into bad habits by frequent repetitions of the same work. Young pianists should give a good new look at their music from time to time and discover treasures they did not notice before. My Villa-Lobos pieces found great favor in Montevideo. I had to repeat some of them. In Buenos Aires they were met with silence.

Here I cannot omit a little love story which quickened my temperament at concerts, something which was readily remarked by the audience. Far from being an easy affair it was a terribly complicated one. The lady in question was married and lived with her husband and a child in my hotel, the Plaza. There had been a mild flirtation between us on my first visit to Buenos Aires, but I had no access to her because her husband, a wealthy and well-known landowner, had treated me in an abrupt, almost impolite way when I was introduced to them. However, when two hearts beat in unison they always find a way. Thanks to a helping hand, I obtained a first meeting.

We had a slightly complicated plan. Their apartment was visible from my room across the courtyard. When a small green pot of flowers appeared on the windowsill of her bedroom, this told me that the husband was away for a few hours. I had to take an old-fashioned taxi with only two small windows where you sat completely in the dark, which would drive me to a practically deserted street. There my beauty was waiting all in black—everything, shoes, stockings, veil, hat, and gloves, which made her look more beautiful than ever. From there on, with her safely in my taxi, we would drive to an address given me casually by a musician who was telling me of his own escapades. The house was situated in a garden in a popular quarter of the city. The car would drive in and stop at a window through which one stepped into a room. The taxi, of course, had to wait. We were happy there many times.

Coming back to the hotel, letting her furtively out of my taxi to find another one so that she should arrive before me, was an art of timing. Our meetings took place in the mornings and she had to be back well before lunch. After a nice refreshing bath, I would put on a well-pressed suit which she told me she liked, a lovely tie held by my pearl pin, tuck in my pocket handkerchief with a few drops of my English perfume, and with my shoes well brushed by Enrique, enter the grillroom, passing their table to find my small one at the window. One morning she confided to me, "Every time you pass our table at the grillroom, my husband tells me with a confidential air, 'That fellow's a fairy, look how he reeks of perfume. I have it from the best sources.' And he never fails to repeat it."

There was an old English gentleman who had a large permanent apartment at the Plaza. He loved music, came often to my concerts, and had now and then a drink with me at the bar. One day he invited me to his box at the Colón for the premiere of *Salome* by Richard Strauss, sung by a French soprano, Geneviève Vix, who was famous for this role. I felt in the mood for a good dinner before seeing my old friend *Salome* again. I invited my English friend to dine with me before the opera and take our time for a good meal. As my reader well knows, I was always an inveterate gourmet and for this occasion I felt the urge to show my culinary talents. The maître d'hôtel helped me to create a magnificent menu: Fresh caviar with thin crepes (I disdained the thick Russian ones) opened the feast. Then we had an Argentine specialty, a *jugo de carne* in cups—really the boiled blood of beef, but beautifully prepared with pepper and some other ingredients. It was extemely tasty and strengthening; I always had it before my concerts. It was followed by a *pejerrey*, the most delicate fish in the world, found only in these waters. The maître d'hôtel served this with small mussels, mushrooms, and a sauce which looked like mayonnaise but wasn't. Cold duck *en gelée* and endives with French dressing and finely cut truffles gave a good contrast to the fish. The dinner was crowned by a *parfait au moka* accompanied by small cakes from the renowned bakery of the house. This opulent meal was washed down by a tiny glass of vodka for the caviar, by a Corton-Charlemagne for the fish, by a glass or two of a good vintage Château Latour, and finally by a glass of well-iced Château d'Yquem. I told my guest, "I do not think it is right to serve champagne with such a carefully chosen repast."

The maître d'hôtel put a handwritten menu on our table; a few lovely roses added their note of elegance. At the display of all this my guest forgot for a moment his English manners. "This is incredible!" he shouted. "It is unbelievable that an artist should know so much about food. The musicians I have met couldn't tell a fish from a chicken—they never care what they eat as long as there is lots of it. And you, the great pianist, seem to know more about food than a member of White's Club in London!" I smiled with false modesty.

The *Salome* was not as good as we expected. Madame Vix acted well as the vicious daughter of Herodias, but without the vocal equipment to do justice to the music. On our return, a half bottle of champagne at the bar made us forget our disappointment.

The next morning I received a letter from Eugenia Errazuriz, congratulating me on my success. She added, "I always knew you would be rich one day. If you have any money to spare, send me some. I need it for a wonderful poet who is starving." I sent her a thousand pesos immediately.

It was time to return to England for my little tour with Elisabeth

Schumann. I booked a nice cabin with a bath on the English steamer *Andes*, a pleasant boat. After a few farewell parties and a last sad look at the window deprived of the little flowerpot, I embarked with Enrique and many friends came to see me off. As the ship moved out of the harbor, I went down to my cabin. My steward said with a twinkle in his eye, "You have two cabins, sir."

"What nonsense," I said. "I know only of one."

"You are wrong, sir, you have two cabins."

"No," I said, angry now. "I don't need another cabin and I'll keep this one. There must be a mistake."

"Oh no, sir," he insisted with a little smile. "The captain gave orders to open this cabin for you."

This startled me. "What for?" I asked.

"You will see, sir . . ." He opened the door next to my cabin and there was an amazing sight: twelve cases of champagne—144 bottles were piled up in that once elegant cabin. There was a letter from my English friend from the Plaza: "As you showed me that you are the greatest gourmet I ever met, it gives me pleasure to send you this excellent champagne which I kept with many other good vintages in my private cellar." When the news of the champagne got around I became the uncrowned king of the steamer. Every morning after breakfast and until late hours of the night, two bottles of the precious Pommery 1904 were in a bucket at my table in the bar. Ignaz Friedman, the Polish pianist who had been engaged by the new Quesada organization to give concerts in Montevideo and Buenos Aires, was on board. At night we played poker with the young Lord Queensberry and the dancer Maude Alan. My champagne helped the game remain lively until late hours. Friedman, who, as I wrote in *My Young Years*, had been rather unlucky when we played together at Lwow (the piano!), was an unbeatable champion at poker, not so much from having good hands as for his genius for guessing the hands of the others. We would bet and raise our bets, holding apparently high cards. If I raised again he would make a strange proposition: "What about exchanging our hands?" A terrible decision to take. One thing was certain: if I accepted, I became the owner of two sevens, but if I didn't he showed four aces.

By the time we arrived at Lisbon my champagne was finished and the money I carried with me was gone. The last three days before reaching Southampton became a serious danger to my health. From morning till night people invited me—no, they forced me to drink champagne with them. "It is our turn now!" they said, and would not accept a refusal. Friedman generously lent me some money for tips on board. The troubles with my poor stomach, the victim of all this champagne, worries about the losses at poker, and any other disturbing thoughts disappeared from my mind when I left the train in London.

Paul Kochanski with Sophie was standing there, the same, unchanged, just as I saw him last time. Mr. Mitchell had told him of my arrival and so gave me the chance of having one of the most beautiful reunions of my life. We had no time to speak because there was an endless series of hugs, embraces, exclamations, and unanswered questions. When Enrique had managed to find a large car that could hold my big trunks, Sophie asked me, "Did you reserve your rooms?" I said indifferently, "No, I like the Ritz. They know me there." Both looked preoccupied. "Are you sure you have reservations?"

"Don't worry. I always find rooms there."

Then Paul began to look alarmed. "Do you know that there is a state of panic in London. You can't find a room in any hotel for any amount of money. They are building some improvised wooden cabins in the parks for stranded tourists. It is a catastrophic situation." This was bad news indeed. But throughout my whole life, I have been pretty good in emergencies. I made a quick decision. "Enrique," I said, "load the luggage on one of those taxis with a roof rack and when you arrive at the Ritz unload it quietly with the doorman without answering any questions. We will follow you in another car." Upon reaching the Ritz we saw that Enrique had got the luggage safely into the baggage room. We entered the lobby, continuing our animated conversation in Polish. At one point I stopped our talk and told them in English, "Excuse me for a second. I must get my key." With three quick steps I rushed to the desk. "Please give me my keys and those of the room for my valet. I'm in a terrible hurry. I have a dinner party and hardly have the time to dress." The three men behind the desk looked puzzled. "Have you a reservation, sir?" said one in a low voice. "Because the hotel is full." This was the cue for my dramatic outburst. "What do you mean by this question?" I cried. "I had a reservation made six months ago from Argentina and you are not going to pretend now that you don't have it. I know very well that hotels play these tricks in order to accommodate their important guests, but I will not tolerate such a thing, so I want my keys right away." And I screamed at Enrique in Spanish, "Press my clothes and have them ready in a quarter of an hour!" The three men were completely flabbergasted. They looked at each other with suspicious but frightened expressions and held a rapid consultation. They then reached for two keys and said, "Only for one night, sir. Tomorrow you must find other rooms."

"That remains to be seen. I have a good mind to talk to the director about this." With that, I made a smiling sign to my friends and we went up in the elevator to a beautiful apartment with a sitting room and bedroom.

Enrique too had been taken care of. Paul and Sophie were speechless with admiration. Before anything else I called Juanita Gandarillas, who I fortunately found at home. "Juanita darling, I've just arrived from Buenos Aires and imagine my surprise, my best friends in the world, the Kochanskis, whom I've told you so much about, are with me. Can you have us for dinner?"

"I'm thrilled to meet them," this angel answered. "Come as soon as possible."

It took Juanita five minutes to learn to love them forever after and we had a heartwarming family reunion. After dinner, happy and relaxed, Paul told me everything, which I was so anxious to know, about what had happened since we were separated at the beginning of the war. "We left London for Ilgovo, the estate of the Mlynarskis in Lithuania. When the Germans invaded the country, the Mlynarski family fled to Moscow with many of their relations and we too left for the Ukraine to join Jaroszynski, where we thought we were safe for the rest of the war. Karol Szymanowski joined us there and composed some wonderful music for violin with my technical help. With the defeat of the Russians, the Bolsheviks came to power. Then came disaster after disaster! The estates of the Szymanowskis, of Jaroszynski, of the Davydovs, and of Prince Lubomirski were taken by force and ransacked. The owners had to flee. Jaroszynski, Szymanowski, Sophie, and I settled in Kiev, where I began to give concerts. Zosia and I moved to Moscow, where the musicians of the city, political chameleons, received me with open arms as their 'comrade.' I even became very successful. But when Pilsudski liberated Poland we couldn't resist any longer and escaped to Warsaw, where we found the Mlynarskis and all our other friends. The Mlynarskis recovered their estate, but Jaroszynski, the Szymanowskis, and Prince Lubomirski lost everything. London and Paris are crowded with exiles, and," he added, "Karol will be in Paris in a few days."

I recount here the bare facts but we stayed up that night till late hours to hear all the details, all the curious, tragic, humorous incidents. Paul informed me also that my sister Jadwiga and her family had lived in Moscow until the last days of the Tsarist regime. Her husband made a fortune and their eldest daughter, Marila, had married a Baron Wrangel.

The Kochanskis rented a small flat in Cork Street and found another one for me nearby. Before my arrival Paul had been busy re-establishing contact with friends he had made on his previous visits. One of them was Sir Hamilton Harty, a fine musician and well-liked conductor. In the old days Hamilton Harty had been Paul's accompanist in some of his concerts. Now he was delighted to see him again and engaged him enthusiastically to play the Brahms Violin Concerto at Queen's Hall with the London Symphony Orchestra. This was the best way for him to find his place in London. When I asked Mr. Mitchell to find a date for a violin and piano recital at Wigmore Hall, he was delighted. "I shall do my best to find some nice concerts for you. What about a few oysters?" For once he had success; Paul liked oysters too.

It was a short but lovely season for us in London. Paul had a huge success with his concerto and the news of it even reached America. Paderewski's last manager, George Engels, was present at this concert and proposed right away a short tour for him in America for January. I introduced the Kochanskis to all my new friends and Lesley Jowitt gave a lovely party after his concert.

My tour with Elisabeth Schumann was artistically very satisfactory, as I had the joy of hearing her beautiful singing brilliantly accompanied by Ivor Newton. Mrs. Bergheim's marriage to the Mexican-born widower whom she met on a cruise caused a great change in our relations. Her new husband did not like me. He was obviously afraid that I might have a share in her will.

The sonata concert which Paul and I gave at Wigmore Hall came off beautifully. We played our three favorites, Beethoven C minor, Brahms D minor, and the César Franck, as freshly as if the six years of our separation had not existed. The hall was full, all our friends were present, and after the concert we had supper and played chamber music at Juanita's. After my recital with Paul, I was ready to leave for Paris for a short stay on my way to Spain. What a joy it was to know my best friend safely in London and to anticipate the reunion with Karol.

On the Quai de Calais before getting on the train, I went to the book kiosk to find something to read. Most of the literature they had I knew from before the war, but the attendant asked me if I liked poetry, to which I answered, "I love to read it but hate having it read to me." He made me buy a funny-looking booklet in the form of a timetable. He assured me, however, that it was a book of poems about voyages by an unknown poet named Blaise Cendrars. The first one was called "Pâques à New-York," which made me cry; it was a beautiful poem about loneliness, a loneliness I had felt myself.

Paris had the same hotel crisis as London. After a miserable night in a valet's room at the Meurice which they gave me as a great favor (I have no idea where Enrique slept that night), I found next day a room at the Hotel Régina, where my window faced a lovely golden statue of Joan of Arc. Karol was still in Warsaw. I wired him to join me at the hotel, where they promised me accommodation for him.

My first call was to Darius Milhaud. I had last seen him in New York, where he and Paul Claudel had me for lunch on their way from Rio to Paris. He offered in his most friendly way to take me that afternoon to a place where he would introduce me to a few musicians with whom he had formed an association. "They already call us 'The Six—' " he said derisively. "We beat out 'The Five' Russians by one number." He took me that afternoon to a place on the rue Duphot called the Bar Gaya. Inside I was greeted by a display on three walls of posters in different colors saying: "Bienvenue à Arthur Rubinstein," "Vive Arthur Rubinstein, vos amis vous salvent Arthur Rubinstein." I embraced Milhaud, obviously the instigator of this lovely welcome. Auric, Poulenc, Honegger, and the lovely Germaine Tailleferre were there. They were a young and eager lot, all babbling at the same time, calling *"pompier"* all the prewar masters, including even Ravel, and promising a new world of music. We drank soft drinks while their young friend Jean Wiéner entertained us at the piano with the latest American tunes. He played delicate blues and straight jazz very well, as well as hit songs by Jerome Kern, Cole Porter, and Irving Berlin. After a while Jean Cocteau made his entrance. I had heard about him from many quarters. Tony Gandarillas had raved about his charm, intelligence, and poetry but didn't tell me of his personal impact. His body and movements were those of a schoolboy. He was slender and graceful but it was his face which revealed all the things I had heard about him—his eyes, his mouth, and his incredibly delicate hands revealing an intelligence of uncanny variety. There was deep wisdom, childish malice, and something effeminate to be felt in this unusual and attractive and powerful personality. He clearly dominated the whole group.

For me it was one of the most fascinating afternoons I can remember. It meant the first contact with the new artistic world after the war. What I loved best about them was that they loved life and they loved music, which had no secrets for them. They knew it all. I had the good luck to know these artists and their music much better and will have more to say about their work. For the time being, Jean Cocteau and Darius Milhaud honored me with an invitation to join their weekly dinners on Saturdays somewhere in Montmartre. Darius, who accompanied me home, told me many details about his friends. "You will see," he said. "The music of each one of us is completely different; we are independent of each other. We are simply linked by friendship and mutual respect for what we are doing. Jean Cocteau has assumed the role of our spokesman, a role he takes quite seriously, but it flatters and amuses us because he has all the gifts but the one for music."

In my most joyful spirit after the great experience of the afternoon, I decided to have my dinner at Maxim's, where so many memories were still vivid. As I entered the famous establishment I heard a loud familiar voice cry, "Arturo!" Juan Avila occupied a table with a lovely young lady. He would not let me eat alone but almost forced me to join them at dinner, which I accepted in spite of my aversion for disturbing a duo. During dinner (the lady was French and remained completely uninterested in our lively Spanish conversation) Juan gave me a full account of his sensational sale in Buenos Aires. "With the money I made there I came to Paris and took a small apartment. Madame est ma petite amie," said he, smiling at her, and she smiled back. "No entiende nada de nada," he confided to me. "She doesn't understand a thing."

From that night on I led the life of Jekyll and Hyde. The days were devoted to the most important musical matters, to Stravinsky, who was in town, to Karol, who arrived a few days later; but when night came on I was irresistibly drawn into the amusing world of Avila.

First, Stravinsky: Igor had left his family in Switzerland. He was in urgent need of money and came to Paris hoping to find Diaghilev. The house of Pleyel offered him a small studio in their house in the rue Roche-chouart and provided him with a contract for records. He invited me to this studio, where we had a heartwarming brotherly reunion. He told me all about his difficulties, showed me which works were to be recorded, and then asked me, "Did you play in your concerts my *Piano Rag Music?*" I was frank. "Dear Igor, I'm more than proud to own your manuscript but I'm still the pianist of the old era. Your piece is written for percussion rather than for my kind of piano." He did not like my answer. "I see that you don't understand this music," he said a little impatiently. "I shall play it and make it clear to you." He then banged it out about ten times, making me more and more antagonistic to the piece. Now he became angry. A disagreeable quarrelsome exchange followed. "You still think *you* can sing on the piano, but that is an illusion. The piano is nothing but a utility instrument and it sounds right only as percussion."

I was infuriated. "You know well," I replied, trying to hurt him, "that the public at large does not understand and does not like your music. Your orchestra is too loud for them. You remember well what happened to you at the first performance of your *Le Sacre du printemps*. But for some mysterious reason, when I play your music on the piano, it becomes clearer to them and they begin to like it." He laughed derisively. "What nonsense." I went to the piano and played part of *Petrushka*, especially the music in Petrushka's room. "Does it sound like percussion?" I asked him. "Or like music?" Stravinsky—it was so like him—immediately forgot all that had been said and had happened before and became quite professional. "How do you make your bass sound like that? Do you use your pedal in a special way?"

"Yes, of course; my foot catches rapidly the still vibrating bass notes, which allows me to change harmonies in the treble. And," I added fatuously, "your hated piano can do all sorts of things, my dear." Completely serene now, Igor declared enthusiastically, "I shall write for you a sonata made of the material of *Petrushka*." I embraced him with emotion and joy. I took him to dinner and we spent hours telling each other how we had lived during the war. He had written a lot in Switzerland. "You will like a thing I have written with a Swiss writer, Charles Ramuz, *L'Histoire du soldat*. There is some funny violin music in it which will amuse you. I also wrote a large piece called *Les Noces*; it is simply a Russian ritual wedding where one sings, drinks, dances, and instead of an orchestra it is accompanied by four pianos. Percussively," he added with a sardonic smile. He was pleased to hear that I had begun to make my way and was earning good money. "Yes," he said, "you pianists become millionaires by playing the music left to you by the starving Mozart and Schubert and the poor mad Schumann, the tubercular Chopin, and the sick Beethoven." He was right. I always felt that we were vampires living off the blood of these great geniuses.

24

Karol arrived two days later in good physical shape after all he had been through. I already knew all about it from Paul but was burning with curiosity to hear his new compositions. There was a wealth of beautiful violin pieces and three exotic-sounding pieces for piano called "Masques": the first, *Schéhérazade*, written in a Debussyan Oriental style; the second, *Tantrist der Narr*, from a German poem. Tristan, under this false name, tries to steal into Isolde's apartment one night but is readily recognized by the dogs and arouses the suspicions of the household. The music is beautiful but terribly difficult to bring to life on the piano. It demanded orchestration. The third piece, called *Don Juan's Serenade*, dedicated to me, was a colorful and brilliant piece which I played successfully in public. Karol had changed; I had already begun to be aware of it before the war when a wealthy friend and admirer of his had invited him twice to visit Italy. After his return he raved about Sicily, especially Taormina. "There," he said, "I saw a few young men bathing who could be models for Antinoüs. I couldn't take my eyes off them." Now he was a confirmed homosexual, he told me all this with burning eyes. "Paul told you about all the terrible things which happened to us. I'm happy to tell you that I succeeded in bringing my whole family to Warsaw, where from now on I have to look after them. On several occasions we barely escaped with our lives. The peasants murdered a few landowners in the Ukraine and mutilated Prince Sanguszko, so we can thank God that we are all safe. But, Arthur, you won't believe it, but in Kiev, right after the flight from Tymoszówka, I found the greatest happiness—I lived in heaven. I met a young man of the most extraordinary beauty, a poet with a voice that was music, and, Arthur, he loved me. It is only thanks to our love that I could write so much music. I even have a third sonata and a third symphony. Since my flight to Warsaw I lost all contact with him, so you can well imagine how I feel now." I hardly recognized the Karol of old; here was a young man in love for the first time.

It made me sad to learn that Gabriel Astruc had gone bankrupt only a few months after giving Paris the last theater worthy of the great

city. This theater had been his dream, which he brought to life by his increasing efforts to get the great amount of money required. But it was his
ambition to make it a thing of great beauty. It took uncanny energy to get a
Bourdelle to embellish the façade of the building, a Maurice Denis to decorate the ceiling, the great painter Vuillard to contribute a series of masterly
paintings of different scenes of Molière comedies for the foyer of the
Comédie des Champs-Elysées. He had even the luck to have Sem, the greatest caricaturist of Paris, paint a large fresco of famous Parisians in the bar of
the theater—among them the Grand Duke Vladimir of Russia and the
Maharajah of Kapurthala, of whom the proud Parisians liked to say, "Ce
sont des vrais Parisiens." Paris, I believe, is the only city where just to live in
it is considered an honor. They even said of Edward VII when he visited the
city, "Il est très Parisien."

Misia Sert invited me to have tea with Diaghilev, Massine, and Eric
Satie, whom I met for the first time. He was a small man with little hair left,
bearded, and with eyeglasses which sat unsafely on his nose. When he spoke
he would hold his hand in front of his mouth, apparently to cover some bad
teeth, and I didn't know any of his music, but he was generally credited as
the master who had shown the way to "The Six." His *titre de gloire* was
the fact that Debussy took the trouble to orchestrate his *gymnopédies*. His
small pieces for the piano were better known for the witty titles and remarks in the scores than for the music itself. He would call a piece "in the
shape of a pear" or "crescendo if you believe me" (*si vous m'en croyez*) or
where a sudden pianissimo followed a fortissimo, he would ask the pianist
to hunch over the keyboard (*le dos voûté*). On that occasion he struck me
as a wit, full of vitality. With the great help of Misia, who was of Polish
origin, we tried to interest Diaghilev in Szymanowski and his music and we
succeeded. Diaghilev invited Karol and me for dinner at the Continental.

We arrived punctually, asked the desk to telephone his room and
announce our arrival, and sat down and waited in the lobby. After a few
minutes we saw the great man appear at the top of the staircase to the
second floor and come slowly down toward us, followed by a young man.
Szymanowski, who had been waiting indifferently, looked suddenly as if he
were about to have a heart attack. He scared me. But in less than a second I
saw that his face was composed again, although there was a tragic expression in his eyes. Diaghilev greeted us graciously and introduced the young
man as a new collaborator. Karol murmured something and we went to
dinner. I suddenly knew what was wrong; when the young man came down
the staircase I saw on Karol's face who he was, and the dinner became a
game. Diaghilev showed that he had an inkling that something was in the air
and the young man, mortally afraid of losing his position, had to play the
extremely difficult role of someone who had never met Karol before. And

Karol was torn between the wild urge to speak out and the knowledge that the young man would immediately be dismissed and that Diaghilev would have nothing more to do with Karol. I had to play the part of moderator and keep the conversation flowing. The arrival of Stravinsky saved the situation. He involved Diaghilev immediately in a long discussion about their plans, which allowed the other two actors of the drama to exchange a few short glances of recognition. Two or three furtive meetings were all Karol succeeded in arranging, but I think it was a sad end to their love.

I dragged Karol one afternoon to the Bar Gaya because I wanted him to meet a few of the young musicians. They received him with respect and politeness, but I felt right away that they had nothing in common. Only Honegger showed a real interest in knowing Karol's work. The Saturday-night dinners there were most enjoyable, with Cocteau the driving force, rarely allowing anybody else to open his mouth. But it was well worth listening to him because I am sure that nobody, except perhaps Oscar Wilde, was a more brilliant conversationalist than Jean. During one of these dinners, after one or two cognacs too many, I addressed my direct neighbor, Jean Hugo, the grandson of Victor Hugo, in a whining voice: "I admire your grandfather so much. I saw *Marion Delorme* and *Ruy Blas* at the Comédie Française with Mounet-Sully. I saw *Les Misérables* on the screen. I pass with the deepest respect his monument on the Place Victor Hugo and walk up and down the avenue Victor Hugo constantly aware of his name, but I never read one blessed word he has written."

"Neither did I," said Jean Hugo.

Poulenc played to me much of his piano music and I picked some of his pieces right away for my repertoire. They were refreshing in their subtle simplicity. Because they always seemed to remind you of something, I sometimes accused them of being simple pastiches. But later I learned better. Poulenc was one of the bravest musicians of his time. He accepted all the influences without qualms but somehow a striking personality emerged. Cocteau had a saying for it: When a great creator copies, his copy becomes an original. Honegger's and Auric's music I heard only later, but I was proud to have a major piece by Poulenc dedicated to me, *Les Promenades*.

On my visits to his studio, Stravinsky played to me parts of his *Noces* and *Coq et le renard*, which was commissioned by the Princess Edmond de Polignac. He usually had a piano score of his works but the latest ones he had to read from the full score, asking me to take over the upper parts, which gave me much trouble because of the constant changes of time signature. While banging the piano he also sang with big accents on the changes of meter. After several such performances I discovered that simply counting to four never failed me. We dined often at some bistro, mostly alone, as

Karol spent evenings with his Polish friends and admirers. Stravinsky took me to a Russian variety show called *The Bat*. Its director, Nikita Baliev, was a marvelous showman. Before the curtain rose, he used to address the public with witty remarks that put them immediately into a good mood. There were sketches with biting comments on the political situation and especially about the Communists. Between the sketches, to vary the program, he would offer some dancing and singing. The greatest success was obtained by a silly polka, played on an accordion by a bearded comic and danced by the most voluptuous blonde imaginable. A Rubens but with curves that were anything but flabby, she would appear showing most of her charms and would leave the audience agape. On a few evenings after the show we had the luck to have this beauty and her best friend, Vera Sudeikin, the wife of the painter, for supper at Fouquet's, where I was the happy host.

A letter from Gabriella Besanzoni announced that she would be arriving with her sister for three days. "I took this short vacation," she wrote, "to see you again after our long separation." It was a nice surprise. I was happy to be able to show her the beauty of Paris—if I hadn't been a pianist, I could have been an excellent guide. As her train was due in the late afternoon, I prepared a nice program for the evening. I reserved a table at Maxim's, a place which was familiar and where the food was good; here she could be sure not to find salads made of worms. After dinner I knew that there would be only one thing that could attract her—the Folies-Bergères, the world-famous variety show, which ever after would remind me bitterly of this fatal night. I was ready to leave for the Gare de Lyon when the telephone rang. It was Stravinsky. "Arthur, I need you. Come as quickly as possible, it's urgent," he said in a muffled voice as if somebody stood with a pistol behind him. "It is absolutely impossible tonight, Igor, but I can come first thing in the morning."

"No, no," he continued in Russian, "you don't seem to understand. I must see you tonight." I told him in a few words my story about Besanzoni and how utterly impossible it was to let her down, but he seemed not to take it in. He even interrupted me and said in earnest, "Arthur, it is a question of life and death." This last sentence and his voice alarmed me. I began to feel for certain that he was facing some grave danger and that he counted on me to save him. I had no choice so I went to see Karol for advice and help. He was rather skeptical: "I think Stravinsky is pretty indiscreet to demand this of you." But he didn't convince me. "Karol," I implored, "I ask you, I beg you to do something for me, something which I know you hate to do more than anything, but I think you owe it to our friendship. You are the only person who can save my face with Mme. Besanzoni and her sister. She would never pardon me if I didn't handle it in the most delicate way. I reserved a table at Maxim's. I shall give you plenty of money to give them the best food and drink, all the champagne you like. You would have to take them later to this box [I handed him the tickets] at the Folies-Bergères, where you can put them in front and sit behind and sleep. I will do my very best to join you there. Karol, if you do this for me I shall never forget it. Tell them the truth and tell Besanzoni how unhappy I am to do this to her." The poor fellow gave in. I knew he would have rather gone to jail. I rushed to Stravinsky's hotel. He hardly took the time to greet me and simply said, "Let us go somewhere where we can be alone." As it was dinnertime, I thought of one of the private rooms at Lapérouse restaurant on the Quais, where I sometimes took one of these rooms for another kind of company than that of this ominous evening. When the maître d'hôtel entered to take our orders Stravinsky dismissed him with "Come back when we ring," and then he poured out the whole story.

"Since the beginning of the war, I have lived in constant fear of not being able to provide for my family. Our estate in Russia was confiscated and we lived mostly on the money from there. Diaghilev couldn't pay his debts. He was himself, you know, in dire trouble. Your generous help from America paid my arrears and was soon gone. And here I am living mainly on promises for the future. Thanks to Mr. Lyon of the house of Pleyel, I have a place where I can work. Diaghilev has commissioned an opera-ballet, which I hope to finish next summer for his new season. But now I can't see any way out. But all this would not discourage me; for this I always had enough strength of character. But I live in deadly fear of an incurable illness." And then he lowered his voice and told me in a deeply confidential tone: "I fell in love with a woman and found out to my despair that I have become completely impotent." At that I laughed loudly. "You are crazy, Igor. It has happened to me more than once. The emotion of the first approach paralyzes your physique. So don't give it a thought."

"Arthur, I got this morning to a point where I was ready to finish my life. And my instinct told me that only your cheerful presence could prevent me from losing my control. Just to tell you all this makes me feel better already."

I rang the bell and ordered a good dinner with a bottle of vodka. "Misia Sert," I said, "is a woman of great resources. I have no doubt that when I talk to her, she will find a way to give you solid financial help. Diaghilev and his ballet couldn't have survived the war without her help. As to your fear of illness, it takes a good checkup and I could swear that it will give you the assurance that you are perfectly well. You wouldn't have the strength to work, your good appetite, and your usual vitality if something were really wrong with you. As to your fear of impotence, it makes me laugh. I know how to cure it." With the excellent dinner and two or three small glasses of vodka I succeeded in cheering him up. After one cup of coffee I said, "Now you must do something for me, Igor. Let us go to the Folies-Bergères and join my abandoned friend, and Karol is probably losing his mind with boredom." He meekly acquiesced. We reached the famous music hall just before the end of the show. In the box sat Gabriella, changed into a fury. Her sister didn't dare to greet us and Karol looked like a schoolboy punished by his master and forced to stay after school for hours. Besanzoni said in an icy voice, "Mr. Szymanowski, take us home." Karol gave me a helpless glance and escorted the ladies out. Igor assisted at this scene with regal indifference. He said quietly, "Where shall we go now?" At that point I was fed up with the whole thing. "I'll take you to a famous bordello, 12 rue Chabanais; that will cure you." He followed me without a word.

At this famous institution I said to the sous-maîtresse, "Call Madeleine." And when this beauty arrived, I told her, "Madeleine, take care of this gentleman." It was the first time that I did not participate but simply waited. After half an hour, Stravinsky appeared in triumph and said appreciatively, "Cette femme est géniale." So ended a difficult day.

Next morning, I received a letter from Gabriella: "Arturo, ho capito tutto.* You are a dirty pederast. I already had my doubts in America but now I am sure. Your lover showed us clearly that he hated to be with us and not with you. I hope I shall never see you again, Gabriella." She departed the next day and I saw her only years and years later when she was married to a Brazilian multimillionaire and I was married to Nela Mlynarska. She came to my concert in Rome and congratulated me on both my playing and my wife.

25

All during that time in Paris, I was constantly asked to play. Darius Milhaud, visibly impressed by the fifteen triumphant concerts in Rio de Janeiro, spread my fame in exaggerated terms, but I preferred to rest comfortably on my Brazilian laurels because I knew my Paris well. This

---

* Arturo, now I understand everything.

intelligent, fickle, not too musical and therefore dangerous public would easily tire of an artist unless he causes a sensation. They pretend to know beforehand what to expect from him. "He is only good for Beethoven," they would say of Artur Schnabel, "but otherwise he is a bore." A second-rate pianist would be acclaimed as *"sublime dans Chopin."* At a concert of Alfred Cortot they would wait with impatience for the moment when his memory would fail. I had learned a good lesson in England when I was stamped a salon pianist whose only forte was Spanish music. I was made to suffer from it for years. And so, at musical reunions at Milhaud's or at Poulenc's, I refused to play anything of my repertoire, amusing them instead with lovely tangos and songs by López Buchardo, Brazilian sambas and other folkloric tidbits, which they enjoyed tremendously and which didn't hurt me.

Ignacy brought me sad news from home. My mother's health was failing, but, he added, my parents had received the gold pieces from Ordynski and my sisters were offended by the food I sent to them. "For whom does he take us," they apparently said, "to send us milk and such things?" I regretted that I hadn't sent them caviar. That they might have appreciated.

Stravinsky recovered from his gloom and thanks to Misia Sert he was provided with a sum which helped him to spend the summer in Biarritz, where he intended to work on his new assignment for Diaghilev, a sort of ballet-opera, *Mavra*. The libretto was by his young collaborator. Karol left for London to join the Kochanskis and I had to give a few concerts in Spain before our reunion in London.

My first concert was in Pamplona and was to be followed by Madrid, Valencia, and Barcelona. The night before my departure on the Sud-Express, I had a wild night in the company of Avila and two charming ladies. It began with a dinner at Maxim's, continued in Montmartre, and finished at the Abbaye de Thélème, the only place where you could find real food in the early morning. I returned to my hotel at seven just to take a bath, dress in a hurry, and leave for the Gare d'Orsay. Enrique had packed everything and we had just time to jump onto the already departing train. I had a seat in the crowded lounge car, where there was so much of the passengers' hand luggage that one could not move his feet. I was in a state of collapse, unable to sleep or doze or eat anything. It was a painful twelve hours. After a lengthy customs and change of train at Irún, I finally reached San Sebastián late at night. A taxi took us to the Hotel María Cristina; when I rang the bell an old man in shirt sleeves opened the door and said that the hotel was closed, as it is usually empty for the winter, but he could give me a room for the night.

After Enrique unpacked my pajamas and toilet things and left for his rest, I suddenly realized that I was famished. I hadn't eaten anything for the whole day. The old man told me there was no kitchen and nothing to be had in the hotel. By then it was one o'clock. Everything was closed in town. "But," he said, "the Casino in front of the hotel is open all night and they have a restaurant." There was nothing else to do but follow his advice.

When I entered the hall I heard loud cries: "Arturo, Arturo, what are you doing here?"—some of my best Spanish friends. They took me to the restaurant, made me eat and drink much more than I needed, and wouldn't hear of my going to bed. "There is a good game going on," they said, "and there are some lovely women around the roulette table." I started to play. My good-luck number 29 came out twice in succession. Greatly cheered by this unexpected success, I continued playing and began to lose. This I couldn't tolerate. When my pocket money was gone I rushed to the hotel for my gold pieces. Only a few of them. I lost them too and went back to the hotel to get the rest of them. Toward morning everything was gone except the small sum I needed for the hotel and the day in Pamplona. The train for Pamplona was leaving at nine o'clock in the morning, which gave me less than two hours to sleep. The old man and Enrique had a hard time getting me on my feet. Seated half dead in the first-class compartment, I begged a fellow passenger to wake me at Pamplona if I happened to fall asleep. He forgot and woke me only at the last moment, when I was in danger of continuing with the train to Zaragoza. I jumped out of the moving train in a panic, found Enrique, and we drove to the Hotel La Perla on the square in front of the Teatro Gayarre, where I had to play.

A charming old lady was at the desk. It was one o'clock. I begged her to let me sleep undisturbed until five o'clock and explained the reason. She promised. Enrique unpacked in a hurry and I hopped into bed and in less than a minute was asleep as if I were dead. About a quarter of an hour later there was a loud knock at the door. I woke up with a start. "What is it!" I screamed in fury. "Los Señores de la Filarmónica."

"Please come back to fetch me for the concert and for heaven's sake let me sleep; otherwise there will be no concert!" My head fell on the pillow and I slept again right away.

An hour later, loud knocking woke me up and practically made my heart stop from the shock. I jumped out of the bed to kill my torturer. When I opened the door I saw three serious-looking gentlemen with concerned expressions on their faces who said, "We must see you right away." So I let them in. "What is it?" I asked.

"You see," they said timidly, "there is no concert. We tried in vain to let you know through your manager but we see you didn't get the message." Had I been much younger I would have begun to cry. But all I could do was to ask them how I could get to Madrid. I already had my ticket. They said, "A bus can take you this evening to Alsasua, where you will have to wait until two in the morning for the Madrid Express to arrive from Paris."

Alsasua was a small station and the *fonda** was closed after midnight, so I settled down in the cold for the long wait. But here something touching happened which can only happen in Spain. Two men from nowhere approached me, asked if I was Arturo Rubinstein, and said rather shyly, "We knew from the papers that you were going to Madrid tonight, and as this station is so inconvenient, we permitted ourselves to prepare you a little supper in our office. We are the *telegrafistas* of the station." They gave me cold ham and cheese and coffee, chatted happily, and even admitted that they had never heard me play. Their lovely gesture compensated a lot for the Pamplona disaster and all it involved.

26

In Madrid, Manuel de Falla came to see me at the Palace Hotel with a portfolio. It contained the long-expected composition I had commissioned him to write for me. He gave it to me with a shy smile. "It is rather long. I wrote it in the spirit of my *Amor brujo*, which you liked so much. As I was writing it, I could hear you playing it in my mind. Please accept this manuscript of the *Fantasía Bética* and my dedication with my friendship and gratitude for your appreciation of my work." We went solemnly to the piano, where he put the precious manuscript on the stand and played it for me with great difficulty, stopping here and there to make a passage clearer to me. I then took his place at the piano and tried to read it at sight. I had a hard time. The piece had many technical problems with its stylized flamenco character, complicated imitations of the guitar, and a few too many glissandi. I thanked de Falla effusively and promised to learn it. I decided to present it as soon as possible at a concert in a suitable provincial town in Spain. We celebrated the occasion with two cups of chocolate each at the Mallorquina.

I had lunch with Elisabeth Asquith, Margot's daughter, who had mar-

* Buffet.

ried Prince Antoine Bibesco, the new Rumanian minister to Spain. He was a man of great culture who had written some good plays and could boast of his great friendship with Proust.

Back in London it was lovely to be with Karol and Paul together. We chatted for hours, exchanging stories of things which had happened to us and making plans for the immediate future. Paul was looking forward to his first appearance in America. I had a few minor concerts provided by R.E. and some better ones which I arranged by myself. We both looked at Karol with the same thought in our minds. "Why don't you come with us? I know everybody in New York," I said. "You could show your opera to Bodanzky, who has great authority at the Met. There are conductors who might like to give first performances of your works, and as London and Paris have nothing to offer for the moment, we think that it would be a great opportunity for you."

Karol was not easy to handle. He suffered from agoraphobia and was exceedingly reserved with strangers. He also had an aversion to showing his works to musicians who had not already heard of him. He would say, "I hate to pass exams at my age!" All this did not make my task easy, but he had the confidence of a child in both of us; he felt safe in our company. And so the four of us left full of hope for the New World.

Alexander Siloti, a famous pupil of Liszt and for many years conductor of a symphony orchestra bearing his name in St. Petersburg, succeeded in escaping from Soviet Russia via Scandinavia with all his family. In London, he made a habit of coming daily to have a friendly visit with Paul and me. In spite of the great difference in our ages, he offered us the familiar "thou," as we were always speaking Russian, and showered on us tiresome arrangements of Bach chorales and toccatas for the piano. Before we had to leave for America, he brought me one morning a long letter in an opened envelope addressed to Rachmaninoff and said to me, "Artur, I want you to add some of your own words to this letter. As you know, Rachmaninoff is my cousin. With his great name, it would be easy for him to help me to get concerts or a professorship or a place as a conductor. My letter explains everything, but it would help if you put in a word of your own about my actual activity, my fine arrangements of Bach, and whatever you and Paul might think of me."

I was not particularly happy about this mission. Rachmaninoff had never shown a special interest in me. When I arrived in New York, I succeeded in making an appointment through Rachmaninoff's secretary and one morning I appeared at his home with the fat envelope in my hand. The Russian master received me very politely, made me sit down on the other side of his desk, and quietly took the letter without comment. After reading the twenty-odd pages he turned to me without a smile. "I say: Can one recommend Siloti as a pianist?" He dismissed me politely without another word on the matter. I hasten to calm my readers' disappointment about Rachmaninoff's behavior, reassuring them that in spite of his cruel opinion, Siloti obtained the master class of the Juilliard School and was highly regarded by his fellow musicians in America.

Sophie Kochanska, who had a gift for organization, found a charming apartment on the East Side in the Thirties which Paul and I took for three months. It had convenient accommodations for all four of us. Karol had a nice room on the courtyard—he hated noise. Sophie got us an Italian girl who cooked and looked after the apartment, while Enrique served the table and looked after our things.

The neighbors on our floor were a charming young couple; Mrs. Wendell was a lovely young lady from New England and her husband a manager of a New York bank. We became friendly after a short while and gave dinner parties for each other. One afternoon, on leaving the house, I saw a striking beauty walking ahead of me. She was tall and slim and so unusually elegant that I followed her, trying discreetly to pass by her. Reaching the corner of the street, we both had to stop. Here I could admire not only her fine, dark-eyed face but her great distinction as well. She ignored my obvious attention and crossed the street, leaving me gaping.

At the Wendells' next dinner there was a surprise for me. "This is my sister, Mrs. Hay," said Ruth Wendell. And there was the very lady I had followed in the street. Mrs. Hay reminded me with a charming smile of my indiscretion on the street. "I must admit I was rather flattered because I knew who you were." Clarence Hay, her husband, was the only son of John Hay, Theodore Roosevelt's famous Secretary of State. Poor Ruth died a very young woman of a horrible illness but the Hays remained among my best friends in the world and Alice Hay, now a widow, never lost her beauty and her bearing.

Paul's debut was a sensation. He played the Brahms concerto conducted by Walter Damrosch with the Symphony Orchestra. I had never heard him as inspired as on this evening. His manager, George Engels, had no difficulty in exploiting this success and Paul was right away in great demand by the most important orchestras and could look forward to a full season. As for myself, R. E. Johnson provided me with nothing better than the Commodore and Biltmore musicales, concerts given in other cities by some women's clubs and the like. Fortunately my personal friendship with a few conductors like Pierre Monteux, Joseph Stransky (!), Alfred Hertz, and Ysaye in Cincinnati helped to keep my name in some esteem. Socially I continued to be the frequent guest of what New York called its Society; the Cornelius Vanderbilts, Mrs. Lanier, and my old friend from the Draper epoch in London, Hoyty Wiborg, constantly invited me for lunch or dinner. I introduced them to Paul and Zosia, whose main talent lay in winning the friendship of the great, the rich, and the famous. Paul did not share her snobbish mania. He loved, above all, the company of musicians and a good game of bridge or poker. Szymanowski loathed both going out and playing cards. He loved to be left alone to his composing and made friends with a few young musicians who learned to love his music: Alexander Steinert, Wladimir Dukelsky, and two young violinists who enthusiastically included Karol's violin pieces in their repertoire. He did show his opera *Hagith* to Artur Bodanzky but without good results. Karol's music was foreign to his Wagnerian background and held no promise for a success at the Metropolitan, where only the well-established operas were welcome. Pierre Monteux, the best musician among conductors, immediately recognized the beauty of Karol's Second Symphony and put it on the program for his tour with the Boston Symphony for the next season.

A young Cuban manager asked me to give three or four concerts in Havana, which I accepted gladly, remembering my so brusquely interrupted success through the fault of dear R. E. Johnson. Karol accompanied me, as I thought that it might amuse him to visit this exotic island. This little incursion into my American season proved to be great fun. Karol was fascinated by the irresistible rhythm and dancing of the Cuban sambas. I allowed him to attend only one of my concerts, in which I played some of his pieces, knowing how he hated to sit alone in any public place. At night we went to the famous gambling casino, where the money I lent him for good luck brought him a nice pile of Cuban pesos. We returned to New York refreshed by the experience and with cash in our pockets. Paul had good news for us: George Engels had organized a fine tour for the next season for him and he had received an offer to become a professor at the Juilliard School of Music, considered the best in the country. He accepted it on condition that he would be able to continue his concerts.

There was an exceptional event, which I have kept firmly in my memory. Prokofiev played the world premiere of his famous Third Concerto under Walter Damrosch. Sitting in the conductor's family box, Karol and I were electrified by the extraordinary originality and beauty of this work. I must quickly add that it was one of the few occasions where his performance was just the right one for the work—technically perfect and this time with a beautiful tone. The public responded with indifferent applause, but I am happy to have lived long enough with the knowledge that this work is played brilliantly by all the pianists to enthusiastic audiences.

The four of us left on the same boat which had brought us and we landed in England, where the Kochanskis remained while Karol left for Warsaw.

Mr. Mitchell began to adopt some of the bad habits of R. E. Johnson. Instead of getting concerts in serious cities like Liverpool or Manchester, he had for me a string of seaside resorts where my public consisted of retired officers back from India and their wives and asthmatic old ladies taking cures. After a few such experiences in Hastings, Eastbourne, and Bournemouth, I became sick and tired of it. I was impatient to return to Paris.

27

Very, very sad news awaited me there. Ignacy told me that both of my parents had died. My poor mother had died of cancer and my father, whom I had never seen ill, survived her only by two months. He had died from pneumonia, which seemed to be only a pretext. He simply couldn't survive the death of his wife after fifty-two years of marriage. I was very unhappy. I had been looking forward to being able to send them on some cure but all this was shattered. Ever since my days in Berlin our ways had been separate. I had seen my whole family casually for a day or two when I went to Lodz for a concert, and then I would sense a secret link with my father's character, I felt love and gratitude toward my good brother Staś, and I was somehow attached to my sister Jadwiga.

I left for Lodz right away, leaving Enrique in Paris. Great changes had taken place since Poland had resumed an important place in the family of European nations. We had a president occupying the old royal castle, and Pilsudski, the worshipped hero, as head of state. I found my birth town greatly impoverished. The good days during which the textile industry had given my town the name of a second Manchester were gone. They had lost the immense Russian market and had to seek new ones in postwar Europe, which was so greatly impoverished. The reunion with my family was a very sad one. The presence of my parents had always lent a patriarchal touch which was now missing. Our apartment was occupied by my brother Staś, as before, and by two aunts, one a widow, who was my darling Neomi's godmother, and the other the wife of Nathan Follman, the uncle who wrote the famous letter to Joachim when I was three years old. Staś had lost his prominent position with the Russian bank where he had worked for years. My second brother, Tadeus, the engineer, was married, and had two little girls but was in bad financial shape. My youngest sister, Frania, had a husband, Leo Likiernik, who was a gambling addict and had constant difficulty providing for his family. His daughter Jadwiga was an excellent pianist and had won a gold medal at the Warsaw Conservatory, and his son was studying medicine but had to leave the university because of the growing anti-Semitism there. Hela and her three children lived in Warsaw. The only successful member of the family remained my brother-in-law Maurice Landau. He had fled with his family to Moscow at the beginning of the war and he made a considerable fortune there; when the Communists came to power he lost everything but succeeded in taking his wife and children to Berlin, where he managed to get in touch with a celebrated upstart millionaire, Stinnes, who helped him to become rich again rapidly. He bought one of the largest textile factories in Lodz and another one in Zagreb in Croatia, and installed his family in a comfortable apartment in Nice, where he retired, leaving the management of the factories to his son. Staś got the job of cashier in the factory but was soon on bad terms with his nephew, who had inherited from his father only the worst parts of his character along with an additional touch of cruelty and extreme egotism. Staś had plans for a business of his own and even found a partner. I gave him the money he needed for entering this partnership, but his partner cheated him, disappeared with the money, and left poor Staś to take back his job at the factory. I can only say I was happy to be able to help my nephew Likiernik to finish his medical studies at Montpellier, where he graduated brilliantly, but back in Warsaw the university authorities didn't grant him the so-called "nostrification," so that he could not exercise his profession in Poland. He, his charming sister, and his parents all perished later in Hitler's concentration camps with the rest of my family, except for a few nephews and nieces who escaped the holocaust.

28

Warsaw and Lodz had two enterprising managers. The minute they heard of my arrival they came forward with proposals for my reappearance in both towns. I agreed to come back sometime in the future but insisted that I be paid in dollars, as the new Polish zloty was dangerously fluctuating.

I left for Spain for two concerts in Madrid. The second one, in the Teatro Real, I gave as a gesture of gratitude for what Spain had done for me and turned over the receipts to Queen Victoria Eugenia for the charities of her choice. In need of rest, I went to Seville for the *feria* for the third time.

As usual, I found a nice room and my *cordobés* hat and a valet's room for Enrique at the Hotel de Madrid. The manager told me that Seville was enjoying the greatest affluence of all time because the King and Queen had arrived to stay at the Alcazar Palace. As before, I rented an open carriage with two mules for my stay and drove with my *cordobés* on my head, like a proud *sevillano*, to the *feria*. The crowded *casetas* took charge of me right away. I had to pose for a photographer cranking a street organ. They took photos of me dancing the *sevillanas* and with an eternal glass of *jerez* in my hand. The next day, the biggest *corrida* took place with Gallito, Belmonte, and Gaona, and I was lucky to get a good seat in the *barrera* from the Duke of Alba, who always had some spare seats. The first day finished in an orgy at the Venta de Antequera with flamencos, *jamón serrano*, and more *jerez*. I returned completely exhausted to the hotel, where a telegram awaited me: "Arrive with a friend tomorrow ten o'clock in the morning. Please reserve me two rooms. Greetings, Alma Gluck." I fell on the floor in terror and in this position I remembered the whole thing. At a large dinner at Mrs. Lanier's, I had been seated next to Alma Gluck, the famous soprano of the Metropolitan Opera House, wife of Efrem Zimbalist, the violinist. She was a good-looking, charming young lady. Usually it is difficult to find a topic of conversation with your neighbor at a dinner, and I am always careful to choose a nice neutral, noncommittal subject, especially with professional people. And so, on this fatal night I was extolling the wonders of the *feria* of Seville thousands of miles away—a topic that was completely safe. To round off my madrigal about Seville I finished by saying, "You ought to come to see the *feria*. It is something one shouldn't miss." I remember very well her answer: "If I should decide to come, would you take care of me?" To which I gallantly answered, "Without boasting I can assure you I am the best guide for such an occasion." I also remember that, unfortunately, I mentioned the beauty of the Hotel de Madrid. I want my reader to trust that I always try to behave like a gentleman; this was a difficult occasion to prove it. As there was absolutely no room to be had at the hotel, or anywhere else, I decided to give her mine, which had two beds for the two ladies, and I would take the miserable one reserved for Enrique, whom I eventually sent out to sleep in the street. I asked the maître d'hôtel to prepare a lovely table for three with the famous red carnations on it and to give especially good service at breakfast. I rang up the secretary of the Duke of Alba to see if by any chance he had two extra seats for the *corrida* for one of the most famous singers of all time and her companion, who were arriving by surprise and would hate to miss the famous attraction of the *feria*. By a sheer miracle, he did have two more *barreras*. Tired to death after the sleepless night, my body feeling as though it were a barrel of *jerez*, I took my mules and drove to the railway station. Alma Gluck waved from the open window and, followed by a lady whose age I could judge as between forty and sixty and who had three prominent golden teeth, descended from the train. I greeted them with all the grace I could muster and after getting her luggage led them proudly to my carriage. To express timidly my not too small resentment for this unexpected intrusion, I said bitterly, "You should have given notice of your charming arrival two or three weeks ahead. I forgot to mention in New York, the city is overcrowded during the *feria* and so all I have to offer you is my room, which fortunately has two beds, so that you can share it with your friend." They were not interested in hearing where I would be myself but showed disappointment in not getting two separate rooms. After my delicate reproach I said, all smiles, "A lovely Sevillian breakfast awaits you in the patio of the Hotel de Madrid, which I described to you so nicely, you remember, Alma?" Alma answered in a businesslike tone: "Before we go to the hotel, I must go to the bank."

"To a bank?" I asked.

"I never have cash on me—I want to take out a checkbook. My bank sent a note to a bank on Sierpes." (I forget the name.) I tried sweetly to dissuade her. "I can lend you all the money you need for your stay and you can give me an American check." But she wouldn't hear of it. She repeated sternly, "Arthur, drive us to the bank." Driving in this case became a joke because the calle Sierpes, where this bank was, does not allow carriages, so we had to walk. At the bank we found two young employees who were playing cards and looked annoyed when we stopped their game. Alma delivered a document to one of them and asked for a checkbook representing the sum of money advised by her bank. Both employees turned toward me. "Don't you know that today is a holiday? There is no one here except us, and we are leaving too in a moment." Alma did not know a word of Spanish but understood their gestures and asked me to insist on getting the checkbook. They became alarmed and began to look for the letter from New York, which after a long while they failed to find. A little shoe cleaner, who sat on the steps of the bank, said, "Such documents are always put in a special drawer there to the left." They followed his advice and eventually found the letter. The young man said he couldn't deliver the checkbook but could give her the money and suddenly asked me for my signature on a paper he produced. Upon my declaration that the money was hers, they asked, "Pero usted es el marido?"* and after my negative answer, they drily said, "We can't give you anything without the signature of your husband." When I translated that, Alma went into hysterics. "This country is in the Middle Ages. I never heard of such an outrage. Let us go immediately to the American consulate!" There was nothing to do but obey; we drove to the American consulate, where the consul, receiving Alma Gluck's card, invited us immediately into his private drawing room and called in all his family to meet the celebrated singer and get her autograph. Her complaint about the bank made no impression, but he told her, "The consulate can lend you all the money you wish." I dared to hope that she would immediately take the train back to Paris. "Well, all right," she gave in. "This is one country which I will never visit again." And she accepted the money from the consul. Out in the street she said gloomily, "Well, Arthur, let us go to that hotel of yours for that delicious breakfast you talked about." At the hotel we went straight to the patio, but the breakfast, the table, and the carnations were gone. They had waited in vain for three hours. We had to wait another two hours until lunch was served. When she calmed down finally, I told her proudly of my good luck in obtaining fine seats for the bullfight that afternoon. Her companion, who until then had not opened her mouth, now showed her three golden teeth, enthusiastically clapping her hands. "How exciting!"

After lunch, the two ladies rested in my room while I tried to doze in one of those hard Spanish chairs of Cordovan leather.

My carriage drove us to the ring, Alma Gluck beautifully dressed and looking proud next to the fake Spanish hidalgo with a red carnation in his lapel. Her companion fortunately did not open her mouth. I introduced the two ladies to the Duke of Alba, who greeted them graciously, pretending even to have heard Alma Gluck—a thing I would bet he had not. When the King and Queen arrived, the Queen beautiful in her mantilla and high comb, the great parade of the toreros began. It was a wonderful sight. The three great matadors, in their costly gala costumes, short trousers, and beautiful silk stockings *couleur de chair*, were followed by the banderilleros and the heavy picadors on horseback with their legs protected by pounds of heavy leather. The mayor gave a sign and the signal was blown on the trumpet to begin the fight. A powerful dark bull, who had been penned up for hours in the dark, dashed into the blazing sunlight and attacked furiously everything he saw. After a few graceful movements with the *capas*, the two picadors rode in. It was still the unhappy time when the horses were unprotected, so in most cases the poor animals were left dead on the

* But you are the husband?

arena floor when the infuriated bull with his sharp horns lifted both horse and rider in the air. When this happened, Alma gave a wild shriek: "Murderers, murderers!" She shouted at the crowd, jumped out of her seat, and made a sign to her companion to follow. But her placid friend loved the show and said quietly, "I stay here." And so, poor me, again I was the victim and had to run after the enraged singer, who was by then being insulted by some of the public. "Callese, sinvergüenza." I had to take the bitterly sobbing Alma to the hotel, where she went up to her room. I, of course, dashed back to the arena to see the rest of the show.

In the evening a completely transformed Alma Gluck appeared in the lobby for dinner in a white dazzling evening dress. She looked quite beautiful. She smiled at me with an irresistible charm and said, "Poor Arthur, I did give you a hell of a day, didn't I?" After a delicious meal of fresh *langostinos* and other Sevillian specialties, I invited my guest to a long fine flamenco session at the Venta de Antequera, where I always found my cabin and my flamencos ready for me. Alma left her companion behind both because of her behavior at the bullfight and to please me.

At the Venta, everybody fell in love with her. She was the life of the party, trying to dance a *sevillana* with me, not too badly, and taking the *jerez* bravely like a man. She adored it all. The next day was devoted to visiting this unique city. The huge cathedral, the largest in Spain, with the grave of Columbus, impressed her by its sheer proportions. And the beautiful Giralda tower, which we bravely climbed, gave her a full picture of the majestic Guadalquivir, the Torre del Oro, the Moorish Alcazar, and the beautiful park of María Luisa. But late at night the visit to the Barrio de Santa Cruz enchanted her with its mysterious unspoiled ancient architecture and its romantic atmosphere. When we arrived at the small square I repeated the silly phrase of the official guides: "Here is the bench where Doña Elvira met Don Juan." This brought tears to her eyes.

Alma Gluck left Seville thanking me with a warm kiss for an unforgettable time.

After she had gone, I received a flattering invitation. Guglielmo Marconi, the inventor of the wireless radio, had anchored his yacht *Electra* with its scientific instruments on the Guadalquivir in front of the Torre del Oro. We had met in London at parties and I remember having mentioned my intention of going to the *feria*. Someone must have given him my address and the invitation was to be a guest on his boat for the two days of his stay. I was highly flattered, in spite of being sure that he needed me mainly as a guide.

There were two women on board. One was a ravishing beauty, a young sister of an English lord. The other functioned as her "duenna," but she was all but that. She was the wife of the then famous actor Sir Charles Hawtrey and one of the well-known mistresses of Edward VII. We had fun; my talent as a guide was at its best, but I can remember one disagreeable moment. My highly recommended thick Spanish hot chocolate with *churros*, an Andalusian specialty to be dunked in the delicious nectar, turned out to be a horrible disaster. At the first sip we spat it all out with disgust. On this day, they had nothing but goat's milk, the smell of which is unbearable to any civilized palate. I screamed at the waiter, "This is goat's milk! Shame on you! Don't you have cow's milk?"

"I'll bring it right away." He brought three fresh cups of chocolate. At the first sip we spat it all out again; the man thought he could fool us and we wouldn't know the difference.

Lois, the young girl, was a dangerous flirt. That night after a great flamenco session, Marconi caught us in a passionate, long kiss and made a horrible scene. This didn't upset Lois too much, though, and Lady Hawtrey enjoyed it all thoroughly. This lady, near eighty, had the erect figure of a woman in her thirties; young men would follow her in the streets but when they saw her face would almost faint. I had to take her to dancing places in London and Monte Carlo, where she never stopped dancing with professional dancers whom I had to pay. She compensated for this annoying habit by telling me all the naughty secret stories of her affair with the King of England.

Back in Madrid, I received a sensational letter from Juan. "Monsieur Hebertot, the present director of the Théâtre des Champs-Elysées, offers you an engagement for three recitals during one week with different programs at the equivalent in francs of $400 a concert." How Juan knew Hebertot and how he succeeded in getting this offer I learned later. I sent my acceptance by telegram. This was to be my second debut in Paris— seventeen years after the first premature one, which the optimistic Gabriel Astruc had dared to call a "gala." This time I felt that I had to give a decent account of myself.

Paul arrived from England to join me for a few recitals, playing violin and piano sonatas in some of the principal cities of Spain. This introduction helped to get him many engagements in the future.

29

Back in Paris, Juan introduced me to Mr. Hebertot, whom he had hypnotized into believing that my appearance there would be the greatest thing which could happen to him. This man of the theater prepared the way for my concerts beautifully with sensational announcements in the press and important interviews. The same old devilish Juan found out that the owner of the plush Majestic Hotel, a Mr. Tauber, of Austrian origin, was a passionate lover of music and had had Busoni as an honored guest for weeks at his hotel. Busoni, in gratitude, had dedicated to him his delightful Fantasia on *Carmen*. Mr. Tauber, impressed by my coming concerts and by my famous name (still due to Anton and not to myself), gave me a beautiful apartment on the ground floor of the annex of the Majestic on the rue La Pérouse, consisting of a large living room, a fine bedroom, and a vast, most modern bathroom—the whole at a ridiculously low price. It became my headquarters for a long time to come.

The house of Pleyel sent me a nice piano for my apartment and a beautiful-sounding concert grand for the Théâtre des Champs-Elysées. Gabriel Astruc very intelligently had made it possible for the theater to be transformed into a perfect concert hall with a set continuing the architecture of the hall and with a covering in the form of a shell over the stage giving perfect acoustics. My three programs were carefully chosen. I began the first one with the majestic F major Organ Toccata of Bach, brilliantly transcribed by D'Albert, followed by the Chopin B minor Sonata. The second part finished with *Albaicin* and *Triana*, which were wildly acclaimed, so I added as encores *Navarra* and the *Fire Dance*, which received ovation after ovation. For many years they would never let me finish a concert without playing one or both of these pieces. This phenomenon occurred in Japan, Australia, Italy, and Scandinavia, and in my own country the Poles had a fanatic love for these Spanish pieces.

These three concerts also contained the *Carnaval* and *Symphonic Études* of Schumann, the second volume of the Brahms-Paganini *Variations*, the Liszt sonata, the *Waldstein* Sonata of Beethoven, some Scriabin, Prokofiev, and Szymanowski, the *Barcarolle*, some études and a nocturne or two of Chopin, the *Mephisto Waltz* of Liszt, five or six pieces by Debussy, including my favorite "Ondine," the six short pieces of *O Prole do Bebe* of Villa-Lobos, and, finally, the Polonaise in A flat of Chopin.

The three concerts turned out to be very successful. Hebertot succeeded in gathering the *"tout Paris,"* the real one and not the sham one of my first debut. Besides the elite of the true music lovers, I had Stravinsky, Milhaud and his colleagues, the most important critics, Isidor Philippe and Marguerite Long, the much feared professors of the Paris Conservatory, not to speak of all the pianists present in Paris. Many of them came to all three concerts. Overnight I earned the title which remains to this day: "Artur Rubinstein est un vrai Parisien."

The critics treated me well, practically without exception. The Villa-Lobos pieces were acclaimed. My Chopin found some detractors, who found it brilliant but a little dry. Paderewski's exaggerated sentimentalism and Alfred Cortot's too delicate conception were still considered the true way to play the Polish master, and Cortot's treatment of Chopin as the weak tubercular artist was still in public favor. My own conception of Chopin was always based on the conviction that he was a powerful, masculine creator, completely independent of his physical condition, just as in the case of Beethoven, who was weak and ill while creating his greatest masterpieces. The A-flat Polonaise of Chopin has more pride and heroic impact than any composition by Liszt.

After the concert, the artist's room was invaded by enthusiastic well-wishers. I even received an unusual present that night. A lovely American actress, whom I had met in the United States, came backstage and said, "Your playing enchanted me. I would like to give you a present but I have none to offer except myself. If you would like to spend the night with me, you can have me." It was a great night.

Those concerts made quite an impression in Paris. *"Le tout Paris"* is a sort of a power that can make or break an artist. It was my luck that they adopted me. I was showered with invitations, among them one from the Baroness Edouard de Rothschild, who took a great interest in successful Jewish artists. She offered me an attractive fee for giving a concert for her guests in their beautiful house, which had been built by Talleyrand at the corner of the Place de la Concorde and the rue St. Florentin. I agreed to play but not to dine, as I never eat before playing. The party was magnificent; she invited no one but real music lovers and fine musicians besides the whole large Rothschild family. I played more than I intended and felt at my best. After I finished, Baron Edouard took my arm and led me to a small salon where, helped by the butler, he served me caviar and vodka and some wonderful remains of their dinner. He didn't leave me until I had finished and we joined the guests. Baron Edouard was a great gentleman of authentic aristocratic distinction. More than some members of the oldest families of France, he proved it during the Second World War. Obliged to leave France and all his wealth, he arrived with his wife in New York on the first flight of his life, invited my wife and me to a dinner at a modest hotel, and behaved in his role of host exactly as he did on that first evening in his palatial home. Ever since the first contact, I was considered a friend of the whole family and after my marriage their friendship included my wife and my children.

30

After my second concert, Denis Davydov, the eldest son of Madame Nathalie, came to see me. He told me the sad story of his family after their flight from Russia. "My mother, my brother Vassia, and I are now in Paris. My father has found employment at the Monte Carlo casino." In a hardly audible voice he added: "My mother and Kiki, my little brother, you remember, were taken to prison, where she saw with her own eyes how Kiki was shot in the courtyard. They let her go after a few days and she joined us here. But she has never recovered from this terrible shock."

That same day, I went to see her, and found this cheerful, artistic lady changed into an elderly woman with an unalterably tragic expression on her face. She seemed glad to see me again, never mentioned the tragedy, but asked me if I could find work for her at Coco Chanel's. "I hear that she is very kind toward us Russian exiles." I promised, of course, to do all I could.

The first thing was to ask Misia to advise me how to approach Coco Chanel on the subject. "Can she model?" asked Misia. A terrible question. I had to tell her the whole story and she reacted nobly. "Coco might use her as a receptionist or in the accounts department."

She went to work on it right away and obtained Coco Chanel's promise to receive Mrs. Davydov. When I brought the good news Madame Nathalie said, without changing her expression, "Thank you, Arthur. When the moment comes, will you take me to that rendezvous?" I promised.

When I went to fetch her I saw a poignant picture. This grand lady of my Verbovka memories stood there with a makeup so grotesquely exaggerated that it made her look like an old prostitute. It was all the more tragic because she thought it made her look young, and I had not the courage to make the slightest remark about it. Coco Chanel, who really did feel for the Russian exiles, did find something for her, but she did have the courage to tell her to take off that horrible makeup. Mrs. Davydov came to my next concert and later on to others and visited me after, always with the same set expression. One day, I heard the sad news: she had taken a great overdose of barbiturates and had been found dead in the morning with the photo of Kiki in her hand.

Right after my last appearance, a young concert manager visited me at my hotel. He struck me as being enterprising and energetic. Greatly impressed by my success, he offered to take over the management of my concerts in France for a small percentage and said he had no doubts that he was the right man for me. As I had always heard that the two or three known managers of Paris were old men who were contented to run the affairs of a few well-established artists and showed no interest in any newcomer, I agreed to sign a contract for three years with Mr. Marcel de Valmalète. He immediately obtained offers from the Lamoureux Orchestra and the Colonne to be soloist for the next season and advised me to give at the same time two or three recitals at the Salle Gaveau. "Why this small Salle Gaveau?" I asked. "Can't you get the beautiful Salle des Champs-Elysées again?" He answered, "You can have the Salle Gaveau for nothing if you play the Gaveau pianos." His answer gave me a nervous shock. It brought back to my memory my unhappiness at the first contact with this woody, toneless instrument. "I couldn't consider any other piano but Steinway," I told him sternly. He answered with a malicious smile: "French customs do not allow importing. You have only the choice of Gaveau, Erard, and Pleyel, and I advise you strongly to take the Gaveau, which has now a dynamic manufacturer. His instruments developed a better tone while the others have not improved since Chopin and Liszt." Well, poor unfortunate me, I followed his advice. True enough, my Pleyel at the Champs-Elysées lacked power but had a beautiful, human tone, whereas the Gaveaus I tried had more power, a better action, but a cold sound. I had to fight them for some years to come. But all this was still in the near future. For the moment I was bathing in my fresh Parisian glory, accepting all the invitations for luncheons, dinners, parties, dances, and restaurants. My spare time I used for seeing all the worthwhile plays, a good opera or two, and would finish the night in Avila's company or at the recently opened Boeuf sur le Toit, which was managed by a man called Moïse, Jean Cocteau's friend. It succeeded the small Bar Gaya as the great meeting place of musicians, paint-

ers, and writers. Léon-Paul Fargue, Picasso, and Jean Cocteau himself liked
to take me on drinking bouts in which treasures of wit, brilliant repartee,
sharp criticism, and amusing stories kept us wide awake till early hours.

This late spring in Paris was one of the most beautiful I had ever seen.
The lovely old chestnut trees in the avenue du Bois were a majestic sight.
The boulevards were crowded with happy tourists, young men walking
with their arms around their girls, stopping from time to time for a passionate kiss. The café terraces were filled with people talking all languages and
sipping cool drinks. At night, the rue Pigalle in Montmartre was invaded by
noceurs ever hungry for new sensations. The Russian cabarets were the hit
of the season, with Russian ex-generals in a different kind of uniform as
doormen. Inside, Caucasian dancers, dressed in native costumes with wasp
waists, dancing on their toes in soft leather boots, excited the French ladies
to distraction. Montparnasse was becoming rapidly the rival of Montmartre.
Here you saw mainly painters, sculptors, and their beautiful models spending their nights at La Coupole, La Rotonde, and Le Dôme, drinking Pernod
and wolfing down their food after a day's work. There you could see
Modigliani, my dear, dear friend Moïse Kisling, and the sickly Soutine and
Gottlieb having discussions about art which ended in fist fights sometimes.
Years ago there had been, in the early hours in the Bois de Boulogne, a real
duel between Gottlieb and Kisling, which was the sensation of the day,
having been watched by hundreds of Montparnassians, partisans of one or
the other. Neither of them had any idea about fencing but lashed out at
each other with ferocious temperament. They wouldn't stop even after
drawing blood, and both landed in a hospital. After being released they
reappeared at La Coupole in triumph, reconciled and friends forever.

31

One night I invited Avila, his lovely girl friend, and two young
Frenchmen for supper at the Abbaye de Thélème. "Arturo," said Juan, "the
Abbaye is dead now. Everybody goes to a new place, Le Jardin de Ma
Soeur, in a small street near the Etoile. I shall order a table for you because
it is very difficult to find one."

We entered the place, which had a small garden with a large lawn and a dance floor in the center surrounded by tables, practically all of them occupied. Thanks to Avila, we got a table near the dance floor. The restaurant provided us with an excellent supper. The champagne was properly chilled, the band was very good, and we danced each in turn with our only female companion. Juan never danced but kept us in stitches with his wit and told stories brilliantly. Around three o'clock, I asked for my bill; the maître d'hôtel announced that it was paid. I objected to that, hating to have my bills paid by people not known to me. But the maître d'hôtel reassured me: "Our director offers you this supper." I felt like meeting the generous host to thank him personally. The director turned out to be a woman by the name of Elsa Maxwell. Small and fat, she spoke French haltingly with a dreadful American accent. Her face was that of an ordinary charwoman. Hair of a nondescript color was kept in a bun. Her only attraction lay in her eyes, which showed a sharp, alert intelligence. She was dressed in what she thought was an evening gown and which looked anything but that. She reminded me that we had met and I suddenly remembered where and how it happened. In New York on my first visit just after the war, I had taken part in a gala at the Metropolitan Opera House for the Red Cross. Mary Garden had been the special star. Prokofiev conducted one of his early works and, as far as I remember, Mischa Elman played and so did I. At rehearsal time, there was a fat little lady around who was in charge of the gala. Mary Garden swore by her. "Nobody can run this gala better than that little woman; I tried her in Chicago." Without noticing it, we had all become dependent on her for every detail: the right lighting, the best placement for the orchestra, a higher piano stool, not to speak of free tickets for our friends. She knew to perfection how to distribute the boxes of the famous Diamond Horseshoe. The Vanderbilts sat on the right in their usual best box. Other privileged boxes were sold to the Astors and Goulds. Otto Kahn and his family kept their special box, as he was president of the board, and she put the Rockefellers in a not too conspicuous box; Gatti-Casazza had invited his star singers to his directorial one. The programs, which were to be sold by young ladies of New York society, were printed in beautiful type on specially chosen paper. Many pages were filled with advertisements by different firms. All this huge preparation had been done by Elsa Maxwell. "Now I am running this restaurant," she said to me. "I succeeded in a short time in making it into the best place in Paris." Then she added with a mischievous air: "But I'm afraid that the owner will soon be bankrupt. My method is a very special one. Every day I preside at a huge table in the center to which I invite the most famous personalities in town at the moment. The other day I had the Prince of Wales and his lady friend, Douglas Fairbanks and Mary Pickford, and some members of the highest French aristocracy. As I became your fan, dear Arthur, on that night at the Met, I am happy to have had you and your friends as my guests tonight."

During the years between the wars, this little lady became the toast of Paris, London, New York, Rome, and Venice. Her uncanny vitality was contagious. The old, blasé, lifeless wives or widows of millionaires became puppets in her hands. She would play bridge with old Mrs. Belmont and with the wealthy American wives of French aristocrats and invariably made nice sums of money which she would spend generously on young penniless artists. She would give fantastic parties, for which she always invented a theme, at the Ritz in Paris, at the Danieli in Venice, or at Claridges in London. These parties were invariably paid for by some stranded American millionaire from the dark provinces. She would promise him that he would meet the elite of Paris and the delighted provincial American was only too happy to pay for such a privilege. Considered as just another guest at Elsa's party, nobody paid much attention to him and those in the know sometimes took bets on who was the one who had paid for it all. I wouldn't exaggerate in calling those parties sensational. Elsa always had a surprise up her sleeve. Before one of her grand dinners, she would send out two rented buses to fetch her usually unpunctual guests. They had to come at whatever stage in their dressing they happened to be. You saw lovely women arriving in their underskirts with unzipped backs or in bedroom slippers, men half shaven with soap still on their faces, some duke or marquis minus white tie or in his shorts. Delivered of the usual social constraint, the guests in these ridiculous attires dined practically in the dark and it all made for a riotous time.

I remember a small dinner for twelve at the Duke and Duchess of Gramont's organized by Elsa. That morning she sent me a note by messenger, saying: "Please give the man a nice photo of yourself signed: 'To darling Molly with love and kisses from Arthur,' and send it straight back." I complied, knowing that something was afoot.

This dinner she transformed into a brilliant detective story. We were told that there was the body of a murdered woman in the bedroom and we were asked to find the murderer. Every one of the guests was gravely suspect. After dinner, the twelve of us, transformed into Sherlock Holmeses, had to find the guilty one. My Molly was, of course, the murdered woman. Another man had half a ticket to a cinema dated the day of the murder, the other half being in the bag of the poor victim. There were enough clues to lead to the arrest of all of us. After two hours of a most amusing search, the Duke of Gramont was found out to be the culprit. The murdered woman lay in bed beautifully half undressed with a horrible red mark on her lovely breast.

Elsa's masterpiece was the treasure hunt in London which was so daring that it provoked angry protests in the papers. A very wealthy American, Mrs. Moore, had rented Norfolk House, the proud seat of the first Duke of the Realm, for the summer. Elsa had arranged a huge supper party for her starting at any time late at night. The idea was the following: Each participant had to pay ten pounds; the collected money was put into a sealed envelope as a prize for the winner. The program called for couples, husband and wife or wife with a friend, to chase through all of London hunting for clues to the location of the treasure. Lesley Jowitt was my partner and my driver. We were sent to Hyde Park Corner; there we found a letter which said: "Proceed to War Monument," then to one of the lions at Trafalgar Square, followed by one or two other places I do not remember. But I do remember an almost naked woman at the entrance to the Tower of London who was chained to a wall and finally we were sent to the supper at Norfolk House. The Prince of Wales with a lady companion was one of the participants.

In the great hurry, a little damage was done to the wreaths and flowers laid at the war memorial. The shouting, gay laughter, screams at finding the letters startled many Londoners from their peaceful well-earned sleep. Lesley and I were not the winners but we did get there in time for the most magnificent party, where we supped and danced till around seven in the morning. The papers commented on the damaged flowers and on the terrible noise in the middle of the night and on the Prince of Wales's participation. It was the talk of the town for some weeks.

Elsa Maxwell considered the whole thing the major triumph of her career. She tried to repeat a treasure hunt in Venice but did not count on the pride and fury of the Venetians, who got wind of what was coming and gathered in the Piazza to give a sound beating to the first participants. The rest of them fled in panic to their hotels.

Over the years Elsa and I became great friends. She never failed to invite me and later Nela, my wife, of whom she was very fond, to any event she organized. She loved music and musicians, especially the famous sopranos of her time, like Mary Garden, Geraldine Farrar, later Tebaldi, and quite especially Callas. For me, she sometimes played the role of concert manager. She would telephone me: "Consuelo Balsan, ex-duchess of Marlborough, née Vanderbilt, plans to give a big musical soiree and would like you to play. I managed to get a fee of 25,000 francs for you" (a huge fee in those times). Of course I accepted. The soiree was excellently managed by Elsa. She invited the right people and I had the honor of meeting Paul Valéry that night. The next morning Elsa sent me a letter with a check for 15,000 francs. "Dear Arthur," she wrote, "I kept 10,000 as my percentage for the deal. I'm sure you don't mind." And I didn't mind it at all, knowing that she used all her money to help people in need.

Another time she called to say, "My old friend Mrs. Belmont wants to give a small party for the birthday of her son William K. Vanderbilt. She dreams of having you play and would consider it the nicest present she could offer him. She is ready to pay 40,000 francs. Please, please accept it." It was a royal fee all right, but I was nevertheless very astonished at Mrs. Belmont's idea, having heard in New York from the estranged wife of William K. Vanderbilt that he hated music. However, it might have been pure malice. I offered to send my concert piano for the occasion. But Elsa reassured me: "They have a fine instrument. You'll love it." This was a strange party, I must say. We were not more than eight at dinner. The guests, all Americans, were rather dull and when the birthday cake arrived with its candles, we duly sang "Happy birthday to you," then proceeded to the large living room, where Elsa announced pompously: "And now Arthur Rubinstein will play Chopin." I went ceremoniously to the piano, tried a chord or two, and stopped in panic. It was an old ruined Erard with hardly any sound left. I was just going to get up and express my regrets at not being able to play when Elsa ran up to me and whispered in a terrified voice, "Please, please play, I just sold them the piano." I had not the heart to let her down. I received my check, minus her commission, which amounted this time to 20,000, but I guessed that she must have been hard-pressed for money. I write this story in homage to a remarkable woman who exploited the rich but gave to the poor, whose family and age nobody ever knew, physically so completely unattractive, without any particular gift, but endowed with a powerful vitality which brightened for half a century the lives of hundreds and hundreds of fine people.

32

The season in Paris was as brilliant as ever. Eugenia Errazuriz had a new apartment on the avenue Montaigne. The drawing room had nothing but two pictures by Picasso, a portrait of her daughter and a wonderful landscape.

She showed me with pride her chairs. "Ah! Ah!" she said. "Beautiful chairs. These are the chairs which one hires in the Bois de Boulogne and I was lucky to be able to buy them. I like rooms *vacíos*. Ah! Ah! I hate silly things lying around. You will meet my friend the poet to whom I gave your money. His name is Blaise Cendrars." I did meet him. "You moved me to tears with your 'Pâques à New-York', I exclaimed. I won a friend after my heart.

I saw much of Stravinsky, who had begun his work on *Mavra*, now in a peaceful mood. Poulenc invited me to have tea at his apartment. "Germaine Tailleferre will be there with a young pianist who wants to play the Chopin mazurkas for you. You will also meet a charming lady who sings my songs divinely and plays the piano very well." The pianist, Youra Guller, indeed played some mazurkas with fine taste. But all my attention was absorbed by the other lady, a beautiful young woman, small, dainty, and extremely well dressed with an angelic expression on her small round face, lovely blue eyes, little mouth, red like a cherry with full lips, and delicately shaped straight nose; she was the wife of Dr. Jacquemer, the grandson of Clemenceau, and she was the daughter of the famous dress-maker Madame Jeanne Lanvin. She asked me in an irresistible voice to play something and for once I obeyed immediately and played my beloved *Barcarolle* better than ever on a lovely-sounding Pleyel. She had tears in her eyes. When we walked out into the street, I begged her passionately to have lunch with me. She refused at first, making difficult excuses, but finally accepted my invitation for a few days hence in one of the restaurants in the Bois de Boulogne. The day before our lunch, I received a telegram saying that, to her regret, she couldn't come. I met her again some time later in the company of her new husband, the very good-looking Count Jean de Polignac, the younger brother of my old friend the Marquis Melchior. "Arthur, you are the godfather of our marriage. Jean and I were in love for a long time and he was, of course, the best friend of my first husband. He dined with us on the evening after you moved me so much with the *Barcarolle*. When I announced my intention to lunch with you, my husband had nothing against it but Jean lost his usual calm, burst into a violent rage, and shouted at me: 'I shall not tolerate you being alone with this man. He runs after every woman in Paris.' This brought about a dreadful scene between the two men which ended in our divorce. So you see, now, thanks to you, we are happily married!" We became lifelong friends. Jean died after the Second World War and Marie Blanche gave evenings of music in the studio of her beautiful house, where Poulenc would show us his new concerto or play with Jacques Février his sonata for two pianos, and Henri Sauguet and Georges Auric performed their new ballets composed for Diaghilev. Sometimes we heard the hostess singing a few songs in her small but pure silvery voice. The listeners were mainly musicians.

I had met Jacques Février at my concerts at the Théâtre des Champs-

Elysées. He had come to the second of the three escorting Debussy's widow. He told me that she had said, "Il a joué 'Ondine' mieux que personne." This little phrase rang in my ears so encouragingly that, for the rest of my career, whenever I played Debussy I included this beautiful prelude. Jacques Février is a good pianist and an excellent musician and the best sight reader I ever met, which brings me to compare the different ways of learning music at the best music schools in different countries. In my opinion, the Conservatoire de Paris, in spite of some dated methods, still offers the most solid preparation for the career of a musician. The yearly public examination is judged by well-known performers of every instrument and one of the important features of this examination is sight reading from manuscripts of specially composed pieces. All French instrumentalists I have known are past masters at this difficult skill. In my opinion this reading at sight is of prime importance for talented music students. It whets the appetite for reading all the music available, develops a better discernment in their own tastes, and enables them to make a judicious choice of the pieces they are going to perform in public. These must be pieces which "talk" to them, which reveal to them their most intimate secrets. Many pianists perform at their concerts music which they do not understand or particularly like, only because these pieces are much in demand and recommended to them by their managers. I know of great conservatories where the gifted pupils are induced to start races with difficult pieces to see who can play them faster.

My long experience taught me that your only way to success, young pianists, is to pour out your own deep emotion into the music you really love and understand. When that happens an antenna reaches the public and makes them share your emotion even if they have never heard the piece or have a dislike for it. Music is a sacred art. Those who are born with the talent for it ought to feel that they are humble servants of the great immortal creators of music and be proud to be the chosen ones to transmit their heavenly gifts to humanity. Those who take these immortal works for vehicles for the promotion of their commercial success are traitors to this sacred art.

During that Paris season I heard many concerts. The four major orchestras, the Conservatoire, the Lamoureux, the Colonne, and the Pasdeloup, gave interesting programs with famous artists as soloists and still played all at the same hour on Sunday afternoons. It was a difficult choice to make, which annoyed me greatly. Recitals were sparse. And so I had to be satisfied to hear Alfred Cortot or the Scotchman Frederic Lamond, whose main attraction was his supposed resemblance to Beethoven, but who never performed this composer to my taste. Of course, there was always a Risler, a Thibaud, a Casals to fill my heart with joy. The young

"Six" became very active. Honegger's novel symphonic work *Pacific 231* and the oratorio *King David* were in demand. Milhaud used polytonality to excess but wrote some beautiful music based on the folklore of his native Provence, such as the *Suite Provençal* and fine chamber music. Germaine Tailleferre published a lovely little piece for two pianos. All these young musicians had great respect for the modern American jazz. A few tours that some of the famous American jazz bands made produced a sensation in all the European capitals and exercised a great influence on the new works of European composers. Jean Wiéner, our friend from the Bar Gaya, could fill the Salle Gaveau with a recital of the latest American tunes and included Stravinsky's *Piano Rag Music*, which was received by the public with the same favor as the rest of the program. Even the ultra-modern Schönberg had a sensational debut in Paris. His *Pierrot Lunaire* was played by an ensemble which included Milhaud and Poulenc and was received with loud boos from one part of the audience and wild ovations from the other. Ever since the premieres of *Pelléas* and *Le Sacre du printemps*, such a reception assured the composer of lasting celebrity.

Diaghilev's long exile from Russia had created a sort of divorce between him and his native country. After the war, much influenced by Jean Cocteau, he commissioned ballets by Auric and Poulenc. Apropos, I remember a funny incident. Strolling along the rue de Rivoli, I met Jean Cocteau, who asked me, "Tu vas chez Misia?" I was just back from a weekend at the Melchior de Polignacs' at Reims, where we had had orgies of *écrevisses au champagne*. "No, I am not invited," I answered.

"This is absurd," he said. "Come with me, she will be delighted to have you. She has Diaghilev, Massine, and Eric Satie to hear a ballet by Milhaud which he will play four-hands with Auric and hopes to have included in Diaghilev's next season." This sounded too interesting to miss. We entered the Meurice, where Misia had a lovely apartment, and found the company already assembled. I was heartily welcomed by everybody but Milhaud and Auric, who showed great disappointment at seeing me. While tea was served Cocteau took me to another room. "Arthur," he said, "please don't make any remarks after hearing the music. Milhaud composed the ballet which he calls *Boeuf sur le toit* using nothing but Brazilian tunes, most of which he composed by himself, but there are also some popular ones from Brazil and he is deeply alarmed that you might reveal it in front of Diaghilev, as you are the only one who might recognize them." I promised, crossing my heart, not to say a word. We settled around the piano and Milhaud and Auric gave us a lively performance of this most engaging music. Diaghilev and Massine listened impassively, as they always did on such occasions.

The first words came from Diaghilev: "Est-ce que tout cela est original?" Milhaud, with the expression of a schoolboy caught copying his neighbor, answered weakly, "Practically everything . . ." That did it. It was fatal. Diaghilev had had to pay royalties for the tunes of living composers that Stravinsky had used lavishly in his ballets, so he had an alert ear for anything of that kind.

At one of the Elsa Maxwell parties, I was introduced to a very remarkable person—the Princess Edmond de Polignac, called by everybody Princess Winnie. Her maiden name was Winnaretta Singer, and she was the daughter of the multimillionaire manufacturer of the famous sewing machines. She had three brothers with unconventional names. One of them was Paris Singer, who financed and lived with Isadora Duncan. The second was Washington Singer. I have forgotten the name of the third one—it might have been London, New York, or Rome! All three were shrewd businessmen and ran the many factories with great success. Their sister was a woman of many talents. She copied paintings by great masters so well that they could have been taken for the originals. She also was a good pianist; we once performed the *Valse romantique* for two pianos by Chabrier brilliantly for her friends. Her palace on the avenue Henri Martin had a real concert hall with frescoes by José Maria Sert and there she had introduced to her friends first performances of works by Stravinsky, Prokofiev, de Falla, Poulenc, and others which she had commissioned. She also owned one of the most beautiful palaces on the Canale Grande in Venice, to which she graciously invited me to spend a few weeks at the end of the summer. I was her guest in this heavenly city for several summers in succession. The princess had another trait: she was the stingiest woman I ever met in my whole life.

33

The Kochanskis had left for Vichy, where Paul needed a severe cure for his stomach. I promised to visit them for a few days on my way to Biarritz, where Stravinsky was going to write the promised sonata from *Petrushka*, for which he needed my presence. When I arrived in Vichy, Paul and Zosia took me from the railway station directly to their doctor, saying, "It will do you a lot of good to follow our cure for a few days, and the doctor is expecting you." I followed them very reluctantly, feeling in no need of a cure. The doctor examined me for a few minutes in the most perfunctory way and wrote out his plans for me. "At seven in the morning, drink two glasses of the same waters as your friends at the well, after which you will get a water massage with a hose." I obeyed. I joined my friends in this abominable drink, after which they accompanied me to the building where I was to get my massage; they had other things to perform. A strong man in a bathing suit ordered me to strip and stand erect at a certain distance and he aimed the hose at me. He began watering me like a flower bed with a strong stream from the hose, changing the temperature from time to time. This procedure embarrassed me to a high degree because, quite unexpectedly, it produced a sexual excitement instead of the soothing cure. That did it. For me, these kinds of cures were over forever. I left for the hotel, where I had two large cups of coffee, eggs and bacon, and three croissants with marmalade, and smoked a big cigar. My poor friends submitted to a cruel program for the whole of each day, which resulted in my hardly seeing them at all. They took naps while I had my lunch and went to bed for the night when I was beginning to think of dinner. My evenings and often half of the night were spent gambling happily or unhappily at the casino. After a few days of this "cure" I left for Biarritz.

Stravinsky was already there. Some admirer had offered him a small villa in a place at a short distance from the town called, strangely, Chambre d'Amour, which offered everything but rooms of that sort. I was lucky in getting a nice apartment at the Hotel du Palais consisting of living room, bedroom, and bathroom on the ground floor with large windows just a few feet from the sea. I had a nice upright piano sent from Bayonne and so was able to work at some new repertoire. Enrique had a small room nearby. In the afternoons I visited Igor, who was working on *Mavra* but took time off for his arrangement of *Petrushka*, which he showed me page by page as he composed it. I sometimes dared to show him a trick or two to make it sound better with my specialty for using the pedals and by advising him to alleviate the texture by leaving out some secondary stuff from the orchestral score. Sometimes he visited me in the afternoons to show me pieces of *Mavra* or his progress with *Petrushka*. In the evenings my frivolous and pleasure-seeking ego came to life. I took my dinners, rarely alone, mostly in good company, at the Café de Paris, then famous for its culinary excellence. From there I proceeded to the Casino de Bellevue, then tremendously "en vogue," filled with my friends from Madrid, San Sebastián, and Paris. Its only rival was the casino of Deauville, but their seasons were different, so neither lost its rich clientele to the other. I loved to play roulette and also chemin de fer at a friendly table. A confirmed night owl, I stayed there until closing time. It was not so much for winning but for the atmosphere which reigned at that casino. Most of the gamblers were friends or acquaintances who knew how to win or lose with extreme elegance. Whenever I entered a casino I took a certain amount of money with me, ready to lose it just for the pleasure of defying fortune. I was happy if I could bring this same sum home and considered it a miracle if it was accompanied by some new money.

One night I was lucky enough to win 20,000 francs and bring them safely to my hotel room. Before going to sleep I counted them proudly to make sure that I was not dreaming. Next morning, sipping happily my second cup of coffee, I told Enrique, who brought my pressed clothes, of my good fortune of the night before. After my bath, dressing with the help of Enrique, I picked up my things from the table to put them in my pockets, among them the pile of money, which for the sheer pleasure of recalling my good fortune I counted again. I found only nineteen bills of a thousand francs instead of the twenty I knew I had won. I counted again. I looked around the room, under the table, supposing that a gust of wind had blown a bill away, but to no avail. Finally I asked Enrique if he had had to pay someone for me with this money. He answered that he hadn't. "You must have made a mistake counting it last night." Then I was sure. It could only have been Enrique who had taken it while I was in the bathroom. "Have you taken the money?" I asked him point-blank. He denied it but I saw that he was frightened. "Enrique, I have always had confidence in you," I said, "but this time you have to prove that you haven't taken the money. I want you to empty all your pockets." After a short hesitation he produced the bill.

It made me very unhappy. I had always thought that Enrique was not only a valet but a friend. But I remembered suddenly occasions when small sums and some gold pieces in Mexico had been missed by both Besanzoni and myself. But I never allowed her or myself to suspect Enrique. I said to him sadly, "I shall not denounce you to the police, but you must leave right away. I do not want to see you ever again." I had great difficulty in getting over my disappointment because I had grown quite fond of the little fellow. When I told my story to Stravinsky he said with a sardonic smile, "All servants are born thieves." This did not encourage me to look for a new valet.

One of the next mornings, after a long night at the casino, I woke up with no feeling in the fourth and fifth fingers of my left hand. This kind of thing had often happened to a whole hand after having slept with it in a bad position. At such moments I would put the other hand on my heart for a moment and the blood would flow back into the sleeping hand. That morning I used this method again but without success. The two fingers were dead. They felt like two pieces of wood without connection to the rest of my hand. I became panic-stricken. I was in perfectly normal health and couldn't find a reason for such an anomaly. All I could think of was that, when playing roulette, my hands had a tendency to become stiff and slightly bloodless from the excitement of watching the ball turning around before falling into the number. In these instances a glass of cognac would help. There was also the close proximity of the sea with its strong salty air, and I had the habit of sleeping with wide-open windows and this might have had a bad effect on my hands. I was scared to death of seeing a doctor. I couldn't face hearing the fatal news. Nor did I confide in anybody for fear of its reaching the press. I decided to announce a concert in San Sebastián, hoping against odds that in such an emergency my poor fingers would find their life again. I relied on the experience of all my career that high temperatures, toothaches, headaches, catarrhs, coughs disappeared during the two hours of a concert and came back only after it was finished.

This concert in San Sebastián was sold out. Even the Queen, who was on a visit there, was present, and I had to begin my first piece with my two fingers as dead as ever. I can say now after all those years that this concert was the most awful of all I have ever given. I had to play the whole program with eight fingers and two pieces of wood, hitting the bass notes hard, which could have broken my fingers without my noticing it. The public was aware that something strange had happened to me, but had grown so attached to me that they applauded as heartily as ever. After returning to Biarritz I was sure that my career was over.

One or two days later, as I was having lunch at the Café de Paris, a young and charming American lady whom I had met casually at the casino sat down at my table and proposed quite naturally to have lunch with me. To this complete stranger on her way back to America, I confided my terrible tragedy in a conversational, quiet way. "I must give up my career as a concert pianist and try to find a place as a piano teacher in the United States because I have lost the use of two fingers in the past two weeks and can't play anymore in public." She laughed incredulously. "What nonsense," she said, "your hands look as natural as ever. I can't see a trace of anything wrong." When I explained to her exactly what was the matter with my fingers, she told me after we had our coffee: "I will take you right away to my Japanese masseur. I am sure that he will find the way to help you." I left with her immediately with my heart beating. Any help offered me was a blessing after having refused to speak about it for all this time.

The Japanese masseur was a young man with thick glasses. He pulled up the shirt sleeve of my left arm and began touching my arm in all sorts of places. He found a spot which he pressed with insistence. After a little while of doing this, he picked up my two fingers and gave them light delicate touches up and down for quite a while, then returned to the spot on my arm, and I began to feel a living throb in my two fingers. After about a quarter of an hour of his repeating this exercise I felt the blood coming back and I found even my poor fingers hurting me from the many merciless knocks I had given them in my despair. Well, I cried and gave a long embrace to my savior and a longer one to the lady.

I felt reborn and began to practice in the morning with new enthusiasm. Stravinsky had *Petrushka* ready. He was, fortunately for me, a pedantic copyist of his own works, so unlike Beethoven, whose copyist probably ended up in a madhouse. The manuscript of this *Petrushka* sonata was a regal present, written meticulously in a short, nicely bound book. To make it he used his own invention for drawing the staves—a roller with five tiny wheels squeezed between movable holders. When dipped in ink they rolled the staves he needed, neither more nor less. If he wanted to add something above, he could diminish the space between the wheels to make smaller lines. He was quite proud of this clever gadget. The first page of the book contained the title and the date written in beautiful calligraphy and below was the dedication in Russian: "To my friend Arthur, a great artist, in full ownership," and his signature. It contained three movements: "Danse Russe," "Chez Petrushka," and "La Semaine grasse." His transcription was brilliant. You could hear the whole orchestra. But it was very difficult to perform. When I made some remarks about a few passages which might retard the dynamic progress of the piece, he said, "Play it any way you like. I give you carte blanche." I took advantage of his permission but never made a record of it because I knew my Igor. In a bad mood he might announce: "Rubinstein betrays my work when he performs it." Stravinsky was not very happy with his work on *Mavra*. He tried to compose it in an operatic, easily accessible way. "It sounds like Verdi," he told me. But it wasn't true; it was still Stravinsky, but not quite the authentic one. The work was unsuccessful and soon disappeared from public performances.

Igor's private life was made difficult by a fat, bearded brother-in-law of his who had arrived in Paris with a beautiful daughter, counting on the help of his famous relative, who, lacking other resources, turned to me for assistance. It was a complicated affair. Mr. Bieliankin, this was his name, had acquired for a small sum the estate of a Polish revolutionary who had been sent to Siberia and his property confiscated. The government of free Poland returned it to its rightful owner without any compensation for Mr.

Bieliankin. Now, in Paris, he complained bitterly about this "screaming injustice. They had no right to take it away from me! I bought it legally and am ready to become a Polish citizen." I had to suppress the urge to laugh, but Igor took it quite seriously. "Arthur, you know the Polish ambassador in Paris, don't you?"

"Yes, I do," I said. "He is the head of one of the great families of Poland—the Count Zamoyski."

"In that case," Igor continued unperturbed, "he will certainly understand the injustice done to my brother-in-law and make it clear in the right quarters."

"I have strong doubts about it," I said, receiving looks from the two men as if I were a traitor. They wouldn't let up until I promised to take them to the embassy and present the case to the ambassador. My visiting card, asking the count for a short audience, was taken to him by a secretary and he received me, after a few moments, alone. I asked my two companions to wait. When I told the story, half seriously, half ironically, to our distinguished diplomat, he roared with laughter. "Quel toupé!" he exclaimed. Then he added, "I shall advise the finance minister to give this man the amount he paid in rubles in our new zlotys. It will probably be just enough to pay for a good dinner."

When I told my two companions the result of my insistence for justice they departed in a fury, leaving me behind. I consoled myself at the nearby Fouquet's with a café Liègeois accompanied by a good cigar.

In Biarritz, where Mr. Bieliankin arrived shortly after Igor, he besieged his brother-in-law with demands for help which poor Igor had no means of satisfying. I was again called in for consultation. Looking at his big bulk and the long grayish beard which made him look like a Russian Orthodox pope, I could hardly advise him to become a professional dancer in a nightclub. It was useless to think about anything connected with music, because clearly Bieliankin felt no interest in art. After many proposals were discussed and reflected on, I asked him if he had a preference for any particular occupation. "I lived most of my life on the land and never took up a profession."

"Were you particularly good at anything?" I asked, becoming a little tired. Suddenly he became enthusiastic. "I loved to cook!" I was always fond of good food and so became interested again. Suddenly an idea came to my mind. "Would you be able to run a restaurant?" He clapped his hands. "I always dreamed of having one." I thought of the great success of the Russian places on the rue Pigalle. "Why not open one in Biarritz? It is full of nothing but rich gourmets and *noceurs*. If you could find a convenient place in the right spot and open a typical Russian restaurant which could stay open until late at night, with a casual accordion or balalaika player during dinnertime, I could be of great heip to you."

He began to sweat with emotion. "Your idea is fantastic," he said, "but where shall we find the money?" I informed him that I knew three or four Russians who had married wealthy women and that he himself could easily find funds from some bank or institution by persuading them of the great financial success of this kind of nightclub in Paris.

One could hardly believe it, but in a few days he found the necessary investors and I was glad he left me out of this part of the project. He also located without any difficulty and at a low price a nice place which had been a restaurant before but had gone bankrupt.

"When you get it ready," I told Bieliankin, "I will help you launch it by putting on a brilliant dinner and inviting my friends in Biarritz and San Sebastián. They can give you sensational publicity and fill your place if you succeed in offering them the right Russian food. They all know the rue Pigalle and the other Russian places in Paris." As most of my friends were just the right people for this sort of thing, I had no difficulty in gathering twenty guests, including some couples who loved late nights, some titled friends from Spain, and some professional French gourmets.

Bieliankin and I spent a long afternoon planning the menu. I proposed to begin with blinis and pressed caviar, which real connoisseurs prefer to fresh caviar, often too salty. This goes with vodka. He screamed, "Smirnovka. Smirnovka of course!" An authentic Russian borscht was to follow and as entrée a Caucasian shashlik brought in on still-burning skewers with rice à la Russe. "The wine must be a fine vintage of Bordeaux." Here Bieliankin made a stern face of disapproval. "The only entrée worthy of such a dinner is roast suckling pig." At this, it was my turn to make a face of disapproval. "I hate that dish," I said. "In Russia and Poland butcher shops exhibit their poor little heads on large dishes to attract the customers. I always had to close my eyes so as not to see this barbaric sight."

My objection was overruled. "We must have suckling pigs, we must, we must!" he cried, wringing his hands. "I am a master at preparing them. The shashlik," he said with marked disdain, "is not Russian. It is a Caucasian dish without any taste."

As he was the cook, not I, he won. When I mentioned cheese, he laughed grimly. "We don't like this stinking thing on our Russian tables." But he proposed a dessert: an ice-cream concoction with rum, which Bieliankin said was a Russian specialty—a pure lie, as I had enjoyed the same dish in the most chauvinistic French restaurants. This last tidbit had to be accompanied by good vintage champagne.

The opening night was a much greater success than we expected. I forgot that people who hear of an elegant gathering to which they are not invited are ready to commit minor crimes to be present anyhow, and so it happened that night. The place was full and Bieliankin was obliged to serve smaller portions than he had intended to satisfy his newly born clientele. One detail gave me satisfaction: half of my guests refused to eat the suckling pigs, saying that they had eaten too much caviar, blinis, and borscht. Bieliankin even succeeded in finding for a small fee a penniless Russian accordion player, a little man with a shaven head who played Russian tzigane romances with a sad air which provoked enthusiastic bravos from the utterly unmusical diners.

Stravinsky was absent from the feast, for the reason, I assume, that the author of *Le Sacre du printemps* did not care to be congratulated on the roast suckling pigs cooked by his brother-in-law. But I, being no relation to Bieliankin, received with pleasure warm thanks from my friends for a wonderful evening. Next day a very disagreeable surprise was in store for me. Mr. Bieliankin presented me with a bill which amounted to such a large sum that it took all the money I had on hand to pay it and obliged me to obtain some fresh money by selling some of my Argentine bonds with great complications involving banks in Biarritz, Paris, and Buenos Aires. I had hoped that Bieliankin, out of simple decency, would charge me only the actual cost of the dinner. Instead of which, he put in some deluxe prices which I had innocently advised him to charge his future rich clientele. Half of the bill was for those damn pigs. When I rather sharply objected he was ready to cry. "If you only knew the trouble I had to get them! I had to ring up Bordeaux, I had to ring Toulouse! I almost had to order them from Paris! You don't know the trouble I took, the amount I spent in phone calls, and you say they are overcharged!" I gave up; I realized that I had to do with a rather cynical, ungrateful, and passionate lover of suckling pigs.

His establishment became a big success. He called it La Boîte Russe. Later on, he installed a dance floor and it became the last refuge of the inveterate *noceurs*. I had the elegance not to complain about the whole affair to Igor, who had heard the other side of the story and was proud of the culinary and financial talent of his brother-in-law.

Stravinsky remained in his Chambre d'Amour to finish *Mavra*. I returned to Paris, where I found Paul and Zosia back from their cure at Vichy.

34

It is common knowledge the political situation after the great victory over Germany had begun to deteriorate. The bombastic oratory and complete ignorance of the situation outside the United States on the part of two American senators succeeded in persuading both houses of Congress to prevent the entry of the United States into the League of Nations created by the great President Woodrow Wilson. This absurd action condemned the newly born union of nations which promised the restoration of lasting peace after the inhuman tragedy of the world war. The unspoken motto of the League of Nations was: "This war was fought to end wars forever."

Woodrow Wilson could not survive the rejection of his own people and died soon after. The young League of Nations also died miserably after a few years from its impotence to enforce its charter.

After sending Kaiser Wilhelm II into exile, Germany became a republic with its seat in Weimar—the Weimar of Goethe and Liszt—but soon a heavy unrest prevailed. Austria lost its whole empire after the victory of the Allies and became a small state with Francis Joseph's grandnephew, the Emperor Karl, occupying a shaky throne.

The victorious Allies had been all but ruined by the great effort and the many young countries created by the Fourteen Points of Wilson desperately needed the help of America. In all justice, America did help as generously as she could.

The immense Russian Empire, instead of responding to the right meaning of the word "communism" by giving complete freedom to its citizens and allowing them to share judiciously in the wealth of the country, fell under the most abject dictatorship ever imagined. The Duma composed of nobles and bourgeois had overthrown the Tsarist regime by forcing Nicholas II to abdicate but was too weak to resist the growing power of Lenin with his inflammatory way of arousing the mob. The Duma led by Kerenski attempted in the North and South to restore order and create a liberal republic in the Western sense but were repulsed by Trotsky and his Red Army. Only Pilsudski succeeded in beating the Red Army during a short war in 1920 and made the Russians pay for the invasion of Poland.

35

I had a short stay in London, where both Paul and I gave recitals at Wigmore Hall and some other concerts of no importance. We saw much of the Gandarillas and I managed to take in, accompanied by Lesley, a few good plays with Gladys Cooper, Gerald du Maurier, and Sir Charles Hawtrey; also one or two operas at Covent Garden. William Jowitt, then already a K.C., never joined us. "I have to study a few briefs," he would say as an excuse. One evening, entering by surprise to bid him good night, I caught him studying carefully the difficult crossword puzzle of *The Times.*

A joyous surprise was in store for me: Chaliapin appeared in town. In spite of being adulated in Russia by the Communists and the men in power, he suffered from the cruel injustice done to all of his old friends, left Moscow at the first opportunity, and never returned. In London he was received with open arms by the Covent Garden directors and all opera lovers. He had to appear in *Boris Godunov,* his best role, a fortnight after his arrival. I spent my time with him whenever I could, and was happy to advance him some money which helped him to buy some much-needed clothes. "Artoosha," he said, "they say one still needs here a top hat. Will you take me to a shop where I can get one?"

I was always proud to be a customer of the most famous hatter in the world, Lock's, whose shop on St. James's Street stood for more than two centuries and had never changed. The window display showed shabby hats of an old epoch, the original iron shutters were still there, as well as the tired old wooden sign, and, inside the shop, some sand was strewn on the floor. The present owners made a careful choice of their customers, who included, besides the royal family, the great of the realm. I took Chaliapin straight to Lock's and intended to persuade them to accept one of the greatest singers of the world as a customer. As he entered the shop and looked around, I saw suddenly a furious expression on his face. He left the place immediately, called loudly for me, and made quite a scene in the street.

"Artur," he said, "I accepted your money, which you will get back after the first performance, but I never expected you to take me to a dirty shop made for beggars. I have not fallen that low yet." It took a long and difficult explanation of the real facts and he believed me only when I showed him a row of elegant white hatboxes inside: "HRH The Prince of Wales," "The Duke of Norfolk," "The Duke of Westminster," and so on. A surprise which not only reassured him but rather frightened him too.

Chaliapin's appearance in *Boris Godunov* was the sensation of the season. He became the idol of the proud London society. Lady Diana Cooper, Lady Howard de Walden, and others would shower him with flowers daily and precious gifts from Fortnum and Mason, which Fedja and I consumed smacking our lips.

Before leaving England, I had a lovely concert with Lionel Tertis at Wigmore Hall. He introduced to me some young English composers who wrote charming things for the viola for him—Arthur Bliss, the most talented one among them, John Ireland, Frederick Delius, and Arnold Bax enriched English music. I later played a concerto by Ireland with Sir Henry Wood conducting. It was good music in a genuine English idiom. Tertis became famous and England was proud of him. His transcriptions of the Delius violin sonata and of Elgar's Cello Concerto and his superb one of Bach's Chaconne, which he played in G minor, were masterpieces.

It was time to leave for the United States. The Kochanskis and I embarked again at Liverpool and after a fair crossing arrived in New York. I returned as usual to the Biltmore and Zosia found a pleasant apartment in the East Forties.

36

Paul became full-time professor of the Juilliard School of Music. With Efrem Zimbalist, he gave master classes and Paul's very special pedagogic talent soon became a great asset to the school. His concert tour was scheduled for later that winter.

R.E. had some engagements for me in Connecticut, Baltimore, and another one of those damn musicales in Washington. But there was also a concert with Monteux in Boston and we played the Chopin F minor Concerto. My old friend from London, the great painter John Sargent, came to this concert, took me for supper afterward, and invited me to visit him the next morning at the Public Library, one of the imposing buildings of Boston, where he was painting the frescoes in the great hall.

He also took me to the private gallery of a great art collector, Mrs. Gardner, who used to keep insistent tourists away from her museum, showing only to her friends the masterpieces she had assembled with the help of the famous connoisseur Bernard Berenson.

R.E. even made me play in two university cities in Colorado, where the important Denver manager Arthur Oppenheimer engaged me. It was his wife, though, who took a great liking to me. I had been their guest in Denver at the time when Heifetz gave a concert to a sold-out house and the Oppenheimers and I attended. "Arthur," my namesake said, "you must introduce me to Heifetz because I want to get him for my own series." I complied and made them happy as Jascha accepted their offer, at a high fee of course.

In New York, I gave one recital of violin and piano sonatas with Paul. On that occasion, Ernest Bloch, the Swiss composer, honored us by entrusting us to give the first world performance of his violin sonata. We played it from the manuscript. The composer assisted at our rehearsals, giving us precious indications about tempi and other details. On the other hand, he listened carefully to Paul's advice on possible improvements for the violin part and changed one or two places for the piano on my suggestion. At the concert he himself turned my pages. We played the work with great élan and the public liked it. When we made the composer take a bow, they gave him an ovation and then began the usual comedy of hugs and handshakes between composer and interpreters for the benefit of the innocent audience. Later, in private, Bloch gave us the real warm thanks for our great effort.

I was also engaged as soloist again by my friend Alfred Hertz in San Francisco. The San Francisco manager's name this time was Irving Oppenheim, a charming fellow. But here again, his wife, Blanche, was my main supporter. He had a recital for me in San Francisco, another one in Oakland, and also an appearance at the University of California in Berkeley. Oppenheim invited me to the first football game of my life, a yearly event between U.C. and Stanford University. He drove me to Stanford's huge stadium—80,000 spectators—who frightened me not so much by their number as by their behavior; I thought I was in the middle of a war between the two universities which might end in murderous fights. The supporters of each team were yelling like mad at the smallest advantage or disadvantage of the game. Each team had a few lovely girls who, in graceful boots displaying most of the rest of their legs, danced and shouted in a frenzy whenever one of the players got an advantage. Their yell consisted of a syllable which at first I took for a solfège exercise, but I soon discovered my mistake; it was "rah," not "re." Oppenheim, a placid gentleman in ordinary life, behaved like a wild man from the jungle. He shouted the most obscene insults against the Stanfordians, jumped up, often hurting my foot, and was soon hoarse with enthusiasm whenever his alma mater scored a touchdown.

Stanford won, and we drove back to San Francisco, two sad, beaten men. I also had a second engagement in Portland, Oregon, this time with orchestra. It had been arranged between the conductor and myself to play the Beethoven G major, but two weeks before the date of the concert I received a telegram: "The committee would be grateful if you would agree to play the Rubinstein D minor Concerto instead of the Beethoven." This change angered me. My suspicious nature made me guess why they wanted it—the same two names on the bill might give the idea to some innocent concertgoers that it was still the old Anton playing, or that the Arthur was the composer. I sent back a short telegram: "I would rather you called me Arthur van Beethoven for the occasion." They got the message.

This concert had a disagreeable aftermath. The owner of a department store and his lovely wife invited me for supper after the concert. During this meal at a small table, the beautiful leg of the lady and my own nervous one were drawn magnetically toward each other. This electrifying link encouraged me to invite her to lunch with me the next day. My train was to leave late that night. She accepted and added: "I shall take you after lunch to our house in the mountains. It has one of the loveliest views of the city." Luncheon was gay, with stories of my life amusing her greatly, and we settled happily in her Oldsmobile, which she drove herself, with me sitting next to her. The road had big piles of snow on both sides which made our drive up the rather steep road somewhat difficult. When she noticed that I was a little worried, she laughed, saying, "I'm a good driver, you know." Our gay conversation soon became rather flirtatious; suddenly I grabbed her small head and gave her a hard kiss. It became evident that it was her first experience of this kind. She let go of the wheel and closed her eyes, and the car, with us inside, fell on its side into the thick snow. We climbed out rather painfully and the new situation looked rather grim. "What shall we do?" I asked nervously, thinking of my train and her husband. She answered, "You must run down and ask for help. There is a garage at the bottom of the road." My concert legs were used to pedals and not to running down slippery roads full of snow. In constant danger of slipping, I reached the wretched gas station after a good half an hour. It took us a dreadful three hours to get safely back to town. Fortunately we returned before alarming the husband and missing my train. Both of us never forgot the fatal kiss, but as usual, with time, it turned into a good story.

When I got back to New York, Paul was preparing for his own tour. He found a fine accompanist, Pierre Luboschutz. Chaliapin arrived in New York, prepared to sing at the Metropolitan Opera House after his triumph in London. When I telephoned him on the morning of his arrival, he begged,

"Artoosha, come and have breakfast with me." I drove in a hurry to the Astor Hotel and went up to his apartment. Still dressed in his robe, he embraced me in the best Russian way, clapping my back and kissing me three times on the cheek. He ordered a regal breakfast for two—eggs and bacon, croissants, all the jams and marmalades, cheeses, and whatnot—and told me delightful stories about London, and I countered with my own about New York. A short fattish man was shown in whom Feodor introduced to me saying, "He's my agent here, a shrewd little man, a Russian Jew. Beware of him." The man smiled and sat himself comfortably in a chair near the window without being asked to have even a miserable cup of coffee. After we finished eating, Chaliapin asked, "What are you playing now? I want to go to your concert."

"My tour is finished," I told him regretfully. "But I'm working just now on a piece which will amuse you to hear. Stravinsky wrote and dedicated a sonata to me made out of *Petrushka*."

"Ho, ho!" he cried in delight. "Please play some of it for me right away!"

I opened the lid of his piano and started banging out joyously the "Dance Russe." Chaliapin, who knew and loved the piece, did not allow me to stop until I had played most of it. Then he hugged me enthusiastically. "You are great, you are great!" he screamed. "Sol," he said to his agent, using the familiar "thou," "you heard something good, eh? . . . This fellow knows nothing about music," he said to me loudly.

A few days later, R.E. called and asked me to come and see him. "A feller called Hurok, a smart cookie, came to see me. He's running some concerts at the Hippodrome, ha, ha; that damn place has five thousand seats, so he can offer expensive artists at cheaper prices. Now he wants you to take part in a concert with Titta Ruffo, who will be the star. He wants you to fill up the program with a few piano pieces. I asked for five hundred dollars but that s.o.b. brought it down to three hundred and I think you should accept it. It's good for you to be heard by a big audience." I accepted, of course. The little man, so shabbily treated by Feodor, was Sol Hurok, the Hurok whose name became almost a synonym for success.

Titta Ruffo's concert, where I was the assistant artist, took place at the Hippodrome, the place where New Yorkers were treated to circus shows with wild animals and trained horses. No wonder that the place stank of horse manure. I was ashamed for the composers to have their works heard in such a place, but Hurok was successful at presenting the greatest stars of the moment to full houses at lower prices than Carnegie Hall.

That night Titta Ruffo was not in good voice. His troubles with his throat had begun in Mexico and soon forced him to give up his career. But I had never been in better form. To Mr. Hurok's astonishment, this evening Titta Ruffo's arias were given a tepid reception while the good *Navarra* with the *Fire Dance* as an encore were received with the kind of ovations I got in Buenos Aires or Madrid but never yet in the United States. This concert was a consolation to me after many disappointments.

Paul hated the parties Zosia constantly gave in their apartment. Tired from his lessons at Juilliard, he liked a quiet evening with close friends, a little game, and then early to bed. His stomach bothered him and he badly needed his cures during the summer. He made arrangements to spend part of the following summer in Evian on the Lac Leman, a well-known place for cures—well located for me to take some nice excursions, for instance to do some gambling at the casino and to visit Geneva.

Before leaving New York, I asked George Engels if he could take over the management of my next tour without any guarantee, strictly on percentage. He accepted my terms. I felt no misgivings in leaving R. E. Johnson and Lulu. Our contract was void anyway and he did not feel that he had much to offer me. I left for Paris this time alone, as the Kochanskis had decided to live in New York permanently.

37

Valmalète announced two concerts at the Salle Gaveau and six or seven in the provinces. At my first recital at Gaveau with a good-sized audience, I gave the first performance of *Petrushka*, played my own way, making it sound as I heard it by the orchestra more than as a piano piece. The public adored it. The second concert was sold out in one day and we added a third one. The suite of *Petrushka* helped much to further my career in Europe, as this piece was in great demand, and wherever I played, it had to be repeated at the next concert. My European fees could not be compared with those in America. The war had devalued most currencies, although I was still able to lead the life of the good old spendthrift I was. But my bank account was often empty. Whenever I felt a pinch in my pocket I rapidly arranged a new tour in South America, from whence I could return with a good pile of money.

Ernesto de Quesada had engaged Paul Kochanski for Argentina and Uruguay with a guarantee and paid traveling expenses too. I decided to join Paul on this tour, partly because of my ebbing finances but also to be of some use for Paul's debut on this new continent. I wrote to Ruiz to make dates for me for September but asked Mr. Pellas to have a few dates in Rio de Janeiro at the end of August.

My nice apartment at the annex of the Majestic was again ready for me. Mr. Tauber, this most generous of all hotel directors, said, "I keep it always at your disposal. In your absence, I never let it for more than one or two nights."

At tea at Eugenia's one afternoon, I met Blaise Cendrars again. His sense of humor was sometimes sardonic, often cruel, but always witty and original. He could make you laugh and cry at the same time. Though he was physically the opposite of Jean Cocteau, the two of them had this last trait in common. I was proud of our friendship, and he was a great poet and writer.

Picasso dropped in that same day. "Arturo," he said, "why didn't you let me know that you were back?"—as if it had been a week and not five years since we had seen each other. He had become after the war the most celebrated, most admired painter, and that was the reason why I was a little shy about calling him up or visiting him. "Would you like to come to my nasty apartment on the rue La Boétie? I can show you some of my pictures and give you a good cup of coffee." Needless to say, I was delighted.

The next afternoon I climbed the two flights. He was expecting me, opened the door himself, and led me straight to his atelier. It was a nasty apartment, all right, and I could well imagine that he would still prefer to live in the shabby, dirty Bateau Lavoir of Montmartre than in this middle-class bourgeois apartment. What he called his atelier was a typical kind of salon, like the waiting room of a dentist, but as he was Picasso, it became quite naturally Picasso's atelier. Dozens of canvases were stacked facing the wall; a bare table and brushes of all sizes stood in some earthenware containers. The table itself was dirty with paint. The walls were bare except for a few odd pages of magazines tacked up and some large photos of strange sculptures. Here and there on the floor were some wooden specimens of Negro art representing men with overlong torsos, short legs, with their sex prominently displayed. But there was also an easel next to the window, and the only real beautiful thing in the room, a painting by the master, was on it: a guitar on a chair, a bottle of wine on a small table, and a newspaper and glasses. The background was his balcony with its commonplace ironwork. Picasso gave to this banal subject a life and color which astonished me. It took me some time to realize what a masterpiece it was. I did not say a word and he liked it. "I hate empty words," he said. "There is nothing you can say about paintings. You love it or hate it, but there are no words to explain them."

After the Second World War, when Picasso's pictures fetched astronomical prices, a wealthy American millionairess was allowed into his atelier to see his pictures. She stopped at one, pointed at it, and asked the master, "What does this picture represent?"

"Two hundred thousand dollars," said Picasso.

On my practically daily visits I watched Picasso painting the same subject I had seen that first day over and over again. Despite my shyness, I couldn't resist questioning him about this. "Are you painting this subject on commission? Is there a great demand for it?" He looked at me with dismay. "What a stupid question," he said. "Every minute there is another light, every day is different too, so whatever I paint becomes always a new subject." This was a great lesson to me. I suddenly realized that when I repeat the same piece at my concerts I always feel that I am playing it for the first time.

He was unhappy with his marriage. Olga Kochlova, a dancer of the Diaghilev troupe whom I knew well from the days in San Sebastián, was a stupid Russian who liked to brag about her father, who she pretended was a colonel in the Tsar's own regiment. The other dancers assured me that he was only a sergeant. She had also been an avowed virgin. Picasso saw in her an ideal model and she sat for him but did not know that this included landing in bed with him. On this occasion the painter found stubborn resistance. "I'm a virgin!" she cried proudly. "And I shall never submit except to my husband." Picasso was torn between his desire and his better sense for some time, but the poor man succumbed—they were married; she even gave him a son and it was too late to undo his great mistake. This little dancer had an iron will, and it was she who forced him to live in this miserable apartment on the rue La Boétie. He told me all this with growing anger. "Arturo," he said, "help me to get away from this damn place—let's spend the evening together." I was delighted to initiate him into the night life of which I was a past master and at which he soon became adept. I remembered a night when we sat happily in a new fashionable nightclub. That evening I had refused an invitation for dinner by a countess, pretending to be ill. A few minutes later the countess, accompanied by friends, entered the club and looked at me with deep disapproval! I was never invited by her again. On other nights we were joined by Jean Cocteau, Derain, Ansermet, Léon-Paul Fargue, and once even by Avila, whose cynical philosophy of life fell on dead and angry ears. When he left our table, their verdict was: "This fellow ought to be hanged."

One morning Stravinsky joined me at my breakfast at the Majestic and poured out his usual complaints about the difficult time composers have earning money. "You have it easy," he said bitterly. "You play a few pieces and they hand you a good sum of money." I became a little impatient with these repeated accusations. "Igor," I said, "you play the piano abominably.

Your tone is so hard that it could make me hate my instrument. Why don't you write an easy concerto and play it in public? I can vouch that you would get engagements from all the orchestras to appear as soloist. The whole world would flock to hear and see the greatest living composer." My suggestion did not fall on deaf ears. Besides being a genius, Stravinsky was a shrewd businessman. He took my advice and wrote in a few weeks his Concerto for Piano and Wind Instruments. It was a clever work, adroitly written in a percussive way but with a singing andante sounding rather like a pastiche by Bach. When the news got around that such a work existed and that the author was willing to perform it, the managers of most European orchestras made him good offers. Here I can proudly declare that I launched Stravinsky's career as a public performer, first as a soloist, then on a tour in America with a wealthy violinist, Samuel Dushkin, for whom he composed pieces for piano and violin. Much later he emerged as a conductor, proclaiming his superiority in his own works over other conductors.

Paul and Zosia arrived for their vacation and together we enjoyed the early spring in Paris. Misia, who had married a Catalan painter, José Maria Sert, gave many lunches and dinners at which we met many interesting people. Coco Chanel, the shining star of the haute couture in France, became Misia's constant companion. This extraordinary Coco, who had had a difficult past, learned quickly in her new friend's company the ways of the *"grand monde"* and opened a salon in the rue St. Honoré, where she received everybody worth knowing. There were rumors of a great flirtation between her and Stravinsky; nobody knows how far it went. All I know is that once, after one of her large dinner parties in the garden of the Ritz, she asked for a glass of water and Stravinsky, in a playful mood, or maybe in a fit of jealousy, filled a large glass with vodka and brought it to her. Coco drank the strong alcohol practically in one gulp, stood up, and fell on the floor. She had to be carried up to her bedroom. There were no serious consequences. Another, more pleasant episode of their friendship was when Coco Chanel financed Diaghilev's production of Igor's lovely ballet *Pulcinella*.

Misia's brother Cipa Godebski and his wife, Ida, and their charming children, Mimi and Jean, used to receive every Sunday in their small apartment on the rue d'Athènes the most brilliant gathering of musicians and writers. Ravel was their best friend and it was for Mimi and Jean when they were children that he wrote *Ma Mère l'oye*. Later his great work for orchestra *La Valse* was dedicated to Misia.

Paul badly needed a short cure before our tour to South America. The three of us left for Evian and found good rooms at the Hotel Royale, where the management was kind enough to let me put a small Gaveau into one of the reception rooms downstairs so I could practice behind locked doors.

Paul used it as well to rehearse with Luboschutz, who had joined us. As in Vichy, I ignored the cure, took my Evian water only at meals, but worked earnestly on a toccata by Bach-Busoni in C major, on the *Les Adieux* Sonata of Beethoven, and on the Fourth Scherzo of Chopin. In the restaurant at a neighboring table sat a beautiful young brunette, always alone, apparently taking her cure. Once in the reading room she asked me about an item in a newspaper, which I explained to her. So I started a conversation and found out that she had an *ami sérieux* in Paris and had come ahead of him to Evian, where he was going to join her in a fortnight. From then on, the reception room where I worked was used a few times for other exercises and I loved this charming intermission between Bach and *Les Adieux*.

The arrival of Sacha Guitry with his new wife, Yvonne Printemps, was another pleasant surprise. Sacha had become since the time I'd known him in my young years a most successful author and actor, and his wife was a beauty with a voice of unparalleled charm and a fine comedienne, who helped him in no small measure in his brilliant plays. We would spend our afternoons and evenings together in the salon with the piano, sipping our coffee and enjoying Sacha's biting wit and quick repartee. Yvonne sometimes sang her hit songs to my accompaniment and Paul amused us with his stories and imitations. It was a glorious fortnight.

For the trip to South America the Kochanskis and I embarked at Cherbourg on an English liner and to my joy I found Nena Salamanca on board. We invited her to join our table at meals and by the time we arrived, she and the Kochanskis were like old friends.

There was also a Spanish pianist and composer from Barcelona aboard by the name of Joaquín Nin. He had made a name for himself with pleasant compositions in the popular Spanish idiom and was on his way to give concerts in Buenos Aires. One could call him a good-looking man; he was well built, had a face with regular features and, as a special attraction, a beautiful head of hair. He was evidently proud of it and wore it in the fashion of the 1830's—not unlike Robert Schumann—gracefully covering his ears and falling over his collar in a neat, straight line; evidently he was conscious of his looks. At meals he sat alone at a table with a serious book about music in his hand and when he joined us at coffee his conversation was always on a very high plane. When I asked him about his program for his forthcoming recitals he said, "I'm playing composers of the pre-Bach period, as well as some Spanish music by Padre Soler and Albéniz." I exclaimed joyfully, "*Iberia!*" His face took on a disapproving expression. "*Mateo* Albéniz." I had to admit shamefully that I never heard of this namesake.

The passenger liners for South America have an old custom. They give you a baptism when you cross the Equator for the first time. You had to appear in bathing trunks or stripped to the waist at a place on the deck where a half dozen sailors in the same attire awaited you. Two of them would lead you to a tank filled with water, pick up a huge brush dipped into some liquid soap, and smear it liberally all over you—eyes, nose, ears, and mouth included. After this operation, they dunked your head brutally into the tank and let it emerge again only when you were almost ready to give up the ghost. After this barbarian rite, they would hand you a paper signed by the six sailors testifying that you had legally passed the line. Of course, it was always an occasion for much screaming and laughing, especially when passengers made any attempt to defend themselves. The novice Paul Kochanski along with some other victims submitted in terror but accepted the torture gracefully. Joaquín Nin, another novice, refused categorically to be baptized. He told us in a grave tone, "I'm at work on a serious composition and do not intend to join this tomfoolery." His pompous rejection of this innocent ancient custom irritated us, so we decided to give him a well-deserved lesson. Nena Salamanca, a Mrs. Supervielle, the cousin of a famous Uruguayan writer, Zosia, Paul, and I filled a big bucket with salt water and went on tiptoes to his door. "Quiere tomar una taza de te con nosotros?" (Would you come for a cup of tea with us?) When he opened the door, the whole bucketful of water was poured over his head. "Ahora tiene su bautizo!" (Now you are baptized all right!) I have never seen anybody get so furious. His hair seemed to be more precious to him than it was to Samson. He slammed the door without uttering a word and when we saw him the next day at lunch, we could only guess from his appearance that he had spent the whole night putting his hair back in order.

38

I disembarked at Rio de Janeiro and the Kochanskis and my other companions continued south. I was going to join them later. Pellas turned out to be a good manager. At the Teatro Municipal, I found my public again to my liking and apparently they found me to their liking too. I had Brazil all to myself; no other pianist showed up this time.

Mr. Carlos Guinle and his family invited me to a great dinner in my honor. He was the owner of the new modern hotels, the Copacabana Hotel and casino; whenever I mentioned anything I had seen or heard of in Brazil, I found out that he owned it. In Rio they lived in a real palace surrounded by a beautiful garden. Neither he nor his wife was particularly musical, but they had heard me at my recent debut in Paris, to which some friends had invited them.

This dinner was a grand affair; the guests were bankers, owners of coffee *fazendas* and of whatever else Guinle did not happen to own. Apart from all this, Carlos Guinle was a gentleman of the best kind and his wife, Gilda, was a beautiful and charming hostess. After this party, I became a frequent guest in their house.

Petrushka became the main attraction of my program and in the concerts that followed I often gave as an encore the "Danse Russe." My performance of the *Les Adieux* Sonata, which I tried out in Rio, was well received; above all, my conception of Chopin was becoming more and more liked and understood. I omitted Villa-Lobos this time, remembering the disgusting booing of his work on my previous visit. However, I made it known in my interviews in the papers that his pieces were enormously pleasing to audiences in Paris. Villa-Lobos came immediately to my hotel, the Gloria Palace, a new elegant building on the bay with a view of the Sugarloaf. He showed me many new compositions, many of them for the cello, which was his favorite string instrument. He also let me hear some beautiful new songs in which he treated the voice in a completely novel way.

On free evenings he would take me to nightclubs where I heard at last Brazilian sambas played as Villa-Lobos told me they should be. He pointed out some instruments I had never seen before: different kinds of flutes and piccolos, strange brass instruments, and, most interesting of all, all sorts of novel percussion instruments. There were shakers and devices for producing sounds which I couldn't begin to describe. The effect of all this was terribly exciting, but whenever I expressed my enthusiasm Heitor said disdainfully, "We have even better bands and players than that. Wait till you hear the little flute in this next place."

Lunching with me one day, he burst into bitter accusations against his country for its complete indifference and strong antagonism toward his work. "I'm writing and writing and all this becomes nothing but paper lying on the floor, never heard or performed in public, and yet I feel it is good music. If only I could leave this country and show my work in a city like Paris, I am sure to be understood." The success of his little pieces in Paris gave him great pleasure but he commented, "They are nothing—I have so much more to show." And he began to exaggerate in his usual way. "I have thirty quartets, fifty-two concertos, trios, poëmas, dozens of choros, some for great orchestras with soloists and organ." It made me feel as if Schubert and Mozart had done nothing to compare. He and Milhaud were the most prolific composers of my time.

After a good dinner at the Guinles', sipping the delicious Brazilian coffee and smoking a fine Havana cigar (the Brazilian cigar-makers showered boxes and boxes of cigars on me which I never smoked), I suddenly asked my host, "Would you like to be celebrated after your death? Carlos," I continued, "the Archduke Rudolph, the Prince Lichnowsky, and Count Waldstein would have been forgotten if they hadn't had the good luck to understand and love the music of Beethoven and play a great role in his life as his benefactors. Their financial aid enabled the great genius to write his master works free from cares; these gentlemen and a few others like them now have a great name in the history of music. Carlos," I repeated again, "right here in Brazil lives an authentic genius, in my opinion the only one on the whole American continent. His country does not understand his music yet, but future generations will be proud of him. Like all great creators, he has no means of making his works known in the world unless he is helped by some great Maecenas. I thought of you first of all, knowing your understanding, your patriotism, and your great generosity. The composer is Heitor Villa-Lobos, a future famous name in the history of Brazil, and if you are ready to help him, your name will always be linked with his."

Guinle was very impressed. "Your great opinion of him is sufficient for me and I shall be happy to do what I can for him."

After obtaining his promise, it was easy to reveal to him what I had in mind. "Villa-Lobos must go to Paris. It is the only place where his work can get a hearing and be appreciated. This means staying in Paris for at least one year, giving a few concerts of his works and finding a publisher."

"How much does he need?" Guinle asked me. This question was too abrupt for me. "You ought to discuss it with him."

"Well, tell him to be at my office tomorrow at three in the afternoon." I took both his hands and thanked him warmly.

Heitor was a proud man. He did not shed tears of gratitude when I told him this story. "These people don't know what to do with their money," he said. But the next day, after his meeting with Guinle, he changed his tone. Guinle had given him an unexpectedly large sum, with no strings attached, covering all his needs for at least a year. After telling me the good news, Heitor gave me a hug for the first time.

On my previous visit to Rio, at the Hotel Palace on the Avenida Rio Branco, I had been awakened early one morning by something which I thought was a bombardment of the city. I had been about to run and hide in the cellar but I was told by my quiet waiter that they were busy dynamiting a high hill behind the hotel. They were throwing the whole hill into the bay to gain a large section of land for government buildings and a new American Embassy. The future airport was built using the same device.

The new American ambassador, Mr. Morgan (not related to Pierpont by the same name), adored music and gave lovely supper parties after my concerts. One morning, the day of my third recital at the Municipal, I woke up and couldn't move my body. My heart stopped with panic—I thought I was paralyzed; my hands didn't obey me, the fingers could hardly move. I rang the bell with a superhuman effort. Fortunately I had not lost my voice. When the waiter came, I told him to get a doctor immediately and to call Mr. Pellas about it. Both arrived very shortly. I told the doctor that I couldn't move. He and Pellas lifted my upper body several times up and down and that made it possible for me to get out of bed. All I wanted was to see if I could still play. My fingers responded feebly.

It was a day of torture. I had never canceled a concert through my own fault. Slowly, by and by, I recovered some of my movements; I could take a few steps on weak legs, I could eat without help. My hands felt a little stronger and I could play but it sounded like the performance of an old, feeble man. Dressing for the concert was almost an acrobatic exercise. I had to adopt difficult positions for putting on every article of clothing. Finally, with the help of Pellas, tired out as if I had already given ten concerts, I reached the artists' room. My concert began with the *Symphonic Études* by Schumann. The first chords I struck were probably inaudible; I hardly heard them myself. But then, like so many other times, the miracle happened again. At the first variation I recovered my full energy and was my old self again. It was a good concert and after my despair of the whole day, it is easy to imagine my wild euphoria.

Mr. Morgan had a supper for me. This time, he set up a round table in the garden of the embassy for his many guests. He put on his right and next to me a most beautiful woman, who had a lovely complexion, a fine straight nose, a sensuous mouth, and a pair of blue eyes with a spark of vitality. She was French and was married to an American who sat at the other side of the table. I then noticed that her intelligence and her conversation were worthy of a Cocteau. I fell madly in love with her in less than a minute. I declared it immediately to her in a whisper and after the fish I implored her to let me see her again alone. She received my passionate declarations with a charming smile and repeated softly in her golden voice, "Attendez la fin du diner." When the ambassador gave the sign to rise from the table, my beauty gave me a warm kiss on my lips and waved to her husband. He promptly arrived with a wheelchair. She had been stricken with polio and couldn't walk. Her name was Louise de Vilmorin and later she became a well-known writer. Her poetry and several good novels were published, some of which were made into films. After her divorce she returned to Paris and a few years before her death she was going to marry André Malraux, De Gaulle's Minister of Culture.

39

In Buenos Aires, I was happy to learn that Paul had had a great success in both the capital of Argentina and Montevideo, where, to his joy, he found Mora, his old roommate, and Fabini, his other pal from his happy days in Brussels. Szymanowski's violin pieces, written for Paul and with his help, were so well received that he had to repeat them, especially the *Fontaine d'Aréthuse* and a brilliant tarantella which still belong to the repertoire of today's violinists. These pieces are more accessible to the public than his piano compositions, which are much more complicated and not easily understood.

Paul and Zosia were fortunate in having Nena Salamanca as a traveling companion, because as soon as they arrived she opened the door of her parents' house to them and introduced them to her friends, among whom were many useful people. The Mitres and the Gainza-Pazes, who owned *La Nación* and *La Prensa*, saved Paul from the ominous "visits."

The flowerpot and its owner had disappeared from the Plaza. My lovely friend now lived with her husband and children in a flat in the center of the city. I met her here and there but the days of our excursions were over. However, our colorful love idyll suddenly took a dangerous turn. Upon my arrival I was shown to my old room at the Plaza and rang for the valet; the valet who appeared was none other than Enrique. I told him sternly not to dare come to my room again. On an impulse I went down to see the director and told him that I did not want to be served by Enrique because I had discharged him from my service for good reasons. "Do you think it advisable to dismiss him?" he asked me.

"No, but put him on another floor."

The man did not take my advice and Enrique lost his job. A week or so later, I received an urgent personal note sent by special messenger. It said: "A terrible thing has happened. Your valet approached me in the street and demanded a large sum of money for not telling everything to my husband. I don't have that kind of money and am desperate. What shall I do?" And she signed her name. This was a hard blow. I had a difficult decision to make; I could very well manage to find the money but I knew that a blackmailer never stops demanding more if he is successful the first time.

La Señora Elena de Martínez de Hoz was a very influential person. I heard her once affirming that she could obtain anything she wanted from the President down to the chief of police. I telephoned her and told the whole story without giving the name of my friend but letting her know that she was a member of one of the best families in Buenos Aires. La Señora Elena was in the lobby of my hotel in less than half an hour. Without losing any time, she took me out to her car and we drove to police headquarters, where her friend the chief of police was expecting us at her request. I told him everything I knew about Enrique, including some difficulties he had in Spain with his military service and some unpaid debts. The officer smiled. "It is an easy case. I'll have him arrested this afternoon and I am sure to give you good news before dinnertime." It was not an empty boast. He did even better than I hoped. He threatened Enrique with twenty-five years in prison for blackmail, extortion, and other misdemeanors. "I asked him if he would prefer to be tried for these crimes in Spain, where the laws are more severe. But if you sign, I told him, a declaration that whatever you threatened to reveal about a certain person was nothing but a lie for obtaining easy money, I could see my way, thanks to your old benefactor Mr. Rubinstein, to be more lenient and let you go after a month in jail." The cowardly Enrique signed everything as he was ordered and the case was closed. I kissed both hands of Señora Elena in gratitude for her noble help. One can well imagine with what pride I informed my poor friend that we had closed the case successfully. I wrote her a note, which a messenger came to fetch next morning. In her note of thanks she called me not only the greatest pianist in the world but the greatest hero who ever lived. I blushed reading it but liked her to feel that way. There was a little unforeseen sequel to this. Stories of this kind cannot remain secret, so rumors soon spread that Doña Elena was trying to save the honor of her daughter, my brave and charming friend Nena Salamanca, who fortunately never heard anything about it.

40

My new manager, Ruiz, organized a good series of concerts for me and managed cleverly not to let them interfere with Paul's appearances. But this time, I found a serious rival.

Edouard Risler, a great pianist whom I had admired in Berlin, where he was one of Arthur Nikisch's preferred soloists, had just been sent by Quesada to Buenos Aires. His representative, a German, Mr. Ernst Schrammel, announced ten concerts for him, playing the thirty-two sonatas of Beethoven. Such an undertaking could not fail to impress the music lovers of Buenos Aires. As an old-timer, I had no novelty to offer but *Petrushka.* My programs still consisted of Schumann, Chopin, and Albéniz with a sprinkling of small pieces by Scriabin and the *Valses nobles et sentimentales* of Ravel. In all truth, I must declare that my concerts were still sold out and my public as enthusiastic as ever.

I heard three of the Risler concerts. He played some young sonatas, the *Appassionata, Les Adieux,* and the great *Hammerklavier.* To this day, I have never heard anybody play these sonatas as beautifully and movingly as Risler. He played them naturally, just as they spoke to him, revealing the highly romantic nature of these masterpieces. I was never convinced by the intellectual and almost pedantic conception of Artur Schnabel, the ac- knowledged specialist in these works. He sounded to me as if he were giving lessons to us in the audience, whereas the adagio of the *Hammerklavier,* the "absence" in the *Les Adieux* Sonata, and the D minor Op. 31 No. 2 made me cry when played by Risler. One seems to forget that Beethoven was the first composer that one could call "romantic," which means simply that he used his creative genius to bring out in his music his despair, his joys, his feeling for nature, his outbursts of rage, and, above all, his love. With his unique mastery, he expressed all these emotions in perfect forms. Nothing is more foreign to me than the term "classic" when speaking of Beethoven.

As usual, there were two hostile groups: the Rislerites and the Rubin- steinites. "Rubinstein can't begin to play Beethoven," proclaimed the fol- lowers of the French pianist. "Listening to nothing but Beethoven is a bore. He wouldn't dare play Chopin or Albéniz after Rubinstein!" asserted my loyal public. Risler came to one of my concerts and we both laughed backstage about our passionate partisans. On that occasion, he made a witty remark: "I loved your playing. I don't usually go to hear pianists. When they play badly they bore me, but when they play well, it annoys me." Then and there we decided to give a great concert for two pianos. Ruiz and Schrammel got together to arrange it in the big Colón Opera House. Our astonished followers filled the theater in breathless expectation to watch a musical duel between two antagonists. All the musicians were present, among them Ignaz Friedman and Felix von Weingartner. We played, after a few careful rehearsals, with full understanding, the lovely D major Mozart sonata, Schumann's *Variations*, the Saint-Saëns *Variations on a Theme by Beethoven*, and finished with the brilliant transcription of *España* by Chabrier. The concert was a colossal success. There was even a comic incident. The page turner in his enthusiasm threw the music sheet on the floor turning a page too vehemently. Everybody laughed, and we had to start from the beginning. After the concert, having earned a pile of money, we invited Friedman and Weingartner for supper in my apartment at the Plaza. After coffee, Friedman proposed a little poker game, during which our fees were halved. "I feel I played the third piano tonight," said Friedman.

Weingartner irritated me by an impudent remark: "I can't understand why my compatriots do not engage me to conduct operas or concerts."

"That is strange," I said. "I thought the Germans loved you for having signed the manifesto during the war declaring that the life of one German soldier was more important than a bombarded palazzo in Venice." The Allies had accused the Germans of vandalism because they dropped bombs on this beautiful city. Weingartner retorted, "But I am an Italian! I was born in Stresa!" A typical German turncoat!

After our appearance at the Colón, we repeated our succcessful exploit again in Buenos Aires and in Montevideo. Our happy music making silenced our partisans.

The great Risler was unfortunately a compulsive gambler. We were in Montevideo on the day of one of his solo recitals. He invited my friends Kolischer, Mora, and two others for lunch, which we greatly enjoyed, all of us telling story after story which made him laugh tears. At one point he said earnestly, "I'm sorry to have to break up this charming reunion. I always take a long siesta before my concerts." We excused ourselves for staying so long and left in a hurry. Kolischer and I decided to drive out to the Municipal Casino on the outskirts of the city. When we entered the still-empty gambling room, we saw a lonely silhouette—it was Risler. At the end of the tour, I had to lend him the money for his ticket to return to France. I met him again another time in Buenos Aires in the company of his charming daughter. That time he left with his money safely in his pocket.

41

Paul missed the Risler concerts, as he was on tour at the time. The Kochanskis returned to New York and I left for Paris, finding again with pleasure "my" apartment at the Majestic ready for me. Valmalète made me play in Brussels and some other cities in France besides giving a recital at the Salle Gaveau. Music in the French provinces was still at a very low level. Large cities like Lyons, Bordeaux, and Marseilles had small organizations with a handful of subscribers calling themselves proudly Les Amis de la Musique or Sainte Cécile. They would give subscription concerts in small salons which could not hold more than two hundred people—more, to me, like a poor man's copy of the "soirees" in the aristocratic salons in the Paris of old.

In Marseilles, I had the occasion to be soloist with an orchestra in the old Salle Pratt, which was really a shaky wooden shack. All through the performance I was afraid that we would end up buried by the collapsing building. In any case, the quality of the orchestra and conductor deserved it. On the other hand, most of the larger cities had opera houses, some of them excellent. I could add that the musical life in Italy was very similar.

I had on my calendar for this small tour the town of Epinal. The fee was so small that I wouldn't have accepted it if it weren't for my wish to visit nearby Nancy, the town where the Polish King Stanislas Leszczynski, the father-in-law of Louis XV, lived as viceroy after losing his throne and to whom the city owes a great debt. He endowed it with a beautiful square still called Place Stanislas and surrounded it with some of the noblest buildings in France. I decided to stay in Nancy for the night, take a taxi to Epinal for the concert, have it wait, and return right away afterward to Nancy, where I had heard of an excellent restaurant. In Epinal, in the building where the concert was to take place, an elderly gentleman was waiting for me. He wore a shabby overcoat and a hat of a nondescript color, and, if I remember well, he was unshaven. "I'm the president," he said, "of Les Amis de la Musique and we are proud to have you." The hall had a good Pleyel and chairs for not more than a hundred people, which were all filled. I played an eclectic program, bits of this and bits of that, but the real applause was for my good old friend *Navarra*. The president thanked me in such warm terms that I felt ashamed to rush off in a hurry as I had intended. "Could I offer you a cup of coffee in a place I have seen next to this building? I have friends expecting me in Nancy but I shall make them wait a little while," I said.

"Mon cher maître," the man answered, "I hardly dare to suggest it to you, but would you honor my wife and myself by having a cup of tea at our house?" I had not the heart to refuse his invitation and was ready to climb any amount of floors. "Do you live far from here?" I asked.

"No, I live in this next street to the left." We walked, and as we turned into his street, I saw a beautiful modern building. "This house must have been built by the architect of the house in Paris of the Vicomte de Noailles. It looks like a copy of it."

"You are right," he said, "it is the same architect. It is where we live."

We entered a palatial hall covered with tapestries leading to one of the most beautiful salons I had ever seen. An elderly gray-haired elegant lady presided over a lovely silver tea set. The walls were covered with pictures by Cézanne, Renoir, some of the finest Degas, and three or four early Picassos. He introduced me to the lady, "ma femme." Flabbergasted is a weak word to describe what I felt. It serves me right, I thought, a lesson for my blasted snobbism. I was well punished for my hurry to return to Nancy, which would have deprived me of the chance to admire all the wonders of his collection of paintings, books, and the many other things which he showed me. "I hope we didn't detain you for too long," he said. "I told your chauffeur to wait at our door." I departed red in the face with shame. When I told my friends in Paris about my adventure they all laughed loudly at me. "He is the richest man in France, the famous Chevalier."

Between concerts, Paris was a paradise to come back to. I felt more a part of Paris than people who were born there, simply because they were Parisians by birth but I was one by choice. There was not much time before the dreaded return to America and so I made the rounds of the night places where the exclamations of my friends—"Arthur, comme c'est bon de te revoir"—were music to me. Avila was to be found as usual at Maxim's. This time he was in the company of a young man from Chile, good-looking but rather shy. They were on their way to Italy, Juan told me later. "He's terribly rich but, as you saw, still afraid of life. I will try to give him my own sort of education for becoming a man of the world. We will have two lovely girls with us. One is my new friend. I made her leave her husband

and I shall provide the young man with a Chilean beauty who ran away from her husband on her own. She will teach him love and how to enjoy other pleasures. Of course, he will be paying for all of it; it's the least he can do."

I left for London for a short season of concerts. Mitchell arranged one in Oxford, an interesting city to visit. The Czechoslovakian minister, Jan Masaryk, the son of the President of the new republic, offered to drive me and my friend Lesley Jowitt in the embassy Rolls-Royce. We had become good friends on my first visit to London after the war. He showed us around the great city of learning, which impressed me with its fine old colleges and its noble architecture. The concert took place in the Town Hall at 8:15. My first piece was the C major Toccata by Bach-Busoni followed by the *Appassionata*. In the middle of the last movement, a young student came running toward the platform and made me stop. I was startled. Suddenly the clock of the Town Hall began to strike nine o'clock with no less vehemence than the famous Big Ben in the London Parliament. When it was over the student asked me with a smile to continue. I played the movement from the beginning. Later I was informed that they always tried to have the intermission before nine o'clock but this time the first part of my program was too long. I continued in dreadful fear of the ten o'clock bell but finished happily about two minutes before. We drove back in a gay mood to London, where we were given a tasty supper at the embassy.

My by now yearly appearance at Wigmore Hall was well filled with a music-loving public and all my friends. On this visit I made a new friend, the Countess Rocksavage, who later became the Marchioness of Cholmondeley. A striking Oriental beauty, the granddaughter of the Baron Gustave de Rothschild, her father was a Sassoon, a wealthy Jew from India. I met her at the house of Ilona Dernbourg, who was in her youth a famous pianist under her maiden name, Eibenschutz. She never missed a concert of mine. A few years ago, when I was reading the eight volumes of Max Kalbeck's most complete biography of Brahms, I found that she had been a famous pupil of the master, had played his works to his full satisfaction, and, even, did not displease him physically. It gave me a feeling of belated pride to know that she had approved of my playing.

After seeing some good plays with Lesley and playing some chamber music at Juanita's, I returned to Paris. Instead of practicing and preparing programs for America, I became enmeshed in some complicated love affairs. The beauty who danced the polka in *The Bat* and who in the company of Vera Sudeikin often joined Igor and me at supper was the one, I discovered, who had driven Stravinsky almost to suicide. She visited me often at the Majestic and was, of course, always welcome. More often than not a dinner or supper party would end by my getting involved with some lively young married woman who apparently needed a diversion from the routine of marital life. Of course, one should not forget that a French husband would feel dishonored if he remained faithful to his wife, and I am sure the wives were well aware of it.

I was lucky enough to see a beautiful play at the Comédie des Champs-Elysées, Marcel Achard's *Jean de la Lune*, played by the great Louis Jouvet, who also directed it, with Michel Simon and Valentine Tessier. The play was a light comedy imbued with poetic atmosphere which brought laughter and tears at the same time. Two or three nights later at one of the nightclubs, a young couple approached me to compliment me for my last concert. It was Marcel Achard and his lovely wife, Juliette. I poured out happily my admiration for his play; we sat down together and became close friends from that day on. I danced half of the night with Juliette, and Marcel introduced me to Jouvet, Valentine Tessier, and to Henri Jeanson and some other friends of the theater. I missed the Diaghilev season because of my departure for New York.

42

Mr. Engels proved to be a good manager for Paul but not for me. Apart from two or three violin and piano recitals with Paul, he made me play in half a dozen odd places around New York without giving me a chance to appear in the great city itself. Fortunately some conductors who were friends of mine had me as soloist at their concerts. My fees this time were even lower than those which R.E. used to obtain for me. With much idle time on my hands, I spent my days in New York visiting theaters and followed my growing passion for the cinema, which with its sensational new development was no longer silent.

While Paul was on tour, I sometimes helped Zosia at her tea and supper parties. There was a particularly brilliant one. The Duchess of Rutland and her beautiful daughter, Diana Cooper, who played the virgin in Max Reinhardt's production of *The Miracle*, and Prince Yussupoff and his wife, the niece of Tsar Nicholas II, were there. He was the one responsible for the death of Rasputin. The Cornelius Vanderbilts, the Fritz Kreislers,

Walter Damrosch and his family, and a few French and Polish writers on a visit to New York also came. Misia Sert and her husband arrived in New York for the opening of the exhibition of his work. To add a special touch to the vernissage, Paul and I played two sonatas for the guests. This exhibition brought Sert a commission to paint frescoes for the large restaurant of the new Waldorf-Astoria, which became the famous Sert Room. The other commission, a much more important one, was for the frescoes at the huge entrance hall of Rockefeller Center.

I saw much of Paul Draper, who had left his brother's house and found a quaint little bungalow in Greenwich Village. He had a good piano and we made music sometimes. He introduced me one day to a beautiful little blonde who, he said, wanted to be an actress. We were sipping coffee when she asked me to play something. "I'm not in the mood," I said.

"Will you play if I stand on my head for you?" I laughed. "That might persuade me." She promptly turned upside down; her skirts fell all over her, exposing her bare secrets. After this engaging exercise, I played, of course. She was Tallulah Bankhead, who, whenever she saw me again, would always offer to repeat her exploit for the same prize.

A telephone call woke me one morning at the Biltmore. "Arturo?"

"Juan?"

"Yes. I'm at the Ritz."

"Can you lunch with me at your grillroom?"

"I was just going to ask you to invite me," he answered. At one o'clock we sat down to a good meal. The story he told me during lunch was really worthy of Avila.

"You remember, Arturo," he began, "my plans for Italy? Well, Cousiño, the two ladies, and I left for Venice, where my Chilean friend quickly learned about the birds and the bees. He soon even became an expert. As to myself, old hand at the game, I fell in love with this divine city. After two weeks of our quadruple bliss we left for Florence, which revealed itself as another paradise on earth. We saturated ourselves with the beauties of this city and with the Italian pasta, avoiding, of course, the abominable wine. Florence had a wonderful exhibition of art then. Aside from the beautiful paintings, they showed a unique series of Arezzi tapestries which were for sale. The sight of them awakened my genius for finance, which you well know, Arturo, after my success in Buenos Aires. I did not lose any time. I persuaded the innocent Arturo Cousiño to buy them all. It cost him a couple of million (liras, of course), which means that it didn't ruin him. 'I will sell them at a handsome profit,' I told him, 'and pay you back with a good percentage.' The poor fellow fell into the trap and here I was with a fabulous fortune in my possession. But I found a serious obstacle: Italian law prohibits exportation of its works of art. I don't want to tell you by what means I got them out of the country, but they are now safely in customs right here in the port of New York. Cousiño took our two friends back to Paris. And here I am! But here is my new problem—I need two thousand dollars to get the tapestries out of customs. Can you lend me this money, Arturo?"

His request frightened me a little. First of all, I did not have enough cash on hand and was not about to sell any of my bonds in Argentina. Secondly, I was sure I would never see that money again; and so I refused his request with a lot of false excuses. "I shall have to find other ways," Juan said, a little disappointed. I did not see him for a few days, but one morning he called and invited me for lunch at the same place. I accepted with great relief, presuming that he had been successful in finding the money. I found him gay as a lark. "You would never guess in a million years who got the tapestries out of customs . . ." Enjoying for a moment the suspense, he then said triumphantly, "The customs officer! I promised him a good little profit after the sale." Seeing my mouth gaping with astonishment, he said calmly, "Now I must find a buyer. You might help me with this, as you know by now all the American millionaires."

This new request was again not to my liking. I told him earnestly, "I'm known here only as a pianist, not as a dealer in prohibited goods." Two days later, he sent me his Spanish valet, a genuine Leporello, with a letter asking me for three hundred dollars. "I have the jaundice," Juan wrote, "am in bed, and do not have the money for the doctor." I went to see him, found him in his room at breakfast, a little yellow in the face but otherwise quite alert. "I think," he said, "I will soon be able to give you back this money if my new plan works out." This new plan, as I learned from him later, was the most devilish one which had ever been conceived; and here I have to ask my reader to believe every word. Juan found out that the wife of President Menocal of Cuba was staying at the Ritz with her pretty maid. His stratagem was the following, in his own words: "I asked my valet to make love to the maid, and after obtaining her favors and getting into the right intimacy with her, to tell her that his master, the descendant of the great Avila who helped to build Havana, is in grave financial stress after the collapse of his bank. I gave him these last instructions: Make the maid promise not to say a word of it to her mistress." I laughed at his nonsensical scheme. "What good is that?" I asked.

"Wait and see," he replied. Late in the evening he called. "Madame Menocal sent me in an envelope ten thousand dollars, anonymously." This was too much for me. I dashed to the Ritz to see this money and, by Jove, he had it. At our next luncheon at the Ritz grillroom an acquaintance of mine sat at a neighboring table—Mr. Benjamin Guinness, the millionaire brewer, whom I knew from London. He introduced me to his charming daughter sitting beside him, saying, "She never misses your concerts." After I introduced Avila he invited us for coffee at his table. Avila described to him in vivid colors the treasure he had brought to America. "Are they for sale?" Mr. Guinness asked. "Yes," answered Avila indifferently. "Two American customers are very interested in them."

"Could I see them?" asked Guinness.

"If you want, I can show them to you in the storage." And they made an appointment. I will finish this long story quickly. After some bargaining, Avila sold the tapestries to Benjamin Guinness for $200,000.

With this fortune in his pocket, Juan left with his valet for Venice, where he rented an elegant apartment in one of the great palazzi. It took him no time to establish himself as one of the great hosts of the city, receiving at his table the proud Venetian society and the foreigners of rank who lived in the city of the Doges. It goes without saying that this story was a hit at every luncheon and dinner I attended.

At that time an English show called *The Charlot Review* was the sensation of New York. Everybody raved about it. It took me a week to get a single seat in one of the back rows, where I neither heard nor saw very well. But even so, I fell under its spell. For three days in succession I went back to see it, standing behind the stalls and enjoying it to the full. It is difficult to explain the reason for the triumph of this unsophisticated and not very original review, but what made it was the absolute contrast with the American deluxe shows like the Ziegfeld Follies and similar entertainments, where the public felt greater satisfaction in calculating the enormous expenditure in decor, costumes, and performers than in the offering itself.

The Charlot Review was just the opposite: very simple, no expensive costumes, just the few necessary items for each sketch. But it was intelligent and was played by an elite of English actors. It was the debut of Beatrice Lillie, Gertrude Lawrence, Jack Buchanan, and two or three other famous actors, all of whom later became the life and soul of the English and American stage. Noël Coward wrote the music and was also the young unknown author of several of the sketches. My enthusiasm for the two leading ladies was so persuasive that after a short introduction they accepted an invitation to dine with me at the Ritz Grill. I fetched them at the modest Algonquin Hotel, where they were roommates and best friends. Both were endowed even offstage with unbelievable wit and humor. So all through dinner I roared with laughter even when they told me of the poor financial condition of English actors. Nevertheless, they were happy about their success in America. I would take Bea Lillie to dinner any night I was free. She was the prettier of the two, but Gertrude was not only a comedienne, she was a great actress too. But for all their friendship, Bea would confide to me: "You know, Gertie is really my understudy, but I gave her a chance to have one or two sketches of her own." A very feline remark. Before my departure for London, Bea Lillie entrusted me with letters for her husband and little son and begged me to tell them about her success. "I hate to brag, you know," she said. "It sounds silly and they don't believe you."

I gave a concert with Frederick Stock in Chicago and something really disagreeable happened. It was the first recital in a long time for me in Kimball Hall. On the afternoon of my recital, I went to see the piano as usual and found to my dismay a middle-sized Steinway with not much sound. Thinking it had been put on the stage by mistake, I asked the hall attendant to bring up the concert grand. "There isn't any other piano but this one, which was sent by Steinway's for your concert." This gesture of the Steinway people in Chicago infuriated me; I considered it a slight on my standing. "What about that concert grand in the corner?"

"This is a Mason and Hamlin which Ossip Gabrilówitsch played last night with great success."

"Could I try it?"

"Certainly," he said. This Mason and Hamlin turned out to be one of the most beautiful pianos I ever had the chance to play. "Could I use it tonight at my concert?" I asked anxiously. "Of course. These people will be delighted if you play their instrument." With the help of this piano, I gave an excellent account of myself.

Upon my return to New York, Mr. Urchs, the head of the concert-grand department at Steinway, wrote me a rude letter in which he accused me of having committed an act of disloyalty to his firm and announced that henceforth the Steinway pianos would no longer be available to me. This was a heavy blow. Of all the many makers, Knabe was the only one who readily offered his instruments for my remaining concerts. I presume that for the Knabes it was a sentimental memory of 1906, but for myself it was again a heavy fight with a reluctant keyboard.

After that I stayed a few days in the Windy City to be present at the premiere of *The Love for Three Oranges*, an opera by Prokofiev commissioned by Mary Garden, then the director of the Chicago Opera. The work enchanted me by the striking variety of the music. Often funny or lyrical but always masterly, it was profoundly *musical*; I, for one, love the sarcastic vein in Prokofiev's music, but on first hearing it was difficult for the audience to accept it and so unfortunately this fine work had only a few performances. I arranged for myself the March from this opera and played it often in concerts with great success.

Before leaving for Paris, I went to see Mr. Engels and gave him a piece of my mind about the bad way in which he was handling my affairs. Instead of finding some reasonable excuse and giving me a rightly expected promise to do better next time, he became rude. "It is not my fault," he said, "if you are no good at the box office." And he added with a cynical smile, "You have a way with the women. Why don't you make love to the wives of the managers? That might get you some concerts." I slapped him twice across his face, slammed the door behind me, and swore in a raging fury never to return to the United States.

43

Neither Engels nor I spoke about the incident to Paul, because I did not want to harm the good progress he was making in his career. A few days later, I left for Paris, happy to inhale again the air of this wonderful city. Valmalète had been active and received me with good news: "The Count San Martino invites you for two concerts at the Augusteo in Rome, and the Società del Quartetto in Milan wants you for a recital." Concerts in France were also more numerous and paid better fees.

I was happy to learn that Villa-Lobos had arrived in Paris and had prepared a concert of his works for the Salle Gaveau in May. I did not know where to find him and had no time to do so, but I made sure I would be in Paris for his concert.

My recital at the Gaveau was sold out in two days. As usual, Valmalète gave me my concert itinerary with all the details of fees, trains, and hotels. I was astonished to find that the fee for Toulouse was twelve thousand francs, double the other fees. "Is this a mistake, or am I going to play in Toulouse in a special place which holds a bigger crowd?" I asked Valmalète. "No," he replied, "it is the Théâtre Capitol, where operas and plays are given, and I am sure you will like it. It is the best theater in town." I was puzzled, but also glad, hoping to get a similar engagement as well endowed as this in the future.

In Lyons the concert was under the same auspices as last time, but

Marseilles heard me in a cinema with good acoustics. Then it was the turn of Toulouse, where I had never played before. All I knew about the city was that it provided France with good tenors and had half of the name of Toulouse-Lautrec. I arrived in the morning on the day of the concert. No one was there to meet me, so I found a taxi to take me to the hotel, where my room had been reserved by Valmalète. "Has anybody telephoned or is there a letter for me?" I asked the porter. There was nothing. After a good breakfast, I went to the theater to see the piano and meet the director. The piano was inaccessible, as they were changing the set of the previous night's performance. Nobody was there but the porter and the stagehands. After a long wait, I returned to the hotel for my lunch. Still no sign from anyone. I was beginning to feel uneasy about the whole thing. There was no mistake about the date. I had seen a poster at the theater confirming it. After lunch, I went up to my room for a rest but in reality to wait for something to happen. In the late afternoon, after a cup of tea, I returned to the theater, where I found a piano in good shape standing in its proper place on the stage, with a good bench and even the tuner, who was taking good care of it. But no director or anybody else to talk to except the porter, who knew nothing about anything. There was nothing else to do but dress for the concert and get to the artist's room of the Capitol Theater all by myself. When the time came to begin my recital I found backstage only the firemen and the stagehand in charge of the lights. Another stagehand told me, "Quand vous voulez, monsieur," which meant it was time to begin.

There was a nice audience but this large theater was far from being full. Only a few boxes were filled but the gallery was crowded. The people listened well and evidently liked the way I played the long and serious pieces of the first part. During intermission, I became impatient. I asked with a stern voice, "I want to see the director right away, or someone responsible for the concert, otherwise I shall not continue."

They shrugged their shoulders. "Nobody is here." But when they saw me putting on my coat they became nervous and tried to calm me. "Where is your director?" I asked in real anger. "Has he left the city, or is he sick somewhere?"

"No," one man answered meekly, "he is in his office upstairs." This made my blood boil; he had been here all the time. I screamed, "Show me the way to his office!" I knocked at the door at the end of a corridor which they showed me. "Entrez!" I heard. I opened the door to find a man sitting at his desk wearing a bowler hat. His coarse face with long mustachios was enraged as he looked at me. "Un joli coco, your Valmalète," he said rudely. "He made me lose a lot of money with his promise that you would fill the house and make a fortune for me." He laughed with bitter irony. I asked calmly, "How much did you lose?"

"Ho-ho, I'm out three thousand francs, thanks to this coco."

"Well," I said, "take those three thousand francs off my fee, and another thousand for a little profit, but there is one condition."

"Aha!" he shouted. "I know your kind. You want another contract right away, but you won't get me this time."

"This is not my condition," I said.

"Then what is it?" he asked.

"The condition is that you get up from your seat, take off your bowler hat, and greet me in a civil way."

The man looked suddenly about a head smaller. He jumped to his feet, the bowler hat flew off his head and onto the floor, and he rushed up to me. "Mon cher maître, I never meant to offend you!" I said, "That is not true. You are terribly rude and I hope to tell this story one day in order to warn my colleagues about men of your kind." Valmalète's comment was: "C'est un sale type."

On one of my returns to Paris, I learned that Toscanini was conducting a gala concert at the Théâtre des Champs-Elysées. Dressed in my dinner jacket, I went to this great musical and social event. The maestro gave us a wonderful performance. During intermission, I visited my friends seated in their boxes, all dressed up beautifully for the gala. In one of the boxes sat a young girl in everyday dress with a hat on and two elderly ladies behind her. When I passed by, the young girl whispered, "That is Rubinstein, that is Rubinstein." Flattered by her interest, I gave her a little condescending smile. After the concert I found myself on the vast staircase near this young girl. "You did not recognize me," she said with a strong Italian accent. "You must excuse me for that," I answered politely, "but I meet so many people on my tours that it is difficult to remember them unless they are close friends."

"But you played for my mother," she said a little impatiently. This made me angry. I was often accosted by daughters who pretended that I had played whole nights for their mothers while I was well aware of the very few times that I played in a private house. I was going to give that pretentious young girl a lesson. "No," I answered impolitely, "I never played for your mother, you must be mistaken. I never played for anybody's mother." She got red in the face. "Si, si, you played at Villa Savoia." Villa Savoia? I remembered two hotels of that name and I do not play for people at hotels. But suddenly I stopped in terror. Villa Savoia was the residence of the Italian royal family. I stuttered meekly, "Su Maesta la Regina Elena?"

"Yes," she laughed happily. "E la Principessa Maria," said one of the old ladies. Then we all laughed.

My return to Rome became a memorable event. Since Mussolini had become the dictator of Italy and revolutionized the easygoing ways of the

Italians of the prewar days, I was afraid I might find a different kind of public. Instead, I was deeply touched by the reception I received at the Augusteo; the theater was filled to the brim and all my old friends were present. I feel the urge to express in this book my love and my gratitude to this most beautiful and noble country which since my first appearance through these last years has never let me down. I cannot remember a single concert without an enthusiastic welcome. I played in Italy year after year except during the Second World War, and all these visits remain among my most precious memories.

Villa-Lobos had a brilliant debut at the Salle Gaveau. He presented some of his larger things for orchestra, some with voice, but I don't remember the titles. This concert was a great success without any doubt. The somewhat savage quality of his music, the unorthodox development of his ideas, and the novel treatment of his songs and solo instruments intrigued and pleased the Parisians. There were many important musicians in the hall—Prokofiev and Ravel, I remember, among them. These two showed a respectful interest in the music of the Brazilian, but Florent Schmitt, who was also an influential critic, became a steadfast follower of Villa-Lobos.

Carlos Guinle and his wife were present in a box. At the end of the concert Heitor received an ovation from an audience consisting of many Parisians and a large number of South Americans—among them, the same Brazilians who had booed him in their capital but had changed their minds in Paris.

When I went to embrace him, I found him happy and proud of having had the good idea of coming to Paris.

He rented a flat on the left bank of the Seine, he told me, and slipped me a card with his address and a strange invitation; I read it: "Mr. Heitor Villa-Lobos is at home the second Sunday of each month." It was nicely engraved, but in addition to that, in his own handwriting: "Bring your food with you." He explained to me the reason for this. "Carlos Guinle told me on my last visit to him in Rio that I must have a nice apartment and have a *jour*. I didn't know what he meant, but he explained that one must do this in Paris in order to win friends. When he arrived in Paris he had his secretary make up these cards and also envelopes with the addresses of people to send them to. There were so many invitations that I was scared to death that all the money would go if I entertained them with food and drinks as Guinle recommended to me. So I found that it was better to ask them to bring whatever they wanted and it worked out beautifully." And he was right. At the first *jour* at which I was present, I saw well-known personalities arriving with a sausage or some good cheese, ham, and some bottle of wine or cognac, for which Heitor found good use throughout the weeks in between. At lunch with Carlos Guinle, a few days after Heitor's debut, I said, smiling and very pleased with myself, "You see, Carlos, I was right, wasn't I? Villa-Lobos will leave a great name behind him." Guinle listened, not very convinced. "Do you doubt it?" I asked him, quite alarmed. "No, no," he replied, "you were right about him, of course, but he annoyed me a little. I made a special effort to be here for his debut and asked him for a box and you know what he did? He sent me a bill for it." I blushed for my friend's big blunder.

Stravinsky told me with great satisfaction that I had given him the right advice. "I have already played my concerto in the Scandinavian capitals and more concerts are coming. I am also invited to give a few conferences at Harvard University and I might have a few appearances in America." I asked him about Diaghilev's season. "Don't speak of him," Igor answered, "he is only out to 'épater son public.' He produces ballets by Auric and Poulenc and God knows who else. Are you going to London?" he asked me.

"Yes," I answered. "I have some concerts in June."

"I have an interesting proposition from Koussevitzky at that time in London. Where do you advise me to stay?" I said, "The Kochanskis and I have a nice flat for the season. Why don't you stay with us? There is a room for you and we would be only too happy to have you."

He accepted our invitation with pleasure. Koussevitzky was in great need of a first performance of a work by Stravinsky as a main attraction for his season. Stravinsky had an octet for wind and brass ready and entrusted it to Koussevitzky for a good sum of money. During his stay with us he assisted at the rehearsals of his work and seemed satisfied with its progress. At this premiere in Queen's Hall, he asked me to sit with him in the first row of the balcony. Koussevitzky began the concert with a large work I have forgotten. This was followed by the octet. When the eight gentlemen with their wind instruments arrived on the stage, taking their standing positions in front of Koussevitzky, the public was obviously prepared for music like the hymns one hears in church or by a slightly modernized Handel. When they heard the first strange short phrases by the woodwinds they took it for granted that the piece was written as a parody of the music they were expecting and accepted it as good fun. When the moment came for the trill in the bassoon, laughter broke out. Koussevitzky, who was not one of the bravest of men, instead of stopping the performance and addressing the audience with a few words, assuring them that it was a serious work in the modern idiom, smiled maliciously and even had a twinkle in his eye as he looked over his shoulder at the laughing audience. Stravinsky squeezed my arm so that it remained blue for a couple of weeks and uttered an obscene name for the conductor, making me leave the hall with him.

This evening's event had nasty consequences. Stravinsky accused Koussevitzky in the press of being completely incompetent with no idea what to do with his work. The offended conductor retaliated bitterly that Stravinsky had shown the greatest satisfaction with both his conducting and the musicians at all the rehearsals, and now wanted to throw the responsibility for the terrible flop of his work on himself and the wonderful players. The whole story was pretty disagreeable, especially since on top of the public quarrel, the Kochanskis and I had to listen repeatedly for over a week to all the invectives in the Russian and French languages from the infuriated composer.

44

Stravinsky returned to Paris, and Paul and Zosia left for Aix-les-Bains, where I joined them soon at the charming Hotel Bernascon. This lovely resort in the heart of the Savoie on the shore of the Lac Bourget served all purposes; it was good for specialized cures, had one of the best golf links, a casino for idle gamblers, and the most wonderful food imaginable. The small but elegant theater in the casino offered good shows and concerts by some fine artists. Lesley Jowitt and Sylvia Sparrow arrived, the former with the pretext of hearing my own concert there and the latter to take some lessons with Paul. Both remained a couple of weeks. After their lessons, Sylvia and Paul played golf and Lesley sat with me at the gambling tables. The idyllic days of Aix-les-Bains passed too quickly. The Kochanskis had to return to America, the two ladies left for London, so I took this chance to accept the invitation of the Princess de Polignac and visit her at her palazzo in Venice.

Ever since my first visit, arriving at that city was like leaving this planet for a dreamland. At Mestre, my heart began to beat faster. Upon arrival, the *motoscafo* of the princess awaited me, and we went speedily through the small canals and emerged suddenly onto the majestic Canale Grande, stopping at one of its most beautiful palazzi. The Princess Winnie received me most graciously and showed me to a room with a high ceiling and a window on the canal. The other guest was Lord Berners, a gentleman musician who wrote in his moments of leisure quite good professional music; well read and witty, he was excellent company.

It was a great experience to enter into the private life of Venice. Overnight I became a Venetian, not any more the tourist looking around for good bargains, held in disrespect and viewed with irony by the proud citizens. I was given a key to the entrance door of the palazzo, which gave onto a narrow street where only two persons could walk side by side. And yet, this tiny street led after a few steps to the Accademia, where you can see the masterpieces of the divine Carpaccio. I used to slip in on my way to the Piazza San Marco to admire again and again these great paintings. During my stay at the palazzo, the Piazza became like a huge private salon and there every day at Florian's I would meet with my new friends, the descendants of dozens of Doges and other aristocratic Venetians. Distinguished visitors to the city were thoroughly scrutinized before being accepted into our group. Gossip was the mainstay of the conversations, often conducted in whispers with sly eyes darting to neighboring tables. It was very enjoyable to sip a Punt e Mes with soda and ice in the company of the Titianesque beauty Contessa Annina Morosini and Princess Winnie, listening with amusement to the malicious blabber around us. At one o'clock the Florian side of the Piazza was deserted and everybody rushed to his most important occupation, lunch. Where to go and what to order was the gravest decision of the day. Not only did it involve the food, but it provided a new theme for conversation at the apertif with the same company before dinner: whether the *scampi alla grilla* was fresh at this place, or the spaghetti really al dente at that place . . .

After dinner, the Piazza was abandoned to the tourists. Distinguished Venetians remained in their palazzi and were to be seen again at great parties given by one of them or by one of the noted visitors I mentioned before. During the opera season they showed themselves in all their glory in the boxes of that most beautiful Teatro Fenice. They left the cinemas to the ordinary tourist and the merchants of Venice.

As the Princess Polignac never obliged her guests to follow this program of the day strictly, Lord Berners and I went our own ways. I found here and there some lovely things to buy, not the trash that Avila sold in Buenos Aires but the solid and fine Venetian leather goods. But in reality I was a tireless visitor to the San Marco Cathedral, the Palazzo Ducale, and other favorite sights. After these long strolls on foot, I loved to sip the fifteen or twenty drops of the strongest coffee in the world at Florian's again, watching the pigeons being overfed by the generous tourists and going diligently about their own naughty occupations.

New guests arrived at the palazzo. Jean de Polignac with his lovely wife, Marie Blanche, brought with them their charm and their happiness. It made me proud to be the godfather to their marriage. Our hostess, who did not like to have large luncheon or dinner parties (it was too expensive), would invite people for tea to meet her relations. At one of these small receptions she introduced me to the Principessa Palladini of Rome. She was beautiful in the true sense of that word, with a delicate round face and a pale complexion. She parted her shiny black hair on one side and let it fall freely to cover her ears in a curl. Her dark eyes were shadowed by long lashes and heavy eyebrows and they looked at you with a bit of haughtiness but with a touch of humor as well. I'm not good at describing feminine beauty but Princess Winnie told me later, "She's one of the most beautiful women in Italy." The Principessa spoke perfect French with a peculiarly modulated voice, using knowingly some coarse words which sounded funny when uttered by her. When Lord Berners asked me to play a part of *Petrushka* in the adjoining salon, the Principessa came in rolling her eyes in fake ecstasy. "J'adore la musique," she said, and to prove it she added, "In Rome I take daily singing lessons." But it was said in the tone of the usual high-society babble. Frankly, I began to dislike her in spite of her charms. After her departure the comments about her were not too favorable, but there was unanimous admiration for her beauty.

Venice, I discovered with joy, was a very musical city. Two of Verdi's finest operas had their premieres at the Fenice. Monteverdi, Benedetto Marcello, and Vivaldi and Frescobaldi were the proud glories of the city. That year they held an international festival of contemporary music presided over by Richard Strauss, who conducted a concert. Fritz and Adolph Busch conducted most of the others. Many famous musicians of the time came to the city to take part in or to attend these concerts. The Piazza saw the small silhouette of Toscanini taking his daily constitutional at a swift pace. The Italian masters Malipiero, a Venetian himself, Pizzetti, and Respighi were sipping coffee at Florian's.

One day Manuel de Falla lent an unintentional comic touch to the scene. Living in mortal fear of contagious diseases, he was badly bitten by mosquitoes, and instead of using some soothing lotion, he pasted small pieces of white cotton all over his face and bald head. A score of small children, shouting with delight, took him for a super clown and one can imagine the amazement of the musicians sitting at the café tables at the sight of poor de Falla trying to escape from his little pursuers. They ran a joyous race with him around the Piazza until he collapsed in a chair at Florian's, where we tried to protect him from the enthusiastic children. In the evening he had a great success conducting the suite of *El Amor brujo*.

From a purely musical point of view, this festival did not leave a great impression. The works chosen did not represent the authors at their best. They seemed to have a lack of confidence in this first international meeting after the war. But Venice continued to have these festivals of contemporary music until the Second World War.

With autumn in sight, it was time to leave this paradise. "From now on, you must come every year to stay with me at the palazzo," said the Princess Winnie at our farewell. I never accepted an invitation with greater satisfaction, nor expressed my thanks with more conviction for the hospitality I had received.

45

It was always a new pleasure to return to Paris, but as much as I admired the Ville de Lumière for its early spring, the early autumn held a much greater promise. The opera, the theaters, the symphony concerts were now crowded with happy Parisians who, after repairing their livers, came newly disposed to take in all the shows with fresh enthusiasm and attack their livers anew to their heart's delight.

Many good surprises were in store for me. A letter from an enterprising impresario in Istanbul, Mr. Arditi, proposed concerts in Turkey, Greece, and Egypt, places which I was burning to visit. A telegram with my acceptance was sent in a hurry. My tour began in Spain but I had a nice free month in Paris. The theatrical season was the most interesting one I can remember. Besides *Jean de la Lune*, which had a long run, I saw a magnificent performance of *Crime and Punishment* from the novel of Dostoevski by a marvelous actor, Harry Baur, and young Pierre Fresnay, the most promising among the young actors. Marcel Pagnol, unknown until then, caused a furor with *Topaze*, followed by the great plays about Marius with the phenomenal Raimu and Fresnay, which remain unforgettable. In my modest opinion, the picturesque life in the popular quarter of Marseilles was brought out by him with a keen wit, a unique sense of humor, but above all with a kind of tenderness unequaled in the history of the French theater. A new kind of actor was born with Victor Boucher. He looked like any ordinary Frenchman you might see on the street, but provoked Homeric laughter on the stage with the tiniest gesture and the unsmiling expression of his face. Whatever he played became a roaring success. I shall never forget a scene in a comedy by Flers and Caillavet; in the second act, he sits with his host and best friend at the latter's house during a weekend in the country. Both drink hard and by and by get into teary declarations of their eternal friendship for each other. "You and I are brothers . . ." says Boucher, just short of bursting into sobs. "I would give you my life, all I have is yours and I know all you have is mine. When I sleep with Emilienne [his host's wife] I think of you all the time," and he falls into his arms crying bitterly. A priceless scene.

Lucien Guitry, reconciled at last with his son Sacha, began to take part in his son's brilliant and highly successful plays. The trio of Lucien, Sacha, and Yvonne Printemps became the toast of Paris. As an old friend of Sacha, I was invited to all of them. One was *Le Grand Duc.* Lucien gave a caricaturesque portrait of an exiled member of the imperial family of the kind he knew only too well in real life. For years Lucien Guitry had been the main attraction of the French company of the Théâtre Michel in St. Petersburg. The Grand Duchess Maria Pavlovna, the wife of the Grand Duke Vladimir (*un vrai Parisien*), was, as rumor had it, in love with the French actor—she never missed a new role by him. The grand-ducal couple often had supper with the actor after his performance. To one of them, which took place in a private room of the best restaurant in the city, Guitry brought his mistress, a pretty dancer called Balletta. A gay mood reigned during the supper. After enjoying a few glasses of champagne, the Grand Duke felt an urge to pinch the generous posterior of the dancer. Guitry's sharp eyes caught this indiscreet gesture and, promptly overcome by an invincible impulse, he slapped the face of his Imperial Highness. The Tsarist police ordered the actor to leave the country within twenty-four hours.

Guitry never returned to the scene of his early triumphs and Sacha's play was a nostalgic recollection of those times and characters. It was played to perfection by the famous trio, with my old friend Jeanne Granier in the role of the singing teacher of Yvonne Printemps, who, God knows, didn't need any because her voice poured out its beauty as naturally as a nightingale. I had the pleasure and the honor of introducing Marcel and Juliette Achard to Sacha and Yvonne at a supper in a private room of the Café de Paris. Sacha and Marcel became close friends and years later it was Marcel's courageous gesture to pronounce a eulogy over Sacha's grave. Sacha Guitry died after the Second World War, abandoned by many of his friends who could not pardon him for his behavior during the Occupation.

Diaghilev's season recovered some of the éclat of his early conquests. *Pulcinella* by Stravinsky, made with music by Pergolesi, was a great success. Stravinsky with his mastery knew how to handle the lovely old melodies of the Italian but added to it his own savage rhythm. *Les Biches* by Poulenc was enormously pleasing; the music exuded something of a perverted quality and Marie Laurencin's set and costumes caught this atmosphere perfectly. Auric too contributed a ballet, *Les Fâcheux*, inspired by Molière; it had only a succès d'estime. Diaghilev, this old devil, did find a real hit again: *La Boutique fantasque*, Respighi's brilliant arrangement of Rossini's *Soirées musicales*, which in this new form sparkled with its charming witty tunes. The tarantella alone held us spellbound. André Derain had never done anything better than the decor and costumes for this delightful ballet.

One afternoon, while strolling near the Rond-Point, I met Picasso. "Let's have a cup of coffee."

"No," he answered, "I'm going to the Salon at the Grand Palais. Come with me if you like."

I was very flattered to be seen at the great yearly exhibition of paintings in the company of Picasso. But at the same time I was afraid of upsetting him by my complete ignorance. I have always been a passionate visitor of art galleries; pictures like "The Man in the Golden Helmet" by Rembrandt in Berlin, the Velázquez room in the Prado, the "Danaë" of Titian in Naples, and the Raphael Madonna in Dresden always had a deep effect on me. I looked at the Impressionists, who were then coming into their own, with good understanding, and I felt a great admiration for the Picassos of that period. But I knew nothing about the technique of painting.

We walked into the Grand Palais, where hundreds of paintings hung close together. He explained nothing to me. He walked through the rooms seeming to see nothing at all. I didn't dare to open my mouth. But suddenly he stopped in front of a painting which showed some fruit lying on a table. I thought he would give me a great lesson in technique. Instead his eyes became round and he pointed a finger at an apple. "Look at this apple!" he exclaimed. "You could take it in your hand!" That was all he said about the whole exhibition.

It made me very happy to hear the greatest painter of our time speak so simply about art, which held no secrets for him. Art must be easy or impossible. Why does everything Mozart wrote seem so simple? The way to this simplicity is hard labor but it must never seem like labor.

46

In Madrid this time, I included in one of my three recitals, at which Queen Victoria Eugenia was present, *Les valses nobles et sentimentales* by Ravel—a work I loved to play but which presented some difficulties to an unprepared public. The last waltz, which Ravel calls "Epilogue," contains a nostalgic review of the whole work and dies out at the end, leaving the audience in doubts about when it is over. I asked Arbós and de Falla to applaud at the right moment. My concerts were sold out as usual, thanks to my faithful followers, but this time they gave me a bad surprise. I put the waltzes into the program just before the last number, the Twelfth Rhapsody of Liszt, which is a standard favorite of any public. After a few bars of the waltzes, I heard a hostile murmur in the front rows of the theater. With each waltz it grew to an angry protest. I heard things like "Disgusting," "This is not music," "He should be ashamed to play such a thing," and so on. Being endowed with a bad temper, I couldn't take this without getting into a rage. When the last note fell unheard by the noisy audience, my friends gave me their promised applause but it was shushed with fury. I looked at them all with murder in my eyes and began with a crash the rhapsody of Liszt. I owe here to my reader a little information about the Spanish temperament. As I've mentioned before, they are from birth passionate lovers of bullfights. For centuries they have been used to watching every move of the torero. They boo him and insult him for the least imperfection, but a moment later two or three brave close approaches to the bull are received with screams and shouts of wild enthusiasm. They bring this same temperament to concerts. And it happened on this occasion. After a few bars of the rhapsody, I heard again the ecstatic sighs of full approval and after the last chord an ovation broke out as if I had never played the waltzes at all. But I remained the only one who had not forgotten. I got up, cold as ice, gave a curt nod, and went backstage ready to go home. The ovation grew; they wanted the usual encores, but I asked sternly for my coat and hat. The manager implored me to play again but my only concession was to nod again on the stage near the door. I knew I was facing danger; Spaniards are quick to get angry. "You are risking your life if you don't play an encore," said the manager. "All right," I said, "if they want an encore they will have it." This time I walked up to the piano, bowed to the enthusiastic audience, and as usual announced my encore: "I shall repeat *Les valses nobles et sentimentales* of Ravel." My words were received in stupefied silence, the Queen left her box in a hurry, and then pandemonium broke out. I found to my surprise many young supporters who appreciated courage. They shouted, "Bravo, Rubinstein, this is the way to treat old imbeciles." The "old imbeciles" answered by threatening them with their fists. A regular battle began. "We shall teach you!" screamed the young ones. They blocked the doors. "Nobody shall leave this theater until he finishes." This resulted in real fighting, with blows exchanged, while I quietly continued to play. The scandal was commented on in all the newspapers in Spain and for at least five years no music by Ravel was performed. A few years later, a small city where I had refused to play because it had no decent hall and a bad piano invited me to give a concert and allowed me, if I wanted, even to play something of Ravel!

47

The Balkan countries washed away the bad impression of the experience in Madrid. Istanbul proved to be a treasure for the sightseeing maniac I was. I enjoyed all it had to offer to my heart's delight. The many remains, still well preserved, of the Byzantine empire, the magnificent Turkish mosques, the hundreds of slender minarets, and the sharp contrast between Istanbul proper and Pera, built by the Genoese, fascinated me, awakened my old interest in Byzantium and its conquest by the Ottoman Empire. Yet, before taking in the sights, I had to visit my impresario in Pera. Mr. Arditi received me in his office in the presence of two other visitors. He spoke perfect French but his conversation with his friends, which I believed to be in Turkish, sounded familiar to me. I heard distinctly some Spanish words spoken with a strange accent. Mr. Arditi smiled, seeing my astonishment. "We are Sephardic Jews and we speak the Spanish of the time of the Inquisition." When they found out about my great link with Spain they treated me like a brother. "Your two concerts," he said, "take place in our nice French theater, and we have a fine piano for you. Our public consists mainly of Greeks and Armenians. The Turks do not care for your kind of music."

My two programs had Bach and Beethoven, Chopin and Spanish music, and *Petrushka* for the many Russian émigrés from their mother country. My hotel, the best in Pera, bore the name of its owner, Tocatlian, an Armenian. It had comfortable rooms and a fine French cook. Mr. Arditi took me to the theater, where both the piano and the acoustics proved satisfactory. Strolling back to the hotel on the main street, my eye caught in a shop window something which would make me faint if I were still ten years old. It had a small mountain of Turkish halvah, the dream of my boyhood.

The whole of Pera had the look of a provincial city in France. The only sign of the Genoese invasion was a tower of extraordinary beauty in the purest Renaissance style. Both of my concerts were very well received by an audience which behaved like that of any European city and showed their understanding by the warmth of their applause—cool for Bach, respectful for Beethoven, familiar with Chopin, excited applause for the novelty of the Spanish music, and the old well-remembered Russian ovations by the émigrés for *Petrushka*.

Mr. Arditi was well satisfied and used the publicity for Greece and Egypt. "I would like you to give three concerts in Athens instead of the two announced, and for Egypt, where I had arranged only two appearances for you in Alexandria, I shall add now a concert in Cairo which I had not planned." This was a gift from heaven. I would have been so frustrated to have been in Egypt without seeing Cairo. After the first concert, a charming Armenian couple, who became my friends after hearing me play, offered to be my guides in Istanbul. We crossed on foot the long, always crowded bridge to the capital of Turkey. As a great reader of the novels of Pierre Loti, who described the mystery and fascination of the city and the Bosphorus, I was somewhat frustrated by Kemal Pasha's abolishment of the fez. Instead I saw many Turks wearing the well-known English cap but with the visor turned round to the back. When I asked my companions the reason for this, they said, "They were so used to feeling the fez going up in a straight line on their foreheads and the visor became a hated obstacle to them."

Mr. Pekmezian, my Armenian friend, a short, neat-looking man in his sixties with a small head and clean-shaven face, his remaining hair well cared for, was a man of culture, well-off but retired from business. He led the pleasant life of a lover of music, books, and good food. His wife, Sappho, was a very pretty young woman of Greek descent, of which she was very proud. I had dinner at their house near my hotel and when I was invited to use their piano for practicing, I became a daily guest.

Apart from all these nice things, I must mention one disturbing element in this story. Sappho felt a passion for cats. There were more than thirty in the house. As much as I love dogs, cats make me nervous with their sudden leaps and the expressionless shortsighted way they look at you. So the minute I entered their house I became a constant object of curiosity for these inquisitive felines. Two of them would jump suddenly onto the top of the piano while another one sat down next to my soft pedal. My appetite was paralyzed by the envious but disdainful attitudes of at least a dozen of them who were allowed by the lovely hostess to remain in the dining room. So no wonder I enjoyed the company of the Pekmezians best out in the street.

On the way to the basilica of Santa Sofia, turned into a mosque by the Turks, Mr. Pekmezian told me the horrifying story of the slaughter of the Armenians ordered by the last Sultan of Turkey, Abdul-Hamid. "Blood was running in streams from Pera to the Bosphorus and my brother and I were saved only by a friendly Turk. Thanks to Kemal Pasha, we were allowed to return to our houses."

The visit to Santa Sofia was a great disappointment. The Turks had spoiled the interior of this temple by replacing the beautiful ancient stained glass with some cheap modern multicolored imitations. Huge inscriptions in Turkish in large letters were written all round the walls and the beautiful floor was covered by prayer carpets of doubtful provenance. Even the lovely minarets outside Santa Sofia were not in harmony with the main building. But this visit remained my only disappointment. The palace of the last sultan, now accessible to visitors, contained the most beautiful collection of China porcelain in the world. The rich ceremonial attire of the successive sultans was hanging on view. I know I sound like a page from *Baedeker* but I cannot help it. I might only mention the fantastic contrast between the Turkish part of Istanbul, with the endless galleries, its huge covered market, the many coffeehouses with the nargileh-smoking Turks of the old regime, and ancient Constantinople, where you are reminded at every corner of the long and glorious story of Byzantium.

Mr. Arditi gave me the schedules of my next concerts. I was to play first in Egypt and then in Greece. Between my concerts in these two countries I had a week free. "Is it far from Alexandria to Palestine?" I asked Mr. Arditi. "You can get from Alexandria to Jaffa in a few hours by boat," he answered, and found a way for me to visit Palestine for two days and still be in Athens in time for the first concert. It made me happy to see the old soil where, thanks to the Balfour Declaration, my Jewish brethren on the Diaspora for two thousand years found a place again in their homeland.

I arrived in Alexandria on the day of the concert. Arditi's agent took me to the Theatre Alhambra, used ordinarily as a cinema. The city itself had no character whatsoever. The once unique lighthouse was now just like any lighthouse anywhere. You could imagine that Alexander the Great would have created any other city in the world rather than this one. There was no imaginary smoke from the famous burned Bibliotheca Alexandrina. The city, as I found it, had nothing to show. It was in the hands of Greek and Italian merchants of cotton and cigarettes. I met there quite a few rich Jews with English titles bestowed upon them. One of these, the Baron Menasse, was a great benefactor of the city. But I did get a moment of joyous surprise: The native Egyptians wore the fez. It was lovely to watch this red headgear with the black tassel which reminded me of my concert in Brooklyn with the Freemasons.

At both concerts I had all the Italian, Greek, French, and Jewish music lovers but not one fez was to be seen. I met quite a few interesting people whom I saw again later after King Farouk's downfall, as exiles in many cities.

The train from Alexandria to Cairo takes a night through a dusty desert. The Alexandrian agent who accompanied me took me to the new, very luxurious Hotel Semiramis on the bank of the Nile, which overlooks this unique river. Upon arrival at the hotel, the porter gave me a letter from the British governor-general in Egypt inviting me for lunch. His name was Sir Percy Lorraine. The name was familiar to me, and I suddenly remembered that we had become good friends in Buenos Aires when he was staying on the same floor as Avila and me and would often join us to visit places of amusement of the *porteños*. He certainly has made a fine career, I thought, and I rushed to get ready for the luncheon. Sir Percy was a handsome, distinguished Englishman with a flair for good music and good fun. He was still a bachelor and had two friends staying with him—a Prince Demidov, the last Tsarist ambassador in Athens, and Sir Ronald Storrs. Sir Ronald was my friend from London—Lesley and Cristabel had had him often for dinner—and an amateur pianist and organist, well versed in music. The luncheon was graced by lively and interesting conversation. Prince Demidov, who still lived in Athens, invited me to lunch on my visit to the Greek capital, and Sir Ronald told me with satisfaction that he had just left the post of the first governor of Jerusalem, which the English occupied after the war. "In my farewell speech," he said with a grin, "I mentioned regretfully that I had not contributed much more to the welfare of the country than my predecessor Pontius Pilate." His sally was received with loud laughter. Sir Percy amused his guests with some stories about Avila. After my second-rate concert that night, Sir Ronald handed me a few letters. "This one is for the editor of the best Hebrew paper and this other one for the president of the Zionists of Palestine. The other three are for my good friends you might like to meet." This time, I decided to make use of these letters.

On the bank opposite my hotel you could see British battalions still in control of the country. The beautiful mosques, the hundred minarets, and, above all, the museum of old Egyptian art fascinated me to such a degree that I forgot about the concert I had to give. It took place in a much shabbier theater than the one in Alexandria and was far from full. But I paid no attention to this; my mind was entirely set on seeing the Pyramids and the Sphinx.

For a better understanding of these famous sights, I hired an official guide, who wore a lovely fez and a long robe with beads hanging around his neck and another string of beads with which he played incessantly. We went through all the routine of sightseeing. A little boy, for a few coins, had to run up the whole height of the Cheops Pyramid for my benefit. I had read when I was young in Berlin all about the many, many years it took to erect this huge construction stone by stone, of the nine hundred lives lost in the work, and other stories. But now, being face to face with it, I forgot all these details and only became aware that old Cheops certainly did not deserve this exaggerated effort. My guide did nothing to whip up more respect and awe in me for these monuments because he was chiefly occupied in trying to sell me all sorts of trash which he produced freely from his pockets. He showed me beads of Chinese amber, visibly fake, proclaiming them unobtainable treasures. Then he took me away from the other tourists to show me secretly fake Egyptian objects, claiming to have obtained them with no little danger from some pharaoh's tomb. It goes without saying that all this fell on deaf ears, to the disappointment of my dragoman. The only thing I did agree to do to his remunerative satisfaction was to ride an Arab horse for a while; he claimed it was his own and he was honoring me by allowing me to ride it. On subsequent visits, in good company, I learned to appreciate and love this country infinitely more.

I sailed from Alexandria to Jaffa on a smelly boat in rather high seas. Arditi's secretary, who spoke Hebrew, helped me to find a hotel in the new town of Tel Aviv, then still a suburb of Jaffa. The hotel, if you could call it one, was a small villa with two floors and half a dozen guest rooms. Mine, fortunately, had a bathroom attached. In front of the villa a flower bed and some trees brightened the view. Tel Aviv had a half dozen or so nicely paved streets with similar villas, young trees, and genuine green lawns. Beyond that there was nothing but a desert of fine sand.

Our small-town Jaffa had three strictly-kosher restaurants. My companion took me to the best one, as our hotel had no food to offer. At the other end of the place was a large table occupied by a few men in European clothes engaged in a conversation in Hebrew in a quiet, distinguished way, so different from the gesticulating jabber of the Yiddish jargon. Arditi's secretary, pointing at them, informed me: "Do you see those three gentlemen in the center? Sir Ronald's letters are for them and at the end of the table sits the editor of the Hebrew paper which is published in Tel Aviv." Very pleased with this news, I sent him to fetch the letters at the hotel and when he returned with them I walked up to the table, introduced myself, and said with great satisfaction, "I brought some letters for you from a friend of yours," expecting to give them a nice surprise and at the same time make them learn more about me. But while reading the letters their faces dropped in dismay.

"Storrs? This English anti-Semite?" said the editor. "Didn't you know? He was out to make an Arab colony for England of our Israel."

I felt ashamed. "I knew him in London strictly as a lover of music and brought you these letters in good faith, convinced that he was your friend."

"A friend!" They laughed bitterly. "May God keep us from such friends!" My discomfort was a little soothed by the agreeable surprise that they knew all about me. "Arthur Rubinstein! We heard much about you, you are a famous pianist and a good Jew." The atmosphere became friendly in spite of Storrs, and after a second helping of the excellent gefüllte fish, I offered to give a concert for their benefit. "A concert? We would love nothing better, but we have no hall."

"Have you a piano?"

"Yes, of course. We have a Jewish professor from Moscow who has a very good instrument."

"This little Tel Aviv doesn't have many people, so I think that any large room would do."

They laughed out loud. "Few people! Ha-ha, if we announce your concert you would be astonished!"

My companion entered the conversation. "Haven't you an empty hangar in Lydda?" he asked.

"Yes, but there are no seats."

"I think that a Jewish public would listen to Mr. Rubinstein even standing up." The idea caught fire. Before I knew it, a concert was arranged for the following night and the editor rushed to have it announced in large letters in the evening edition.

The next day was a busy day, transporting the piano and rushing back and forth between Tel Aviv and Lydda. Trying out the acoustics, I found an abominable echo. "Don't worry about it," said one of the organizers. "When the people are in, the echo will disappear."

More than a thousand people attended that concert, standing up. I played well because I felt that they were listening with all their hearts. Both the audience and I were so deeply immersed in the music that it took us some time to hear the rain, softly at first but then coming down with such earsplitting force on the metallic roof of the place that I had to stop the concert until the storm passed. But it did not break the spell and I finished to the great satisfaction of my listeners. The organizers were happy to receive a nice sum of money for improvements to the city. We left for Athens by boat with good memories of my first visit on Palestinian soil.

48

On the approach to Piraeus, my heart skipped a beat at the sight of the Acropolis, the majestic remains of the great history of the Greeks to which every cultured human being owes a debt for its gifts to the civilized world. I couldn't wait to visit the sacred sights. Unfortunately, daily routine always demands its own, so we had to go through the chores of getting to the Hotel Grande-Bretagne, unpacking our luggage, and having our lunch. My first concert was announced for the next day, so I refused my companion's request to visit the theater and the piano, receive interviewers, or look over the program, but forced him instead to get a taxi and take me to the Acropolis. After climbing the steep hill we reached the famous summit where the Parthenon and the Erechtheum were so near that I could touch with trembling hands their beautiful columns. I spent the whole afternoon in awe of these old temples of perfect beauty and returned with regret to my daily life.

The porter of my hotel handed me a message from Prince Demidov, who expected me for lunch on the day after my first concert, and I found in the lobby a gentleman waiting for me. His name was Mr. Frieman, a Polish pianist who had established himself in Athens as a piano professor. I kept him for dinner, at which he gave me all sorts of useful information about musical matters in Greece. "They are music lovers," he said, "but completely disorganized. Your concert will take place in an ugly and dirty theater with excellent acoustics. I have some gifted pupils and you would honor me by accepting a meal in my home and listening to some of them. We have here a young Polish pianist from Lodz who came on my invitation to be my assistant. Unfortunately, he is in the hospital with a severe case of tuberculosis. His fiancée, a young Greek pianist, an ex-pupil of mine, looks after him with touching devotion."

I offered at once to visit my unfortunate young colleague from the town of my birth. Next morning, finding the theater and the piano not as bad as I feared, I went with Frieman to the hospital. The young man, whose name was Baratz, was in his late twenties; his red cheeks and teary, sad eyes indicated a high fever. At the foot of the bed sat a lovely young girl, his fiancée, who thanked us warmly for our visit; she wiped his brow constantly, giving him drinks and holding his hand with a touching expression of love. He was handsome and charming and had heard me play when he was a young boy. He talked haltingly but intelligently about composers and pianists. After a while, the young girl asked us to leave; she accompanied us into the corridor, where she told me with great emotion, "He could be saved, I am sure of it, if we only had the money to take him to Davos. The climate in Athens is slowly killing him." And she began to cry. I was deeply saddened by this visit and remained so until the concert. The young girl, Marika Papaioannou, was present and came backstage seeming to be much impressed by my playing. "He plays like you, he feels like you," she said. "Oh, if we could only save him." My decision was made. "I shall give you the money to take him to Davos. It can last for a few months. If you should need more, I will see to it somehow that you get it." She gave me a long embrace without saying a word.

Frieman brought most of his pupils to my concert, proud of the success of his compatriot. I noticed a lovely little girl among them and so promised with a lighter heart to listen.

The luncheon at Prince Demidov's took place the next day at one o'clock. As he had forgotten to give his address, I asked at the desk if they had it. The porter went out with me to give the address to the taxi driver in Greek, a language of which I did not understand a single word. At a quarter of one, the taxi set off for the address he had written. We were driving down the very long main avenue of the city. This worried me a bit, as the porter assured me that I would get there in a few minutes. But after at least a quarter of an hour, the driver left the paved streets and entered a shabby section on the outskirts of the city; this maneuver also took quite some time. Finally we entered a narrow street and stopped at a house which no acquaintance of mine would wish to inhabit. What a strange idea, I thought bitterly, to invite me for luncheon if he is reduced to living in such miserable conditions. I paid off the taxi and rang the bell. When nobody answered, I knocked at the door, which was violently opened by a barefooted woman who looked more like a witch than a servant. She asked me something very loudly in Greek. I could only repeat: "Demidov, Demidov, Prince Demidov," to which she replied by slamming the door. Here I was, almost half an hour late, lost to the world on a hot sunny day. There was nothing else to do but start walking and find the street with the hospitable pavement again, and that took another quarter of an hour. But fortunately I found it. At a slow, tired pace, I came nearer to the center of the town when my old deus ex machina once again called on me. A large limousine stopped beside me and a charming voice said in French, "Aren't you Mr. Rubinstein whom we heard yesterday with such pleasure?" And seeing me somewhat disheveled with my shoes dusty, he asked, "Are you in trouble? Can we help you?" To make it short, on hearing my bitter complaints about Prince Demidov, they laughed heartily. "He has a beautiful house around the corner from your hotel." I screamed in rage at the porter of the hotel, but he said that he gave the right address and that the driver must have misread it. I asked the director of the hotel to telephone the prince and tell him about my sad adventure. I didn't have the courage to do it myself.

My second concert had a much larger audience. *Petrushka* and later *Navarra* won out again. My artists' room was invaded by well-wishers; Prince Demidov accepted my apologies in a most gracious way, and a young banker, Mr. Stefanides, insisted on taking me to his home for supper with an irresistible enthusiasm to which I promptly succumbed. I found in his beautiful house a milieu of high culture devoted to the arts and, what pleased me most, a deep feeling of love and pride in being the descendants of the world of Homer, Socrates and Plato, Sophocles and Aeschylus, and so many other giants of mankind. Driving me back to my hotel, my host and new friend suggested that he take me on a two-day tour to show me the famous theater at Epidaurus and the Corinthian Canal. "I wish I could take you to Delphi," he said, "if you only had the time."

"I burn to see the Pythian oracle but an unimportant concert calls me back to France." The excursion to Epidaurus was accepted with joy. Arditi's agent went back to Istanbul. In the early morning I visited Frieman and three or four of his pupils played for me. A fattish young girl with a German name showed talent. The lovely one performed an allegro of a Mozart sonata with an enchanting smile but with a superficial approach. Yet I kissed her a few times on her lovely cheek—certainly not for her performance. In the afternoon Mr. Stefanides arrived at the hotel in his limousine to fetch me. "Take a bag for one night's stay. I brought with me some other necessary stuff." Our goal was Nauplia, where we planned to spend the night. The landscape we passed reminded me of Italy, but there was the sky, the Greek sky, which was a kind of penetrating blue one cannot describe. Its unique brilliance must have inspired the great architects of the temples and the columns with their varied forms, the shiny white, not to be seen in any other place.

After a short visit to some interesting ruins of this ancient city we took our meal at the restaurant of our hotel. Stefanides gave his orders in a meticulous way, got up from his seat, and left for the kitchen. The boiled fish was fresh and delicious. Before the next course, which was beef, if I well remember, my friend disappeared again into the kitchen. The meat tasted even better than the fish. When I expressed my astonishment that the food here was so much superior to that of the Hotel Grande-Bretagne, Stefanides smiled, obviously pleased. "I brought some fresh butter in a container with ice and smeared it myself on the pans for both the fish and the meat." He accepted with great pleasure my admiration for this display of a fine gourmet.

The next morning we visited Epidaurus, the well-preserved arena in the form of an amphitheater with its innumerable tiers of stone benches. Stefanides pointed at a few symmetrical stone slabs and explained: "On these stones stood the actors who played the immortal dramas of Sophocles and Aeschylus and the satires of Aristophanes to thousands of spectators."

"But how could they be heard?" I asked incredulously.

"Stay here without moving," he said. "I shall climb to the top of the arena, and when I reach it, whisper a few words."

I obeyed. When he came down he repeated the words which I had whispered. "I heard them as clearly as if you had sat next to me." This proved to be a demonstration of the perfect knowledge of the laws of acoustics that the ancient Greeks possessed, but to our everlasting regret did not transmit to the musical world; their secret could not be rediscovered.

We returned that evening to Athens, and I had to leave next morning for Paris by the Orient Express, which ran twice a week. The hotel porter accompanied me to the station to help with tickets, luggage, and porters. He began to annoy me with his constant demands for money. I hoped to get a bill for all his expenses at the end, but he did not see it this way. Frieman arrived, accompanied by his gifted pupil, her father, and Marika. The girls held two lovely bouquets, evidently meant for me. We were soon engaged in a lively conversation in German, French, and Polish, interrupted constantly by new demands for money from the porter. "There is an additional sum to pay for the luggage"; then: "I need it for the porters"; then: "I gave a tip to the conductor to give you a good seat." Then came the change for himself. All this while we were talking about music, concerts, my next visit, and other topics. Suddenly, without warning, the train began to move and picked up speed. I jumped swiftly into the last car with nothing but my cane over my arm. In their great surprise, the girls remained with their bouquets in their hands, and I waved at them and went in search of the compartment that contained my hand luggage. I walked from car to car as far as the engine and back, searching every compartment for my belongings, without success. It was a bad situation. Even the ticket and my passport were in one of my lost bags. I guessed with fury what had happened. The money-greedy porter simply forgot to have my baggage loaded on the train, and here I was without my coat and hat, with nothing but a cane. The only thing I could do was to leave the train at the next station and return to Athens. The conductor, whom I asked about the schedules with the help of a French-speaking passenger, informed me that our next stop was Thebes in two and a half hours and the return train to Athens went by late in the evening. I left the train and felt as miserable as Oedipus deprived of his eyes. A little boy who understood my signs led me up a hill to the city, now a modern, dirty provincial town. I was searching for a car to take me back to Athens when a powerful open limousine turned a corner with a shriek and stopped violently in front of me. Frieman, the father, and the two girls, still holding their flowers but covered with dust, showed me my luggage, wringing their hands in despair. "We tried to catch your train and missed by a few minutes!" Thanking them effusively, I seated myself comfortably between the two girls and we drove back to Athens at a slower pace. At the Hotel Grande-Bretagne, I was prevented by Frieman from slapping the face of the frightened porter and invited the company to a good dinner, which we enjoyed after washing and cleaning up. Marika was leaving the next morning with her fiancé for Davos. The other girl, whose name I learned only then, was Gina Bachauer; she won fame in later years as an excellent pianist. I spent three more delightful days in the Greek capital without much regret for the lost concert in France. At the Stefanides' I met some good friends of theirs who opened their houses to me and remained my faithful followers at all future appearances in Greece.

49

Princess Edmond de Polignac sent me an invitation to a concert at her palace on the avenue Henri Martin, where Prokofiev was to play his Third Concerto with an orchestra. "*Le tout Paris*" filled her huge music room, where a platform was set up for the performers. I found myself

seated next to Princess Palladini; I had met her at two dinner parties and
had become better acquainted with her. She greeted me with questions
about Prokofiev which I had no time to answer, as the concert was just
beginning. I listened, again entranced, to the beautiful work, splendidly
played by the composer. It was received with polite applause by the elegantly dressed audience, which included, I noticed, Stravinsky, Nadia Boulanger, Poulenc, and Auric.

We were just getting up when the Italian princess turned toward me
and said in her singsong voice, a little impatiently, "I suppose that you don't
want me because you've heard some ugly stories about a love affair of
mine." For a moment I was speechless; but I suddenly realized what it
meant. "Will you come with me to my apartment?" I whispered, my heart
beating. She asked quietly, "Where do you live?" When I told her she
added, "Go home and wait for me." She arrived a little later. I took her late
that night back to her own hotel.

I spent the whole morning amazed by what had happened the night
before, trying to find the answer to this completely unexpected situation. It
couldn't be anything else, I thought, than a caprice of a beautiful woman
who couldn't tolerate my indifference. During the whole day, I made no
attempt to reach her. At dinnertime the telephone rang and the now well-
known singing voice said quietly, "I'm dining out, but shall come after
dinner. Wait for me," and she put down the phone. We spent every night
together until her departure for Rome. Her days were occupied by fittings
for her wardrobe and her social obligations. When I gave her the date of my
next concert in Rome she said, "I shall give a big dinner for you. I want you
to meet my friends. Are you going to be in Paris this spring?" she asked.
"Yes, as I have to prepare for my tour of South America." She suddenly
showed great interest. "Which part of South America?" When I said Brazil
she became quite excited. "I always dreamed of seeing Rio de Janeiro. I
would love to go with you."

"That would be wonderful!" I said, not taking it very seriously. "Rio is
enchanting. I know it well. I've been three times and have given many
concerts there."

"Well, you can count on me," she said. "I adore traveling."

After a week, she left Paris.

When she was gone, my life resumed its usual pace: concerts in Paris,
London, and other places, a lunch with Cocteau, a night at the Boeuf sur le
Toit, enjoying the company of Fargue and the Achards, dinner at Coco
Chanel's and Misia Sert's, a visit to Prokofiev, and a good play. I heard
nothing from the princess, nor did I write to her. But when I arrived in
Rome to play a Chopin and the Saint-Saëns concerti under Molinari at the

Augusteo, I found a letter from the princess with the invitation for a dinner written in the usual terms, except that at the end of the letter she added: "Je t'embrasse tendrement."

The dinner took place in their palazzo with her estranged husband present and a few couples from the Roman aristocracy whom I had met before, together with some new distinguished personalities. Among them was a charming lady, Countess Pecci-Blunt; after exchanging a few phrases with her, an everlasting friendship was born. The Princess Carla was a perfect hostess. She chose her guests strictly among people who liked music and had heard me play, which right from the beginning of the dinner created an animated atmosphere in which I was treated as the central figure. I took leave with the others, thanking my hosts for the wonderful evening, and returned to my hotel, the Excelsior. The next day, which was a Tuesday, I had two good rehearsals with Molinari. On Wednesday there was another rehearsal and in the afternoon, the concert. I had always felt it a privilege to play in the Augusteo ever since my first concert there. The way the Roman public treated me invariably brought out the best in me. They felt it and showed their appreciation in a heartwarming way and we never failed each other. Unfortunately, Mussolini, who did some fine work in excavating and restoring neglected ruins of old Rome and showed them to their best advantage by clearing the surrounding area, in his fervor included the destruction of the Augusteo Hall, built on top of the mausoleum of the Emperor Augustus, in order to restore the tomb to its original form, which is of little interest to the visitor. In doing so, he deprived Rome of a unique center for music. Since then, the orchestra of Santa Cecilia has tried out several theaters without finding the right acoustical conditions, and only in the last years was it able to obtain permission from the authorities of the Vatican to use the Sala Conciliazione, where I have played every year since, either with orchestra or solo. My public remained just as faithful as at the Augusteo but both the audience and the musicians couldn't help feeling as if there was a little incense in the air.

The not-too-large artist's room after the concert at the Augusteo was filled with my old and new friends. Carla took me aside and said, "Take me to dinner. I shall come in an hour to fetch you at the hotel."

"I shall wait in the lobby," I answered. I had a hard time explaining to the Count San Martino why I couldn't have dinner with him; I pretended to be terribly tired with no wish to dine.

After changing clothes, I waited for well over half an hour in the lobby; then a chauffeur asked for me and told me "la Signora Principessa" was waiting in the car outside. When I mentioned that I was afraid for her and for myself to be seen together after I had declined to dine with San

Martino, she sang out, "Je m'en fiche." But she did take me to a small restaurant on the Piazza Navona where I doubt that any of our acquaintances would be seen. We had nothing but a soup and a pasta, drank some white wine from Verona, and returned to the Excelsior, where she dismissed her car and followed me to my room. "How will you get home?" I asked.

"Do not worry. You call the porter for a taxi and I shall go down when it arrives." I had never known a woman more indifferent to gossip about her behavior and with more self-assurance in difficult situations.

My friend Mimi Pecci-Blunt gave a dinner for me, and Carla left me a note at the Excelsior asking me to take her. Mimi treated us as if we were married and all the others took it naturally. Roman society felt no prejudice against amorous intrigues among its members.

I had a lovely concert in Florence. It took place in the Sala Bianca of the Palazzo Pitti, a beautiful and dignified setting for music. Florence was a stronghold of classical music. Alessandro Longo, who had edited with meticulous care the complete edition of keyboard works of Scarlatti, was a Florentine. A fine pianist, Ernesto Consolo, and the gifted composer Castelnuovo-Tedesco were members of the committee which organized the Sala Bianca concerts. I played there several times with great satisfaction and the knowledge that no phrase was lost on the attentive ears of these Florentines. However, my appearance at the ancient Società del Quartetto in Milan was of a different character. The audience of the noble Sala Verdi of the Milano Conservatory was made up of conceited subscribers, ever ready to compare me with other artists. On the stage, facing me, sat the professors of the conservatory and their director, Ildebrando Pizzetti, whom D'Annunzio called poetically "Ildebrando di Parma." He also called Debussy "Claude de France." Fortunately a good number of young music students lent life to the concert. Milan as a city had nothing much to offer except the Duomo— that miraculous work of man. Even the world-famous Scala as a building has not the beauty of the Fenice or the grand air of the Teatro Massimo in Palermo.

Back in Paris, I found the chestnut trees of the avenue du Bois showing the first tender green of their new leaves. The whole city felt the promise of its lovely spring. The welcome of my friends warmed my heart. I was born with a very precious gift: to be able to see the world in which I live always with new eyes. Life was and remains a fairy tale for me; I thank providence daily for being allowed to be part of it.

50

There was much music to be heard that spring. Villa-Lobos, after a considerable success in Portugal, came back to Paris and showed me some interesting new works he had written. Fortunately Max Eschig published many of his early pieces, which made it easier for me to learn some of them. A German pianist, Walter Gieseking, made a sensation in Paris with his very personal approach to Debussy and the critics unanimously proclaimed him the ideal interpreter of the French master. The bitter pill that a German should deserve this honor was swallowed more easily thanks to the fact that his mother was French. I went to one of his concerts and was enchanted by the unearthly, delicate climate he created in his treatment of this impressionist music. My own conception, however, demanded more meat, if I may express myself in this crude way. He evoked invariably a magic background, but the action was missing.

Cortot, Thibaud, and Casals formed a trio which remained unforgettable to the fortunate ones who attended their great feasts of music. The Opéra and Opéra-Comique lived mainly by the endless repetition of *Faust*, *Carmen*, and *Manon*, not always performed as they deserved to be.

The small hall of the Agriculteurs was honored by some fine concerts by Kreisler and the great Busoni, who played his recent transcriptions of Bach, including the famous Chaconne for solo violin, which he enriched with an accompaniment befitting the simple notes and chords of the violin. The work became a masterpiece for the piano. In my opinion, Bach himself would have approved. As for the organ toccatas and pieces written for harpsichord, Busoni had an uncanny way of reproducing the sound of these instruments on the piano, so that you thought you were hearing the original.

I heard another concert in this hall which was moving and funny at the same time. The two venerable masters Saint-Saëns and Francis Planté gave a two-piano recital. It was touching to hear these two fine artists playing with a technical perfection seldom attained by younger pianists. At the same time, they made us laugh at the way they behaved—as if they were alone together in a room. "Bravo, mon vieux!" would say Saint-Saëns after the other had played a brilliant passage. "Ah, quelle élégance!" Planté would exclaim when Saint-Saëns rounded a phrase beautifully. As to myself, I gave two recitals at the Gaveau with my by now faithful public, feeling more and more that they were becoming the expected yearly social event and not the evenings of pure musical emotion which I tried to convey.

Avila's tapestry fortune seemed to be ebbing, for from time to time his valet would come with an urgent request from his master for a loan of a few thousand francs. His note was usually accompanied by an invitation for dinner for that same night. Besides his lovely mistress, Juan gathered together some of our Spanish friends who were in Paris at that time. I was always proud to feel that I shared financially in his hospitality.

On the way home, my friend Marcelino Narros told me an interesting little story. "One of the better couturieres in town runs a little business on the side. She provides some *femmes-du-monde de la haute bourgeoisie*, whose husbands are not rich enough or are unable to pay their bills, with wealthy foreigners who are willing to pay for their dresses in return for an amorous hour or two. The shop has a comfortable apartment for such occasions. The owner, terrified of any scandal, is very strict in choosing foreigners on a short visit to Paris, and only if the lady in question is well assured of their discretion." The Marqués Narros seemed to have enjoyed the favors of some particularly charming person. When I asked with great interest, "Can you give me the address of the place?" he answered, "I would have to introduce you myself without giving your name. She is very suspicious and inquisitive."

We arranged a rendezvous for the following afternoon shortly before closing time. A few ladies were still in the shop. At the sight of Marcelino and me, one of them opened the door to a boudoir and invited us in with a smile. After closing the door, she asked Narros unsmilingly, "Who is that gentleman?"

"He is an old friend of mine from Madrid and is here for two days. He would like to talk to you some more," he said in a meaningful tone. She scrutinized me for a moment and then said, "All right, sit down and wait for me." She accompanied my friend to the door and came back. "It is a little late," she said. "There is one lady whom I can send in and if you like her she will stay with you. If you don't, all you have to do is bid her goodbye when I come back in the room." After a while an overdressed woman entered, heavily made-up in an attempt to cover her already tired features. I had no use for her. After a short conversation about the weather, the first woman returned and I stood up to leave with a short nod. While I was waiting for a while alone in the room, she came in again, this time with eyes shining. "You are lucky, very lucky. Just this moment a most lovely young woman has arrived. Beautiful and intelligent. She is a pianist, a *premier prix du conservatoire*." I managed to conceal my surprise and a moment later a really enchanting young woman came in. She had what the Parisians call a *charmante frimousse*—a small head with vivid blue eyes, an upturned little nose, and a well-shaped mouth—and she used no makeup. She was rather tall and slim with fine curves. She began to talk in quick fluent French, informing me that she was a pianist, had finished the conservatory, and needed some clothes for her concerts, which, she added smilingly, her husband couldn't afford. By then, the shop was closing. The woman came in and offered us a room with a bed behind the boudoir and brought us some port and biscuits. My lovely companion undressed in no time, bade me do the same, and we found ourselves lying on the bed. After some short moments of bliss, we took a sip of port, lay down again, this time quietly, and my lovely partner started to chatter again. "Do you like Cortot? I think he's getting tired, what with his memory and all that. I like Iturbi, good fingers." And then: "Brailowski plays some Chopin very well and others less well. Have you heard Gieseking? Isn't his Debussy divine?" She named every living pianist but me. I must admit it vexed me. I presumed that I had begun to be well-known too. After a short silence she said, "I've heard that Rubinstein is *épatant*, but I have never heard him." Hearing that, I was overjoyed, forgot the whole situation, and shouted, raising my hands up high: "It's me! It's me!" She uttered a cry and looked at me with wild terror in her eyes and the whole thing turned into a tragedy. She threw herself on the floor, crying spasmodically, "I knew it! I knew it! I am ruined. I had it coming to me. I shall kill this woman for inducing me to do it for her nasty clothes. My husband is a good musician whom you probably have met or will meet." She uttered all this while crying incessantly and beating her head with her fists.

It took me a whole hour to calm her. I swore by all that's holy that I would keep the secret buried in me and finally succeeded in taking her to a nearby café where we might have met casually, and treated her as a young pianist who had introduced herself to me and joined me in a conversation about music. I never saw her again and never knew who her husband was.

Paul and Zosia joined me for a week in Paris. Paul had just had a tour in Spain and I, too, accepted a few concerts there managed by Quesada, who came to Paris to make up with me, explaining at length the unfortunate incident in Rio. "The directors of the Municipal Opera refused to let you play in their theater if I would not quietly agree to their shameful practice." He departed to prepare our concerts, happy to be working with me again in Spain.

I remember on this occasion a little musical exploit all of my own. Arriving in La Coruña, I received a musical score and a letter from Enrique

Arbós. "Please play with me the *Variations symphoniques* of César Franck, which is in great demand. If you have never played it I wouldn't mind if you read it from the score. You will do me a great favor by accepting my request."

The concert in Madrid was in two days and the only rehearsal was one hour after my arrival on the day of the concert. All I could do was to learn it on the long journey, as there was no time to try it out on a piano. I boarded the train with the score in my hand and studied it by reading it carefully many times, putting in practical fingerings and trying difficult passages on my lap. Upon arrival I only had time to wash up and rush to the rehearsal, prepared to play it from the score and study it meticulously with the orchestra. Seeing two critics and half a dozen music students sitting in the hall at the rehearsal, I suddenly decided to play the piece by heart, thinking: If my memory betrays me, I'll go on playing, I'm sure to find my way again. Well, I played the piece through without a stop but with many unfinished details. However, I had the rest of the day to work on it. And for once I did not leave my piano for about six hours, interrupting my work only for a sandwich or two. At the concert, we gave a very good performance of this beautiful piece.

My South American tour was to begin at the end of May, and I planned to be back at the beginning of August. At the end of April, I received a wire from Carla: "Arriving with my maid day after tomorrow. Please reserve apartment next to yours." Fortunately the apartment was free. She arrived in Paris on time with a large quantity of luggage and her first question was: "When are we leaving?" My surprise that she meant what she said about going with me was mixed, I must admit, with a feeling of being flattered that a lady of her standing would risk her reputation by traveling openly to these still young countries, where her appearance with me might be considered scandalous. At the same time, I felt proudly that this adventure resembled the story of Liszt and Madame d'Agoult.

51

Carla's maid was efficient and very devoted to her mistress. She also showed a great respect for me because her brother was one of the cellists of the orchestra at the Augusteo. We traveled to Marseilles to take a French ship to Brazil. Our cabins were comfortable and the French food was excellent. Carla loved the sea, which was always quiet and smooth when one was going south. She took part in all the pleasant activities the boat offered; we would have tea accompanied by the dreadful music, we would dance after dinner, and she submitted with grace to the baptism at the Equator. We arrived at Rio after a sleepless night full of excited anticipation of seeing the wonder of the most beautiful bay in the world at sunrise.

The first timid rays of the sun shimmered on the hills and mountains in and around the city. As an old visitor, I pointed out to her the original beauty of the Sugarloaf, the amazing Corcovado with the Christ blessing the city, forming a cross with outstretched arms, the endless Copacabana Beach, and so many striking points visible from the boat. My manager, Mr. Pellas, who greeted us at the quay, began by congratulating me on my marriage; when he was told of his mistake and was duly introduced to the princess, he seemed to want to congratulate me even more sincerely. He drove us to the Gloria Palace, halfway between the center of the city and Copacabana.

Mr. Pellas announced only three recitals at the Municipal Theater, as it was taken for all the rest of the season. The three recitals were sold out, thank goodness; I was afraid that my playing of Villa-Lobos instead of the more popular composers might still be remembered. Instead, my Chopin recital, the last of the three, pleased the audience particularly, which gave both Pellas and me the courage to give two more concerts in an old theater which had once served as the opera house.

After the first concert, Carlos Guinle invited me for dinner. I said yes, for the time being, ready to cancel my acceptance if Carla showed the slightest sign of dissatisfaction at my going alone. But she laughed it off. "Je suis ravie de pouvoir me reposer et lire un peu. I do not like to be invited by complete strangers."

I accepted two or three invitations without her, saying, not without hypocrisy, "I want to give you a chance to be rid of me for an evening." At my concerts, Pellas always reserved her a seat in the director's box. In compensation, I made many excursions with her, and took her to cabarets where I had first heard the splendid Brazilian music with Villa-Lobos.

In São Paulo, where I played twice, she had a better time. At the first recital some Roman friends of hers turned up and we had a pleasant supper together. Professor Schiafarelli invited us for dinner and the entire family praised her beauty and charm. We returned to Rio for the two additional concerts and we sailed for Buenos Aires right after.

The "exclusive" society of the capital of Argentina gave me slight shivers when I thought of the grillroom at the Plaza and the sordid curiosity of everybody there. I feared our stay might make us feel miserable, so, before disembarking, I made a quick decision to ask Ruiz to reserve an apartment consisting of a sitting room and two bedrooms at the Palace Hotel, which was in a less fashionable part of the city. The clients of this hotel were mostly traveling businessmen who never stayed longer than a day or two, unlike the aristocratic Plaza, where most guests were residents.

My first four concerts were at the Odeon on subscription. As a novelty, I brought the *Fantasía Bética* of de Falla, which suffered the same fate as in Paris. My public was too used to the dynamic impact of the *Fire Dance* and missed it in this longish work. But I was pleased to notice that my performances of Chopin were liked more and more. More often than not, the gallery screamed for Chopin instead of *Navarra*. Carla came to the concerts, sat deep inside the director's box, visible only to me, and read a book during my performances. I couldn't blame her, as she had already heard most of my programs in Brazil.

Our life in this great city was uncomfortable and complicated. In Rio, I had at least been able to show her the beauty of the city. Our hotel had been elegant and rather empty and, all in all, Rio did not pay much attention to her presence. Not so in Buenos Aires. Here, right at our arrival, her presence became known and the gossipmongers and reporters went to work. At a cinema, at a restaurant, or in a shop on Florida Street, we would be noticed and commented on. And it goes without saying that I had to appear alone at the table of Señora Susana and the Martínez de Hozes, where I did not particularly enjoy the ironic compliments on my "spectacular conquest." "Que don Juan Tenorio, nuestro Arturito!" Señora Susana would exclaim. The Martínez de Hozes showed even a little snobbism; they knew very well what she represented in Europe. One morning, Carla showed me a letter which she had found under the door, in which an anonymous admirer offered to liberate her from her boring pianist and promised her a really good time. We were certainly not happy there. In consequence we started quarreling about unimportant matters, such as a movie or something I liked to eat and she didn't. These divergences brought out my malicious tongue, and we ended up with Carla leaving the room, not to be seen again until the following morning. Fortunately I had to give concerts in a few provincial towns, Rosario and Córdoba, and a few concerts in Montevideo. I went by myself and left her alone in the hotel, probably bored and maybe brooding.

I finished my season by giving two concerts with orchestra at the Teatro San Martín. Both were imposed upon me by Ernesto Drangosh, the ex-pupil of Barth, who insisted on appearing with me in public. On this occasion I discovered how jealous he had been of my concerts with Risler. I was glad to finish this tour as soon as possible. This time I found an Italian boat bound for Genoa; Carla, to my astonishment, told me that she would have preferred a French boat. On this journey she became difficult, sometimes staying the whole day in her cabin or sitting on a deck chair and reading for hours, often leaving me to have my meals by myself on the pretext that she was not feeling well.

We reached Genoa on a very hot day and had to stay there a night, as her train to Rome and mine to Paris did not leave till the following morning. During that night at the Hotel Colombo, Carla asked me quite unexpectedly, "If I got a divorce, would you marry me?" I remember well my embarrassment in the face of such a question. "Certainly not," I answered, trying to make it sound casual. "You cannot mean it seriously. It is impossible for me to imagine the famous beauty Carla Palladini under the name of Mrs. Arthur Rubinstein, the wife of the not too famous pianist. Besides, I could not love you without being able to have you live in a palazzo as you have done all your life. I could not provide you every year with the wardrobe to which you are accustomed." I said all this in a light tone. Carla took my answer badly; I saw by the expression on her face that she was hurt by my refusal to marry her. The next morning we went our separate ways.

I was determined not to marry. My long experience with women proved to me that a lover has the advantage; he shows himself to the object of his love in the best light and only at moments chosen by himself. He need stay with her neither too long nor too little; his courtship can remain fresh, he sends her flowers at the right time. He succeeds by being discreet, and, whenever the right moment comes, passionate.

Now look at the fate of a husband. He is always around even if she wants to see less of him. Or else he is never home when she needs him most. Perhaps he snores at night, or looks tired and disheveled in the morning, or has bad bathroom manners. He has to share with her her worries, make her share his own; they have to discuss money matters, the cost of living, children, servants, etc. I see love life and married life in this way.

52

During these August days in the summer of 1924, the heat in
Paris became unbearable, so I was more than delighted to find a short note
from the Princess Polignac inviting me again to Venice. The princess received me as if I were a steady resident of the palazzo, and had the delicate
thought of putting an upright piano in my room, which was, this time, at the
end of a long corridor. "You can work night and day if you like. Nobody
can hear you in the palazzo."

The first two weeks I took great advantage of this privilege. The date
of my three concerts in Warsaw, after an absence of eleven years, was
approaching. At the first concert I had promised to play the Chopin E
minor and the Tchaikovsky concerti with Gregor Fitelberg conducting.
The two others were recitals where I was going to use my well-tried war
horses, enjoying in advance the surprise they would bring to the fickle,
malicious, but well-beloved public of the capital of the newborn free Poland. I refreshed my repertoire for this occasion by a new look at the music,
but now, as before, there were neglected details which required long hours
of practice. Since the old days in Zakopane in 1904, I had changed my
habits very little when I learned new pieces. By reading a few times a work
which I wanted to include in my repertoire, I was able to grasp clearly, in
my own way, the intentions of the composer. (I often use the expression "It
must speak to me.") I see it as a whole work, not giving too much importance to fragmentary passages which can often break the sweep of the
whole. At the same time, my memory would absorb the piece unfailingly.
There are three kinds of memory: visual, aural, and memory of the fingers.
Mine was visual and performed best while playing, when I would actually
see the printed music and turn the pages in my mind. I was always greatly
helped, of course, by my knowledge of the form of the work. All this enabled me to present the new piece to the satisfaction of any general public.
But critics and musicians who knew every bar of what I was playing could
easily discover the imperfections in certain technically difficult spots, which
I never took the time to practice note by note. This dreadful negligence
remained with me until the years when the recording industry required all

the notes to be played properly and faithful to the text. At the same time, it taught audiences to expect from live performances the same faultless execution.

I was the only guest at the palazzo. The morning after my arrival, the butler who brought the breakfast to my room announced that La Signora Principessa was lunching out and asked if I desired to take my own in the palazzo. I was rather pleased to be free to sample some Venetian tidbits in a nice *taberna* such as La Fenice or Martini's. Just before lunch I met all my friends of the year before at the Piazza and watched the arrival of seven giants, all well over six feet tall, very elegant and very aristocratic. When they approached our tables, they obscured the sky. The princess introduced me to them; these giants were the Count and Countess Robillant, their four sons and a daughter, descendants of the powerful Venetian family Mocenigo, who provided Venice with seven Doges. To meet this family was both an honor and a pleasure; their daughter Olga, who married the Portuguese Marques de Cadaval, remains a close friend to this day. At Martini's I had some delightful *scampi alla grilla* and my favorite dish, spaghetti. After a long stroll, a visit to Carpaccio, and a cup or two of the strong Italian coffee near the Rialto, I returned to the palazzo. Princess Winnie was waiting for me in the lovely balcony turned into a loggia which was attached to the side of the palace overlooking a garden belonging to the neighboring palazzo. With her lower lip in its customary crooked position when she spoke, she said in her strongly disguised but still faint American accent (apparent both in French and Italian) "I hate formal dinners. As we are alone, I ordered a light snack and coffee with some pastry." The snack consisted of cold ham, salad, and some ice cream. She was pleased to find out that I didn't care for wine. "I never drink alcohol myself," she said, "and I think that painters and pianists should beware of it."

After dinner, in possession of the key to the back door, I strolled back to the Piazza, sat at Florian's to hear the municipal band, set up in its center (it was Sunday), play some overtures and potpourris of favorite operas. The next morning the butler asked me again if I would like to have my lunch alone at the palazzo because the princess was lunching out, but a friend at the Piazza took me instead to a yet unknown trattoria near the Freccaria, the Colombo. There we ate a delicious fresh *aragosta* with the right kind of mayonnaise. When two more days passed with the princess always lunching out, I became a little alarmed. As far as I knew, she had introduced me to all her friends at the meetings at the Piazza, as well as foreign visitors. Why then, I thought, does no one care to invite me, knowing that I am her guest? Unbeknownst to her, I began to spy on her at lunchtime and found out that she took her meals alone at a miserable trattoria on the way to the Rialto. After discovering her secret, the next day I invited her to lunch with me at the new restaurant, the Colombo. She accepted my invitation with pleasure. Henceforth, I became her proud host at lunch and made her enjoy, as much as I did, the various rather expensive *crustacés*.

One day, after working longer than usual on the difficult Fourth Scherzo of Chopin, I arrived at the Piazza shortly before one and saw Carla sitting with a group of friends on the terrace of Florian's. She answered my surprised greeting in her quiet singing way: "I stay at the Danieli." She went on to lunch with some relations of hers but agreed to have tea with us. On our way to the trattoria, Princess Winnie said, "Elle est belle mais un peu loufoque" (she is beautiful but a little off). When I brought Carla down to the *motoscafo* that was waiting for her she said, "Come to the Danieli at eleven tonight, straight to my room," and gave me the number. I accepted with misgivings about the management of the Danieli, but was brave enough to risk it. As usual, I found her indifferent to my apprehensions, saying with perfect calm, "If somebody comes, I shall send him away." I did not see her the next day until late in the afternoon. "J'adore le Lido," she said. "Venice is too humid and has too many mosquitoes," and she introduced me to two charming young men who were her companions for the day—one the Duke of Verdura, a Sicilian known as Fulco, the other one Count Branca of the Fernet Branca firm. This trio spent every day at the sea resort, except when there was a tea party at the palazzo. I cannot say that I was jealous, but still I must admit that I felt a certain vexation at her capricious ways with me. Unaware of it, Carla asked me how long I was going to stay in Venice. "About two weeks more," I answered. "I have to be back in Paris before I leave for Warsaw."

"Well, let us go next week to Gardone. You will like Lake Garda and we can go by car from Mestre." Taking my acceptance for granted, she joined the others at tea. Before leaving, I proposed to Princess Winnie that she invite all her friends for a little concert I would play for them. "This is a small token of my gratitude for offering me this divine city in your wonderful way." Her lower lip went down even further. "My palazzo is your home forever." She gathered about fifty persons, all my good friends by now, and I played nothing but pieces I knew they would like to hear.

Two or three days before leaving for Gardone, I met Carla at the Piazza on her way back from the Lido. "Let me come up to your hotel room tonight," I proposed.

"No, it is too uncomfortable, but if you want me you can take me late at night to your room," she said placidly.

"This could be not only uncomfortable but dangerous too. I feel sure that the princess would not appreciate this intrusion on her hospitality."

"We can do it very quietly," Carla said with a conviction that I didn't share. However, my dislike of appearing a coward in her eyes made me give in. At about one o'clock at night she joined me at the Piazza and we walked quietly up to the back door of the palazzo. I opened the door with my key, but fearing that the noise of her high-heeled shoes might be heard by the servants, I carried her upstairs, where she took her shoes off, and we walked into my room like burglars. Even in bed, I had to shut her mouth several times when I saw she was about to treat me to her sonorous singing voice. With the best will in the world, I couldn't call it a night of love. I gave out a long sigh when I saw her safely to the door of her hotel.

We left for Mestre separately and then continued together in a comfortable car to Gardone. We reached a pleasant hotel in the afternoon and took two adjoining rooms overlooking the lovely peaceful and slightly sad Lake Garda. Gabriele D'Annunzio, the hero of Fiume, lived in a sumptuous villa on the lake but remained out of sight. That night was spent quietly; we both needed a rest.

The next morning after a rich breakfast of coffee, prosciutto, and orange marmalade, we hired a *motoscafo* and made a tour of the lake. There at one point I was struck by a strange vision: a famous picture by the Swiss painter Arnold Böcklin which bore the title "Die Todesinsel," the Isle of Death, a reproduction of which I had seen in practically every other house in Warsaw and Berlin, was suddenly here, alive before my eyes. The painter couldn't have created it anywhere else. I must confess that I was never an admirer of this painter, but his picture affected me very much. It did convey the feeling of a deserted island which could hold nothing but death. Rachmaninoff composed a beautiful symphonic poem inspired by this picture and gave it the same title. My own nervous system must have had a premonition when I felt the lake to be sad.

My story made a great impression on Carla. The thought of death was constantly present in our minds and often in our conversation. Our gay escapade lost its charm and purpose; we spent these few days taking our meals in gloomy silence and our conversations were about anything but love. Without declaring it, we were both glad to return to our homes, she to Rome and I to Paris.

53

I began to work hard on my programs for Warsaw, but at the Majestic dozens of invitations awaited me. Germaine de Rothschild wanted to have me for lunch, writing: "Edouard [her husband] loves to hear your stories and appreciates your culinary taste." Unfortunately, Edouard had his lunches at twelve-thirty—the bank required his early return; but for me it was much too early, as I never had my breakfast before eleven.

The Melchior de Polignacs often had me for dinner. One of them was given in honor of Josef Hofmann and his first wife, who was closely related to Nina de Polignac. Melchior gathered for this occasion a few of the young "Six"—Honegger, Poulenc, and Germaine Tailleferre—as well as a few families of the *grand monde*. Hofmann tried belatedly to conquer the capitals of Europe, which he had neglected for many years, playing exclusively in the United States. His name was known, but nobody had actually heard him play. No wonder that after the great dinner he was besieged by the young musicians and by some lovely young girls with requests to play something. He hated to do it but finally succumbed to their indiscreet insistence. He chose "In der Nacht" from the *Fantasiestücke* of Schumann —the worst choice he could have made. This difficult piece taken out of the context of the work sounds rather weird and after the many drinks he had had his playing sounded even more strange. Many wrong notes and a short gap in his memory made his performance a ghastly experience. His listeners looked at each other, bewildered by this sample of the "great Hofmann." The whole thing saddened me terribly. Out in the street, I gave a piece of my mind to the young musicians. "I can assure you that, at his best, he is *still* the great Hofmann and the only thing I can reproach him for is to have yielded to your unhealthy curiosity." Nevertheless, the impression he left that night hurt him considerably when he made his Parisian debut playing the *Emperor* Concerto of Beethoven at the Champs-Elysées for the veterans of the war. The audience behaved as if they were bored and condescended to allow him one bow. Backstage, where I went to greet him, he introduced me to the Maréchal Pétain, who was still the war hero and who had come to thank Hofmann as president of the Veterans' Association.

After a few amusing evenings with Eugenia Errazuriz, Jean Cocteau, Cendrars, and the Achards, the time came to leave for Warsaw. Before the train stopped in the new capital of the great and proud country, my heart began to beat rapidly. All the memories of my early years came back to my mind. I was apprehensive about learning what the war had done to my friends but, at the same time, terribly excited to see my beloved Warsaw free from the Russian scourge.

When I arrived, the Moszkowski brothers, Richard Ordynski, and Alexander Szymanowski of the old days took me to the Hotel Europejski, which had fresh paint and new furniture in the rooms. The lovely restaurant had been left intact, though, to my great pleasure. It was good to feel that I could order my favorite dishes without waiting to be invited, and to pay with my own money.

I was anxious to hear everything about Pola in detail. It seemed that her parents lived now in a palatial house of the Poznanskis on the Aléja Ujazdowska. At the beginning of the war, Pola had made up with her family and lived with her daughters in her parents' house. Frederic, as usual, had a separate apartment where he gave piano lessons and was composing an opera. It made me happy to know that Pola had her daughters with her again after the great heartbreak of their separation, which I had caused. But it was terribly sad to think that we could never see each other again, as this was the condition on which her family took her back.

Warsaw looked gorgeous to me. The old Royal Palace was now inhabited by a Polish President; the Belvedere Palace was now the seat of Pilsudski and no Russian words were to be seen anywhere. The officers walked with a swagger in their dashing uniforms and the women looked more beautiful than ever.

In the afternoon I saw Karol, who was in a better mood than the last time I had seen him. The University Jagellon, of Cracow, had bestowed upon him the title of Doctor Honoris Causa, the highest honor the country could confer. There was also good news for me. He was working on a symphonic piece for piano and orchestra. It was not to be a concerto proper but a symphonie-concertante. He promised to bring it to Paris when it was ready.

On the morning of the concert, I had the one rehearsal. The Tchaikovski went quite smoothly; Fitelberg used the right tempi, watched me carefully, and even had good words to say for my playing of the cadenzas. In the Chopin, however, he became negligent and treated the tuttis carelessly and indifferently. When I complained to him about it he answered drily, "There isn't anything there for the orchestra. Chopin could write only for the piano." One of our old quarrels ensued.

"It's *you* who are a poor musician, only good for the loud pieces of Richard Strauss, and you love best the vulgar bits in them!" I cried.

The victim of our quarrel was Chopin. However, at the concert, the orchestra itself played the tuttis with more care, knowing the work so well. The hall of the Filharmonja was sold out, and all my old friends who had survived the war were there as well as the critics. The rest of the public came to hear "the great favorite of Spain and South America, the man who earned millions in the United States, the toast of Paris and London," etc. etc. I knew my Varsovians well; they remained the snobs they were during the Russian times. They admired me for taking so long to play in my own country; as long as I can remember, whenever I had to leave for Vienna or London, I would notice their satisfied smiles—"He has better things to do than stay in Warsaw"—and it always irritated me. Well, with all my modesty, I must report that this evening was a great triumph for me. The two recitals were sold out right away. My telephone at the hotel rang the whole day with requests for tickets, which I had no way of satisfying. My recitals gave me the chance to surprise them with my Spanish repertoire, completely unknown to them. *Navarra* and the *Fire Dance* were again the winners and I couldn't get away without playing them at every concert. I received $500 in American currency for each concert, a great fee in those times. The critics published most flattering accounts, save one—a Mr. Piotr Rytel, professor of harmony at the Conservatory, who not only disliked my playing but denied me any talent at all.

The new manager of the concert hall in Lodz, whose name was Karol Rubinstein (no relation), offered me the same sum for my recital in the town of my birth. This time my concert was not a family affair. The real public of Lodz, the one seen only on great occasions, filled my hall. There were hundreds of distinguished-looking men and women I had never seen before. My large possessive family had always made me feel that there was no one worth knowing in that great city. As a matter of fact, I had never been in the house or apartment of anyone who was not a member of my family.

Mr. Karol Rubinstein immediately announced a second concert, which was even more successful because the stage was filled with more than a hundred people sitting closely around me. My two aunts and my brother Staś, who now lived in my parents' apartment, gave after both concerts the same kind of parties that we had when my parents were alive. It was exactly like the good old times but I could not enjoy it, feeling an unbearable regret for not having my parents there to witness the success of their prodigal son.

I left Lodz to spend another few days in Warsaw. Now, happy to have found an honorable place for myself in the country of my birth, I spent a whole day doing something I had been looking forward to for a long time. With my pockets full of well-earned American dollars, thanks to my concerts, I undertook a grand tour to pay the debts from prewar times I owed to creditors who had had faith in my future. One can well imagine the pleasure with which I paid good old Styczynski of the Victoria Hotel. His happy surprise at this unexpected windfall was so great that I thought he was going to give me the whole hotel as a present. My tailor had changed hands but the new owner had the bill ready and took the money with the offer to make me some clothes at a discount. I thanked him, saying that I was now in the hands of a London tailor.

The creditor I was most anxious to repay was Dr. Goldflam, who had vouched for me at a credit bank for a loan of 500 rubles. The other guarantor of this loan, Mr. Leon Bernstein, the father of Sophie Meyer, had died during the war. The dear doctor received me, as if the years had not passed, with words of high praise for my concerts. He showed me his new acquisitions in bronze and never mentioned the purpose of my visit. When I finally reminded him of my debt, with my apologies for having let him down because of the war, he accepted the full amount. The death of Mr. Bernstein had obliged him to pay the entire 500 rubles himself; this information I received from Antek Moszkowski. He handed me the bank's receipt, looking as though he were the debtor and I the creditor.

Joseph Jaroszynski dined with me at my hotel. I was a little afraid of this meeting, of having to listen to his powerful voice shouting bitter complaints about the loss of his estates and his fortune, but I was wrong. After our warm embrace we sat down and he used his loud voice to discuss with the same enthusiasm of old, the Spanish pieces I had played at my concerts. When I said a few words of regret about his misfortune, he replied, "There are many of us who lost all our possessions in Russia. But we are compensated now by being proud citizens of our own free country." This brought tears to my eyes.

After dinner, in my room, I gave him all the dollars I could as a small token for what he had done for me. He took it as if it were a gift and assured me that he lived very happily and that he had married. "She is lovely and a very talented painter, we are very happy." Before I left, he brought me a present, a rather large object wrapped in two or three newspapers. "Here is a wonderful present for you!" he shouted happily. "It is a stone from the road to Zelazowa-Wola!" (Chopin's birthplace). I took it gratefully but almost fell to the floor with the weight of it and decided secretly to leave it at the hotel in a safe place.

One morning the telephone rang. The lovely voice of a woman asked me, "Do you remember a young girl by the name of Mania Szer?" Of course I remembered: she was my first love when I was nine. "Yes, I do," I answered. "What happened to her?"

She answered in a subdued way, "I am Mania Szer, and I have been married for many years. I am staying at this hotel for two days. If you have a free moment, I would love to see you again after all these long, long years."

I was thrilled. Everything came back to my mind all at once. She accepted my invitation for lunch and agreed to meet me in the lobby.

There it took me some time to recognize her. She had grown rather tall and wore a long winter coat and a hat with a veil covering her face. However, when she lifted the veil, I saw the same Mania Szer, the one from a Persian miniature, with the same lovely nose and mouth and the beautiful dark eyes.

She followed me in silence to a small restaurant, where we were practically alone. There she told me quietly of her sad lost youth with an unloving and unloved husband. She finished by saying, "I lived only for my daughter, who died two years ago, killed in an avalanche in the Tatras. Now I have nothing to live for." There were no tears, only a mask of deep despair. I kept quiet for a long while, then I said, "Do you know that you were my first love? Do you remember Inowlodz?" And I began to tell her the whole story, how I rode a horse to impress her, how terribly jealous I was of a red-haired boy with whom she danced constantly, which enraged me. "Do you remember when you tried to kiss me after I played something for you and how violently I rejected it because I wanted you to love me and not to pet me as the talented little boy."

She was blushing with excitement and her eyes were shining. "Do you know," I continued, "that I watched your window for hours from my aunt's apartment, which faced your house, even if only to catch your silhouette or a glimpse of your hand moving the curtain? I left for Berlin heartbroken at the thought that I would never see you again."

She listened to all this with her head bowed, wiping her eyes. After a short silence, she said in a very low voice, "I knew all that. Girls always know when they are loved. The red-haired boy you were so jealous of was a stupid boy but he danced well. And back in Warsaw I felt your love constantly around me."

We had both reached a high state of emotion. I took her hand, kissed it several times, paid the bill, and we left the place hand in hand. We drove to the hotel, and I took her to my room, where we fell into each other's arms, both feeling that we were accomplishing something long overdue.

We parted with a warm embrace. She was returning to Lodz the next morning and I had an appointment with Karol that evening. I went to a flower shop to send her roses with a few words of deep emotion and upon my return that night I found some flowers from her with the single word "Dziekuje," in English, "Thank you."

Karol took me to a new café, which was also a sort of a tearoom, called Ziemianska. On the way, he informed me, "You will meet a few brilliant young writers and poets. You will not easily find their like in the world." And he was right. A large table in a corner of the place was already occupied by his friends. When we approached, he introduced me to them; and I shall name them all because each one of them belongs to the elite of contemporary Polish literature: Jan Lechon, Antoni Slonimski, Jaroslaw Iwaszkiewicz, Casimir Wierzynski, and last but not least, Juljan Tuwim. We were soon joined by another remarkable writer, Boy-Zelenski, the son of the composer Ladislas. He wrote poems in the style of nursery rhymes fustigating the new bourgeoisie, pedantic academicians, snobs, and women of light morals and little brains. He was widely read and some of his clever verses became maxims that are still in popular use. Also, this remarkable man found the time to translate brilliantly all of Molière, Balzac, and many other French masterworks. The last to arrive was my old friend Franc Fiszer. The minute he sat down his stentorian voice dominated everyone else and his witty and original sallies provoked volcanic eruptions of laughter. If Fiszer had published half of his funny, yet philosophical remarks, he could have been one of the most widely read writers. But he disdained putting a single word in writing, declaring proudly, "I would never lower myself to besmear with ink a beautiful sheet of white paper."

Thanks to Szymanowski's introduction, this unique company treated me right away as if I were one of them. Tuwim told me, "We are in some way related. My mother and your sister Jadwiga were inseparable friends as young girls and when I was four or five years old my mother used to take me to the station to watch your family seeing you off on your way back to Berlin. Mama used to say to me, 'You see this Artur, he's already a famous pianist and what will become of you?' I hated you until I heard you play, but now you are my pianist." We embraced to celebrate our friendship and drank immediately to our brotherhood, addressing each other by the informal "thou."

Juljan and Jaroslaw were the only ones who loved and understood music. The others had not much use for it but this never kept us from remaining in close contact from then on.

Count Alexander Skrzynski had become the Minister of Foreign Affairs, so I went to the State Department to present my respects to him and was received most cordially by this true nobleman. He said, "I am glad to see that both of us have made good progress since we last met in Rome!" Before I left I received a precious present from him—a Polish passport with a diplomatic visa. "This will facilitate your travels," he said.

Karol told me all about the new developments in the musical life in Warsaw. "Emil Mlynarski is now the sole director of the Opera and has succeeded in raising it to the highest European standard. He produced my *Hagith* with fine singers, but the critics, my archenemies, called it maliciously a German opera in the style of Richard Strauss, but this didn't deter Mlynarski and he has promised to put on the new opera I'm working at, *King Roger*. You will be amused to learn that the Conservatory has asked me to take Mlynarski's place as its director. I'm terrified at the very thought. You know how little suited I am for this bureaucratic position, but I am afraid I shall be forced to accept it because of my desperate need for a steady income. You see, Arthur, I now have to provide for my whole family. My brother Felix tries to find work as an accompanist—you know he plays the piano quite well—but with little success. My poor mother is an invalid who needs a nurse to look after her. My sisters Nula and Zioka are still unmarried and live at home. Stasia, the singer, is divorced. She often performs at the opera and gives concerts, but her fees are scarcely sufficient for her needs. So this is my present situation." Until his premature death at the age of fifty-four, my poor Karol was the victim of his family; his love for them was very similar to Chopin's love for his family.

Richard Ordynski was now a director of films. He showed me his lovely apartment facing St. John's Cathedral in the old part of the city. "Next year when you come back you must stay with me," he said, and he insisted so much that I had to accept.

I saw little of my sister Hela. She was present with her family at both concerts in a box I reserved for them and had coffee with me in the tearoom at Lourse.

I promised the Filharmonja to come back the next year for two recitals and accepted Karol Rubinstein's offer for a concert in Lodz. The Cracow manager, Teofil Trzcinski, proposed a whole tour for his city and Lwow, as well as six or seven smaller cities in the old Austrian part of Poland.

On my way to Paris, I stopped in Berlin for half a day to select a Bechstein concert grand for the palazzo in Venice at the request of the Princess Polignac. Since its bankruptcy after the war, the house of Bechstein had been taken over by the banks to which it was indebted. The new owners kept the factory as busy as before, helped by the great name of Bechstein, but the quality of the instrument was not the same as in the old

*A Monsieur Claudel son lecteur profondément ému et reconnaissant
Rio 1918   Arthur Rubinstein*

Photograph of
Rubinstein taken
by Paul Claudel, 1918

With Pastora Imperio and
Manuel de Falla, 1917

With Paul Kochanski in Venice, 1932

With Karol Szymanowski (right) and
Paul Kochanski en route from America, 1922

A portrait of Winnie the
Princess de Polignac, by
Jacques-Emile Blanche, 1941

Pastora Imperio

Stravinsky and Winnie on the balcony of the Palazzo Polignac, about 1925

Party in Warsaw: Rubinstein linking arms with wives of music professors; Karol Szymanowski (2nd from right, 2nd row) Bronislaw Hubermann (3rd from right, 2nd row); Gregor Fitelberg (extreme right, front row)

Nela in 1928

Mr. and Mrs. Arthur Rubinstein,
just married, 1932

A picture of Rubinstein
in Buenos Aires

With Nela at Zakopane, 1932

A mi querido amigo Manuel de Falla su admirador entusiasta de siempre —

Artur Rubistein con Eva y Pablo.

Cordoba 20.8.40

Accompanying
Eva dancing

A painting of the house
in Paris at Square
Avenue Foch by Felicya
Kranz.

...mily outing with (left to right) Johnny, Eva,

The drawings
Picasso did
of Rubinstein
in 1958

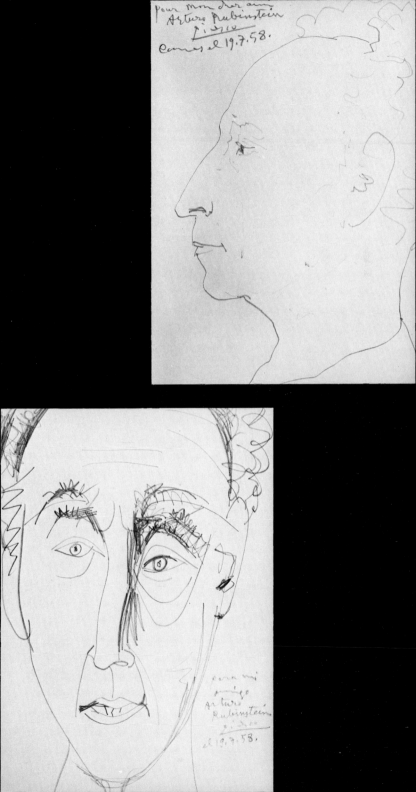

Rehearsing with the Jerusalem Symphony Orchestra, conducted
by Alexander Schneider, Independence Day, May 1975

Playing at Symphony Hall, Boston, 1959

Recording in the RCA studio with Eugene Ormandy

Rubinstein at 90

Rubinstein at 92

days when each piano was carefully examined and tested before its sale. I was lucky enough to find a concert grand of good quality with easy action. I had it sent to Venice right away.

54

At the Majestic I found many letters, most of them from managers in countries where I had never played before. There was one from Zagreb, now part of Yugoslavia, in which I was offered five concerts in the larger cities of this interesting country. Rome had a new concert manager, an energetic lady from Trieste, Clara Camus. Thanks to her, I now had the opportunity to visit a few fascinating old cities of which I had always dreamed. The Augusteo in Rome and the Santa Cecilia concerts remained in the hands of Count San Martino. Belgium too opened its doors wide for me: Brussels, Liège, Antwerp, and Ghent wanted to hear me. Turkey, Greece, and Egypt now became places which I visited as if they were old friends.

One morning, to my happy surprise, I had a call from Pola. She had just arrived in Paris, with her two daughters, she told me, and would I care to see her again after all this time? I invited her right away for lunch. We were happy to see each other. I kissed both her hands several times. All through luncheon we exchanged a flood of news of the years since we were last together. She gave me all the details of her family: "My husband died last winter, and when the war began, my reconciliation with my parents took place and I could live with my children again, thank God." Then she smiled. "They are, of course, grownup ladies now. I am afraid to have you meet them. My mother has been telling them since their childhood that you are Satan incarnate and made them swear that they would never lay eyes on you." We both laughed. "As a matter of fact, they are coming to fetch me here!" Pola had not changed much; she was a little heavier but kept the pure features of her charming face with its small nose and kind, sweet eyes. When I took her down to the street, two young girls were walking up and down on the opposite side. When they saw us, they made as if to run away, but suddenly thought better of it, crossed the street, and were duly introduced to me. I knew, of course, that that would happen; young girls couldn't possibly resist meeting Beelzebub, Lucifer, or Satan. The two girls showed a sympathetic indulgence toward the man who had deprived them of their mother for a few important years of their lives.

I saw Pola again a few times before she returned to Warsaw.

My first visit to the new Yugoslavia was interesting from every point of view. Although Serbia and Croatia were now united under the euphonic-sounding new name, they were still two distinctly individual countries. In Zagreb, the capital of the former, I felt an atmosphere akin to Poland. There was, of course, the link of Catholicism, but even without that, the city could easily have been situated in some Polish province.

My manager was a Croatian Jew, an elderly man whose burning patriotism embraced both Croatia and the country that had dominated it, Hungary. He had a young wife, very tall, rather heavyset, and very beautiful. All through the tour he never left my side but he rarely brought his wife with him, which I much regretted, as he also talked me to death in four or five languages. I listened to his talk about the war, of which he spoke with a vast knowledge of the political situation. I agreed with him on most things, with one exception: I felt that Croatian audiences were even more reserved than Polish audiences, whereas he called my concerts "the triumph of the century" and re-engaged me on better terms. In Belgrade, the Serbian capital, I found much more receptive audiences, Russian style: easily enthusiastic but rather fickle. I also played in provincial towns of both countries where concerts were still a novelty. Nothing was lost on me. I could read and understand both languages, as Croatian has much in common with Polish and Serbian sounds and reads like Russian.

My next concerts were at the Società del Quartetto in Milan and in the small hall of the Benedetto Marcello Conservatory in Venice. This was my first appearance in Venice and my audience was practically the same one that the Princess Edmond had gathered for me at the palazzo. A few professors and a flock of students made up the rest of it, so it was very much like a family affair. My playing was received accordingly and I felt that my real debut in Venice was yet to come. I left by the Orient Express for Istanbul; Mr. Arditi had prepared new appearances there and in Athens. My friends the Pekmezians took charge of me for lunch and dinner in their house with their cats and all, but they also gave me the chance to practice the new pieces I had prepared for these concerts: some Szymanowski, Villa-Lobos, and some dances from *The Three-Cornered Hat* of de Falla, which I had arranged for the piano. One day, Sappho Pekmezian took me for a boat ride on the Golden Horn and showed me the wonders of both shores.

Arditi proposed another visit to Tel Aviv for a concert. "They have a hall now," he said. "It only holds a thousand people, but they will be happy to hear and see you again." I agreed, in spite of my fear of being late for the Christmas and New Year festivities in Paris to which I was invited and to which I looked forward with joy.

Tel Aviv had grown since my previous visit. It had begun to look really like a small town, with new construction everywhere, while Jaffa already looked like the Arab quarter of Tel Aviv. The hall was not very attractive to look at but it had good acoustics. It was sold out before I arrived. It was a good concert; my love for my people made me play my heart out to them. During intermission I heard a clash between the police and a crowd of young people who had tried to force their way into the hall. The local musicians and two or three professors exiled from Russia gave me a small supper, toasting me in turn with every sip of vodka. As I was frightfully shy about speaking in public, I hated to be toasted because it was such an effort to stutter out a simple thank-you. This shyness of mine was a strange contrast to my irresistible passion for talking and telling stories and jokes in good company; but the minute I was expected to make a speech, my tongue became paralyzed.

I left for Greece the next day. There, in Athens, Marika told me the sad news of the death of her fiancé. "He was happy in Davos with its pure air, and the kindness of the doctors and nurses give the poor patients hope that they will recover their health." Her voice faltered. "He died suddenly after a heavy loss of blood. Such a great talent and wonderful person dying unjustly before his time." I stayed in Athens just for the concert, which I gave under the spell of the sad news.

Suddenly I received a telegram from Clara Camus imploring me to play in Palermo on December 30. "They offer you another concert in Messina on the 28th to make it worthwhile. They pay a good fee. Please, please accept."

I had a hard time making a decision. A *réveillon* in Paris was terribly attractive. The French treated it rather more like a Mardi Gras than a religious festivity. Maxim's was the ideal place, with a gorgeous supper of foie gras, turkey, and fresh truffles and plenty of champagne, followed by dancing in the darkened room until the early hours of the morning. The tango was still the dance à la mode and you could clutch your partner with all the passion you had in you. Yes, it was hard to give it up. But with all my lust for life, I have always maintained a deep respect for my profession and never allowed myself to miss a concert except for circumstances beyond my control. And so, with a heavy heart I took the train to Messina.

The journey was not as simple as it sounds. At some station in Calabria they put the train on a ship which goes across the channel to Messina and I arrived at seven in the morning on December 28. A charming young man greeted me: "I'm the representative of your Palermo manager, who asked me to be entirely at your service."

A taxi took us to a hotel, where we settled down to a hearty breakfast. After I had finished my cigar, I said, "I'd like to see the hall and the piano." He suddenly became serious. "We have a great problem. There is no concert grand available, but there is a French lady who lives near Messina and is the owner of an Erard concert grand. She is very proud of her instrument and doesn't like to lend it for concerts, but I feel sure that if you ask her personally as a favor, she will not refuse." The idea did not appeal to me very much, but as I mentioned before, I was professional and understood that there was no other way.

A taxi took us to her house in less than a quarter of an hour. She was expecting us, and after a stiff, half-smiling handshake, led us to the room with the piano, which was covered with a heavy velvet cloth. This French lady, over sixty, was very tall, extremely thin, and dressed all in black with a high stiff collar around her neck that gave her a haughty expression. "I know what you want," she said in a husky deep voice, "but I can allow the piano out of my house only on condition that you send at least three professional men to transport it and set it up on the concert platform. I've had bad experiences before, and am willing to give in this time only because some friends from Paris wrote me some nice things about Mr. Rubinstein." After my companion's solemn promise and my effusive thanks, we left this forbidding person, but not before she made me sign her guest book and the program.

On the way to the hotel, I complained to my young man of the impossibility of visiting Taormina and seeing the beautiful Etna, about which my friend Szymanowski had raved so much. Hearing this, my companion suddenly became wild with excitement. "But I can make it possible for you!" he shouted. "It is quite easy. I can hire a small Ford, and if we leave at nine o'clock, we can reach Taormina by noon, see everything you want, lunch there at the famous San Domenico Hotel, and be back at least an hour before the concert, which is at six-thirty!" His enthusiasm was contagious; I clapped my hands with joy and said, "While you go for the car, I will lay out my concert clothes and wait for you downstairs."

He arrived in an old beaten-up Ford convertible with the top down. As I looked at it with a certain apprehension, our little driver smiled and said, "This car was driven sixty thousand kilometers without a hitch." Mildly reassured, I drove off with him. The road to Taormina had probably never been repaired since the disastrous earthquake, and it felt as if we were driving over a potato field. The monotony of the long ride was charmingly interrupted from time to time by some playful boys who amused themselves by throwing pebbles at us. One took aim at my neck and struck me a good blow. In spite of everything, we arrived shortly after twelve in the central square of Taormina. Now it began to rain and the sky turned black, but my companion, pointing at a particularly black cloud, said ecstatically, "There is Etna, when the sun comes out." As the sun did not come out, we ran to the nearby San Domenico, and found the big doors closed. When we rang the bell, a porter opened the gate and said coldly, "closed until April." We lunched in a smelly trattoria on overcooked spaghetti. However, I found a bargain there. A man was selling some beautiful amber beads and I bought a string for only a thousand lire which was cheap for genuine amber. Then we drove back. The driver put up the top but during the whole drive we were annoyed by the torn, flapping plastic windows. Back in Messina, before we reached the hotel, my young man left me, saying that he was going to the hall and that I should dress and wait for somebody to pick me up. I arrived well after five o'clock with barely time to shave, wash up, and dress for the concert. In the entrance hall sat two young ladies who jumped up from their seats when they saw me and tried to talk to me. I said politely in my best Italian, "Impossible. I must rush and get dressed." They insisted. "We must see you, even if only for a moment." I waved them away and went toward the elevator. They ran after me. "I must talk to you," said one of them. "It is most important!" I now began to get really angry. "Don't you understand? I have a concert in half an hour!" The lady began to cry. "That is just it," she said. "There is no concert. My husband, who accompanied you to Taormina, forgot to get the men to transport the piano and now the public is sitting there and there is no piano on the stage." I was stupefied. "Can't you get them now?"

"No. We've tried hard the whole afternoon, but they are unavailable!"

Now I understood why he left me on the way back to the hotel; he must have suddenly remembered. He never showed up again. To make this long story a little shorter, I took the train that same night and arrived the next morning in sunny, beautiful Palermo.

A middle-aged gentleman with very black eyes and hair met me at the station, and instead of shaking my hand he was wringing his own hands about the lost concert in Messina, shouting, "Che vergogna! Che disgrazia!" I knew well how to console him. "Don't blame him too much," I said. "The young man showed so much enthusiasm for this beautiful island and I like him for it. For that reason I have decided not to claim my fee for the lost concert." At these last words a broad smile illuminated his face. After thanking me for my *collaborazione* he said proudly, "I love my Sicily too

and I shall be honored if you allow me to show you the beauty of Palermo."
This time I said with a smile, "I would rather make sure that the piano is on
the stage and that my concert will take place tomorrow."

He took me to the Teatro Massimo, the largest opera house in Italy. I
found a good instrument on the stage; it was well tuned and produced a big
tone, but the enormous size of the theater frightened me. "Are there enough
music lovers in Palermo to fill this theater?" He answered, "Do not forget
that the greatest genius of music, Bellini, was born on this island." I acknowledged this declaration with an approving nod, being a bit afraid of the
Sicilian temperament.

After we left the theater, he took me on a long tour of the city. I
admired the Monreale monastery, the churches and palaces, somewhat half-
heartedly. I had seen more beautiful things in Italy itself. But I was enchanted with my hotel, the Villa Igiea, a most romantic place with a
beautiful garden leading straight to the sea and full of some great memories.
Wagner is supposed to have worked there on his *Tristan and Isolde* after
the unhappy ending of his romance with Mathilde Wesendonk. That night,
before retiring, I strolled through the gardens thinking, remembering, daydreaming, and humming the sad music of the English horn at the beginning
of the third act of *Tristan*.

The concert went well. The man was right; the audience almost filled
the huge place, but it was more mundane than musical. Fortunately that did
not affect me. The night in the garden had inspired me. I was still completely absorbed in its beauty as I made music. I left Palermo by boat for
Naples, where I undertook the long journey back to Paris.

55

Ever since I had abandoned the United States, my concert activities in Europe had been developing considerably and wherever I went I
pleased enough to be invited again, but I must confess with sorrow that I
was not very proud of myself. The dissipated life I was leading, my constant
preoccupation with the opposite sex, the late hours spent nightly with my
intellectual friends, the theaters, the shows, the rich food at lunch and
dinner, and, worst of all, my passionate attraction for all of this never

allowed me to concentrate on my work. I prepared my concerts using the large repertoire I had accumulated but without the urge to play better, without referring to the text, relying entirely on my fine memory and my cleverly acquired knowledge of how to use certain encores to arouse the audience to the right pitch of enthusiasm. To put it in a nutshell, I couldn't boast of one single piece which I played entirely faithful to the text and without some technical shortcomings. For the reader who might be dismayed by this confession, I feel compelled to add a few words in my favor. My genuine great talent for music and my very special gift for my instrument were always there intact. With all the terrible flaws I have just mentioned, I never played a piece without feeling a deep emotion and a deep love for it, and when (and this is a great gift from heaven) I am inspired, this emotion and love reaches the public. More often than not, perfection in every detail, obtained by many hours of hard work, leaves the audience cold because the very essence of the meaning of music is missing.

It was fun to see my friends again in Paris and a pleasure to see that they had missed me at Christmas. However, I had to leave for England for a short season of concerts which Mr. Mitchell, after a few dozen oysters, had arranged for me. There is no point in writing about them, as it was Bournemouth again, with a second-rate orchestra, and some neighboring seaside resorts. It goes without saying that I rushed back to London as quickly as I could.

One morning the telephone rang and a charming young lady I had met at various parties invited me to a dinner of a very particular sort. "I don't know if you remember me," she said. "My name is Audrey Coats." How could I forget her, one of the most beautiful women in London? "There will be only four of us. The Prince of Wales and my friend Mrs. Dudley Ward." And she gave me the details: the day, the address, and the hour of the dinner.

"I accept gratefully this very flattering invitation, especially coming from a lady I have admired for quite a long time. But I am rather anxious to know if the Prince of Wales is a great music lover." I heard her laugh.

"He is the most unmusical person in the world! But I told him things about you which made him want to meet you."

This dinner turned out to be an amazing surprise for me. I expected to be introduced to the most typical kind of Englishman, the heir to the throne, naturally allergic to foreigners and unmusical to boot. Instead I found a cosmopolitan young man with a great joie de vivre.

"Please don't ask me what I think of Wagner. I know nothing about music," the Prince said, but added with a smile at the ladies, "I know that you have other interests as well." From then on, things became easy. After the first sip of sherry, I fell into my bad old habit of telling stories and anecdotes, to which he was more receptive than any Englishman I had ever met. The two ladies joined in our merriment and at the end of the dinner the Prince invited the three of us to a variety show then in vogue. At the theater a large box was opened for him. His aide-de-camp, a nice young gentleman, was expecting us there. The show was good and from time to time the Prince laughed so uproariously that his aide whispered to him that people in the nearby boxes were complaining, which made him laugh even more. We ended up the night at the Embassy Club, where we danced in turn with each of our ladies. Although I am by no means a snob, I must admit that this evening gave me a great deal of satisfaction. But my surprise was great when on the morning after my concert in Brighton I received a telegram saying: "His Royal Highness the Prince of Wales invites you to dine tonight at eight at St. James's Palace"—signed by the aide-de-camp. Well, well! was all I thought. I took the earliest train possible to be there in time to change and arrive punctually at the Palace.

This dinner, for the same four of us, felt like the continuation of the first one, except that one was aware of sitting this time in the same room where many English kings had thrown their chicken bones over their shoulders. The Prince was a most gracious host, giving all his attention to filling glasses and whispering orders to the two butlers. Again I fell under the charming spell of our small company, and I hasten to mention how extremely pretty, witty, and intelligent our ladies were. This time, though, at the end of the dinner the two ladies left us alone for drinks and a cigar. During our tête-à-tête the Prince displayed his gift for languages; besides English we spoke French, German, and even Spanish, which he had picked up recently in South America. He told me quite frankly how dull the life at court was and how it bored him. "I love to travel," he said, "because it is my only means of getting some fresh air after the stuffy atmosphere of our palaces." I thought of that remark when he abdicated his throne.

When we joined the ladies he clapped his hands. "Let's go right away to the Embassy Club and have fun!" We danced, drank, and ate again until late hours. It was well after two o'clock when we left the club ready to go home. The Prince turned to me and said, "My dear fellow, they tell me that you are so good at the piano. Why don't we drive to the Palace, where you could play us a piece or two if you like."

Unaccustomed as I was to being asked to play in this fashion, I could not refuse a request by the heir to the English throne, so the four of us drove back to St. James's Palace. As we passed the gate, the two yeomen of the guard slammed halberds and snapped to attention. Inside the Palace there were no servants. The Prince, like any other English host, took me to a place to wash up and "powder my nose" and showed the ladies where they could leave their coats. When all that was done, he took us to the large drawing room, where I saw to my astonishment a whole set of percussion instruments for jazz. In another corner of the room stood the piano, if you could call it that. It looked rather more an ancient piece of furniture, green with a gilded rim, the top painted with a bad imitation of Watteau, perched on thin legs in Louis XV style. When he saw my bewildered eyes, the Prince smiled and said, "My mother, the Queen, arranged this room and thought that this piano would fit in well with the rest of the decorations." I opened the lid, curious to see who the maker was, and found an unknown name in brass letters in relief with sharp corners which grazed my little finger. The Prince said again, "I know the history of this piano. It was built for the wedding of Queen Victoria, which explains the rich decoration on it." By then I was pretty intimidated by this formidable museum piece. I opened the top, which reposed on a shaky staff, and thought quickly which piece could produce enough of a sound to satisfy the unmusical ear of His Royal Highness. Aha! I thought. The good old Polonaise in A flat of Chopin will do the job. I settled down on a strange antique bench and tried to find the pedals with my feet and began to play. The beginning sounded spindly but when I played the first big fortissimo chord, something terrible happened: the right leg gave way, the lid slammed down with a horrible noise, and the notes I had played remained stuck. This performance provoked more laughter than any anecdote of mine ever did. It took several minutes before the Prince calmed down. "This great performance calls for a drink!" He brought the whiskey, ice, glasses, and soda himself and poured them out for us. Only then did he find some words of excuse. "I'm sorry that happened, my dear fellow. I should have had a decent instrument for you."

I took the ladies home and discovered that they were rather shocked by the whole mishap because they felt a little guilty. "I should have warned you," said Audrey. "I've seen this piano before." But this time my sense of humor won out. About two weeks later, Audrey Coats telephoned. "The Prince of Wales has a new concert grand for you and asks you to come for a drink this evening and perform something for him on an instrument you like to play." I must say I was flattered and even touched by this unmusical future monarch who had taken the trouble to acquire an expensive piano just to hear me play. On that evening, besides our two lady friends, there were some half a dozen personalities whose names I forget but who were evidently invited because they loved music. I played the *Appassionata* and a nocturne and waltz of Chopin. My performance pleased his guests but I doubt that the Prince enjoyed it himself—at least I didn't see him yawn. Outside the gate of the Palace stood four men I knew well because they usually transported my concert grands. When I asked them what they were doing there they answered, "We have to take the piano straight back. They need it for a concert tomorrow and the manager sent it only because the secretary of the Prince said it was for you." So, after all, I did not win out.

In later years, whenever I met the Duke of Windsor, his first sentence after greeting me was always: "Have you broken any more pianos since I last saw you?"

Life in London at that time was even more brilliant than in Paris. The English are hospitable by nature. There was hardly a day when I was not invited to a lunch or dinner but above all to interesting parties where one met, besides the elite of London society, men like H. G. Wells, Augustus John, Noël Coward, and Somerset Maugham. There were gay theater parties where half a row would be engaged by the host after a dinner, with the evening finishing at the Savoy Grill, where most actors could be seen having supper after their shows. When midnight was past, and the English law didn't allow you to have drinks in a public place, we had a little refuge called the Eiffel Tower in Bloomsbury. You had to know the special series of knocks which opened the door only to friends and there you would find Augustus John on his way to getting dead drunk, Iris Tree, Syrie Maugham, and my good companions Lesley Jowitt and Cristabel McClaren. The Sitwell brothers, Osbert and Sacheverell, joined us sometimes. I reciprocated the many invitations by offering them all wonderful chamber music at Sylvia Sparrow's studio, where the old pals, Sammons, Tertis, Warwick Evans, and Salmond would provide rich musical fare after a good supper. The hours of music with my friend Tertis and the others were the only ones worth remembering. The concerts at seaside resorts and the recitals at Wigmore Hall were not sufficient to inspire me. I was still awaiting the occasion to play with the right enthusiasm for the great London public.

56

One day in Paris, Valmalète announced: "The Casino in Cannes wants you as soloist for a concert with orchestra. Would you mind if the conductor is Reynaldo Hahn?" I answered: "I know that he conducts Mozart beautifully, so I have nothing against playing with him, but find out which concerto he wants to play." Reynaldo Hahn telephoned me himself. "What would you like to play?" he asked.

"The B-flat Concerto of Brahms, but how shall we play it with a casino orchestra?"

"I don't know the work," he said, "but I do admire Brahms, so it would be a great occasion for me to get acquainted with the concerto." I wondered what would be done to the poor concerto by the casino orchestra. After Cannes, I had to play in Florence, Perugia, and Rome. I wired Carla giving her the date of my arrival and she sent back a loving telegram saying she was looking forward to it.

Unbelievable as it sounds, Reynaldo Hahn turned out to be a brilliant conductor. He made the concerto sound as if he had known it for a long time and he let me play out my part freely. The next night, there was a gala at the casino. My friend Lady Cholmondeley was there and we sat together, talking about Reynaldo Hahn, who was a friend of hers. To our regret, he had left already, so we could only exchange our impressions of him. We came to one conclusion: nobody could be more charming in a salon when talking, telling stories, and singing with his small but mellow voice his own and other French songs. Leaving the casino I met in the cloakroom a friend from Madrid who announced that he would be going to Rome. I told him that I would be playing there in a few days and hoped to see him at my concert.

My recital at the Palazzo Pitti in Florence was more interesting than ever because, aside from the usual distinguished personalities, the daughter of Wagner, who, however, bore the name of von Bülow, was present. She told me some interesting things about her pseudo-father, about his playing and his wit. She showed me her album and the inscription by Hans von Bülow: "Bach, Beethoven, Brahms, tous les autres sont des crétins." Then, smiling, she turned a few pages and showed me what her friend Moritz Moszkowski had written: "Meyerbeer, Mendelssohn, Moszkowski, tous les autres sont des chrétiens." We both laughed heartily and I signed my name modestly neither as a *crétin* nor as a *chrétien*.

A motorcar took me from Florence to Perugia. The more we advanced, the more beautiful the landscape became. The old city of Perugia is built on a steep hill; nothing along the road prepares you for the mysterious charm of this city. The car takes you to a hotel, an elegant building painted red, situated on a square overlooking miles and miles of the Umbrian plains and forests. You walk up the indifferent main street with its shops and cafés and find yourself suddenly in the purest Cinquecento surroundings. There is the old palazzo, now turned into a museum, where the paintings of the great sons of the city, Perugino and Raphael, are on view among other masters. Two ancient fountains give vitality to the square.

The promoter of concerts in Perugia was the wife of Mr. Buitoni, owner of the famous Perugina chocolates, a lover of the arts and a noble-minded lady. She endowed this small city with the best music. Famous German orchestras, choirs, and soloists of the very first rank were heard thanks to her generosity. Clara Camus had told me all this but she omitted to tell me where I was to play and that was the best of all. I played right in that hall where all the glorious pictures were hanging. A rare inspiration for any artist! That afternoon I played my best. I would have hated to leave this city without giving the wonderful lady the wish to hear me again. I declare not without pride that Perugia has wanted me back every time I have visited Italy.

After the concert, Mrs. Alba Buitoni invited me to her splendid home, where there was no one but her husband and father. We spent hours and hours talking, agreeing or quarreling passionately about this or that piece of music or this pianist or that violinist. It was one of my most rewarding concerts in Italy. Early the next morning she lent me her large Fiat for the drive to Rome.

At the Excelsior I was astonished not to find a telephone message from Carla. When I called up her palazzo the butler told me that La Signora Principessa was lunching at the golf club. This surprised me. Her wire had indicated that she expected me that morning. I lunched by myself and called again in the afternoon, only to receive the same answer. It seemed incomprehensible, but I tried to understand that her husband needed her for some special occasion. Toward the evening I decided to drive to her palazzo and wait for her while practicing my concerto on her piano, to make up for the wasted day. It would be my only chance before the rehearsal next morning.

When the butler opened the door, Carla's maid rushed to greet me with a strangely frightened expression on her face. She repeated nervously that her mistress was out, which made me suspect that something was going on. I declared coolly that I would work on the piano while waiting for her mistress.

I had played through the whole concerto when I heard voices coming from Carla's bedroom. Thinking it was the maid, I passed through the large living room and entered the adjoining bedroom. What I saw was not the maid but Carla and my friend, the Spanish count whom I had seen in Cannes, sitting on the bed all dressed up. I was boiling with rage. I dashed up to Carla, shook her violently, and threw her on the bed, shouting, "Why this disgusting comedy!" My Spanish friend stood and put up his fists ready for a fight, but I pushed him off, saying, "I need my hands for the piano and not for breaking your bones." At that moment, the maid and the butler, terribly alarmed, rushed into the room, afraid that a murder might be committed. But I walked out quietly, took my coat and hat, and as usual after great emotion, once out in the street thought of nothing but a good restaurant for my dinner. The grillroom of the Excelsior was good enough and I enjoyed my beloved *spaghetti al sugo di carne* and a fresh *aragosta* with mayonnaise, followed by two or three cups of the precious coffee (equal to about half a cup in Paris) and a good Havana cigar. I went up to my room. On the way, the man at the desk handed me a letter and said that it had been there since the morning. The letter was from Carla and explained the whole thing calmly and nicely. It was one of those unforeseen quid-pro-quos and I felt sorry and rather ashamed of my behavior.

The next morning, Carla called me. The belated letter explained it all. I said a few words of apology and she said she was sorry to have hurt my feelings.

The concert at the Augusteo was a special occasion for me. I played for the first time in public the C minor Concerto of Beethoven with Molinari conducting. I remember this concert particularly well because I feel a special love for this concerto and had, at last, the chance to play it with a fine orchestra. I remember the cadenza by Clara Schumann which Barth had recommended to me and which I had never liked. The original cadenzas by Beethoven were discarded by all the pianists in those times and these wonderful originals came into their own only many years later. But my happiness in playing this work must have been so great that it reached the audience; it turned out to be one of my best concerts in Rome. The composer Ottorino Respighi and his lovely wife, who was a fine singer, came to embrace me after the concert.

Mimi Pecci-Blunt also came in to invite me for dinner the following evening. It was a great dinner for at least twenty guests, all members of Italian society, many of whom I had met in Venice, Milan, and Florence; now they had all converged on Rome for the high season. I was one of the first to arrive and received a slight shock when I saw Carla entering with my dear Spanish friend as her escort. They were greeted by the others as though nothing had changed. As to myself, recovering my sense of humor, I treated them like an old married couple.

57

A few days later, after a recital in Madrid, I heard wonderful news. Sergei Prokofiev was in town and invited me to join him at a concert in which a young violinist was to perform the world premiere of Prokofiev's Second Concerto. It took place on a Sunday morning at eleven in a great cinema rightly called the Teatro Monumental. I arrived ahead of time but found Prokofiev already sitting in the box. "I am glad you could come. We will be all alone here. I have the score with me and if you like you can follow the music with it."

I was thrilled to hear a new important work by him; I had not heard one of large dimensions since his famous Third Concerto for the piano. Paul Kochanski used to play the First Concerto, which, although a youthful work, in my opinion was not one of his best.

The hall was practically empty, which made me furious with Arbós. I bitterly resented the fact that he had the honor of presenting a major composition by one of the three or four greatest masters of the day and did it in this manner. He could easily have found a way of doing it at the Teatro Real, as well as making it an evening concert. While I was ruminating on all this, Prokofiev sat next to me, completely indifferent to the surroundings, with the score open so that we both could follow it easily. Arbós conducted first some work which I have forgotten, followed by Sergei's concerto. He informed me that the violinist was a Belgian of means who had commissioned the concerto for the right to give the first performance of it. "He is not very good," Sergei said with a sad smile, "so I am rather glad that not too many people are present. When I heard that you were here, I called you because I am very keen to hear your opinion."

The violinist appeared. It is difficult to describe him; he looked like any man you might see in a bank waiting to cash a check. However, he had learned the concerto. When I heard the solid beginning with the fine theme well played out and developed, and the orchestra making it sound clearly and nobly, I knew I was hearing a great Prokofiev. The music flowed quietly and melodically, the development had nothing of the usual sarcastic touch, and then the second subject came in as if sent from heaven. Even the worst violinist would not be able to spoil the noble line of this melody. I became excited, very moved, and whispered to Prokofiev, "Brahms could have written it! It almost sounds like him!" Sergei smiled broadly, showing all his teeth. "Da! Da! In this case I learned a lot from him!"

In all three movements I didn't hear one bar which let me down and this in spite of the labored and uninspired playing of the violinist. When it came to an end, the three hundred or so people applauded with great respect, with more warmth for Arbós than for the poor soloist, and didn't take the opportunity to pay homage to the great composer who had honored them by his presence. Prokofiev himself seemed to be satisfied with Arbós and the orchestra, did not blame the soloist, and was delighted with my obvious enthusiasm. He accepted my invitation for lunch at a typical old restaurant on the Plaza Mayor, the beautiful square in the old part of the city. We had Arbós and his wife and two musician friends of his. The meal was exuberantly gay. Arbós treated us to some of his best anecdotes, at which he was a past master. Prokofiev laughed tears and seemed to be in the best of moods. He even said quite earnestly, "I *like* my concerto!" He had to return that night to Paris and I had another week in Spain.

58

Practicing and studying at the Villa Majestic was not easy. I was constantly interrupted by telephone calls, messages, and now and then a visit from Avila's Leporello asking for money. Besides this, there was not a day without some invitation to a meal or a play or a concert. If, by any chance, a day was free, I invariably felt the urge to invite a charming lady for lunch.

These luncheons often turned out to be disappointing. As a confirmed gourmet, I liked to take the lady in question to a restaurant known for its duck Rouennaise or *homard à l'Armoricaine* or some other elaborate dish to show off my knowledge of the culinary art. So, to give an example, I proposed Larue on the rue Royale, which the lady readily accepted. When we were happily seated at a table, I called the maître d'hôtel and ordered their marvelous *homard à l'Armoricaine* for two. "It takes about forty or fifty minutes to prepare, so I suggest a few oysters or some caviar."

She stopped me violently. "Please, Arthur, order your lobster for your-self. I will have a green salad and some raw carrots with lemon, no oil—that is all I ever have for lunch. As you know, I like your company and shall gladly wait for your famous dish." I had to give in, a little reluctantly, but I hated to forgo my *homard* just because of the feminine mania for keeping slim, so I ordered it only for myself. While she munched her salad, I tried to keep her amused during the long wait. Finally the maître d'hôtel, assisted by two waiters, began to work before our eyes on the lobster, which had already been prepared in the kitchen. It was wonderful to watch the three men handing each other the ingredients, pepper and salt, a drop of cognac, mixing the sauce, adding carefully a little butter and fresh cream to the dish set carefully on a burner. When all was ready the three doctors, I mean the three waiters, deposited it with loving care on my plate. The maître d'hôtel filled a spoon with the precious sauce and poured it slowly in a circle over the rice and the crimson and gold *crustacés*. The whole delicate operation was watched by both of us with awe and admiration. As soon as I took my first bite, smiling at my companion with delight, she picked up a fork and said condescendingly, "I must try a bit and see why this dish makes you so happy." After swallowing it she exclaimed, "This is divine," and began to devour the best part of it, leaving me a claw and an empty shell. I describe this scene because two or three other charming ladies repeated this misdeed until I learned the lesson and always whispered to the maître d'hôtel, "For two, please . . ."

In 1925 there was good news from Warsaw. The Polish government had decided to give a festival of Polish music in Paris, to take place at the Opéra and the Salle Gaveau. The date, if I remember correctly, was the last week of June. I was asked to take part in both events; three pieces of Chopin ending with the Polonaise in A flat at the Opéra, where Emil Mlynarski was to conduct the rest of the program, and the Concerto in F minor of Chopin at the Salle Gaveau under Fitelberg. Of course I accepted with joy. In November of the same year, I was engaged also to play in Warsaw, invited by the Filharmonja. It made me happy to feel that I was wanted in my own country. Valmalète had announced a concert at the Salle Gaveau, which we planned to be a Chopin recital, but in view of the Polish Festival I had to change the program. This, I thought, was a good oppor-tunity to present in Paris the *Fantasía Bética* of de Falla as a first world performance of the composer whose *Fire Dance* had made him so popular. The rest of the recital consisted of works I had played often before. The expectation for the new work brought a crowd to the Salle Gaveau. I was much applauded for my Beethoven sonata and for a large work by Schu-mann, but de Falla's *Fantasía*, which I played after the intermission, fell somewhat flat. I had been right in finding it a vastly enlarged *Fire Dance* but without the impact of its model, interrupted unnecessarily by a short intermezzo which sounded as if it belonged to another piece. To make it worse, the coda, which he tried to make as brilliant as the end of the *Fire Dance*, is badly written for the piano. It might be much more effective if played by an orchestra. I was sorry to have let down my friend, who had dedicated the work to me and attributed its poor reception to my own performance.

The Polish Festival was a strange affair. After regaining her freedom, Poland was keen to show her own artistic achievements without interference from her three indiscreet neighbors who had dominated her for a century and a half. As a matter of fact, the years under their yoke had both tragic and comic consequences for the cultural heritage of Poland. The Polish identity of many great Polish men and women is often contested. Nicolaus Copernicus, born in Torun, was claimed by the Germans during their occupation of the city of his birth. Joseph Conrad Korzeniowski left his country, which was under Russian rule, when he was twenty and went to England, learned the English language, joined the merchant navy, and dropped his difficult Polish last name, keeping his other two. As Joseph Conrad he became one of the foremost English writers, despite the fact that, when we met, I heard him speak with a strong Polish accent. Marja Sklodowska, after finishing school in Poland, went to Paris to study physics and chemistry, making her living as a governess. She became the discoverer of radium with the help of her husband, Pierre Curie, winning the Nobel Prize twice, the first time together with her husband and the second time alone as the sole discoverer of radium. The French adopted her as one of their own but she also kept her Polish accent.

In the case of Chopin, there is the undeniable fact that his father, who was born in France, came to Poland as a young man, fought with the Poles for their freedom, established a Polish family, and never went back to France. Some French claim their 50 percent of Chopin's blood but they try to ignore that Chopin himself until his last breath proclaimed in his words and in his music his deep love for his mother country.

The program of the Polish Festival at the Paris Opéra was a miscellaneous affair. In the first part there was a short work by Mieczyslaw Karlowicz, followed by the First Concerto of Szymanowski played by Paul Kochanski. I finished the first part with four mazurkas of Szymanowski dedicated to me, the Ballade in F major and the A-flat Polonaise of Chopin. That was the serious part of the concert. In the second half, Emil Mlynarski showed his Warsaw opera-ballet proudly in *Pan Twardowski, Halka*, and a dance by Mlynarski himself, followed by Polish popular songs for chorus.

The Festival was a great success. The French did not mind this kind of program, as they were used to worse with their six-hour shows for charity. Mr. Mlynarski came out with honors. One of my memories of this concert was meeting his son Felix, who had fought at the age of sixteen in the war against Trotsky's army. He contracted tuberculosis and died a few years later in Zakopane. Emil Mlynarski was pleased with my performance. "I'm going to conduct two special concerts in Warsaw and Lodz next year. Will you be my soloist?" I accepted delightedly.

Another Festival concert took place a week later at the Salle Gaveau. Fitelberg conducted the Third Symphony of Szymanowski and I performed the F minor Chopin Concerto. At that concert, Ravel honored us with his presence and George Gershwin was there too. Gershwin, with whom Paul and I had become acquainted, often used to see us and play his latest songs during my last year in America. I asked him if he was planning to stay in Paris, and he said, "No, I tried to get some lessons from Ravel, but finally I didn't." Later on, a story went around that Gershwin had asked Ravel for lessons. To that the French master replied with the question: "How much do you earn a year from your compositions?" Gershwin replied modestly, "Oh, between one hundred and two hundred thousand dollars."

"Then I must ask *you* to teach *me* how to compose."

There was a big reception at the Polish Embassy, where I met for the first time Eve Curie, the younger daughter of Madame Marie Sklodowska Curie. She was a beautiful young girl, with dark eyes in a small round face, slim and elegant and remarkably intelligent. She told me that she was a pianist, had studied with Alexander Brailowski, and had recently given a concert. Quite naturally I became interested in seeing her again and she accepted my invitation for lunch.

It was a long lunch and she agreed without hesitation to share the menus I ordered. She told me, not without bitterness, that she would never play in public again. "I meant to make a modest debut. I wanted simply to see if I was ready for a career, but I was outraged by the behavior of the audience. Huge bouquets of flowers were given to me before I had even started. Every number received an ovation, quite uncalled for by my performance. At the end of the concert, more flowers still and more ovations. It was all a tribute to my mother and nothing else. Now I have agreed to be the music critic of the weekly *Candide*, where I am free to express my opinion. I think I can be of better service to music than if I played in public under such conditions."

She told me how difficult her life was. "My older sister Hélène has become a great scientist like my mother and she too married a professor of physics and chemistry. Since my father's death in an accident I live alone with my mother. Early each morning my mother leaves for the laboratory, comes home exhausted from her work on radium—its rays are detrimental to her health."

I shall not give more details about the life of Marie Curie; Eve has given her a beautiful tribute in her biography of her mother. I became good friends with Eve, who often would lunch or dine with me, and I tried to lift her out of her depression. "At home, my mother receives only old professors, her friends, and I want to live. I love life, music, the arts, and people, and I feel very lonely."

One day, Eve invited me to lunch with her mother at her apartment on the Ile St.-Louis. Madame Curie, small, very erect, with a little head, was unmistakably Polish. She wore her brown hair in a chignon and was gray at the temples. I bent to kiss her hand with deep respect, but she didn't allow me to and pulled her hand back quickly, evidently disliking gestures of that kind. We spoke Polish, which Eve also spoke fluently. There was nobody else for lunch, so the three of us went to the dining room. Madame Curie was pleased to hear that I knew her sister well, the wife of Dr. Josef Dluski. I told her of the concert I had given in Zakopane as a benefit for his sanatorium. Before we were served, she gave me a small lecture on the merits of Communism. "France and Poland have much to learn from it," she said. I did not dare to argue, having learned from Eve about her mother's political convictions. At that moment, the maid came in with a large plate of cold lobsters and a mayonnaise sauce. Madame Curie frowned. "Why these luxuries?" she asked her daughter rather sternly. Eve blushed with anger. "Mr. Rubinstein has often treated me to these *crustacés*, for which he has a predilection." It took me the entire luncheon to awaken some kinder thoughts in Madame Curie about me, in spite of her evident dislike for the way I dressed and for my love of expensive lobsters. She looked at me with kinder eyes after I told her of my hard beginnings and of the poverty of my parents.

Eve left with me, feeling a little uncomfortable about the reception given me by her mother, but she moved me with a little story about her. "You see, Arthur, Mother was disappointed because I wanted to become a pianist and not a student of physics like my sister Hélène. But the other day, my heart broke when I saw her pale and tired in the morning leaving for the laboratory with her poor hands badly burned by the radiation. I begged her to stay home but she wouldn't listen. I insisted on taking her for lunch to a good restaurant near the Institute and you know what she said? 'I don't dare to be seen in public in my poor clothes and hat with my elegant and beautiful daughter.' " I cried.

59

Early that summer I spent a few lovely weeks with Paul while Zosia went to Warsaw to see her family, and we made the rounds of the nightclubs, rather more those of Montparnasse than Montmartre. We both liked the company of Moïse Kisling, a brilliant young Polish painter who was the life and soul of the cafés and cabarets in Montparnasse. After a few drinks, Kisling would become violent. The slightest remark that he disliked earned the offender a punch in the nose. Once he fought off two policemen with a few well-placed uppercuts but they let him go because he was jolly and charming at the same time. And he had a heart of gold.

The Kochanskis and I decided to spend the beginning of the summer in St. Jean de Luz as the nearby Biarritz with its casino and other attractions was too tempting for both of us. We took an apartment in a villa, had a small piano sent from Bayonne, and worked in the morning either together or one after another. Our afternoons were also devoted to music in the house of some good friends from Bordeaux, Mr. and Mrs. Emile Blanchard, where both Ravel and Jacques Thibaud felt at home. We made music in many ways; Ravel would try out with me a few pages of a new piece four-hands. Paul would play his arrangements of Stravinsky's *Pulcinella* to Ravel's delight and the de Falla songs, which we all thought sounded better on the violin than when sung. I accompanied Paul and Thibaud for as much of Bach's concerto for two violins as our memory permitted. It was a good month of music for all four of us and ended all too quickly. The Kochanskis left for Warsaw to see their families before returning to the United States; Ravel left to finish his new composition at Ciboure, his birthplace. Thibaud joined his family in Biarritz, where he owned a villa, and I left via Paris for Venice to enjoy anew the hospitality of the Princess Polignac.

The new piano had arrived. Princess Winnie was delighted with its beautiful tone and easy action, although I myself found it rather woolly. This, of course, was because of the humidity of Venice; nevertheless, it was a pleasure to work on it.

The other guest this time was Violet Trefusis. She had the lovely room next to the great hall and I remember well the day I first met her. The previous spring, Princess Winnie had invited me to lunch on behalf of Violet Trefusis. "She is a charming woman, very intelligent and a good friend of mine."

By some bad luck, I had forgotten the date and it came back to me only when the lunch was already over. Ashamed of having let the princess down, I rushed to the address she had given me to apologize to Mrs. Trefusis. The butler told me that the guests were gone but that he would announce my visit. I had been waiting a few moments in a little garden in front of the house when Mrs. Trefusis appeared, having evidently interrupted her siesta, for she wore a robe and her stockings were falling loosely over her shoes. She took the affair of the missed luncheon very lightly. We chatted about nothing and everything for a long while and parted as old friends.

One morning after breakfast, I went to the Bechstein and began practicing the Fourth Scherzo of Chopin. A door opened and Violet Trefusis appeared, her long hair down, wearing nothing but a bra and a petticoat, shouting enthusiastically, "This is my favorite scherzo!" At that moment, Princess Winnie appeared from a side door and screamed at Violet, "How dare you appear like that in my salon!" and pointing a stern finger at her: "Go right back to your room!" The terrified Violet disappeared in panic.

Violet was, from a psychological point of view, one of the most complicated persons I have known. When in the company of typical housewives, she would carry on a conversation of the most banal kind, but her talk would become strikingly intelligent when she gathered around her table men and women of quality—a Stravinsky, a Léon-Paul Fargue, a Poulenc—who would listen to her with interest. Even physically there were striking contrasts. She could, as on that morning at the palazzo, look like a strumpet, but at a great dinner party she would be one of the most distinguished ladies. Her face was not beautiful; she had a funny nose that always reminded me rather of a pig, which spoiled her otherwise good-looking face. But her figure was full of curves, a little plump, but because of that very sexy, and she moved lazily and engagingly. To put it in a nutshell, I liked her.

The Bechstein piano inspired me to work more assiduously than the little upright had during previous seasons. The social life in Venice was more animated this time. I was invited to several great palazzi, such as the Mocenigo of the Robillants, where the young Olga charmed me with her talk about music. Her mother, Clémentine, was still a famous beauty. Giuseppe Volpi, Mussolini's Minister of Finance, and his wife and daughters invited me several times for cocktails. On one occasion, Mr. Volpi, a powerfully built good-looking man, produced a Polish newspaper. "There is an article about me and I would be grateful if you would translate it." I quickly looked it over; it was a most insulting diatribe against my host. The first three words must have worried him: "Volpi vel fuchs" (in German the third word means fox and would be a Jewish name). Seeing me blushing with embarrassment, he insisted on learning what followed. Well, the indiscreet Pole said that Volpi was an upstart from some African ghetto. I translated, laughing it off. "It must be someone who wanted money from you and you didn't give it to him." He slapped me on the back. "You guessed it!" I didn't enjoy my cocktail that day.

60

I left Venice at the beginning of October for the Villa Majestic again. One day a friend of mine, Madame Jeanne de Marjerie, called me: "Arthur, I have found a lovely place for you. If you feel like it, let us drive up and look it over." On the way to Montmartre, she told me that Pierre Fresnay had left it in order to live with his parents.

She came to fetch me in a taxi and we reached the Butte by the steep rue Lepic, stopping on the Place Ravignan opposite the famous Bateau Lavoir, where Picasso, Max Jacob, Juan Gris, and many other painters had ateliers during the starving early years of their careers. Jeanne opened the gate to a house, stopped at the loge of the concierge, a dark-haired disheveled woman, and asked her to show us Mr. Fresnay's apartment. A few steps led to a small gate to the left and there was a ravishing little garden. In the center of it, a small round fishpond, surrounded by five tall acacias, chestnut trees, and lilac bushes, charmed the eye. Along the wall was a flower bed. To the side two white steps led to a sort of bungalow, built in the latest modern style in complete contrast to the modest old Montmartre houses which surrounded the garden. The inside of the bungalow, now bare, consisted of a long, narrow living room with a window at each end, one looking onto the garden and the other onto the Bateau Lavoir. Just off the living room was a small alcove used as a bedroom with a door to the bathroom. There was a rather unusual annex; three small rooms on the ground floor of the big house behind the bungalow were included in the lease. The rent was so low that my apartment at the Villa Majestic seemed to cost a fortune by comparison. I was so wildly enthusiastic about this place that I grabbed Jeanne and we danced a jig in the garden. The disheveled concierge arranged a meeting with the owner of the house for the following day. We were both punctual and he was waiting for me in the small garden. After shaking hands, he handed me his visiting card, which read: "André Bloch, Ingénieur de l'Ecole Polytechnique." This impressed me very much. He was a middle-aged man with strong Semitic features and looked like a modest businessman. We signed the lease and had a drink to celebrate— some dreadful red wine served by Judith, the concierge. He said he was a close friend of Pierre Fresnay. "What a pity that little bitch left him. He is very unhappy now. He loved this house and I hope you will too."

Before starting to do anything to the house, I invited Eugenia Errazuriz to look at it and give me some advice (without Jeanne, of course). She looked around approvingly, pointing a finger where the bed had to be. "Ah, Ah! Red! Red! The spread must be red! And the curtains, gray! Like wall! Gray! Ah!" Jeanne was astonished to see me adamant about these colors. "I did not know you were so interested in these things!" she said with a certain admiration. She went to work rapidly on the decoration and furnishing, submitted plans, made small drawings, and ordered things from her usual providers. "I get everything cheaper," she said, "because they like dealing with me and I'm good at auctions at the Hotel Drouot." Jeanne was brilliant and artistic; I paid her for her work, of course, although she wanted to do it for love. "I adore decorating. It is my passion. My husband, who is a snob, does not like me to do it, so don't tell him!" Sometimes she would call urgently: "Come right away, there are six beautiful antique dining-room chairs in a private sale. You must buy them!"

In a fortnight I was able to move into the unfinished apartment. It had a double bed, a piano, and an antique bedside table. The three rooms in the house behind had yet to be decorated and we decided to make a dining room of the one on the left, a kitchenette of the narrow one in the middle with the door that led onto the corridor, and save the one on the right for a future servant. For the present, Judith the concierge brought my breakfast to my bed and I had my meals in town as usual. By and by, we found a heavy old Spanish oak table for the dining room and a graceful one for the living room, which began to look richly furnished with the six embroidered chairs. I left Jeanne to finish the work while I went to Poland and asked her to try and find some help, a man or a woman. I left toward the end of the year.

61

For my two recitals in Warsaw the houses were full of loyal followers. I played much Beethoven, Schumann, and Brahms, the four mazurkas of Szymanowski, and some Liszt. I played Chopin only at the second recital and not too much of it. However, the audience forced me to play the indispensable *Navarra* at both concerts as well as de Falla's *Fire Dance* and my own arrangement of "The Ride of the Valkyries." I went back to Warsaw every year from then on. The two recitals were followed by concerts in Lodz, Cracow, Lwow, and three or four smaller cities in the old Austrian Galicia.

For my stay in Warsaw, I accepted the hospitality of my friend Richard Ordynski. His "guest room" was unfortunately not very comfortable; he made me sleep on a strange couch which bulged up sharply at the head. It was far too short for me and with a pillow under my head I slept practically in a sitting position with part of my legs dangling over the bulge. Ordynski seemed satisfied with this arrangement; the one bathroom was next to his own very comfortable bedroom, where he slept in a fine double bed. His breakfast was extremely frugal; a maid would arrive rather late in the morning, stay for two hours, and serve us tea in tall glasses with rolls and butter. That was all. Ordynski would then ask me cheerfully, "Where are we lunching?" and join me at the excellent restaurant of the Hotel Europejski very punctually for lunch as well as for dinner—as my guest.

Sophie, the daughter of Mr. Bernstein, who, with Dr. Goldflam, had helped me to get the loan from the bank before the war, had married Stanislaw Meyer, the son of a rich businessman. She was back from Berlin, where she had studied with Barth. She had intended to make a career but gave it up after her marriage.

She used her apartment for giving big receptions for artists who came to Warsaw and invited the right people to meet them. She created a real salon which was well known in Warsaw.

In Cracow and Lwow, I found all my friends again and they were happy to see me getting on in life. Lwow was still the one city which preferred my conception of Chopin to that of other pianists.

After this short and strenuous tour, I rushed back to Paris, anxious to return to Montmartre and to the first home of my own I ever had. Jeanne de Marjerie knew of my longing to see my books around me and had shelves built for them all around my bed and in every free space in the living room. When I put my precious books carefully in order where they belonged, I looked at them with tears in my eyes. It was the first time I had seen them on shelves since Berlin. Jeanne had done exactly what I asked; the bedspread was made of beautiful dark red velvet, the gray curtain was of a not too heavy material and when it was drawn it gave me the comfortable feeling of being in a small cozy room instead of an open alcove. Lying in bed, I learned an acrobatic feat: to draw books off the shelf with my toes. I had brought from Brazil a rather large number of butterflies of a fantastic blue pinned on white cotton and encased in thin black frames. They looked lovely on the wall opposite the books and on the windowsills. When the carpets were in place at the beginning of January, I took advantage of the yearly sales, on Jeanne's advice, and bought at the fine Maison de Blanc all I needed for the dining room, towels, and other linens. China, silver, and glasses began to fill the cupboards in the little kitchen. It was a heavenly feeling to have one's own apartment and be at home at last!

At a luncheon with Jeanne she asked me, "Arthur, would you like to have a real valet, one who could do everything, look after your clothes and prepare you a good breakfast?"

"Yes, but he will probably cost a fortune!" She named the price and, with the low rent, it was an amount I could well afford.

Next morning, Judith knocked at the door. "There is a gentleman to see you." In came a strikingly good-looking young man of around thirty, well dressed and with the best of manners. It took me quite a while to realize that this was the promised valet. His French was impeccable, he spoke softly and respectfully; in short, he was what the English called a gentleman's gentleman. François Delalande was to stay with me for a number of years to come and, to this day, I never had better service. From then on, life smiled at me. Packing, traveling, receiving guests, getting a taxi, everything became easy. François never took a day off; he asked only for permission to go out if he was sure I didn't need him, but that was all. When a lady needed his help, he was never at a loss. There wasn't a spot he couldn't remove. If something was torn he could sew it and he was always ready to do the right thing in unforeseen circumstances. There was once the case of a suspicious and jealous husband who came to surprise his wife at my home. François heard him asking Judith about me and hurriedly took me and the lady in question to the kitchen door and out through the corridor into the courtyard. I didn't know that a passage existed which linked the courtyard to another street, ten minutes by car from my home.

I used to have my breakfast in bed while reading the morning paper or a good book. To dress was no trouble, everything was prepared. The suit was pressed, the socks and shoes were on the floor in just the right place to be slipped on in no time, my toothbrush had the toothpaste on it and lay on the glass with the mouthwash, the shirt and the tie were ready, and all the things for my pockets were laid out in order. When I was ready to go out, he had a taxi waiting for me.

Sometimes, though, I got into trouble. The Polish ambassador in Brussels, Tadeusz Jackowski, whose charming wife was a well-known ex-actress, used to give me lovely parties after my concerts in the Belgian capital and even obtained a flattering decoration for me from King Albert, the hero of the war. One day, his wife called me on the telephone: "We are in Paris for a short visit and would like to see you." I seized the occasion to reciprocate so much kindness on their part. "Would you and the ambassador have lunch with me the day after tomorrow at one o'clock at Larue, an excellent restaurant?" She accepted delightedly but added: "Would you be so kind as to let us lunch at the Ritz? I doubt if the food is as good as at Larue but I'm burning to see the famous Olivier at work. Yesterday we saw *Le Sexe faible* by Edouard Bourdet and I want to see this man in real life." I said yes, naturally. The play was then the biggest success of the season. It was about a maître d'hôtel at the Ritz who was a unique specimen of his profession. He would lend money, could arrange a passport, could make or destroy marriages, provide a homosexual with a young friend, a lesbian with the right woman, get tickets for sold-out shows—there wasn't a thing he couldn't do. Bourdet's play was a masterpiece of a portrait of Olivier at the Ritz and his actor was Victor Boucher, who was unforgettable in this role.

I invited the counselor of the Polish Embassy in Paris and his wife to lunch with us. And here I must confess a dreadful thing: I forgot all about it and it was François who reminded me of it when I rang for my breakfast well after eleven o'clock. I hardly had time to shave, wash, dress, and get a taxi, hoping not to arrive too late. Of course, there was no time to order a table or do anything about the luncheon itself. This time I was in a spot. As everybody knows by experience, the more you rush, the slower you get ready. And the worst of it all was that François had a hard time finding a taxi. I finally left at ten minutes to one. The more I urged the taxi driver to speed up, the more traffic he found in his way. It was a nightmare. But as often happened before, I had a sudden inspiration: I ordered the taxi to drive to the entrance of the Ritz at the rue Cambon. By then it was about ten past one. I threw my coat and hat at the woman in the cloakroom and ran through the long passage leading to the front of the Ritz on the Place Vendôme, stopped for a moment to get my breath, and entered the elegant lobby, where my four guests were sitting waiting for me with gloomy faces. Seeing them, I clapped my hands. "Here you are!" I exclaimed, showing great astonishment. "Didn't I tell you I would be waiting for you in the bar on the other side? I thought you had forgotten my invitation. Fortunately, I thought of looking for you here. And now," I said with fake despair, "you sit here without the drinks I ordered at the bar!" I called the waiter in the lobby. "Please bring four glasses of dry sherry—I had mine"—I smiled to them—"and while you have it I shall see the maître d'hôtel and find out if my table is ready."

In the restaurant, I caught Olivier by his arm, pushed a fifty-franc note in his hand, and whispered, "I have the Polish ambassador and his wife as well as the counselor to the embassy and his wife—we are five—have an elegant luncheon ready in the shortest possible time, flowers, wine, and all."

"No trouble," he said.

I came back and, smiling, said, "Lunch will be ready in a few minutes." I sat down and cheered them up with some funny stories about the night before. They had just finished their drinks when Olivier appeared and said, "Monsieur est servi."

He showed us to a table in the restaurant, beautifully decorated with flowers, a bottle of white wine in the ice bucket, a bottle of fine Bordeaux in a basket, a neatly handwritten menu in the place of the ambassador's wife. We had an excellent hors d'oeuvres served with tiny glasses of Polish vodka, *quenelles de brochet à la Lyonnaise, canard à l'orange, salade d'endives, plateau de fromages,* and *parfait de café.* My guests complimented me constantly on my taste and the great care I took in ordering this meal.

The wife of the ambassador had her eyes glued to Olivier, studying every gesture he made. When we reached coffee, served in lovely small cups, she said to me, with an air of great disappointment, "This Olivier is just an ordinary maître d'hôtel like all the others in Paris or Brussels. Bourdet must have invented this character from beginning to end." At this I bit my tongue till it bled to restrain myself from screaming at her: "Damn it! He just did for me one of the best tricks Bourdet makes him perform!" They never learned the truth. When I paid my bill and thanked him, Olivier said with an indulgent smile, "Ce n'est rien." He had given me a table ordered for later by someone else.

62

Valmalète had an offer from Vienna for a recital at the great Musikvereinsaal. I was very happy to play again in the city of Mozart, Schubert, Beethoven, and Brahms. I remembered my prewar concerts with pleasure. There was now a new manager there, Mr. Hugo Knepler, who must have advertised my concert with special care, for I found a good house. I was flattered to see in a balcony facing me Emil von Sauer and his young wife (I don't know if she was his number four or number five). I remember having played at that concert the rondo Prokofiev dedicated to me. It is from the music of his ballet *The Prodigal Son*, and when I told him I loved a particular piece from it, he transcribed and arranged it for me. The public received it with indifference, but Emil Sauer showed great interest.

As Mr. Knepler and I were satisfied with each other, I promised to come back again for a second concert. He did have one irritating habit: Just before I went onstage to begin the concert, he would ask, "The first number is the *Appassionata?*" and when I nodded yes, he would sing out the theme in the most speedy tempo, as if it were a street ditty. I could have killed him.

"The Danish State Opera Orchestra wants you for a symphony concert at the opera," Valmalète told me. I was very pleased to hear that. I had a great wish to play both in the Scandinavian countries and in Holland, which were known to be very musical.

"It is known that playing in Copenhagen with some success opens the door to Sweden and Norway and even Finland," I said. "Please arrange two recitals at my own risk in the hall, which, by the way, I've heard is one of the best in Europe."

I looked forward to these three concerts. A few weeks before the date, Valmalète wrote me that the Copenhagen orchestra wanted me to play *Nights in the Gardens of Spain* of de Falla. I telephoned him: "I shall play it gladly, but only, you must tell them, on condition that I can play another important concerto in the same program." My preference was Brahms B flat or Beethoven G major, as they would be a great contrast to the de Falla piece. The *Nights in the Gardens of Spain* for orchestra with piano obbligato is not a real solo part and it couldn't possibly awaken interest enough to hear me in two further recitals. Valmalète transmitted my demand; the answer came: "We heard that Rubinstein is only good in Spanish music, so the de Falla work is all we want." I was enraged. It was like a slap in the face. "Send them to hell! Cancel the two recitals!"

"You can't do that. I can cancel the Opera concert but you would have to pay an indemnity to the recital hall."

"Never mind," I said. "I would rather lose all my money than give in to these people." About ten years later, Fritz Busch engaged me as soloist with the Radio Orchestra in Copenhagen. I played the Saint-Saëns concerto followed by a sold-out recital and well-paid engagements in Stockholm, Oslo, and Göteborg, which became my followers for the rest of my career; but I always stubbornly refused to play with the Opera Orchestra of Copenhagen.

A committee in Geneva invited me to join the jury for a piano competition to take place after my concerts there and in Lausanne. It was interesting because there were to be only four judges—the other three were Ernest Schelling, Professor Pembauer from Munich, and Alfred Cortot.

About a week before that competition, I had a rather bad accident. As I was coming home late from a party, dressed in a dinner jacket with a light coat over my arm, my taxi was hit violently by a big car which was coming on the wrong side of the street on the Boulevard de Clichy. The impact was so strong that I lost consciousness. A policeman, helped by some passersby, took me to the nearby Hôpital Lariboisière. I came to, after having had an injection against a concussion, to find a big wound on my scalp which had to be sewn up, and my white shirt was soaked with blood. After the treatment the doctor advised me to sit down for a while before going home. I did so, fearing a hemorrhage, but when the doctor was gone, I asked if I might leave. A passing nurse said sternly, "You must stay here until you are allowed to move."

I sat there, feeling faint from time to time, but did not dare to disobey. At about six o'clock in the morning an elderly woman, shuffling along, dragging her slippers, made herself comfortable at a small table, beckoned me with her finger, and when I approached, asked me coldly, "Do you have the money to pay me? It's twenty-five francs." So this was the reason why they made me wait so long! A policeman who showed up felt sorry for me, put me into a car, drove me home, and helped me to undress.

The doctor had put a big white bandage around my head and ordered me to keep it on for two weeks and then come back to have it removed. I felt a little seedy the next day but recovered quickly from the shock. The large white bandage made me look rather conspicuous but I showed it off with a certain pride, playing the brave sufferer.

One of the men who had brought me to the hospital remained there to see how I felt, and when I thanked him, he said, "I noticed a strange thing: when the impact occurred, you had both hands wrapped in your coat." I must have developed an instinct to protect my hands, for in every moment of danger, instead of using my hands for defense, my immediate reflex is to hide them. I left for Switzerland with bandage and all, and in both Lausanne and Geneva, the stage manager had to prepare the public for my appearance, assuring them that the music was all in place behind the bandage.

When I joined my colleagues of the jury at the competition, my spectacular headdress gave me certain privileges. Professor Pembauer was constantly preoccupied with my comfort, looking for the best chair, or trying to get a pillow under my head. The competition ran for three days because of the large number of participants. It was a dull affair. We heard immature playing and often a complete lack of musical gifts. Then, on the third day, a pianist appeared whose name was already well known in the concert field—Claudio Arrau. It did not take two minutes of his playing before we began nodding to each other, smiling with satisfaction. "Cela c'est un pianiste," said Cortot. He received the prize, which was a Bechstein concert grand. I had first heard about his talent in Chile, where he had been a child prodigy, so I was wondering why he entered this competition. It was like a race between a thoroughbred and some cart horses. After it was over Schelling gave us a supper in his sumptuous villa on the lake.

A few weeks later, Mr. Henri Rabaud, the director of the Paris Conservatory, invited me to be on the jury for that year's "Concours du Conservatoire," the great public annual event. I found out that it was Cortot who had recommended me for this honor. The jury this time consisted of Cortot and myself as outsiders, Mr. Rabaud presiding, and three or four professors of the Conservatory. This *concours* is not an easy matter either for the candidates or for the jury. On this occasion, all the eight pianists had to play the F minor Ballade of Chopin and then read a piece of music at sight from manuscript, specially written for the *concours*—a long and tiring business. A fifteen-year-old boy named Dreyfus showed genuine talent, whereas the others presented little interest. Late in the afternoon, Mr. Rabaud invited the jury to follow him into a room where we would vote after a long exchange of views. We were unanimous about giving the first prize to the young Dreyfus. He won after only one year at the Conservatory. Reluctantly, we gave a second prize to a young man who played his Ballade properly but without inspiration. One *accessit* was given to a performer who showed promise, and that was all. We were ready to leave when Mr. Rabaud addressed us with an appeal for our consideration: "There is a young man [I forget his name] who won a second prize after his first year at the Conservatory. He is now in his fourth year and so competes this year for the fourth and last time. Our rules oblige a recipient of a second prize to win the first prize or nothing if he enters again. This boy has a family without means who supported him with great sacrifices and expect him now to be able to support himself and even help them in turn. That will be possible only if he wins the first prize, which opens the door to lessons and other remunerative activities. As it stands, he will leave the Conservatory with nothing to show. I appeal to you, gentlemen, to consider his sad situation and concede him, even against your convictions, the first prize."

There was a moment of silent consternation around the table. Then Cortot replied, "In my opinion, art is a temple where only the chosen are allowed to enter. Personal circumstances have no place in the temple and should not be pitied." I felt he was right. I would gladly help the poor fellow with money, or with a recommendation for any possible work, but a first prize to an undeserving performer seemed to me a betrayal of our role as a jury. Cortot's protest was accepted.

Out in the street a small crowd was waiting for us. They were the families of the losers. When they saw us, they began to scream: "Murderers!" "Assassins!" "We ought to kill you, heartless beasts!" Some of them spat at us. I swore to myself never to take part again in a jury of the Conservatory.

63

After a restful summer spent partly in Deauville and a few weeks in Venice, I returned to my home in Montmartre, where François helped me with the transformation of the primitive washing place into an elegant modern bathroom. I was preparing my autumn season of concerts. Richard Ordynski arrived in town and told me that he and an important group of Polish actors had been engaged by Paramount Pictures to dub into Polish one of their very successful films. "I have a wonderful idea, Arthur," he said. "We have a free day next week and it would be wonderful if you gave a luncheon for our actors, whom you admire so much." It was true, there were three or four men and women among them who were my favorites of the Polish stage. I called François for a consultation. "Do you think it possible to have twelve persons for lunch in this place?"

"Certainly, sir." he said. "It is still warm and I could set up a large table in the garden."

"Well, then," I said to Richard, "invite them in my name on that free day, but not before two o'clock, because I have to order the luncheon from different places in town and it usually takes time for it to be delivered and prepared."

For two days before the lunch, I was busy ordering a sumptuous meal: lobsters from Prunier, ducks from Larue, and the then famous raspberry tart from Edouard of the rue Daunou. I also took care of the wine, vodka, and cognac. François had to get the table, chairs, and all we needed from a caterer, including the coffee.

I was looking forward to my first party in my home and to having as my guests the actors I admired so much. On the day of the luncheon, at nine o'clock I received a call from the Baronne Germaine de Rothschild. "Cher Arthur, I hope you did not forget the luncheon today at twelve-thirty. Please don't be late because Edouard has to be at the Banque de France early." I almost fainted. I had completely forgotten I had accepted this invitation about two weeks earlier. I saw no way out of it, so I answered with an assumed cheerfulness, "Certainly, chère Germaine, I shall be on time." I dressed in a hurry, saw the man arranging the table and chairs in the garden, and ordered François to take care of the flowers, and remind the different places to deliver the things on time. Leaving at noon for the rue St. Florentin, I said, "Have everything ready for two o'clock, but if I am not back on time, tell Mr. Ordynski that I telephoned and was held up at a bank, and that I would be back any minute."

This was a day to be remembered! Gargantua, Rabelais' creation, could not have devoured more food than I did. Edouard de Rothschild was not only a great gourmet, but a gourmand as well. His table was famous for having the finest food in town and the menu always offered a lavish assortment. He liked my company because I appreciated this and also because my stories amused him. This lunch began with a *saumon fumé*: "Il n'est pas salé. Vous le trouverez excellent,"* said the baron. Then came *perdreaux rôtis sur canapé* with a very original salad made of celery, apple, and truffles finely cut up with a delicious sauce which I cannot describe. After this dish

* It is not a bit salty. You will find it excellent.

from heaven came the *plateau* of cheeses. The baron picked a big piece of one special one and forced me to eat it, praising it in a way that did not admit refusal. The last course was a *parfait de glaces*—it was filled with powdered chocolate, a specialty of their table which I couldn't refuse, even on my deathbed. As it was getting late for both the baron and myself, I succeeded in doing without the coffee. It was almost two o'clock and I dashed home in a taxi and found my guests with a nervous Ordynski in the garden. I received a hungry welcome. François whispered, "Everything is in order, sir." I put the two lovely ladies next to me and the Lucullan feast— the first for them, the second for me—started off with gorgeous fresh lobsters, with well-cared-for mayonnaise with the right amount of pepper, to the great satisfaction of my guests. A few sips of vodka helped to loosen the tongues of the great actors and every new course was received with an ovation. The bottles of wine were emptied in no time and the cognac gave the final touch to this culinary orgy. I may assure my readers that I didn't leave the table hungry. To this day I lose my appetite when I think of it.

Ordynski was happy to accept the thanks of the actors for organizing this feast. He addressed me in a voice heard by everybody: "My dear Arthur, you must stay with me again when you come to Warsaw." They nodded their approval of this generous offer.

The season was particularly brilliant. I remember especially some masked and costume balls. Being at that time much in demand, I was invited to most of them and enjoyed them to the full. There was, of course, the annual official ball at the Opéra, where we all appeared hiding our personalities in black dominoes—eyes and noses covered by black masks. The game was to recognize people in this disguise. It was fun to see Germaine's delight when I whispered, "This beautiful silhouette in the elegant domino can only be Germaine." We danced a lot after this and took a table for two on the balconies outside, where supper was served. The two orchestras never stopped playing one-steps, waltzes, and my favorite tangos.

Another brilliant ball was given by Mimi Pecci-Blunt, who had a lovely house and garden on the other side of the river. She called it "The Ball in White." The guests were invited to wear costumes of any kind but they had to be white. I decided to appear in the gorgeous disguise of a maharajah, which I found at a theatrical costumers, who also took care of a lovely black beard and mustache and made me up in a light brown color. A splendid white turban covered my head, and to make it more spectacular, I affixed in front the best of my diamond pins, of which I had a considerable collection. A London jeweler in Bond Street employed a specialist for these pins, many of which were given to me by friends and others I had specially made for me. I had a lovely horse, a little Scottish terrier with eyes made of rubies, a donkey, a camel, a mouse, a lion, a cock, a bull, a pig, and many others. In later years, when my children were small, I used to wear a pin for their benefit which would indicate my humor for the day. They screamed with delight when it was the lion, the horse, or the dog, but were pretty ashamed of me when it was the mouse, the pig, or the donkey. I always tried to be honest about my mood.

The ball at Mimi Pecci-Blunt's was wonderful. There were white clowns, white harlequins, white Columbines, and there was even a Scotsman who wore a white kilt, white tartan, stockings, shoes, a little cap with ribbons, all white. The dance was one big whirl of white. We were served a supper of mostly white food by servants dressed as cooks with tall white hats. This ball was the talk of the town for quite a time.

Valmalète announced three recitals at the Salle Gaveau, for which I prepared the *Promenades* of Poulenc, dedicated to me, and the *Saudades do Brazil* of Milhaud and I repeated the four mazurkas of Szymanowski which I had played at the Polish Festival. The public liked the *Promenades*, to my astonishment, but disapproved of the Milhaud and Szymanowski pieces. It did not discourage me. Both of them had a hard time before the public took to them.

Jeanne de Marjerie arranged a supper for me after the first concert at the house of a friend of hers, Dominique André, a charming hostess. Her guests were the famous writers Henri de Régnier, Abel Hermant, and Jacques de Lacretelle, along with the young Jacques Février, Jeanne, and myself. It was one of the most delightful evenings imaginable. The meal was enlivened by the most brilliant conversation and later, in the drawing room, Jacques and I played all sorts of things four-hands and I then played, to their delight, the best tangos and Strauss waltzes of my repertoire. Late that night, we followed the hostess to the kitchen and had scrambled eggs and coffee.

We had the pleasure of gathering again at Madame André's house after the second concert, where we had even more fun this time. Misia Sert gave a supper after the third concert with Poulenc following my performance of his *Promenades*. Coco Chanel and the dancer Serge Lifar were there and they all talked a lot about a young pianist who had made a sensation at his debut in Paris. Misia told me, "He succeeded in getting out of Russia with two friends of his, a violinist and a cellist. His name is Vladimir Horowitz. He had a colossal success in Germany and played in Paris while you were away. You must hear him whenever both of you are in Paris." Lifar added, "He played as an encore the dance from *Carmen* so fantastically that I was ready to jump up and dance it." It made me laugh. I couldn't believe that a serious pianist would play *Carmen* at a concert, but I was very impressed by their enthusiasm and promised myself to hear him as soon as I could. I was glad that my own three recitals were full, even sold out, with people standing. It was time to leave for Warsaw to play with Emil Mlynarski, and then Cracow, Lwow, and Lodz.

64

I arrived in Warsaw on a cold morning, drove directly to the Old Square, and climbed the two flights to Ordynski's apartment while the driver helped me with my luggage. Richard received me with kisses and hugs but had not thought of changing the horrible couch which my dangling legs resented so much. That same morning I had a rehearsal with Emil Mlynarski. In both Warsaw and Lodz, I would be playing the G major Beethoven Concerto and I felt a particular pleasure playing under his direction. He was always calm and made his observations with extreme politeness. He moved his baton with perfect rhythmic precision and achieved the best results without exaggerated gestures. He approved of my conception of this concerto which I had loved ever since I heard it played by D'Albert.

I had Ordynski, as usual, as my guest for lunch and dinner at the Europejski and rested that night as best I could on the dreadful couch. Thinking of the concert, I looked forward to showing my so devoted public in Warsaw that I was not a mere virtuoso, charming them with a *Navarra*, but a musician who could do justice to the best concerto of Beethoven.

Sophie Meyer appeared at the rehearsal to invite Mlynarski and me for supper after the concert, but the conductor declined. "I have the premiere of *Parsifal* next week," he said, "and have to study the score. This concert with Arthur gives me a little rest from constantly rehearsing and preparing the opera." But I did accept her invitation, as I knew I would find most of my friends there.

The concert began with *Leonore* no. 3, followed by my concerto and, after the intermission, the Fifth Symphony. The concerto had an unexpectedly great success, which made me very happy. During the intermission the door to the artist's room opened and three Graces entered, three Polish beauties. The one with darker hair had the most beautiful eyes and a melancholy expression. The tallest, who was very blond, showed great vitality and charm, and the last one looked at me with daring coquetry. She felt sure of her charms.

The tallest one came forward and said, "I'm the daughter of Emil Mlynarski," and introduced the one with the beautiful eyes: "This is my sister Alina," and pointing at the last one: "This is my cousin Hela." It came as a surprise to me to learn that Mlynarski was the father of these two beautiful young girls. I had known for years his eldest daughter, Wanda, now the wife of the pianist Wiktor Labunski; his two sons I had met in Paris.

These three young girls had the charm and the authentic something which always attracted me so much to Polish women. By some instinct, though, the tallest one, the one they called Nela, was the only one I looked at, as if the other two were not in the room. After the introductions, acting as speaker for the three, she said some kind words about my playing; it was the first time she had heard me. When they were ready to leave, I begged them to come back after the concert. "My friends Staś and Zosia Meyer are giving a big party tonight. If you would like to come I shall ask them to invite you." They smiled without answering. When Emil Mlynarski had taken his bows after the symphony, the artist's room was invaded by friends and admirers. The first to come in was Zosia Meyer to get her fur coat and rush home. When I asked her to invite the three Mlynarski girls, she looked at me with surprise. "They probably begged you to have them invited but you know better than that. We can't have such young people at my party." I had to restrain my rage and not say, "If you feel that way, I shall take them for supper and give up your charming party." When the three Graces reappeared, I told Nela that Mrs. Meyer was sorry not to be able to have them, to which Nela said with a proud smile, "I knew she wouldn't have us."

I hated the party and left early. The next night I took the train for Cracow. The beautiful old capital of Poland received me this time as cordially as Warsaw. I now felt completely at home in the country of my birth. Lwow, though, was the only town which loved my way of playing Chopin. My recital this time consisted entirely of works by the Polish master and was, I am happy to say, a huge success. Back again in Warsaw, I begged Karol to telephone Nela Mlynarska and ask if the two of us could come for tea. The three girls invited us that same afternoon for tea and cakes served in a boudoir of the large Mlynarski apartment, which took up the whole left wing of the Opera House. Nela played the hostess. And again this time, as with Pola in the old days, both of us, Nela and I, felt the *coup de foudre*. We fell in love. Right away we became shy with each other. She accepted my invitation to dine at the Europejski but brought her cousin with her, and Ordynski joined us as well. We finished the evening in a box at the Opera and we forgot which opera it was. Her father invited me for lunch. As his wife was away in their estate in Lithuania, Nela took her mother's place,

Alina being rather aloof. After lunch Nela danced most gracefully a Mazur to my accompaniment of a Chopin mazurka. She dreamed of becoming a dancer and told me that she often joined in the exercises of the Opera ballerinas.

The time came for the concert in Lodz, where I was to play the G major Beethoven Concerto with Emil Mlynarski conducting the recently created orchestra of my birthplace. Our train left at eight in the morning on the day of the concert, arriving just in time for the rehearsal. The night before had been a heavy night for both of us. Mlynarski had given the premiere of *Parsifal* at the Opera, which finished at one in the morning, followed by a long supper given by him for the singers. For my part, I had accepted a great party in my honor after a brilliant literary cabaret show by Tuwim, Lechon, and Marian Hemar, which was a colossal success. In it they even made good fun of me. Later on they gave me some private entertainment with food and drinks. It was five in the morning when Ordynski reached his bed and I his couch. One can well imagine the state in which poor Emil Mlynarski and I arrived at the station at a quarter to eight, with formidable hangovers. We gave a tip to the conductor so that he would leave us alone in a first-class compartment to sleep at least until our arrival. At that moment, a well-known piano professor of the Conservatory, Josef Turczynski, came running up to us shouting joyously, "Here I am! Every week I go to Lodz for lessons. They begin at nine in the morning, but I succeeded in shifting the hours for today in order to be with you! Usually I leave the night before!"

He was just about to jump into our compartment when the gray-faced Mlynarski said to him in a low, sweet voice, "Zozio [Turczynski's nickname], we have to sleep. Please go to hell."

We did manage to rest a little but not nearly enough and we were practically asleep during the rehearsal. Fortunately the orchestra was well prepared by their usual conductor, and after a good afternoon's rest, we gave a decent performance. Nela appeared at the concert. I knew she had come for me and I was intensely happy. After the concert I had to face a dramatic situation; Emil (we now addressed each other as "thou") invited me for supper with his daughter at his hotel, but I had to take care of my family; they would never understand any deviation from our usual customs and I had to whisper to them that it was exceedingly important for my musical future to be on the best possible terms with the powerful Emil Mlynarski and promised to come home as soon as I could get away. The supper was a little tense because Nela could not understand why I couldn't stay with them the whole evening. But the next morning in the train I explained to her as clearly as I could how difficult it had been for me to be

with her at all. We talked and talked, standing in the corridor, and exchanged our first words of love. There were many things I had to tell her. I
begged her to meet me the next morning at eleven in the Lazienki Park on a
bench under Chopin's monument. I was to leave for Budapest the day
after.

The rest of the day and a sleepless night were spent at Ordynski's
apartment. I wanted desperately to marry Nela—yes, I wanted to marry.
She was the image of what I always loved and admired so much in Polish
women. It was true, she was beautiful, slim, and very well built, a small fine
face with the bluest eyes, like turquoise, an irregular nose, small beautifully
shaped ears, a fine forehead crowned by a mass of dark blond hair. Her
most striking feature was her long slender neck, which gave her a proud
bearing; but she was just eighteen and I was going to be forty in three
months. I did feel that she loved me. I was even sure of it. Could I take her
away from her young life spent in the loving care of a large family with
admiring uncles, aunts, and cousins, with her ambition of becoming a great
dancer, and bring her to my world and what I knew through my sad experience of the frailty not only of marriage as such but even of marriage based
on love? Would she be able to resist my so good-looking Spanish friends or
my hundreds of rivals for the favors of attractive young married women?
Men are afraid of young girls, they can bring them trouble, and I hope that
my readers remember my point of view about the difference between a
husband and a lover.

Next morning I found myself in a very nervous state. I had a decision
to make at the meeting in the park. Down in the street I could not find a
taxi and had to take a slow horse cab, which made me late for the rendezvous and still more nervous. But my decision was made. I was going to tell
Nela exactly and honestly what was on my mind.

I found her at the entrance to the park, hurt by my being late even
after my explanation. We walked to a bench and sat down without exchanging a word. I told her my love and my great wish to marry her, but then
continued with my misgivings and my terrible fear about the difference in
our ages and especially about her being so very young. "My darling, if you
love me well enough to be able to wait until I am sure that it is the right
thing for both of us to marry, I will be the happiest man in the world. One
thing I can tell you right away: you are the only woman in the whole wide
world with whom I would like to have a daughter."

She listened to me in silence and then said softly and sweetly, "I shall
wait." I left for Budapest with happy thoughts and filled with love. The
concert in the capital of Hungary was highly interesting in every way. I
played the B-flat major Concerto of Brahms, conducted by Ernö Dohnányi.
The public liked it but the approval of Dohnányi made me even more

happy. He invited me for a lunch the next day at which I met his beautiful wife, a famous Viennese actress, Elsa Galafres, who had left the great violinist Bronislaw Hubermann to marry Dohnányi. There I also met Zoltán Kodály and Béla Bartók. I was proud to be in the company of the three greatest musicians of Hungary.

Budapest enchanted me with its beauty, the Danube seeming to me much more proud and blue here than in Vienna, and the old town, Buda, overlooking the river from a hill, was truly a majestic sight. Pest, the modern town, had something of both Paris and Vienna. I spent the whole afternoon in a famous French tearoom where from four o'clock on you could see all the Hungarian beauties—but I had no eye for them. I sent a postcard to Nela just to let her know that I thought of her all the time. On the way to Paris, I stopped in Vienna for two days to see Mr. Knepler about future concerts and went to a delightful operetta by Leo Fall with Max Pallenberg, one of the greatest comics in the world. I was happy to come back to my dear rue Ravignan, number 15, in Montmartre and not to some hotel. It was good to see my books, my butterflies, my nice chairs, my red-covered bed again, and some lovely flowers that François had put around.

65

Friends began to call, among them Misia. "I'm glad you're back, Arthur. Come for tea. I have a nice surprise for you." Misia had guests; I remember her brother Cipa and Alexander Steinert with his young wife. All of them were very excited. Misia announced proudly: "You will hear an amazing record: Vladimir Horowitz playing the Third Concerto by Rachmaninoff." She piled up the three or four records on her turntable and we heard the most brilliant performance. It certainly was the finest record I ever heard. Misia noticed with pleasure the astounded expression on my face. "He is even better in concerts. He is going to give a recital at the Opéra. Are you going to be here?" On the date she mentioned, I was playing in London and I would miss hearing him again. I must frankly admit that the great ado and excitement about Horowitz gave me a little pang of jealousy. My staunchest friends and supporters, my most loyal admirers were now talking of nothing else but young Horowitz.

A little deus ex machina in the person of Villa-Lobos lifted my morale considerably. He arrived one morning with a manuscript and shouted from the door: "Rubsten, Rubsten! I wrote for you a long piece which is so much like you that you could have written it yourself!" I laughed at this exaggerated statement but when I saw his dedication on the first page of the manuscript, I was deeply touched. "Rudepoêma, pour piano solo à Arthur Rubinstein. Mon sincère Ami, je ne sais pas si j'ai pu tout à fait assimiler ton âme avec ce Rudepoêma, mais je le jure de tout mon coeur que j'ai l'impression, dans mon esprit, d'avoir gravé ton tempérament et que machinalement je l'ai écrit sur le papier, comme un Kodak intime. Par conséquent, si je réussis, ce sera toujours toi le véritable auteur de cette oeuvre."*

Heitor grabbed his manuscript out of my hands after the big hug I gave him, and rushed to the piano to play it for me. It was a very long and very complicated piece of music. The "Rude" of the title did not have the English meaning. In Brazil it meant "savage." When I asked him if he considered me a savage pianist, he said excitedly, "We are both savage! We don't care much for pedantic detail. I compose and you play, off the heart, making the music live, and this is what I hope I expressed in this work." We read it, playing it in turn with great difficulty, but I did recognize that it was a most original and in places a very beautiful work. It certainly made me want to learn it, I spent that whole day with Villa-Lobos, took him out for dinner, and we parted late at night.

On my return home, I put the *Rudepoêma* back on the piano stand and read it through again, this time undisturbed by the presence of the composer. It appeared to me to be a monumental attempt to express the origins of the native Brazilian *caboclos*, their sorrows and joys, their wars and peace, finishing with a savage dance. The idea of this work is somewhat similar to *Le Sacre du printemps*, but with the difference that whereas Stravinsky's work is clearly explained and each piece has a perfect form, Villa-Lobos' great opus is a vast improvisation, as are all his large orchestral poems. However, his immense gift for musical invention often compensated for the lack of form and his refusal of discipline. He remained a master in his shorter compositions, especially his piano pieces and songs. I personally could not describe him better than as a rough genius, an uncut precious stone. His generous dedication of the *Rudepoêma*, naming me in such flattering terms the co-author of his work, is really erroneous; my own talent as an interpreter is mainly based on my need for understanding the structure of a musical work.

---

* My true friend. I do not know whether I have really been able to assimilate your soul with this *Rudepoêma* but I vow with all my heart that I feel I have engraved your temperament, writing it mechanically on the paper like an intimate film. Therefore, if I have succeeded, you are the real author of this work.

Life in Paris, with its irresistible charm, again took hold of me. I was too weak to resist its temptations. Daisy Fellows, the beautiful niece of Princess Winnie, gave a brilliant ball, calling it "Le Bal de Tête," at which the guests had to appear as somebody else—a most original idea which made this ball one of the most amusing I remember. To give an example, the Countess Salverte (the well-known mistress of the pretender to the French throne), who looked like a twin sister of the famous dressmaker Jean Patou—and as one can imagine the obvious thing happened. The latter appeared as the Countess Salverte and the countess as Jean Patou and it was anyone's guess who was who. Princess Winnie de Polignac was grotesque as the fat bearded Tristan Bernard, who this time might have found it difficult to make a witty remark at this horrible caricature of himself. But she was pleased with herself, repeating to every newcomer, "Je suis Tristan Bernard." Henri Bernstein represented himself with a mask of his head made of papier-mâché placed comfortably on his crown while his own face was covered. As for myself, I chose modestly to represent King Alfonso XIII of Spain. The costumer who helped me previously found the right wig and characteristic mustache, which made my face look as much like his as possible. All I had to do was to stick out my bottom lip. We all tried to play our roles gaily until late hours, but were happy to find our own personalities again.

Christmas and New Year's celebrations were duly observed with late nights, foie gras, truffles, champagne, and all the rest. This kind of curriculum did not help my fingers to play with more precision. The telephone would constantly interrupt any attempt at playing a work from beginning to end.

I remember one afternoon, after a lunch in town, some friends came to my place. They wanted to hear the Liszt sonata which I was then preparing for a concert. In the middle of the piece, the telephone rang. One of the listeners lifted the receiver and put it quietly on the table. When I finished he hung up. A moment later, it rang again. I called François and said impatiently, "Tell whoever it is I'm not in." We all watched him. "Monsieur est sorti," François said. He listened for a moment and then said with great conviction, "No, you must be mistaken, Monsieur was not playing, it was me dusting the keyboard." We laughed heartily knowing that the caller had distinctly heard a good part of the sonata.

My mind was constantly in Warsaw with Nela and occupied with the thought of marriage. Deep in my heart I had hoped for a word from her reassuring me that she would wait, as she had promised, until I felt free of apprehensions and doubts. Not hearing from her disquieted me terribly; with all my hatred of writing letters I would have written her myself but a letter from me would only have repeated what I had said last time in the park. If I only could have felt like saying to her, "Yes, I am ready, I want you. I want to marry you right away!" I would have sent the message triumphantly with flowers. Instead, many little signs made me feel more insecure than ever. Now and then people would say unexpectedly, "When do you think you'll marry Nela? We hear it will be soon. There is great excitement about it in Warsaw." When leaving Warsaw, I was convinced that our love and the question of marriage would remain our secret.

For two or three months I was giving concerts in Spain and Italy, Brussels, and for the first time in Antwerp, Ghent, and Bruges. These cities gave me a deep artistic pleasure. In Antwerp it was the atelier of the great Rubens, kept as he left it; in Ghent I saw the triptych by van Eyck. After seeing the Madonna of Raphael in Dresden no painting since has touched me as much. The castle of the Duke of Flanders, which stands intact in the very center of the city, is akin in dignity and impact to the Tower of London and the Castel Sant'Angelo in Rome. Bruges "La Morte," as the poet calls it, is far from dead. It has the lifework of Memling and numerous canals that flow through the city with sweet melancholy past centuries-old houses. On one of these canals I saw from my boat some women making lace in long black dresses with the white caps you know so well from the old Flemish pictures. I regretted that Vermeer had not immortalized this scene.

On my return to Paris, I found an invitation to lunch from Misia. She had good company: Coco Chanel, her beautiful niece Mimi Blac-Belair, and Pierre Brisson, the brilliant drama critic of *Le Temps*.

"I have a pleasant surprise for you," Misia said. "After the recital which Horowitz gave at the Opéra with great success, I asked Rouché, the director of the Opéra, to follow it up with a recital by you. He just let me know that he has a date for you in May." I was too proud to show the intense joy the news had given me in front of the guests, but after the lunch, alone with Misia, I gave her a great hug in gratitude.

66

For this great event I prepared my program very carefully. If I remember well, I began with the *Appassionata*, three or four important works by Chopin, and after the intermission two or three pieces by Debussy, two Spanish ones, and I finished with *Petrushka*.

My concert at the Opéra made me very happy. It was the first time since my "second debut" at the Théâtre des Champs-Elysées that I was heard by a large Parisian audience, and this time in the finest theater in France. My success was greater than I expected. The public did not leave until I had played three encores. Among the friends who came backstage to congratulate me was a slim young man slightly taller than me, rather good-looking, who addressed me in Russian: "My name is Vladimir Horowitz," he said. "I heard you in Kiev when I was seven years old. That was my first concert." I expressed my regrets that I had not yet heard him and learned with pleasure that he was going to play at the Champs-Elysées in a few days. We had lunch together and he told me a great part of his life story. "My teacher was Felix Blumenfeld, the uncle of Karol Szymanowski. I gave many concerts in Russia." Then he told me at length how he and his friends Milstein and Piatigorsky succeeded in escaping from the difficult life in the Soviet Union. In Paris, we had a friend in common, the young composer and conductor Alexander Steinert from Boston.

The concert in the Champs-Elysées was crowded. I managed to obtain, at the last moment, a *strapontin*. I do not remember the whole program, but I shall never forget the two Paganini-Liszt études, the E flat and E major ones. There was much more than sheer brilliance and technique; there was an easy elegance—the magic something which defies description. He also played two major works by Chopin, the *Polonaise Fantaisie* and the *Barcarolle*, both masterly performances even if they went against my conception of Chopin. The greatest success of the evening was his encore, his own arrangement of the dance in the second act of *Carmen*. He brought the three repetitions to a shattering climax which made us jump up. When he had played his final encore, in a high state of excitement I rushed with the others to see him backstage. While he was dressing, his admirers, among them most of my friends, were shouting enthusiastic comments at each other and I was the loudest. Horowitz came out of his dressing room sweating and pale and received the great homage with regal indifference. When I came up to him he said, "Ach! I played a wrong note in the *Polonaise Fantaisie*." I would gladly give ten years of my life to be able to claim only one wrong note after a concert. On the way out, one lovely and very musical lady, a great friend of mine, said, "Arthur, pour la *Barcarolle* il n'y a que vous." This little sentence stuck in my mind for a long time.

Alexander Steinert invited me for dinner and wrote: "We are having Horowitz and don't forget that I have two lovely pianos in my drawing room." It was the first of many night-long sessions of music at Steinert's home; we played, Horowitz and I, everything at hand—works written for two pianos and arrangements of all sorts, such as the *Capriccio Espagnol* by Rimsky-Korsakov, lots of Wagner, whose music Horowitz was just begin-

ning to know, *España* by Chabrier. Sometimes Jacques Février, the fabulous *prima vista* reader, took my place at the second piano for things like
En Blanc et Noir of Debussy which both Horowitz and I had trouble
reading. But we had our revenge with the "Fêtes" from Debussy's *Noc-*
turnes. By then Horowitz and I were close friends. We called each other by
our first names with the familiar "thou" and he would come some mornings
to my place to consult me on his repertoire of effective encores; but I began
to feel a subtle difference between us. His friendship for me was that of a
king for his subject, which means he *befriended* me and, in a way, used me.
In short, he did not consider me his equal. It caused me to begin to feel a
deep artistic depression. Deep within myself, I felt I was the better musician.
My conception of the sense of music was more mature, but at the same
time, I was conscious of my terrible defects—of my negligence for detail,
my treatment of some concerts as a pleasant pastime, all due to that devilish
facility for grasping and learning the pieces and then playing them lightheartedly in public; with all the conviction of my own musical superiority, I
had to concede that Volodya was by far the better pianist.

67

         Carla called one morning to say: "I am in Paris and would love
to see you again and I have many things to tell you." I invited her right
away for lunch, feeling no grudge against her. She looked as beautiful as
ever, used her charm and her singsong voice to the best advantage, and told
me, with her sweet indifference, about her short love affair with my Spanish
friend. "He is so stupid," she said, "that I couldn't bear the sight of him
another moment. But I long to hear you play again." She flattered me. Well,
our friendship, lame as it was, continued. She liked to have me judge her
new dresses and hats. We would see a good play together, we continued to
be invited out together by our mutual friends. From Nela, no sign. Once,
while taking her back to the charming little house she had rented for the
season, I told her in a casual way, "Carla, I fell in love with a young Polish
girl. She is only eighteen but I want to marry her."

         "Oohh!" she said in her best singing voice. "Your old mania for Polish
women and for having a daughter!" And she laughed it off with an ironic
smile.

Paul and Zosia arrived and I gave a great cocktail party in their honor in my little garden. Afterward, when only a few friends remained, Paul and I played sonatas which were a balm to my heart. Together we made pure music. We planned to spend part of the summer together. Paul told me of the sensation both Horowitz and the Spanish pianist José Iturbi had caused in New York. It did not astonish me. The United States had certainly never heard piano playing of this kind before. As to myself, I had a large tour in view for the late autumn which would begin in Warsaw—and I thought of it with a trembling heart. I was almost sure that this time I would propose marriage to Nela. It was constantly on my mind.

One morning Sophie Kochanska called me up. "I have something disagreeable to tell you. Bronislaw Mlynarski came to see me and asked me if I knew what your intentions are with regard to his sister Nela. Do you intend to marry her? She is very disturbed about your silence. What shall I tell him?" This classic intervention of a brother in defense of his sister, reminding me sternly of my promise of marriage, upset me very much. It was the first time such a thing had happened to me. There were two English girls, at different times, I could have married; we talked about it but it always remained strictly between us. Nobody else knew or heard anything about it. This time, I felt suddenly trapped by the whole Polish population. I was glad to go to Warsaw for a concert and have the chance to find out what all this meant—whether Nela herself had instigated it, which I doubted with all my heart, or if it was just one of those horrible intrigues which are born of nothing. I for myself had decided to marry Nela; she was the only one in the world I wanted to marry, but only if I could be sure that she loved me the way I needed to be loved, completely and faithfully. Her silence and the indiscreet behavior of those around her disquieted me. I told Zosia to answer Nela's brother for me that the date of my marriage with her would be decided only by the two of us with no interference from anybody.

Carla asked me about my plans and about my concerts. "Are you coming to Rome?"

"No," I replied, "I have a lovely tour beginning with Warsaw, then Bucharest, Greece, Tel Aviv, and Egypt."

"Oohh! What a dream of a tour. I always wanted to see Greece and Egypt. Princess Marthe Bibesco has invited me to stay with her; her husband is a relative of mine and they live near Bucharest. When you play there, I could join you."

Her proposal did not appeal to me very much. I remembered our South American tour without pleasure and I did not expect to derive much satisfaction from visiting these romantic places with Carla after what had happened to our love affair. For the time being I said, "Well, if you would like to see Greece and Egypt, I am a good guide."

That summer the Kochanskis had gone for a cure and I went to Venice for a good rest before my tour. Lord Berners was again the other guest. We had many talks about music and we were joined at the Piazza by a highly intellectual Russian; there was nothing I enjoyed more than an intelligent exchange of points of view about the burning question of the reasons for our existence. Quite naturally, it never led to any conclusions but it was good to explore the different facets of it all. When alone, my thoughts were constantly occupied with Nela and the problem of marriage. My self-esteem was at its lowest. The pianistic exuberance and the technical ease of Vladimir Horowitz made me feel deeply ashamed of my persistent negligence and laziness in bringing to life all the possibilities of my natural musical gifts. I knew that I had it in me to give a better account of the many works which I played in concerts with so much love and yet with so much tolerance for my own lack of respect and care. It came to a point where I seriously considered giving up my ambition of a great pianistic career to become a piano teacher, giving concerts here and there, especially in places like Spain and South America, where my public accepted me unconditionally, just as I was. I knew that I was born a true musician but instead of developing my talent I was living on the capital of it.

On my return to Paris, I prepared for my forthcoming tour starting in Warsaw and decided to present my case truthfully to Nela. My plan was to go the following year to South America and pile up enough money to be able to provide my future wife with a comfortable living, because, besides using up the capital of my talent, I was still the spendthrift of old and always lived luxuriously on the last concert I had given, so that my bank account was always nearly empty.

Carla called one morning to ask, "When are you leaving for Warsaw?" When I gave her the date she said casually, "This is very convenient for my trip to Rumania. I can leave for Warsaw with you, stay for the concert, and be right on time in Bucharest. I'll wait for you there and we can continue your tour together." It gave me a shock. Nothing could have been further from my mind than the thought of having Carla in Warsaw. I rushed to see her.

"I would be glad to show you Athens and Cairo but I do not want you to go to Warsaw."

"Why not?" she asked, playing the innocent.

"You know very well why not," I said impatiently.

"But we don't need to be together," she said in her best singsong. "I shall stay in a hotel and you can stay in another one or stay with your friends." It became impossible to argue with her. My final word was: "You will be on your own if you go to Warsaw. I do not want to be seen with you."

Well, we did leave on the same train. I had wired Ordynski of my arrival, asking him not to tell anybody about it. At the station, Carla took the omnibus of the Hotel Europejski and I took a taxi. Richard told me that he had received an invitation for me for a party that night at the British Embassy. "Mrs. Max Muller called herself and I accepted for you. She said she had met you in Rome and was very enthusiastic about your concert." I did not dare to get in touch with Nela by telephone and even less to pay her a visit without knowing if I would be received. I counted on my concert the next day, where I was sure to see her and could ask her then to meet me. In the afternoon, I called up the Hotel Europejski to find out if Carla had a good room and if they were looking after her. Instead of answering my question they connected me with her right away. A cheerful voice said, "You know, we are both invited to a party at the British Embassy. They know me well from Rome. Please fetch me at nine o'clock, it is a buffet affair." This was just the sort of situation that I feared, but there was nothing else to do but escort her there. My only hope was that Nela in all probability would not learn about it.

When Carla and I entered the great reception room, the first people I saw were Emil Mlynarski and his daughter. My heart froze. The ambassador and his wife greeted us in the Roman fashion, like a couple of old friends, and began introducing us to the guests with great relish. Emil Mlynarski gave me a warm handshake but Nela turned her back. It was one of the rare moments in my life when I felt miserably unhappy. I did not pay any attention to Carla for the rest of the evening but almost forced Nela to follow me to a corner where I could talk to her. She looked at me with icy indignation and only squeezed through her teeth the words: "I have nothing to say to you."

"You have to listen to me," I said, impatient now. "I shall call tomorrow afternoon and explain everything. You have nothing to reproach me for." She answered with a bitter smile but agreed to receive me. She and her father left shortly afterward. Carla and I had to stay on, as she was the guest of honor. On the way to her hotel she said, "C'est cette petite blonde que tu veux épouser? Je pensais que tu aimais les Polonaises, mais c'est une boche."* I snapped back, "She is the very quintessence of the Polish girls I love."

"Mais c'est une boche," she insisted. I could have killed her.

After a horrible sleepless night—and this time certainly not due to Richard's uncomfortable sofa—I had my coffee early and went reluctantly to the concert hall of the conservatory where my recital was to take place to try out the piano and the bench as usual. But I had no thoughts for

* It is that little blonde you want to marry? I thought you liked Polish girls, but this one is a boche.

the concert. After a quick lunch in a café I rang the doorbell of the Opera apartment of the Mlynarskis. My heart was pounding as I was shown into a large room where Nela sat alone in a corner. She didn't utter a word. I began by telling her clearly the real facts about Carla and me, from the very beginning up to last night. "You can see that it couldn't be called a love affair anymore. When, after a long separation, I saw her again in Paris, I told her that I was in love with you and wished to marry you." To prove it I told her Carla's malicious comment about her. These last words produced in Nela a human smile at last. From that moment on we began to exchange our doubts and our disappointments, our indignation about the interference of others and all the suffering it had created for both of us. Nela said, "How could I trust you, how could I believe in your love when I heard from everybody around me that you jump from one love affair to another, that you don't take women seriously, that you tell everybody that you are an inveterate bachelor? But still," she said, "I would have ignored it all if you had written a single word. You asked me to wait for you but do you realize what it is for a young girl to wait for a man of your reputation who doesn't take the trouble, over such a long time, to reassure me that he meant what he said, that he *was* the man I had begun to love."

I was silent for a while, deeply ashamed. "Yes, my darling," I said, "you are right, you are absolutely right. I was a fool not to realize all this, not to understand it. I can see now what you went through, abandoned and left to yourself, having promised to wait for my decision, surrounded by people who don't take me seriously, and without a word of reassurance of the warm love I felt for you the whole time. I have little to say in my defense. True enough, I was a confirmed bachelor until I saw you." I told her about my past, about the darkest hour in Berlin and how I discovered my unconditional love of life. "From that moment on, my dearest, I was determined to live every moment to the fullest, but instead of developing my musical gifts I led the life of a sybarite, an epicurean." I reiterated my misgivings about the faithfulness of married women. "But in the depth of my heart I know that you are the only woman in the world I want to marry and I want a daughter by you. But to make it possible I must be able to provide you with the comfort you deserve, so please, please wait for me. Don't give me up."

Nela sat still, but I saw love in her eyes. When I mentioned the gossip and her brother's intervention she denied violently having had anything to do with it. "Zosia lied to you," she said. "My brother would never have done such a thing and if he did say anything she certainly distorted the meaning of it. But I feel I have to tell you something. There is a young pianist, Mieczyslaw Munz, who wants to marry me. He is terribly in love with me. He sends me flowers and letters. He even gave up a tour in Japan to be near me. I told him that I was in love with you but I admitted that I do not believe you mean to marry me."

I became terribly upset. "You can't marry him, Nela, you love me, don't forget it. I must leave now, I have a concert tonight. It is terrible for me to play in this state. I shall come again tomorrow afternoon. I can't let you marry a man you don't love."

The concert was a disaster. I played the program to the bitter end but the feeling for the music I played was not there. Carla sat placidly next to the Mullers and I could see Nela sitting next to some girl friends of hers, whispering to them, paying little attention to the concert.

My visit the next day was a sad one. I kept on imploring her to wait for me. I told her of my plans for South America. "After my return I feel sure I will be ready." I used all the tender words I knew to tell her my love and she finally consented to wait for me.

68

Carla left for Rumania by herself and I took the next train for Bucharest. This tour, which could have been so pleasant and interesting had I been alone, became difficult due to a series of disagreeable incidents. It was mainly my fault because I couldn't get the possibility of losing Nela to my young rival out of my mind. My concert in Bucharest took place at the Atheneul, a lovely and dignified concert hall. In a box facing me sat Carla and the Prince and Princess Marthe Bibesco, the well-known writer. Their presence displeased me because Carla had remarked to me that they did not like music. I remember having performed on that evening two concertos, I don't know which, and the *Variations symphoniques* of Franck at the end, which had a great success. After the concert the Bibescos and Carla came backstage to invite me for dinner the following evening at Mongoshvoia. The prince told me, "Your hotel porter will give the right information to the chauffeur of your car; in any case, everyone knows where it is." The time for the dinner was eight o'clock. Carla had told me wonders about that place, and of how famous it was for the palace itself and its surroundings.

Among the many autograph hunters, a young music student and his fiancée came back just to thank me. "We are both studying with Madame Musicesco." They didn't say their names, but many years later, after his death, I learned from his widow that the student was Dinu Lipatti, whom I deeply regret never having heard while he was alive, but whose records live with me and move me whenever I listen to them.

The porter of the Atheneul Hotel ordered a nice car for me to take me to the dinner at the Bibescos. As he opened the door of the car he said with a smile, "It is a half-hour drive but it is worth it! Everybody in Rumania knows this place."

We reached the outskirts of the city in about a quarter of an hour and then got on a road which seemed endless. We had been driving along for about forty-five minutes when I touched the shoulder of the driver and asked him, by gestures, if there was still far to go; it was getting late. Instead of answering, he stopped the car at some little house where one saw lights, obviously to inquire where we were. When he came back he made a helpless gesture. We started driving around, asking here and there but without success. It turned darker and was getting later and later. I was livid with anger and exhaustion, and helpless, not knowing the language. In one particular moment of exasperation I thought only of one word, which is known in many languages, and I shouted it: "Canaglia, canaglia!"*

We arrived at Mongoshvoia at nine-thirty. If I could have spoken Rumanian, I would have ordered the driver to go back to town, but I first owed it to my host to make excuses for my incredible delay. When I was shown into the great salon, I found the prince alone. Boiling with rage, I mixed my excuses with bitter complaints about what I had endured with the chauffeur. The prince, instead of showing some compassion for the state I was in, enjoyed my story and burst into loud laughter. This offended me. "I'm glad you find it so funny." I left the room, grabbed my coat and hat, ran out to the driveway, and screamed at the driver: "Hotel Atheneul, Bucharest!" The man lifted his cap meekly and we drove home in silence.

My dinner, back in my room, consisted of a cold glass of milk and a cracker with some bad cheese.

Two days later, when we met at the railway station, Carla greeted me with a giggle about the incident. "When you left in such a rage, my Aunt Marthe was furious with her husband and has asked me to express her apologies to you." We finished by laughing the whole thing off.

Athens welcomed us with a glorious blue sky. The manager of the orchestra drove us to an annex of the Hotel Grande-Bretagne, as there was

---

* "You dirty scoundrel" is perhaps the nearest to "Canaglia," but it is really impossible to translate.

no room in the hotel itself. This annex was a large villa which the great Prime Minister Venizelos had sold to the hotel. "Your first rehearsal takes place tomorrow at eleven o'clock and I'll fetch you at ten because the conductor wants to discuss the concerto with you." It was the G major of Beethoven and the young conductor's name was Dimitri Mitropoulos. I listened to the manager distractedly, as I was thinking only of a quick lunch and a tour of the Acropolis with Carla.

We climbed the steep stone steps with amazing alacrity and then we stood in awe. Carla's silent emotion made me very happy; she did have a real sense of art and beauty. For hours we visited the Parthenon and the Erechtheum. I showed her those female statues for which I had a very special admiration and which are clad modestly in front but expose their naked *kallipygos*.

We returned to the hotel in a state of euphoria. There was a telephone message from Sir Percy Lorraine, now the British ambassador in Greece. I called him immediately. "We will be delighted to hear you again, Arthur. I want you to know that I am married to the daughter of my colleague in Italy, whom you may have met in Rome. Can you dine with us tomorrow?"

"I would love to," I replied, "but I'm not alone. I am here with the Princess Carla Palladini. Would you mind having us both for dinner?" There was a short silence.

"Please hold on for a moment. I shall ask my wife."

After some time, I heard, "She would rather have you alone," in a slightly embarrassed voice.

I was embarrassed too. "In that case, I'm terribly sorry but I will not be able to come." I did not say a word to Carla, but I was very annoyed.

At the rehearsal next morning I met Dimitri Mitropoulos, a slim young man who greeted me in a charming way. "I was a pupil of Busoni," he said with a proud smile, "but my playing was not good enough to make a great career as a pianist, so I chose to be a conductor. I am very happy indeed to have you as a soloist." Our rehearsal was a bit difficult. Mitropoulos was hectic in his movements and the not too good orchestra did not follow his baton with precision. We repeated the concerto three times before we were satisfied that we would give a proper performance at the concert.

Marika Papaioannou was at the rehearsal. She had been studying with Schnabel and was now preparing her programs for a concert. I heard her play with great pleasure; it was the performance of a *musician* not just a pianist.

In the afternoon, Carla went by herself to the museum. I was about to have a rest when my friend Stefanides appeared. Cordial as ever, he gave me a big hug. "How long are you staying in Athens?" he asked.

"Three more days," but I added confidentially, "I did not come alone this time. Princess Carla Palladini is here with me." Stefanides jumped up from his chair. "Princess Carla?" he said. "I knew her well in Rome! I think she is the most beautiful woman I ever saw! Where is she staying?"

"Right here with me."

"You are the luckiest man in the world!" he exclaimed. I smiled fatuously.

"Don't be modest about it; she is lucky too." I liked that better. He would not leave before Carla returned. When she joined us he greeted her almost tearfully from emotion, kissed both her hands, and exclaimed, "You are more beautiful than ever!" Carla recognized him right away and was very pleased to see him again.

"Dear Princess," he said, "will you do us a great honor and dine at our house with my friend Rubinstein the day after the concert?" Carla looked at me and when I nodded she said, "Yes, with great pleasure, I will be delighted to meet your wife."

The second rehearsal, the following morning, went much better and, pleased with that, I invited Mitropoulos to lunch with Carla and me. He spoke Italian better than French, so our conversation was in that language. That night we had a good audience for the concert, but I was unhappy with the orchestra and the conductor. Fortunately we did finish together. The public was lukewarm but two encores saved the evening for me.

The Stefanides' gave a great dinner; we were at least twenty. The guests were members of the diplomatic corps and the Greek government and personal friends of the host. Carla and I were among the first to arrive, and soon after, Percy Lorraine and his young wife were announced. It is easy to guess how I relished the situation, especially because Carla was honored as a special guest. Stefanides introduced his guests to her, the Lorraines among them. Sir Percy shook hands with her most politely but his wife gave her a cool nod. Carla addressed her: "You probably don't remember me, but I saw you dancing in Rome at one of those boring balls for young girls!" And that was their only exchange during the whole evening. Carla, of course, did not know of the snub she had received. We stayed until the last guests were gone. Then our host, happy as a lark, toasted Carla in exuberant terms with the last glass of champagne.

We left for Alexandria the next day. Arditi's agent had made all the arrangements. My concert took place that same evening. The audience, as usual, consisted of Greeks, Italians, and Jews with a sprinkling of French; French, however, was the predominant language in the city. As Carla was anxious to visit Cairo, we left the next morning on the first train. This time I was lucky to find rooms for both of us at the famous Shepheard's Hotel, right in the center of the city. I was delighted to be playing this time in a real hall, the large Aula of the American College in Cairo; at this concert, I saw, in addition to the European colonists, a red fez here and there. The next day I put myself into the hands of an elegant guide dressed in Arab fashion in a long colorful robe with a collar of beads. He manipulated constantly another string of amber beads with his hands. He was good-looking and behaved with a mixture of servility and imperious authority. He took us to the Pyramids and showed them off to us as if they had been built for his own pleasure, as though he himself had sacrificed all those thousands of men without turning a hair. It was obvious that he was trying to impress the beautiful Italian lady. Every word he said was underscored with meaningful glances of his dark eyes. I enjoyed this scene more than I did the Pyramids; I had seen them before and they had not impressed me too much the first time either. The same little boy, or perhaps it was another one, ran up the hundred steps, for money, and we turned to the Sphinx, who kept her secret more impenetrable than ever. We went back to Shepheard's just in time for lunch, which I enjoyed more than the sight of the Cheops Pyramid. Shepheard's was famous for its haute cuisine; the chef would come up to your table himself and offer you anything you could want—for a good price, of course. While we had our coffee, the guide waited impatiently outside. "I shall show you three beautiful mosques," he said, adding, of course, "The finest in the world. But after that if you are not too tired I will take you just outside the city to the farm of my father, who raises thoroughbred Arab horses." We thought it would be polite to accept his offer and drove out to the farm in a taxi. On the way, the guide explained that his father relied on contributions from tourists to breed these horses. I paid up a good sum of money, but it lowered my respect for his father's standing in the world.

The "farm" looked like a casual setup for this sort of occasion. There were two or three uninhabited wooden shacks and a shaky enclosure in which there were three good-looking Arab horses. A poorly clad elderly man appeared from nowhere; the guide gave him an indifferent clap on the back and ordered him imperiously to show us the horses one by one. A handsome black stallion was saddled; we did admire this beautiful horse. The guide said emphatically, "This horse needs to be *ridden* to appreciate his true beauty."

"Let me mount," I said. "I like riding and it would be a new experience." I had never ridden a thoroughbred. Carla looked at me in astonishment. She whispered in Italian, "Think of your hands!"

"Do not worry." Clad as I was, helped by the guide I caught the stirrup with my left foot, adjusted my trousers comfortably in the saddle, and took hold of the bridle gently to give confidence to the horse, then tapped him lightly with my heel and off we went. Count Potocki's lessons came in handy. I made him trot for a while, then a short gallop, and after a few tours around the farm, stopped in front of Carla and the guide. I jumped off and said casually, "Yes, I enjoyed my ride." Both were rather open-mouthed and I had to do a good deal of explaining to Carla about why I showed such a command of horses. She was certainly much more impressed by this exploit than by my concert the night before. That evening at our dinner at Shepheard's a few people came up to congratulate me on my concert, among them two Frenchmen I had met in Paris, and I invited them to have coffee with us. Both were in Cairo for business and knew the city well. When Carla left us for a moment, the two Frenchmen invited me for a tour of the famous Cairo bordellos. "You will see a unique show."

I said, "But I couldn't take a lady with us."

"Out of the question, for heaven's sake!"

My old curiosity got the upper hand and I decided to join them. When I told Carla that I was going out with my two acquaintances she wanted to come too, but I refused and was adamant. She slammed the door angrily.

The three of us visited all sorts of places where some horribly unattractive women, mostly Arab, performed the most degrading acts, meant to excite us but producing just the opposite effect. I returned late that night, thoroughly disgusted, and went straight to bed in my room to rest after the day's exertions.

Rather late next morning I went down to breakfast expecting to find Carla but she was not there. When I knocked at her door she let me in; there was a fury in her eyes I had never seen before. I became aware of a strange fact about her: I had never seen her cry, ever. She was actually the only woman in all my life whom I had never seen in tears. The horrible scene in Rome, the many small quarrels, the many disagreeable times in South America when I was obliged to go to parties leaving her alone in the hotel, left her dry-eyed, without the slightest sign of self-pity. This time she was enraged as I had never seen her before and I felt disgusted and humiliated to see her taking so much to heart my leaving her out of the vicious spectacles of the night before. On the boat which took us to Brindisi, we hardly spoke to each other, and there, in Brindisi, after a cool handshake, she took the first train to Rome and I the first one to Paris.

69

Back at 15, rue Ravignan, I found everything in order and François brought a bundle of letters which took me a long time to read. Valmalète had sent proposals for concerts in France and Mr. Mitchell had some dates for minor appearances in England—most of them, as usual, on the seaside. Quesada wanted me to play all over Spain, and in Italy, besides the Santa Cecilia concerts, I was offered concerts in several cities where I had never played. I put off my decisions until the next day and enjoyed a wonderful dinner at Larue. Later on at the Boeuf sur le Toit, I found Auric, Fargue, and Cocteau and told them some amusing stories of my travels.

As Easter approached again, there were parties, lunches, and dinners. This constant merry-go-round caused me moments of great depression. So many concerts in small cities, always using more or less the same programs, began to wear out my natural love for music. It had become purely routine and I was thinking of nothing else but accumulating as much money as possible with the modest fees I received. And it is sad to admit that the money I gained this way served for nothing else but to pay for my extravagant way of living, to send expensive flowers to hostesses who had invited me to dinner, to buy elegant clothes, and to pay for taxis day and night. There was a funny paradox in the fact that whenever a lady, be it a Rothschild or any other, met me for dinner, she always liked to say, "Arthur, I hate to have my chauffeur waiting for me. If I send the Rolls away, could you take me home?"

"Certainly, with pleasure!" I would reply. "I have thousands of taxis waiting for me."

I began to hate to be alone. My seeing Nela again at that fatal reception at the British Embassy had left me with a bitter taste; I was prepared to propose marriage to her in spite of all the gossip and Zosia's interference, which had quite naturally irritated me in no small degree. I was asking her to share her life with a man twenty-two years older who was far from rich, whose artistic success was still limited, and who lived in a small bungalow on the hill of Montmartre. I fully understood her indignation at seeing the man she was ready to marry arrive in Warsaw accompanied by a beautiful lady whose love affair with me was well known, especially in Warsaw with its vicious passion for gossip. Now all my hopes were centered on the conviction that Nela loved me, but her revelation of the possibility of her marrying Munz shattered my plans. This Polish pianist had arrived in New York the year I left the United States forever. He had immediate success, which even then gave me a slight pang of jealousy, with his perfect technical equipment, and being a conscientious worker, he had made a brilliant career and became prosperous and free of care. In my eyes he was perfectly entitled to want Nela for a wife. He could offer her all she needed and was her elder by only a few years. I felt more paralyzed than ever for writing; to remind her of my love seemed preposterous. But on the other hand I was starving for a letter from her with reassurance of her love—the only thing that mattered; but she was too proud to write, and I admired her for that. Unfortunately I was proud too. Ever since my early years I had adopted a philosophical point of view that it is useless to ask for any favor from anybody unless you can make him *want* to do it for you without your having to ask.

All these thoughts gave birth to a certain revolt in me. The faithful acclaim I found in Spain, in Italy, and all over South America made me realize that my talent and my personality must have some secret power which enabled me to keep their enthusiasm alive for so many years. This revolt became a strong determination to show in some way that these countries could provide me with enough money to show Nela that she would not be marrying a pauper. And so, the spendthrift which I was began to economize. I gave all the concerts in Europe which were offered to me but this time I kept as much money as I could and went even so far as to open a *bank account* in the Banque Transatlantique on the Boulevard Haussmann, which represented a powerful bank in Argentina. I wrote a long letter to Francisco Ruiz to arrange as many concerts as he could in Argentina and Uruguay. I wrote another letter to Pellas in Rio de Janeiro to do the same for Brazil. This time I set aside three full months for concerts in these countries, not counting the two long voyages.

I embarked on the *Andes*, a British steamer I knew well, armed with a dozen books to read on the long crossing. Before sailing I had had a wonderful surprise in Paris. Karol Szymanowski had written a Symphony Concertante for piano and orchestra and dedicated it to me. The work was beautiful. It was his first large work in the Polish musical idiom, and it was music after my heart. He had promised to send me the first printed copy.

On the boat I spent whole days sitting on the deck reading. Next to me sat a bulky gentleman occupied in the same manner. Our books made us acquainted. He was Emile Vandervelde, the leader of the Belgian Socialist

Party, a famous statesman. We often interrupted our reading with interesting conversations about politics and I was happy that he listened to my modest remarks with great interest. Halfway through the voyage we were both finished with our supply of books, so we promptly exchanged them and started reading afresh. We were both winners. I learned a lot about the state of the world and he was entranced by the marital dramas in French novels which he had never read.

As we approached Rio, the wonder of this city moved me as at my first view of its unique beauty. I took up my quarters at the Copacabana Hotel, a glorious place right on the world-famous beach. My friend Carlos Guinle had built it and installed a gambling casino. Pellas succeeded in arranging an extensive tour for me with six concerts in Rio, two of them in the Municipal Opera House and the other four in the old opera house.

Carlos and Gilda Guinle invited me for a dinner to welcome me. All their friends were there to greet me in the most cordial way. I felt that they were happy that I was alone this time in Rio. They gave me astounding news: "Gabriella Besanzoni married Enrique Lage, the greatest shipping magnate of Brazil." I was open-mouthed. "When did that happen?" I asked.

"Two years ago."

"Is she in town?" I asked a little nervously.

"No, she left for Rome to stay with her family." I gave a hidden sigh of relief.

My opening concert went well. The *cariocas* remembered me after my absence of four years with the same love as before. On this occasion we became even closer to each other because on my previous visit I had played with less abandon; then I had felt constantly nervous about Carla's presence, but now I thought of nothing but music. During intermissions I like to be left alone in the artist's room, but this time Pellas came in and announced, with respect in his voice: "The sister of Mrs. Lage would like to see you." For a moment I didn't know who he meant, but then I remembered Gabriella's sister Adriana at the Folies-Bergères on that fateful night in Paris. When Pellas showed her in she exclaimed, "Dear Arthur, what a joy to see you again!" We exchanged fraternal kisses, but when Pellas left, she became aggressively flirtatious. It was quite evident she wanted to find out what her sister Gabriella and Carla Palladini saw in me. In the old days, when I felt free, I wouldn't have minded showing her what she wanted to see; but now I remained a cold fish. She did not show up again.

Villa-Lobos didn't come back to his country until much later, in triumph, as the world-famous Brazilian master. Then, sponsored by the government, he founded the Brazilian Academy of Music, of which he made me an honorary member. At the great ceremony of investiture I replied in Portuguese to Heitor's speech. That same night we laughed heartily, remembering our first meeting at that poor cinema, his rude behavior, and the utter disdain in which he was held by the musicians of Rio.

After the last concert there I left as usual for São Paulo, but this time I played not only in the capital itself but in several smaller cities in that province. I even had a chance to spend a weekend at a coffee *fazenda*, which impressed me not so much with what I saw there as with the exquisite taste of the freshly ground coffee itself; its aroma reached me across three or four rooms. Its only rival is the coffee of Bogotá, Colombia. Italy, too, can provide you with a fine cup of coffee but it takes them a good half hour there to give you no more than a dozen drops.

I went further north to Salvador and the province of Bahía and even to Recife and Pernambuco. It was there, sitting in a café reading the local paper, that I learned of the tragic death of Frederic Harman, of my ominous Berlin and Warsaw days, from a heart attack while conducting the overture of *Die Meistersinger*. He fell dead on the podium during the passage he most loved.

I remember particularly the state of Minas Gerais, which means "general mines" for its deposits of diamonds and other precious stones. Its capital has a lovely name, Belo Horizonte, and in recent years the new federal capital, Brasília, has been established in Minas Gerais. I was happy to put a good amount of money into a bank in Rio de Janeiro at the end of my Brazilian tour.

70

In Buenos Aires I was sad to learn that my dear motherly friend Doña Susana Quintana had passed away, and her death left a void in the city. In a way she had been the sponsor of my success in Argentina. Her daughters continued to invite me to their house but the warmth and goodwill that the dear old lady felt for me, so soothing and relaxing amid the turmoil of my activities, were lost. There was more sad news about the bankruptcy of Mr. Martínez de Hoz, in whose house I had found so much hospitality and help. The whole town spoke of nothing else. This family was one of the most socially prominent in the city and was extremely rich. Their estate in the south, Chapadmalal, called an *estancia* in Argentina, was the pride of the country. Mr. Martínez de Hoz used to go every year to England to buy livestock. One day he made me attend a sensational sale of pedigreed bulls called short-horns, at which he became the proud owner of a champion bull for 100,000 pesos. There was an improvised dinner party after that at which the cook, by mistake, slaughtered a champion fowl instead of an ordinary chicken. When I visited them this time, the household was in an uproar; the house had already been sold and the family was moving to an apartment near the Plaza Hotel. Fortunately, two sons of Mr. Martínez de Hoz were married to millionaire heiresses and so, in some miraculous way, Chapadmalal remained in the hands of the family.

Luís and Nena Salamanca were both in town. This whole disaster in which my sympathies were so much involved had one result which gave me great moral satisfaction. Luis Salamanca, a very distinguished descendant of an old Spanish aristocratic family, married Nena for money, as was the habit among the impecunious sons of noble families who would have felt disgraced by professional work. During the first years of their marriage Luis treated his wife in the most careless and egoistic way. The *beau monde* of Buenos Aires was often outraged by his behavior at their social gatherings. More often than not, he would enter a salon, take a look at the guests, and say loudly to his wife, "Esto es un aburrimiento" (This is a bore). At the first opportunity he would leave his wife with the guests, find some room with a comfortable couch, take his shoes off, and go to sleep until it was time to return home. His misbehavior was so widely known and laughed at that some people were disappointed when he behaved properly. Now, when his wife was no longer the heiress to a great fortune, the true blood of the aristocrat showed itself; overnight, Luis Salamanca became the most attentive husband, took full care of his wife, gave her a home in Madrid, and obtained for her the coveted title of Lady-in-Waiting to the Queen.

One day, having coffee in the Plaza, I saw my friend of the flowerpot signals. She astonished me by passing by indifferently, although she was well aware of my presence. After all these years I found it unnecessary to be discreet and went up to her. "Don't you recognize an old friend?" I asked, slightly hurt. She was as beautiful as ever. She answered with indignation: "I shouldn't even speak to you after the insulting way you treated me the last time you were in Buenos Aires." I was speechless with astonishment. "When I telephoned your room," she continued, "a woman told me in the most offensive terms not to call again and threatened to throw me out if I tried to see you." Good old Carla! I had a hard time putting things right and only after a long while did she consent to sit down and resume our old friendly relations.

The day of my arrival I had worked out my tour in Argentina and

Uruguay with Francisco Ruiz. I agreed to play in most of the provincial towns and demanded a high fee, which was often granted. Buenos Aires and Montevideo made the largest contribution toward the sum I wanted to accumulate, which was exactly a million French francs. This amount I thought would enable me to give my future wife a pleasant way of life. The least I could offer. It is on purpose that I have not mentioned the quality of my playing at these performances; as far as I can remember, I played with more care. I practiced before each concert and in general gave a good account of myself. But my mind was set on the money I was making and not on the music. And I would like to declare that this was the only time in my life that music ceased for a while to be the very pulse of my existence. After every concert I greedily added up the earnings and watched carefully how much I still needed to make in order to reach my goal. At the same time I was living more modestly than on my previous visits. I took my meals in some modest restaurants in the center of the city and only from time to time allowed myself a nice fresh *pejerrey* at the grill of the Plaza.

My frugal way of living extended even to refusing the usual supper parties after my concerts. I preferred a modest snack in my room. The only companions I liked around me were friends connected with musical matters. Rafael González, an excellent pianist and teacher, with his charming wife, Victoria, became the closest friends I had in Buenos Aires. There was also Germán Elizalde, a man of culture and a passionate lover of music, whom I saw almost daily. Thanks to him, I met two sisters of my unforgettable Amelia Luro, who, during that strange summer I spent at Caux with the Harmans, had sung tangos so sweetly that they still ring in my ears. We used to go together to cinemas and to some concerts given by a newly created orchestra that had Juan José Castro as permanent conductor. The program announced the arrival of Fitelberg as guest conductor. Returning from Rosario, I found that Fitelberg had already given one quite successful concert and I arranged with my friends the Gonzáles' to hear the second one. I promised my friends that they would hear a fine performance of a large work of Strauss.

Fitelberg began with a Beethoven symphony, which did not come off very well, and then after intermission the *Heldenleben* of Strauss. During the intermission, we went backstage to meet him. We found him not very happy about the Beethoven. "This orchestra has much to learn," he exclaimed. Then he smiled at me and said, "I have news for you, Arthur: Nela Mlynarska married Mieczyslaw Munz in Warsaw. I thought that might interest you . . ."

It was a terrible shock, of course. For a moment I froze, but the news did not surprise me. For months I had been weighing that possibility constantly in my mind. But it finished something in me. More cynically than ever before, I felt *après moi le déluge*. I just didn't care about anything. I thanked Fitelberg with a smile for his news, didn't tell my friends about what had just happened to me, and decided to return on the next boat to Paris.

71

Alone in my room I couldn't sleep for hours trying to find out if I had lost her through my own fault. There is one hard, egoistic trait in my character. I am not able to love without being loved in return. So writing to a girl that I loved her, begging her to wait until I was ready to marry her, knowing that she was considering marrying another man, went completely against my nature.

An English steamer took me to Cherbourg. On the long voyage I spent my time reading in my cabin or on deck, exchanging a few words with other passengers only at mealtimes. *Don Quixote* completely absorbed me. I had read it in French and tried to learn Spanish with it, but the *castellano* of Cervantes' time caused me great difficulties. But now it was a pure joy to live again with this great book which gives such a lesson of deep human values, with its divine humor that brings tears. I owe a great debt to Cervantes: he was better company at this time than any friend could be.

It was the beginning of September and Paris was still empty. I found nothing better to do than go to Deauville and play baccarat instead of the piano. I was sure to win: "unlucky in love, lucky at cards"! Deauville, Biarritz, and Cannes were the only places where I liked to gamble. I went not so much to win or lose money as to enjoy the atmosphere of an ideal private party. We were all *habitués*, smiling and talking to each other but without being personally engaged. We sat around the baccarat table in good company, losing our money with elegance, giving a congratulating smile to the winner. The great season of Deauville was over; only the usual flock of confirmed gamblers remained. The boardwalk and the bars and restaurants around it were empty. Only a few people were to be seen in the streets. The jewelry shops were closed; but the gaming tables were crowded.

Dressed in my dinner jacket, after a quick dinner I entered the casino's graceful building and was confronted by three severe gentlemen in charge who asked me for my passport, made me sign a card with my particulars, and then I had to pass by the discreet draftsman who drew rapidly a profile of everyone who passed the severe requirements.

Gamblers are never hungry. A dinner or supper is lost time to them. While the croupier is shuffling for the new deal they rush to the buffet, eat two cold hard-boiled eggs and a sandwich of anything from cheese to caviar (depending on their winnings) washed down with a glass of beer or champagne. When the croupier has the shoe made up again, they rush back to their seats. Following the custom, I had my eggs and, as my money was still intact, two sandwiches—the reader may guess what kind!

I had taken a large sum of money (100,000 francs) with me and I left at seven in the morning without a penny. I walked to the hotel fighting a cold wind, paid my bill, waited two hours in the station for my train sipping bitter coffee, and arrived in Paris utterly exhausted.

Next weekend I took the train back to Deauville, this time with 300,000 francs obtained from the Banque Transatlantique by giving the order to sell some of my Argentine bonds. I was determined to wait for a seat at the big table; it was the only way of recuperating my losses.

The season in Deauville cost me over half a million francs. I considered this great loss of money to be my wedding present to Nela.

72

The Kochanskis arrived from Zakopane and stopped off for a few weeks in Paris before returning to the States. Zosia complained that Paul had refused to take his annual cure and I did find him looking pale and tired but with the same vitality as ever. "I am exhausted," he conceded. "Karol is writing a beautiful second concerto for the violin and needed my help for the solo part. We spent hours and hours working at it but I feel happy to be of any use to him." During his stay we were constantly together. We went often to Misia's, where we liked to play sonatas.

At 15, rue Ravignan I gave a small party and Paul and I played for our friends. It began as a cocktail party but I kept the most musical of my guests for a buffet supper and they stayed until late that night listening to stories and enjoying Paul's brilliant imitations of famous artists.

Paul's presence worked miracles for me: thanks to him I calmed down and lost the bitterness of the last weeks. A few days before leaving for New York, Paul came alone to see me, "about a serious matter," he said. "I'm going to be rich, Arthur, and I want you to become rich too. There are now ways in America which make it easy for people to make fortunes by buying stock on Wall Street on credit with a small initital deposit. I put up ten thousand dollars for stocks which are now worth one hundred and fifty thousand and their value grows day by day. I wouldn't dream of selling yet because my broker assured me that it will soon reach a half a million dollars. Why don't you do the same? I am sure you can easily put up the initial sum and I can do what is necessary for you."

His story seemed to me a fairy tale. I was greatly impressed with what he told me but was far from being convinced. "You know very well, Paul, that I can spend a whole night playing chemin de fer, that I can get excited by roulette, and we both like to play poker, and you remember our famous piquet game in Warsaw where we won a hundred thousand rubles which we never meant to pay." We laughed heartily. "But you see," I continued, "all these games are played with me *present*. I hold a hand, I put up my money on a certain number at roulette, I decide myself if I shall outbid my partner at poker or bridge. But I do hate to put one single dollar into something over which I have no personal control. Your story about getting rich so rapidly frightens me a little. It seems so completely illogical. In every game, if you win it means someone else loses. But here, everybody appears to be a winner." I not only refused to get involved in his scheme but warned him from my heart not to trust his broker. "These men can be dangerous." Paul laughed all this off. "You have no imagination, Arthur. You will never make real money." Well, I never cared about money itself, only for the things it could provide. At our farewell, we both stood by our own convictions.

Ernesto de Quesada proposed by letter a short tour in Mexico. "My agent," he wrote, "can offer you three concerts in the now completed Teatro de Bellas Artes. He has also planned some concerts in Puebla and Monterrey. All these concerts are on a percentage basis, which will be very profitable for you as your name lives in their memory here after your famous twenty-six concerts in 1919. You have a choice of several fine boats sailing for New York at the beginning of January and the trains from New York to Mexico City are better now and quite safe. The revolution is over and the country is now becoming prosperous."

I liked the idea of going to Mexico again, and this time without danger, so I accepted Quesada's proposal. I filled the time before my departure for Mexico with the usual round of concerts in Spain and Italy and made a prolonged stay in London, where I spent Christmas and New Year. At a luncheon at the Cholmondeleys', I mentioned my Mexican tour. "When are you going?" asked Lady Cholmondeley. When I said it would be in January, she exclaimed, "we are sailing for New York in January. Rock [she always called her husband Rock, short for Rocksavage, since their marriage] is going to play polo for England against the American team—we are sailing on the *Majestic;* can't you take the same boat?" I liked the idea, the date was just right, and I found a nice cabin.

It was an amusing voyage. The Cholmondeleys invited me to join their table at meals, during which I learned all about the game of polo. "All my polo ponies are on board," he said, "and I was lucky enough to find these English players; one of them has the highest handicap, which is 10, and the others have 8 and 7." He didn't mention his own handicap. All this was very interesting, but I must say that Lord Cholmondeley did snub his teammates during this journey. He never invited them to join us but sometimes at coffee he went to their table to discuss horses, stableboys, etc.

There was also a famous person on board, Vladimir de Pachmann, the Russian pianist. He was an old man now and was on his way to his last tour of the United States. I remembered him from my Berlin days, when I heard him in several concerts playing quite beautifully short pieces by Chopin and Schumann, but pieces in larger forms were scarce in his repertoire. Well known as a comic character, with his very large round bald head on a short body, he would stop in the middle of a trill, lift his fingers, which continued to trill in the air, and confide to the public with a wink: "Very difficult, very difficult!" After a successful concert, he would stop the applause and affirm loudly, "There are only two pianists in the world: The other one is Godowsky." Dozens of stories circulated about his clowning, probably not all of them true but always very funny. I had been introduced to him in Berlin and since then he had always treated me in a most friendly way, giving me tickets for his concerts, and so it was not astonishing that, knowing I was on the boat, he invited me to his cabin. I found him in a luxurious suite consisting of a living room and two cabins, one for himself and the other for his secretary and his wife. He received me lying in bed but was quite alert and in a good mood. He smiled at me with his typical clownish expression, let me sit down on the foot of the bed, and said in a whiny way, "I'm an old man and have to lie in bed—this terrible sea, this terrible sea!" And right away, he added, laughing, "But Pachmann plays better than ever!"

I became his daily visitor, enjoying his funny ways, and later at lunch or dinner I amused the Cholmondeleys' with my imitations of his funny faces and with stories about him. They would roar with laughter and one day Sybil exclaimed, "Arthur, I must meet that man, you must make it possible." I was a little doubtful about it, but I had to try.

At my next visit to the old pianist, I told him, "There is a lady, one of your great admirers, who is terribly anxious to be introduced to you." He made a disgusted face.

"A lady? I'm an old man, I'm in bed, what can I do with a lady?"

"She is the Marchioness of Cholmondeley. Her husband is a Chamberlain of the King." His face became more sour.

"What do they want of me, Chamberlain, lady, March . . ." I felt I had to give him more details. "She is the granddaughter of the great banker Baron Gustave de Rothschild." My gambit produced an expression of admiring wonder.

"Rothschild?" He rubbed his thumb and forefinger together. "Very rich!" he said. I nodded.

"All right," he said. "Bring her tomorrow at noon. I will get out of my bed."

Sybil thanked me effusively. At noon next day, I knocked on Pachmann's door. It was opened by his secretary. "Please take a seat, the Maestro will be right with you." We waited a good quarter of an hour. The door opened and Vladimir de Pachmann entered in a black frock coat with silk lapels, stiff white collar, and a tie, in black shoes, and with diamond rings all over his fingers (he was a famous collector of diamonds of different colors). He shook my hand and then, pointing at Lady Cholmondeley, he asked a little too loudly, "Rothschild?" Sybil blushed. She did not know that this name had done wonders with the Maestro. He walked up to her, made a short bow, and looked disapprovingly at an emerald brooch that she wore. "Bad stone, your emerald," he said, "but look at my beautiful diamonds!" and he spread out his ten fingers, which were covered with them. Sybil was so scared to death by this whole show that she was unable to utter a word. She stood up, whispered a few polite, inaudible words, and left the cabin, followed by me.

At lunch she tried to tell the whole story to Rock but laughed so much he couldn't understand a word of it. For years it was enough to pronounce Pachmann's name for her to burst into uproarious laughter.

I decided to take the train for Mexico the day after our arrival in New York. I did not want to see anybody, not even Paul; he might try all over again to convince me of the great sums to be won on the stock market. The one person I did want to see again was Paul Draper after those many years, so I took a taxi to the last address of his I knew. There I heard the sad news: my poor old friend had died a few months before after a terrible attack of delirium tremens.

It was a long journey to Mexico City but quite comfortable. I was able to read the whole time in the lounge car, sipping coffee and smoking cigars.

The Mexican capital seemed to be a different city this time; busy, smiling crowds in the street, tall modern buildings on the wide main avenues, and a large square with a monument to an Aztec hero.

Ernesto's agent was very competent. He took me to the best hotel in town, where I found a comfortable room and bath with all the modern conveniences. We lunched at a very engaging Spanish restaurant with the name of Prendes, which I adopted henceforth on all my visits to Mexico. My friend Manuel Ponce gave me a brotherly welcome but was about to leave for Paris, where he wanted to continue his studies in composition. My concerts this time were of quite a different nature than the ones during the revolution. The audience was now composed of the new prosperous bourgeoisie and many foreigners, mostly Americans who had come to help develop the natural resources of this wealthy country, rich in oil and minerals. All these changes had taken place in less than ten years. The Teatro de Bellas Artes was built of marble with a regal staircase leading to the auditorium. The ground floor was given over to exhibitions of paintings and sculptures and other cultural activities. I felt as if I were playing in a new city for the first time, which sounds rather absurd when one thinks that I had played twenty-six times in six weeks only ten years before. But I must state with deep satisfaction that my new Mexican public, like that of Rome and Madrid, became staunch and faithful to me. At the third concert, I heard cries of "Come again, come again!" which touched me very much.

Monterrey and Puebla had now become industrial cities, but in both places I found a greater love for music than before. After my many visits to North, Central, and South America, I came to the conclusion, and this is my very personal opinion, that the Mexicans and the Brazilians are by nature the most musical people on the whole continent. They are, of course, far from having the vast musical education of the United States or Western Europe, but they are *born* musical. I found the same phenomenon in Russia. The Germans *learn* music more thoroughly than other people but they do not have a *natural* understanding of music they have not learned. Russian peasants walking home from work sing a cappella; they guess the right harmonies, the right intervals, and sing by instinct.

In Mexico City I found a letter from Cuba written by an unknown concert manager—at least he called himself so—who urged me to give two or three concerts in Havana on my way back to Europe. With the soft spot in my heart that I always felt for Cuba, I accepted his proposal. On the way to Veracruz, I passed through the state of Yucatán, the land of the Mayas, the most advanced civilization of ancient Mexico. It is still the state of which Mexicans are most proud.

When I landed in Havana, a young man, my correspondent, met me with great demonstrations of friendship. "You don't remember me," he said, "but I met you once when I was working for Braccale. I studied music but had to give it up for the simple reason that I didn't have enough talent. But now I try to bring fine artists to this island and you are the first I wanted to present."

In my hotel room, discussing our concerts, I discovered that he did not know much about what it takes to be a good manager. I found myself in the situation of having both to play concerts and manage them too. I was mainly occupied with the posters for the streets, with the publicity in the papers, with finding the right piano, the right stool, and a tuner, who like many of his colleagues was usually drunk; no little activity for a man who should be mainly occupied with Bach, Beethoven, and Chopin. My young manager was, however, an expert on cigars and he knew the best places for coffee. During a lunch to which I invited him, he revealed to me the fresh little crabs, a specialty of Cuba.

My first concert took place a week after my arrival. With all the work we did to prepare it, it was successful. I played with pleasure, my audience was most appreciative, and the second concert was sold out. Between Mexico and Cuba I made a nice little pile of money and arrived in New York just in time to sail to Europe.

73

The change of climate and atmosphere cheered me up considerably. I arrived home in good spirits and resumed my life in Paris at its gayest. I saw all the new plays with the unique Victor Boucher, Max Dearly, Jules Berri, and Harry Baur. If I remember well, Sacha Guitry produced the *Mozart* with the role of the young Wolfgang Amadeus delightfully played and sung by Yvonne Printemps. Reynaldo Hahn wrote music which was just right for this little comedy. I was also an assiduous follower of the cinema; Hollywood and its stars were at the peak of their fame in the 1920's and 1930's. The lavish productions which cost millions of dollars were impressing the whole world. The stars of both sexes became idols; one spoke of them intimately: Garbo became Greta; Dietrich, Marlene. There was Clark, there was Gary, and, of course, all of them were topped by the little man called Charlie. Chaplin would come to Europe and be invited by the Duke of Westminster for weekends. When one of these stars happened to be in Paris, crowds followed them in the streets and made their lives miserable. The whole thing was contagious. Highly intellectual people, academicians, and even poor pianists like myself fell for Greta or Ginger like everybody else. I remember seeing six times in a row *The Gay Divorcee*, which enchanted me by the incredibly beautiful dancing of Ginger Rogers and Fred Astaire to the music of Cole Porter. Fred Astaire's small, dry toneless little voice had a quality that reached your heart right away. His little songs could touch me more than a famous soprano or tenor at the opera.

At the Boeuf sur le Toit and at other so-called intellectual nightclubs, conversations about the recent Prix Goncourt or the newly discovered Kierkegaard or about the latest ballets of the Diaghilev company gave way to heated quarrels about who was the greater star or which film was better.

All this sounds as if I never touched the piano. Well, the truth was quite the contrary. Sir Henry Wood, during my last visit to London, had given me a score of a concerto by the English composer John Ireland. "My dear Rubinstein, why don't we give the first performance of it?" I promised to consider his proposal, took the score home, read it, and liked it. This music was fresh and had a subtle English flavor to it; and it was well written for the piano. So, in spite of the feverish social activities in Paris, every morning after breakfast I was at the piano learning this charming concerto. Sir Henry gave two full rehearsals to the work, which helped me to become quite familiar with it, and the performance was a success. I was proud to have overcome my natural laziness and to have shown the English my good understanding of their musical idiom.

At this concert a man named Fred Gaisberg reminded me of our meeting in the United States. "I don't think you remember me," he said, "but I am here working for 'His Master's Voice' gramophone company and I wanted you to make records for us." I laughed, "Don't try to persuade me. The piano sounds like a banjo on records. In the old days in America I refused to have anything to do with it."

"Well," he replied with a smile, "will you at least agree to have lunch with me at a nice place?"

"Certainly! If I refuse to make records I have nothing against a good meal." We made a date; he fetched me in his car and we drove for a long time. I asked him, "Is this restaurant a special place in the suburbs?"

"Yes, indeed. I'm taking you to Hayes, where we make the records."

"So this is kidnapping? Instead of giving me something to eat you will point a gun at me and force me to make a record, eh?"

"Don't be scared," he laughed. "We will give you a very good lunch, but what will happen after is in God's and your hands." We reached the imposing factory building after a good half hour and went straight to the restaurant. The food was astonishingly good for a place of that sort. Gaisberg introduced me to some interesting musicians who were busy recording, and then came the attack. "Please, please, Mr. Rubinstein, play just one piece of your choice. We swear it will not be published and we can play it back to you right away so you can judge for yourself how it sounds." I could not resist for long. After my coffee and a cigar we went to one of the recording rooms where they had a Blüthner piano. It was not a concert grand, and when I objected to playing it, Gaisberg said, "Try it and we will see . . ."

Well, this Blüthner had the most beautiful singing tone I had ever found. Suddenly I became quite enthusiastic and decided to play my beloved *Barcarolle* of Chopin. The piano inspired me. I don't think I ever played better in my life. And then the miracle happened; they played it back to me and I must confess that I had tears in my eyes. It was the kind of performance I dreamed of and the sound reproduced faithfully the golden tone of the piano. (These were the first recordings made with the electronic process.) Gaisberg had won.

This was a very important day; a new life began for me. From then on and up to now as I write, public concerts alternated with serious conscientious work in studios specially built where I would sit at the piano all by myself and play with great care, and at times with inspiration, while in another room, invisible to me, three or four gentlemen were busy perpetuating my performance on turning discs. In the beginning our records preserved our true performance, unaltered, with wrong notes here and there or a phrase which we could have played better. We were not allowed to hear back what we had played right away; the recording had to remain untouched until a matrix could be processed. Of course, we were allowed to repeat a piece until we thought we couldn't do it better. For my part, I was always apt to choose a performance with a spark of inspiration even if it had some not too noticeable imperfections rather than a too careful note-perfect version.

Right there in Hayes, Mr. Gaisberg proposed a contract for five years and I was ready to sign it.

A few days later I left for Glasgow to play with the Scottish Orchestra the Brahms B-flat Concerto. The conductor was a young Englishman of Italian descent, John Barbirolli. He played the cello but like many other cellists he had become discouraged with his instrument's limited repertoire and began a successful career as a conductor. With him, it was a case of

love at first sight. We felt our music the same way and inspired each other
with our phrasing. For once I could play the concerto with closed eyes—I
never had to look at him. The concert was a great experience in my life.
The public in both Glasgow and Edinburgh must have felt it because they
gave a great reception to both of us. John and I became close friends.

74

   François woke me up one morning: "Princess Edmond de Polignac wants to speak with you."

   "Cher Arthur," she began in her nasal voice, "I would like you to give
a concert in my house. All my friends would be delighted to hear you."
After a little pause, she added, "Of course, quite professionally. What is
your fee for these private appearances?"

   I always hated to discuss money with friends. "Chère Princesse," I
answered, "it will be an honor and a pleasure to play for your guests and
even more so for you, but please discuss the terms with my representative,
M. de Valmalète." I liked the idea of playing at one of her famous musical
gatherings; she always invited people who were earnestly interested in
music. That same afternoon, Valmalète came to see me. "I'm highly disturbed," he began. "The Princess Polignac called me up. She inquired about
the fee you take for concerts in private homes. When I told her that it was
your usual fee for concerts she became quite angry. She almost shouted that
it was quite impossible; she doesn't sell tickets to her guests, and it would be
an entirely private affair, she said."

   I listened with growing indignation. "This is an outrage!" I exclaimed.
"Here is one of the richest women in Paris and she begrudges me the
miserable fee you are getting for my concerts." Valmalète became red with
anger. "You are quite right! The French impresarios are stingy enough but
this American millionairess beats them all." We decided to insist on my
fee.

   Well, my reader may not believe it, but she refused to pay this amount
and the deal was off. Quite naturally, this nasty business cooled our relations considerably.

   One morning I received a letter from the princess. "Cher ami, a Greek gentleman, a friend of mine, would like to visit you; he has a proposal to make." I promised to receive the gentleman the next day. This visitor turned out to be a diplomat who lived in Paris. He said, "The Princess Polignac was kind enough to encourage me to ask you to play in my house at a party I am giving in honor of our exiled King George."

I answered him very politely that I would be glad to do it but that he should get in touch with Valmalète about the fee. He thanked me warmly. "I shall go and see him right away," he said, and left delighted with my acceptance. I telephoned Valmalète immediately, informed him of this affair, and asked him to charge the Greek gentleman two thousand francs more than my usual fee. Valmalète was only too glad to do it. A few hours later he called. "This charming gentleman came in person and agreed to pay with an air of finding it quite reasonable. He agreed also to pay for the transportation of the piano of your choice."

This party was successful in every way. My concert pleased the guests, especially King George of Greece, who loved music and had heard me in England. Princess Winnie was one of the guests. At the buffet after I had played she told me, "You see, cher Arthur, I did provide you with the fee you demanded," adding with a malicious smile, "And you even took good advantage of it!"

I lost sight of Stravinsky, who had taken my advice too seriously and was now spending more time on concert tours than writing new music. But one day on the express train from Brussels to Paris, I met him sitting in the lounge car. After a few hugs in the Russian style, Igor said, "I took the train from Amsterdam, where I played my concerto last night with a huge success." We took a table for two and were served lunch. Igor drank a half a bottle of red wine and talked all the time. I hardly opened my mouth, drank nothing but water with my lunch, and felt tired after a long supper the previous night. "You know, Arthur," Igor said, "my technique has much improved, and you know to whom I owe it? To Czerny, who was the greatest composer for the piano." I was too tired to stand up in defense of Chopin or Schumann and gave up in view of his categorical conviction.

"I am writing now some music for piano and violin," he went on. "A young American violinist, Samuel Dushkin, has arranged a tour in the United States for both of us, and I'm also busy on a Capriccio for Piano and Orchestra. You will like it, Arthur. I shall make the piano sound in my own way and thanks to Czerny I can handle it."

He had two glasses of cognac with our coffee and continued giving me enthusiastic accounts of his present and future activities. Just before arriving in Paris he was silent for a long moment, became suddenly sad, and in a low voice said in Russian, "Ach, the devil, I sometimes think that all my work is just pure rot . . ." We left the train. I did not comment on anything, I was tired.

I had still two concerts to give, one in Toulon and the other in St. Raphaël. I gladly accepted both dates, not for the sake of the money, which would barely cover travel and living expenses, but for the pleasure of spending a few days on the Mediterranean in good company. Denise and Edouard Bourdet had a house near Toulon and promised to spend a week there, the only reason being to have the Marquis Melchior de Polignac and me staying with them and to be at my concerts. Denise's very pretty sister, Giselle, was coming from Bordeaux to join the party. After the concert in Toulon they were going to accompany me to St. Raphaël. On the way, we had an invitation to stop a day and night at Hyères from Marie-Laure de Noailles. All this promised to be great fun and the concerts themselves played a minor role.

The Bourdet party was a constant feast for five days—excellent food, much champagne, dancing, playing poker, with hardly any time for sleep. On the day of my concert in Toulon the Bourdets showed me this lovely city with the warships of the French fleet. The streets full of sailors with red pompoms on their caps and, of course, a rich luncheon given by Melchior de Polignac. On top of it, I found a piano in not too good shape, so I must frankly admit that I remember this concert with no pleasure. My usually very musical companions did not notice it; it belonged to the program of fun. Two cars took us to Hyères, where the Vicomtesse de Noailles, a famous Parisian hostess, gave a great dinner for the occasion. We danced till late hours and proceeded the next morning with drawn fatigued faces to nearby St. Raphaël.

The concert was to take place at three o'clock in the afternoon. We sat down to a short snack beforehand in the hotel. Then something dreadful happened to me: I suddenly discovered that I had forgotten the program I had to play that very afternoon. My professional pride did not allow me to reveal it to my friends. I asked casually, "Edouard, have you seen the advertisement of my concert anywhere in the street or in a newspaper? I always like to verify the exact printing of the details before going on the stage." He asked politely for the morning papers but without success.

I went to the desk and asked the porter anxiously, "Have you by any chance yesterday's newspaper?" He smiled. "No, we always destroy it." By then, I had become terribly nervous. It was time to leave for the hall.

My friends left for their seats in the audience and I dashed up the steps leading to the wings of the cinema where the concert was to take place and asked the first stagehand I saw, "Get me my program right away! I heard there is a mistake printed in it."

"I don't think I can find one." It was time to begin the concert. I said with rage, "I shall not go on the stage before I see this wretched program!" By then I was out of my wits—I was on the verge of simply running away and finding an excuse later. Three men came running with programs in their hands. I was so relieved that I tore the first one before having time to even look at it. But the second one I read carefully.

When I think back on it, it was a good punishment and an admonishment for the lighthearted, superficial way I was beginning to treat concerts. From then on, concert days became sacred days, treated with utmost care and love.

75

Paul and Zosia arrived in the spring of 1929, this time for a few weeks. Paul had succeeded finally in bringing his whole family from Leipzig to Paris. He had lost his father some time ago and set up his mother and younger sister in a small but nice apartment on the left side of the river. His eldest sister was married to an artist, a specialist in miniatures; he made excellent little portraits not unlike the miniatures of the eighteenth century and both Paul and I were lucky enough to persuade friends to sit for him and acquire these little pieces of art. I sat for him myself and liked my little portrait, which I lost during the war.

Paul arrived in excellent shape, still raving about his gains on Wall Street and still trying to induce me to take his advice, but I was obstinate and refused. Playing the stock exchange meant simply gambling and my losses at Deauville still smarted. "I hope you converted some of your gains into real money and have it in the bank, Paul," I said.

"Are you taking me for a fool? My broker assured me, and all my friends are of the same opinion, that stock will be climbing still for a long while. America has never been so rich as now. It is a great opportunity for everyone." I listened without conviction; Wall Street was an unknown world to me.

I gave a cocktail party in honor of Paul and Zosia; it made me happy to see how popular he had become and how they loved his playing and his great personal charm. Zosia tried hard to win the friendship of Misia Sert and Coco Chanel, but to no avail. However, they were the exceptions, be-

cause I have never known anybody who knew better how to insinuate herself into the good graces of people she needed. She was a virtuoso at
matchmaking; she would introduce a charming, good-looking, but idle
young friend to a famous heiress and see to it that the all-important matri-
monial contract was duly signed. Denise Bourdet, before leaving, took me
aside and addressed me with great conviction in her voice: "Arthur, why
don't you give a great party in your lovely place here? Nobody could do
it better than you." These so very flattering words went like a dart into
my ambitious ego; right then I decided to do it. It was a warm June which
promised to last and there was no great risk in giving it in the open.

I went to work on this project with fantastic energy. Denise helped me
to send out the invitations. My list included over a hundred guests but I
could count with certainty on about eighty. It was to be a grand dinner with
entertainment. The food and drinks I took into my own hands with the help
of François. I also had my own ideas about the entertainment part. In a
small bar in Montmartre where I sometimes took a last cup of coffee or a
weak Scotch and soda, there was a nice little man, good-looking and well-
mannered, who would come to your table and do odd tricks like picking
your watch out of the pocket of the barman and bringing it back to you
with a charming smile or making five knots in your handkerchief and un-
doing them with one little pull on the two ends or taking a pack of cards out
of your hair, always with the greatest dexterity and elegance. I engaged him
for the party on condition that he show his tricks at a certain distance from
my guests, with cards and knots and not with the contents of their pockets.
I also engaged two Chinese boys who amazed me with their act at the Cirque
Medrano. One of them would climb on a table held tightly by the other,
bend backwards, and pick up with his mouth a full glass of water from the
floor and drink it while recovering his equilibrium. I hired both boys for a
small sum of money to come to my party after their show and perform this
little act. So far, so good, but I was set on providing my guests with a dance
floor and band to play.

I had no idea how to go about such a thing. Here my friendship with
Elsa Maxwell came in handy; I called her up, explained the plan, and heard
her say cheerfully, "I have everything you need; I'll bring a man with me
this afternoon who will take the measurements of the place and I'll tell you
about the band." She and the man started measuring the space for the dance
floor, ignoring my presence, and then she said quite casually, "I telephoned
Le Touquet. They have the best band at the moment. I could get them here
for you for three hours' work but it will cost you a good bit of money!" It
was indeed a big sum of money, but I suddenly remembered that I might
have risked two more bancos at the big table and lost it; here I would have

something I wanted in return. I wondered what percentage Elsa got from the band, but it didn't matter.

I went with François to Potel et Chabot, a famous caterer, and spent a couple of hours choosing all we needed: the buffet, tables and chairs, and all the setup for the meal and the right amount of help.

I looked forward to this party feeling like a shy debutante. I never felt as nervous before a concert as on that night. Denise and Elsa Maxwell came late in the afternoon and helped me put the names of the guests at their places. If I remember well, I had seventy-five to eighty guests seated at dinner. Elsa did well with the band; her arrangements were perfect. A specialist put magical lighting on the branches of my trees and the night was warm with no wind.

All my friends were there. The first to come were Paul and Zosia, to whom the party was a surprise. Out of pure vanity and remembering their lovely parties in New York, I wanted to show them what I could do on my own. My darling Paul even innocently brought his violin, thinking we might play a sonata or two. My guests were a composite of all the elements of Parisian society: aristocratic and plutocratic, artistic, intellectual and bohemian. All the Polignacs I knew, the Faussigny-Lucinges, two Princes Poniatowski with their wives, Dolly Radziwill and La Rochfoucauld and others representing the Faubourg St. Germain; the Rothschilds, Lazare and Weil, came. The Académie Française was represented by at least half a dozen members. But there were also the Serts and Godebskis, the Bourdets and Henri Bernstein, Eve Curie, the minister of Poland Anatole Mühlstein, Moïse Kisling, Jean Cocteau, and the Achards. Stravinsky was absent and Picasso had no evening clothes. The critic of *Le Temps* Pierre Brisson, Serge Lifar, Jean Bérard, and many others I can't remember at this moment all came. It was a perfect, beautiful party. The different groups were delighted to get acquainted.

The dinner of my own choice was highly praised. I had at my right Princess Winnie and at my left Germaine de Rothschild. My little magician charmed everybody by the way he performed his rather well-known tricks. The dinner was barely finished when the Chinese appeared. Everybody gathered around them and was duly flabbergasted by their act, to which they added a few other demonstrations of the fantastic dexterity of their hands. And then . . . the ball started! The band from Le Touquet was composed of five players who gave us their full repertoire of one-steps, waltzes, tangos, and even the popular French Javá. From the beginning of the fete, the whole neighborhood was aware of it. All the windows of my house were wide open and full of spectators. The Place Ravignan in front of my little garden began filling up with people from everywhere; I must say

here in honor of this crowd that they behaved beautifully. One heard no
voices of protest but frank amusement and applause for the performers.
Our Javá was caught up by the people in the square and danced with relish.
I sent François and two of my waiters with a few bottles of champagne to
regale the spectators at the windows. Toward the morning hours the police,
always nervous about unexpected gatherings of crowds, appeared. When I
informed them that it was nothing but merrymaking, they accepted a glass
of champagne and departed happily. At about seven o'clock in the morning,
only a few of my guests remained. Eve Curie, Mühlstein, Henri Bernstein,
and the Kochanskis. Everything became calm around us; the men were
cleaning up and making order when Paul and I decided to play the Brahms
Sonata in D minor, listened to in grave silence by the half-drunk survivors
of the party. While François was supervising the cleaning up, the rest of my
guests and I decided to drive out to the Bois de Boulogne for breakfast.
With a lot of coffee and eggs *sur le plat* our spirits were fully restored and
we enjoyed the lovely morning reminiscing about all the nice, comic incidents of the party.

This night was the high point in the life of the spendthrift Arthur
Rubinstein.

76

One day, Zosia gave me news of Nela, in spite of my never
broaching the subject. Her descriptions of Nela's married life were full of
malicious innuendoes. "They live in Cincinnati, where Munz is teaching at
the College of Music, but since Emil Mlynarski took the post of professor
of conducting at the Curtis Institute in Philadelphia, Nela spends more time
there than with her husband in Cincinnati. Whenever she is in New York
she comes to see us, mainly to ask my advice about clothes. Arthur, she
really thinks of nothing else but clothes." It was not difficult to discover in
her little story the distortion of facts. A friend of Nela would have told me
the same things in a flattering way. I listened to Zosia's news without
comment, showing no interest.

I told Paul about my decision to sign a contract with "His Master's

Voice" to make records and tried to persuade him to go with me to London and meet Fred Gaisberg. But Paul said, "I have better things in view. In America we have the great firm of Brunswick, the famous manufacturers of billiard tables, a company worth millions which is now engaged in producing gramophone records. They've already signed up Josef Hofmann and have big plans for me. This means huge publicity over the whole United States while the English records are still little known in America." I did not insist.

Horowitz was in town and telephoned me one morning. "What are you doing today?" he asked. I took his hint. "Come to the rue Ravignan and I will take you out for lunch." He immediately agreed. I was still in my dressing gown when he arrived. After a friendly hug he sat down at the piano and played for me all sorts of little pieces. "This last movement of the Haydn sonata makes a fine encore, eh?" Seeing that I was not quite convinced, he wanted my opinion on other odds and bits for encores. He was astonished that I showed no taste for encores that were prepared. I myself gave my encores spontaneously, choosing them according to the climate of the concert and my own inspiration. But I certainly never knew beforehand which encores I would play. Well, I gave him a good lunch at Fouquet's, after which he left for some chores, but he returned to be taken for dinner and later on to one or two nightclubs. A day like this became the usual program in our friendly relations.

Jascha Heifetz was another visitor to Paris. He expressed a great wish to see me, invited me for a drink in his room, where I found some of his American friends, and made a date with me for the following morning to take him to the shops where I had bought different things which he was anxious to acquire as well. Ever since our first meeting in New York he could not keep his eyes off a special golden chain I had for keeping my keys, a cigar cutter, and other items safely in my pockets, which I had ordered at Mappin and Webb. My ties and matching pocket handkerchiefs apparently also gave him sleepless nights. I began to be afraid that he might try to steal François from me. The only thing he did not envy was my career at that point. Both he and Volodya Horowitz called themselves my friends: Horowitz showed his friendship by accepting without difficulty my hospitality, Heifetz by earnestly taking my advice on the right way of living, but both treated me as an inferior in our profession from the heights of their American-dollar superiority. As a matter of fact, I never envied either of them their great success and I took it for granted that Heifetz was the greatest violinist of the time, who never touched my heart with his playing, and Horowitz, the greatest pianist, but not a great musician. On such premises our trio got along together quite well.

An attaché of the Polish Embassy called me up one morning: "Mr. Rubinstein, I am proud to announce to you that the French government bestows upon you the order of Chevalier de la Légion d'Honneur. We have your decoration at the embassy at your disposal." This was a great honor indeed. The Légion d'Honneur was the only decoration which required the unanimous vote of its members; it could be vetoed by a single vote.

That afternoon, I left for the embassy to find out when the ceremony was going to take place; according to the custom, a high French official would pronounce a citation and pin the decoration on my lapel and plant kisses on each cheek. When I asked the porter if I could see the ambassador, he opened a drawer of his table, took out a little package wrapped up in brown paper, and handed it to me. "His Excellency left this for you," he said. The package contained a little box with the medal and the document signed by the Minister of Culture.

I was deeply hurt by the rude behavior of Mr. Alfred Chlapowski, the Polish ambassador; for a moment he turned the honor into a dishonor for me. I took the package, went home, called François, and made him open the box and the citation. "François, read out to me loudly what it says and then pin the medal on my lapel." I omitted the kisses.

Every year the students of the Académie des Beaux Arts would hold their traditional ball, which was unique. For that one night, the municipal authorities would close their eyes to any excesses perpetrated by the youthful temperament of the budding artists. The ball was held in the vast Salle Wagram, where boxing contests and other sporting events usually took place. The name of the ball: "Le bal des Quat-z'arts." The committee would provide a theme—"Ancient Rome" or "Ancient Greece" or "Carthage"—but the students invariably gave it the same interpretation, painting their bodies a dreadful red or brown color and turning their faces into bewhiskered ancients. All the beautiful models of painters, sculptors, and engravers were invited. Outsiders who tried to penetrate into the ballroom had to show their invitations, which were closely scrutinized. If a fraud was discovered, the person might be thrown out into the gutter.

A Polish sculptor, a good friend of mine, had provided me on two previous occasions with invitations. I didn't mention it then, as it was one of many other balls and feasts, if of a less violent character. This time I am describing it only because Jascha Heifetz begged me with great insistence to take him to this ball. My sculptor friend was reluctant about a second invitation. "You are one of us. Art is your profession, but who is this other guy?" he asked. It was fun to discover that Jascha Heifetz was not yet the universal celebrity he thought he was; but when I gave my friend his particulars he understood that Heifetz was "one of us" too.

The three of us had dinner, after which the sculptor took us to his atelier, covered us with nasty paint, and commanded us to go home, remove our clothes, shoes and all, put on some sandals (he lent us two pairs), and pin some cloth around our middles with safety pins. Heifetz, who needed help, came with me to my home, where François helped both of us get ready for the ball. We left in a taxi for the Salle Wagram; approaching the hall, we saw yelling ancient Romans, who had evidently already nipped various alcohols, arriving from all directions, some of them in open carts, scaring innocent passersby. We entered the hall after two powerfully built students of the Beaux Arts had looked our cards over carefully. We were astounded to hear that a Maurice de Rothschild was thrown into the gutter when he insisted on being let in.

The huge hall was packed. There was a round platform in the center. The girls, mostly models, were in flimsy tunics which accentuated their nude bodies to advantage. A blaring band played one-steps, waltzes, Javás, but to no avail; the dancing couples simply clung to each other in tight embraces, ignoring the tune and rhythm without shame. The progress of the night led to a sequence of licentious behavior. Many tunics were left in an improvised wardrobe in a box of the gallery. The dancing changed into other exercises, executed with art to the finish. It was a Roman orgy, all right, but I think that the imagination of the Parisian students surpassed that of the ancient Romans they chose to emulate. Heifetz, slightly terrified, kept his eyes wide open. When he saw a lovely model being raped on the platform by two enterprising students (who, of course, were pretending) he was all ready to go home, afraid of the police arriving to arrest the perpetrators of the "crime." I calmed him down and took him to the wardrobe box, where they also served some black coffee; there a strange scene took place: a woman in her forties in charge of the wardrobe was willingly having her virtue abused by at least half a dozen brave *amateurs*. I was highly amused, but Jascha Heifetz almost fainted. He begged me to leave toward six in the morning and we found ourselves in the street. Now our flimsy clothes made us shiver with cold. "Aren't you hungry, Jascha? I'm dying of hunger."

"Yes! I'm hungry too." The only place that could give us some decent food at such an hour was the Abbaye de Thélème on the Place Pigalle. A taxi took us there; when we entered the restaurant there was only one table occupied—by an elderly gentleman and two prostitutes, one on each side of him, with two ice buckets, one with a magnum of champagne, the other with some fading flowers. The gentleman exclaimed, "Rubinstein! What happened to you?" I explained in a few words the reason for our appearance, introduced Jascha, whose name he knew quite well, and we settled at a neighboring table for supper.

By that time, our paint had become a mass of dirt, our cloth had lost its color, and we looked as if we had escaped from a prison in this disguise. Albert, the manager, who knew me well, treated us to a delicious snack. It was only then that I recognized the gentleman at the other table. I shall give his name because he was certainly a picturesque personality. He had two brothers. One was the Cardinal Merry del Val, the highest official at the Vatican after the Pope. The other was the Chilean ambassador at the Court of St. James's in London. Our neighbor was evidently the black sheep of the family but he certainly was the most charming of the three brothers. Domingo Merry del Val had absorbed a lot of champagne, which accounted for his poor choice of companions. But he was elegant enough to offer them flowers. When he saw me finishing coffee he suddenly exclaimed with wild enthusiasm, "You two great artists, why don't you play something for these charming ladies!" We were completely baffled but with some sense of humor left, we rose to our feet. I went up to the piano and, I don't know how, but Albert produced a violin for Jascha—a member of the band must have left it there. We played some easy stuff that we both knew very well, after which Mr. Domingo Merry del Val said solemnly to one of the prostitutes, "Give these flowers to these two great masters. You will never in your life hear anything like that." The woman obeyed and was ready to kiss our hands. At that moment, Albert approached Jascha and said to him gravely, "Vous savez, jeune homme, qui a joué ici? Le grand Kubelik!" Jascha gave him a grimace for a smile and that was our night at the "Quat-z'arts."

77

The Kochanskis left for Evian for a short cure before returning to the States and I joined them there. Paul's accompanist, Pierre Luboschutz, was with us, and I took a friend from Chile, a pretty and charming young lady. There we found Raimund von Hofmannsthal. The five of us had our meals together and were kept in stitches by Paul's stories and imitations. He was funnier than ever, but I was worried about his looks; the cure did not seem to agree with him. When I asked him about it he avoided straight answers but declared himself to be satisfied with the treatment. At our farewell, I felt very sad. I always missed Paul very much; his presence would have prevented me from doing many things which I loved to do but were not good for me.

After my return to Paris that same year, 1929, the papers announced the death of Sergei Diaghilev in Venice. The whole of artistic Paris was in mourning. The loss of this great magician of beauty bereaved our hearts; we were suddenly aware of our great debt to him for the years of unforgettable enchantment and excitement which this great man bestowed upon us so generously. Young composers became orphans and dancers cried at the news.

Princess Winnie had invited me to spend the end of the summer at her palazzo and upon arrival I went in a gondola to the cemetery and put some flowers of gratitude on his grave.

Stravinsky and Vera, who was now his constant companion, were in Venice. I found Igor very much shaken by the loss of the man who had played such an important part in his life. Many admirers came in great numbers to pay homage at his grave.

I left Venice after having given my annual bread-and-butter concert at the palazzo. The princess invited friends of hers who lived permanently in Venice: the Robillants, Annina Morosini, the charming musician Giorgio Levi and his wife, a few local artists, and the director of the Fenice. She had also two young English girls, Sheila Ponsonby, who later married the Duke of Westminster, and Hilary Wilson, whose father was the owner of the Wilson Steam Line. Hilary became a lifelong friend; she married later Lord Munster, had no children, and was completely involved with music, studying the piano with Solomon, a splendid teacher. In later years she helped young musicians most generously.

Back in Paris, I had a long conference with Marcel de Valmalète; it even led to a mild quarrel. "Please, mon cher ami," I said, "give more serious attention to the quality of the concerts you obtain for me. I am getting tired of unmusical, small audiences. I want to play only where there is a real feeling for me. You see, a concert in Rome, Florence, Madrid, Barcelona, or the capitals in South America inspires me." Valmalète smiled a little contemptuously. "Don't disdain small places and low fees. You can always earn enough for a good dinner or two." His arguments fell on deaf ears and I was steadfast in my refusal to play in cities that were not to my liking.

The few weeks of vacation that I gained were most welcome. My lifelong passion for books could be indulged again to my heart's delight. I strolled in and around the rue Jacob, where one could find treasures in out-of-print books, biographies and history, or interesting correspondence between authors and musicians. With my heart beating with joy when I came across a rare find, I could forget my lunch. I shall always remember the day I discovered a Russian book shop where I found the first edition of all the works of Dostoevski, a lovely edition of the plays of Chekhov, and *War and Peace* and *Anna Karenina* with beautiful illustrations. I heard that Bernard Shaw published a few volumes of his reviews as a music critic and was heartbroken to be told that they were out of print. All my friendly book shops had standing orders to reserve missing editions for me when they became available again. My small bungalow was overcrowded with the constant influx of reading material. Some more sophisticated theaters such as the Comédie des Champs-Elysées, Théâtre Antoine, Théâtre de l'Oeuvre, and Théâtre de l'Atelier had bookstalls where books by the authors of the plays being performed were sold, but they also took subscription orders for special, more beautifully bound editions. I remember having bought in this manner the complete illustrated works of Musset, Daudet, Baudelaire, Verlaine, and even Courteline. My good friends in Poland were constantly on the lookout for rare books in the Polish language; thanks to them I became the proud owner of the *first edition* of *Pan Tadeusz* by Mickiewicz, the great Polish bard. In Cracow they found even an old chronicle in its original rough leather binding secured by a lock with a key. Many new books were sent to me by their authors with kind inscriptions; they had heard of my devotion to literature and felt appreciation for it. During this short vacation I hardly touched the piano and was reading night and day. Sometimes when I woke up late after having read until the early hours of the morning, François would serve my breakfast on my bed and I would not get up until I finished the book. I can assert without any exaggeration that I forgot all my troubles and pains and lived these weeks in full euphoria. It was then that it became clear to me that the great books were my ideal friends for exchanging views on abstract matters. I felt happy when I found in some of them ideas akin to mine, and my mind would become feverishly engaged in defending my theses against strong attacks on my own convictions. Certain books, like certain music, remained companions of my inner self and will for as long as my mind remains clear.

One morning, I read with horror of the Wall Street crash. At first I did not grasp the whole importance of this news; I had often read about "black days" at the Stock Exchange, of unlucky investments in this or that stock, but it took me days to understand that this time the whole American economic system had collapsed like a castle made of cards. I became suddenly aware of what it would mean to my Paul but there was no way of knowing to what extent he was affected. I hoped against odds that he had had the foresight to save his own investments. Being without news I did not dare to communicate with him; it might have hurt him after all my admonitions and misgivings, so I had to be patient until I could find out from him what had happened. In town one spoke of nothing else but there was no visible change in the way of living in Paris. Anyway, it made me more conscious of the value of money. I wrote Ruiz and Pellas to arrange a tour in Brazil and Argentina for the next season; it would give me the means to find out what had happened to my own investments in Rio and Buenos Aires.

The concerts in Spain and Italy were as successful as ever but this time I took great care with the accounts, as I played in both countries on percentage. Still every day the newspapers printed terrifying news of hundreds of bankruptcies, of dozens of suicides, and of millions and millions of people out of work; it seemed to be the end of the American wealth, so envied by the whole world. Everywhere the United States was being blamed for its irresponsibility in allowing people to build huge fortunes on empty speculation.

My Chilean friend, a relation of Juanita, wanted to visit Andalusia. My tales about the *feria* at Seville and about Granada excited her imagination. "But I will not go if you are not my guide." I could never resist a woman's whim and I always had a passion for taking people to the right places, showing them the best pictures in a museum, the best restaurants in the city, and I was particularly proud to be able to point out some beautiful item which was not to be found in *Baedeker*. Ernesto de Quesada arranged in a hurry two or three concerts in Andalusia with ample time for Seville and Granada. All I remember of this little tour is the night in Seville when I was lucky enough, thanks to my friend Juan Lafita, to gather the best flamenco singers and guitarists to play for us. My lovely Chilean lady showed a great dislike for this sort of entertainment; she made me leave in a hurry and later, out in the street, burst into a violent attack on these players. "How can you stand this dreadful yelling, Arthur, you, such a refined musician! I call them barbarians and nothing else." A great part of my friendship for this lady was considerably weakened that night. I was happy when I had delivered her safely back to her home in Paris.

The mood of the Parisians for Christmas and the New Year was a little subdued this year. The American financial disaster began to be felt all over Europe. The chauvinistic Frenchmen suddenly resented the absence of American tourists with their easily spent money. Winter resorts, hotels, and restaurants complained about their great losses and many were closed. All this spread a gloomy cloud over Europe. Bad news came from Germany; after the assassination of the great liberal leader Walther Rathenau, the country lived in constant unrest. Poland was in constant trouble over the very artificial "corridor" at Danzig, unsatisfactory to both sides.

In early spring, the Kochanskis arrived in Paris and Paul told me all about his poor shattered hopes for a fortune; he was bitter about it but fortunately he kept his morale intact. He had been intelligent enough to keep his losses limited to his original ten thousand, so he was without debts and still had his salary from Juilliard plus a few concerts in view. I suggested we give some concerts for violin and piano sonatas in England and eventually in Spain. He liked the idea very much and we decided to do it the following spring. They left, this time for Zakopane.

On my return to Madrid for another appearance there, I became rather upset by an unrest I felt all over Spain. There were talks about violent disagreements between the King and Primo de Rivera. The country was divided in their opinions.

Just before my concert, the Duke of Santo Mauro came to see me at the Palace Hotel. "I have come on behalf of Her Majesty the Queen, who asked to be excused for not coming to your concert tomorrow. She does not leave the Royal Palace these days. The Socialists are committing acts of violence. You and I know how dangerous these horrible people can become." I learned only then how the political situation had deteriorated.

A rather absurd paradox happened after the duke's visit. A young musician who was a devoted admirer of mine arrived with a piece of music in his hand. "This is a great present for you from the Socialist Party of Spain. It is the first draft of the new revolutionary hymn."

I have never felt more keenly how fond the whole of the Spanish people was of me. Here I was considered a staunch monarchist and there "one of them" by the Socialists.

Fred Gaisberg called me up: "Are you willing to make a record of the B-flat major Concerto of Brahms? A good orchestra and the conductor Albert Coates are available on [such and such a date]." I was not only willing, I was thrilled by the idea. The date was just a few days before my departure for South America.

The morning after my arrival in London, Gaisberg took me to the hall where the recording would take place. It was an ugly, completely empty large room where once some popular balls were held. "I have a fine Bechstein for you." This did not sound reassuring, as lately I had had difficulties finding really good instruments. It was also impossible to see Mr. Coates before the recording, as I had hoped. We were given only two days for this longest of all concertos with its four movements, and the result was completely unsatisfactory. Everything seemed to be against us; the piano had a good sound but it was slightly out of tune and the tuner was not able to fix it. Mr. Coates conducted at the opposite end of the room, far away from me, so of course I had as neighbors the percussion and brass instruments at the back of the orchestra. In these circumstances there was no way of establishing a close contact between conductor and soloist, and neither of us liked any of the sequences we played. I considered the two days of hard work a useless effort and begged Gaisberg to destroy the takes. If I remember well, I said to him, "Our contract contains a clause where I have the right not to allow a record I do not find acceptable to be issued." Gaisberg promised. I departed for South America very disappointed.

The tour this time left nothing but unpleasant memories in me. Both in Brazil and in Argentina, I gave fewer concerts and they were not always sold out. It was pleasant to see all my friends again, just as warm as ever, but here too I felt the shadow cast by the American debacle. However, the bank in Rio and the Credito Argentino remained the same; I gave a sigh of relief.

On my return from South America, I heard with dismay that Karol had spent a long season in Davos, the famous place for tubercular patients. I had not known that his health needed that kind of cure but when I got back he had returned to Warsaw.

78

Fred Gaisberg had betrayed me; my record of the Brahms concerto was on sale. In my anger I was ready to break off our contract. "You have no reason whatever to get so angry. Musicians like it and the sales are promising," said he, adding that Albert Coates had nothing against the issue of this wretched disc. Henceforth I promised myself to be more careful.

Gaisberg had great plans for my future recordings. "Why don't you give us your Spanish pieces which have been so successful in your concerts? What about *Navarra*, *Triana*, and the *Fire Dance?*" My answer was very evasive. "I want you to know," I replied, "that I play these pieces in my own fashion. It is rather more the synthesis of the musical content than all the notes." He wouldn't listen to me and insisted on these pieces, so I finally promised to take a new look at them and see if I could take the responsibility. "His Master's Voice" now had excellent studios at Abbey Road with the most modern equipment. Work there became pleasant and efficient; the small restaurant on the premises was just right, so that one didn't lose too much time on food. When I was ready to make the *Navarra* record, my friend Hoyty Wiborg, who adored this piece, begged me to let her watch me do it. When both Gaisberg and I warned her not to make the slightest noise, she swore that she would even stop breathing. The piano was good, this time a Steinway, and I attacked the piece for all I was worth. I had never given a greater smash to the middle section and I was happy not to have missed one single note (of the notes of my choice, of course). But before I had time to give the last forte chord, Miss Wiborg shouted a loud enthusiastic "Bravo!" and spoiled the record. I wanted to kill her. It was only after the fourth performance that I allowed them to issue the recording.

A great political upheaval was taking place in Spain. In 1930 the whole of Catalonia and central Spain were threatened with a revolution. The Army was under the order of a fanatic general who was ready to fight to save the monarchy, but the King, a confirmed liberal, could not tolerate his country being involved in a bloodbath. He announced in noble terms his abdication and left the country with full honors on a Spanish warship leaving Cartagena for Italy. The Queen and the children left for Paris. The old Infanta Isabel, a much beloved figure to all the people, was asked by the revolutionary committee to stay in her palace with the promise that her position would be honored as before. The grand old lady declined. "My place is near my king," she said. She left a day later, accompanied by the Infanta Beatrice of Orléans, to join the Queen in Paris. Upon arrival, she went to bed and died two days later.

That same year, after a few concerts on the Continent, I came back to London to make more records. I found a nice flat in Bury Street. I tried out a few Spanish pieces but did not decide whether to allow them to be issued or not. However, I did begin serious work on the nocturnes of Chopin. Mr. Mitchell, who had me play in two or three cities, was preparing on my request a recital for Paul and me at Wigmore Hall. It turned out to be one of the best concerts we ever gave. We played the *Kreutzer* and C minor Beethoven sonatas and the Brahms D minor. Fred Gaisberg was enthusiastic: "Why don't you record sonatas for us?" he said.

"Why don't we!" I asked Paul, delighted with the idea. Paul answered a little evasively, "I have a verbal understanding with the Brunswick Company, so I don't know if I am free to do this." I invited both of them to lunch the next day at the Savoy Grill. Gaisberg reassured Paul about his obligations to Brunswick, especially when he learned that they did not set dates or repertoire for recording. While we were sipping our coffee, Fred suddenly banged his fist on the table. "Why don't you boys come with me to Abbey Road right now and record the Brahms sonata you play so beautifully!" Paul and I exchanged glances. "Should we risk it just like that on the spur of the moment?" I laughed. "Paul, I think we've played this sonata over a thousand times. We could perform it under chloroform."

The three of us landed at Abbey Road and went straight to the studio, where we found everything in readiness for recording. This devil Gaisberg had prepared it all very cleverly. Well, I must admit even at this late hour that we gave the sonata a fine, spontaneous performance. Paul never played the slow movement more beautifully and even the difficult last movement went off without any false notes.

After these first recordings I fell into a happy mood which involved a few amorous adventures not worth telling about. One was on Avila's instigation and the other one involved a very beautiful Polish lady who was generous enough to accompany me on a short Spanish tour. I finished my summer in Biarritz with many excursions to St. Jean de Luz and San Sebastián for a luncheon with Ravel and my friends the Blanchards. We also went to a sensational bullfight with Gallito and Belmonte. On that occasion I won a colossal moral victory over the most reluctant and reserved misanthrope, the Marquis of Cholmondeley. He had come to Biarritz for an innocent golf match. One day I met him in the street and persuaded him to accompany me to San Sebastián for this famous bullfight; he must have had a very soft spot for me to have accepted at all because in London whenever I mentioned bullfights he seemed ready to be sick. And that was not all; that same evening, he actually entered the Casino Bellevue with me to watch me play chemin de fer, a thing he stubbornly refused to do for his wife when they stayed in Cannes. And he liked it! Sybil could hardly believe her ears when she heard the story, and for the rest of his life, whenever I lunched or dined with the Cholmondeleys, he would evoke this incident with great gusto.

Four

Marriage and Family

79

When the 1931–32 concert season began, Warsaw and Lodz were again on my schedule. I had to accept Ordynski's hospitality as before; it seemed to me that the fatal sofa was destined to make me pay for my sins. On top of it, the heating in the room broke down and I shivered with cold. "There is a concert tonight by Gregor Piatigorsky; it might interest you to hear him." I was glad of this opportunity, having heard that he had escaped from Russia at the same time as Vladimir Horowitz and Nathan Milstein.

The hall of the Filharmonja was far from being full; there were rows of empty seats. At the cloakroom, where I left my coat and hat, I saw a familiar face; it was Nela, and she was alone. I greeted her cordially and kissed her hand. It was the custom in Poland to kiss the hand of married women only. She responded by treating me as a good old friend. After a few banal questions—"How have you been?" "How is the family?"—we entered the hall. When we saw the many empty seats we discarded our tickets and sat down together.

Piatigorsky played very beautifully; he was certainly the best cellist I had heard since Casals, but somehow the unexpected meeting with Nela interfered with my paying full attention to the music. After his performance Nela took me to the artist's room and introduced me to the great cellist. This very good-looking artist turned out to be a charming man. Right then, our close friendship began.

Back at the cloakroom I asked Nela, "Would you like to have a bite with me?" To which she answered, "Everything is closed at this hour but if you like we can go to Adria, a very nice place for dancing."

In this elegant, large dance hall, we found a nice table and were joined by Nela's friend Miss Halina Lilpop and by Richard, who had the gift for always finding out where I was. I danced with Halina and then with Nela, who danced beautifully. While we were waltzing happily, she asked me half seriously, half jokingly, "Well, would you marry me now?" I answered in the same tone, "Certainly, you should know that."

From that moment on, we fell into a new attitude: we began a serious flirtation. I took her home to the rue Wawelska, where her parents, now back from Philadelphia, had a nice apartment. Emil Mlynarski was afflicted with the severest arthritis, she told me, and was condemned to spend his days in a wheelchair; but he had not lost his wonderful vitality. "He even likes to give lessons in conducting to young musicians who know how much they can learn from him." Before she left me, we kissed for the first time.

After my own concert, I spent my few free days in Warsaw in Nela's company, mostly at Wawelska, where her parents gathered around their table almost daily, with the proverbial Polish hospitality, their friends—such as Roman Jasinski, a brilliant young pianist, who, besides being a man of high culture, could make us die with laughter with his comic improvisations. On the day before my departure I asked Nela to lunch alone with me. I chose a new restaurant on the beautiful square of the old city of Warsaw which had opened recently on the first floor of the house owned by descendants of Foukier, the proud owners of a wine cellar dating from 1765—it was famous for its centuries-old Hungarian Tokay. With great difficulties I reserved a small table for two. Ordynski had left early for a studio where he was making a film and I took great care to fetch Nela on time in a taxi which took us to the restaurant. My intention was to find out what was on her mind; was she returning to America or did she intend to divorce and did she really want to marry me?

We had just ordered our meal when Ordynski appeared. "I was *sure* you would lunch here today!" he said, smiling and happy. "I hurried my filming to be on time. What are you having?" Nela and I hated him in unison, and our welcome was the most hypocritical gesture of our lives. He robbed us of our only opportunity to exchange views about our future. I had to leave that same afternoon for Lodz and then return to Paris, where I resumed the life of the inveterate bachelor my friends knew me to be.

80

The Christmas and New Year festivities were approaching. I made plans to spend the *réveillon* with the Achards and New Year's Eve with the Bourdets, who were going to take me to different parties that night. After Christmas Eve I received a picture postcard from Zakopane. It read:

"Why not spend the St. Sylvestre here with us? We have snow, ice, a good drop of wine, and dancing in store for you—Nela." This card with its not too engaging temptations changed my plans. I found false excuses to get out of the Bourdet parties and sent François to buy railway tickets and sleeping accommodations for Cracow, where I had to change trains for Zakopane. I arrived on December 30 in the afternoon and found Nela waiting for me at the station.

She took me to a charming villa. "I reserved a room for you," she said, "in this *pension de famille*. My cousin Irka manages it. My sister Alina is here too. The food is simple but quite good, so I hope you will like it." Of course I liked to be in the same place as Nela.

At dinnertime I was duly introduced to everybody; there were three or four other guests in the villa and I liked both the dinner and the company. Nela's beautiful sister treated me rather indifferently but her cousin Irka received me with a charming show of hospitality. After dinner I took Nela to the Morskie Oko, as her card had insinuated that she would like a drop or two, and there I ordered a bottle of champagne to be put into an ice bucket. While the waiter was filling our glasses, Nela suddenly declared, "I don't drink champagne." This vexed me a little. She might have said it earlier. Somewhat resentfully, I managed to finish the bottle by myself while we were talking. It took three hours, however. Our long talk brought back to us our first awareness of our love; we felt happy to be starting again from the beginning. On that blessed night we forgot everything which had happened since that beautiful first moment.

The next morning, New Year's Eve, at breakfast, Nela appeared in her skiing outfit and declared cheerfully after our good-morning kiss, "I'm going on a skiing expedition with my friends and shall be back before dinnertime." And with that, she left. I fell into a stupor of rage. So she makes me come all the way from Paris, makes me abandon my friends, to sit and wait for her a whole day while she is off cavorting with friends on skis. Fortunately I have the happy gift of never being bored by myself. And so I spent the day in the excellent company of a book I brought from Paris. At luncheon there was another agreeable distraction; a very good-looking lady with beautiful dark hair appeared and, as I found out later, had the room next to mine. She seemed to be impressed to see me there because all through the meal she stared at me. When Irka introduced me to her, she told me flattering things about my concerts in Cracow.

I went out to the Morskie Oko to reserve a table and a bottle of champagne, whether Nela liked it or not, for the New Year's Eve ball and to order some flowers. Nela returned toward dinnertime and during the meal entertained me with vivid descriptions of the beauty of the snow, of

the fantastic sunset, and the great sport of skiing. After dinner she disappeared to dress up for the dancing. We arrived at the Morskie Oko an hour
before midnight. The place was packed, and the dark-haired lady was sitting
with some friends at a neighboring table.

After some Polish hors d'oeuvres and vodka we danced. Then we
settled down for the supper; I had the champagne uncorked and said sternly
to Nela, "I have always greeted the New Year with a glass of champagne.
I'm even superstitious about it." Just before midnight Nela became aware
that the dark-haired lady had never taken her eyes off us and particularly
me. "Do you know her?" she asked me irritably.

"Yes, I met her at luncheon." Nela did not like that. When the band
stopped and the New Year was announced through a megaphone, the usual
pandemonium took place—screaming, shouting, kissing, drinking, and
wishing Happy New Year in the darkened room for a long while. Nela was
not happy. The lady's glances angered her. She took it out on me, accusing
me of having provoked this lady's behavior. I answered bitterly, "Of course
I will pay attention to a beautiful woman if I am left alone for the whole
day." To which she replied coldly, "I'm going on another excursion tomorrow." This started a scene. We exchanged a few angry words and Nela rose
to her feet, went for her coat, and left. A nasty beginning of a New Year. I
remained proudly in my seat, finished the champagne, and asked the manager where I could find a skiing instructor.

It happened there was one at the ball. After a few words with him he
agreed to take me to the nearest hill early the next morning. I left with him
before breakfast in my heaviest shoes and he lent me a pair of skis and
poles. I followed his instructions with great care, fell down about a dozen
times, lost my skis, but learned enough to move around pretty confidently.
My legs were always very strong.

At breakfast I was alone. Apparently there was a general hangover
and I saw Nela only at luncheon. She said to me curtly, "Our expedition
takes place the day after tomorrow." We were slow in making up, but,
helped by the absence of the lady, we finally had our Happy New Year with
great hopes for the future.

The next morning I went to the best shop in town to buy the full
equipment for skiing. I felt rather ridiculous seeing myself in the mirror
with a woolen cap and pompon over my hair, a thick sweater which made
my shoulders look like a prize fighter's, and baggy pants and thick stockings. Somehow—and I never shall understand why—they forgot to sell me
the right boots. My own seemed to be the proper ones, but they were not,
and gave me a lot of trouble. When I got back to the villa I announced
proudly to Nela, "I shall join your excursion tomorrow!" She took it as a

joke and laughed but was pretty astonished when she saw me in my ridiculous outfit ready to go.

A sleigh took us to the foot of a high hill. This was a hard time for me. I tried to imitate the others walking up at an angle but lost those goddamn skis two or three times on the way. When we reached the summit, our companions gave a shout of triumph, pointed at a little hut down the other side, and said, "Let's go down for a good hot grog and sausages." And down they went zigzagging happily, Nela along with them. I hated to be left behind, and seeing them all safely entering the hut, I made ready to join them and shot straight down the hill, proud of holding on sturdily. But here came the catastrophe. When I reached the bottom my vertiginous speed did not allow me to put on the brakes, so my whole body shot into the air. My head and half of my trunk were buried in the snow with my legs sticking out. Nela and two fellows who were still outside the hut ran to help me, terrified, thinking I was dead. As a matter of fact, I was incredibly lucky to have fallen into a great mound of snow, because a stone might have killed me on the spot. When my face emerged it was covered with blood. It was more spectacular than serious, simply that the impact had burst the skin. Everybody took great care of me in the hut, where after three hot grogs I was laughing happily at my exploit and a little tipsy to boot.

For the next few days I went skiing with Nela and Alina on smaller slopes where I could show my progress to better advantage. My concert manager from Cracow heard that I was in Zakopane and suggested a concert in the old capital within three days. I accepted gladly, happy to fill my purse again. Nela remained in Zakopane but I was surprised to see my youngest sister Frania in the hall. After the concert Teofil Trzcinski paid me my full fee in dollars. Some good friends came to greet me and Frania entered the room after the others were gone. "Leo has been gambling again," she said to me, "and has lost everything. Please, please help me because I am desperate." I gave her my freshly earned dollars and returned with empty pockets to Zakopane.

Nela made plans to leave for Dresden, where she intended to study dancing with the famous Mary Wigman. Nela had made quite a name for herself as a dancer in Warsaw. She had given a recital of solo dances of her own invention with music of her own choice, which was a great success, and for years I was reminded of it by the Countess Joseph Potocka, who was the president of the charity to which Nela dedicated her performance.

I left Zakopane with regret; I did not know it then but it was the beginning of a new life for me.

81

In Paris I was telling my closest friends of my intention to marry a young Polish woman. "Tu n'y penses pas," said Denise Bourdet. "What will you do, you old Parisian, with a girl from the wild steppes?" I tried to describe Nela. "She is very intelligent, you know." They laughed. "And I find her beautiful," I said with greater emphasis. "Tu ne vas pas nous épater avec la beauté de cette étrangère."

"And she is very simple!" I said a little impatiently. "She is a talented dancer." They did not even laugh but dismissed it with deprecating gestures. And then I added a little indifferently, "She's not spoiled like Parisian women, and she even has a great talent for cooking." At that, both Bourdet and Marcel Achard exclaimed enthusiastically, "You lucky devil! You lucky devil!" They were now ready to accept Nela in hopes of a good dinner.

After two weeks I left for Istanbul, Greece, and Egypt. These three places, so different and so interesting, I loved better each time. There was always something new to discover. The Pekmezians with their cats in Istanbul and the good Stefanides, Frieman, and Marika made me feel as if I had always lived there. My public in these places, always the same, were now friends and not critical ticket holders.

A rough crossing got me to Alexandria, where Arditi's representative expected me. Again I played for my Greek, Italian, and Jewish audience—not a red fez to be seen. My program for Cairo was ambitious this time: I was going to begin with the difficult B minor Sonata of Chopin, followed by six études, continuing after intermission with *Petrushka* and some Liszt. Ten minutes before going on the stage, I was handed a telegram: "Am ill in the hospital [she gave the name and address], please send urgently some money, Nela."

I sat down, thunderstruck. Horrible thoughts came to my mind of all sorts of possible illnesses. The uncertainty was absolutely unbearable. A minute later I had to play the B minor Sonata of Chopin. Here my deeply professional nature won out again. I played the sonata with more feeling than ever before. Any strong emotion, be it from the illness or death of a person one loves, of unbearable jealousy, of deep loneliness, of any tragic event, always makes me play better in a concert. Playing is a moral life jacket. All through the concert I was making music with all my heart. I even gave two encores. But sitting again in the artist's room with the telegram in my hand, I decided on the spot to leave for Dresden. Arditi's agent had seen the expression on my face when I read the telegram and noticed how despondent I was after the concert. He seemed to fear that I was ready to commit suicide, for he never left me until he saw me safely in my room. He arranged my journey to Dresden and took me the next morning to the bank to send the money by telegraph.

I reached Dresden after an interminable voyage and rushed with my luggage and all to the hospital. I was told that Nela was home again at the address she had given me in Zakopane. A few minutes later I rang the door of her pension, was shown to her room, and there I found Nela smiling happily with surprise at seeing me in Dresden. "I am glad you came," she said. "I was afraid of some dreadful symptoms which turned out to be nothing at all." We feasted the good news with a warm embrace and right away made plans for the evening. I left my luggage at a nearby hotel and took her for dinner at a good restaurant. Looking over the theater page, we found out that they were giving *Parsifal* at the Opera. The paper said it was sold out but we decided enthusiastically to try our luck. At the box office I used an old stratagem I had used in Paris. I said that I had been sent to write a review about it for Poland but had forgotten to reserve tickets. The man quite visibly did not believe me, but sold me with indulgence two seats in the gallery which had been returned. We climbed up the four flights and sat down breathlessly to hear this great work in the same famous opera house in Germany where Richard Strauss had had all his premieres.

Von Schuch was the conductor and we listened to the music of the first act with a great emotion. However, the second act annoyed us; the music and the singing of the fat German flower girls who tried to seduce poor Parsifal made us laugh. From then on the endless solo of Gurnemanz, which was about to come on, seemed more than we could endure. In a spontaneous gesture we ran down the staircase and took refuge in a nearby café where for a long time we discussed our future.

I invited Nela to accompany me to Prague, where I was to have my next concert. "I would like nothing better," she said, "but I must go to Berlin to see my poor father on his way to Dax, where he will try a cure for his terrible arthritis. The train coming from Warsaw stops for half an hour at the Schlesischer Bahnhof. I want to kiss him goodbye and wish him luck."

"I shall take you to Berlin!" I said. "It is time I introduced myself to your parents as your fiancé." She was a little uncertain about that. "My father might be quite happy about it, he was always fond of you and believed in your talent, but my mother will exclaim, 'That's all we need!' when she hears about us."

Anyway, she agreed to my plan. We arrived in Berlin just in time to go to the station and wait for the train to come. Nela rushed up to embrace her mother, who was standing at the open door of their sleeping car. I followed her slowly and received a cold handshake from Mrs. Mlynarska. Her husband was sweet and tender to his daughter and had some friendly words for me. He smiled bravely in spite of his cruel pains.

When their train departed, we left for another station to take our own train for Prague. We settled in our comfortable sleeper for the night. At daylight, I woke up and dressed quietly. Nela was still fast asleep when the train stopped at Pilsen, the city of the famous beer and the arms factories. I left the train to buy a morning paper and saw in front of our car a man selling hot sausages; the best sausages, usually called "frankfurters" or "wieners," really come from Czechoslovakia. I grabbed a pair greedily, covered them with delicious mustard, and finished them in less than a minute. Before I swallowed the last bite I held a second pair in my hand. I had the courage to wash it down with a stein of the precious Pilsen beer, I who never drank beer in my life. I was just reaching for the third pair of sausages when, looking back, I saw Nela's face at the window showing stern disapproval. I quickly dropped the third pair back on the stand like a boy caught in a little mischief. An ominous sign of my marriage!

We reached Prague an hour later at eight o'clock in the morning. As the concert took place that same evening, we decided after settling in our room at the hotel to go to bed again; we both needed a good rest after the visit in Berlin and the night on the train. I was sound asleep when the telephone rang on a table out of my reach. I jumped out of bed and said "hello" in an unkind tone. A cheerful voice of a man answered in German. "My name is Sonnenschein" (sunshine indeed!). "You must remember me, we went together with Emmy Destinn to the zoo in London, where we laughed so much when you imitated the monkeys in front of their cage." I remembered Destinn and the monkeys but not Sonnenschein.

"Yes," I answered evasively, "what can I do for you?"

"Last night Ravel gave a concert with Marguerite Long playing his concerto. He knew that you were playing tonight and was terribly sad not to be able to stay over. They are leaving this morning for Paris. Ravel kept on regretting that you missed his concert and that he will miss yours." I could hardly believe my ears; for as long as I knew Ravel, he never expressed regrets of any kind and showed a complete indifference for everybody around him. So it is easy to understand how touched I was by this great demonstration of friendship toward me.

"When are they leaving?" I asked anxiously.

"At ten-thirty. If you hurry up you could see him off at the station. They are leaving by sleeping car for Paris."

It was ten minutes to ten. In spite of Nela's protests, I dashed into my clothes, down in the elevator, and caught the first taxi available. "To the station, quickly!" I cried to the driver. We reached it at ten-twenty. I ran to the hall and asked the way to the train. "Take tunnel number three." I ran down one staircase and up another staircase. It was the wrong one. "It's number two," I was told. Down again and up again, breathless. Then I saw Ravel standing in front of his car. I rushed up to him expecting a cordial welcome with many handshakes and maybe even a hug. But I received neither. Ravel seemed to be not even aware of my presence and muttered dreadful insults against Marguerite Long, the famous French pianist. "Idiote! Cette idiote, she always forgets something! She lost the tickets, this idiot." And he went up and down with increasing rage. The train was about to leave when the poor Miss Long shouted triumphantly, "I found them, I found them!" At that, Ravel jumped alertly up the steps and disappeared into his compartment without even looking at me. The train left and I stood there muttering much harder insults at Mr. Sonnenschein and returned to the hotel, where I found Nela still comfortably resting. I told her my story without much pride. She was nice enough not to laugh.

There was a note from the French Embassy, written by Audrey Parr, the French wife of an English diplomat whom I had met in Rio on my first visit. She was a beautiful woman with the purest Greek profile, and I remember that Claudel had been in love with her at that time. "Cher Arthur," the letter said, "I'm staying with the French ambassador and his wife and we are all going to your concert. We would be delighted if you could come for a cup of tea at five o'clock. Please call me." I telephoned my acceptance. "I'm here with my fiancée, dear Audrey. Could I bring her? I would like you to meet her."

She answered on behalf of the ambassador, "Yes of course, with pleasure."

I began my concert that evening with the difficult Toccata in C major by Bach arranged by Busoni. I practiced it for an hour on the piano in the restaurant after lunch when everybody had gone. Some guests came back and listened to me hard at work as though it were a concert.

We arrived punctually at the embassy and were shown into the salon, where Audrey introduced us to the host. A few other guests were present. The moment we sat down I started a vivid, colorful account of the incident with Ravel. "Ce crétin M. Sonnenschein will pay for it!" I continued. Audrey Parr stood up suddenly, interrupted me, and with a loud voice introduced me to one of the guests. "M. Sonnenschein . . ." she said. A cold wind blew through the room. Sonnenschein mumbled some indistinct words amidst dead silence and I tried to laugh the whole thing off in a horribly artificial way, after which we left in a hurry.

I do not recollect this concert with much pride. In the big, half-empty hall the Toccata sounded with an echo and I played the rest of the program with less than inspiration. Nela sat alone in an empty box. Audrey Parr, accompanied by the ambassador and his wife, came to congratulate me, which made me feel still worse about my playing. Sonnenschein stood silently in the door without daring to approach.

After the concert we were given a free day in Prague and two tickets for the premiere of an opera by Hans Pfitzner. The opera was a heavy post-Wagnerian work, the singers not good enough to hold our attention, but there was one element which was outstanding—the rhythmical impact of the orchestra and the splendid sound it produced. In the program I found the name of the conductor, George Szell. Neither Nela nor I had heard of him. "Here is a great conductor," I said with deep conviction. How right I was!

The next morning I said to Nela, "I have some lovely concerts in Italy. Wouldn't you like to come too? Invite Alina on my behalf. She would make a lovely chaperone. My first concert is in Verona but we could meet in Padua and spend two days in Venice." Nela accepted happily.

82

Nela returned to Dresden and I to Paris. This time I prepared my program for Italy with greater care, especially the Beethoven Concerto No. 4 and the Tchaikovsky concerto for the Augusteo. I spent the two weeks almost incognito, lunched and dined by myself, and finally left with François for Padua, where we arrived an hour before the train which was bringing Nela and her sister. I saw them both emerge from their car, Nela fresh as a daisy and her sister looking somewhat funny wearing a student's cap with a visor. After Venice and Verona we proceeded to Rome for the great event at the Augusteo.

Here I could show off my immense popularity in the Eternal City. In the crowded Augusteo the thunderous "bravos," the rush of the audience to the platform to hear my encores at closer range, left Nela and her sister speechless. They had never seen that kind of a success before. Count San Martino, proud of me, invited me and the two sisters to the finest club in Rome for supper.

The next morning I was called up by an Italian friend of mine who was now one of Mussolini's ministers. "The Duce wants to meet you," he said, "and will send a car to fetch you this afternoon and take you to the Palazzo Venezia, where he will receive you." I was very flattered by this invitation, having heard that Mussolini played the violin and was interested in music. I expected my friend to come with me and introduce me to the Duce but to my astonishment the car arrived only with a chauffeur. It took me to the palazzo alone. At the well-guarded entrance, two men looked me over, took out from their pockets what I suppose were some photographs of me, and then escorted me to the famous reception room. It was well known that Il Duce received his visitors sitting at his desk at the far end of the room, which permitted him to scrutinize them on their long walk to the desk. Being used to appearing in public, I walked up with my usual quick steps without being especially impressed at meeting this formidable personality. Mussolini rose halfway to his feet to shake hands and I said a few polite words in French, knowing that he spoke it fluently but not as well as I did, which would help me, I hoped, *in petto*, to dominate the conversation. But he won. "My friend told me," he said in Italian, "that you speak our language very well, so let us talk in Italian." I felt right away in a state of grave inferiority. My Italian at that time was good enough to give orders at the restaurant or at my hotel but not for leading a stimulating conversation. "I hear that you play in many countries with great success," said Il Duce. I responded with a modest smile. "How do you manage to get your fees, since the Wall Street disaster, with all the countries making difficulties in allowing money to be taken out?"

I was a little astonished at this turn of our conversation. I tried to explain to him in my halting Italian that concert managers have a way of facing the situation. "In Spain, it is more difficult, I hear," he continued, "but as far as I know, all the European countries have severe laws about the money situation." By now, I became very impatient and a little vexed. I thought we were going to talk about music and not about money matters. I said in the best Italian I could summon, "Noi altri guadagnamo sopra tutto dei cuori più tosto che i soldi."* Mussolini clapped his hands and ex-

---

* We win hearts above all, rather than money.

claimed, "Bravo, bravissimo!" My phrase sounded to me like an aria of Verdi, but it won the day.

When my visit was over, he stood up, accompanied me to the door, which he seldom did, and the next morning I received his photo with the inscription: "Con admirazione al grande artista Arthur Rubinstein, Benito Mussolini." And that was not all: my friends told me that in his next speech from the balcony of the Palazzo Venezia he used with great emphasis my operatic phrase on the crowd below.

Shortly after this Roman victory, we left for Naples and there embarked for Palermo, where the Villa Igiea gave us beautiful accommodations. Even François had a room on the seafront. We arrived early in the morning. After a long rest, Nela and I strolled in the garden. It made me happy to see her share my predilection for this place. Alina took it for granted, constantly preoccupied with her own comfort as she would be in any other place in the world. At our *table d'hôte* meals she had the irritating habit of putting the left-over fruit into her bag and taking it to her room. I begged her not to do it but she didn't pay any heed. When I prepared enthusiastically to show them some particularly beautiful place, or a palazzo, she would force Nela to accompany her to a shoe shop and stay there until it became too late to do anything else, and my poor Nela did not dare to refuse.

I played again in the Teatro Massimo, which was filled by the subscribers of the Società Musicale of Palermo. Nela sat in a box opposite the stage with the president of the Società, the Baron del Monaco, a great music lover. A patriotic Sicilian, he showed us many of the beauties of this city which were not known to everybody. His only defect was that he was cross-eyed; you never knew if he was looking at you or at something else. Del Monaco offered to have me play at the Teatro Massimo any time I wanted to come.

Nela decided to accompany me to Tunis, where I was to give a concert. We were both excited at the prospect of seeing Hannibal's Carthago or rather what remained of it. Alina decided to return to Rome and wait for us there. I gave her the money for her expenses, happy to be rid of her for this small price. The last night in Palermo there was a full moon out of a fairy tale. I took Nela for a walk in the garden, our nostrils filled with the aroma of jasmine. We strolled down to a bench near the sea and it was there that we felt with certainty that we belonged to each other.

We reached Tunis in the happiest mood. The town itself looked like a French provincial city but its population was more Italian than French, although the latter gave it a characteristic imprint. The country around was pure Africa. The place where once the powerful Carthago threatened the existence of Rome was now an empty space with some sparse reminders of Hannibal's empire. But the countryside was beautiful and the bay of Hammamet was a paradise for tourists.

My concert was received by a heterogeneous public with a great politeness. Only my Spanish pieces brought a warm response. We returned to Palermo to take the boat for Naples but there was a telegram from Alina asking urgently for more money and so Nela decided to embark on a small seaplane that had been in service for a short time between Palermo and Rome. I admired Nela's intrepidness but tried to dissuade her. She wouldn't listen to me and so I let her go alone, not so much from fear but from not wanting to see her sister again.

Nela decided to give up Dresden, where Hitler's methods were beginning to be felt. "I shall stay with my parents in Warsaw," she declared. In the beginning of the spring I had a small tour in Spain.

"It would be wonderful to show you Spain," I said to Nela. "I'm sure you will love it as much as I do. For me it is my second homeland after Poland." She hesitated for a moment but then she said yes. Our meeting place was Barcelona.

It was a lovely week. My friend Eusebio Bertrand was enchanted to learn that I was going to marry and feasted my fiancée in the best manner: a great luncheon with his family and an interesting excursion to the monastery of Montserrat, the place of the Holy Grail in Wagner's *Parsifal*. Bertrand's daughter Mercedes, a very musical and charming young girl who never missed my concerts, was about Nela's age; there was also Isabel Marfá and the three became friends immediately.

The concert in Barcelona was not one of my best, but my public did not fail me, even if I was at my worst. We sailed for Palma de Mallorca, where I had promised to give a benefit concert to help with the expenses of a monument for Chopin. A priest, Padre José, was collecting money for this purpose from many artists who came to the island. My recital took place at Valldemosa, where the piano was placed at the open door of what is supposed to have been Chopin's cell. Wherever the cell was did not matter much but Chopin's soul was felt in the air. The padre had seats for the public this time in the long passage and both the audience and I were deeply moved. Most of the pieces I played had been composed right there. A composer born in Lodz, Alexander Tansman, who had made a great name for himself in Paris, was present at that concert and had supper with us. He told us some sad stories about his marriage and seemed to be very unhappy. After the concert I showed Nela the beauties of the island.

The padre took us the next day to the boat for Barcelona and promised to go to work on the monument. Nela and I went up to the deck for fresh air and a talk because I noticed she was gloomy. "I feel guilty about Munz," she said. "Tansman's sadness made me think of him. Shouldn't I go back to him in these sad times?" I became quite upset. It took me quite a time to calm her pangs of conscience and when we arrived in Madrid, where I took her right away to the Prado museum, she was herself again.

We went to the Prado on three consecutive days and I impressed her with the Escorial, this most severe and overpowering monastery where Philip II ended his life. In Madrid I could show Nela what the Spanish people meant to me, and she now understood my love and gratitude for this country. I hated leaving Spain without showing Nela Seville, the city of song and the *guitarra*, which the Andalusians call "honey and carnations" (*miel y claveles*), but the austere Castilian calls it the *España de la pandereta* (Spain of the tambourine). There were only five days left for me before an important date in Paris. The porter of the Palace Hotel, whom I asked to get train tickets, suggested, "Why don't you take a plane? There is a service between Madrid and Seville and you can be there in less than two hours." Without asking Nela, I obtained two tickets for the plane, which was leaving that same afternoon. As I was secretly envious of Nela for being the first to fly, I said casually, "I hope you don't mind that we are flying to Seville. I love to travel by air." She took it for granted.

At the nearby airport we entered a wooden structure where four other passengers were awaiting the plane. When the time came I followed Nela bravely onto the small plane but my heart was beating rapidly with expectation and, let us be frank, fear. We six passengers were seated three by three on benches opposite each other. We looked at one another with anguish in our eyes. When the motor started and the small plane began to rise in a very shaky way, I thought that our last hour had come. But after a short while it straightened out and suddenly my heart swelled with pride and exaltation at being able to look down on our poor planet with the eyes of an eagle. When we passed victoriously the Sierra de Córdoba, I felt sorry for the poor mountain climbers who risked their lives at every step to reach the summit. But when we began to descend, circling dangerously and seeing the earth upside down, I clutched Nela's hand in white terror. A few minutes later when we landed safely, I managed a smile and said to Nela, "It was lovely, eh?" She was not taken in.

Since that day I have flown a million miles between and above the tallest mountains, enjoying it more than any other conveyance for its comfort and even luxury.

At the hotel I communicated immediately with my old friend Juan Lafita, this man who represented the ideal prototype of an Andalusian. We didn't lose a moment; a long visit to the Cathedral, the largest in Spain, then we climbed the beautiful Giralda tower, walked up and down the gay Calle de Sierpes, and Lafita made us rest in three or four cafés, where he absorbed glasses of dry *jerez* and we a hot thick chocolate. After dinner he took us proudly to his beloved Barrio de Santa Cruz, entirely reserved for pedestrians. The next two days, thanks to my friend Juan, we enjoyed all Seville has to offer: a bullfight and two nights spent with the best flamencos on hand. Nela's enthusiasm and understanding for the Andalusian way of living made me want to show her Granada, but I had only two days left. "Are you willing," I asked her, "to leave tonight after supper and drive the whole night? We could reach Granada early in the morning, see whatever we can in one day and take the train for Madrid that night." She liked the idea.

I rented a decent car and we drove off at midnight. Nela slumbered practically all through the night. We reached Granada at five in the morning. The first glimpse of a deep red sun emerged from the Sierra Nevada while the city lights were still burning. Later, after a quick lunch and coffee on the terrace overlooking the other side of the city now in full daylight, I showed her meticulously all there was to see, the Alhambra and all, and we took the night train for Madrid.

There we parted. Nela made the long journey to Warsaw to get her divorce and I returned to Paris to wait for her.

The second Polish Festival was more brilliant and more elaborate than the first one. This time, two great international figures gave solo recitals within the framework of the Festival: Paderewski and Wanda Landowska, both with recitals at the Théâtre des Champs-Elysées. A third concert was an orchestral one at which Fitelberg conducted the Violin Concerto by Szymanowski played by Paul Kochanski, and I played four mazurkas by a young, very gifted Polish composer, Alfred Gradstein. The mazurkas were modern but kept a very pure Polish character. I liked them very much and obtained a big success for them. Paderewski and Cortot attended in a box at that concert and were very impressed by Gradstein's composition. After the concert I succeeded in interesting Germaine to help Gradstein compose his piano concerto by giving him a monthly allowance.

Paderewski's concert was typical of his public appearances. He made us wait as usual, and when he finally appeared, executed his famous deep bows a dozen times, and then settled down to a Chopin program. I cannot remember all of it, but the A-flat Polonaise, with which he finished the recital, had his fists banging the bass notes without discrimination. Then something strange happened. The public was applauding without much enthusiasm, politely awaiting an encore; when Paderewski reappeared, he bowed almost to the floor until the applause grew stronger and stronger, then he settled down and played four encores in succession without letting his public leave the hall. It remained in my memory as a sad concert.

Wanda Landowska had a genuine triumph. A long-time favorite of the Parisian public, she showed her absolute supreme mastery of the harpsichord.

There was a curious aftermath to the Festival. Paderewski invited Szymanowski, Fitelberg, Kochanski, and me to a lunch in his private rooms at the Hotel d'Orsay. To my astonishment, he put Karol to his right and me to his left; a gesture which was against the rule, as Fitelberg, being the conductor of the Festival and the oldest of our company, should have had the place of honor. Paderewski's renewed warm feeling toward me touched me very much because all through the years, since my visit to Morges, I had felt he was angry with me after the unfortunate item in the Russian newspaper in St. Petersburg when a gentleman asked me for my opinion of Paderewski. I had said with full conviction: "Paderewski has a personality of such genius that he would have been just as famous without playing the piano." The man published simply: "Paderewski, in the opinion of Rubinstein, is a great man but a bad pianist." I heard that this little item reached the master. Now I was overjoyed to hear that Paderewski was asked whom he considered the most talented of the young pianists and he unhesitatingly mentioned me.

Nela got her divorce certificate in Vilna with the help of a school friend. Mieczyslaw Munz behaved in the most noble way; in spite of the deep unhappiness he felt about losing her, he did all in his power to give her her freedom. In a little more than a week, Nela arrived in Paris, free to marry me, and I put her up at the Hotel Scribe. Now she became my official fiancée and was duly introduced to most of my friends.

At a concert at the Agriculteurs which we attended more out of duty toward some friends than out of pleasure, I had the occasion to introduce Nela to Misia Sert. Misia, in her brusque way, sized Nela up, liked what she saw and "ordered" her to change her hairstyle right away. Nela obeyed and continued to take all the advice Misia could give her. Misia, on the other hand, often said, "I wish you were my niece rather than Mimi, who irritates me too often." I was pleased to have found for Nela this maternal support.

Robert de Rothschild gave a great luncheon in our honor at which he, his family, and his guests loved Nela at first sight. She was right away declared to be "très parisienne" and in no time she felt at home in Paris.

We used to have lunch at the rue Ravignan. François was on friendly terms with the wife of a baker nearby who roasted a chicken in a masterly way. Edouard of the rue Daunou provided me with his famous raspberry tart. Nela was very much impressed with my luncheon; it must have reassured her that I had a great appreciation for the art of cooking. After lunch we often had long talks and I told Nela about my feelings concerning marriage. "Every day, we have to find out anew if we want to marry each other, and never take each other *for granted*."

Marcel and Juliette Achard took to Nela right away. We became anxious to get our marriage license as quickly as possible, and found out to our disappointment that Paris demanded more than a month while English laws required only two weeks of residence. We had no choice—it had to be London.

The Kochanskis arrived from Zakopane and decided to spend the rest of their vacation in Le Touquet. Paul seemed pleased about my marriage to Nela and said to her, "I warn you, I shall kill you if you don't make him happy." Zosia was cool, if not hostile, and was rather evasive when I invited them to the wedding.

83

On a rainy day we took the train to Calais, where we boarded the boat train and had to endure the usual ordeal of dreadful smells on high seas. Nela in her warm coat and a lovely brown hat dragged me up to the deck to get some fresh air. To give her head more elegance, I lent her my diamond horse tiepin to replace her own hatpin. We were walking hand in hand when a terrific gust of wind swept the hat, pin and all, into the sea. Nela looked at me in despair; I was glad that I didn't know how to swim, otherwise I might have been tempted to retrieve it gallantly. My poor fiancée reached Dover with her beautiful hair very windswept. At Victoria Station, I took Nela in a taxi to the Mayfair Hotel and I rented the same flat in Bury Street again.

The next morning, I took the necessary steps for our wedding and was told that July 29 was the first legal date on which we could marry.

Gaisberg telephoned one morning: "Arthur, I have a wonderful project for you to make a record of the Tchaikovsky concerto with Barbirolli and the London Symphony Orchestra. The date is fixed and the studio ready. Will you do it?" For a moment I was taken aback. The wedding and everything connected with it had taken my mind off my music, and I suddenly became ashamed. "Yes, I will do it, Fred, and with joy." I went right away to work on the concerto, particularly on the dangerous octaves of the first movement. On the day of the recording, I felt fit and happy. John, the orchestra, and I were inspired. We finished the whole concerto in two days. Gaisberg promised to let me have a proof of the record as soon as possible.

My friends opened their warm and generous hearts to Nela in that true English way which had always touched me so much. Lesley helped Nela in every way, just as a mother would have done. Sybil Cholmondeley had us for a small luncheon and suddenly announced: "You must let me give you the wedding reception. I hope you will not mind if Rock is not present. This occasion will be the first time that I have opened my house, as we never had more than ten or twelve people to lunch or dinner." Her invitation was gratefully accepted by me and I was proud to give Nela the proof that, in some way, I was well liked in the great city of London. In spite of the many expenses in view, I decided to ask Nela's brother Bronislaw to be my best man at the ceremony. He was delighted to come, especially to London, which he loved and where he had good friends. I reserved a room for him at the Savoy and was glad for Nela to have a member of her family present.

Two nights before the wedding, we received a regal present unforgettable for me. Sylvia Sparrow had married a lawyer from Plymouth, a Mr. Caunter, who had been wounded in the war. He was left a cripple and could walk only in a bent position. The present for the two nights was music in their home, pure divine music. Jacques Thibaud, Tertis, and Salmond, with Sylvia casually as second violin, played with me two whole nights all the chamber music we loved best. We played the Brahms quartets, a Schubert trio, the Dvořák quartet, the Fauré quartet, a Mozart quartet, the great *Archduke* Trio by Beethoven. Jacques and Lionel played some of their pieces with my accompaniment and we basked in this musical euphoria. Sylvia, emulating Muriel Draper, offered us tasty cold suppers during our rests. I am afraid that Nela, in spite of loving the music, was a victim; she was not too strong at that time and needed her sleep, but she took it bravely.

One morning, Lady Cholmondeley gave us bad news: "Your party has to be on the twenty-seventh, my dear," she said, "because on the twenty-eighth my household leaves for Norfolk for the summer." This was a blow, but I did not give in. "All right," I answered, "we shall be married on the twenty-seventh." By some clever manipulations on my part, I made the registrar accept the date of July 27. The Polish ambassador, Mr. Constanty Skirmunt, Lesley Jowitt, Ruth Draper (who was appearing on the London stage at that time), and Bronislaw Mlynarski were the witnesses. On the great day, the wedding took place at three o'clock in the afternoon at Caxton Hall. Nela was taken care of by Lesley from early morning and she was in good hands. At nine in the morning, I rushed to Asprey's to get the wedding rings. I saw there only one client at such an early hour. It was Queen Victoria Eugenia of Spain, who, funnily enough, was the first to congratulate me on my wedding.

I put on my elegant cutaway which I used at concert matinees, my top hat, white gloves, and took Bronislaw to lunch at Quaglino's restaurant in Bury Street, only three houses away from my flat. We both felt terribly nervous. I was suddenly panic-stricken at the thought of losing my freedom and he was still slightly nervous about his sister's divorce. We drank two strong whiskeys to calm our nerves, before our food was served. The drinks untied our tongues and on the way to Caxton Hall, Bronek sang the praises of his sister. The ambassador and Ruth Draper were already there and after a while Nela appeared in a long dress, with a new hairstyle and a large hat. She had a bouquet of tuberoses which I had sent her and the rather unattractive room was decorated with the red carnations I had ordered. The ominous question of the registrar was duly answered with a loud "yes" from both of us, the witnesses signed the register, and Lesley invited us to her house for a rest and a glass of champagne before Lady Cholmondeley's party. It was I who drank most of the champagne and I went to the piano and played all the well-known wedding marches and a few improvised ones to boot. I rented an open limousine, which took us to Kensington Palace Gardens.

When we entered the house, the huge drawing room was full of people and many of them were out in the garden, which bordered Kensington Park. It was one of the largest receptions I have ever seen. All the available ambassadors and their wives were present, many members of the British government, the arts were strongly represented by famous musicians, writers, actors, and painters. The only person who was not at the feast was Lord Cholmondeley who had left that same morning for the country. Two enormous buffets were covered with champagne in buckets and lovely things to eat. Everybody seemed to want to drink to our health, to which I had to respond with at least one sip of champagne. Nela, fortunately, abstained from drinking. When the time came to leave, I could hardly stand on my legs. I have never drunk so much in my whole life, before or since. After warm thanks and embraces for our hostess, we entered the open limousine to drive as man and wife to my flat in Bury Street. The newspapers had sent reporters and photographers, who besieged us at Caxton Hall and at the reception. To our great surprise we saw our pictures on the front pages of the last editions in the evening papers. Our wedding day finished with a dinner at Quaglino's, where I was really drunk for the first and last time of my life. My head turned all the time and I could only mumble. All I remember is Gertrude Lawrence, who came over to our table to apologize for not coming to our reception. Her apologies seemed to last more than an hour; I was trying to stand up but dreamt only of sitting down again.

Next morning, in spite of my splitting headache, I felt depressed by Paul's absence at my wedding. I knew Sophie was responsible. It might have been a belated revenge for my refusal to be at her wedding; but I did not miss her, I only missed him.

We took to Paris a shower of presents. Sybil gave Nela a beautiful diamond-and-sapphire brooch. Margot Asquith and Elizabeth Bibesco gave us an ancient Egyptian cat of great beauty. Christabel gave me an autographed letter by Chopin, Lesley, a golden antique watch chain, and there were many others which I cannot remember. In Paris, we found a pile of packages with wonderful presents. I remember Germaine de Rothschild's diamond clip for Nela, rare books, other books with dedications, and lovely gifts of all sorts from all my friends. The only person who did not give us anything was Princess Winnie de Polignac, but she invited us to spend a few weeks in Venice at her palazzo.

My own wedding gift to Nela was to be a nice diamond ring. Robert de Rothschild, whom I asked for advice, sent me a jeweler he knew well who brought me a few cut diamonds to choose from and then have the stone set in platinum by Cartier. I chose a fine cut emerald-shaped stone, accepted the price, and went to the bank the next morning to have the money sent from Buenos Aires as usual. To my great shock, the director of the bank informed me that my money in Argentina was blocked and could only be used in the country itself. This was bad news indeed. I had spent most of the money which I had earned in Europe on the lovely times in Italy and Spain, on the not small expenses for Nela in Paris and London, the invitation for her brother, and the wedding itself. I telephoned Valmalète and asked him to arrange some concerts at once for me for the needs of the rest of the summer. He promised to do his best. "But now," he said, "go to Evian, where there might be an immediate chance." Nela was not much impressed by my sudden show of poverty. She had become used to these changes and was ready to leave for Evian.

We settled at the Hotel Royale, so well known to me, and enjoyed breakfast the next morning on our private balcony. A telegram arrived; it was Valmalète announcing a concert for me in Deauville the next day, another two days later in Le Touquet, and a third one in the same Evian. At the same time, a charming letter from Germaine was forwarded to us inviting us to spend two or three weeks at her villa in Cannes. We wired right away our enthusiastic acceptance. My old deus ex machina did his work again, enabling me, with no money, to offer my wife the most precious kind of honeymoon in Cannes on the Côte d'Azur and in Venice, the paradise of honeymooners.

Valmalète was nice enough to drive us to all three sea resorts for these concerts, which were an unwanted intrusion on my honeymoon. What was worse, they didn't fill my pocket with gold, but only the means to spend the next months without worries.

Germaine received us in her lovely villa with her warm hospitality. Our stay was slightly spoiled by continuous attacks by millions of mosquitoes which would not allow us to sleep, eat, or move without being engaged in a constant fight with them. I will always remember an unfortunate picnic on a small island off the coast. Germaine insisted on having it in the right tradition. Germaine, her daughter Jacqueline with her husband, Nela, and I arrived at the wretched island after a rather rough crossing and settled under a kindly-looking tree which, as we noticed too late, also lent its hospitality to an anthill. I think it is unnecessary to state whether we enjoyed our meal, but I can say that we were very happy when we were back in Cannes again.

After the two weeks of Germaine's sweet hospitality and an unbearable heat wave, the Orient Express took us straight to Venice. The beginning of September was the ideal time for the City of the Doges. The princess was generous enough this time to send her *motoscafo* to fetch us and assigned to us the privileged room overlooking the Canale Grande. The very large four-poster bed was welcome after the long journey, and after a good rest, we felt ready to enjoy to the full all that this divine city had to offer. The princess was pleased to see me happy with my bride. "She is right for you," she said, and from that day on, she included Nela in her friendship for me. Nela, for her part, was fascinated by the very attractive but complex personality of Princess Winnie.

To make my stay perfect, Paul arrived with Zosia. He even brought his dog Lucky with him. Poor Paul poured all his love in that dog who gave him the warmth he so much needed. Of course, we spent the time mostly together, but it was heartbreaking to see Paul refusing to enter the Ducal Palace or the Accademia "because I can't leave Lucky behind, he would feel lonely." Both Nela and I were worried about Paul; he had lost his usual humor and did not enjoy his food. We would end up sadly by playing our old piquet game in his hotel room, and this was Venice for my poor Paul. His departure for America made me very sad, knowing I would miss him very much. Our friendship was essential in my life.

84

An agent of Soviet Russia's cultural department came to see me at the rue Ravignan proposing that I give a few concerts in Russia. When I asked him about the fees, he smiled benevolently. "We will pay you one thousand rubles per concert and all traveling expenses first-class and sleeping cars. We will take care of everything else, hotels, transportation, etc., etc. You will be able to use the rubles to buy many useful things for which we will give you an export license." When I mentioned my wife, he added, "Of course it goes for both of you." I liked the idea of living for a month without having to touch my own money, but Nela was a little hesitant. She had dreadful memories of the First World War when her family fled to Moscow before the German invasion of Lithuania. She was barely six years old when she had to go through the whole tragedy of the war and the Communist revolution. "Darling, it will be interesting to see what has happened to this country which we both know so well, and as the relations between Poland and the Soviet Union are now very friendly, there is no risk for us." We decided to accept, and I signed the contract.

We took the Nord Express to Warsaw, where we had to change trains for Russia. When we reached the German frontier, a man entered the train and walked up and down the corridor staring at us. In the dining car, where we sat down for breakfast, we began to feel frankly uncomfortable; all eyes seemed to look at us disapprovingly. We did not know it yet, but this was the beginning of the Hitler era. We spent the whole day sitting in our compartment and gave a big sigh of relief when we reached the Polish frontier. We found Warsaw in a nervous state about the latest developments in Germany—the early moves of Hitler, the unsuccessful putsch with General Ludendorff in Munich, and his book *Mein Kampf* with its violent attacks against Socialists, Communists, and Jews, which were derided in the beginning. The Poles were mainly preoccupied with the Danzig corridor (this artificial bridge between the two countries). Now the great success of the National Socialist Party, already called Hitler's Nazis, looked like a terrible threat to peace.

We took the train to Moscow in a gloomy mood. Soon enough we were struck by the stark difference between the Western world and Communist

Russia. At the Polish frontier station, polite customs officers in neat uniforms were expediting our luggage quickly and efficiently. At the restaurant, the buffet offered an attractive variety of the Polish culinary art. All the tables were occupied by people engaged in animated conversation; one heard laughter just as anywhere else in Poland. When the train slowly entered the Russian side of the frontier, even the landscape looked bleak and dreary. At the station itself, heavily armed policemen dressed in unclean khaki uniforms entered the train and rudely took our passports; this reminded me of my first impressions of the Tsarist Russian frontiers. The customs officers scrutinized our luggage for well over an hour. When we were finally allowed to enter the canteen for a glass of tea, there were two pots of faded flowers on the buffet, but no food in sight. The waiter, wearing a dirty apron, put two glasses of pale-looking tea in front of us. When we asked for lemon he answered rudely, "No lemon." Our fellow passengers who occupied the other tables sat in silence looking around with fear in their eyes. This discouraging prelude was a good preparation for what was to come.

After a very long journey we reached Moscow in the morning. A bearded man clad in a leather jacket and a peaked cap was expecting us and welcomed us on behalf of the Soviet department of music. After a polite exchange he told us in Russian (which Nela and I spoke fluently), "I am assigned to escort you," and he added with a sarcastic smile, "I shall be constantly with you." It sounded more like a threat than an offer of help. He took us to the Hotel National, which I knew well from previous visits. The once elegant hotel now looked shabby and dilapidated. The old elevator functioned on and off. Right away, Nela started looking for "unwanted guests" in the bed and worked quite a while on the bedclothes. As to the bathroom, it gave us quite a lot of trouble. There was no plug in the bathtub. The tap in the washbasin was perforated on top, so that when you turned it on, you were showered all over with water. Nela managed to find a way of channeling the water into the basin.

The food situation was tragicomic. You were offered bread "but no butter" one day, or there would be butter but no bread on the next. Something essential was always missing; most irritating of all was that the so-called restaurant workers were completely indifferent to all these shortcomings. Our imposed companion expressed with deep conviction that life in the Soviet Union was ideal. He would laugh at our complaints. "But what about the slaves working in the capitalist countries?" "Capitalists" and "imperialists" were used in every phrase he pronounced. I would have loved to hear his opinions on the terrace of a café on a boulevard in Paris.

I found in my dressing room a letter written in Russian. When I opened the envelope, I looked from habit at the signature. As unbelievable as it sounds, the letter was signed by Muriel Draper. She told me that she was staying in Moscow as an envoy of the Communist Party of the United States, had learned Russian, as I could see, and would visit me after the concert. I had told Nela all about Muriel, so it was amusing for me to watch the confrontation between them. As Muriel insisted on speaking Russian, she made me laugh and that angered her. I never saw her again, nor did I wish to.

My first concert took place in the large Tchaikovsky Hall of the Conservatory. The piano was an old Steinway, not too well reconditioned. I cannot remember the whole program, but I feel sure that I played *Petrushka*, on which I counted very much, and my best Chopins. The hall was full, but I did not know if the tickets had been sold or given away. The Russians are fundamentally musical. They are totally involved in a performance, engaging their hearts and souls. They are easily moved and excited, but just as easily discouraged and disappointed. My playing pleased them immensely, especially my conception of Chopin and the pieces by Albéniz, which were new to them. *Petrushka*, however, was received with a cool polite applause. My encores—*Navarra* and de Falla's *Fire Dance*—provoked wild screams and ovations. The old attendant of the artist's room, who had been at his post since Tsarist times, said to me with a deep sigh, "No tea, no lemon, no cakes anymore. There is nothing left to live for." It was the only sincere phrase I heard during all my stay in Russia.

After the concert, my first visitor was Harry Neuhaus. We were both shouting with delight and hugging each other after our long separation. He was now the director of the Conservatory and this was a very high position indeed. It made me happy to hear that, as Karol and I were often worried about his whereabouts. He accepted our invitation for supper at the Hotel Metropole, the only restaurant, which was frequented mostly by foreign ambassadors and tourists. Our Russian companion, who in reality was assigned to spy on us, took us there in his car and declared that he would wait for us to take us home. I remembered the restaurant well from prewar days; it remained the same but was in a state of neglect. Harry was waiting for us and we settled down for a well-deserved supper. Nela and I were famished. While we were ordering, an attaché of the Polish Embassy, Henryk Sokolnicki, rushed up to our table. He was a good friend of Nela's and she seemed pleased to see him again so I invited him to join us. He told us that the whole embassy had been at the concert and that the ambassador, Mr. Stanislaw Patek, intended to give us a reception, to which he would invite Litvinov, the Foreign Minister. The four of us fell into an animated conversation in Polish.

Harry revealed the reason why *Petrushka* fell rather flat at the concert: "You see Arthur, the public knew every tune of *Petrushka* by heart, and as they had never seen the ballet in Russia, they thought it was a simple potpourri of Russian folklore. As it is rather long, they felt a certain disdain for it, in spite of your playing it so brilliantly." I must add that Harry gave me a great pleasure finding my playing in full progress. It was late when we finished our supper. "Please have lunch with us tomorrow, Harry," I said on parting. He accepted, and our Russian, who had dozed in the lobby, took us home.

In the morning, Harry's shaky voice came over the telephone: "I spent the night at the G.P.U. [the Russian secret police]. They wanted to know why I was driven home by an attaché of a foreign embassy, so I do not dare to come to lunch." I hardly saw Harry for the rest of my stay in Moscow. He was even afraid to accept the official invitation to the reception at the Polish Embassy.

The party turned out to be very interesting. It gave me an opportunity to meet the new generation of Russian musicians, who besieged me with questions about the musical life in the rest of the world. All they knew and heard was about strikes and revolutions, the cruel attacks of police against workmen, and other such nonsense. Litvinov had kind words for me, which obviously impressed our spy-companion, who then showed greater respect and more attentive service.

My next date was in St. Petersburg, now called Leningrad. I was quite excited at seeing the old capital again with its memories of the Anton Rubinstein Piano Competition, of André Diederichs, of its luxury and its beautiful palaces and churches. We arrived early on a bitterly cold morning and were driven to the old Hotel d'Europe, which had become shabby and neglected after being one of the finest hotels in Europe. The concert hall was still the same, except that it had changed its name from the Hall of the Nobility to the Philharmonic. The piano was excellent and to my joy I heard that Prokofiev was in town. My first concert took place the evening of our arrival and was a genuine great success. The audience in Leningrad was much warmer than the one in Moscow, and seemed to be the same as under the Tsarist regime. The people were better dressed, had better manners, and during intermission I was served, as of old, tea and cakes. Prokofiev came to the concert, was pleased to see and hear me, and spent several hours with us the next day at the hotel. Our conversation revolved around the state of music in Soviet Russia. "The appreciation for music is at its lowest just now. They went so far as to prohibit the playing of Chopin in public for some time, under the pretext that its 'extreme sentimentality' was detrimental to the character of the Russian people. As for myself, I am still considered the exponent of decadent music of the Western world. Fortunately, my fellow musicians have kept some respect for me."

My second concert took place two days later.

Odessa and Kiev were the next cities. The train would take eighteen hours to get to Odessa. Our steady escort took us to the station, and there we saw a sad sight: dozens of people, men, women, and children, lying around on the floor of the large dirty hall, exuding a dreadful smell, which indicated a long stay. They were obviously waiting to be allowed to leave for some unknown destination. We found the Polish consul and his wife in front of our car with some flowers for Nela. While we were talking to them a porter put our luggage into our compartment. When I went in to see if everything was in order, I saw to my dismay that it was a compartment without sleeping arrangements. I jumped right down to complain to our escort about the mistake, but he answered coolly that there was a priority for some officials and that we would have to sleep the best we could. This enraged me. My contract stipulated clearly our right to the usual sleeping accommodation. I shouted to the porter, who was waiting to be paid, "Get our things down again, we are not going." The porter obeyed, and my man became nervous. "I think at the next station you will have the sleeper. These officials will probably leave there." This was too much for me. I shouted at him, "I know you are lying, like everybody else in your country." The Polish consul and his wife became ashen pale with fear. They were afraid of the worst, but my man became meek. "Please, please believe me. You will get the sleeper at the next station."

"Then you have to come with us and prove it." The poor man had to resign himself. We took him along, and two hours later at a longish stop, he managed to get our accommodations, but he had to wait the whole night to get back to Moscow. That taught him a good lesson.

We arrived in Odessa early in the morning on the day of the concert. Two kind professors from the local Imperial Conservatory took care of us at the station and brought us to the hotel, but they had sad news for me about the piano for the concert. "It is a prewar instrument, but I feel sure you will make the best of it." In spite of their warning, I was distressed by the state of the piano. To my great pleasure, however, the concert went better than I expected; even *Petrushka*, which was so coldly received in Moscow, found a really enthusiastic reception here.

The director of the Conservatory agreed to have supper with us at the good old Hotel d'Angleterre, now deteriorated like all the others. "What a shame that our piano students couldn't hear you. We had seats for only a few. One of them is an extremely gifted boy of thirteen. He dreams of playing for you. Could you possibly come tomorrow morning and meet our students? We would consider it a great honor." It was difficult; our train for Kiev was leaving in the early afternoon, but Nela encouraged me to do it. "I shall pack and be ready when you return from the Conservatory." I always loved young piano students. There were many things for me to tell them, ideas to share with them, and I simply enjoyed their company. After a few exchanges, the director introduced his talented pupil. A short, red-headed boy shook hands timidly and went straight to the piano. With the first bars of the *Appassionata* by Beethoven, I felt I was in the presence of a true God-given talent. I wanted to hear more and he played the still little-known *Jeux d'eau* by Ravel like a finished master. I kissed him on both cheeks and took his name, which was Emil Gilels. I wrote it down carefully because I was determined to tell Harry Neuhaus about him. I came back to the hotel in an exultant mood and raved to Nela about this wonderful boy.

There was a touching scene at the station when young Gilels appeared wearing only a light coat in the bitter cold, with two of his fingers poking through holes in his gloves. He held tightly three roses which he offered to Nela. A gift which probably meant he would go without lunch. Back in Moscow, Harry was so impressed by my account of Gilels that he made him come right away to the capital, and provided the means for him to enter the Moscow Conservatory. Well, I had the honor to be on the jury of the Queen Elizabeth competition in 1938, at which we unanimously gave the first prize to the master pianist Emil Gilels. I learned later from Sviatoslav Richter of another curious incident. At a reception in New York, he told me quite casually, "I happened to be at your recital in Odessa when you played *Petrushka*. I was studying art then, but your playing convinced me that I should become a pianist, so in a way, I owe you my career."

We arrived in Kiev after a few hours in a smelly train. The local "comrade" in charge of music affairs took us to the onetime best hotel in town—the Continental. It was heartbreaking to remember the lovely days with the Davydovs, with Jaroszynski, and not see the gloomy aspect of the city and, even worse, of the hotel. Nela, who was visiting the city for the first time, was so appalled that she could hardly believe my tales of the charm of this capital of a province where so many prominent Poles had lived, where Balzac found his Madame Hanska, where Liszt found his Princess Wittgenstein née Iwanowska. Anyway, we did not give in and tried to make the best of it. My concert took place in the same old hall where twenty years before I had played to the elegant elite of the city. Fortunately, the shabby and smelly audience still showed its born love for music and listened to me with attention and approval. Here, too, *Petrushka* earned an ovation.

The next day, I took Nela for a walk to show her the beautiful Church of St. Michael, with its green roofs and golden onion-shaped cupola. The exterior was just the same, but the inside was desecrated in a dreadful way. They had turned it into an anti-religious museum. The famous icons by

Rublev were no longer to be seen. We left in disgust and it made us suddenly feel the bitter cold more acutely. "Let us find a place where they sell vodka freely," I said to Nela. Buying food freely was impossible in Soviet Russia; things could only be had in the shops of the Soviet syndicates. My own position as a foreign artist was that of a *spets* (special worker), which meant that I could buy food in a place assigned to this kind of worker. While in Moscow, I went to one of these places, and upon showing my special card, I was asked if I wanted a kilo of fish or a kilo of caviar. I shall let my reader guess my choice! We ate that caviar for two whole days until Nela began to hate it. "Everything smells of caviar, the whole room is full of it. I can't bear it." And so I gave the rest of the tin to the wildly enthusiastic maid. The shortage was so great that the man who brought us our tea asked us timidly if he could use the remains of our lemon when we had finished with it. We had brought lemon with us from Poland together with other provisions which we had heard were lacking in Russia.

Nela suddenly shouted, "I see a shop with alcoholic drinks which seems to be open." Here I could spend my rubles. To our satisfaction, there were many bottles on view. A salesman with an indifferent expression on his face sat behind the counter. On my request for a bottle of vodka he waved his hand in a negative way. "No vodka left," he said, "but you can have a Caucasian wine." Seeing our disappointment, he seemed to feel sorry for us. "We have received a shipment of hundreds of bottles of a kind of cognac. If you like, I can sell you some." At the sight of a bottle, Nela and I became speechless with amazement. It was the most expensive and finest drink to be had in Poland. The great Polish families sometimes kept barrels of Starka, as it was called, for more than a century in their cellars. The bottle the man showed us had a Polish label. It had arrived straight from the cellars of a Prince Sanguszko and was eighty years old. A small glass of this liqueur was then worth three dollars in Poland. We managed miraculously to ask casually if we could buy a certain number of these "strange bottles" to give to friends. He replied smilingly, "As many as you want. A good drink keeps you healthy." He brought up as many as we could handle between us. I am sure we took more than a dozen to the hotel. Their real value was greater than all the rest of the rubles I earned in Russia.

The last city of the Ukraine was Kharkov, with its memory of my visit to Koussevitzky after the Anton Rubinstein Piano Competition in 1910. Here, as in the rest of Soviet Russia, the public at my concerts consisted of the upper crust of the Communists, those who had ready money for the tickets. The real music students and music lovers, who lived on their miserable earnings, could not afford to come to the concert.

The Polish consul general turned out to be an acquaintance of Nela's from Warsaw and invited us to spend the whole day at his apartment, where

I was able to practice and his wife saved us food in the best Polish manner. For our part, we gave our hosts the unexpected royal gift of a bottle of Starka, which was received with enthusiastic acclaim. The taste of it was even better than we had imagined. After the concert, which left me with no memories, we spent a gay evening at the consulate.

The following day, something quite unusual happened which has never been repeated since. During the inedible meal they offered us at the hotel, we decided to uncork a bottle of the precious Starka. This helped us to wash down the oversalted, hard-to-swallow herring, and by and by we actually finished the bottle—just the two of us. My readers might think that an ambulance had to take us to a hospital, but they would be vastly mistaken. Fresh as daisies, we went to the consulate for coffee; I went to the piano to practice and Nela played bridge with the family; if I am not mistaken, she emerged the winner.

Moscow was our last stop and my concert there gave me a whole free week, which we spent in the various theaters, where we lived the really great unforgettable moments of our stay. The so-called Artistic Theater of Stanislavski and Nemirovitch-Dantchenko, my beloved experience from the old days in Moscow, remained the same, and even better. Stanislavsky had died, but his partner added operas to the repertoire of his theater, where the singers also had to be accomplished actors. We saw *Eugene Onegin* by Tchaikovsky, sung and *acted* magnificently. We saw *The Cherry Orchard* by Chekhov as produced by the author himself.

I have a few memories of another kind from my return to Moscow after the First World War. There was the interesting visit of Vladimir Horowitz's father, who came to tell me flattering things about my concerts but mainly to inquire as to the whereabouts and success of his son. Naturally enough, my news about his son made him very happy.

The other visit was one of a very sad kind. Mr. Alexander Zatajevitch, who was for years the chief of cultural matters in Warsaw under the Tsarist rule, often used to come to the Hotel Victoria to exchange views about the latest concerts. A great admirer of Rachmaninoff, he had made me a gift of the first printing of the First and Second Concerto of his beloved master and friend. He made me sight-read them in his presence. Now in Moscow, I saw an old miserable man. His clothes looked threadbare and he was shod in nothing but galoshes. He told me heartbreaking tales about his life and the misery of the remaining upper class of old. "I think," he said, "that I am better off than others." Nela presented him with some unobtainable items such as good soap, needles and thread, a couple of lemons, some tea and coffee, and a dozen lumps of sugar. I could hardly bear the sight of him crying when he accepted them.

There was another deeply moving scene which showed the tragedy of the once wealthy and powerful. At one of the theaters, we were given seats on the aisle of the last row. Two old ladies with fine aristocratic faces and demeanor were standing next to us among others who evidently only had tickets for standing room. Both Nela and I quite spontaneously stood up and offered them our seats. They first resisted our offer, but finally sat down. During the first intermission, something poignant happened: One of the ladies opened her shabby handbag, took out with a trembling hand two large crackers, and offered them to us. We felt that it was their meal for the evening but we took them so as not to offend them.

Before leaving for Poland, we tried hard to invest our remaining rubles in some worthwhile objects. Unfortunately, the Soviet government put up two kinds of shops—one for the internal commerce, where you could buy things with rubles, and the other, called *torgsin*, which was the most important, where one could acquire goods with American dollars. Some of these goods had been stolen from the palaces and houses of the rich by the Communists. There were even dishes, cutlery, and napkins from the Winter Palace of the Tsar. We looked at these riches with hungry eyes, but without the necessary dollars. In the other shops we found nothing but odd and rather silly ware. I remember buying three back scratchers with ivory hands, a mute piano which the salesmen pretended belonged to Anton Rubinstein, and all sorts of worn-out brocades and material which Nela acquired half-heartedly.

There was also a book shop and there I emptied the shelves with delight. Most of the books had poor bindings and bad printing, but fortunately the texts remained unchanged. I now needed a new suitcase to carry them in. Mir and Mirilis, once the largest department store of Moscow, was now empty of goods. All it had to offer were the classical Russian toys. In a dark corner they had half a dozen suitcases, not made of leather, of course, but some unknown material. We were happy to get rid of the heavy weight of the books we were carrying and filled the case with them. Out in the street, I had a dreadful surprise: The two sides of the case fell apart and all the books landed in the snow. Luckily we were near our hotel, so the discomfort was not too great.

At the last minute, I wanted to use my *spets* card to get some fresh caviar, but Nela's disgusted expression stopped me. "I can't endure that smell in our luggage," Nela said, and so I gave in. A few months later we dined at Maxim's. "What would you like to order, Nela?" I asked her. After a short hesitation she said, "I would like some caviar." I couldn't help laughing when the maître d'hôtel dished her out carefully a teaspoonful! "I like my caviar only when I feel like it," she said imperiously.

The high moments of my stay in Russia were seeing Prokofiev and Harry again and the evenings at the theaters. Also, to my great satisfaction, the official concert agency insisted that I return.

85

On our way to Paris, we stopped in Warsaw, where my in-laws offered us the hospitality of the small apartment next to theirs, where Nela's brother, Bronislaw, used to live before he married. It had a piano in the room, which was very welcome.

Valmalète wrote that the orchestra of Bern in Switzerland wanted me to be the soloist in one of their concerts if I would perform the Liszt E-flat Concerto. I had never played this piece before but was very keen on appearing for the first time in the capital of Switzerland. I bought the score, read it through carefully, and decided to accept the engagement. I became quite enthusiastic about this beautiful and so masterfully constructed work and learned it by heart in less than three days. As usual, I practiced for no more than three hours a day.

To my delight, on one of my quests for books and things, I found a charming portrait of Paul Kochanski in an antique shop; it had been painted in Brussels while he was studying there. It hung proudly in my homes until the Second World War, when I lost it together with all my other belongings.

I arrived in Bern the night before the concert. My only rehearsal was to be at ten the next morning. I remember an amusing prelude to this rehearsal: Feeling very nervous about this "premiere" of the Liszt concerto, I dressed at seven o'clock, had a quick breakfast, and rushed to the hotel lobby, which had an old piano, mainly to decorate the room. Here I started to work with terrific intensity on the many hazardous passages in the concerto. When I stopped, I found the room full of elderly people, women knitting and the men reading morning papers; they had listened the whole time to my practicing. I don't want to keep the reader uncomfortable about the result of this concert, which turned out to be exceptionally good. They engaged me again for next season with the additional offer of a concert in the very musical city of Zurich.

In Paris, very great news was waiting for me—Nela was expecting a child. I embraced my wife with tears in my eyes. "It will be a daughter, it will be a daughter," I cried.

Ever since adolescence I had felt a deep desire to have a daughter, as I have in my nature a passion for women. A daughter is your own daughter, even if she hates you, and this very fact of *belonging* calms a possessive mind.

The Christmas and New Year's Eve festivities took on another color for an expectant father. This time, it was I who became oversolicitous, urging Nela to rest, while she suddenly showed an unusual vitality. Number 15, rue Ravignan changed overnight from a bachelor's den into a solid home for a family. There was suddenly a kitchen with a stove and all the necessary utensils, a maid appeared from nowhere, and my chic little dining room was turned into a nursery.

Horowitz came to town from Milan and was quite astonished to have a good lunch at our home instead of being taken to a restaurant. "You know," he said half mockingly, "you give me a good example. I want to marry Wanda Toscanini." I took it as a good joke. While he was in Paris he continued his old ways, played me his latest encores, and spent the rest of the day in our company.

A little later, I learned with astonishment that he did marry Wanda Toscanini. We sent him a wire of good wishes.

During the next season, he appeared in Paris again alone and always spent the whole day with us. Late one night, when we took him to his hotel and were parting, he said very amiably, "Will you lunch with me next Sunday?" I was flabbergasted! It was the first time that I heard him invite anybody. "Well, well," I said, "this is quite an honor, Volodya, but unfortunately on Saturday night I am playing the Tchaikovsky concerto with Mengelberg in Amsterdam and there is always a supper afterward, so I couldn't be back before Sunday afternoon."

"But if you don't go to the supper, you could take the night train," he said. I did not like to disappoint the Concertgebouw directors and disliked the night train, which arrived in Paris at seven in the morning, but Nela was on his side: "Arthur, we cannot refuse Volodya's first invitation. We can easily give up the supper and be here on Sunday morning."

This very concert in Amsterdam remains in my memory. At the rehearsal, Mengelberg gave me a hard time. The whole morning he had been rehearsing a long work by Max Reger. After an intermission there was hardly any time left for the Tchaikovsky. "Don't worry about it," he said with a heavy Dutch accent. "The orchestra knows the concerto and I know it too."

"I know it too," I said impatiently, "but the question is, have we time to know it together?"

"We don't need to play the whole thing through," he said, "only just the few places which are important." I gave in, but I was not happy about it. We settled down to the rehearsal. The beginning went well, but he stopped the orchestra and picked up another part of the concerto. Then, when we came to the cadenza, he stopped us and began to munch a cake, which he had the cheek to deposit on the piano. "Play a few bars before the end of the cadenza," he said. I did so, but he missed the orchestra's entrance. I politely played the bars once more and he missed it again. He angrily stopped the orchestra. "Are you playing the first or second version of the concerto?" he asked me.

"The last one, of course," and then, turning to the orchestra, I said, "Another Rubinstein hated the first version before me, as everybody knows."* The whole orchestra laughed at this remark and Mengelberg said curtly, "Please play it again." This time he put his nose into the score and we played it through.

The concert was a great success. Mengelberg remained on the stage, listened to my encore, and kissed me in front of the audience. It was getting late and Nela and I rushed to the train. We arrived home at seven o'clock in the morning, had a quick breakfast, and lay down to await the call from Horowitz. There was no call. At eleven Nela impatiently telephoned the Prince of Wales Hotel. He had forgotten his invitation, had decided to go to the races, and offered us, as a compromise, a snack in his room. His behavior both irritated and amused us. We dressed and drove to his hotel, where in the lobby I wrote him a short note which I remember well: "Dear Volodya—I hate to interfere with your wish to go to the races, so I invited Nela for lunch in a good restaurant and she accepted." Out in the street, I said to Nela, "The poor fellow will feel pretty bad and will probably send you some lovely flowers." We lunched in the Bois, saw a movie, and returned late in the afternoon to Montmartre. There was a call from my manager: "Horowitz's manager asked me to tell you that he didn't like your letter. As I do not know anything about it, I am simply relaying the message." Now I became really angry. "Tell your colleague to inform his client that I do not want to hear from him again—I am fed up with him." For many years to come, we were not on speaking terms. Here and there, I would meet his wife, with whom I would exchange a few polite words, but we never mentioned his name.

Two eminent German managers, who had fled from Hitler's threat to Jews, joined Valmalète's concert agency, as they were not allowed to

---

* Tchaikovsky had dedicated the first version to his friend Nicholas Rubinstein, who disliked the work so much that the composer changed the dedication to Hans von Bülow.

establish themselves independently in France. One of them, a Mr. Friedrich Horowitz, had been the manager of Vladimir Horowitz (no relation) in Germany. The other one, Dr. Paul Schiff, who had a well-known agency in Cologne, heard me in a concert at the Salle Gaveau and again as soloist with an orchestra, and was frankly astonished at the way Marcel de Valmalète was handling my career. I decided to do something about it and found to my agreeable surprise that Valmalète himself advised me whole-heartedly to appoint Dr. Schiff as my new manager. As the titular head of the agency, Valmalète had a share in the percentages to be earned by Dr. Schiff.

As if by magic, my career changed overnight. There were engagements in store for me in Stockholm, Göteborg, Oslo, Copenhagen, and many cities in Holland. Dr. Schiff dissuaded me from playing again in the Salle Gaveau.

Still, with all these improvements in my European career, I needed the money which was blocked in South America. My future status as a father made me feel acutely responsible for the well-being of my family. I planned for Nela to have her child near her parents in Warsaw. "Would you be able to accompany me on a short tour of Brazil and Argentina this summer?" I asked her. "I could begin it in May and be back in time for us to leave for Poland." She agreed quite happily. "There will be plenty of time to get back. I don't expect to have the child before the end of August."

I made my usual preparations for the tour. Both Pellas in Brazil and Ruiz in Buenos Aires promised to do their best to keep the tours as short as possible. Cook's travel agency recommended the newest German deluxe steamer and promised a nice cabin with bath. I was rather reluctant at the idea but Nela persuaded me to take it. "I used to take the German boats from New York to Bremerhaven," she said, "and they are the most comfortable and have the best service."

This took place at the beginning of 1933, when alarming news about the continued progress of Hitler's party was pouring in. The climax came when he became Chancellor of the Reich with the senile President von Hindenburg's consent. Excerpts from Hitler's book *Mein Kampf* were being publicized and in it I discovered with terror not only the threat to the Communists but the deep fanatic hatred of Jews. He encouraged brutal attacks on Jews by his special guards.

I immediately canceled my reservation on the German steamer, telling the clerk at Cook's to let them know that, as a Jew, I would have nothing to do with anything German anymore. The clerk promised to convey this to the German line. A week later, I received a private letter from the president of the line, assuring me of the deep respect and gratitude he felt toward the

Jews, to whom the line owed its existence and great financial success. He finished his letter by begging me to reconsider my decision. "I can vouch for myself and my crew and I am sure my passengers will feel it an honor to have you on board." His letter persuaded me; if a man in such a high position dared to write a letter of this kind, there must be some decent Germans left. The president kept his word. We were treated and served as splendidly as everybody else and had nothing to complain about. Our cabin stewardess, who had served for years with a German family in Bremen, had nothing but invective for Hitler's prejudice toward the Jews. "He must be mad," she exclaimed, "to close his eyes to the truth of the generosity and patriotism of the German Jews."

In spite of all this, we kept apart from the rest of the passengers and spent the whole long journey playing word games. We became such experts that we chose to play in four or five different languages. The passion with which we played intrigued our fellow passengers.

On our arrival in Rio there was the same scene that had amazed me so on my first visit. This time, I could share with Nela the Sugarloaf, the beautiful Christ on Corcovado, the same incredible blue of the sky and the sea. Pellas had reserved for us a charming apartment at the Palace Hotel, with windows overlooking the bay and the Municipal Opera House across the street, where I was to give my concerts. As we could see the box office, we played games guessing which passersby would stop at the box office and which would walk on. We became quite passionate about this little game and insulted those who let us down.

Carlos Guinle sent flowers for Nela and invited us for dinner the same night. He and Gilda, his wife, gathered their whole family to celebrate our marriage and the coming child. All the women of the Guinle clan offered their friendship to Nela and did everything to make her stay comfortable.

My concerts went well, as by then I had won a nucleus of followers who listened to my playing as though they were my personal friends.

A similar reception awaited us in São Paulo. Here we enjoyed the hospitality of the Schiafarelli family throughout our whole stay. The Brazilian season was financially less successful than the previous ones, clearly because the financial crash in the United States had had repercussions in the whole of South America.

Anyway, we left in high spirits for Buenos Aires. It would be fun to see the faces of my friends at the sight of the confirmed bachelor married and close to being a father. As I expected, Nela was right away adopted by everyone. Nena Salamanca and Victoria González took full charge of her and reserved the services of the best gynecologist in town. At the first visit, the doctor assured me that everything was in order and that there was nothing to worry about. My role as a debutant of fatherhood was often laughed at. My complete ignorance of these matters even led me to ask the old manager of the Odeon, who was a multiple father and grandfather, how one knows the precise moment when the birth will occur. The man was a little confused. "I must confess I never knew, but the women are unbelievably clever about it. Be patient, everything will happen at the right time."

In my ignorance I did a horrible thing to my poor Nela. After a particularly successful matinee concert, I invited Rafael and Victoria González and some young enthusiasts for a cup of chocolate at the splendid Confitería de Paris. Nela was then in her ninth month. The talkative Latins raved about the concert, which made me offer them some champagne. The party became longer and louder when we suddenly saw Nela burst into bitter sobs. Scared to death, I asked her what the matter was, and she said through her tears, with the voice of a little child, "I'm so tired, I'm so tired." We all jumped to our feet; I rapidly paid the bill and took her home. When she was safely in bed she said quietly, "You did not realize what an effort it was for me to sit all through the long concert in that hot theater and then you had the bad idea to make me endure your friends, all of them talking loudly at once." I blushed in deep shame and could only stutter, "I swear this will never happen again."

My other, much less important preoccupation was with the money I had at the bank. The director received me very politely in his office and gave me full information. "Nothing has happened to your stock. As usual, we invest your income from it, only the law does not allow the money to be taken out of the country. While you are here, you can do what you want with it." That last statement greatly reassured me. I had enough money for any eventuality.

Francisco Ruiz arranged my tour better than ever and, unlike my Brazilian tour, I had full houses in Buenos Aires and many towns in the provinces wanted to hear me.

Nela was of course thrilled when I arranged an evening for her in the house of Mastrogianni and his wife, who had become my friends. We listened to Brigidita accompanied by López Buchardo, who was now her husband.

At the end of one of my concerts at the Colón, a little man found his way into the artist's room. "I was born in Lodz," he said, "came to this country as a boy, and am now well established as a furrier. I have a good proposition for you. The American financial crash is having strong repercussions in Argentina. People are not buying expensive furs anymore. As I heard that you cannot take your money out of the country, I could sell you a full-length chinchilla coat at a greatly reduced price. Ten years ago I would not have considered selling it for under twenty-five thousand dollars but I can now let you have it for eight thousand. You can easily sell it for three times that amount in Paris, where the market is still very much alive." His proposition seemed to be a brilliant one and the little man born in Lodz, revealing himself as a great music lover, convinced me.

I bought the precious fur right away before he had time to change his mind. When I showed it triumphantly to Nela she was rather critical about it. "The furs as such are beautiful, but the style of the coat is out of fashion." When I explained to her that the coat was nothing but an investment, that I felt sure Coco Chanel or Madame Lanvin would buy it at a high price, adding that I badly needed the money in Europe, she appeared to be satisfied. She wore it only once, for an opera at the Colón, and it was duly admired.

Mr. Julio Roca, the Vice-President of Argentina, was well disposed toward me and obtained permission for me to receive a monthly allowance abroad from my deposit in Argentina.

As time went on, Nela was dreading the long journey which would take her to Warsaw for the birth, as we had planned. When I expressed my misgivings about it to my friends, they laughed. "Arturo," they said, "in our country every family has at least half a dozen children, all in good health, so you have nothing to fear if you stay." That night, Nela and I made the great decision. She would continue to follow the orders of the doctor and I would take on all the concerts I could, to provide the right money for my baby.

From that moment on, Nela assumed the role of the classic expectant mother. At night in bed, she surrounded herself with an arsenal of knitting material and said to me, "I will knit in both blue and pink, just in case." Besides all that, some books appeared on the bed. "What are you reading?" I asked with curiosity. "Oh," she replied in a casual tone, "I am studying Spanish. I would hate not to understand what the doctors and nurses are saying about me." She was so diligent at these two activities that I was often fast asleep while she was still working. Her extraordinary gift for languages came once again to the fore. In less than two weeks she mastered Spanish well enough to communicate with the service and in restaurants with ease. It was a pleasure to see my friends amazed at it.

My readers are probably astonished at this point about the complete silence concerning my music. Well, I must reassure them. I worked less than ever due to my imagined preoccupations as a future father, but I never played better at concerts. The divine art of music is the only one which gives us interpreters the means of transmitting our deepest emotions to receptive listeners. The Argentine public felt my subtle state of inspiration and the success in both Argentina and Uruguay was greatly heightened by it. Ruiz said, not without being personally interested, "Don Arturo, you could come back here every year for at least fifty concerts." My poor Nela accompanied me once or twice to Montevideo, where she wanted to meet my friends, but suffered agonies on the abominable night boats.

Late one afternoon, Nela told me quietly, "I think you must take me to the hospital right away." Nena Salamanca had a room prepared at a fine clinic in the Calle Santa Fe, so all we had to do was announce our arrival. Nela's midwife took charge of everything and led Nela to her room. I asked for, and obtained, a room next to my wife's and waited nervously for things to happen. After a while, Nela appeared at the door and danced a few steps of a mazurka, probably to reassure me, but it was a little thoughtless.

Some time later, the midwife told me that the birth would soon begin, and although she tried to dissuade me, I insisted on being present. We went into the labor room, where the midwife, helped by nurses, made all the arrangements for Nela. Some time passed and then I heard groans which soon turned to loud complaints. I dashed to the bed, took hold of Nela's hand, and tried to calm her by stroking it. Then, suddenly, my poor Nela gave out the most inhuman screams which went on and on with increasing power. I squeezed her sweating hand and, near to fainting, closed my eyes. I felt as guilty as an assassin. Even now, I can swear that it was the most terrifying moment of my whole life.

Then we heard the unique sound of the newborn human body. At that moment, I cried spasmodically and would have collapsed if the nurses hadn't taken me to a chair. "It is a little girl," the midwife said. I laughed and cried. The midwife bathed the baby and the nurses began to take care of me. I swallowed a pill and had my head soothed with cold water. When I could gather my forces again, I said indignantly, "Why don't you look after my poor darling?" Here something incredible happened. Nela, completely calm, said in her normal persuasive way, "We must have another baby as soon as possible. It is bad for her to be an only child." I was speechless.

While I was kissing my wife with all my tender gratitude, I had a shy look at the little red body which was my daughter. The midwife told me about Nela's exceptional courage: "She wouldn't accept any anesthetics, or pills to calm her. She insisted on wanting to hear the first cry of her baby." It filled me with pride and admiration. When I saw my Nela lying quietly in her room with the baby in a little cot next to her bed, my heart was filled with an unknown happiness. "I have my daughter, I have my daughter." I sang out to myself. The wish of so many years was fulfilled.

Nena and Victoria came to embrace Nela and brought flowers, but they did an unforgivable thing. They failed to inform me that my poor Nela needed a private nurse to take care of her and the baby at any time of the day or night. I thought, in my innocence, that this was the duty of the nurses of the clinic. My poor Nela, on this night of her extreme fatigue, had to take care of the little one all by herself; she rang for the nurses in vain. I had intended to spend the night at her side but she insisted on my going to bed and I obeyed. However, I couldn't close my eyes for hours, reliving the horrors and the joys of the day.

I woke up at lunchtime, opened the door carefully, and, seeing Nela asleep, walked out to buy flowers and a little gift to commemorate the date of August 18, 1933. I also bought some morning papers, which Nela liked to read to improve her Spanish. Nela, looking lovely and fresh, allowed me to give my daughter a long, long look. "Please take a photo of her," she said, and made me take her camera. I took a few snapshots under Nela's instructions. She suddenly exclaimed, "They are giving your beloved *Meistersinger* tonight at the Colón. You must go and hear it." I objected to any thought of leaving her alone, but finally gave in—not without great satisfaction.

The performance was splendid. Frieda Hempel sang Eva and her great song for Hans Sachs in the third act made me cry. I was in a particularly vulnerable state that night. When I came back to the clinic and gave Nela a vivid account of the performance and especially of the Eva by Frieda Hempel, we both exclaimed almost at the same time, "Let us call her Eva. Besides, it is such a lovely name."

After a few days we returned to the Plaza, and Victoria found a nurse for Nela. After two more concerts we began to prepare for our return to Paris. My well-informed friends advised me to buy objects in gold and even English gold sovereigns. I followed their advice and soon found myself in possession of two hundred gold sovereigns, a golden chain for Nela, and some jewels for her which were mainly in gold.

Nena Salamanca had a good proposal: "An English nanny whom I know well and who for many years has been in charge of the children of my friends, dreams of going home for her vacation but cannot afford it. If you pay her trip she would look after your baby while you are on board." We both jumped at the idea.

The next morning, Miss Billington, the very prototype of an English nanny, came to meet us and see the baby. She looked at little Eva with the ecstatic eyes of one who has never seen a baby before. I made arrangements and was lucky in finding the right cabins on a French steamer going to Marseilles; we embarked happily two days later. Most of our friends saw us off with flowers and tidbits for the journey.

At teatime in the lounge on the boat, we suddenly heard a loud altercation between Miss Billington and the waiter. When I approached her table she said indignantly, "Mr. Rubinstein, this boat has nothing but China tea to offer. I couldn't stay on a steamer which does not provide Ceylon tea. I would rather get off at our next stop and return to Buenos Aires."

Her evident determination greatly alarmed me. "Miss Billington," I said, "I solemnly promise you that I will find your tea in Montevideo on our three-hour stop." I certainly had a hard time fulfilling my promise. At least ten shops did not even know what kind of tea they had. However, I found it at the last minute just before sailing. Once on the high seas, every afternoon Miss Billington arrived with the sleeping baby in a cot next to her, settled down for tea, and demanded imperiously, "Hot water, please. I use my own tea." The other passengers thoroughly enjoyed this scene.

We had on board a famous Spanish flamenco dancer, Antonia Mercé, called "the Argentina" (she was born in that country); I greatly admired her. One day on deck she looked at our baby for a long while and said prophetically, "She will be a dancer." It was a happy trip for the "young" father.

In Paris, before she left for London, I took Miss Billington on a sightseeing tour of the city which she has never forgotten. She is now retired in England and we still keep up a friendly correspondence with her.

86

The Kochanskis arrived from Warsaw, where Paul had played the first performance of the Second Violin Concerto by Szymanowski. He had worked at it with Karol in Zakopane and wrote the cadenzas. The night of the concert my poor dear Paul was so weak that he had to play seated. For quite some time we had begun to fear the worst. Now, when I saw him, I received a terrible shock. He had lost weight, his face had a strange grayish color, and his beautiful almond eyes had lost their shine and their spirit. His pathetic effort to appear cheerful made me want to cry. It was terrible to see my only and best friend in this hopeless condition.

Misia Sert invited the Kochanskis and us for lunch and Nela decided to bring our baby in a carry-cot. Paul gave Eva a long sad look, took my hand, and we both had tears in our eyes. They left the next day for New York and that was the last time I saw him; he died of cancer in January 1934 in New York at the age of forty-seven. I have had to survive all these long years since deprived of a friend I could never replace.

Quick decisions had to be made. Nela said, "My mother writes that Karola, the nurse who looked after Wanda's boys after their birth, is now free. I can't think of anybody better for our Eva. The best thing would be for me to go with the baby to Warsaw and engage her right away, while you make the necessary changes to our home." I certainly had to make many alterations to enlarge our home.

With my usual luck, I succeeded in paying off the shoe craftsmen who occupied the workshop situated under my bungalow in the rue D'Orchamps in front of the famous Bateau Lavoir, where so many painters began their careers. Jeanne de Marjerie came to my rescue; accompanied by a young man, she looked at the place, and after a short consultation between the two, they appeared to be sure of what to do. I left it in their hands. In no time, the large room was cleaned up, the walls and ceiling painted a soft beige. When it was ready, a wet patch suddenly appeared on the wall. The young man exclaimed, "We must panel the room." When he saw me rather startled, he said, "Don't be afraid. We can use a cheap wood which will look the right color. It will not be the usual dark paneling but it will give a gay warm feeling to the room."

As it was not too expensive for me, I accepted his offer. The small space between my alcove and the bathroom was going to give way to a narrow spiral staircase and the rest would be used for closets. The bathroom I was so proud of remained untouched. When I first moved in, I had had it painted with a black lacquer paint with white on the inside of the bathtub and washbasin. I had borrowed the idea from Juanita Gandarilla's beautiful bathroom in London, which I always admired. I also owe to her my love for bath essences which perfume my bathroom. Soon, I was ready for Nela's and the baby's return, this time accompanied by the family nurse she was so anxious to engage.

Karola was a little fat Polish peasant in her forties, illiterate and completely devoid of intelligence. She soon became devoted to both of us and looked after the baby day and night, washing and feeding her without respite. Accustomed to the French ways with servants, we suggested she take Sundays off, but she answered almost in tears, "Please, please let me stay. I have to wash the diapers all the time." She had one little habit which both annoyed me and made me laugh: at the slightest opportunity, she would take off her shoes and walk around barefooted, even in the presence of guests!

For my next recording sessions in London, Nela took the baby and Karola to our usual flat in Bury Street. The next morning, I accompanied Karola, who was pushing the baby in the pram, to St. James's Park, which was nearby. When I settled them in the shade of a big tree, I said, "Look, Karola, there is Buckingham Palace, where the King and Queen live, and look how green the park is." She answered happily, "Yes, this is the perfect place for me to hold the baby out."

One night, after recording Chopin's nocturnes, I took Nela to the Savoy Grill for supper, where we met the lovely Yvonne Printemps with Pierre Fresnay, the great French actor, whom she had just married. Yvonne had left Sacha Guitry. "I couldn't endure anymore his ferocious jealousy and the way he made me work. He would wake me in the middle of the night to repeat with him rapidly some dialogue for the next play, or make me do it while I was dressing or even during meals. After this, life with Pierre is a paradise," she said.

When they heard that our new baby was with us in London, they insisted on seeing her right away. The four of us entered the nursery on tiptoe. Nela put the light on and they both looked at our sleeping baby, Yvonne with tears of envy and admiration. When little Eva woke up and began to cry bitterly with fear, our late guests fled from the room and it took Karola a long time to calm her.

Before returning to France, I worked on my recordings. At this time, records were made on wax, which did not allow the performer to hear his work played back during the sessions. We could get proofs only when the matrix was ready. It was rather frustrating to have to play without being able to judge the quality of the performance.

My next concert was in Brussels; Ysaye had asked me to play with him for a charity. The program included the Franck sonata and we each had to give some solo pieces. Queen Elizabeth and the lovely Princess Marie José, who played the piano well enough to be able to perform the Schumann concerto, were both there. The old master and I entered the hall of the Conservatory to a warm reception by the audience. I settled down for our sonata, which we were to play by heart. Ysaye gave me a nod to begin. I played the four bars of introduction softly in the right tempo when I saw to my horror Ysaye standing still without putting his violin to his chin. I repeated the four bars with more insistence and nothing was to be heard from Ysaye. I was beginning my little prelude for the third time when the master gave me an imperious signal to stop. Then he addressed the public more or less as follows: "I cannot begin to play this masterpiece without telling you my emotion at being able to pay homage once more to this immortal master and my dear old friend, César Franck." He gave them a longish account of what he thought of good old Franck and then, after having had his say, he gave me a nod to play my wretched four bars again. With the violin safely settled under his chin, he gave another glorious performance of the sonata.

The reason for this unexpected improvisation was a sad one. At the moment when he should have begun, poor Ysaye had an attack of trembling in his right hand and could hardly hold the bow. The speech allowed him to recover. Only a few days later this poor great master had to undergo the amputation of his right leg, which was infected and could not be saved. When I visited him after the operation he said cheerfully, "Quand va t'on donner notre prochain concert?" But he died a few months later. He was the violinist I loved most and he was a man of great generosity and charm.

87

One morning the Paris papers brought out a story which almost made me fall off my chair. Juan Avila was the unfortunate hero, but this time one of his typically crazy adventures had an unhappy ending. It had been quite some time since I had last seen Juan, but I had heard that he had become a heroin addict. Lately, he changed names. It was the Spanish custom for husbands to adopt the titles inherited by their wives and Juan's estranged wife had become a marchioness after her father's death. Juan promptly seized the occasion to become a marquis. In his new glory but in dire need of money, he met another notorious personality on the Côte d'Azur, but this one was an authentic duke, a grandee of Spain and related to the King. His link with Juan was that he too was eternally lacking money and had no scruples about such matters.

Here was a beautiful occasion for Juan to tap his inventive talent again and he came up with a masterly plan; the drug which was ruining him was now going to make him wealthy. Juan became acquainted with a very rich man in Nice whose sideline was renting cars at a high price. Avila soon learned how to cunningly exploit the fantastic snobbism of this man. "I am the aide-de-camp of a duke who is going on a secret mission to Paris. We do not want to be seen on trains or on any other public conveyance. A great sum of money is awaiting us in Paris. All we need now is a comfortable Rolls-Royce to take us, with frequent breaks in our journey, to the capital. You will have to instruct your driver to pay all our expenses until we reach Paris. His Highness has promised to pay your driver regally and might even consider a Spanish decoration for you." The man fell over himself with thanks and agreed to all the conditions with humility. And so our two heroes spent the most luxurious fortnight traveling in small stages and stopping a little longer in places famous for their culinary art. My imagination followed with delight Juan's relish of it all.

Mantes, a small town near Paris and their last stop, was where they met their nemesis. The French police somehow or other became very interested in the luxurious, leisurely, and expensive way in which these two "regal personalities" who never opened their purses were traveling. So they decided to investigate before our two friends reached Paris, where they might easily slip through their fingers. On opening their suitcases, they found a large quantity of heroin. Their trial revealed that they had abused the good faith of the poor snob and were completely impecunious. Their authentic foreign titles saved them from prison and they were condemned to expulsion from French territory. Their widely publicized case greatly amused the Parisian readers. We, the friends of Juan, duly appreciated his infernal cheek. "This is good old Juan again" was our comment.

A year or so later, on the day of my concert in Monte Carlo, I saw a lonely figure walking around the big flower bed in front of the Casino. It was Juan. "This is the only spot where I can live which smells of France," he said with a sad smile. He did not tell me how he made his living.

My last meeting with him was again spectacular. I was on a tour in Morocco, and at my concert in Casablanca I stopped after the first movement of a sonata to allow the latecomers to enter the hall. Among them I noticed a gentleman in an elegant dinner jacket wearing a white carnation in his buttonhole. I was delighted to see it was Juan; his appearance implied that he was allowed to live again on French territory, as Morocco was still under French rule. During intermission, Juan visited me in the artist's room, where Nela was thrilled to meet him. "I am so happy you can live in France again, Juan," I exclaimed. He laughed. "No," he answered, "things haven't changed. I now live with my sister in Tangiers, which is an extraterritorial city, but when I read that you were playing tonight, I had to come to see and hear you again." We had him for supper, of course, at which he kept us in stitches with his account of his famous exploit. "It was a glorious occasion," he said with a greedy look, "to learn all about French cooking."

At the end of the supper two policemen appeared. "I was waiting for you gentlemen," said Juan. He had to pay for his latest intrepidity with three days in prison.

When the Spanish Civil War broke out, Juan could not resist. He joined the Spanish troops of Morocco who went to fight under Franco, and he was killed in action. This was a beautiful end of a life led to the full, and his own immoral but courageous philosophy was untarnished.

88

My tour of the Balkan countries and Egypt was more interesting this time, as I had the occasion to introduce the historical marvels of these countries to Nela. Her presence made me look at all these wonders with new eyes. It was the first time that we saw Tutankhamun's grave at Luxor and admired the beauties of the Temple of Karnak. Our marriage was, of course, duly feted by my friends.

In a cinema at Istanbul we saw a German film in which a singer amazed us by the volume and beauty of her voice. Her name was Gitta Alpar. By a strange coincidence, I was glossing over a Berlin newspaper in the lobby of our hotel and found the announcement of the premiere of an operetta in which Gitta Alpar was the star. On the spur of the moment we decided to go to Berlin and take in the show on our way to Warsaw. I made all the arrangements, wiring my usual hotel for the tickets.

We arrived in Berlin looking forward to the show with great excitement. A big disappointment was in store for us. The voice sounded like a deflated balloon and there was nothing left of the sparkle and beauty. The show itself was boring to boot, so I took Nela to my favorite café, Unter den Linden, to recover our senses; there you could always find a gay and animated atmosphere.

That night, however, only a few tables were occupied. When we settled down, there was a strange silence in the room and we felt all eyes were upon us. I paid in a hurry for our two cups of coffee, which we hadn't drunk, and we returned to our hotel. This was the beginning of Hitler's danger-laden era. We were relieved when we finally reached Warsaw.

Mr. Patek, the Polish ambassador in Moscow, informed me that the Russian authorities had invited me to give two concerts in Moscow and one in Leningrad. I readily accepted for the sheer pleasure of playing for the wonderfully receptive Russian audiences again. Nela remained in Warsaw at her parents' with Karola and the baby.

I found Moscow more interesting this time. Everybody was talking about the great success of the opera *Lady Macbeth of Mzensk* by the young Shostakovich, who had already shown his great talent in his First Symphony. My new help-guide and spy all in one arranged for me to see the opera on the night of my arrival. I was thrilled by this stark cruel drama taken from a Russian novel of the same name and set to music of great power and beauty.

My first concert took place the next evening at the Tchaikovsky Hall of the Conservatory. That morning I had a call from Artur Rodzinski. He was a conductor who had begun his career as an assistant to Emil Mlynarski at the Warsaw Opera. He had lately become conductor of the Los Angeles Symphony Orchestra and had been invited to conduct a special concert in Moscow. At my recital I played *Petrushka* again, with more success than the last time. Rodzinski, who was hearing this work for the first time, was so impressed that I invited him for supper. Our conversation turned, of course, to Nela, whom he had known for years, and her school friend Halina Lilpop, whom he intended to marry; but when I mentioned my enthusiasm for Shostakovich's opera, he shouted excitedly, "This is what I have really come for. As New York has heard about it, I am simply dying to be the first to bring it out. Will you help me?" he said. "Let us go to see it together and you can introduce me to the right person. All I want is to get the score in my hands. As I don't know Russian, I beg you to be my interpreter." I promised to do all I could, chiefly because it would give me a chance to hear the opera again with a fellow musician and we could discuss it together. I enjoyed the opera still more the second time, watching Rodzinski's enthusiasm. He was so keen on getting the score that he wouldn't leave me in peace until I obtained it for him. Of course, they knew that it was important for them too to have the opera produced by a man of Rodzinski's fame.

With my pocket full of unexportable rubles, I decided to make the most of them. I found in a shop with a whole variety of goods a fine sable skin which I knew Nela could use for a cap. They also had some lovely pieces of Persian embroidered silks, but I was disappointed to learn that I would have to leave them behind. This time, the book shop had fine illustrated editions which I was allowed to take out of the country. Only one volume of an old Elzevier could not be taken out. I prepared a strategic plan for the customs. The sable skin was squeezed into my pocket and covered by a large handkerchief. The precious Persian brocades were concealed by a heavy coat which I threw nonchalantly over my left arm. I had the books casually spread out in my suitcase, but I left the Elzevier on top. I knew that the train would stop for at least an hour before being allowed to leave for the Polish frontier.

The customs officer made me open my two suitcases. One had nothing but my clothes and shoes but the other contained my books. The man examined my clothes with great care, taking some of them out in order to search my pockets. This took quite a while before he turned to the other case. His sharp eyes fell immediately on the Elzevier—not a difficult discovery, as it had the original binding. He picked it up and looked at me severely. "You can't take this book out of the country," he said.

I put on a most astonished expression. "But they sold it to me. I paid for it."

"They should have told you that this volume is not exportable."

"But then you must give me the money back. I paid for it," I said indignantly.

"I cannot do that. It is not in our power."

Now I played the furiously offended man. "So you think I must make you a present of it?"

"Don't use such a word. We don't care what happens to it. We only know it cannot go with you."

"If you don't let me keep it, I demand that you send it to the Polish Embassy in Moscow and have them keep it for me."

He shrugged his shoulders. That enraged me. "I gave concerts in your country, I was paid with your rubles, which cannot be exchanged or taken out of the country, and when I at least want to have some good books for it you try to take them away from me." It became a small riot. Two other officers approached and wanted to know what it was all about. I complained to them bitterly. "This officer will not allow me to take a book which I want to have and which I paid for with your legal money, paid to me for my work." I pulled out my passport. "I was engaged to give concerts as a *spets* and trusted that I would be treated as such, but I see it is not so. In this country which protects workmen, you want me to have worked for nothing." The three men tried to appease my growing rage. Finally, they promised to send the book to the Polish Embassy. At that moment the whistle blew. I said, "You must give me a receipt for this." Now they were in a mad hurry. My first man scribbled something on a piece of paper, closed my suitcases, and ran with them to put them on the train. The others urged me to follow him. "Hurry, the train is leaving," they told me. I obeyed but pretended to do so reluctantly.

When the train left Soviet Russia for Poland a fellow passenger came into my compartment, which was empty. It was Dimitri Mitropoulos, who was returning to Greece after a successful tour in Russia. "You terrified me," he said. "I observed the whole scene from a distance and I was afraid they might arrest you." At which I threw my coat on a seat, showed him my precious brocades, then freed the beautiful sable skin from my pocket, and told him with a broad smile, "I played that big comedy on purpose. I put the book in full view where any fool would find it, thus not giving them time to search me more thoroughly." We feted the victory of my strategy with fine Polish herrings and vodka in the elegant Polish buffet, which was laden with the best food Poland could offer. Nela was delighted with the brocades and the skin, which was just long enough to be made into a lovely cap.

Emil Mlynarski had a guest for lunch, Michel Kondracki, a gifted composer, so he told me. My poor father-in-law sat at the table in agony. When my little baby, Eva, was presented to him she patted his bald head in the typical babylike way. It was tragic to see the terrible pain it caused him.

Our conversation at table revolved around our plans for the summer. The young Kondracki offered a suggestion: "My mother-in-law owns a chalet in a lovely spot of the Savoy mountains; it is a peak above St. Gervais. She has rooms to let and could easily accommodate you in two spacious rooms." The price he mentioned sounded agreeable to my ears. Since my young days I have always been concerned about long, inactive summers. Kondracki helped us to make the arrangements right away and a few days later we returned to Paris with Karola and the baby.

One morning Nela revealed that she was expecting again. This time my paternal pride and joy were mixed with a slight apprehension, but Nela calmed me. "Darling, don't get nervous about it. It does not make me an invalid. As a matter of fact, I feel better than ever in this state."

Mr. Mitchell had two concerts for me in England and this gave me the occasion to make some records. The last time I had recorded in London, I was conscious that this was going to change my future musical life. There was a heavy price to pay for not being taught by a Leschetizky or, better still, a Busoni, after Barth. I was much too young to take my musical education into my own hands. Of course, this is not an excuse for my laziness, which is an inborn vice. But in my heart I felt a great need for guidance by a musician who would be what Dr. Altmann had been to me in my Berlin days. He had tutored me for three hours a day for five years, thus leaving enough time for my musical studies. Instead of treating me with the customary dry discipline, he had a miraculous way of initiating me into the flowers of literature in many languages which I could later enjoy in the original version. He guessed my thirst for an intelligent approach to philosophy, religion, politics, which later became of invaluable help to me.

Unfortunately, in matters of music I received the necessary dry discipline but without an understanding of the deep needs of my talent.

Now speaking of my first recordings, I remember how appalled I was when I heard the first proof of my performance. I suddenly realized that when I played in public, I gave out my inspiration and feeling of the moment, which prevented me from listening to myself critically, being too involved in my actual performance. Then, listening to my proofs, I became aware that I could really learn something only from myself. From that moment on, the first hearing of a proof became an all-important lesson.

89

Nela wanted a car; she was proud of her driving. "We spend too much on taxis," she said, "and it would be more economical to buy an inexpensive car. I know that you could pay for it in monthly installments." She convinced me, but I insisted that it should be a Citroën. "I know Mr. Citroën personally," I said. "He married a Miss Goldfeder from Lodz and if I can buy the car from him personally, he might give us a better price." And he did sell the car to us. It was a neat little car which satisfied Nela's experienced eye. Two or three days later, she drove me proudly in our new Citroën straight out of the factory. Sitting at the wheel she felt that Paris had become her real home.

Our life in Montmartre became much easier and she climbed the steep rue Lepic with gusto, stopping at the curb in front of our home.

Nela's love and knowledge of cars was contagious. I became slightly jealous of the fact that my own wife drove better than any taxi driver, so one day I decided to get a driver's license myself. For two weeks a taxi took me every morning to the driving school at Porte Maillot. My teacher put me behind the wheel and asked me if I had ever ridden a bicycle. "Yes," I answered. "Only once, but I fell off right away and never again touched this dangerous vehicle. I always hated to expose my hands except when absolutely necessary, but I did know how to take the turns right and left without difficulty."

My teacher had a strong preference for showing me how to park. I went through agonizing moments when he made me stop and back into a small space between two cars. My heart stopped each time I made the attempt, as I felt quite sure that I would destroy both cars. Luckily everything went well and I found out this was because the car had dual controls and my professor never let me get into trouble. He showed me how to accelerate, which I learned with relish, but when I asked him how to stop he said, "You simply take your foot off the accelerator and the car will stop by itself." Soon we were rolling happily down the avenue Foch and back again. I began to love my lessons, except for the devilish parking business. One morning, my teacher said solemnly that he had arranged for my examination on such and such a day and thought I stood a good chance of passing it. Before leaving, he gave me a little booklet about the highway code. The inspector, an elderly man with a grayish beard, showed a marked impatience, which made me feel nervous and insecure. To my satisfaction I parked without a hitch, but when he made me drive around the monument of the Place Blanche, he suddenly screamed, "Stop!" I promptly took my foot off the accelerator but the car continued to roll. "Stop!" he screamed, which made me angry. Fortunately at that moment the car stopped by itself. At the end of the examination the inspector wrote something on a card and handed it to me without a smile. The card said: "You have the right to try again in three months." I came back home complaining bitterly to Nela, "This fellow hated me from the beginning. He was evidently an anti-Semite. He did not give me the driver's license in spite of my brilliant parking, which I did in your manner." Nela said, "You will do better next time."

A few days later, I had a concert in Brussels. A lovely day in late spring gave Nela an idea: "Would you mind if I drove you all the way down?" I was, of course, delighted. I felt completely safe with Nela and I loved seeing something of the French and Belgian landscape, which trains never allowed me to see. After one of those unexpectedly fine luncheons which Michelin gratifies with a star, we reached the Belgian frontier. From then on, the road was paved with cobblestones, which slowed us down. On a long straight stretch of the highway, I felt an urge to show Nela that I did learn how to drive and that I was well able to hold the wheel. She was a little uneasy about it. "You can always take over again," I reassured her. We changed seats and I took the wheel, happily singing gay tunes to the rhythm of the dancing car on the cobbles. Suddenly, as if out of nowhere, a large cart pulled slowly by two horses, one behind the other, came out of a side road. I took my foot off the accelerator, but it was too late. A small catastrophe would have happened if Nela hadn't stopped the car immediately. When she took over again, I sat meekly next to her up until our arrival in Brussels.

After the concert, we returned safely to Paris and began our preparations for the summer. Nela adored the idea of driving me, with Karola and Eva in the back of the car, all the way to our destination, St. Nicolas de Véroce.

We drove gaily for two hours until a car in front of us stopped dead in order to avoid a dog. Nela managed brilliantly to stop a few inches behind it, but another car hit us from the rear. We looked around, terrified, to see if anything had happened to Eva and Karola, but we were most fortunate— the child slept peacefully. Our poor car, however, was badly bruised. We had to spend a few hours in Dijon having it repaired and were finally on our way to Nantua, where our Michelin indicated with three stars the presence of one of the great culinary places of France. Michelin proved to be right; we had one of those fantastic meals of *écrevisses à la sauce Nantua*. Then we proceeded, gaily singing, toward our ultimate goal. From the kindly village of St. Gervais, the spiral road became narrow and the little house stood at the top of a peak a thousand meters above sea level.

A friendly elderly lady and her rather good-looking daughter greeted us very cordially and showed us to our rooms. One was a bed-sitting room with a convertible sofa and next to it was a smaller room for Karola and the baby in her cot. Two other couples were also staying there. Kondracki appeared at dinner after a shooting expedition and formally introduced us to his wife and his mother.

After an almost sleepless night due to the narrow sofa, which constantly threatened to throw me to the floor, we began to worry about the question of a piano. Kondracki had an upright piano, which he offered to place in a stable, which was quite close to his house. As I intended to work mostly at night, Nela put four candles in the candlesticks attached to the piano. I found a comfortable chair, brought a bag full of music to the stable, and wrote down different projects for programs.

From the beginning of our stay in St. Nicolas, our life was rather original, often amusing, and always interesting. I liked to hop down after lunch to the village of St. Gervais, where I promptly discovered a most attractive tearoom with the best cakes one can imagine. Nela came later to fetch me in her car, had a nice cup of chocolate, but left the cakes to me. Often after breakfast we would climb some little neighboring rocks where we found to our amazement our beloved Polish mushrooms called *rydze*, which are reddish and lie flat on the grass; the French think they are poisonous but in Poland they are considered a great delicacy. Our little Eva had her first birthday right there in St. Nicolas on August 18, 1934.

Nights now belonged to me. After the household was ready to retire I would walk to the stable, close myself in, and begin a strange musical life, a life which was completely new to me. In a way, it was a revelation; the simple fact was: I discovered the joy of practicing.

As readers of my first book well know, my childhood practicing was a cheat and a fake. I used to make silly noises alternately with the right and left hand, while actually enjoying a good novel accompanied by chocolates

and cherries in season. Later on, my facility allowed me to learn in no time
a concerto, a sonata, or some shorter pieces, which I dared to play in concerts with the greatest aplomb, covering technically difficult passages with
an intelligent use of pedal or with some dynamic impacts which gave the
innocent listener the idea I had played the piece to perfection. The frequent
repetitions of so many pieces, at so many concerts, helped me greatly to
learn them better and better each time without any special effort. The irony
of it all was that since the very beginning of my career I had often been
severely criticized in the press for my lack of depth in playing Beethoven,
my insufficiently poetic approach to Schumann, a certain dryness in my
treatment of Chopin, but never, never, never was there any doubt expressed
about my technical perfection! It came to the point of my being conscious
that I was the only one who really knew about the miserable state of my
pianistic technique.

These nights in St. Nicolas became the turning point in my approach to
my art. I felt suddenly an intense physical pleasure when I succeeded in
playing the étude in thirds by Chopin in a clear decent way without pedal
and without getting too tired. I began to work seriously on the fingers of my
left hand, which I had always neglected abominably. Now I wanted to hear
all the notes clearly articulated, gaining a hold on the reluctant fourth
finger. I repeated endlessly an unimportant passage simply to gain more
respect and confidence in my poor left hand, feeling the fourth finger becoming alive and independent.

I took up the most frequently played pieces of my repertoire one by
one, and gave the greatest attention to all the passages which I had neglected for so long. After a few nights of that kind of work, which sometimes lasted until two or three in the morning, I discovered a half dozen or
more listeners who settled quietly down around the stable night after night.
It was rather reassuring to find out that my dry practicing was somehow still
making music.

Our little Eva was a pure joy to watch. For her first birthday her
mother crowned her head with a wreath of flowers and took photos while
the child was bravely climbing a little rock without help.

Our stay was interrupted by concerts in Aix-les-Bains and Chamonix,
where we drove in the jolliest of moods, waltzing down the road.

My daily walk down to the tearoom resulted in our getting a wonderful
maid for Paris. She was a pretty brunette who served the whole tearoom
with such extraordinary efficiency that Nela could not resist proposing that
she come with us to Paris; to our joy, she accepted our offer right away.

Before we left St. Nicolas, I must confess blushingly that I tried once more to get a driver's license, hoping that the little town of St. Gervais would not find much fault with my achievements. I took the spiral way down, proudly and all by myself, entered the village of St. Gervais triumphantly, where the inspector awaited me, and we began our nice examination drive. All of a sudden, my car was surrounded by a furious flock of sheep and I remained completely paralyzed, not knowing whether to go backward or forward or kill some of them, until the inspector helped me out. Of course, no driver's license for me. I consoled myself in the tearoom with more cakes than were good for me while receiving expressions of pity for my lost battle with the sheep.

On our return to Paris with the new maid, we found a room in the house for François and gave her his room. It was at that time that I received a visit from a Mr. Strok, a well-known impresario in the Far East. He was the only one who arranged tours in Japan, China, and the Philippine Islands. Holland was offering me twenty concerts on the island of Java, where, as in Holland, an institution called the Kunstkrink existed. Mr. Strok offered me a tour in Japan of not less than twelve concerts beginning in April 1935, concerts in Shanghai, Peking, and Tientsin in China, and, if I had some time left after my tour in Java, he suggested a few interesting and well-paid concerts in the Philippine Islands.

The whole proposition was more than attractive to me. I was lucky enough to find a way of reaching Tokyo from Paris by a sleeper; accommodations were provided for both of us round-trip, allowing a stopover for two concerts in Moscow and one in Leningrad on the way over and another on our way back. For once, the ruble, so useless on my previous visits, would now pay the full price of this enormous trip, first class! To have taken a boat would have cost a great deal of money and I would have lost at least a month just sailing, whereas the journey by the Trans-Siberian took only ten days.

With my born thirst for adventure, for change, and for knowing the world, this was indeed a brilliant opportunity. Java wanted me for the whole month of June and part of July. The society arranged a standard fee of $300 per concert and Mr. Strok offered me decent fees. I was becoming more and more enthusiastic about the whole plan; it meant six months of well-paid concerts and the most interesting itinerary one could dream of.

Nela was expecting the child in the second half of January and assured me that she would be quite able to join me on this fantastic tour. She would leave both babies in Warsaw in the best of care under the supervision of her mother, who could not take charge of them herself because Emil's health was deteriorating rapidly. His dreadful incurable arthritis began to break his resistance but this true gentleman never lost his sense of humor. He would joke about his death and warn his family not to leave the doors open when they went to the funeral. "Thieves wait for those occasions, so please take care."

Dr. Schiff had an unusually great number of concerts for me at this time. There were two in Stockholm, one in Göteborg, and one in Oslo; besides, there was Rome again. I promised to record all the polonaises of Chopin for "His Master's Voice" and had three or four concerts in England in connection with the recordings.

Nela stayed in Paris for Christmas and New Year's, which we feted in the good company of Marcel and Juliette Achard and some other friends. About that time a curious person suddenly emerged in our lives; she was a Pole from a modest background, and by some strange circumstances became the nurse of an old American millionaire who married her before dying and left her his whole fortune. This happened just before the famous economic crash of 1929 and she was then known as Mrs. Irene Warden. Overcome by the sudden fortune which fell into her hands, she had the childish habit of going to the bank and asking the director to pile up her fortune in front of her. For a while she wouldn't invest that money because of an old peasant instinct. This not only saved her whole fortune in the crash, but allowed her to multiply it by buying up later the best Wall Street values at a cheap price. She then became the richest Polish woman. As a bachelor, I had met her in Cannes, where she had invited Paul and Zosia for a stay at the expensive Carlton Hotel. She showered presents on both of them and wanted to include me. By some instinct I resisted because I hated her complete lack of manners and constant bragging about her riches. True enough, she did help a lot of people, being quite generous, but linked it with an ugly way of reminding the beneficiaries, most likely in public, of her gifts. Quite naturally, she was courted by men with the highest Polish titles who wanted to rebuild their fortunes, which had dwindled due to Pilsudski's severe new laws. Prince Radziwill of Nieswierz, named by Liszt as the most fabulous palace he had ever visited, and Count Potocki of Lancut were candidates for Irene's hand. But she finally settled on an Italian, Count Cittadini, who was then the counselor of the Italian Embassy in Warsaw. She rented the most lavish apartment available on the Aleja Ujazdowska and divorced very soon because of the extreme sadism of her husband.

Nela met her at Misia Sert's and she immediately became most friendly with both Nela and me. One day she made Nela promise to stay in her beautiful apartment in Warsaw while she was in America and have the baby there. I was not overenthusiastic about the idea, but seeing that Nela accepted it with great joy, I had not the courage to dissuade her.

So, at the beginning of January, Nela left for Warsaw with Karola and

Eva and took possession of the luxurious apartment, which was perfectly equipped with the necessary staff, including an excellent cook. As she told me later, she became a constant hostess to her friends, treating them to her favorite dishes, especially the fattening Lithuanian dish called *kolduny*.

During that time, I was giving concerts which Dr. Schiff and Mr. Mitchell had arranged for me. At the end of January, I began my work on recording the polonaises of Chopin. On my birthday, January 28, 1935, Dr. Nahum Sokolow, the famous Zionist and a highly respected personality in London, gave a diplomatic dinner at which the British Foreign Secretary, Sir John Simon, the Polish ambassador, Count Raczynski, and the minister of Czechoslovakia, Jan Masaryk, the son of the creator of the Czechoslovakian Republic, were present. The talk was mainly about the dangerous ascendance of Hitler, his strange political moves, like the unexpected pact of friendship with Poland, his victory in the Saar plebiscite, his extremely violent anti-Semitic laws, brutally inciting the destruction of Jewish property and shops and depriving German Jews of all human rights. The gentlemen talked intelligently but they did not offer the slightest approach to any energetic protest against Hitler's dangerous activities.

Somebody mentioned my birthday and I was treated to a polite little toast with good wishes from these gentlemen. When it was time to go home, Jan Masaryk offered to take me in his car. On the way he said, "What about a glass of champagne in my embassy and a good piece of cake in your honor? The staff are still awake and will be happy to join us." I accepted with enthusiasm simply because Masaryk was one of the people after my own heart. There was nothing of the typical diplomat in him. He was free and outspoken without a trace of hypocrisy, but the nicest thing about him was the fact that he was really fond of me. In no time, he improvised a lovely warm birthday party. He filled our glasses with champagne and they all toasted me from their hearts. At one moment, Masaryk left the room, came back after a longish while, and said, "Arthur, I have a present for you." I protested in the usual insincere way, but I was very curious to see the gift. He took me to the telephone in the corridor and said, "This is my present." The dear man got Nela on the phone. She was already in the hospital. She said with a weak and tired voice, "I think the moment has come, it might be a present for your birthday."

I said, "I finish the polonaises tomorrow. Please let me know right away." I ended up by wishing her all the good luck and love, etc., and I kissed Masaryk on both cheeks for this most wonderful present.

The next morning, I started my work on the last two polonaises. The A-flat one went off brilliantly, and after two takes I was satisfied. After lunch, I played the last, most difficult one, the Op. 44 in F-sharp minor. I was very inspired and played it better than ever before, but unfortunately in my élan I struck two false bass notes. I was miserable and even furious to have lost such an exceptional performance, as of course I was obliged to play it again. Nervous as I was, I declared, "I will do that tomorrow. Now I couldn't possibly repeat this beautiful piece as well as before." They begged me to take a rest and have another try, but to no avail. I took a taxi and hurried home to my flat, and ordered tea with delicious English crumpets. Then the telephone rang. Nela's much stronger voice announced triumphantly, "Arthur, we have a son. He is beautiful and weighs more than eight pounds." I shrieked, "Hurray, bravo, darling, thank you"—all the silly words which came to my mind. I decided there and then to have that F-sharp minor polonaise issued, faults and all, because it was fun for my son to know what his father was doing while he was born.

Unfortunately it took four days to have a chance to see my newborn child. I had concerts in Göttingen and Stockholm and four days later a concert with orchestra in Rome. I decided to fly from Stockholm to Warsaw and leave for Rome from there. Upon arrival in Warsaw, I found my family back at Madame Cittadini's apartment, Nela flourishing and already on her feet, and the lovely little baby was blond and sturdy. I remember a funny moment when I was practicing my concerto for Rome in the drawing room; a yell came from the baby's bedroom which practically deafened me, I couldn't even hear my playing. For the next year or two, he announced his hunger with the same kind of yell, later using the Polish *"Njam!!!!"* I was pretty proud to have a strong little Rubinstein for a son. We decided to call him Paul in memory of my beloved friend.

Two days later, I took a Polish plane for Berlin and changed there to an Italian one for Rome. The planes at that time were still pretty small, could not take more than a dozen or so passengers, and flew rather low, so that with every hill or valley they jumped up or down. The passage through the Austrian mountains was rather trying and we felt happy when the plane descended to land in Venice for the first stop. However, the landing proved to be extremely dangerous. A heavy rain had flooded the small airport, and when the plane finally came to a halt, we gave a big sigh of relief. After two long hours in the waiting room, the pilot came in and made an announcement: "I advise you strongly," he said, "to take the night train for Rome, as we are not sure whether the plane can take off from the flooded runway."

I asked the pilot, "Are you taking a train too?"

He answered, "No, I am obliged to take the mail to Rome tonight."

There was something in my nature which always made me take a dare. A risk attracted me. Taking the train would get me there nicely on time for my rehearsal, but I chose otherwise. "Would you take me with you if I wanted to get to Rome tonight?"

He smiled. "Of course, you have the right to come."

Half an hour later, the three of us—the pilot, his copilot, and I—were sitting in the plane. As they attempted to take off, my heart stopped beating, but the plane took to the air and off we went on one of the most dreadful flights of my life. Passing between the formidable Apennines, we endured some bumps which seemed like crashes. All the movable objects on the plane were smashed on the floor. When the danger of the mountains was over, the pilot declared candidly, "I hope we will be able to see the Tiber clearly. It is our only hope if we want to get to Rome safely." As I am still alive while writing this, the reader has the proof that we did see the Tiber, and the plane landed solidly on the soil of the Eternal City. My risky little exploit was nicely commented on in the papers, which added more enthusiasm for my not too fine performance of the Tchaikovsky concerto.

When I returned to Paris, there was a tragedy going on. Jeanne, the brilliant maid, had fallen head over heels in love with François. I do not know what his amorous response was, but on my arrival Jeanne gave me her account with tears and told me she had decided to return immediately to St. Gervais. There was no way of dissuading her. She became a fury of jealousy, love, and deception. As a matter of fact, François married a few months later and his bride was a milliner who lived in the house. For the time being, however, he promised to stay and look after us. He packed me up carefully and I left for Warsaw to start on the great adventure with Nela.

In the meantime, Nela had managed to rent a little villa in Otwock, a short distance from Warsaw, where it was supposed to be very healthy. The way to the house was not paved, but was covered with thick sand. The villa had a living room with a piano and enough rooms to accommodate the children with Karola and Nela's first cousin (Irka's sister from Zakopane), whom she put in charge of the household. There was even a large double bedroom for us, and the price for the length of our absence was very reasonable. In spite of the fact that my poor mother-in-law hardly dared to leave her husband's bedside, she promised to keep a watch over our small family.

Five

A Great Oriental Tour

90

At the end of February, well equipped for the long expedition, with the right clothes for all changes of climate, we took the train for the Russian frontier, where, after a long check of passports, visas, and tickets, we were finally allowed to take the first-class sleeper. The car was certainly one of those which I had used about twenty-five years earlier on some trips in Europe.

When the train moved, Nela went to work with unbelievable energy to rid our compartment of an overwhelming mass of lice, fleas, and cockroaches. When she thought she had won the battle, she soon found out that this was only the beginning. We hardly closed our eyes until Moscow and we did not dare to take our clothes off, except for our shoes.

In Moscow, our usual "guide" was expecting us, but this time he was accompanied by two members of the Polish Embassy staff. One of them was Henryk Sokolnicki, an old friend and flirt of Nela's. The two recitals were given in a smaller hall, after which I received the two first-class tickets to Tokyo and return to Paris.

In Leningrad, to my immense astonishment, the hall, which I was told was sold out, was almost empty. I remember that I played with a certain anxiety and felt nervously that something unnatural had happened. There were no encores, not for lack of appreciation, but for some mysterious reason. When we returned to the hotel, Nela told me the horrifying facts. Kirov, Stalin's best friend, the comrade chief of Leningrad, had been assassinated three months previously, and that Stalin had just begun a widespread purge of suspected dissidents. "A woman in tears," she said, "whispered to me that thousands and thousands of people were taken by the police and will be sent to Siberia. She told me there was not a family who had not been victimized." This was terrible news. We couldn't wait to return to Moscow. Officially the whole affair was hushed up. Even the Polish Embassy did not want to give us any information.

Back in Moscow, we were brought to the station by our guide and we saw heartbreaking scenes of the misery of the Russian people under the

Communist regime. About fifty people—men, women, and children—were sitting on the ground, waiting for days for the chance to leave, helping themselves to hot water for some tea from time to time; it was a tragic sight. Our sleeping car of the old Belgian company Wagon Lit seemed to be even more ancient than the one which had taken us to Moscow. This time, it was going to take us to Vladivostok, or the old Port Arthur, in eight days. Nela's battle with the bugs had to be fought every day. The washing facilities were so unspeakably disgusting that we felt nauseated just thinking about it. The daily breakfasts, luncheons, and dinners insulted our aesthetic sense. The man who served us seemed never to have washed or changed his clothes. The tablecloth was full of suspicious spots and we only used the paper napkins which we brought with us, not being able to use the ones provided for anything in the world. The food was a tasteless mess of something pretending to be fish or meat, one never knew the difference.

I remember that at a station where we stopped, some peasant women, mostly elderly and covered too lightly for the bitter cold, offered us some fresh roasted chicken and country cheese. They were mercilessly beaten up by the policemen who caught them at this little private enterprise.

One day, it was probably the fourth, we both lost our patience. At lunchtime, I asked our waiter, "Will you allow my wife to cook eggs, which we have with us and which she knows how to make to my liking?" I have never seen a more astonished expression, but taken by surprise, he agreed. Nela apparently showed them in the kitchen what it meant to cook after having cleaned her utensils meticulously beforehand. She then easily obtained a clean tablecloth from the astonished servant and produced the food she had cooked for the two of us. Overnight, to our great amusement, the whole atmosphere of that dining car changed. All the tables had clean linen and the three waiters looked washed for the first time in years and wore spotless aprons.

Another triumph awaited Nela: a co-passenger, an engineer with whom we talked from time to time and who had tried in his Communist innocence to make us admire the "beautiful brand-new sleeping and dining cars," as he called them. "Do you have cars like this in the West?" he asked proudly. We were too kind to disappoint him. One day, he was taken ill. People were talking about it and Nela inquired what the matter was. Having an unusual instinct for diagnosis, she guessed what was wrong with him and treated him and helped to restore him to health in no time. From that day on, the nasty bourgeois with their silk stockings and ties were changed into the most important, highly honored passengers on the train. Everybody wanted to show us his appreciation.

I must mention that on the long Siberian journey we saw nothing but the hard snow and sometimes the long line of a dark forest and the frozen Lake Baikal. Our co-passengers showed us some miserable huts and said with pride, "You don't have such beautiful buildings in your country, eh?"

On the eighth day we arrived at a station called Mandjuria. We were told it was a frontier with Korea. We waited for the customs to come, but after quite a prolonged wait nothing happened. We were even aware of a strange silence around us and all of a sudden the train moved. It was then that we dared to leave our compartment and ask for some information. We passed a few cars without meeting a living soul and it became evident that we were all alone except for the engine driver. After half an hour of this, the train stopped at a small station and was immediately invaded by a swarm of Japanese police and others. The policemen asked us politely to leave the train and enter a little building while others took care of our hand luggage and the rest of our baggage. The two policemen took us to a room and made us sit down at a table which was occupied by at least a dozen or so Japanese Army officers. They had an English interpreter and interrogated us for an hour about what we had seen of the Russian Army. As we finally succeeded in convincing them that we really had not seen anything, they allowed us to go for some refreshments.

Our passage from Mandjuria to this small station was of historic significance: Russia handed over to Japan her previous hold on the stretch from Mandjuria to Harbin on that very day. It was strange to feel that we were already in Japanese hands. There was a short stop in Harbin and we spent the night in Seoul, the capital of Korea, then occupied by Japan, and proceeded the next morning to the port of Fusan, where we boarded a boat that took us to Shimonoseki. There we took a train right away which brought us to Tokyo in thirty-six hours. The train was slow and stopped constantly, but the sleeping car and all the other commodities were absolutely clean and we were splendidly attended.

A telegram was sent by us from Harbin to inform Mr. Strok of the date and time of our arrival. One can well imagine our consternation in finding nobody expecting us at the station. We were speechless and lost in the world like a couple of orphans. I remembered vaguely that when the last severe earthquake occurred in Japan, the only building in Tokyo which remained intact was the Imperial Hotel. We gathered our belongings, found a good clean taxi, and pronounced clearly: "Imperial Hotel," which the driver fortunately understood. We were looking forward to seeing the famous Japanese cherry blossoms, for which Strok in Paris had prepared us, but were disappointed to find sharp cold and snow on the street. Our car stopped at a white two-story building with the name printed in English. I walked up shyly to the reception desk, fearing that the hotel might be crowded, but was astounded when the man announced in his broken English, "Your loom, sir, leserved, piano inside," and he took us to a very nice large double bedroom with an engaging bathroom. There was, indeed, a shiny Japanese upright piano in the corner. The receptionist even understood the precious word "breakfast" and, thank goodness, they served us a very tasty one with good coffee, toast, and English marmalade.

After breakfast, humming and singing, we took turns occupying the bathroom, which we had been dreaming about every night after the daily battle with the fleas on the Trans-Siberian. I spent a beautiful moment in the bathtub with piping-hot water and emerged gloriously clean, with my hair violently washed and my face shaven as never before.

We lay down happily for a good rest, when I suddenly saw the piano, wardrobe, and a table sliding from side to side. "Do you see what I see?" I asked Nela. Her frightened look gave me the answer. Fortunately the movement stopped after a minute or two and it turned out to be only a reminder that we were in Japan, where they endure constant and severe earthquakes.

We were dozing peacefully when a nervous knock at the door startled us. I got out of bed and went in my pajamas to open the door just enough to see who was there. It was Mr. Strok, who instead of looking guilty for not having received us upon our arrival, began to shout at me with indignation: "You came on the wrong train," he shouted. "I expected you to arrive at three in the afternoon by the Train Deluxe from Osaka." I let him in, and we exchanged explanations. Apparently, our telegram from Harbin mentioned simply the day of our arrival from Shimonoseki but no time. The train he mentioned was a much quicker one and he not only was prepared to come to the station but had organized hundreds of people to welcome us in grand style. "The ambassador, his wife, and the whole Polish Embassy are coming, as well as about two hundred persons who will bring flowers and gifts on behalf of 'His Master's Voice,' record dealers, and the usual crowd which likes to welcome and see off personalities." We became pretty upset.

"In my opinion," I said to Strok, "the only thing to do is for you to go and explain by megaphone that we have already arrived and are resting from the long journey at the hotel."

He made a very sour face at my suggestion. "I only know half a dozen words in Japanese and the whole thing would be fatal for business." Suddenly his face lit up. "We still have a few hours. If you dress and take two or three bags with you, we could go by train in an hour to Yokohama, where I will make it possible for us to take the express to Tokyo and simply pretend that I went to welcome you in Yokohama."

Of course, this sounded like a French farce, but just because of that, we liked the idea. "Yes," we both exclaimed practically at the same time. "You will see how well we will play it up." We dressed in our best clothes, put on our traveling coats, hats, and mufflers, and filled three suitcases with light stuff. Secretively we stole out of the hotel, drove to the station, and took the train to Yokohama a quarter of an hour later. The hour of this trip was spent in planning the best way of playing our little comedy. When the great express train arrived, we had some difficulty in getting aboard without paying for sleepers all the way from Osaka. But the half dozen words Strok knew were sufficient to allow the conductor to enjoy the farce with us, and it was in this mood that we made our final glorious entrance into the capital of Japan.

Mr. Strok had not exaggerated. There was a crowd of certainly not less than a thousand, screaming, shouting Japanese words of welcome, among them some good old Polish ones too. Our great triumph, of course, was that we looked so marvelously clean and fresh. The Polish ambassador and his wife were even beginning to annoy us with constant exclamations of wonder and admiration at seeing us in such a state after the abominably long journey we had endured. We might have let them in on our sham arrival, but we were enjoying our colossal success too much. Strok even went too far; he showed us off to the people, smacking his lips and yelling, "Have you ever seen two people arriving like that straight from Paris?" There was a great shaking of heads from a thousand people.

We had a very hard time defending the door of our room against the ever indiscreet interviewers who wanted nice things to write about our nightshirts on the well-used beds. Our only punishment for this comedy was that we were starving, but we had to pretend to unpack and do other chores before emerging for the meal.

The next day was devoted to a serious preparation for our concert tour in Japan. The first event was a concert with orchestra, conducted by the Viscount Konoye, a younger brother of the Prime Minister, Prince Konoye. My piece was the Concerto in B flat by Tchaikovsky. The first rehearsal took place the next morning. The orchestra was made up entirely of Japanese musicians with the exception of a German concertmaster. It was not of the very first rank, but could stand comparison with quite a few provincial orchestras I had played with. The Viscount proved to be an expert conductor. He had studied music in Leipzig and New York and spoke perfect English. The only thing which rather frightened me was that whenever I had to play one of the long solo passages of the concerto, all the Japanese players dropped their heads in deep slumber. My pianistic pride was rather hurt when I saw musicians going to sleep during my brilliant cadenzas, which in Europe received spellbound attention. But my astonishment turned into amusement when I discovered that the Japanese fall asleep on the spur of the moment as soon as their hands are not occupied.

One morning, while waiting in the lobby for the car, a distinguished-looking Japanese gentleman walked excitedly up to the information desk and obviously tried to find out if a certain person was in or out. On receiving a negative answer, he sat down on the other end of the couch on which I was sitting and in less than half a minute dropped his head backward and began to snore open-mouthed. When the person whom he came to see entered the lobby, he immediately jumped to his feet, fresh and alert. The Japanese capacity for sleeping anywhere at will was so well developed that men and women standing up in buses, holding on to the rails to keep their balance, slept in this position probably until they reached their destination.

Nela, with her feminine shrewdness, soon discovered the Japanese genius for imitation. "Arthur," she said, "you could order a dozen shirts copied exactly from your London tailored one and the price for the dozen would be less than for one from London. I intend to have them copy two or three of my best dresses, choosing the lovely Japanese silk. The price is ridiculously low." Well, I had eighteen shirts ready in less than two days and four pairs of shoes which were perfect replicas of my English hand-made ones.

After the second rehearsal, which promised a good concert, Nela and I went to the Ginza to do some window-shopping. When we reached the famous avenue, we stood for a moment gasping in astonishment. All the cherry trees on the street were covered with perfect pink-and-white blossoms, even though snow was still on the ground. We began to believe in some miracle of nature until we entered a shop where an English-speaking salesman explained with proud laughter: "These chelly blossoms are papel." I must attribute it to a very special trait of the Japanese character in not accepting that the weather had failed them; they were so determined to see their cherished blossoms on time that they had to teach nature a lesson. We fully admired this.

Strok had arranged an evening for us in a private room of a club where one hired a few geishas. "This is one of the official attractions of Japan," he said with a smile. Nela, who as a rule disliked it if I showed any interest in women, was curious about this entertainment. Like most Europeans, we had enjoyed *The Mikado* by Gilbert and Sullivan and were all familiar with Madame Butterfly; for us, the word "geisha" represented a pleasant un-known world of pleasure. Strok took us to the comfortable room with a very low round table, made us take off our shoes, which we had to leave outside, and we sat cross-legged on cushions. Three geishas appeared dressed in beautiful colorful kimonos, their hair was most elaborately made up, and they wore gold sandals held by a strap between their toes. So far, so good, but suddenly Nela and I gave each other a significant look of disgust. All three girls had rotten teeth, partly black. This little disclosure killed all possible pleasure. Their program consisted of singing and dancing and serving us a meal. They began with unbelievably slow movements of hips, arms, and hands, which they called a dance, while singing with a white colorless voice a Japanese refrain which we were treated to whenever something was sung or played all over Japan:

It was a miracle that we did not fall into a dead sleep during what seemed the longest half hour of my life. Then, with their tiny steps, they disappeared and emerged again with some dishes and chopsticks. Nela learned very cleverly to use these damned things, but I could never master them. A geisha was kneeling close to each one of us, giving us a better look at her teeth, and tried to help us with the food. Now things began to irritate me seriously. My own geisha, seeing that I was not very interested in the food or gifted in handling the chopsticks, became cheeky. She picked up pieces of some indescribable something with my chopsticks and actually tried to put them into my mouth by force. I could not endure that; she was treated to an angry look and a not too tender slap on her chopsticked hand. Strok saw the light, paid the bill in a hurry, and we left, happy to breathe fresh air and forget those teeth.

The concert was brilliant. My success was genuine enough to promise a good tour. Unfortunately, there was a very sad moment in store for us. A wire announced the death of Emil Mlynarski. We knew, of course, that there was no hope of his recovery, but this sudden certainty of his passing did give us a dreadful shock. Still, the tour had to go on.

We did go to the great show of the Kabuki, a drama lasting five or six hours in a crowded theater. We were slightly shocked to see female roles played by men, and during lengthy love scenes we couldn't refrain from laughing when the man lover bellowed at his paramour as if he were threatening her with death while his partner used a voice which sounded an octave higher than any actress I ever heard and spoke so meekly that we feared he might be killed at any moment. The whole audience wiped their eyes, deeply moved, and we were told later that this had been one of the most moving love scenes of the Japanese theater. During the long intermission, everyone there would invade the shops which sold a great variety of mementos—it was a Japanese habit never to visit anyone or return from a short absence without bringing a gift neatly wrapped in a nice cloth.

With all that I have been describing, the Tokyo of 1935 gave us the strong impression that it would soon become one of the world's capitals.

At my first recital in Osaka, Tokyo's rival city, a disagreeable incident occurred. The day before the concert, I agreed to visit the city's first piano factory, where I found mainly upright pianos, two or three baby grands, and one rather large pretentious instrument with a not too good tone. As usual, I was asked to sign my name in their visitor's book and make some nice comment. I politely complied and wished them the best of luck, in writing, for the development of this important industry. On the concert day, I tried out the Hamburg Steinway in the presence of a good tuner, whom I left to his work. At the hall, before the concert, I found lovely flowers and the usual little present in the artist's room. When it was time to begin, the local manager came in about six or seven times, saying, "Whenever you are ready." I pulled myself together and walked out, onto the stage, bowing three or four times to the very warm and large audience, and full of confidence approached the piano. But what did I see? Instead of my Steinway, there was the local manufacturer's piano ready for me. I felt a wild rage surging in me, walked off the stage, and shouted so as to be heard by the audience: "Bring out the Steinway immediately or there is no concert." The man was scared to death, the Japanese piano was removed in a second, and three minutes later, not more, I sat down and started my concert with more enthusiasm than ever.

I also gave recitals in Nagoya, Kobe, and the wonderful old capital of Kyoto, the only town which maintained some of the proud tradition of old Japan. Women mostly wore the old-fashioned kimonos and there was no sign of any imitation of European ways as in Tokyo. There we saw an old traditional play, which was rather more a variety show with singing and dancing. The musicians would sit one by one surrounding the audience, at some distance from one another, playing with no conductor and looking straight ahead. However, they never failed to start and finish together. We liked the result.

The Japanese temples were all ancient and gave the whole city an appearance of great dignity. Later on, in the company of the Polish ambassador and his wife, we visited Nikko, the great shrine where certain abbots of Nikko were buried. For the three born Catholics and the full-blooded Jew, it was startling to witness the existence of a religion completely foreign to us which inspired so much faith in millions of highly intelligent and civilized human beings.

The Marquis Tokugawa, a descendant of the famous Shogun dynasty, a Japanese gentleman and an authentic Samurai, showed a great interest in

my concerts and seemed to like our European music. Our first friendly
meeting was immediately followed by an invitation to spend a weekend at
his estate near Tokyo and we gratefully accepted. It was a marvelous opportunity to learn about the private life of a distinguished Japanese family.
He picked us up in his car late one afternoon and in less than an hour we
entered a beautiful park leading to his house, which had little of the usual
Japanese architecture. He showed us to a very comfortable apartment consisting of a large bedroom and living room; then he took us down and
introduced us to his wife, who wore European clothes as he did. After quite
a good dinner, he and I remained in the dining room while the ladies left for
the drawing room in the English fashion. After a good cigar and much new
information about ancient and modern life, we joined the ladies. Before we
retired, he announced: "Tomorrow, after breakfast, my wife will be glad to
perform for you our ancient tea ceremony, which has been a custom here
for a thousand years."

The next morning, after a good breakfast served in our rooms, we
dressed to be ready for the ceremony. In the large reception room, we saw
some preparations being made and after a short while the lady of the
house appeared, looking quite regal in her classical kimono. Her hair
was most artistically arranged, as on the old Japanese prints. She gave
us an admirable performance. The same gracious lady who had received us
the night before with the charm of a hostess in a house in Mayfair changed
into the traditional wife of a Samurai. She gave us four deep ceremonial
bows, then went quietly to a large cushion and knelt down on it slowly and
elegantly. A maid appeared with the tea set on a large tray and put it down
with an exaggerated slowness on a very low little table in front of her
mistress. Now, an unbelievable show began; I do not intend to exhaust my
reader's patience by describing every single moment of this tea ceremony, so
I shall simply give a quick synopsis.

The ceremony has served for centuries to test the nerves of the
Samurais ready to leave for battle. Their farewell cup of tea was supposed
to be served with an extreme slowness. This slowness had developed, in
time, to such a degree that what we saw could have been taken for a
practical joke. Let us count a little: Picking up a dainty napkin took about
ten minutes, the approach of the lovely hand with the napkin for the teapot
took, I would guess, ten minutes; it probably took the same time for the teapot to get near one cup. To fill it, a good three minutes, ditto the other cups.
By that time, I became greedy and wanted to taste the precious beverage,
but when I reached out my hand, she gave me a severe look of disapproval.
I shamefully dropped my hand and waited patiently—oh God, how patiently—before I could hold the precious cup. This unbelievable display of

slowness had a funny effect on me, because, as I remember, I did not dare to take the cup to my lips in less than three minutes. When the ceremony was over, both Nela and I gave out one of the biggest sighs of relief of our whole life. But, of course, infected by our easy European hypocrisy, we exclaimed with enthusiasm over the wonderful performance. My hosts were satisfied, but I think their approval was also slightly hypocritical.

I do not intend to write about my concerts, but the audiences that filled the halls listened with evident attention—and showed no desire to sleep. The music I played must have meant nothing to them except sudden fortes or pianos and at each instance their expressions changed. The comic relief in this little drama between the public and me came invariably at the end of any piece I played; there would be a deep silence and the uncomfortable feeling that they did not know whether I meant to stop or continue. The moment I gave them the green light, there came a hearty applause. Mr. Strok, for one, thought it was a highly successful tour. It was time to leave for China, where Mr. Strok's family, his wife and two daughters, lived in Shanghai and helped him with his work.

We arrived in Shanghai after a pleasant voyage on a Japanese steamer. Strok's family had arranged everything nicely for us and from the beginning made our life in China comfortable and interesting. Shanghai, lying at the basin of the Yangtze Kiang, was considered then the most important industrial center of China. But I was struck by an unhealthy political situation. The city was in the hands of France, England, and America. Our hotel was situated in the French quarter, where the avenues bore the names of Clemenceau, Briand, and Poincaré. The people in the street spoke French, and French police were directing the traffic. A short walk brought you into the Shanghai England. To make it more picturesque, Hindu Sikhs, beautifully turbaned and wearing their spectacular black beards, represented the English police force. The American quarter was immediately recognizable by skyscrapers.

For days, I did not see anyone who resembled a Chinese. The Strok family answered my questions as to the whereabouts of the Chinese with an expression of disdain; in the south of the city, they said we would see millions of them in unpaved streets and cramped quarters which could only be described as slums. I must admit that these descriptions killed our interest in visiting the sad-looking rightful owners and inhabitants of the city.

My three recitals took place in a theater and the public was made up entirely of Europeans and Americans. I really had no pleasure in playing for them. There was, of course, a certain nervous state in the whole of China because Japanese armies were mounting a siege on the other side of the Chinese wall and took threatening positions everywhere they could to harass China.

Our next town was Peking, the capital. We arrived there by train early in the morning on the day of the concert. The very comfortable French-owned Hotel de Peking had a nice apartment reserved for us. The manager told me with pride that my concert would be given "dans notre salle de Fêtes." At breakfast in our room, we received messages by letter and telephone as though we were in America or Paris. John Alden Carpenter, the rich composer from Chicago, declared that he had a house where he had been living with his wife for a year to work peacefully on his new compositions. His first wife was a remarkably artistically inclined person. She had created a women's arts club which had begun to put on important exhibitions. After she died, Carpenter married a great family friend, Mrs. Ellen Borden, the famous owner of the greatest American milk company. At that time in America, you couldn't look around for long without seeing Elsie the cow.

I was pleased to find these good old friends in such an unexpected place. They happily offered to show us everything worth seeing in the old Chinese capital. On the day of the concert, however, I wanted to be left alone, and it was only after a light lunch that I went to see the hall and the piano. When I asked for a tuner, nobody understood what I meant, but the director of the hotel informed me that there was no tuner in town. I entered the nice-looking, rather large ballroom, which was on the ground floor, and there stood the piano on a clean-looking podium, but when I opened the lid, I discovered with horror that it was an old Schiedmeier. I ran my fingers over the keyboard and found out for the first time in my life that even with the best will in the world I could not give a concert on this instrument. The organizer and director of the hotel were appalled when they heard me say emphatically that the concert could not take place. They screamed and argued. "You can't do it to us. We are responsible. Ambassadors are coming from Nanking, the seat of the government." The organizer even began to threaten me about the consequences, but this time I was adamant. This went on all afternoon and the two men were in despair about how to notify the public that the concert would not take place. But still, there were the important diplomats who had probably already left Nanking.

Suddenly, out of nowhere, a young American who lived in the hotel introduced himself to me. "I hear you have a problem, but why don't you ask Mrs. Lyon to lend you her new Steinway grand?"

"Who is Mrs. Lyon?" I asked.

"She is the wife of the American consul here and the daughter of Joseph Grew, the American ambassador in Tokyo, whom you must know."

I did know her father, who had been very kind to me in Tokyo, never missing a concert.

We went to a telephone booth, where he got the lady on the line in less than three minutes. After excusing myself for calling I told her that her father had been so nice to me and that I was sad to inform her that there would be no concert because of the abominable piano I had found in the hall. "If they can postpone the concert, would you be kind enough to lend me your piano?"

She answered enthusiastically, "But of course I will let you have the piano and please don't give up the concert. You will have it on the stage in less than a quarter of an hour."

"No, no," I answered quickly. "If you send the piano by men who don't know how to handle it, they might ruin it."

"Let me worry about that," she said, and rang off.

The young American and the two unhappy men received the news with joy. I was the only one who was worried about the porters. We sat down apprehensively and suddenly we heard a chorus, as it seemed, which had started up a singsong in the streets. It became much louder in the lobby of the hotel. Then we heard some twenty voices singing quite near and rhythmically: "cling clang tium tium clung cling clung clung," and about twenty coolies entered the room carrying, on ten huge bamboo poles, a Steinway grand with the legs and pedal well attached, using the singsong to keep their steps in order so as not to collide, as they couldn't see each other. The forty feet of the men moved rapidly toward the podium, they slowed down their singsong to walk up the steps, and when they deposited the piano without any noise, their heads and shoulders emerged from under the bamboo poles, which they removed quietly. I don't think they had ever received a larger tip than on that evening. They left, rather ran happily out of the hotel without singsong and without rhythm.

The concert went gloriously well. An elegant entirely European and American audience gave me a big ovation. It was good to see old friends. There were the Carpenters and Mr. Hoppenot, who was now the French ambassador. After the concert it was fun to reminisce about the good old days in Rio during the war when Hoppenot was Claudel's counselor. He and his wife decided to stay in Peking and spend the following day with us. Mrs. Lyon was a most charming young lady who was devoted to music. I thanked her effusively for making the concert possible. Later on, the Lyons became good friends and at one time they were even posted to Paris.

The next two days were spent visiting one of the most beautiful and interesting cities in the world. There in the streets I was struck by the unexpected beauty of the young generation of Chinese women, who were no longer being subjected to the abominable torture inflicted upon their feet as they were in ancient times. In contrast to the Japanese, the Chinese women were tall, slim, and had a wonderful bearing. Besides, there was something strangely exciting as they wore long skirts with a slit up one side so at every step you saw a well-shaped leg and thigh.

The Carpenters took us to the Forbidden City, previously forbidden during the reign of the Chinese emperors, but now very accessible to tourists. The buildings, in pure Chinese style, were intact. Inside, there were many priceless objects to be seen. I remember blushing with shame when the man in charge showed us an empty wall and said quietly, "On this wall hung the most extraordinary piece in the whole of China, a big piece of jade, so artistically carved that one could never find an equal. It was broken up and taken by the Germans, English, and French who came to fight the Boxers." It was humiliating to find out that French, German, and English soldiers had played the role of vandals.

Madame Hoppenot took Nela and me to the famous Chinese shopping center. It was rather late in the afternoon and the streets were completely dark, but the minute we took our first steps, bright lights appeared in all the windows, right and left—the famous jewelers, displaying their beautiful jade of the right deep green color, beads of all kinds, and many artistic, very desirable objects. We acquired quite a lot of things in Peking and left happily for Tientsin, another large city, where I had a concert. It had nothing of Peking's beauty and I must admit one thing angered me. At the largest square there was an important monument and I could hardly believe my eyes; it was good old Queen Victoria sitting on a white marble chair. What the devil she was doing in Tientsin, God only knows.

Here, as at previous concerts in China, my public seemed to come from London, Paris, and New York. Our next stop was Singapore in Malaya, where the Stroks in Shanghai had arranged an appearance. We left Tientsin by train and then took a steamer in Shanghai for Singapore. I was pleased to find myself so near Java, where the great tour of the Dutch Kunstkrink was awaiting me. We stayed at the famous Raffles, one of the small group of hotels like the Ritz in Paris, Shepheard's in Cairo, and the Savoy in London. When we reached the hotel, sweating in the infernal heat, we recovered our senses after a long shower and dressed in the lightest clothing. We settled happily on the famous terrace filled from morning to night with white people enjoying a large variety of multiple drinks with which they pretended to fight the heat. Suddenly, I heard a loud voice shouting "Arthur!"; it was Noël Coward, who had arrived the night before. He invited us to his table, offered us two tall glasses of gin and tonic, and tried in vain to explain to us why he was there, which was quite unnecessary, because, as I knew him, he wasn't quite sure of it himself. His presence, with his charm and wit and his genuine love for music, gave me a new shot of enthusiasm for my Singapore concert. It took place in the Victoria

Hall, a pompous severe-looking English building. British flags guarded each side of the platform, which had a large organ at the back whose pipes looked threateningly like disguised arms. The Steinway was exceptionally good.

Unfortunately, an hour before the concert, Nela came down with some dreadful food poisoning and I left for the hall terrified at leaving her alone. I was afraid I wouldn't be able to play, but again, as so often before and after, my professional musician's blood came to my rescue and I played better than ever. Noël's show of enthusiasm, clapping and shouting louder than anybody else, helped me in no small way.

At the end of the concert, the audience, completely dominated by Noël, gave me the sort of ovation which meant they were expecting several encores. The organizer of my concert, who was also manager of the Victoria Hall, was waiting for me in the wings and asked me with a terribly anxious expression on his face, "Do you intend to play something else?"

"Certainly," I answered, "if the public insists." And I gave a nice short Chopin. The response became even warmer, and the man, now nervously trembling, asked, "Are you going to play again?" This time he scared me. I told him, "Is it better not to play? Shall we go?"

"No," he said with trembling lips, "go ahead, go ahead and play, go ahead." I began to be really frightened. In these faraway English colonies, anything violent could happen, and I distinctly felt that some horrible danger was in the air. When I left the platform after my second encore and the applause did not subside, the man clapped his hands in despair and asked me, "Is that the last one?" This was too much. "What is the matter with you?" I said. "You are frightening me. Tell me what happened, you must tell me, I am terrified." He answered with a trembling voice, "You see, after each concert I have to play the national anthem on the organ, and each time I get this terrible stage fright." I was speechless for a moment, and then laughed my head off. The laughter became much stronger later, on the terrace of Raffles, when I told the story to Noël. The evening finished happily. Nela was peacefully asleep and I was told that a doctor had soothed her pains and given her a sleeping pill.

The next day, we sailed for Batavia, which had the beautiful and rightly called Hotel des Indes. For luncheon and dinner they served a *rijsttafel*, consisting of twenty different kinds of food, offered in small quantities—pieces of fish and meat, unknown little vegetables, and other eatables. But I must admit that it was not so much the taste which attracted us as the spectacular way it was served. The twenty plates were actually brought to our table by a parade of twenty waiters wearing batik-like costumes, and they repeated the parade several times.

Had it not been for the intense heat, the three concerts in Batavia would have made me feel as though I were playing in Holland.

Nela complained about some pains, which disquieted us both. At my concert in Bandung, the Dutch capital of the island, an Austrian doctor promised to take care of her at his clinic. It was dreadful for me to have to leave her there for three or four concerts, which were given in quick succession; but I managed to find a little plane which brought me every morning to see her at the clinic. Thank heavens, she was cured after a few days and could continue the tour with me.

We reached a little town on the afternoon of the concert. After signing the register in the clean-looking Dutch-run hotel, I asked for the theater or hall where my concert was to take place. The receptionist said, "The concert will be given right here in the hotel."

"You have a ballroom?" I asked.

"No," he answered, "it will be in this very lobby."

I smiled, thinking he didn't know what he was talking about. "This is sheer nonsense," I told him. "You couldn't place more than fifty people here."

"Oh," he uttered rather unsmilingly, "you will have no more than twenty people." Noticing that I didn't take him seriously, he explained in a few words what the whole thing amounted to. Four families of tea planters from the city were so fond of music that they had decided to pay the full fee among them for any of the Kunstkrink's concerts. It made me happy to hear that. Those sixteen persons who came to hear me had the best concert of my tour in Java. Usually a large audience obliges me at the start to fight for their attention, and if I am lucky to be inspired, I win them over, but in this instance these few devotees of music inspired me to give of my best right away. After the concert, we had a little reunion and a particularly enthusiastic couple invited us to spend the next day at their tea plantation. Nela, who was born in the atmosphere of farmers and planters, never lost her keen interest in agriculture and naturally liked the idea.

Having the day free, we were driven the next morning up a steep road to a charming home in the Dutch style with all its attributes. The windows were washed and rewashed to distraction; everything else was nice, but there was one great winner: the tea!

I have always been fond of good tea of a rather light color. We drank it in Poland in tall glasses with lemon and I could easily consume half a dozen to a dozen glasses in succession. I love the English afternoon tea but am completely indifferent to its origin. But here, in this Javanese plantation, I was absolutely overcome by the taste of it with the very first sip of the tea they offered. From that moment on, I never stopped asking and begging my

hosts for another cup of tea. At bridge, which we played after dinner, I
think I absorbed a good dozen cups of tea. Nectar is a poor word for it. I
can solemnly declare that no drink, whether alcoholic, coffee, chocolate, or
even milk, has ever given my palate such complete satisfaction. Nela too
was enthusiastic, but she was so proud of her perfect knowledge as to why
the tea leaves at the plantation were superior to the ones we were used to
that it seemed to her more important than the enjoyment itself. We left
enchanted with our day in the hills.

The tour continued in a rapid tempo, without becoming monotonous;
every town had its own peculiar character. In one, Nela took my concert
clothes out of the suitcase and put my black dress coat on a hanger; when
the time came to dress, she picked up the coat and about a thousand
mosquitoes abandoned it, filling the room with their lovely singsong. We
were horrified and fought them off with anything to hand. I still wonder that
we were not bitten to death by those infernal insects. But again, we won the
battle.

The next city was the hottest of them all, Surabaya, the second-
largest city on the island. Here, our beds were covered by fine mosquito
nets. We decided to undress and spend as much time as possible lying
quietly well protected. But there was something much worse in store for us.
Some huge unknown insects, looking almost like animals, seemed able to
tear our nets to pieces, knocking with great power against them and making
threatening, unbearable noises. It took courage to get up the next morning
and go through all the chores of a concert day. Fortunately, we enjoyed an
unexpected artistic diversion. Not far from Surabaya was the seat of the
Emperor of Jogjakarta. At my astonished question about the existence of an
emperor, a Dutch official told me, "Our government has always kept the
Emperor on his throne in his palace in Jogjakarta, but the offices of our
Dutch governor-general are on the other side of the square."

I asked, "Is the Emperor on friendly terms with the governor?"

"Oh yes," answered my informant. "The Emperor calls the governor
'Uncle.' "

We were lucky to be there the day of the annual National Feast of
Java, when the Imperial Gamelang was allowed to perform in front of the
palace. I was very curious to hear this performance for which thousands of
fervent lovers of this music gathered. All I knew about it was that the Bali
Gamelang had performed at the last World Exhibition in Paris and greatly
impressed Debussy, Ravel, and other musicians who had the chance to hear
it. I was enchanted by this new strange sound, which I could not help but
accept as *music* in the sense that it was an orderly, prepared succession of
sonorities. I could well understand why this music struck the imagination of
the composers.

The last city, Malang, on the extreme western point of Java, was fortunately in the hills, where the heat subsided, and my tour ended in Batavia. I was paid quite well in good Dutch money. Our next stop was Manila, again with Strok, in the Philippine Islands. It was only the beginning of July, and to my joy, I discovered that we had a few free days before taking the Japanese boat for Hong Kong. There, one or two days later, an American boat would be available to take us to Manila. Both Nela and I were very excited about the possibility of visiting the island of Bali, of which we had heard wonders. While we were in Singapore I had mentioned enthusiastically that we might go to Bali. "This is wonderful," shouted Noël. "I shall wire my friend Smith right away, and he will show you everything in the most marvelous way."

There was a plane service between the two islands and I found tickets for the next flight. Two interesting Americans were fellow passengers on the plane, Doris Duke, the rich tobacco heiress, who was on her honeymoon, and her bridegroom, a charming gentleman of European background. We became acquainted right away because they had been present at my concert in Singapore.

I remember one horrible moment on this flight. The pilot, anxious to show us the beauty of the island, flew rather low. The four of us occupied the window seats to admire the landscape. Imagine our terror when, right below us, we saw a horrible huge crater sending up high flames which almost touched the plane. We let out shrieks. Fortunately, nothing happened, but the American went to the pilot's cabin and remonstrated with him angrily. The man replied that he had wanted to give us the pleasure of watching a real volcano at close hand.

A short while later we landed at a small airport of this magic island, and the magic started right away. We left the plane, undisturbed, as though we had landed anywhere in a helicopter. There was a nice road bordered by tall trees, but out of nowhere a long parade of tallish women laden with fruit and other gifts walked slowly and majestically right in front of us. They were beautifully dressed in colorful skirts with bare breasts; they suddenly disappeared around the corner as if it had been a dream. We found out later that there were daily processions of that kind for some religious rite of their own version of the Buddhist faith.

There was a very tall blond young man who introduced himself. "My name is Smith. My friend Noël wired me to show you the island. I shall be delighted to do so." I must confess, I had not expected dear good Noël to send that cable and was overjoyed he had done so. Smith took us to a small hotel, which we found engaging and clean. Actually it was a rest house of the Dutch government.

The next day was entirely devoted to music and dancing. I introduced our American companions to Smith, who allowed them to accompany us, and he really made everything possible for us. He arranged a beautiful show where the most striking thing I remember was an extraordinary dance by a young boy certainly not older than ten. The movements of his hands and feet and head were harmoniously linked with the contortions of his body and there were lovely contrasts. He would give a few leaps and then move very slowly. The dancing was accompanied by a Balinese Gamelang, which was closely related to the Javanese but had some additional percussion instruments. During the day we saw several processions similar to the one in the morning, but with other colors, other gifts which the women carried on their heads, making them walk with a most graceful bearing. To our happy surprise, the climate was hot but agreeably dry.

Later at night, Smith arranged a concert of a male chorus for us. There were two dozen men standing close in front of each other and one line would start a tune, each man giving out a note in unison. This was immediately followed by the dozen men opposite with a note half a tone higher. They would repeat this a few times and then they began to speed up the tempo, finishing with a frantic exchange of these two notes with a long loud trill. I was simply amazed by the dozen singers who sang the syncopated note with unfailing rhythm. I think this was the high point of our visit to this beautiful island.

The next day, the indefatigable Smith drove us around the island with its soft hills, a threatening volcano, rice fields, and amazingly beautiful forests. The whole landscape had a unique beauty which I had never encountered anywhere else on my many travels.

On the third day, early in the morning, we took leave of the American couple, and thanked Mr. Smith effusively for giving us such an unforgettable memory of an enchanted island. We rented an open car, which took us to a landing place where a rowboat could take us to Java in less than an hour. The air was fresh and the short morning drive on a nice narrow road through a friendly forest was a pure delight. From time to time, two or three monkeys peered out at us with an intense look of nervous curiosity. Sometimes, terrified, they would jump shrieking up to a high branch. Others remained on the ground and graciously let us pass.

At the landing place, we hired a spacious rowboat with two oarsmen. A funny thing occurred: While I had shown my brave sea legs smoking cigars on high seas, I was miserably sick in an unsteady rowboat, whereas with Nela, the slightest roll of a big steamer had her running to her cabin in fear of the worst. However, the constant swaying of our little boat seemed to be to her serene liking. At the landing, she jumped elegantly on shore while the two oarsmen had to help me so that I wouldn't fall into the sea.

We took the train to Batavia, where, after a nice farewell *rijsttafel*, we embarked for Hong Kong.

We reached Victoria, the capital, on an exceptionally hot and humid day, all the more painful after the three refreshing days in Bali. We found rooms in the best hotel of the city, where the restaurant was air-conditioned. We had to wait two days for the American steamer which would take us to Manila.

This beautiful island, an English colony, fascinated me. It was more interesting than the enormous cities like Shanghai and Tientsin, where I was so deeply annoyed by the intrusion of Europeans and Americans. Here the English seemed to be at home as in so many other colonies at that time. The natives seemed to give them a picturesque background which sometimes gave the feeling of a show.

At the restaurant of our hotel we were served by a Russian maître d'hôtel, or rather, supervisor. He came to our table right away and tried to convince me that I had met him before. Actually, I hadn't, but pretended, to give him pleasure. From that moment on, he never left our side. After lunch, we went out for a walk. Both Nela and I were very impressed by the visible wealth and importance of the city. "Why didn't Strok arrange a concert here?" I asked Nela. "Isn't it strange?" Just then I saw an imposing music shop with an interesting window display. I said to Nela, "Let's go in and find out what musical life exists in this city." We entered the shop and saw a few pianos and other instruments, as in any provincial city in Europe. I introduced myself to the owner, a very polite Englishman, who said he knew that I had made records and asked me what he could do for me. "Who arranges concerts in this town?" I asked him. He answered with a sigh. "This rich big city is utterly uninterested in music. Four months ago, I tried to introduce a young lady from England who played the piano very nicely. We had a completely empty hall. After this experience. I would not advise you to appear in public in this city. A great disappointment would be in store for you."

We returned to the hotel, tired and hot, and rushed to the restaurant for tea and air conditioning. The Russian appeared again and, making conversation, I told him the discouraging news about the concert life. My story seemed to enrage him. "This man is a fool," he screamed. "He tried to make the people pay money for some third-rate performer. He never had the courage to engage a great artist. I could arrange a concert right here on the roof of the hotel for tomorrow night if you would agree to it." We laughed incredulously, but he became serious. "It is a charming ballroom which could hold two hundred persons. I could charge high prices and fill it to the brim."

I never could resist a challenge. "It would be quite amusing to see what happens," I admitted. He quickly replied, "I will immediately get three or four men from the press to see you and tomorrow morning a short but significant advertisement will appear in the two main papers."

I made up a surefire program in which the Funeral March Sonata by Chopin was the only important work. By Jove, this fellow succeeded. The reporters published vivid accounts of our interviews, the advertisements looked engaging, and the hall was sold out before noon. The governor announced his presence and the Russian told me triumphantly, "Everybody who counts in Hong Kong will be at the concert tonight." When I mentioned the heat, he told me, "There is a wonderful air-conditioning installation." The piano was quite a good Steinway, not a concert grand, but sufficient for the hall. But it was not easy to get into my concert clothes because of the humidity.

When the public had gathered, I took the elevator up. At a signal from the Russian fellow, I went up the two steps to the podium and everything seemed to be in perfect order. The very elegant audience was well behaved and became silent when I began to play. My first piece was a scherzo by Chopin. After a few bars there was suddenly a deafening noise from at least a dozen electric fans which completely drowned out my playing. It must have been a very primitive device and I could barely finish my scherzo against such odds. When I finished I left the stage, which I never usually do before intermission, and made the man in charge stop those fans. When this was done, I returned to the platform, smiled at the audience, and continued my program. As the concert progressed, the fans took their revenge; poor me, who for years have managed to play long and exhausting concerts finishing in all kinds of climates with an immaculate shirt and collar, had my head swimming on this occasion and I was soaked in sweat. During intermission, the Russian had to bring up some ice water and both he and Nela alternately put compresses on my forehead.

Refreshed for a moment, I continued the concert with growing effort. The last piece, a Liszt rhapsody, brought a great ovation and I bowed almost unconsciously. I shall never know how I managed to give two encores, but when I left the hall, I fainted. After I came to, they helped me down to our room, where poor Nela had to tear off my clothes, which were sticking to me stubbornly. She sat me in front of the electric fan, and then had a hard time persuading me to leave that fan and go to bed.

Next morning, I was fresh and fit for traveling again; besides, I had made a good pile of English pounds. My improvised Russian impresario was well satisfied with his own part of the pile and he helped in every way until our departure. On taking leave, he said, "On your way back to Europe, you have to touch down in Hong Kong again. There is always a long stop, so why not give another concert?" Being an indomitable sport, I answered, "Why not?" without giving it much thought.

After three days' unspectacular journey, we reached Manila, the rich capital on the island of Luzon. Strok's representative was a nice-looking Spaniard who told me he had heard about my success in Spain. This was good to know and I felt at home right away. We went to *the* hotel in town, justly called the Hotel de Manila.

After a very nice lunch at the hotel, I received two men who came on behalf of a great Spanish club with an invitation from their president to a banquet in my honor and they also gave me a card which made me an honorary member for two weeks. I was delighted to accept because in my imagination it transported me into any similar club in Spain.

My first concert took place on the following evening. That morning, my local manager took me to a vast theater or cinema, I couldn't say which, an elegant modern building. "You will have the whole Spanish population of Manila at your concert," he said with satisfaction. I found everything to my taste. A good instrument with an easy action stood at the right angle on the stage. There was a comfortable piano bench at a good height. Much encouraged, I felt that I owed it to my audience to be in especially good shape. I arranged with the manager that the stage should be available for practicing that afternoon. "And please make sure that no one is allowed in while I am working." He did as he was asked and we returned to the hotel.

After a good rest, I took a taxi and went back to the hall. A man let me in, and announced that he was going to leave but that nobody would disturb me. "You can easily call a passing taxi when you have finished," he said. I set to work very seriously without giving a thought to the time, and suddenly became alarmed when I saw that I had barely an hour and a half before starting the concert.

I dashed to the doors, hoping to get a taxi quickly, when, to my horror, I was faced with the most unbelievably violent tropical rainstorm I had ever seen, and, of course, the street was deserted. When I returned to the hall to find somebody, I found the door closed. I was all alone. It was one of those stupid situations with no visible hope of help. However, there must be a special god for pianists, because out of nowhere a private car stopped in front of me and I heard a voice say in Spanish, "Can I do something for you?"

In less than ten minutes, I stepped into the hotel. My relief was indescribable; I was convinced that I would end up having to play in my soaked day clothes. Nela, who had felt I was in trouble, had everything prepared. I just had to slip into my evening clothes while munching a chicken sandwich and gulping down a cup of coffee.

This concert remains in my memory. I gave my much-played pieces as if for the first time, and my public responded the way it did in Valencia or Oviedo.

The next day, I realized that I was a great success in this city. The Philippine ladies of distinction swarmed around Nela and gave a tea party in her honor at which they appeared dressed in some regal but exotic garb. It did not look like anything we had seen before. They satisfied Nela's curiosity by telling her that they always appeared on formal occasions in these dresses. They were made of the fiber of pineapple leaves. Nela agreed enthusiastically to have one made to measure and, after two fittings, appeared proudly at a feast with these ladies.

Manila treated us to an extraordinary show of hospitality. The American governor-general, Mr. Frank Murphy, a senator from Michigan, gave us a dinner party at the government palace at which we were introduced to Manuel Quezon, the President of the Senate and future first President of the Philippines.

Doris Duke arrived with her bridegroom on a lovely rented yacht and invited us with Mr. Quezon to a sumptuous dinner on board. A charming couple from Barcelona who were related to some friends of mine in the Catalan capital, offered to be our cicerones of the island. They were lively and we felt on friendly terms right away, so we accepted their offer. His name was Juanito López.

Before my third and last concert in Manila, the banquet in my honor took place at the typical Spanish club. As in Spain and England, the clubs were exclusively for men. The wife of the president had, however, invited Nela and two other ladies for dinner, which was served them in a small salon just off the banquet room.

The president introduced me in a long speech to the eighty-odd members, praising my concerts with exaggeration, evoking grandiloquently my success in Spain, and making much of the honor of having me. His oratorical masterpiece was sheer torture for me, because I knew that I had to reciprocate and was expected to show my gratitude in similar flowery phrases.

Now I must confess I consider myself to be one of the greatest chatterers of this century. In a small group of friends I never give anyone a chance to say a word, but on official occasions when somebody stands up and makes a speech in my honor, and I have only to answer with a "thank you," I am panic-stricken and cannot even open my mouth. This time I was at my worst; with my legs shaking under the tablecloth, I managed to stand up and tried to say something, but my voice failed me, so I uttered the sound of a strangled chicken. The assistants probably thought I was not feeling well, but after a short pause I stuttered out a few words of thanks in the poorest possible Spanish. Later on, however, when the group became less official and some members gathered around the president and me, my talent for chattering came to life again, and I succeeded in making them laugh heartily over a pun or some of my well-chosen anecdotes. Nela often mocked me afterward with her imitation of my strangled chicken voice, which she had heard from the other room.

López was not a member, but we spent most of the remaining time in their company. They were what one calls a jolly couple. López did not hold his drinks well and so, invariably, while driving us home his car would begin to zigzag and his wife would comment reproachfully in Spanish, "No hagas dibujitos." We've used this phrase ever since when a chauffeur doesn't inspire our complete confidence.

My last concert took place in the capital of the neighboring island, Iloilo. "You should know," my manager said, "that a doctor, a very nice gentleman, has invited you and your wife to spend the night in his house because the local hotel is very poor." An invitation accepted without my previous consent was not to my taste, but as usual there was nothing I could do.

A short flight in a small plane brought us to Iloilo, where the climate immediately suggested Surabaya—hot and humid. The doctor, a kind, smiling, brown-skinned man in his fifties, took us to his home, where we were a little startled by the sight of a great number of children staring at us with intense curiosity. There was a large room with an elegant staircase at the right side and many pairs of big brown eyes were glaring at us through the balusters. The doctor commented modestly, "We have nineteen children. I hope they won't disturb you." At that moment, a tall lady, evidently his wife, came in. She was at least seven months pregnant. That did it! Nela and I gave each other a frightened look and whispered a few hard swear words in Polish directed at the Manila manager.

Fortunately, it didn't turn out as badly as we feared. The lunch was served just for the four of us, after which I returned to my professional chores, such as inspecting the hall and the piano and arranging everything to my satisfaction. The city itself held no attraction whatsoever. The concert was listened to by a strange crowd with expressions on their faces as though the police had forced them to come to the concert. They reacted to my music as though I were delivering a long conference in Polish, and they applauded only when somebody gave the signal. With the permission of my readers, I shall comment no further on this concert.

Afterward, my clothes were completely soaked and our hosts allowed me to take a snack in my lightest dressing gown. I did not dare to speak too loudly for fear that my hostess might instantly give birth. During our conversation with the doctor, he revealed with pride, "My wife had triplets twice and twins three times."

Then he showed us to our room. During the day, Nela and I had been thinking that we would see two cots brought into our room for the night, but now, when the time came to go to bed, nothing was in sight. He showed us the two couches with hard leather seats and said, "We sleep this way in Iloilo." He picked up two small pillows and added shyly, "They are not for your heads, they are better used to separate your legs during our hot and humid nights." On leaving the room, he added with a smile, "We call these little pillows 'Dutch widows.' " We remained speechless for a moment, and then we tried skeptically to follow his directions. I said bitterly with some more Polish swearing, "We have a sleepless night in store for us." We took up our positions on these hard couches and, lo and behold, we slept beautifully, right away, as never before.

We woke up happily and were hungry for breakfast, but we decided to spend the last night on Iloilo in the worst hotel rather than in this baby factory. Our plane for Manila was leaving at seven the next morning and we used this as an excuse for moving to a hotel. The doctor, whose noble profession gave him much understanding, helped us to find a modest room in a hotel which didn't deserve that title. Sightseeing was out of the question and we spent the whole day with practically no clothes on, reading, impatient to leave Iloilo for good.

In the middle of the night, something terrible happened. We woke up with a start. The whole wooden structure of the building was shaking as if ready to collapse. At the same time a threatening tropical shower was whipped by the wind with a violence which seemed to destroy everything in its way. We jumped out of bed terribly alarmed, and in an attempt to find out what was happening, we opened the door to discover people running up and down. We were lucky to find the manager and asked him if we were in grave danger. "Not yet," he said. "So far, we are having typhoon number seven and can only hope that it will not get worse."

We returned to our room and waited in terror. The typhoon subsided a little but the rainstorm never stopped. "The plane will never be able to leave," I said in despair. "We are condemned to stay on this godforsaken island." In the early hours, the manager came up and said quite calmly, "Get ready, the bus is waiting to take you to the airport." I think it is unnecessary to describe our relief.

At the airport, we gave the plane a loving look and when the rain lessened, only an hour late, we took off for Manila. It was on this short flight that I said to Nela, "From now on, we must hurry up. We must get home for Eva's birthday." We arrived in Manila in due time but landed in knee-deep water at the airport. Men came to our rescue and carried the six or seven passengers to the bus. Fortunately the storm subsided and we reached the Manila hotel without incident. It was still early in the morning and our American steamer of the Dollar Line was not leaving until late that afternoon, so we had time to fetch the tickets and finish packing the luggage which we had left behind. We sent an anxious telegram to the concert agency in Moscow about our arrival, which was likely to be on August 15.

Nela thought that it would be nice to invite the Lópezes to lunch before taking leave. They promised to come. We washed and changed. The office of the Dollar Line was in the hotel, which made things easy.

When I asked for my tickets and made ready to pay for them, the agent asked me indifferently, "Have you your sailing permit?" At my astonished expression he added, "Have you paid your taxes?"

"There must be some mistake," I said. "What are you talking about?"

He answered unsmiling, "You are on American territory and we are not allowed to give out tickets without a permit showing that you have satisfied the tax authorities about your earnings in this country."

I became very impatient. "I have a manager here who should have told me that, but he never mentioned such a thing." The man turned his back and here I was without the tickets. I ran up to the hotel manager to find out if he really had the right to retain the tickets. "Yes," he said, "you must go to the tax office and show them the income you made in this country." I could have killed my manager, who never showed up but had settled his account with me. It was difficult for me to find out where the tax office was and when it opened. I was waiting anxiously for the Lópezes. When they arrived, we immediately told him about our ordeal. They proved to be much better friends than I had hoped. He said, "Leave it to me." He succeeded in getting a tax man to come to the ticket office by telling him that it was an urgent case, that it was utterly impossible to get the right account of my earnings, as it had to be made out in correct form, and that I had no way of getting hold of my manager, who had promised to see me off. Now this Juanito López really showed his mettle. He told the tax man in elegant terms that he was ashamed at seeing me treated as if I had tried to cheat the American treasury. The tax man remained cool and indifferent to all these explanations, and this so enraged our Juanito that he told the man proudly, "I am a citizen of good standing in Manila. I shall sign my name to a declaration in your words and will guarantee any eventual debt of Mr. Rubinstein's to the United States." At that, the tax collector, the ticket agent, and López went to work, drafted the right statement, and Juanito signed it.

A few minutes later, the tickets were in my pocket and the four of us had a friendly and gay farewell lunch. In the afternoon, this nice couple took us to the port and after quite a few hugs, kisses, and slaps on the back, with thanks and assurances that we hoped to meet again soon, we finally embarked.

We sat on the deck quietly for a long rest after the terrible night and the dread of not being able to leave. Suddenly I felt a pang of apprehension. I turned toward Nela. "Darling, do you realize that we have to count the days carefully so as to be home in time for Eva's birthday? I could not bear to be late for that." Poor Nela! She had lived for weeks longing for the children, waiting feverishly for a wire or letter, and becoming desperate if there was a delay. So now she smiled faintly. "What about me!"

In the evening, while we were sitting in the dining room, a fearful wind began to make the boat rock fiercely. The dining room was empty in less than a minute and we ran to our cabin, where Nela threw herself on the bed and seemed ready to die. I ran up in alarm to find out what had happened from the ship's purser. "This is a typhoon, sir," he answered. "We hope to avoid it. Don't be afraid. It will be an uncomfortable trip, but at sea one is safer from typhoons than on land." This last sentence reassured me very much. I tried to convey the good news to Nela but she wouldn't listen.

After four dreadful days of fear, lack of food, and practically no sleep, we landed in a shaky condition at the port of Hong Kong. The typhoon had subsided for more than a day. We were to lose a whole day on the island before continuing to Shanghai; from there we would travel by train until we reached Warsaw. The boat was slow to come to a standstill and all the passengers were on the deck searching for friends and family or just looking around out of curiosity.

I saw a man in a white suit in front of the crowd waving furiously with a handkerchief. "He seems to be waving at you," Nela said. I gave him a timid wave, at which the man practically jumped in the air with excitement. When our boat came quite close, we both recognized him at the same time. "The Russian headwaiter," we exclaimed.

We were finally allowed to step down and he rushed like a madman toward us, shouting in Russian, "Thank God you are on time." His almost hysterical welcome disquieted me slightly. His next words were: "Have you the program ready?"

"What for?" I screamed.

"We have a concert tonight and it is sold out."

"Whaaat?" I stammered.

"It was understood, don't you remember? I found out from the Dollar Line when you would arrive and announced it so as not to lose time. Everything is ready but the program."

My professional blood came to my rescue. I forgot all about Iloilo, taxes, and typhoons; my thoughts were concentrated on the program. At the hotel, I delivered it to him in a few minutes. The Russian said with a shy expression, "I have another commitment for you. The nearby, very important Chinese city of Canton has a large university and they have offered a good sum of money for a concert tomorrow afternoon. You can get there by train in less than two hours and be back late in the evening."

This made me angry. "We leave tomorrow for Shanghai. We must be home without fail on a special date which I wouldn't miss for the world."

"You will be on time," he said hotly. "I made my plans. The day after tomorrow, the large Italian steamer *Il Conte Verde* is leaving for Shanghai and will arrive before your own boat—and I have your reservations," he added triumphantly. He had a way with me, this Russian good-for-nothing. I followed all his instructions.

Nela, however, showed a certain resistance and decided to let me go alone to Canton. The Russian informed me that my audience would be completely Chinese, mostly students. This made the choice of program difficult. I finally decided on an eclectic one: my Bach Toccata in F major, the Beethoven Sonata in E flat, and then some carefully chosen pieces of a quite different character, like *Petrushka*, Chopin, Liszt with his Twelfth Rhapsody, of course!

The Hong Kong concert was a replica of the first one—not the program, but the atmosphere. This time, my clever fellow found a way to turn on only a part of the air conditioning, which made it possible for me not to suffer too much from the heat. Both the Russian and I were pleased with our earnings.

The next morning, he and I took the train to Canton, a huge, authentically Chinese town. The hotel had a pure Chinese style and there I found a letter addressed to me from the International Rotary Club. The American businessmen invited me to join them at luncheon on a houseboat, and expected a little speech from me. Ever greedy for diversions, I agreed, in spite of having more useful things to do before my concert, which was announced for four o'clock.

On a nice English-looking boat, a large long table was occupied by keen-looking Chinese businessmen presided over by a typical American member of the club. They served a horrible half-American, half-Chinese concoction of chicken and rice, followed by ice cream, hard and cold as a stone. With the first bite the usual procedure took place. When a clear beverage pretending to be coffee was served, my turn was announced by taps of the president's hammer. The paralyzed speaker that I was suddenly found a torrent of compliments for the commercial genius of America and China, and that earned me my first applause of the day.

The concert turned out to be a great experience. The vast assembly hall of the university was packed to the brim with Chinese students. The rector, who received me with the almost servile Chinese politeness, was an Oxford graduate. My piano was astonishingly good. All these circumstances inspired me to play better than at many previous concerts. After the toccata, I received an ovation. Ah-ha, I thought, here is an audience which is ready to give ovations for anything I have to offer. But I was wrong. The Beethoven sonata received a prolonged applause, but after my fiery performance of *Petrushka*, there was a silence; they were not sure whether it had ended and they applauded with indifference. I counted on my Liszt rhapsody, my much-used war horse, but it simply fell flat. They rose to their feet, ready to leave the hall; encores seemed to be unknown to them. I was somewhat hurt, having for once been satisfied with my performance.

Backstage, the rector shook both of my hands with four or five deep bows, and invited me for tea in his private rooms. I was frank with this highly educated scholar. "Your audience seemed to have had enough of me after my first piece, or did they find out in some Chinese books about music that in our part of the world we consider Bach the greatest musician and consequently paid him due homage?"

My slightly ironic question alarmed him. "Oh no no no, you are quite wrong, quite wrong. You see, we Chinese are tremendously gifted with our hands, so great demonstrations of technical prowess or strength in the pieces you played do not impress them at all. But in your Bach, they felt the overwhelming greatness of the music. The ovation they gave you came from their appreciation of the nobility of a music they had never heard before."

His words left a lump in my throat. "What a beautiful lesson to our own audiences with their easy enthusiasm for cheap demonstrations of bravura and speedy fingerwork!"

I returned to Hong Kong in high spirits while my Russian companion burst into invectives against these "Chinese ignoramuses," as he put it. As I got off the train in Kowloon, I saw with pleasure the majestic and brilliantly lit *Conte Verde*. The sight of it made me feel that I was nearer to my Eva's birthday. Nela, happy to see us back, was waiting to have supper with me, which was served us with particular care by our maître d'hôtel–concert manager! During the meal, I happily told her the day's adventures; she, for her part, had been busy making the necessary preparations for our return home. "I wired the Polish consulate in Shanghai," she said, "to send somebody who could help us with our tickets and luggage between the boat and the train. I found out that we arrive on a Saturday, when many official places are closed." Our Russian helped us to embark with our, by now, large amount of luggage and bid us goodbye with great hopes of seeing us back very soon.

Oh, how we loved the *Conte Verde*. It was Europe again. I remember absorbing the greatest amount of spaghetti ever in one sitting and it was just as good as at Savini's in Milan. It was a wonderful rest too.

Early on Saturday morning, we entered the basin of the Yangtze and we were told that we would arrive in Shanghai well before noon; but the ship slowed down and continued to do so in a most alarming way. We didn't seem to make any progress at all, while smaller craft passed us with ease. Noon went by and the situation did not change for two more hours. We began to agonize and almost gave up hope. "We shall never get to Shanghai," I said to Nela, "and if we do not catch the train today, we will lose two whole days." I discovered the delay was due to the low tide.

It was well after three o'clock when we finally disembarked. The Polish vice-consul did wait for us, to our great relief. "We must hurry to the ticket office, which will close in half an hour." He put us into a car, gave the driver the address, and remained at the dock to take care of our luggage. "When you get the tickets, my car will take you to the station, where I shall be waiting for you, because the train leaves in an hour."

We followed his instructions. We dashed to the ticket office, which was still open, asked an attendant where the tickets were, and were told that the man in charge had left for the weekend. "We don't need the man, we want our tickets," I said irritably. "The office is still open."

He led us to a desk and said indifferently, "The tickets must be in a drawer and he must have taken the key with him." Now I began to scream: "I'll break up the drawer. I'll sue the company. We *must* take that train." Several employees watched me with frightened faces. One of them ventured, "He lives nearby. I might try to bring him back." I jumped at his offer and I made Nela drive right away to the station to make all the arrangements for our departure with the vice-consul. "I shall wait for this goddamn fellow and will join you as quickly as I can." I stood in front of the office, fidgeting madly for what seemed hours, and the man finally arrived just as they were beginning to close the doors.

I had a taxi waiting, leapt into it, and kept yelling at the driver to speed up—every minute counted. At the station, I jumped out of the car and almost fell flat on the pavement, but by a miracle I was on my feet again and ran like mad to the platform. I found the train ready to leave and only Nela and the vice-consul standing there. The vice-consul had two coolies in front of the luggage van and ordered them to push it all inside. He already had the labels and tickets for them. Nela stood there speechless. The vice-consul screamed, "Get in, get into the car." When we took the first step, the train was moving. I could only wave with thankful gestures at our compatriot, and I might say without exaggeration that we collapsed in our seats, but felt victorious. According to my careful calculations, if things went smoothly from then on, we would be in Otwock on August 18, our darling's second birthday.

We went humming to the dining car for dinner, passing through half the train, which was filled with people of all nationalities. The Chinese headwaiter gave us seats at a table for four. Our companions were two Frenchmen, typically voluble, who immediately engaged us in continuous conversation. One of them, feeling happy at giving us valuable information, told us with a broad smile, "We shall be lucky if there isn't a delay of three days on this little trip to Tientsin. The Yangtze Kiang is in flooding season and I shouldn't be astonished if our train has to stop here and there for hours or days." Hearing that news spoiled our appetites. The two days' journey to Tientsin became a torture, we were in such fear of being caught by a flood. I shall never be grateful enough to "Ol' Man River" Yangtze Kiang for having allowed us to reach our goal without trouble.

We arrived in Tientsin on a mild summer day. After breakfast in the hotel, I left Nela for the Russian consulate to get our visas and tickets for the return trip to Moscow, but it was not easy to get in and I had to produce my passport to be allowed to enter the premises. After a long wait, I finally saw the consul. When I asked him to deliver the necessary items, he went through a pile of papers and said indifferently, "We have nothing here for you." Seeing the distorted expression on my face, he added, "They usually send them to the consulate in Harbin." This news shattered me completely. I had my whole schedule clearly in my mind and remembered that our train arrived in Harbin at seven in the morning and left again at eight. I addressed the consul: "Could you do me a great favor and telephone your colleague there about my dilemma and ask him if he could help me?"

The man shrugged his shoulders. "I'm sorry," he answered, "but this consulate can't do anything about it, and it is even possible that Harbin has nothing for you either." I returned to the hotel to share my despair with Nela. When we calmed down somewhat, I made my decision. With the help of the hotel clerk, I sent a telegram to the Russian consul in Harbin. It was the first and last time that I wrote a missive using the most imploring terms I could think of; at the same time lying that I had a concert in Moscow on a date which could not possibly be changed and that I would suffer irreparable loss if I missed it. It was a slightly degrading document but in my desperation I had to try anything. We left that afternoon in a gloomy mood. The train was to take us to the Korean frontier, to a village at the foot of the Great Wall. This news revived our spirits.

Upon our arrival, late in the afternoon, the full view of the wall was an amazing sight. "It runs for fifteen hundred miles," I reminded Nela, "and was started hundreds of years before Christ—not, as they taught us, in order to stop cultural development, but simply to protect this highly civilized country against intruders, the Northern Barbarians."

We were happy to learn that we had three hours before leaving again —an unexpected chance to visit the wall. A man who spoke English showed us the way to an Italian restaurant. "For a good tip, the headwaiter will help you. He is used to serving the tourists." We found the place easily and were immediately approached by a happy, smiling Italian. After receiving my little gift, he called a rickshaw and gave instructions to take us to the wall. "He will wait for you as long as you want, and bring you back here," he said to us. We settled down comfortably in this strange vehicle propelled by a galloping coolie—this one was certainly a good runner.

He stopped at a strange heavy iron door. At one side of it we saw steps carved into the wall which went up to the top. Nela clapped her hands when she noticed flowers up there. "I would love to pick some." When the coolie saw us moving toward these steps, he began to scream in Chinese and gesticulate wildly. I understood that he did not want to wait and with calming gestures I indicated that it would not be for long. But the fellow kept on shouting. I became impatient. "Don't worry," said Nela. "He will not leave without being paid." We gaily climbed the steps. When we reached the top, we were amazed at the incredible width of the wall. I think twenty men could have stood in a line across it. Nela happily picked some multicolored nondescript flowers. "I shall press them in a book," she said. The view was not interesting. There was a monotonous landscape with tall plants and shrubs, and so, after a short while, we went down and found our coolie shaking his head incredulously.

On our return to the restaurant, the coolie ran excitedly up to the headwaiter and obviously complained, pointing his finger at us. The Italian wrung his hands and shouted, "Dio mio, Dio mio, they might have killed you, they might have killed you." Later came the explanation. Apparently, Japanese snipers hidden in the shrubs took a shot at anyone venturing on top of the wall, and we escaped death by something short of a miracle. Both Nela and I felt a little shiver at the thought of being killed for picking a few miserable flowers.

We boarded the train for Mandjuria. On the platform we overheard some passengers talking about the almost daily assaults on the train by robbers who, during the summer, could hide in the tall shrubbery. This information, I must admit, put us into a state of terrible fear. After the long tour, I had a large sum of money in my bag; Nela had some too and also her own jewels and the jewels we had acquired. Exhausted as we were, we spent half the night trying to hide our valuables cleverly, but after this great effort we suddenly became afraid that we would forget where we had hidden them, so, in the middle of the night, we put them back where they belonged.

We reached Harbin at seven o'clock in the morning after a sleepless night, not only because of the threat of the robbers but, even more, because we were frightened of being kept in Harbin for three more days with the shattered hope of reaching Warsaw on time. Besides, I had no knowledge as to whether my concert in Moscow could take place on the day of our arrival there or, at the latest, the next day. I had conceived a plan to try and telephone the Moscow concert agency and beg them to help me with the visas for Mandjuria and, if possible, announce my concert for the day of my arrival or the following day.

We left the train, ready for action, when a well-dressed gentleman approached me and asked politely, "Am I right in guessing that you are Mr. Arthur Rubinstein?"

Smiling at him, I said, "Yes, I am, but please don't ask me for an autograph. I am in a tremendous hurry."

He laughed. "You could give me one later. I am the consul of the U.S.S.R. and have come with your visas and all necessary papers for Mandjuria which you requested in your telegram. You look tired, so go right away to the restaurant, give me your passports, and have a nice breakfast. I will bring everything there and we'll get the signatures I need." Well, I had tears in my eyes. I felt like kissing his hand. But here was a born gentleman. Aware of my emotion, he pushed us into the restaurant with authority. Every one of my readers will know how I felt. The breakfast seemed the best we had ever had. He joined us at coffee, had us sign his papers, and when the time came, took us back to our car.

We left for Mandjuria with enough courage to fight the whole world. Mandjuria was now the dreaded Russian frontier. I knew well the men in the long gray coats with pistols in their holsters, the grim inexpressive faces, ready to make our life difficult. Here we were, after almost six months of adventure, loaded with an incredible mass of luggage. I do not remember the exact number but I know that we had no fewer than twenty cases. When all this stuff was lined up on a long bench under the spying eyes of these customs officers, they pointed accusing fingers at our many belongings and ordered us to open them all.

In moments of emergency, I used to get sudden brain waves for a good way out of trouble. I picked up my tickets, pointed at the itinerary, and said, "You can see that we took off from Paris to Tokyo and these tickets take us back to Paris. You can send all this luggage straight to Warsaw, where we have to stop, and you have the guarantee there is nothing in it which might interest your country. All we must take is one little case for immediate needs and the concert. I am a concert pianist and have to play in Moscow on the way."

They were taken aback, and were more amenable now that we would have no access to our belongings until we reached a foreign country. They could now let us go with the few things which did not interest them anymore. We felt great pity for some other passengers whom these unfriendly gentlemen tortured mercilessly with close scrutiny and interrogation. At the buffet, we had two glasses of pale tea (there was nothing else to be had) and were finally allowed to enter the old, old Belgian sleeping car, probably filled with a new assortment of fleas, cockroaches, etc. I shall not dwell on details of this long journey to Moscow; all I can say is that this time the landscape presented many beauties, thanks to the summer.

At various stations, peasant women in picturesque dresses were selling fresh eggs, butter, and fruit without being attacked by policemen. However, there was something very disquieting: our train arrived at large stations several hours late. At every stop, my anxiety heightened. When we approached Moscow, I realized with despair that we were almost twenty-four hours late.

A comic incident enraged me: when our train finally stopped at the Moscow station, a deputation of a dozen or so delegates of the government came to deliver a medal to the two men in charge of the train for their brilliant performance. Both Nela and I laughed angrily for a long while.

The concert manager, who was waiting for us, gave me some soothing news which calmed my wrath. "Unfortunately," he said, "we couldn't find a date for your concert, so we shall have to postpone it until your next visit." The date was August 16, and I begged the man to get us reservations for the seventeenth for Warsaw. He took us to a shabby room at the Hotel National, which we did not mind this time, thinking of nothing but our child's birthday. For dinner, we were served the famous Russian soup called *shtshee*, but on this occasion it was devoid of its necessary ingredients. "There is no bread or butter today," said the attendant; when we asked for coffee, she said, "We only have tea." After dinner, back in our room, came a new shock; the concert manager knocked at our door and entered in great excitement. "Comrade Stalin wants you to play tomorrow night at the Kremlin. We have an International Medical Congress and he wants to honor them with a concert."

I became ashen pale. "This is impossible, this is utterly impossible," I cried. "You must have some pianist or other artists who could do it better than I."

The man was taken aback. The poor fellow had expected me to kiss his hands in gratitude for the high honor. When he asked me why I refused, I told him, "If I do not reach Warsaw on the eighteenth, I shall have to commit suicide." And Nela nodded her head gravely. This dramatic outburst scared him. "Please don't worry. I shall arrange it as best I can," and he left the room. We both gave the longest sighs of relief.

On the seventeenth, sitting safely in our compartment on the way to Warsaw, our hearts were beating fast with happy expectation. Nela had sent wires to her mother and to her brother so that they would know when to expect us. We arrived on August 18, toward evening and right on time.

Nela jumped out to look for her mother and brother. I gathered our belongings, called a porter, and stepped down onto the platform. I stood there with the porter, and there was no sign of Nela. After a short time, I saw her running back in dismay. She shouted, "There is nobody here. I looked the length of the train and there was no one. I searched every corner. They probably didn't get the telegrams, or are out of town." That was a blow. Nela gave some practical advice: "If our luggage has arrived, we can leave most of it at the *consigne* and put the most important into a taxi and leave for Otwock." To our joy, the luggage had arrived with us. With the help of the porter, we followed Nela's plan. He found a taxi and loaded it with as many of our cases as it could carry and took the rest to the *consigne*. We hardly found room for ourselves in that taxi. We gave the address of the villa in Otwock and drove out. We were so burning with impatience—it had become alarmingly late, as we had lost an hour at the station—that we prodded the driver to speed up, but he answered with a critical eye on the luggage, "How can one drive quickly with such a load?" We reached the health resort of Otwock in less than half an hour and the taxi entered the little sand road leading to the villa. Then something terrible happened: The taxi stopped dead in the sand, and although the wheels turned like mad, we were stuck. We all left the car to push with all our might, but in vain. The driver, instead of helping us, cursed and swore. Finally, seeing our despair, he said, "At the nearby station, you can find a horse cab which could do the job." Without losing a word, I ran to that station and there was indeed an old cab with a tired old horse. I produced the right amount of money so that he would work quickly. We galloped to the place where the taxi was stuck, piled the luggage into the cab, and I said to the old driver of the horse cab, "The luggage must go with us, but we can walk." We walked with the driver, who pulled the horse's head, and we advanced very slowly indeed. We must have looked like some lost pilgrims.

When we rang the bell, it was ten minutes to twelve. The door was opened by Nela's cousin dressed in a nightgown and we ran past her to the nursery. Nela put the light on, which woke our little baby from her sleep. She sat up with a start, looked at us with suspicion, studied our photo on the wall next to her cot, and only then recognized that we were we. When Nela threw her arms around her, the child said with a reproachful voice, "Will you leave again?" We turned to the crib where baby Paul was fast asleep and we kissed him without waking him. Nela cried bitterly and I felt like a criminal, but I was proud; it was still before midnight. We couldn't sleep that night.

Early next morning, we dashed down in a hurry to find the child at her breakfast with Karola and Nela's cousin. It was only then that we could call it a happy reunion. Frantic telephone calls came from Bronek and my mother-in-law. They had had bad luck; the very day we announced we would arrive, they had already accepted an invitation to stay with some friends in the country.

I tried to amuse my lovely little baby with her blond curls by telling her extravagant stories. She listened, but did not laugh. After finishing her breakfast, she stood up, took my hand, and said with her sweet voice, "Play something." Two words which gave me an indescribable emotion—my own daughter asking me to play for her. I took her to the living room, which had an old baby grand. I opened the lid and the top, settled her in a comfortable chair, and sat down to play. A short dilemma: shall I play a nursery song, or something serious to remember this moment forever? While still undecided, Eva called out impatiently, "The gra-mo-phone." My emotion turned into great laughter. She showed me a little record player and I learned from Karola which were her favoite records and she listened, clapping her hands.

Little Paul was only six months old and led a peaceful life between sleep and food. For a few days we were a happy family.

91

I went back to Paris alone because Nela had to settle accounts for the villa and pay the debts we had incurred. She also wanted to stay for a short time with her mother, so recently a widow.

As for myself, I found Paris empty, as it was every year in that season.

Most places were closed. Even my manager, Dr. Schiff, was on a probably well-deserved vacation.

One day I received a visit from Bronislaw Hubermann. It was a most interesting meeting. There was a wealth of important matters to talk about. Hubermann was a noble-hearted, remarkable man. Before Hitler, Germany and Austria considered him the greatest violinist of the time. Brahms had kissed him when the thirteen-year-old boy had played his concerto for him. So now, deeply hurt by the attack on the Jews by Hitler's blindly obedient Germany, he wrote an accusing letter to Goebbels which was widely read and commented upon and which Wilhelm Furtwängler repudiated on Goebbels' order.

He poured out to me the reason for his visit. "I have conceived a plan which I hope you will approve. The idea is to create an orchestra in Tel Aviv consisting of the many excellent orchestral musicians who have been expelled from so many cities, not only in Germany but in countries which have followed Hitler's example, like Austria, Poland, Hungary, and Rumania. I already seem to be getting good results, but I must have your help. We are in great need of contributions from wealthy Jews in the still free world and you would have the opportunity on your concert tours to raise funds for this orchestra." I accepted this challenge with fervor and promised to do everything in my power.

After two or three days which I spent preparing our bohemian home for the family, Paris began to fill up again and my bachelor's blood came to the fore. I wouldn't go to bed without duly visiting my old haunts. It was pleasant to resume the old talking bouts with Fargue and sometimes Ravel, who didn't need my replies to his questions. He liked to put the questions and tell himself the answers and go on like that endlessly. I must also admit that the taste of the refined French cuisine made me forget the six months of curry and rice which I did not enjoy but which kept me alive.

Dr. Schiff came back and filled my ears with proposals for concerts. The future looked good! When Nela and Karola arrived with the children, they saw a man refreshed physically, morally, and musically. Nela, with her incredible energy and competence, changed our funny home into a paradise. Our miniature kitchen began to function as if it were Larue's and she even found a Polish cook and a Polish maid. As it was still warm, she put a playpen in our tiny garden, and little Eva, surrounded by her favorite toys, was happily occupied.

On the way to London, the sea between Calais and Dover was particularly rough, and I decided to sit it out on the deck. Suddenly, I found that Rachmaninoff was sitting next to me. I shall quote here a letter of Szymanowski, who wrote to his sister after I had told him of this meeting:

"I know yet another version of a conversation between Rachmaninoff and Arthur Rubinstein concerning me, which took place when they met on the boat. They talked at length and Rachmaninoff was terribly critical of contemporary music, putting down the Stravinskys, Ravels, etc. But when Arthur mentioned my name, he suddenly brightened up and started inquiring about me in a very friendly way, calling me a most charming man. Arthur was triumphant. 'Then you like his music?' he asked. Rachmaninoff replied, 'What? His music is shit, it is the man who is very nice.' "

I can guarantee the authenticity of this interview rather than the other one reported by the *Illustrated Courier*.

The autumn season, until Christmas, kept me busy with concerts. The long Oriental tour, with programs repeated so often, gave me a more solid hold on them; thus I had the opportunity to widen my repertoire, even during my tours. I discovered a trait in my character which was unique in my profession. All through my very long life, I never lost my love for playing in public and all that it involved; the traveling, even uncomfortably, the constant change of cities, hotels, food, climate, I simply adored it all. It went even further than that; whenever I was obliged to stay in the same place for more than two or three months, even if it was Paris, London, Rome, or Venice, to be forced to walk through the same streets, see the same buildings and shops, I began to get irritated. Having visited most of the world, I use the phrase "I never leave, I always return," because everywhere I feel at home.

Dr. Schiff started by sending me to Sweden and Norway, countries which I love to visit in the early autumn, where you see endless forests covered with their golden leaves. The sun is very intense in these northern places and helps one to endure the cold. The Swedes interested me. They were too tall, too reserved, and often too pompous, which was irritating. But these same people could, all of a sudden, show you the most gracious warmth. I think they were made of contrasts. The tall beautiful blond girls passed you on the street without giving you a glance, but you knew that they were passionate enough to engage in free love with the approval of their families.

The same thing happens in the concert hall. They fill the house, sit through the program with stiff attention, listening intently, but at the end, something unexpected happens. They simply go wild, shouting and yelling bravos, shaking the chairs, and behaving in a way which would be unheard of in Naples. Yes, indeed, the Swedes are warmhearted people.

My manager, Mr. Helmer Enwall, invited me to his box for the premiere of *Arabella* by Richard Strauss. He introduced me to the two ladies seated in the front. One was his wife, the other a striking Negress. In those days, it was a tremendous rarity to see a colored person in Sweden, and I was quite startled by the extremely intelligent expression of her face. Her musical taste was astonishing too. *Arabella* was not one of the best operas of Strauss and her judgment during the intermissions seemed to me absolutely right. At one point, when Enwall and I were alone, he gave me all the information. "This is Marian Anderson, the greatest lieder singer of our time," he said. "She is worshipped in Sweden and Finland, where she could fill the hall any time she chooses." He excited me. "Is there any chance of hearing her? I am leaving tomorrow night, but could you beg her to sing for me wherever she chooses?" He conveyed to Miss Anderson my burning desire and she responded as only a great artist would. The next day, in the afternoon, when the restaurant of my hotel was empty, she appeared with her accompanist, who was wonderful, and sang all the most touching beautiful songs I asked her to sing in a way which I cannot describe, but I still have tears in my eyes when I remember it. I kissed both her hands with deep gratitude and never missed an occasion to listen to her.

Norway is quite different. After the spectacularly peaceful separation from Sweden, which dominated it for nearly one hundred years, Norway soon recovered its own remarkable personality, and even began to impress its superiority over its neighbor. The Norwegians began to remind the world of the great era of the Vikings, of their pride in having an Ibsen, a Björnson, and the painter Munch, not to speak of Edvard Grieg, whose music sung out their Nordic souls. They have much in common with the Danes, but Denmark is the most attractive country of the three and it had the most enjoyable capital, Copenhagen. I loved playing in these countries, where I became a frequent visitor.

Six

1937: My Longest Tour and a Triumphant Return to the U.S.A.

92

I remember having played all over Europe during the 1935–36 season and felt with pleasure that my popularity was growing from concert to concert. After New Year 1936, we heard the good news that Karol's ballet *Harnasie* had finally been accepted by the director of the Paris Opéra, Mr. Rouché, and the main role was given to Serge Lifar, who was then director of the Opéra ballet school. This was wonderful news for us. Karol was coming for a long stay in Paris to supervise the rehearsals and be the victim of the newspapers and the radio. I must say, I felt great joy in seeing Karol again after a long time and felt proud for him to have his ballet produced in Paris in the best possible way. When he arrived, his looks disquieted us. He looked more frail and there was a strange sad look in his eyes. He was very nervous and apprehensive about how Paris was going to receive his ballet. My poor Karol, with his agoraphobia, was besieged by boring admirers. He came to our place from time to time for a meal and he was happy with little Eva, who amused him with her precocity.

"Arthur, I brought you a nice present," he said one day. "The first printed score of the Symphony Concertante. You know that I followed your advice and played it in quite a few cities. You will never know what an effort it was for me but I needed the money desperately. The Polish government is terribly stingy with subsidies for music and I have my whole family to support." At that time, I was only able to help him with small sums. I had quite a little family of my own!

I managed to be present at the premiere of *Harnasie*; there were great hopes for it and it was a genuine success. Lifar did his best dancing the difficult main role of the Polish mountaineer and the orchestra sounded very good. There was high praise in the press. Henry Prunières, then the most important music-magazine publisher, devoted a whole issue to Szymanowski, of whom he was a real admirer, and the Polish ambassador gave a large luncheon in Karol's honor.

It was a lively social season all around. Edouard and Robert de Rothschild gave large dinner parties; Misia Sert and Coco Chanel enter-

tained the famous people; the cinemas were overflowing with enthusiasts of
Fred Astaire and Ginger Rogers; balls were given by the embassies.

South America claimed me again for the summer of 1937. I was going
to play in Brazil, Uruguay, Argentina, and Chile.

Dr. Schiff was also very keen on getting me a tour in the United States
but was deeply discouraged when the head of the Columbia Association of
Managers, Mr. Arthur Judson, answered coolly: "Rubinstein is poison for
the box office." Another manager, Mr. Coppicus, wrote candidly: "I might
get him an engagement with an orchestra if he gives two recitals at Carnegie
Hall, and pays for it as well as all the publicity." We had a good laugh
about this one, Schiff and I. Then came an unexpected offer from the
Australian Broadcasting Commission for fifteen well-paid concerts plus all
expenses; I accepted it with pleasure—again I was burning to see a new
country.

This made up a huge season for the year 1937, starting with more than
fifty concerts in Europe, followed by over forty concerts in South America,
and from there, back to Europe by boat to fly from Amsterdam to Australia.

When all these contracts were duly signed, something completely unexpected happened. On my return from a long tour which took me to the
French provinces, Spain, Italy, Belgium, and Holland, with a few concerts
in England, I hoped to have a well-deserved rest with my family, enjoying
the lovely spring in Paris. My nature never allowed me to get used to
anything, so whether it was the exciting spring in Paris or the Polonaise in
A flat of Chopin, it was always new and fresh to me. We were happy in our
rather absurd but so romantic home. It was lovely to watch little Eva
cavorting in her little playpen next to the tiny goldfish pond bordered by
geraniums and begonias.

My little Eva was a capricious child. She was quite lovely and graceful
and showed early a gift for dancing. Whenever she was in a bad humor it
was sufficient for Nela and me to dance a few steps and she would jump
happily to her feet and imitate us with the right rhythm. At four, she started
dancing lessons. Her teacher, the famous Polish dancer Mathilde Krzesinska, was the ex-mistress of Tsar Nicholas II. It was from the balcony of her
palace in St. Petersburg that Lenin harangued the crowds daily. After the
Revolution she married morganatically the Tsar's cousin, the Grand Duke
André, and lived in Paris giving dancing lessons. She was enchanted with
my little girl and after the lessons her husband never failed to produce some
tidbit for little Eva.

One night after dinner, Nela and I went to a neighboring cinema but
on arrival we were told it was full. Seeing my disappointment, a man,
evidently the owner, offered us two seats without letting me pay for them. "I

always have some places for special guests," he said. I asked him, smiling, "Do you like music?" He made an astonished face. "I don't know anything about music, but I am your neighbor and watch from my balcony your adorable child playing and I recognized you as her parents." I thanked him effusively. We felt terribly proud to owe these tickets to the charm of our little Eva.

I can't keep my readers in suspense any longer! The surprise which I previously announced was a telephone call from Dr. Schiff, who told me triumphantly: "I have a well-known American manager in my office who is offering you an important tour. I told him of your reluctance to go to the United States again, but he insists on seeing you in person. He says you will remember him." I promised to meet the man only to please Dr. Schiff.

On entering the office I at once recognized the fat and important-looking middle-aged gentleman as the little man called Hurok, who fourteen years before had heard me play *Petrushka* for Chaliapin one morning in New York and who had engaged me that same season to play at Titta Ruffo's concert at the Hippodrome with considerable success. Now, this meek little man spoke with an air of supreme authority about musical matters in the United States.

After exchanging reminiscences, he took up the matter in hand. "I want to present you in America and I offer you twenty concerts for the 1937–38 season." I laughed. "You are making a great mistake," I said. "I haven't been in America for fourteen years but I feel sure that they remember me quite well. So you intend to present to them a fellow aged fifty whom they heard before and who really didn't make it. As I am very ambitious, I decided never to go back to your country. I am perfectly happy with my success in Europe and South America. By the way," I added, "I am already signed up for the year 1937 for more than one hundred concerts in Europe, South America, and Australia for the first time."

"When do you finish Australia?" he asked, without being in the least impressed by my speech. "Middle of November," I replied.

"Well, that is fine. We can start at the beginning of December and go right through March."

Now I flared up. "Are you ready to pay me enough for your tour to make it worthwhile for me even if I have to come home with a half success like the other times?"

"Let me vorry about it. I will guarantee you a good fee for every concert. First-class travel everywhere for two from Paris and back to Paris. All the publicity and piano transportation. Dr. Schiff and I have already agreed about your fee."

He won me over. After the insulting responses of Mr. Judson and Mr.

Coppicus, it was pleasant to find that an American manager of importance really wanted me. I telephoned Nela to give her the good news. It was always her dream to get me back to America.

When I finally told Mr. Hurok, "Well, it's O.K. with me," in the American fashion, we shook hands, but before parting he said, "I hope you won't cancel concerts like you did once with the Boston Symphony." This made me mad. "You will live to eat your words. This is the most preposterous accusation I ever heard in my life." And he did. In the thirty-seven years of our association, I have never missed a concert through my own fault. It was a unique and famous case in the United States.

When Dr. Schiff was satisfied with the contract, I signed it; Nela was delighted. Suddenly, at that point, I thought of Marian Anderson. My enthusiasm for her had had great results. She had an immediate overwhelming success wherever the managers engaged her on my recommendation. I told all that to Mr. Hurok. "You ought to present her in America," I said. "I vouch for her triumph. She is the greatest lieder singer I have ever heard." Hurok made a sour face. "Colored people do not make it with the box office," he said in his professional lingo. But he was visibly impressed by my insistence. He left for Amsterdam to hear her sing and signed a contract the same night.

As for myself, I was thrilled by the idea of covering half the world in a single year with my concerts. After all, I was a born adventurer.

93

We spent a quiet summer in Mondorf-les-Bains, a health resort in Luxembourg. Before finding an apartment, we stayed one night in the very hotel where, much later, all the condemned Nazis were interned before the Nuremberg trial. It gave us a shiver when we remembered that hotel.

One morning the news of the civil war in Spain came like a bombshell. We sat glued to the radio to listen to all the latest developments. It soon became evident that it was a contest between the U.S.S.R. and Hitler's Germany. In my own opinion, the poor Spaniards were being used as tools by the two big contestants.

Nela and the children were happy in this lovely peaceful village bordering the Moselle River. I was kept busy in the early morning drinking the nasty water of the health spring and later giving a lesson a day to a young American pianist who had been sent to me by my brother-in-law Wiktor Labunski from faraway Memphis, Tennessee. It was interesting to notice that I learned more from teaching than when I studied myself. The compositions which I chose to prepare for concerts were immediately clear to me through my born musical instinct. The music simply spoke to me. But when I heard the same composition played by a pupil whose performance did not convince me, I had to gather my thoughts to explain the construction of the work; to show him the climax and the way to grasp the composer's intentions. After my down-to-earth explanations, I invariably played the work much better myself by adding to my instinct the clear knowledge of what the work was made up of. I worked by myself in a happy mood, having that mountain of concerts in store for me.

Of course, by then, I had a large repertoire for Australia, where I had never been before, and for America, where fourteen years earlier I used only a little part of it. For South America I had plenty of trouble with programs. There I had to face at least six recitals in towns like Rio or Buenos Aires and no fewer in Montevideo and Santiago de Chile; but I could always rely on Albéniz, de Falla, and some good stuff I had accumulated during the last four years.

On our return, Paris looked better than ever to us; mostly for the reason that we too looked better, feeling in wonderful shape from having lost weight—all four of us. Nela became one of the best-known hostesses in town. Her talent for cooking attracted all the gourmets of France to our table. Anyone worth knowing gladly accepted invitations to our Montmartre nest. Famous dramatists like Edouard Bourdet, Henri Bernstein, and Marcel Achard; the painter Kisling, the Polish ambassador and his cultural attaché, Jan Lechon, who was a great poet, were seen at our table surrounded by a bouquet of intellectual and beautiful women.

One day, we gave a cocktail party to which we invited all our friends and acquaintances, numbering more than a hundred persons. Nela also prepared a dinner for a chosen dozen or so of our friends after the party was over. A disagreeable contretemps took place. The American ambassador was giving a cocktail party the same afternoon to which he invited us and very many of our friends, but it was too late to change. Anyone who knows the Parisian's passion for buffets and drinks at cocktail parties will not be astonished that almost all our guests went to both parties. But in the end it was a victory for Nela, as both the American ambassador and the Polish ambassador came after their party was over and were visibly happy when she found room for them at our dinner party. These dinners went on late into the night. There would be some music making, some imitations, and lots of fun.

Nela and I left for London, where I had a recording session with "His Master's Voice." We found England much upset about the death of George V and the ascent of the Prince of Wales to the throne and his too passionate interest in the American multiple divorcee. During our stay, we had a momentous dinner. Lady Sybil Colefax, now a widow, was more of a lion hunter than ever. She called one morning to say, "Arthur, you and Nela must come to my dinner on Wednesday. The King is coming, so please don't tell anybody." I understood; she wanted me to let everybody know about it. We accepted, of course, and I was fascinated to see the charming Prince of Wales appearing as His Majesty, the King of the British Empire. The dinner given by this perfect hostess turned out to be a sort of historic event. It was the last time that the young King of England attended a party before his abdication. We and the other guests were asked to come half an hour earlier than the King, who had to be the last, and so Winston Churchill, Harold Nicolson, the Jowitts, Duff Cooper and Lady Diana, and we were sipping cocktails for a long while. Suddenly the door was opened wide and the King entered accompanied by Mrs. Simpson. The ladies present curtsied to him, but greeted Mrs. Simpson rather coolly. Before we went in to dinner, it was my turn to approach the King and he asked me with a giggle, "Did you break any more pianos since I last saw you?"

Nela was seated at the King's table and I had Mrs. Simpson, Winston Churchill, and Lesley Jowitt at mine. During dinner, I had an amusing argument with Mr. Churchill. The British and American newspapers always irritated me showing off their presumed gift for languages by calling a German "Herr," a Frenchman "Monsieur," an Italian "Signor," and a Spaniard "Señor," but giving all the other nations a disdainful "Mr." I complained about that to Harold Nicolson a little ironically and was overheard by Mr. Churchill. "You see," he said grandly, "our papers are mainly interested in the news of these few countries." This easy reply stung me. "I thought that England is supposed to be vastly concerned, since the last war, about all the other nations, and so I think it would be more polite if they dropped these privileged titles or learned those of every nation. And I can give you some right away. I am really 'Pan' Rubinstein and not a simple 'Mr.'; Stravinsky is 'Gospodin'; a Dutch gentleman is a 'Mynheer.' " The two gentlemen became more attentive to their food than to my lesson and the subject was dropped.

After dinner and coffee in the drawing room, Lady Colefax exploited the situation by saying to me, "Arthur, would you be so kind and play something. His Majesty is anxious to hear you again." The poor King had to nod approvingly, and I, *nolens volens*, sat at the piano. In such instances, I liked to play the *Barcarolle* of Chopin. While I was playing it, the King turned to Nela and said, "I like the *Tales of Hoffmann*; they give it at Covent Garden and my favorite is this barcarolle." Nela repeated this to me later and we laughed a lot. Very soon after this event, the King abdicated for the woman he loved. I met him later quite often when they were the Duke and Duchess of Windsor.

I left London for Amsterdam, where I was to play the B-flat Concerto of Brahms with Monteux and the Concertgebouw Orchestra.

At that time, everybody was becoming more and more concerned about the civil war in Spain; famous writers like André Malraux and Ernest Hemingway joined the leftists in their fight. I had a visit from my friend the Marqués del Mérito from Cordova, who urged me to give a concert in Burgos for Franco's side. It was difficult for me to refuse. "You must realize," I told him sadly, "that all the Spaniards have given me their unconditional friendship. Therefore, I have no right to take the part of some against others." This noble fellow understood my feelings and did not insist.

I gave a successful Chopin recital at the Salle Pleyel. Another interesting concert took place in the wonderful Concertgebouw in Amsterdam. Instead of Willem Mengelberg, its regular conductor, George Szell was to play with me the Beethoven Fourth Concerto. I was delighted to meet him and to play with him, remembering how he impressed me at the Prague Opera. Before the rehearsal, at our first meeting, he appeared to be a musician of the German type, rather than a Czech with a Hungarian name. When I finished my solo entrance in the concerto, he stopped me and said loudly, "Artur Schnabel took it slower." This uncalled-for comment vexed me not a little. After we had played the first movement, there was an intermission. In the artist's room, he took up the score and began to teach me how Artur Schnabel had played the concerto to his full satisfaction. Well, I told him very angrily, "Tell your Artur that this Artur feels it in a different way," and I did not speak to him anymore. At the concert, he conducted the concerto very well but we didn't make up and I left the hall during intermission without staying for his performance of the *Eroica*. Next morning, Nela arrived with Misia Sert, who wanted to show her some special shops and also to hear the repetition of the concert in Leyden that afternoon. I wanted to leave again after my performance but Misia Sert insisted on our staying with her for the *Eroica* and here came a revelation. I had never heard the symphony played as beautifully before or since that performance; the Funeral March made me cry.

All I can remember of the season 1936–37 is an avalanche of concerts with frequent returns to Paris for only a few days' rest, social activities, and preparation of programs, as well as an amusing incident in Rome.

My concerts in Rome were usually attended by Queen Elena and the Crown Princess Marie José, my old friend from Belgium. On one occasion, the Queen invited me to the Villa Savoia, the royal residence near Rome. Surrounded by her daughters, she asked me to play on a Bösendorfer with a hard action. After a few smashing chords, a string snapped. Seeing me disconcerted by this incident, the Queen smiled and said, "I have a nice Bechstein in another room. Let us go there." The whole party moved through three or four large rooms, one princess carrying the heavy piano stool. Everything ended well, as the Bechstein allowed me to give a decent little concert. After an evening concert at the Augusteo, the Queen and the Princess Marie-José gave me a charming supper which they served themselves.

Before one of the concerts, which took place in the casino of Cannes, I had the occasion to visit my poor Karol, who was confined to bed at a clinic in Grasse. It was heartbreaking to see him so wasted away. He had lost his voice, could only speak in whispers, and told me with a sad smile, "If I smoke another cigarette, it will be my end." I made a heroic effort to cheer him up because I needed it just as much for myself. When he heard that I was giving a recital he whispered, "I shall come to that concert. Get me a seat where I could be invisible."

"Can you lunch with me before the concert?" I asked him.

"I shall be happy to sit with you. But I shall be unable to eat your luncheon—only what I am allowed to eat."

The concert took place two days later at four in the afternoon. At lunchtime the porter telephoned that a gentleman was waiting in the lobby. I was in such a hurry to see him that instead of using the elevator, I ran down the stairs. To my horror, I saw Karol throwing away a cigarette when he saw me coming. He smiled faintly. "I was not going to smoke but I am so used to holding it between my fingers." Neither of us ate much at lunch. We sat on the terrace while I had my coffee and he a glass of milk. As I didn't want him to speak, I kept on telling him stories, gossip, pleasant echoes about the success of his *Harnasie*. I kept it up until it was time for me to change for the concert. I ordered a limousine for his return to Grasse and we walked slowly to the casino. The director gave him his own box, which was just behind the piano and invisible to the public. I had never been so nervous before a concert as on that day, in constant fear of displeasing him with this or that composition or the way I was playing it. Fortunately I had none of his compositions in the program, which would have made me dreadfully uneasy about not making the public like it. He listened to the whole recital with a stoic calm. He simply seemed to like to be near me, that is all.

After the concert, we got in the limousine, which would take me back to the hotel and then go on with him to Grasse. I suddenly ordered the driver to stop at a flower shop, where I got out of the car and bought a large bouquet of different flowers. I gave them to Karol with a hug and kiss. "This is to thank you for the great honor of having had you at my concert." He thanked me with his sad smile and I left the car quickly. I felt it was the last time I would see him and I cried bitterly in the street.

Shortly afterward, he was taken by his doctor to a clinic in Lausanne and from there came the sad news on March 29, 1937, that this great composer and my dearest friend was dead. As we all knew that it was going to happen, our first concern was for the expenses the funeral would entail. I had a concert and recordings in London and had to leave the next morning, but Nela, accompanied by our friend Kazimir Kranz, left immediately for Lausanne with a sufficient sum. Upon their arrival they were astonished to find Karol's sister Stanislava, the singer, and some members of the Polish government taking charge. Lechon, as the cultural attaché of the Polish Embassy, had come to attend to everything on behalf of the Polish government. The Polish treasury was always rather tightfisted on subsidies for music. The minister went so far as to complain publicly about Szymanowski's constant demands for money. Karol was the only composer, after Chopin, who could represent Poland proudly all over the world and deserved all the help he needed from this mean government. When he was no more, the authorities trumpeted pompously the tragic loss of their great son. They prepared a Warsaw funeral with an unheard-of mass of publicity. A hundred thousand people were tightly massed to watch the funeral. A special train transported his body, accompanied by ministers and the family, to Cracow for the grand burial at the church at Skalla, where only the greatest of the nation were allowed to lie. They put on the catafalque the insignia of the Grand Cross of Polonia Restituta, the nation's highest honor. What a bitter irony! For years they had made my poor Karol suffer through their meanness and now they were willing to spend a fortune on this big show. And what really infuriated me was the fact that they asked Hitler's government to make the train with Karol's body stop in Berlin long enough to receive military honors.

When Nela came back from Lausanne, we had to begin the preparations for the South American tour. I did mine automatically; the death of my two best and really only friends left a horrible void in me.

The day of the departure arrived. I was downstairs sorting and packing my music and Nela was upstairs with her friend Basia Sienkiewicz-Lafont, who had come to look after the children while Nela prepared for the trip. Suddenly I heard a shrill scream from Basia: "Come up, Paul is terribly ill!" I dropped everything and dashed up the spiral staircase and found little

Paul blue in the face, breathing with difficulty. Nela had him in her arms trying to calm him while Basia telephoned the doctor. The Rolls-Royce which Germaine had sent for us was waiting at the door to take us to the station. When we called our doctor's household they promised to send him to the station right away, but Basia's doctor arrived in a hurry, looked at the child, said that he was suffering from convulsions, and gave him something to calm him; his color came back but he had a very high temperature.

Nela, Karola, and the two children left for the station and I followed in a taxi with the luggage. My poor little Paul vomited violently all over the floor of the Rolls.

At the Gare de Lyon our doctor was waiting for us at the sleeper for Marseilles and immediately examined the child and diagnosed tonsillitis. Since birth, Paul often had terribly high temperatures at the smallest discomfort. The doctor gave Nela instructions for the trip, some pills, and promised to have a colleague expect us at the hotel.

Poor Nela spent the whole night attending to the baby without any help other than my inadequate efforts, because Karola took a cheaper train and arrived two hours after us. Upon our arrival, we went to the Hotel de Noailles and had the doctor in right away. Paul's temperature was lower and after a long examination the doctor said, "I think it is pretty safe to take him on the boat, where the ship's doctor can look after him the whole time." We were greatly reassured. I even took little Eva shopping for some toys for the children.

The ship was to leave late in the afternoon and we found two nice adjoining cabins. Karola put Paul to bed right away and the ship's doctor found him asleep and promised to come back later.

A voice over the megaphone announced that visitors must leave the ship, which meant we were ready to sail. Suddenly a dreadful pang of conscience came over me and I was simply panic-stricken. I couldn't bear the idea of exposing my sick little boy to the lack of care on a ship. I needed to be reassured by a great medical authority. I dashed to the captain's cabin; he was a kindly-looking man. "Please, please help me. Could you delay the departure for an hour?" At the negative expression on his face, I went on imploringly about my predicament and he softened. "Try to get the doctor as quickly as possible because I couldn't give you more than an hour." He must have seen the deep gratitude in my eyes, because he smiled.

With my address book in hand, I asked quickly for a telephone and was shown one on the dockside amid all the ado of leave-taking. Despite my natural dislike of phones, I was incredibly efficient, getting Germaine on the line in a minute or two. She had spoken in Paris about a great specialist living in Marseilles but had forgotten to give me his number; now I begged her urgently to give it to me and fortunately she had it handy. When she tried to ask me questions about Paul, I dropped the receiver without answering and immediately tried to get the professor. A secretary informed me that he was not available because his waiting room was full of patients. I said angrily, "This is a most urgent case, he must speak to me." Two minutes later, I heard his voice: "What can I do for you?" I told him the case in a few pathetic words, imploring him to come right away. "But that is impossible. I am now attending to my private patients."

I replied with a broken voice, "I am a poor pianist who earns his living with concerts. I have a tour in South America, but I shall not sail without your decision."

He asked impatiently, "Mais qui êtes vous donc?"

"Mon nom est Artur Rubinstein."

"Artur Rubinstein, le grand pianiste?" he exclaimed suddenly. "J'accours tout de suite."

I cried! In less than a quarter of an hour he was in the cabin. When I wanted to kiss his hand he tore it away from me. "Je fais mon devoir," he said. Nela quickly told him everything and he examined the child in his most expert way while both Nela and I waited breathlessly for his verdict.

"Vous pouvez partir," he said after a short while. "Don't worry. I shall give the doctor here my instructions. Your boy will recover." He turned and spoke to the ship's doctor.

"How much do I owe you, Professor?" I asked.

"The joy you have given me at your concerts has amply compensated me." It was not his generosity which I admired; my gratitude went much further than that. His prompt help when I mentioned my name gave me a new respect for my talent.

I dashed to the captain's cabin and shouted even before entering: "We are sailing, thank you, thank you." It was still less than the hour and the sirens started screaming.

Little Paul was on his feet two days later and we were happy parents again. This long passage to Argentina gave us a good rest after the hectic season in Europe. The air and the calm of the southern seas gave us fresh energy.

Our friends in Buenos Aires had rented a doctor's apartment for us which we found quite comfortable. The doctor's study became the children's playroom, and we and Karola had a hard time stopping the children from playing with some human embryos in test tubes on a shelf, which fascinated them.

Ruiz arranged a tour which consisted of a few concerts in Buenos Aires but mainly in the provinces. During my absences, Nela remained with the children in Buenos Aires. As my money was still blocked, I continued to invest the sums I made and this time I decided to leave it all there because I felt that it had become unsafe to keep any large sum in Paris. France seemed to be falling under the spell of Hitler. There were many signs of a growing anti-Semitism there.

I had a pleasant surprise in Córdoba, Argentina, where I found Manuel de Falla accompanied by his sister. They had succeeded in leaving Spain when the Civil War broke out. We had a happy reunion. It was fun to see that he still kept his hygienic mania: the minute you shook hands he clapped for his sister, who came with a solution in a bowl, and he quickly washed. The tragic war in Spain made him unhappy. He looked haggard and tired, but continued working on his great oratorio *Atlántida*. He was too weak to come to my concert and wrote me a lovely letter, which is still in my possession.

I was constantly traveling all over Argentina and Uruguay, and whenever I was back we went quite often to the Plaza grill and saw some operas at the Colón.

I still had six concerts in Santiago and Valparaiso in Chile and this time they had a plane service. In those days it was rather dangerous to cross the Andes because instead of flying over them they flew in between them. Nela stayed behind in Buenos Aires.

Juanita Gandarillas, who lived then in Santiago, invited me to stay with her. My flight was not without danger, because when the plane took off from Mendoza, where it always stopped for fuel and also to get information about the meteorological conditions in the mountains, we encountered a sudden fog in a narrow passage and our pilot had to make a most dangerous turn to go back to Mendoza. After an hour's wait, the fog cleared and this time we arrived safely in Santiago.

We had a happy time there, Juanita and I. She had a lovely house, lived there quite alone because two of her daughters were married and the third one, Carmen, remained in London with her father. In her dining room was a large cage with a beautiful multicolored parrot who babbled incessantly. When I asked darling Juanita if this constant babbling didn't tire her, she said sadly, "He keeps me company." She said to me, "How I would like to have Nela here and I think she would be happy to see how our public loves you." She began to urge Nela over the telephone to come. When I joined in, Nela promised to come right away, leaving the children in the good care of Karola, supervised by Victoria González. We were expecting her on the day of my third concert, but her plane had to stop in Mendoza, where she had to spend the night because the passage through the Andes was blocked. The next day, the weather grew worse with no hope of improvement. Nela, getting impatient, gave up and went back to Buenos Aires. We, on the Chilean side, were frustrated by her vain attempt.

I gave my six concerts in both towns to the fullest satisfaction of my public and myself, and the time came to fly back. I had my ticket, but a telephone call from Pan American announced that there would be no flight for twenty-four hours. Mr. Salvati, the director of the Opera, persuaded me to give an additional concert. It was flattering to have the house sold out at such short notice, but I was beginning to feel alarmed about my return to Buenos Aires. Our ship was leaving from there in five days and I had a broadcast concert the night before sailing. The next two days did not bring any change in the weather.

I remember a Saturday when Salvati persuaded me to give an eighth concert in Santiago and said, "On Sunday, you are sure to take off." Sunday meant two days before sailing and one day before the concert. My program for this extra concert in Santiago was made up in a hurry and relied mainly on the most popular pieces of Albéniz and de Falla and the best-loved Chopins. During the intermission of this most successful concert of the lot, Salvati came in to my dressing room and announced triumphantly, "There is no plane tomorrow—we can have a matinee at eleven o'clock." I laughed bitterly. "You will end up by making me play for a few dogs and cats! How can you get a real public overnight?"

"If I put up a poster now in the lobby and announce the same program for tomorrow morning, you will see the same public again, but of course there would be an announcement on the radio and something in the Sunday paper."

Juanita gave a farewell party with her family and some good friends but I was not very happy, feeling trapped by the Andes. As Monday was the day of my concert in Buenos Aires and our departure for Europe was on Tuesday morning, my impatience became desperate. One of Juanita's guests had something to do with tourism and suddenly asked me, "Would you consider flying to Buenos Aires in a German plane?"

"Of course I would," I said, "if it gets me there."

"I know of a plane which will take off early on Monday morning and try to find a possible passage through the Andes. Will you take the risk?"

"I would do anything to get there."

Salvati was right! The next morning a great part of my public was the same as at the previous concert and there were even standing-room tickets sold.

Juanita's friend brought me my ticket on Sunday afternoon. I called Nela, feverishly giving her the news and asking her to watch the time of my arrival by checking with the German airline from time to time. Nela, who lived in anguish these days, was relieved but worried about the risks involved.

We were only six in the small plane, which had two sturdy-looking motors. A tall pilot and his copilot climbed into their seats and we took off at eight in the morning. I was still under the spell of Juanita's touching farewell and felt more sentimental than afraid. After flying for half an hour, we passengers began to be frightened when the plane tried to get across but had to turn back.

After a long unsuccessful search for the passage, we had to go down for fuel. In the air again, the plane was hopping mercilessly up and down, making us feel that our last hour had come. Suddenly, the pilot announced happily, "We are on the other side." Hurray, we were safe! We had to stop in Córdoba for fuel and hoped to reach Buenos Aires late in the afternoon. We found Córdoba covered by a thick fog and had to circle over it with a dangerous lack of fuel.

It was six o'clock in the evening when our plane landed in heavy rain in Buenos Aires. At the bottom of the steps I found Nela crying. She threw her arms around me and held me tight for a long while. The two airport officials who allowed her to come near the plane watched the scene and said, "The lady was so upset we had to let her come directly to the plane."

I had just enough time to get home, have a cup of coffee and a sandwich, change into my evening clothes, and get to the concert by nine o'clock. Nela told me, "The radio was constantly sending out bulletins about the progress of your plane and they scared me to death by making me believe you couldn't make it and that at any moment the plane might crash. The radio also warned the public that the concert might not take place, so now they have probably reassured them," she said, smiling through her tears. I must say that I smiled myself when an hour later I began the peaceful E-flat Sonata by Beethoven in the crowded theater, with the radio broadcasting the concert.

Afterward, we had a long farewell supper with the Gonzálezes and Germán Elizalde. Packing took the rest of the night. Once on board, the children, who had slept during the whole long night, now wanted to play with us, but this time we just fell on our beds like a couple of logs and slept for the next twelve hours.

During this long journey, I was mainly preoccupied with programs and nothing but programs. I placed great importance on programs; I might even add that I became quite well known as a particularly good maker of programs. The public in South America could never hear enough of the Spanish music I offered them and some complete contrasts like *Petrushka*. My way of playing Chopin convinced them completely, which I could not say of Poland.

Now I was facing two continents, far apart from each other: Australia, where I had never played before, and the United States, where after fourteen years' absence I felt like a newcomer. There was a decent piano on board which allowed me to try out a possible repertoire for both countries.

Schedules were so tight that year that I couldn't even get a glimpse of the World Exhibition in Paris. After our arrival, Dr. Schiff gave me the return ticket for Sydney and I had to leave the same evening for Amsterdam to take a KLM plane for Australia.

The journey I had to make would be difficult to conceive nowadays. We were to fly for nine days, stopping every night at dusk and getting up with the sun. We were ten passengers. The plane had two reliable-looking motors and the pilot and his navigator were solid Dutchmen whom we all liked at first sight.

It was fun to see on the map all the interesting, picturesque, and sometimes beautiful places where we would stop for fuel or for the night.

I remember (and I don't know why) that we slept in Athens, where I could go to bed after enjoying once more the beauty of the Acropolis. Then there was Cairo; then Basra, where we flew low enough to feel the sun-baked soil and the oil underneath it. We slept in Allahabad, where I had time to visit and admire the maharajah's beautiful red palace.

The next stop was for fuel in Calcutta. Our landing was dangerous. The airport was flooded and we glided cautiously when the plane stopped and we had to wade into the building. The pilot gave us bad news: "It is impossible to take off in these conditions. The airline will reserve accommodation at the hotel and I only hope we shall be able to take off tomorrow." I, for one, was pleased at this news; passionate for a constant change of scene, I would have liked to have a free day at every stop.

We could sleep the whole night quietly, as there was no question of taking off; it felt good to have a nice English breakfast at the right time and not at five in the morning.

One of my co-passengers had lived in Calcutta and offered me his services as a guide. We strolled through the crowded streets full of wide-open shops where you saw people hammering pretty designs on round metallic plates, making multicolored saris. Quite often we could see some European or American products for sale. The goods were displayed in the open air but the artisans worked inside. All that would have been pretty banal if it were not for a rather picturesque diversion. A large white cow came strolling toward us at an exceedingly slow pace and the crowd gave it free space as if this beast were a maharajah. The cow seemed as interested in the goods displayed as we were and stopped to nibble at this or that without being in the least disturbed. My companion whispered, "A white cow is sacred in India, nobody would dare touch it."

My guide took me out of the center of the city toward more open spaces. We saw a strange house, one story high, where the windows had no panes. As we reached the gate, there was a horrible stench. I looked up at the man in horror and he said, "They are burning their dead. Are you interested? You could go in and see it." I must say, my curiosity was stronger than my disgust and we walked in. There were six tables in a row and on each a burning body, attended to by a man who added wood as fuel from time to time. It certainly was the nastiest way of getting rid of dead bodies which I had ever seen or imagined in my life. This slow procedure was simply revolting.

In the evening at dinner, our pilot declared that the airport was drying out and that there was a good chance for us to leave the next morning. We took off for a short hop to a city in Burma where we were scheduled to spend the night. The next sleeping places were uninteresting, one in Malaya —Kuala Lumpur—the second an island east of Bali—Timor. On our way to the Dutch residence there, where we spent the night, the crouching natives lined the sidewalks chewing a dreadful stuff which made their mouths and chins look as though covered with blood. Timor was the last stop before reaching Port Darwin in Australia. Between the two points there was nothing but open sea, which made us passengers rather apprehensive of the three-hour flight over the Indian Ocean. I was pretty happy when we reached Australia and solid earth.

I went through customs and entered the lobby, where I saw to my great astonishment a large poster on the wall advertising winter sports on the highest peak of Australia, Mount Kosciuszko. I knew my history of Poland pretty well and particularly the life of the Polish national hero Tadeusz Kosciuszko, but I never knew that he had anything to do with Australia! I was rather ashamed of my ignorance.

We took off very early the next morning for Sydney, with one long stop for fuel in a completely deserted place. A curious incident occurred there. A plane landed a few minutes after ours on its way to Europe. I was struck by the sight of a tall sturdy woman who emerged from the aircraft holding an important-looking violin case containing two instruments, used exclusively by soloists who could afford it. I began to be vexed at not recognizing her when I saw a little man leaving the plane; it was Bronislaw Hubermann, the great artist and my old friend since childhood. We embraced and duly enjoyed our surprise. We had snapshots taken of us by his secretary and then Stanley and Livingstone parted.

It was then that I learned that the whole large continent of Australia has no waterways, which accounts for the fact that all the important cities are near the coast. Flying rather low over endless miles of shrub-covered plains, one saw large numbers of kangaroos, frightened by the sound of our motors, hopping several yards at a time.

We reached Sydney at noon. While the plane was moving slowly toward the airport building, I gave out one of the largest sighs of relief. What bliss to find a real bathroom, to unpack one's clothes, and to be a pianist again! When the plane came to a halt, I put my two coats over my arm, picked up my bag with the other hand, and was the first to descend the steps. A half dozen men in formal clothes and two photographers were waiting for me. When I extended my hand cordially, the apparent head of the Australian Broadcasting Commission didn't take it; he stood stiffly, reaching for some papers, and addressed me with a speech. It was an elaborate welcome lasting several minutes. When I thought it was over, another man came forward with a newspaper and began reading out what it said about my arrival. When he stopped, all of them looked at me, awaiting my reply; I would have liked to kill them for it. I felt my usual allergy to making speeches and I stammered a few incoherent words in something which sounded like a borrowed voice. I could see that they were not very happy about it. Only then did they deign to take me to customs and pass-port control, after which two of the men escorted me to a limousine and we went straight to the hotel. In order to be left alone, I effusively thanked the two gentlemen for their help, but they did not budge and kept repeating, "You have plenty of time."

"Fortunately," I said. "I need a few hours to recover from this enormous journey and I intend to have something light in my room and go to bed until dinner."

They looked frightened. "There is a big luncheon in your honor and the guests are arriving in forty-five minutes." This was a blow, but as usual, I did not show it and braced myself to get through that too. I had to shave in a hurry, get some pretty crumpled clothes out of my suitcase, beg the maid to give them a rapid press, which fortunately she could do herself; then I went down to a crowded private dining room.

The two gentlemen seated me in the center of a large table between two ladies. I kissed their hands in my old Polish tradition, but not being used to it, they vigorously shook my hand and almost knocked my teeth out with their knuckles. We were about twenty at the table and the luncheon indeed looked formal with written-out menus and several wineglasses in front of us. A nice hot consommé was being served, which I was about to enjoy, tired and hungry as I was, when the ring of a glass announced a speech; it was the president of the Australian Broadcasting Commission. He addressed me with warm words of welcome but it was rather difficult for me to understand his strange accent. When he finished, I gave him a smiling

nod of gratitude, and reached for my consommé, when there was another
tap of a glass and a different man stood up, declaring he was musical adviser
to the ABC, and started to praise me in the way I most hated. But that was
not the end! The lady to my right jumped to her feet and told me with
fervor how impressed she was with a concert in Bournemouth where she
heard me play the Tchaikovsky concerto. When she took her seat again, all
eyes turned toward me, waiting for my answer. Now I became angry and, I
hate to admit it, I felt sorry for myself; this gave me courage. I stood up,
and said with a clear voice: "Ladies and gentlemen. Your generous words
of welcome touched me very much." Then, changing my tone, with a malicious smile I continued: "But they were unfortunately addressed to a tired
and hungry traveler. You cannot imagine how much I would have enjoyed
them after a good bath and a rest, so please be satisfied with just a big
'thank you.' " My ironic sincerity was much applauded.

Back in my room, I felt exhilarated. It was the first time in my life that
I had spoken with a clear throat and said the truth to boot. My suite (I
mean the elegant gentlemen of the airport) surrounded me, and their
spokesman said in a low timid voice, "Mr. Rubinstein, I know you are not
going to be happy about it but the Sydney Conservatory has been expecting
you for half an hour."

When he saw white fury in my eyes, he added quickly, "The director is
a Russian and a great admirer of yours." The poor man was far from
knowing that I couldn't give a damn, but I knew I had to accept my fate.

At the conservatory, I had a hard time reaching the hall on the second
floor, as the staircase was crowded with girls and boys who greeted me with
great applause.

A fat man with sparse yellow hair awaited me with open arms and
kissed me three times on both cheeks in the Russian manner. After this
osculatory introduction, he took three steps backward, pulled some papers
out of his pocket, and addressed me in Australian English with a Russian
accent. He recalled multiple meetings with me which had never taken place
and, after much praise for my art, concluded by introducing me to the
students as an old friend. Once again there was an ominous silence, expecting my reply.

Irritated both by his lying and by his exaggerated praise, I spoke with
a newfound authority, finding the right words with ease. I explained my
ideas about music and piano playing and (reader, don't laugh) I was even
carried away by my speech! They gave me an ovation.

After a polite exchange with some professors and shaking hands with
many students, I was driven to the hotel, where at long last I had a nice
snack in my room, found the energy to unpack, had a hot bath, and enjoyed
a lovely dreamless night's sleep.

My first concert in Sydney was with the ABC Orchestra under a conductor with a German name and the English "Sir" added to it. I played the Tchaikovsky concerto for my debut. The orchestra was far from being even adequate. The conductor, a good musician, confessed that he had a hard time with his players. Luckily, I seemed to have pleased the audience and, as I found out, my Australian public at large. It made my tour very successful.

After Sydney, where I played both with orchestra and a recital, I left for Melbourne by train accompanied by the dear old spokesman. Melbourne, in the state of Victoria, was a great novelty to me, mainly for its complete contrast to Sydney. The latter felt clearly under American influence. The hotel, the shops and what they offered, the brazen publicity, reminded me strongly of Baltimore or Pittsburgh, while Melbourne struck me at first glance as a nice old-fashioned English city.

The charming hotel was only two floors high, with no elevator, and we were received by a beautiful strong draft from the open windows. Its food was, to my deep regret, as tasteless as in some lost English provincial towns. London, Manchester, Liverpool, and Bristol were clever enough to have a well-cared-for French grill next to the large English restaurant. Here the most serious topic of general interest was horse racing, just as in the old country. Of course I remembered the great Melba, who took her name from this city of her birth, and poor Fritz Müller, my rival during our student days in Berlin. Even my audiences were rather reserved and had a deeper understanding of my music.

The president of the ABC was not happy about the orchestra in Sydney. "We need a great conductor. For your last concert in Sydney you will have Georg Schneevoigt, who begins his tour after yours, but he cannot stay. Do you know of anyone who could discipline the Sydney orchestra, which has the best players? A Toscanini or a Stokowski is, of course, out of the question. We cannot afford them." I found the right answer immediately. "George Szell," I said eagerly. "I can't think of anybody who could train your orchestra better than he and he happens to be available at the moment." He clapped his hands. "Hubermann recommended him with the same enthusiasm," he said. Thanks to both of us, Australia had the privilege of witnessing the transformation of its orchestra by this great master conductor.

After three enjoyable concerts in Melbourne, I left for Adelaide, the capital of South Australia, a quiet distinguished city where my concerts were received with great warmth. Perth, in western Australia, was the last city of my tour before my return to Melbourne for another appearance. On the way back to Sydney, I played in Canberra, the federal capital of Australia, a small newly created town where the English governor-general,

Lord Gore, invited me graciously for a private lunch on the day of my concert. I was received by him and his wife most cordially and I sat between them at the table; there were only two attachés with us. "We are coming to your concert," he said with the English accent of a born gentleman. "I don't know a thing about music, you know, ha-ha, but I hope to learn something tonight, eh-eh?"

I remembered suddenly a subject which interested me: "Landing in Australia, I was taken aback by a poster advertising winter sports on the highest peak of Australia, called Kosciuszko, which is the name of our Polish national hero. I know his life by heart and know that he was never in Australia and had no connection with it whatever."

Lord Gore laughed out heartily. "My dear fellow, ha-ha, it is one of those horrible native names, you know. I have great trouble remembering the damn things."

I timidly insisted, "But the spelling is exactly the same."

"Oh, ha-ha, I know of cases like that, ha-ha. You would be astonished if I told you some of them." I dropped the subject.

The concert was well attended; the audience was made up chiefly of diplomats. During intermission, I received a visit from some members of the diplomatic corps whom I had met in other posts, but suddenly Lord Gore appeared, shouting from the door in great agitation: "I am afraid I made a damn fool of myself, sir. Yes, indeed, I made a damn fool of myself. This name of the mountain which I couldn't remember for the life of me, ha-ha, *is* that of your hero, ha-ha. A Polish engineer reached the summit for the first time and, by Jove, he gave it this godforsaken name." We, and all those present, laughed for a long time.

I played my last concert in Sydney with orchestra conducted by Georg Schneevoigt, with whom I had played before in Holland. He was a Finn, an excellent musician, who, in spite of his old age, showed a great vitality. We gave a fine performance of a Brahms concerto (I don't remember which). Later, in the artist's room, Mr. Schneevoigt asked me, "Have you been to the zoo?"

"No," I said—I couldn't find another answer.

"You have missed the best thing in Sydney. Are you free tomorrow afternoon?"

"Yes," I said.

"I wish I could take you in the morning, but I have a rehearsal. There is so much to see and the afternoon is short because of the zoo's closing time. But you *must* see the laughing birds."

"The laughing birds?" I asked.

"Yes, they are fascinating. They laugh at you insultingly, they mock you. You must see them, you must see them." He slapped his knee.

The next day, I could hardly wait. When he returned from his rehearsal, we had a quick lunch and drove to the zoo. He was right; it is one of the finest zoos in the world, rich in animals you can't see anywhere else.

I made poor Schneevoigt very nervous stopping for ages at the great cage with the kangaroos. For a long time I was fascinated by the platypus, and of course when we reached the little koala bears sitting peacefully on the tree branch and not minding if you take them in your arms. But when I arrived at the huge cage filled with monkeys he almost tore my coat trying to pull me away. "We will be late for the birds." By then, we had walked quite a lot and I was getting tired, but the old man wouldn't give up.

We had to pass a lot of interesting animals before we reached a round, lonely cage with a dozen or so large birds of a dark brownish color, their long beaks resting on their breasts; they looked at us forbiddingly. Schneevoigt nudged me with his elbow, waiting for the big laugh. The birds kept quiet. Becoming slightly impatient and in order to excite them, Schneevoigt gave out a ridiculous little laugh. Nothing from the birds. Now becoming quite angry, the old man began to produce horrible hoarse noises. He even had tears in his eyes and broke into a dreadful asthmatic cough, but these nasty birds never budged and only seemed to look at us disapprovingly. Schneevoigt became hysterical. "I'll make them laugh, I'll make them laugh," he shrieked.

At that moment a loud siren announced closing time. The visitors had to leave the zoo. My companion bowed his head in utter frustration and whispered, "We must go." It was a long way back to the exit. When we turned into the principal alley, something horrible happened. A shrill, ironic, malevolent laughter pierced our ears and I was so deeply insulted that I felt like running back and ringing the necks of the whole dozen of them. Schneevoigt coughed all the way to the hotel.

My last Australian appearance took place in Brisbane, the capital of Queensland, and the day after, I took off for the long KLM flight back to Amsterdam and Paris.

The return trip was just as long and provided some incidents of a new kind—like having a Nazi official as my neighbor on the plane. We began by giving each other murderous looks, but unforeseen circumstances were to make us see things in a brotherly way. I can give a good example: In Rangoon, the capital of Burma, where we had to spend the night, we arrived early enough to be able to see one of the most famous Buddhist temples in the world. The cupola was solid gold. Pilgrims and visitors made their contributions in the form of thin golden pieces. Both the Nazi and I were set on seeing this temple, but there was a condition: you had to leave your shoes behind and walk up a muddy path in your socks. The mud on our feet brought a friendly smile of mutual disgust at our ordeal.

94

My return home after my pleasant success in Australia and with some fresh money in my pocket was particularly happy. Nela enjoyed the tales of my adventures and musical experiences, but was all set on preparations for the most important event, my first tour in America after fourteen years.

I spent much time on my programs for my appearances with orchestra and my recitals. This involved some hot arguments with Hurok by correspondence. His managerial flair made him feed the gallery with the most popular stuff I could dig up. Here I put my foot down and wouldn't let him interfere with my own decisions.

I learned with pleasure that quite a few conductors had engaged me— among them my dear friends John Barbirolli with the New York Philharmonic, Pierre Monteux with the San Francisco Symphony, and Eugene Goossens in Cincinnati. Eugene Ormandy offered three concerts in Philadelphia and Artur Rodzinski (now married to Nela's childhood friend Halina Lilpop) not only invited me for a concert in Cleveland but wanted us to stay with them, which I accepted reluctantly. I never liked to stay with friends when giving concerts because I needed a special diet and disliked disturbing the household by asking for favors like pressing my concert clothes and other things that could be so easily obtained in hotels.

Our departure from Paris was preceded by a painful scene: We had to send our babies accompanied by Karola to Warsaw to remain in the care of my mother-in-law during our absence. At the Gare du Nord, when the train was starting and the children were waving goodbye at the open window, Nela broke down, crying out loudly, and little Eva, aged four, said in a soothing tone, "Don't cry, Mummy, we shall come back," which made poor Nela cry still more.

After a hateful day of packing, when it was impossible to decide what to take and what not to, with our passports graced with American visas we left one morning on the train for Cherbourg, where we embarked on the *Queen Mary*. When I stepped up on the boat, my fighting spirit was wide awake; this time I felt ready for America. That evening in the lounge, where we had coffee after dinner, a very lively little lady introduced herself to us as Blanche Knopf, the wife of the well-known publisher Alfred Knopf. She kept us company during the whole trip, trying to arouse my interest in her great admiration for Benno Moiseiwitsch but, at the same time, fascinating me with her love and knowledge of literature.

Another co-passenger was Mr. William Steinway, who was in charge of the Hamburg factory of that firm. I had met him casually in the early twenties and he now approached me with a friendly smile. "I have heard many wonderful things about you," he said. After two or three days of nice talks, he proposed that I use Steinway pianos for my concerts again. As we both very well remembered our break fourteen years before, I put on a serious expression, being secretly enchanted with his suggestion. "I shall consider your offer very seriously," I answered, "but you must allow me to examine your latest instruments." He earnestly acquiesced and I was quite happy.

We arrived in New York on a cheerful day. Mr. Hurok was at the dock to help us out of the formalities and drove us to the Hotel Ambassador, where we found a lovely apartment. We settled in our drawing room and offered him a cup of tea while we talked for the first time about our immediate plans. "Even before your debut I got you an engagement," he said with a conceited smile.

"Where?" I asked.

"Right here in New York," he answered. "One of these rich ladies telephoned. She wanted to know when you were arriving because she wanted to give you a party. Well, I told her: 'If you want him to play, then there is a fee to be paid.' Well," he added with a laugh, "I got a nice fee out of her."

"It is not a Mrs. Vanderbilt, I hope," I said, remembering my bad experiences with them.

"No," he said. "It is a Mrs. Chadwick. She says she is your friend."

"My goodness," I exclaimed. "Dorothy Chadwick! She is one of my best friends and I wouldn't mind playing for her for nothing."

He made a disgusted face. "If I work for you, you will never work for nothing."

My first concert was set for the next Thursday as soloist with the New York Philharmonic under John Barbirolli; we were to play the Concerto in B flat by Brahms. The program had to be repeated on Friday afternoon, but then on Sunday afternoon it was to be the Tchaikovsky B flat instead of Brahms.

When Hurok was gone, we telephoned Dorothy. "I have invited for you," she said, "your old friends the Damrosch family, John Barbirolli, Helen Hull, Hoyty Wiborg, and of course Sophie Kochanska. I hope you will be pleased to see them again and, Arthur," she added, "I am so happy you will play." I apologized for Hurok's distasteful approach but she laughed it off. "He was quite right. I am glad that you have a real manager."

The party was lovely. There was a fine Steinway concert grand and I played my most beloved Chopins and some Spanish music, which brought an enthusiastic response from the guests. Dear Dorothy—she had helped my friends Szymanowski and Kochanski so much and remained a devoted friend until her death. Now, this kind of pre-debut restored a good deal of confidence in me.

William Steinway telephoned to say that a good number of Steinway concert grands were lined up for me to choose from. I went at the appointed time to the beautiful new Steinway building on Fifty-seventh Street. At the entrance, I found myself in a large rotunda where two or three secretaries were working at elegant desks. On the wall hung a large portrait of Paderewski and one of Josef Hofmann. An elevator took me to the basement, where there was a long walk through a big hall filled with pianos. But at the end was a large closed door. When it was opened to me, I saw a huge room which had the gruesome appearance of a morgue. At least a dozen concert grands were standing in line looking like huge coffins. Mr. Theodore Steinway, the president of the firm, welcomed me most cordially and introduced me to a Mr. Alexander Greiner. "He is in charge of these pianos which travel all over the United States for concerts given by the many pianists who use our instruments."

Mr. Greiner addressed me in Russian. "I come from Latvia on the Baltic and you will be astonished to know that I was a student at the St. Petersburg Conservatory when you had that triumph at the Anton Rubinstein Competition." The two gentlemen opened the lids of three pianos and had me choose the one I wanted for my concerts. "The one you like best," they said, "we will keep at your disposal." I picked one with a difficult action, which means that the keys were resistant, but it had the most beautiful tone.

Ever since my early pianistic days, I have never been satisfied with the simple sound of the piano; it was up to my fingers to produce the tone which sung in me. Yes, I always had to hear a singing tone coming out of this percussion instrument.

The rehearsal went wonderfully well. John's spirited accompaniment was contagious and both the orchestra and I fell under the spell. The concert was a victory; a full house acclaimed us and Mr. Olin Downes, the critic of *The New York Times*, wrote his review in the form of a welcome: "We missed Mr. Rubinstein for too long and are happy to have him back."

Even the Friday-afternoon concert, with its subscribers consisting mostly of rich old ladies, was a genuine success. On Sunday I played the Tchaikovsky, which as usual brought out the special enthusiasm of the gallery but dissatisfied an old critic of the *Herald Tribune*, who clung faithfully to the performance of a favorite of his.

What mattered now was my first recital. Whether you won or lost was of the utmost importance because the whole of the United States waited for the verdict of the New York press.

I chose my program carefully and wouldn't listen to Hurok's suggestions of surefire pieces. I would begin with the Prelude, Chorale, and Fugue by Franck, followed by two of my favorites by Debussy, and *Petrushka*, which was new to New York, and after the intermission the Chopin I loved best, finishing with the Polonaise in A flat.

Hurok's publicity worked wonders. In spite of a tiff we had about it, I saw on the Carnegie Hall poster my concert announced with: "Artur Rubinstein, Prince of Pianists." This unwanted title infuriated me. "What is this 'Prince of Pianists' for and why did you drop the 'h'?" I shouted at Hurok.

"You play the piano and let me make the publicity," he said with an indulgent smile.

"If I had to pay for your publicity," I retorted in my most sarcastic way, "I would say: 'Hurok, God of Managers,' and not just a mean 'Prince.' When will I have the honor of seeing my name in print without a title?" He gave me that chance for my next concert.

The concert took place on a Saturday afternoon, the best time for a recital, and Hurok succeeded in filling Carnegie Hall to the brim. While I was waiting to go out on the stage, he came in and told me with proud satisfaction, "Why, I have all the famous pianists for you in the hall— Rachmaninoff himself, Godowsky, Joseph and Rosina Lhévinne, and all the others who are in New York." At this news, I became conscious of a great change in me. In the old days, I used to die with fear when I heard that a pianist was in the audience, but on this occasion, I was simply gratified to be able to play for them.

As I appeared on the stage, there was a warm wave of welcome which unleashed all the passion I had in me for the music I was going to play and I wanted my listeners to share it with me. I felt this elusive gift from heaven which one calls inspiration.

The Franck was received with a growing and warm attention, after which *Petrushka* became the culminating point of the concert. It was being heard for the first time in America and the program note that it was written for me and dedicated to me heightened the interest. I played it with my usual freedom, as I heard it played by an orchestra and not as a piano piece. The audience burst into an ovation, screaming and shouting bravos. I bowed happily, and leaving the stage for the intermission, I found to my amazement Rachmaninoff standing there all alone, saying in his guttural Russian, "Came now, afterwards crowds." At the same time, he touched his forehead and his heart, indicating with this mime that I had played with brain and heart. The ovation in the hall was growing. "I shall wait," he said, making me go out and bow. When I returned, he said angrily, "Don't play in America dirty stuff like *Petrushka*, they don't like that kind of modern music."

While he was talking, Hurok appeared and shouted, "Go and take a bow. They are screaming." Now there was a roar in the audience. Back in the wings, Rachmaninoff warned me again quietly, "Now and then, small piece modern, that is all right, but not long, horrible piece like this." Hurok pushed me on the stage and the people wouldn't let up. This time, Rachmaninoff said, a little impatiently, "Play encore!" and left.

My Chopin of the second part of the program received a special treatment. Every single piece in this group was applauded, something which never happened when I played a group by another composer. This time I was careful; I played these works with my deepest love but also all the notes were played out to satisfy the American ticket buyers. The Polonaise, which I played with an exceptional fire, brought the house down. Four encores followed and I left the stage with a proud feeling of having won a firm foothold in the United States.

Hurok was exultant. "Aren't you happy with the way my public received you?" Yes, indeed, "his" public was wonderful.

I was more pleased by the reaction of Lhévinne and Godowsky, who both in their own way declared that their early conviction that I would someday amount to something was right.

Mrs. Helen Hull, whom I had known previously as Mrs. Vincent Astor, invited us to a charity luncheon given in aid of the Musicians' Emergency Fund of which she was the president. Her treasurer was an old friend of mine from Berlin, Yolanda Mero, who had married a Mr. Irion, an associate of Steinway. The luncheon took place in the large ballroom of the St. Regis Hotel. There were at least three hundred people and we were invited to sit at the speaker's table. While the rest of the gathering was having their lunch, John Barbirolli and Walter Damrosch nervously pulled out their written speeches, which were many pages long. John read his for a good half hour and Walter Damrosch used his fine voice to advantage. Both told their audience that life without music was not worth living and that each of the greedy lunchers should dig deep into their pockets so as not to let it die out. They were duly applauded, in spite of the length of the speeches and the menace to pockets which their words implied. At that moment, Helen Hull whispered, "Would you like to say a few words, Arthur?"

"Certainly." I jumped at it, fresh from my schooling in Australia. When she announced me and I stood up, I saw poor Nela growing pale and gasping heavily. In my best of moods I painted the short and sad lives of Mozart and Schubert and how they made me feel guilty about my having been showered with favors which I never deserved. Vienna ought to be eternally ashamed of letting them live and die in dire need. Now it basks in their glory and makes fortunes exploiting their names. "Such a crime must never happen again," I said with pathos. "We have, right here, great artists in need and this time we ought to do all in our power to let them live and create in peace." My improvised grandiloquent speech had an unexpected success, especially with Nela, who had a hard time recovering from her astonishment. "Australia did it," I told her triumphantly, "and from now on you will hear me making speeches day and night." As a matter of fact, the Musicians' Emergency Fund was able to pass in secret large sums as yearly income to a few of the now best-known American composers and, to their honor, the great Béla Bartók until his death.

Dorothy Chadwick called me a few days later. "Arthur, I have a great favor to ask you. The owner of the little book shop on the corner of my street tells me all the time about the talent of his young son who is only thirteen years old and he says he cannot afford to buy the boy a piano. Would you consent to hear him play? Because my decision to give him a piano will depend on your opinion." I promised, of course, and she brought the young boy the next afternoon to the hotel. Steinway had provided me with a good piano, so I asked them both to come up to our drawing room.

The boy was not attractive to look at, with a face full of pimples, a mop of curly disheveled hair, and dark eyes scrutinizing me without friendship. After fussing with the stool and trying out the keyboard, he played a prelude and fugue of Bach very well indeed. Three more pieces by Chopin and Liszt convinced me he was already a pianist. "Dorothy," I said, "you can give him two pianos."

Willy Kapell right away became overfriendly with me and tried to amuse me by speaking badly of his teacher, who happened to be my friend

Joseph Lhévinne. When I reprimanded him, he burst out: "He doesn't understand me. I have no communication with him. But if you could take me on, I feel I could make real progress."

I refused, point-blank. "You need discipline, young man, and also to be heard often. I am not the right teacher for you because I give too many concerts, but I shall always be willing to hear you play whenever possible." He left happily and I was satisfied to have helped him obtain a piano.

Walter Gieseking, whom I had heard in Paris as the finest interpreter of Debussy, announced a concert of works by this composer. I went to hear him and was enchanted with his delicate approach and the truly impressionistic treatment of these often elusive pieces. By pure chance, passing the lobby of my hotel, I found that Gieseking was taking part in a so-called matinale at eleven o'clock; an abominable hour for a concert. He must have felt that, too, because the Beethoven, Chopin, and Liszt which I heard on that occasion were far below my expectations.

My next concert I owed to Nela. Mrs. Mary Bok, who created the famous Curtis Institute of Music in Philadelphia, had become very fond of Nela during her stay there with her parents. When my wife wrote her about her marriage to me, and after my successful New York debut, Mrs. Bok invited me to play at the Curtis Institute for the students. At that time, Josef Hofmann, whom Mrs. Bok worshipped like a god, was president of the institute. Fortunately for me, he was on tour when my concert took place in the Kazimir Hall.*

It was a difficult appearance for me. All these young students who filled the hall looked at me as though they would swallow me alive if I disappointed them. Well, thanks to *Petrushka*, I won them over. Hofmann sent me a nice telegram with regrets at not being present—a sign of politeness which he seldom showed.

We invited Mrs. Bok to dinner; in spite of her adulation of Hofmann, she seemed to have liked my playing and approved of Nela's second husband. I think it gave my wife great satisfaction.

---

* The first name of Hofmann's father, in whose memory it was named.

95

Artur and Halina Rodzinski received us in a most friendly way. He was pleased about my success in New York, which he had read about in the Cleveland press. "This will make your debut here much easier," he said. It was to be the Brahms Concerto No. 2 in B flat.

The rehearsal on the morning of the concert went very well, the orchestra was good and Rodzinski, the disciplinarian he was, carefully went through the score in detail. After lunch, he had a long siesta. Nela and I took advantage of it and went to see a film which we were anxious to see. It was a wonderful account of the Dreyfus affair and about Emile Zola, who was magnificently played by Paul Muni. We were so excited about it that when we returned to the Rodzinskis' the Zola story seemed more interesting than the concert. Artur was a little put out by this, but our temperaments were so very different. My excitement over the film made me play the concerto with even more love than in New York and my success was considerable. Later at supper, Rodzinski showed great satisfaction with the reception by the public. "You are certainly going to play with us again two years from now," he said. "We never engage the same soloist two years running." But to my great pleasure it turned out differently. The board of directors simply made Rodzinski engage me for the next season. Soon after that the Rodzinskis came to New York, where Artur was to select players for the new orchestra which NBC created for Toscanini. New Yorkers were happy to have Toscanini back again. Several years had passed since he had left in anger both the Metropolitan Opera and the Philharmonic Orchestra, swearing that he would never return.

From then on, my tour continued far better than I expected. In Chicago, though, a disagreeable incident occurred, but, as usual, it made a good story later. For my debut concert I was to play the Tchaikovsky concerto conducted by the famous Otto Klemperer. Once again, I reluctantly accepted an invitation to stay in a private home. The Carpenters, remembering our meeting in China, insisted on having us. Mrs. Carpenter was an inveterate hostess who gave receptions and parties from morning until night.

The day before the concert, the guests never stopped coming. There were pre-luncheon visits, a large lunch party, some important ladies for tea, a cocktail party of course, a big dinner, and some guests coming after dinner. The hostess was tireless. "Arthur, you must talk to this wonderful man . . . Mrs. X is so keen on meeting you, do sit down with her," and so on and so forth. It was unbearable. Luckily, I managed to slip out to play with Klemperer on two pianos, something he liked to do; he was a good pianist.

On Sunday the concert was to take place at three o'clock in the afternoon. We had a fine rehearsal in the morning. Somebody told me that the Tchaikovsky would be the last number. Back at the Carpenters', Nela informed me that there would be a pre-concert lunch party for twelve. This was too much for me. "Helen," I said, "I cannot lunch with your guests. I shall remain in my room; a cup of coffee would be welcome." The lunch was in my honor, but she noticed my stern expression. "I shall take Nela to the concert and the car will come for you at about a quarter to four."

From my window I watched the cars leaving the house for the concert and felt, as usual, very nervous. Suddenly, the maid ran up and burst into my room. "There is an urgent telephone call from the orchestra hall. They want to know what has happened. You are already a quarter of an hour overdue."

One can imagine my shock. I dashed down the street, fortunately found a taxi, and hurried to the hall. The manager was waiting anxiously outside. "What the devil happened to you?" he screamed. "We had to tell the audience that you had a little accident, and Klemperer is conducting the symphony now instead of after intermission and, I might tell you, he is furious."

During intermission, Klemperer wouldn't talk to me, but when we came out for the concerto, the audience, glad to see me alive and enthusiastic about the symphony, gave us a small ovation. At last, to finish the sad story, our performance elicited a still greater ovation. Ever since, I have been careful about checking the exact time of my appearance.

In San Francisco, my good old friend Pierre Monteux received me with a hug. "Your concert is a special event. It will take place in the Civic Auditorium, which holds ten thousand, and not in the Opera House, where we usually play." I had the G major Beethoven and the C minor Rachmaninoff on the program.

The next morning, Nela accompanied me to the rehearsal because we were apprehensive about the enormous hall. Monteux was rehearsing an overture, and when he had finished he came down to greet us. "It is strange," he said, "the piano hasn't arrived yet. I was forced to persuade the orchestra to take the intermission now instead of at half time. I hope the piano will be here any moment." Well, the intermission was over and there was no piano. The Steinway representatives in San Francisco answered our frantic calls and tried to calm us with a stereotyped answer: "The piano is on its way."

Time was up. The orchestra was assembled on the stage and Monteux said grimly, "I shall have them play the tuttis." But I did not like it. I jumped onto the stage. "I shall sing my part," I declared. And, believe it or not, we went through the whole Beethoven concerto with me croaking the piano part, but it proved to be quite efficient. By the time we finished, the piano was put up on the stage in a great hurry and the Rachmaninoff was properly rehearsed.

Before I finished my tour for Hurok, Quesada, who had left Spain for Mexico during the Civil War, proposed three concerts in Mexico City. As Nela liked the idea of visiting this interesting country, I accepted. Hurok, delighted to have won a strong foothold for me in the United States, suggested finishing my season with a second recital at Carnegie Hall after my return from Mexico. "I booked you solid for next year and there are return engagements in every city where you played."

Mexico was a happy break. I found all my old friends there, reassured in their opinion of me by my success in the States. They were delighted to see me happily married, approved enthusiastically of my choice, and showered us with invitations. It was a short stay and, in every way, worthwhile. Ernesto de Quesada was in his element again. "Arturo," he said before my departure, "I have a good idea. After you finish with Hurok, we could go to Colombia and Venezuela. They are now the richest countries in Latin America and with your great name in Spain and the success in the United States, we could make a lot of money in these two countries."

My adventurous blood began boiling again. "Wouldn't it be fun?" I asked Nela. At that, she made a stern face. "I have been away from the children long enough. The *Ile de France* is leaving two days after your last concert in New York and we should ask Hurok to order our tickets right away." I did not give up. "But we need the money, Nela—this tour has not made us rich."

"It will not take more than two weeks," said Quesada, "and it is really worthwhile."

Nela weakened. "Well then, I can sail back by myself and you can go there alone with Ernesto."

"Darling," I said jokingly, "I will bring back from Colombia a sack of emeralds and throw it at your feet." (Colombia was famous for its emerald mines.) But she was not in the mood for jokes. And so it was a sad parting in New York. The Jean de Polignacs, who were sailing on the same boat, promised to take good care of her.

I flew to Bogotá, the capital of Colombia, where I found Quesada waiting for me. He warned me at the airport that the city was over eight thousand feet above sea level. "Walk slowly, and if you feel your heart beating too strongly, try to sit down and rest." But all his precautions seemed unnecessary because the extraordinary altitude had no effect on me. As in the rest of Latin America, my close ties with Spain were well known and helped me to fill two houses.

Pleased with the money I had earned, I went out to buy the promised emeralds, but the first jeweler I visited informed me that all the emeralds produced by Colombian mines were sent to the United States and there were none available for local buyers. I was not one to give up so easily. The local Polish consul, a kind man, confided to me, "I know two Jewish merchants who emigrated from Poland. I could ask them to call on you and I feel sure that they can help you out."

Two little men speaking Polish came into my room. "Do you have genuine emeralds for sale?" I asked. They smiled slyly. "If one really wants something, one gets it." The silent one brought out of his pocket a bundle which looked like a knotted handkerchief, undid it carefully, and spread out an assortment of emeralds of all shapes and shades. I made a choice quickly, and as the price was acceptable, the deal was clinched. Before giving them the money, I asked them to provide me with an elegant little sack for the emeralds.

Bogotá was rightly proud of its excellent Spanish, spoken with a pure accent, and of its high level of culture. The people I met were even musically well educated.

We flew off to Caracas with Ernesto munching *chirimoyas* and spitting the pips into his paper bag during the whole trip. I didn't like passing the very high mountains within inches of the peaks.

The capital of Venezuela in those days was quite similar to a small provincial Spanish city. Narrow streets, low houses, a proud square with a large theater and a hotel on the other side. In the center of the town, there was the other typical plaza, with benches around the fountain in the flowered center. Venezuela is a proud and wealthy country; proud of having given birth to Bolívar, who delivered the whole continent from Spain, and wealthy with its oil. The population was not very large in those days. Many Jewish immigrants came from Europe, mainly from Germany. Here too I had very good concerts; Chopin, Albéniz, and de Falla always earned the most success.

After my last concert, I agreed to dine with two great lovers of music.

Ernesto de Quesada, who never dined properly but followed his personal diet, joined us afterward. We strolled down the main street and when I noticed an oasis of neon lights at the end, I asked, "What goes on there at this late hour? Are they preparing for a special festivity?" The answer was a bitter outburst: "Festivity indeed!" one of the men said angrily. "We have been invaded by these dreadful Jews running away from Hitler. They own our city. What you see there are cinemas, a café, and two huge department stores—all built and owned by the Jews." This infuriated me. "Did they cheat anybody to do this?" I shouted. "Did they bring their own people to build it? Didn't they pay for it?"

"Of course they didn't cheat anybody," they answered, a little taken aback, "but it is unacceptable to our people to have foreigners establish themselves in such a grand way."

"Then why the hell didn't you build it all yourselves? You have all the means for it with your dirty oil, don't you? You ought to be grateful to them for giving you a glimpse of fine living in this dead provincial town of yours." Quesada tried to pacify me, but I made him accompany me to the hotel without a further word. We left the next morning with good Venezuelan money in our pockets.

On our way back to New York, we had to stop in Jamaica for twenty-four hours. We reached Kingston at teatime and, sitting on the terrace of a little hotel on the outskirts of the city, we enjoyed one of the most beautiful sunsets I had ever seen. The sun was sinking slowly as though bathed in blood, sending out multicolored rays. Suddenly Quesada disappeared and joined me only at dinner in the restaurant. "I arranged a concert for you," he said. "Tomorrow morning at eleven, you will play at the opening of a new cinema. There is money in this town and I couldn't stand being here for twenty-four hours without getting some of it." I was greatly amused that while we were watching the poetic sunset, he was really putting together the whole plan—to visit newspapers and the director of the cinema and to arrange everything necessary for the concert. Without asking me, he had given them the program of my last recital in Caracas, and I played it better this time.

At the airport, Ernesto and I parted. He left for Mexico and I flew via Havana to New York. The Hurok office booked me on the *Normandie*, the luxurious French liner, where I found Sophie Kochanska as a traveling companion.

It was the most enjoyable voyage I can remember. There was everything you could expect of the famous French taste. Besides the restaurant, they had built an elegant grillroom on the upper deck where the price of the meals was not included in the ticket and which gave the impression of a large tent. A good band played during dinner and later for dancing. Naturally, all those with a love of luxury flocked to the grillroom. There was Danielle Darrieux, then at the height of her fame. The still young and brilliant David Niven and the charming Brian Aherne were both unmarried and excellent company.

After tea, there was always a good film in the theater on board, which could stand comparison with any elegant theater in Paris or London. The usual concert for the sailors' pension fund was a brilliant affair; we offered a good program and Danielle Darrieux and two other pretty ladies sold programs and collected contributions from the delighted passengers.

This attractive and most comfortable voyage returning from my first genuinely successful tour in America gave me the opportunity to evaluate what had happened to me and to the United States during the fourteen years of my absence.

Sol Hurok was, of course, instrumental in bringing me back, but, as I soon discovered, my return wasn't due to Hurok alone. During the first terrible years of the financial disaster, the classical music recording industry was at a complete standstill. The first important record produced by the Victor Company happened to be my Tchaikovsky concerto, which had been made in England by its then sister company, "His Master's Voice." It was sold in great quantities to the Americans, who were starving for good music. Thus, my name became well known. Hurok, with his uncanny sense for what the public wanted, was quick to realize that the time had come to present me. In 1937, he was still far from being the world-renowned impresario. He had a small office which was linked with the very powerful NCAC, the great rival of the Columbia Association. However, Hurok was lucky in his choice of collaborators. There was a young woman, Mrs. Mae Frohman, who actually ran the office because her boss was constantly traveling in search of talent. She had an ideal secretary, Miss Anne Opperman. Hurok's son-in-law was in charge of publicity.

The ballet was Hurok's real passion. Serge Diaghilev was his ideal. He was out to emulate Diaghilev and, in time, surpass him. He inherited the Diaghilev company, then called the Ballet de Monte Carlo (where it had been hibernating). His main soloists were Marian Anderson and myself. I can state without exaggeration that the three of us made our great American careers together.

Marian Anderson became the idol of the American public. As a member of the Negro race, she had to endure the humiliation of racial discrimination. In cities where she filled the hall with enthusiastic listeners, she could not find lodgings except in the Negro ghettos. There was no place for her in a decent city hotel. Her case provoked a great outcry and it came to a

Among the stars in Hollywood

With Basil Rathbone (left)
and Charlie Chaplin

With Benita and Ronald Colman

With Myrna Loy (left)
and Hedda Hopper

Rubinstein receiving an Oscar
from Gregory Peck, 1970

Joscha Heifetz (left) and Gregor Piatigorsky, 1949

With Alfred Wallenstein

With Henryk Szeryng at Square Avenue Foch

To Arthur Rubinstein in remembrance of the unforgetable date (October 29, 1944) of our first artistic meeting

(X mas 1944)

Arturo Toscanini

With Andrés Segovia

Arturo Toscanini - a photograph dedicated to Rubinstein "in remembrance of the unforgettable date (October 29, 1944) of our first artistic meeting"

With the winners of the Arthur Rubinstein International Piano Master Competition in Israel, 1974 (left to right) Emanuel Ax (U.S.A.), Seta Tanyel (Austria), Janina Fialkowska (Canada), Eugene Indjic (U.S.A)

With Igor Stravinsky

With Nadia Boulanger

With Pablo Casals

With Heitor Villa-Lobos,
about 1960

With Emil Gilels, 1961

With Daniel Barenboim, 1975

*With Zubin Mehta, 1971
(above right)*

*With Leonard Bernstein (left)
and Isaac Stern, signing
the manifesto against UNESCO
excluding Israel*

With Albert Einstein

With Sol Hurok

With Pablo Picasso

pour mi Arturo
mi amigo   Picasso
el 27.6.71.

With Indira Gandhi

With Golda Meir

Honored by Presidents and the Académie Française

Dressed in the official uniform of the Académie Française

Receiving the Medal of Freedom from President Ford

Receiving the Kennedy Center honors at the White House, 1978: (left to right) Richard Rodgers, George Balanchine, Marion Anderson, President and Mrs Carter, Fred Astaire

Congratulations to Arthur Rubinstein, a great American!

Rosalynn Carter

Jimmy Carter

climax when the famous Constitution Hall in Washington, owned by the Daughters of the American Revolution, was denied to her because of the color of her skin. Hurok quickly reacted. He obtained the right to arrange a concert on the great lawn in front of the Lincoln Memorial, where Marian Anderson was to sing for a charity. It became a great historic event. The wife of the President, Mrs. Eleanor Roosevelt, herself a prominent Daughter of the American Revolution, resigned from the association, proclaiming her indignation publicly and presiding over this concert on the platform with other dignitaries. It was said that a hundred thousand people were present. Marian Anderson's triumph started the great movement which led finally to the civil rights laws. From then on, Hurok established himself as an independent and began his fantastic career as an impresario. My own career greatly benefited from these developments.

I would like to inform my readers now about the musical and cultural life which I found on my third visit to the United States. In my first book, *My Young Years*, I criticized disdainfully the state of things musical there and the year was 1906.

On my second visit, in 1919, the beginning of the so-called Roaring Twenties, the great exuberance of the victory in the war and the importance of alcohol produced by prohibition made it difficult for me to make a clear judgment. I heard bad orchestras with great conductors and bad conductors with good orchestras. There was an evident need for music, but a great lack of discrimination.

Now, in 1938, I found a progress which would have taken Europe a hundred years to make. All over the country orchestras sprung up like mushrooms, supported not as a sheer duty by municipalities, but by a growing enthusiastic love for music by the people of the communities who year after year paid the huge deficits inevitably incurred by every orchestra.

I noticed, too, a growing passion for learning. In addition to the state universities, Harvard, Yale, and Princeton inspired wealthy citizens to build magnificent private universities which rapidly gained renown, and each one had a serious music department. Enterprises of great learning and cultural value appeared overnight.

Koussevitzky created a beautiful center for music during the summer, Tanglewood, an enchanting spot in a large clearing of the Massachusetts forest. It provided the great Boston Symphony Orchestra with a profitable summer season, but Koussevitzky's talent for organization and his inventive mind brought to Tanglewood a free exchange of music making. From morning to late afternoon, small studios were invaded by musicians of all categories, reading with delight chamber music for different combinations of instruments, giving and taking the opportunity to learn this most noble form of music, which was actually meant to be played in chambers and not in concert halls.

This beautiful way of musical life was adopted later by Rudolf Serkin at Marlboro, his lovely estate in Vermont. Southern California was quick to emulate it, and thanks to the semitropical climate, several festivals of this kind could be put on during the year. The famous yearly Bach Festival in Bethlehem, Pennsylvania, attracted a public from everywhere and the high quality of its productions was second to none.

This time, at my concerts my listeners showed a much deeper under-standing. I was happily looking forward to the next season.

96

Nela was waiting for me at the port of Le Havre. The poor thing was looking rather pale after minor surgery. At the rue Ravignan, I was glad to feel my old Parisian self again. When we entered our little bunga-low, with great care I took the emeralds out of my pocket and with a theatrical gesture I threw the little sack at Nela's feet. "I kept my promise, darling, didn't I?" Nela picked it up, and when she opened it, showed no little surprise at the sight of the mass of little emeralds. We planned to have Cartier arrange them into a brooch right away.

A few days later, Nela left for Warsaw to bring back the children and Karola. Left alone, I strolled down to the center of the city and found with dismay that every free wall was covered with threatening slogans against the Jews. They had written about it in America but I could not believe it to be true.

Now in Paris, I found out that dreadful things had happened. Hitler, now drunk with power, having annihilated all his opponents in Germany, had hypnotized his people into blind obedience. His earlier anti-Semitic moves had become cruel humiliating laws. The German operas and orches-tras were obliged to expel Jewish members, but what enraged me most of all was to see all the so-called civilized countries accepting this inhuman treat-ment with complete indifference. Paris knew that Hitler had appointed a special ambassador, Heinrich Abetz, who organized all the anti-Semitic propaganda in France and it had disastrous results.

Even Poland, frightened by Hitler's vituperous speeches claiming the corridor of Danzig, was infected by his diabolical anti-Jewish campaign. Universities introduced *numerus clausus* for Jewish students and assigned them to special benches as a result of the violent demands of the Christian co-students.

Encouraged by the tacit adherence to his ideas by his neighbors, Hitler began to move toward the realization of his deep-seated plans for revenge and conquest. His army occupied the border of the Rhine without the permission of the Allies. As this move met with success, he became bolder and after disposing of Schuschnigg, the Austrian dictator, he entered Vienna at the head of his army; I must say, he was enthusiastically welcomed by the Nazi masses in Austria. To my bitter disappointment, Mussolini, who had talked to me of the racial laws in Germany with great disapproval, suddenly changed his policy.

Everyday life in Paris did not change, however. Nela, the ever practical wife and mother, was set on finding a better home for the family. For a good week or two we searched for a new place to live, but as I strongly objected to living in an apartment with the usual disagreeable neighbors, we didn't find anything suitable. It was disappointing to find ourselves looking mostly at little houses left by doctors or dentists which were reeking of antiseptics.

At that time, Queen Elizabeth of Belgium invited me to join the jury of the Ysaye piano competition in Brussels and I readily accepted. This international competition was a great event of tremendous importance to pianists all over the world. The jury was most competent, consisting of famous pianists like Emil Sauer, Olga Samaroff, Walter Gieseking, Ignaz Friedman, and Nicholas Orloff. Hitler sent a musician who belonged to the Nazi Party to observe the proceedings. Poland decided to send Raoul Koczalski, an ex-child prodigy who was covered with medals when he was six, some of them hanging on his little bottom; he lived in Germany and developed into a very bad pianist. Queen Elizabeth of Belgium, a character of great nobility, who presided over the competition, was always present in her box, this time accompanied by her daughter, the young Queen of Italy, Marie José.

The competitors were pianists of the very first rank. Emil Gilels, my young protégé from Odessa, played both volumes of the Paganini-Brahms *Variations* in a way which left no doubt that he was the outstanding competitor and he did get the first prize. Among the other eleven semifinalists, Arturo Michelangeli, the now famous Italian artist, gave then an unsatisfactory performance but already showed his impeccable technique.

After one of the sessions, I invited Friedman and Orloff to have a bite with me. Seeing Gieseking standing alone, I asked him most amiably to join us. "But don't let the German Nazi come with us," I said in a confidential tone.

"What do you mean by that?" he answered arrogantly, "I am a convinced Nazi. Hitler is saving our country."

This put me into a boiling rage. "Look here, Gieseking," I said sternly, "you had better keep out of my way," and I never addressed him or looked at him again.

After a banquet given by the Queen, we returned to Paris, where I told Misia Sert about Gilels. "Arthur, I want to hear him," she said. We were both anxious to have Gilels and his companion, Jacob Flier, who won the third prize at the competition, visit our house, but in those times it was still a most complicated affair. Both stayed at the Soviet Embassy, not as a gesture of hospitality but simply to have a close watch kept on them, but we knew they would love to come.

When we called the embassy and asked for Gilels, a strange voice answered. It was evidently the man who was assigned never to let him out of sight. "What do you want of Comrade Gilels?" Nela mentioned the invitation for dinner and it was favorably received. "I am their good friend and we never go anywhere separately," he said cynically.

Of course, Misia was delighted to come. Well, we waited for the Russian guests for about two hours. The embassy did not answer the telephone, so we had dinner without them; at about eleven-thirty at night, the three of them appeared. They were exhausted and hungry. "We were late to begin with because the embassy had no car for us and there were no taxis. Finally we found one but he left us cold-bloodedly at the wrong address." None of the three Russians knew a single word of French or any other language. In their despair, they took another taxi and drove back to the embassy, in hopes of getting help, but the place was dark. Flier apparently saved the situation, finding our address and a taxi, so this time they arrived.

Of course, we started by feeding them and it was around two o'clock when Gilels consented to take his seat at the piano and played divinely the Brahms-Paganini *Variations* which won him the prize. The noble-minded Emil then invited his colleague to offer us the joy of the whole sonata of Chopin, which enraged poor Misia, who was waiting all this time to hear more of Gilels.

97

The lovely spring in Paris was filled with social events; we attended balls, luncheons, and dinners and quite often had guests in our own house.

One day, during a luncheon at Germaine's, a young Mrs. Strauss, a relative of our hostess, started talking about houses, as she and her husband were looking for one. We pricked up our ears. "There is a charming house for sale right here on the avenue Foch," said Minka Strauss. "Fred Singer, the nephew of Princess Polignac, rented it for a time but he is leaving for London now and the house is free. Unfortunately, it is too small for us and there are not enough accommodations."

Nela and I exchanged knowing glances. We asked casually the exact whereabouts of the house. Right after luncheon, with the last sip of coffee, we dashed down the avenue Foch, and across the street we found a gate which opened onto a little square; the concierge in charge gave us precious information: Apparently the sale of the house was not yet advertised, but he indicated that Frank Arthur, the well-known estate agent, was looking after it. "If you want to see the house, I am authorized to show it to you even if the residents are there."

We followed him around a little circular garden to a lovely house with three large windows on each of the three stories. There was a small gate and a little garden leading to a glass-covered porch. On the ground floor were the reception rooms, which were quite nice; the second floor had a large master bedroom, two other rooms, and a big bathroom; on the top floor were a servant's room, a wardrobe room, and a guest room. Nela, with the clever eye of a mother, saw right away all the changes that could be made.

We met Mrs. Fred Singer, who was willing to leave much of the furniture and fittings to the buyer, and we left in a daze—for this house was a dream. First thing in the morning, we rushed to the Frank Arthur Agency in the Boulevard Haussmann and were kindly received by my namesake. He told us a romantic story about the house: "From what I hear, a wealthy Englishman bought this house for his Parisian mistress. After his death his heirs decided to sell it as quickly as possible." We wondered what had happened to the mistress but Mr. Arthur didn't know anything about it. "Are you prepared to sell the house?"

"I am not authorized to do so until they give me permission, and the price has not yet been settled." This last sentence made me very nervous; I was in deadly fear that it would be beyond my means. Frank Arthur showed sympathy for my anxiety: "I can give you the telephone number of this family and you might find out more details." He was kind enough to get me the connection and a pleasant-sounding English voice answered the phone. I introduced myself timidly as a possible buyer for the house in question. "We are determined to sell it," the voice came back, "but in these uncertain times it is difficult to know what price to ask in France."

"I am not a man of means, madame, but a concert pianist who has difficulties in living in apartments where neighbors object to my practicing. This house seems ideal for me and my family."

"Would you kindly tell me your name?" she asked. When I told her, I heard a little cry of delight. "Arthur Rubinstein? We heard you recently and enjoyed your recital immensely, so nothing would please us more than for you to have the house." They instructed Frank Arthur accordingly, and we settled the deal before a French notary. Nela and I became the co-owners and we were overjoyed about it.

With an assured future in America, we rented a lovely villa in Aix-les-Bains. Sophie Kochanska was our guest and we even had a short visit from Nela's sister Alina, who had been attending a meeting of Yogis in Holland.

I was lucky to find a good piano for the villa and for once worked with pleasure on a new repertoire. The Italian Concerto of Bach, which I had never played before, and the beautiful Partita in C minor, which I had played very badly for Barth, were my greatest concern. I added the last scherzo, the last ballade, and a few more études to my Chopin. Of new things, I remember the *Bourrée fantasque* by Chabrier, four mazurkas by Szymanowski, and a few short pieces by Debussy and Ravel. I also improved technically some pieces of my old repertoire, in view of the pedantic attitude of the American critics.

We had a lovely party for our little Eva's fifth birthday, with Jacques Thibaud and Marguerite Long as honored guests. I remember that concerts in Aix-les-Bains and Evian interrupted my rest for a few days but they were welcome because long interruptions in my public appearances used to depress me.

Our stay in Aix-les-Bains was extended until the end of September while our house was painted and a few minor repairs were made. Thibaud persuaded me to play in Biarritz, where he lived. "September is our best season," he said, "and we shall have some fun together."

One morning brought news which horrified us: Hitler arranged a meeting in Munich to which he invited the British and French Prime Ministers and, as a special honored guest, Mussolini, after having invaded the Sudetenland of Czechoslovakia, claiming that it was entirely inhabited by Germans. Mr. Chamberlain, the English Prime Minister, previously had had a talk with Hitler at Bad Godesberg to learn about his intentions and had warned him that his incendiary speeches could have dangerous consequences. He came triumphantly back to London, waving a sheet of paper, exclaiming, "This paper means peace." The whole world gave a sigh of relief at these words but the latest news dashed all hopes. Now, as then, the participants at the Munich meeting proclaimed it as a step toward peace but they did not find any echo. Everybody felt it clearly as a great humiliation for France and Great Britain to have accepted Munich following Hitler's blatant behavior after Bad Godesberg.

The Munich conference turned out even much worse than one feared. The Western powers meekly gave in to his demands and Mussolini now joined Hitler as a full partner, becoming soon enough a mere satellite of the Führer.

When the papers revealed that Mussolini had decreed anti-Jewish laws on Hitler's orders, I fell into a blind rage and decided then and there to send him back the decoration he had bestowed on me, explaining my reasons by telegram. I remember the text of it very well: "Deeply offended by your discriminating laws against Jews, I would be ashamed to continue to wear your decoration and I hereby return it to you. Arthur Rubinstein, Jewish pianist." The official at the post office refused to send my wire, but I wouldn't stop at that. After a long time on the telephone, I succeeded in reaching the Minister of Communications, whom I knew personally. He fully understood my gesture, but he advised me: "Before you send your telegram, which I shall of course authorize, as it does not contain any insulting words, you should give a copy of it to the Havas Agency, because the Italian government could state that Mussolini himself annulled your decoration." He was kind enough to do it all for me so promptly that the Italian press published the text of my telegram before Mussolini received it himself.

My message provoked great indignation. In Rome, the secretary of Santa Cecilia wrote that I would never be allowed to appear in Rome again, but other cities, like Milan, Turin, Florence, and Venice, simply sent letters of regret that they couldn't have me this year but they hoped to hear me again soon.

My little trip for a concert in Biarritz in some way soothed my anger. Jacques Thibaud was exceptionally good company; he gave me a charming dinner after my concert and accompanied me to the station, where I took a sleeper to Paris to supervise the work being done on the new house.

After proudly inspecting my new possession, I went back to Aix-les-Bains, where I worked better than ever with more attention to details. My acceptance by America, after so many years, changed my life considerably. Before I returned to New York, Dr. Schiff booked me at the Salle Pleyel, where to my great joy I had a very good house.

Nela and I experienced that special delight in finding, choosing, and loving the things we wanted in our new home. It was thrilling to find nice things like a table, a chair, or a lamp which was the only right one for the place. We had no use for a specific style but chose each object to be in harmony with the others and the rooms were made to warm our hearts. Our bedroom became especially beautiful.

98

I accepted a very unexpected invitation from Antanas Smetona, the President of Lithuania, who wanted me to play in Kowno (Kaunas), the capital of his country, in spite of the fact that Lithuania and Poland had separated after the First World War. Wilno remained in Polish hands and this caused the closing of the frontiers between the two countries, followed by a complete break in diplomatic relations. Therefore, it was indeed a great honor for me as a Pole to receive this invitation. This my first concert in Kowno was also the first occasion for me to visit Nela's birthplace, to which I had so often been invited. She could not accompany me, as the new house absorbed all her time.

I reached Kowno via Warsaw, where I had a concert and where the Lithuanian visa on a special document was sent to me. After my concert, which had the usual success, I read with disgust the reviews of three critics who, instead of criticizing my playing objectively, treated me with anti-Semitic abuse. Mrs. Mlynarska, Nela's mother, came to Kowno for the concert and stayed with her charming nephew Jan Gromadzski. The concert turned out to be a festive one; the moment I appeared on the stage, I felt that the audience wished me well and were pleased that their President honored me by his presence. My program was well chosen without giving too much prominence to Chopin, whose works might have been considered politically provocative. De Falla's *Fire Dance* as the final encore did its duty as always. Mr. Smetona had warm words for me and I expressed high praise for the music-loving Lithuanians.

After the concert, my mother-in-law and her nephew joined me for supper in the happiest mood. The next morning, Mrs. Mlynarska took me to Ilgovo, her family estate, of which I had heard wonders from Paul Kochanski, who had been brought up there and was even present when Nela was born. She herself felt a deep love for the place and never stopped telling me about it.

The house was situated on a small hill overlooking the majestic river Niemen, which we had to cross in a rowboat. It was modest and old-fashioned but imbued with warmth. The large music room pleased me most. I sat in the empty room for a long while and felt the walls ringing with all the music that had been played there. The dining room reminded me of Tymoszowka (Szymanowski's estate), as both contained dark and faded-looking portraits of ancestors. What impressed me most was the huge kitchen with their famous cook Barbara reigning over it, its long wall of copper pans beginning with a huge one and going decrescendo to the smallest; if I well remember, I counted about twenty of them. In this beautiful kitchen and in the cellar filled with fruit, I felt vividly Nela's presence.

The estate was managed by Nela's cousin Henryk Hryncewicz, who lived there with his wife and children. I was shown everything on the estate, the livestock, granaries, and barns, and I loved the old chestnut trees.

After two lovely days being treated like a king in every way, but especially in the culinary art of my mother-in-law and Barbara, I returned to Warsaw and, after a day or two, to Paris.

Nela had done marvels with the house. It looked as if we had lived there for weeks. We began to think seriously about a housewarming party and we chose to have it after a farewell concert before leaving for America. Our guest list was very ambitious; everybody accepted and, as a great surprise, Nela's mother arrived that day for a prolonged stay, to our great joy. There was one disturbing note: Dr. Schiff had accepted a concert in Marseilles for the day following the party, with a flight early in the morning.

The party, I must say modestly, was sensational. *Le tout Paris* seemed to be only too glad to inaugurate our little house. Nela organized it all beautifully and received admiring compliments from everyone. Over fifty people were served at table and every table had its own champagne in ice buckets. Nela was quite proud to be envied for her *savoir faire* by Germaine de Rothschild, herself one of the great hostesses of Paris. Nobody wanted to leave and, as I well remember, the last guests left at six in the morning.

We just had time to change, pack two bags, and leave for the airport. Once on the plane, we fell into our seats and slept like logs immediately.

A tap on my shoulder woke me with a start. To my great astonishment, it was H. G. Wells, the famous English writer. I had met him on two occasions and remember a lengthy talk about politics and the general attitude toward music. We had exchanged interesting remarks about the impact of music on the individual. Now, seeing the sleepy expression on my face, he said smilingly, "I am sorry to have woken you up, but I am curious to know if you have many friends in London." I answered with conceited self-assurance, "I have many friends all over England."

"Well," he said in a serious tone, "if you knock at my door, you will find a very good friend." I had no answer but I was deeply touched and he saw it. Later on, staying at the same hotel, we met again in the lobby and had a long, very interesting talk before we separated for lunch.

The concert that evening was not one of my best and I promised myself never to risk this kind of fatigue before a concert.

99

In January 1939 we returned to New York in excellent spirits, leaving the children in the comfortable new house in the care of their grandmother. Hurok was at the dock to help us through customs and all the rest, but this time we went to a more modest hotel, the Gladstone, on the advice of Sophie Kochanska.

Unlike the previous tour, I arrived this time with full confidence. I felt that the public and the critics were glad to hear me again, and, as a matter of fact, I had prepared my programs with great care. Due to the disquieting political atmosphere in Europe, not many pianists could come to America, but I did have a few formidable rivals who had had a great following for a decade. There were the fanatic followers of the brilliant Vladimir Horowitz, whose marriage to Toscanini's daughter gave him an additional luster. The devotees of German classical music swore by its specialist Rudolf Serkin; Robert Casadesus, the fine French pianist, inherited Alfred Cortot's admirers of the Gallic school. Hofmann and Rachmaninoff were still playing, but made only rare appearances.

As for myself, I still had a long way to go, but I had return engagements everywhere I had played before. My idea of what people call a great career was a very precise and personal one. It might sound preposterous but you reach it when you are offered concerts by managers, conductors, and societies who might hate to have you but cannot afford not to because your public flocks to the box office and fills your hall. This makes you the master of the situation. My first immediate indication of success was that Hurok thought the better of calling me "Prince of Pianists."

The Victor Record Company approached me about recording the Franck Prelude, Chorale, and Fugue and the great C major Toccata by Bach-Busoni. This company was linked with "His Master's Voice" in London, with whom I had a contract, and consequently I did not need to sign any contract with Victor. These two companies used each other's recordings with the condition that the English company had the market for all Europe, Africa, and Australia and Victor had both Americas and Japan. This accounts for my Tchaikovsky concerto being issued in America so early.

I agreed to make those two recordings. My recording engineer was a Charles O'Connor, a nice Irishman to talk to but not to work with. During sessions, he was always in a hurry, whereas I never gave up and would repeat something until I reached the point where I could not improve on it. I was not happy working with Victor. I felt neglected, there was no sign of publicity, and it took a long time to have the proofs of my first recordings sent to me. On the other hand, London's "Master's Voice" treated me regally; they even spoiled me.

It was a strenuous tour; travel by plane was not yet generally used but in those days American trains were most comfortable and attractive. During that season, I covered vast distances, including an extensive tour of Canada. Hurok had so many demands for me from smaller cities that he declared conceitedly, "I let them wait, it will do them good!"

I remember particularly two concerts in the East—in Washington and Boston. In the former, we were invited to stay at the Polish Embassy, where Jan Ciechanowski, my old friend from London and Paris, was now the ambassador. He and his charming Belgian wife gave a beautiful party after my concert at which I met many people who were later to mean much in my life. There was Virginia Bacon, whose vitality and hospitality were second to none and who is, to this day, a friend so close that she simply calls us "family"; Alice Longworth, the brilliant daughter of Theodore Roosevelt, who remembered me from 1906; and many members of the diplomatic corps. My concert at the famous Constitution Hall started a yearly series that continued until my last concert there in 1976.

Boston was another story. I played the B-flat Brahms with Koussevitz-ky conducting and was very warmly received. Later, at a supper in his house, a young man was introduced to me as the critic of the Boston *Herald*. Koussevitzky made a great fuss over him, but the next morning's paper had a terrible review of my performance by him. I was told by friends that he was hated in Boston for his frequent attacks on musicians who were well liked by the public. Fortunately for me, he was fired the next year, but Koussevitzky did not dare to have me before two years had elapsed.

I remember well our first visit to Los Angeles, where this time I was engaged by the Los Angeles Orchestra, whose conductor was Alfred Wallenstein, Rodzinski's successor. Hollywood was, in those days, the center of worldwide interest. The American film industry dominated the international market and dispensed fabulous riches. The great houses of MGM, Warner Brothers, Sam Goldwyn, Universal Studios, and Columbia Pictures were in the hands of multimillionaires. Extravagant sums were earned by world-famous actors like Clark Gable, Gary Cooper, Cary Grant, Ronald Colman, and Charles Boyer. Charlie Chaplin was the world's idol.

Nela and I as inveterate moviegoers felt wildly excited to find ourselves in this Mecca of the cinema. Sitting in the coffee shop of our hotel, we would practically jump out of our seats and pinch each other. "Look at that man," I would whisper, "he was the butler in that film with Carole Lombard." Or seeing an insignificant little blond sitting at the bar, Nela would say, "She played the friend of Barbara Stanwyck in that murder film."

Alfred Knopf introduced us to his half brother Edwin, a film producer en vogue, whose wife, the lovable Mildred Knopf, invited us for lunch with two film stars.

After a good rehearsal of the Beethoven Concerto No. 4 at the downtown Philharmonic Hall, we had our meal at a good restaurant on the way to our hotel, the Beverly Wilshire. At a nearby table sat a beautiful young girl engaged in a serious conversation with an elderly gentleman. Nela disapproved of my looking at her with such attention. "Darling, I look at her because there is the first pretty young woman who evidently is not an actress, belongs to society, and is talking to her father."

The concert went very well; the house was packed and Wallenstein proved to be a perfect accompanist. Many people came backstage to meet me, among them my old friend Bronislaw Kaper and his wife. The four of us had a great reunion at supper and Bronek, as I call him, who was a very successful composer for films at MGM, promised to show us around the studios.

At Mildred Knopf's luncheon we were introduced to her two guests. One was the already famous Olivia de Havilland and the other, her sister, was, to my great surprise, the girl I had admired in the restaurant. She was just beginning her career under the name of Joan Fontaine and indeed became a great star and a good friend of ours.

Thanks to Kaper, we were allowed to watch at MGM studios the take of a scene from *Marie Antoinette* played by the lovely Norma Shearer; it was the scene in which John Barrymore as Louis XV was lying on his deathbed, not daring to breathe. We were open-mouthed at the lavish costumes of the actors and the fantastic replica of Versailles. Later on, when we saw the film, we waited excitedly for this scene, but it never showed up because they had cut it.

Wallenstein immediately engaged me for the next season. And so we left, happily looking forward to our return.

My tour continued smoothly except for a nasty case of food poisoning. It happened on the train from St. Louis, where I had played with Vladimir Golschmann, to Schenectady. Nela remained in New York for these concerts. A bad sausage was the culprit; I swallowed it stupidly, in spite of finding it not to my taste, and I was severely punished for it. As I left the diner for my compartment, a horrible itching started which made me scratch my skin to distraction during the whole night.

When I arrived in Schenectady, I dashed to a doctor recommended by the hotel. He lost no time; after examining me thoroughly he pronounced the ominous words with a worried expression on his face: "It is a giant urticaria." The "giant" impressed me more than the "urticaria," which I did not understand. "I will give you a strong shot to save your life because it is a severe poisoning." His shot was severe too! I had the impression that he was pouring into me a whole champagne bottle of his lifesaving liquid.

My mood the whole day before the concert could not be called a jolly one, but, as usual, sitting at the piano in front of a good audience, I forgot my trouble and gave a rather decent account of myself. But the encores I played reluctantly because the itching became intolerable. Leaving the auditorium, I put my hat on and thought I had taken the wrong one, as it was much too small for me.

I shall never forget what happened to me on the train to New York that night. In bed in my compartment the itching subsided but something strange happened to my head; it began, of course, with the hat but then it was still invisible. When I got up to look at myself in the mirror, I was quite alarmed to see that the whole top of my head was swollen. There was no question of sleeping; all through the night I rushed to the mirror and found that the swelling was rapidly spreading to unbelievable proportions.

The train arrived in New York at six in the morning. Passengers were allowed to sleep on until eight but I dressed in a hurry and in no time was at the Gladstone Hotel, where I woke up Nela by telephone. "Don't get scared, darling," I said, "but you won't recognize me. My head looks like a pumpkin. I shall explain everything." She jumped out of bed, rushed out to the corridor, and seeing me gave a shriek. When I told her what happened, she called our friend Dr. Garbat, who arrived promptly and diagnosed from the door: "Oh, a giant urticaria." It was still the word "giant" I hated with my swollen head. The doctor gave me the consoling news that if I had had that swelling in my throat, I would have been dead by then. "You should stay quietly in bed for a few days and I will send a charming lady who will cure you, but you must accept the treatment without protest."

"I don't protest any treatments," I said sharply, "but I have a rehearsal tomorrow morning and concerts on Thursday, Friday, and Sunday, so there can't be any question of staying in bed."

Dr. Garbat laughed. "You intend to be seen like that at Carnegie Hall?" he asked ironically.

"Yes, indeed. I used to play better with a swollen head." There was no way of dissuading me, I was adamant and won out, but I had to submit to a treatment which makes me blush with shame even now as I write of it. The same afternoon, a distinguished elderly lady arrived at our apartment. She was dressed severely in black with a high collar and a neat black hat. She was a Swedish baroness and she ordered me imperiously, "Take off your trousers and underpants and lie down on your side." When I obeyed, she set out her instruments with elegance and attacked me with the formidable weapon of the enema. Poor me, I was subjected to this degrading "cure" half a dozen times.

When I arrived for the rehearsal, I scared Barbirolli out of his wits. He calmed down with difficulty and then walked out on the stage and explained to the orchestra, "You will see a terrible monster who is going to play the Mozart with us, but I can vouch that it is Rubinstein, all right." My appearance was duly received with little murmurs of dismay, but the minute we started playing, everything was in order again.

There was the problem of dress for the concert, as I was unable to put on my usual shirt and collar. Nela found an ingenious solution by putting a white scarf around my neck and pinning it to my white waistcoat. To add some elegance to this outfit, I inserted my pearl tiepin in the center of this improvised shirt.

At my instructions, there was subdued lighting on me, so that only the first few rows saw with horror my monstrous face, but the music soon calmed them. The Friday-afternoon concert was easier; the public, the orchestra, and even I had become accustomed and we all paid less attention to it, but on Sunday, a comic transformation took place: Thanks to the elegant treatment by the baroness, the swelling at the top of my head subsided, but settled comfortably in huge proportions in the lower part of my face. I looked singularly like a pig with small slits for my eyes, my nose buried, and the ears sticking out from enormous cheeks and neck, and, to boot, I had to play the Tchaikovsky concerto. The exuberance of this work made my head move much more than the Mozart and I felt my swellings in constant movement.

Looking at my program, I saw to my dismay that the opposite page was entirely covered by a sensational advertisement of "the greatest recording ever made—the Tchaikovsky Concerto by Vladimir Horowitz conducted by Arturo Toscanini." Their finished record, which I heard later, was defective both artistically and mechanically.

Fortunately, after less than a week, I was rid of the swelling and the baroness. Life became normal again.

My Chopin recital in New York consolidated my position in that most important city. The American tour kept me busy all through the long season and on top of it I received an urgent letter from Wilfred Van Wyck proposing a tour of South Africa upon my return; the prospect was not only advantageous but whetted my interest in knowing this new faraway country.

The musical world in America was thrilled to have the great Arturo Toscanini back again and the Jews in particular felt grateful for his noble gesture of conducting the newborn Israeli Orchestra in Tel Aviv for a month without remuneration.

My readers will certainly be astonished that now I seem to barely mention my music making and my concerts, but to describe long tours, concert by concert with detailed programs, is utterly impossible. All I can say now is that my playing improved considerably, mainly due to the fact that the American public was more demanding than any other, and also to my recordings, which had to be note-perfect and inspired. The result was that I learned to love practicing and to discover new meanings in the works I performed.

100

In Paris, our children and their grandmother gave us a wonderful welcome; our lovely new house began to grow on me. From day to day, it became more elegant. My dear collection of books found a comfortable home on large shelves. All in all, I felt on top of the world, with two successful tours in America which the snobbish European countries looked upon with due respect.

The season was more brilliant than ever. We were invited to many parties of all sorts. I particularly remember a dinner at the American Embassy in honor of Léon Blum, the Socialist leader and builder of the Front Populaire. There was a nice end to this dinner. Léon Blum, as brother-in-law of Paul Dukas, was extremely musical. He asked me to stay after the last guest had left, which I did, and then the ambassador and Blum begged me to play. It was a lovely long session of music making. We parted feeling extremely happy.

The last great ball of the season took place at the Polish Embassy. It was a lavish affair. *Le tout Paris* came en masse. Ambassador Lukasiewicz asked Nela to dance a Mazur, which she danced better than anyone I have seen. Nela always loved to dance and I often felt guilty that our marriage ended her career. So this time, she brought along her beautiful traditional Polish costume, which she had decorated artistically, and a headdress with multicolored ribbons. The ball started late in the evening in the garden of the embassy, where the ambassador had erected a dance floor and engaged an excellent Polish band. As the ball became more and more animated, Nela changed into her costume. At a signal from the ambassador, the dancing stopped, the orchestra started a well-known Mazur, and Nela and her partner, Count August Zamoyski, gave a wonderful performance of this proudest of all Polish dances. Her success was so great that she had to repeat the dance all alone. After a brilliant supper served inside, we all danced into the early hours. On the way home, I felt sure that all of us had the same tragic thought. This ball ends a happy era—God knows what is in store for us.

France's attitude toward Hitler's constant threats distressed me very deeply. German agents and spies were allowed to carry on their anti-Semitic propaganda without any official blame or interference. French newspapers were publishing the most abominable articles against Jews and in the streets the free spaces usually used for advertising concerts and other events were now filled with insulting anti-Semitic slogans. Poland too, as we heard, made life for its millions of Jews difficult. But life had to go on.

A young fifteen-year-old American pianist from San Francisco came to see me with her mother, who told me that a wealthy lady from her home town had sent them to Paris so that she could take lessons with me; Laura Dubman was her name and she was quite talented. When the mother agreed to wait for my return from Africa and was willing to follow me to Deauville, where Germaine had offered us a villa for the summer, I promised to take her on. The few lessons I gave her before my departure were gratifying; she was intelligent and very musical.

While the family made ready for Deauville, I left for Southampton to embark on a nice English steamer for Cape Town; it was a ten-day journey. When I entered the dining room for the first time, a lady exclaimed, "What a surprise, Arthur!" I recognized her from some reunions in London but did not quite remember her name. When I approached her table, she introduced me to her husband, the Duke of Devonshire. "We are traveling on official business," she explained. "My husband is Undersecretary for the Colonies."

They graciously asked me to join them at their table for meals, which became a great pleasure for me because nobody ever enjoyed my stories as much as the duke. He laughed uproariously at my very announcement that a story was going to be funny.

There was an old lady on board whom they knew from London. They introduced me to her but she asked six times who I was until she understood my name. She was stone deaf. In the evening after dinner, the duke would propose a game of bridge. "We are a nice foursome," he would say, "and of course, we don't play for money." There was nothing else for me to do but sit down every evening after dinner and play bridge with the Devonshires and the deaf old lady. Just to have a little fun, I would announce at every second game a grand slam, to see how much one can lose with a poor hand, and if the game became too boring, I would interrupt it with some storytelling, which never failed to affect the duke in the usual way.

Cape Town turned out to be a charming English city. My local manager was an Englishman who at lunch in my hotel gave me all the information about my tour, the country, its politics, and the Boers.

"Do you know anything about the diamonds?" I asked him, because I was determined to buy some for Nela.

"Yes, indeed," he answered. "If you have the chance to meet Sir Ernest Oppenheimer, who is the president of the De Beers Company, which hold the monopoly on these precious stones, he might help you to buy some at only a small fraction of the price you would pay on Bond Street, Fifth Avenue, or the rue de la Paix." That did it! His answer sent me on the right track and I was set on meeting the formidable Sir Ernest.

I had three lovely concerts in Cape Town. The hall in which I played amused me because it was linked with an anecdote about Paderewski. There were many open windows and my manager told me, "On the day of his concert a bird flew into the hall. That evening, poor Paderewski played with a scared bird fluttering around and above him. He became so furious that he discontinued his tour there and then and left for Europe."

Benno Moiseiwitsch, for whom I had great admiration, also had had a discouraging tour. With his passion for card games such as poker and bridge, he became better known for playing cards than the piano and the press was eager to let it be known.

In my own case, I was lucky not to find birds in my hall and not to be an inveterate card player. My manager affirmed that I was actually the first pianist to find favor in South Africa.

My next three concerts were to take place in Johannesburg, the largest and most important city in South Africa. In addition to looking forward to these concerts, I had hopes of meeting Sir Ernest Oppenheimer, who lived there, but when I arrived I learned that he had left for Kimberley, the seat of the diamond mines. "Don't be disappointed," my agent said, "you are going to play in Kimberley too and there you are sure to meet him."

My first concert in Johannesburg was a genuine success, for my manager immediately arranged three extra concerts, two of which were to be with orchestra. It gave a great lift to my morale and thus a real contact with my public was established. I played my best-loved programs with enthusiasm and won many hearts and many friends.

During the intermission of one of the concerts with orchestra a very elegant lady, escorted by two men, came to meet me. "I am Lady Oppenheimer," she introduced herself. My heart beat faster and I called for a comfortable armchair for the lady. "I want to ask you a great favor," she said.

I was sure she wanted an encore, and I was ready to give her the whole Tchaikovsky concerto. "I will do anything with the greatest pleasure, madame," I said with a servile smile.

"I've heard such wonderful things about you from the Duke of Devonshire, who dined with me yesterday, and he told me that you make the funniest faces he has ever seen. Could you make some for me?"

I was speechless for a moment, then I became angry. "Oh, he liked my faces," I said ironically. "Well, I will try to do my best." And I made two or three of the most dreadful faces, sticking my tongue out and squinting hard. It would have been enough to frighten any child to death. "I hope he meant those?" I asked her with a stern expression. She suddenly realized her faux pas and became overly apologetic. In doing so, she committed a worse one: "You know, I am not musical at all and never go to concerts but I came just to meet you." She left, certainly not as a friend, and I decided to forget about the diamonds.

Johannesburg is one of the richest towns I have visited. Inexhaustible gold mines are right under its soil and I was horrified by the lot of the miners, all blacks, who had to go down a mile to mine them. A law condemned anybody found with a rough diamond on him to ten years in prison. The miners, before being allowed to leave, were subjected to the most humiliating examinations.

Colonel Aaron Kisch, who had lost his leg in the war as an English officer, came from Israel to remind me of my promise to Hubermann to help the new orchestra in Tel Aviv by making propaganda during my tours. He himself was visiting rich Jewish colonies all over the world and collecting money for the orchestra. I told him about my good work in Australia and introduced him to some important acquaintances I had made during my concerts.

He was tiring me a little with constant telephone calls and inquiries about possible contributors when suddenly he came out with a grand invitation to a reception after my last concert. He announced that he would gather in my honor the best people in the town.

After my concert, I arrived in a happy mood at the hotel where the reception was to take place, and as I never dine before a concert, I was craving some food. Kisch received me in the lobby. "We must wait until all my guests are assembled."

There were quite a few of them already there but others continued to flock in. After quite a long while no less than two hundred people were in the lobby. I began wondering and calculating what the cost would be for the buffet and drinks for so many guests. Would it be paid by him or will the orchestra be responsible for it? When I thought that the moment had come to enter the dining room, Colonel Kisch, very elegant in his dinner jacket, made a sign that he was going to speak. Ah-ha, I thought, we are finally invited to follow him into the dining room. But imagine my surprise when he began a long exposition of the difficulties involved in maintaining a first-class full-sized orchestra with a fine conductor at its head. He elaborated on the theme with statistics and full details. His fine speech lasted well over a half hour, by which time I was starving, but the worst was yet to come; instead of finally giving us something to eat and drink, which I needed so badly, he made a great announcement: "Now I give you Mr. Arthur Rubinstein, the great friend of Hubermann, whom he helped from the beginning with his plans. Mr. Rubinstein will tell you with more knowledge and greater eloquence what music played by an orchestra means to the world." And he made me take his place. By then, I had the strong wish to kill him, but I smiled politely and delivered the longest eulogy on music, composers, conductors, performers, and orchestras a hungry man has ever given. Now, almost collapsing, I felt the compensation of a wonderful supper must come, but what actually happened was a real catastrophe: The guests, after thanking Kisch and me politely for our lovely speeches, went quietly home, leaving the two of us alone. "Ah," I exclaimed cheerfully, "how wonderful, we will have our supper quietly." My host made an impatient gesture. "What are you talking about? Everything has been closed in this town for two hours. Anyway, I couldn't possibly eat. I was invited to a lovely dinner before the concert."

The next morning I asked for my breakfast at seven; my hunger had not allowed me to sleep for one minute.

The rest of the tour was strenuous. I had to play in every city of any importance, even in Pretoria, the seat of the central government, which as a rule did not allow concerts to be given in the capital.

Upon arrival in Kimberley, I was very pleased to receive a telephone call from Sir Ernest Oppenheimer, obviously because of his wife. He very politely offered to show me around the diamond mines and I, to put it mildly, jumped at the idea. I had not missed him at the concert, knowing that he was not musical. The next morning his car took me to the mines and we stopped at the offices of the De Beers Company. Sir Ernest, a middle-aged man with charming manners, took me first to the showroom, where I could admire some particularly beautiful diamonds. This was the right moment for me. I confided to Sir Ernest that it was my dream to buy some diamonds for my wife and admitted that the prices of great European jewelers were too high for me. "Are there some jeweler's shops here where I might get them cheaper?" I asked, trying to look innocent.

He laughed. "We have no shops here. Buyers from all over the world come right here to our offices, but I will be glad to send one of my men to your hotel room with a small collection from which you can make a choice and acquire it at wholesale price." He dismissed my thanks with a short "It is a pleasure," and on taking leave instructed a secretary to show me the mines. What I saw did not interest me very much: men were washing some dirty rocks on wire-netting trays.

After my lunch at the hotel, the man with the diamonds arrived and insisted on coming up to my room, where he locked the door behind him. Then, approaching a table, he began unbuttoning his trousers, to my great dismay. Suddenly he fished out a long plastic belt and flattened it on the table after modestly buttoning himself up again. This belt turned out to contain diamonds worth millions. The man began to spread out a number of small packets containing the precious stones, which were wrapped carefully in tissue paper. "These are one carat." In the next bundle were two carats, then three, four, five carats, the last packet containing nothing but ten-carat ones—very expensive, big diamonds. All were beautifully cut and of the best quality. This great treasure laid out before me inspired in me a rapid succession of criminal ideas. The man was small and looked rather weak and my eyes were suddenly attracted by a heavy poker hanging by the fireplace. I could kill him with one stroke of this poker, I thought, sizing him up, but what to do with the body? This was enough, I gave up the whole brilliant idea, but not without having to admire professional assassins who manage such situations so neatly.

I became again the polite prospective buyer. Examining the stones with great care and very much aware of how much I could afford, I finally chose an emerald-shaped seven-carat diamond of a beautiful quality. The price did not empty my pocket and the man told me it was about 20 percent of what one would pay in Bond Street. This allowed me to buy six one-carat diamonds which could adorn some nice earrings for Nela. I paid the man, and when he left I looked proudly at my acquisition. "At last, my belated wedding present," I said to myself.

My tour ended in Durban, the southernmost city. The town struck me as being quite different and very independent from the rest of South Africa. There was a large Hindu population that had a great influence much feared by the other inhabitants. I was impressed to learn that Mahatma Gandhi started out from Durban for his great campaign in India. The audience at my concert was nondescript but it was temperamentally more responsive than in the rest of the country.

My manager was well satisfied with the whole tour and offered me a return engagement two years later. He obtained for my journey home a first-class ticket on Imperial Airways, the British seaplanes. It was a most interesting trip; the plane took off from Cape Town and soon flew over the famous Kruger Park, the largest of the national parks for wild animals. The pilot made it possible for us to see it quite close up and it was fascinating to watch a stampede of hundreds of zebras and a herd of elephants wagging their ears; some giraffes tried to lift their heads higher to see the plane and a flock of ostriches fanned themselves with their feathers.

We stopped near Angola and, after a short flight, in Dar es Salaam—both devoid of interest. The third stop, as far as I remember, was Victoria Nyanza, the first contact with the Nile, with a beautiful view of the highest peaks in Africa. We spent the night in Khartoum, the capital of the Sudan, where the heat was so intense that the bathtub severely burned my posterior and my hands. My restaurant waiter informed me that this heat never subsides. I decided there and then not to return to that damn country. The Nile at Cairo, our next stop, felt like home and from there the Piraeus allowed me to give a loving glance at the Acropolis.

When we reached Brindisi, something very disagreeable happened: Italian policemen came on board and took our passports for examination. Since my angry gesture toward Mussolini, I was none too happy in these Italian waters, but became rather panic-stricken when the policemen brought back all the passengers' passports but mine. I was suddenly sure that they were going to arrest me! It took another half hour of agony before a policeman handed me my precious passport. I presume they asked authorities in Rome whether they should keep me and received a negative answer. When we took off for Marseilles, my final destination, I heaved an immense sigh of relief.

At the port, I saw a charming silhouette of a woman waving a white handkerchief. To my joy, it was Nela, who had come down from Deauville for the welcome. It was one of the nicest returns from a tour and we both felt exuberantly happy. She had a sleeper for Paris, leaving at midnight, and as I arrived late in the afternoon we had a few hours to spend in this gay city. After depositing my luggage at a hotel, we decided to have a jolly good dinner at a restaurant famous for its bouillabaisse. After ordering this favorite specialty I had a fine bottle of champagne uncorked and we sipped it happily until being served.

I had the diamonds hidden in my spectacles case because I knew they would be safer in my pocket than anywhere else. After drinking two glasses of the excellent cold champagne, I suddenly pulled the case out of my pocket and, holding it up to Nela, I asked her jokingly, "How much would you give me for this case?"

She answered nervously, "Arthur, don't drink any more. After this long trip the wine can easily go to your head."

I had another sip of champagne and insisted on my bid. Now she became scared. "You are drunk, let us go."

I put the case back into my pocket. "If you don't make me an offer, you won't have it." And I continued to enjoy my bouillabaisse and drink the wine. I was not drunk, just happy.

Later, when we entered the sleeper, I held out the case to her. "Never mind," I said, "you can have it anyway." Now she became curious, took out my glasses, and felt the hard bundles of tissue paper. "Look out," I said, "don't throw it on the floor." Now, at last, came the climax of our little game. After duly appreciating my little gift, she gave me my well-deserved hug and kiss.

Next day in Paris we went to Cartiers, where we decided on the appropriate platinum setting, and they also made a design for the earrings.

After a few days in Paris, Nela was anxious to return to the children and I was glad to see them. Laura Dubman and her mother were already in Deauville waiting to resume our lessons.

The villa which Germaine de Rothschild put at our disposal was situated between the charming little village of Pont l'Evêque (the cheese) and Deauville proper; it formed part of the Rothschild haras of racehorses. The children were in the care of a new French governess, Mademoiselle Yvonne. My mother-in-law decided to leave for her estate in Lithuania, but a few days later Nina Mlynarska, Nela's cousin, was a very welcome guest. She had a quick witty tongue; she was sometimes a little malicious but was altogether a charming person whom we all liked.

I had a baby grand Steinway sent from Paris and Laura Dubman came every afternoon for her lessons. In the mornings, I worked on the fresh repertoire for America. After my work was done, I used to walk to the casino and play a little chemin de fer, which I did more for the constitutional than for the gambling, as I could not really enjoy the game; however, I never liked to walk just for the sake of walking.

We all lived in a nervous state. Hitler's shrieking voice on the radio was constantly threatening Poland more and more violently and attacking France and England venomously for their alliance with Poland.

One day, Count August Zamoyski appeared in Deauville in his little car and his passenger was a huge dog who couldn't raise his head because the roof of the car was too low. The only person he met upon arrival was the children's governess, Mademoiselle Yvonne, a rather pretty person of a highly sensual disposition. After exchanging a few words, he took her off in his little car and she reappeared somewhat disheveled to serve the children their tea. The count was duly reprimanded by Nela but did not pay much attention.

Another visitor arrived from London, Jan Raue, the husband of Nela's sister Alina. He had been on business in England and brought from there alarming news: "The whole country thinks that war is inevitable." Nela's radio dominated life at the villa; we would listen in helpless fury to Hitler's shouting and we devoured the political news from all available newspapers.

Our great friends Anatole Mühlstein and his wife Diana (the daughter of Robert and Nelly de Rothschild), who were spending the summer in Deauville with their three little daughters, shared our great worry with us. He was a Polish diplomat who during the First World War, when merely an attaché, had remained in Brussels all through the German occupation and published a clandestine paper for the underground movement. He retired from the diplomatic service as counselor with the rank of minister. Now we were constantly in touch with each other. Anatole was always in communication with Warsaw and shared the latest news with me from hour to hour. France and England urged Poland not to move its armed forces while, as I learned from Mühlstein, the German tanks and artillery were surrounding practically the whole of Poland. It would have been plausible if these two countries had been mobilized but there was no sign of this.

I left for two days to play in Scheveningen, Holland. After a nice concert, there was a gay supper with my friends at which we heard the terrible news that von Ribbentrop had just gone to visit Stalin in Moscow, where they signed a secret document whereby Russia would not interfere in Hitler's military undertakings. This was a deathblow to the Allies. We sat suddenly with a somber vision of the future. The next day, I came back with the bad news.

A terrible gloom fell on this gay resort. Toward the middle of August the place suddenly became deserted and everyone returned to their homes. It seemed to me that we and the Mühlsteins were the only ones remaining; the sea air was good for our children.

Nina Mlynarska decided to return in a hurry to Warsaw. "Before anything starts," Jan Raue offered to accompany her back.

Well, one tragic unforgettable afternoon, the radio announced: "Poland has been attacked by Germany from three sides. The German air force has bombed Warsaw heavily at strategic points." This short message was followed by the A major Polonaise of Chopin conducted by Fitelberg and a strong declaration by the mayor of Warsaw that he would defend the city.

From that moment on, we followed the progress of the attack, our beating hearts full of anxiety and anger. The Poles defended themselves bravely wherever there was a chance. They resisted in a fort near Danzig for three weeks until they all fell without surrendering. The whole country fought with indomitable courage, waiting for the French and British counterattack, which, however, never came. The Parliament in both these countries heatedly discussed the pros and cons. They finally decided after four long days, which permitted Hitler to consolidate his gains, to declare war. But there was no sign of an attack.

I suddenly became frightfully nervous about my family. With the occupation of Poland, they must have been subjected to Hitler's terrible laws.

Now a worse blow came to poor Poland: Stalin, who had previously signed with Pilsudski a ten-year non-aggression pact between the two countries, now attacked Poland, treacherously crossing its eastern frontier. The rest of the retreating Polish Army, thinking that the Russians had come to their rescue, fell into this diabolical trap. The "brave" Russian Army occupied a long stretch of eastern Poland in a pushover, without losing a man. This was the end. The Polish government fled to Rumania, taking the country's treasury with them. Most of them later reached England.

Toward the end of September, Hitler overpowered the whole of Poland, which he held until the end of the war with an inhuman cruelty, but he did not interfere with the Russians. We witnessed the whole tragedy over the radio in the now windy, rainy, abandoned Deauville.

I remember one afternoon when the Mühlsteins, Nela, and I were watching the sea from the beach and I felt an irresistible urge to disappear in it. Nela and Anatole must have been aware of it, for they suddenly dragged me away from there.

Seven

World War II, Escape to Hollywood and My American Citizenship

101

We returned to Paris to make our plans. I had expected to see Paris at war—Paris which I so well remembered from 1914—but this time it was a completely different picture. There was no exodus; on the contrary, people were returning to town after their vacations. The only thing which reminded me of the last war was the blackout, but with the difference that night life was as active as ever. War bulletins were issued every morning and afternoon announcing shooting across the Maginot Line without loss of life, but pretending to have efficiently hit important targets. The first days of the war people showed a feverish interest in these bulletins. Heated arguments were exchanged in cafés and comments were made on the success of the day's shooting. However, reading for days the same kind of war bulletins without any progress on either side brought a growing indifference. A phrase in a newspaper describing this war as *"une drôle de guerre"* became a slogan adopted in the whole country and, soon afterward, everywhere else.

The attitude of my French friends and probably the rest of the country was that they had to sacrifice *"la pauvre Pologne"* and by declaring war on Hitler they would keep him at bay: "Nous ne pouvons pas risquer une guerre mondiale pour sauver Dantzig."

A trickle of refugees who were able to escape through Rumania began arriving in Paris. Mühlstein and I were happy to be of some help to them. The Polish Embassy, so friendly before, suddenly became hostile toward Jews. I commented on this new phase sarcastically: "Whenever a country suffers a political setback, the Jew right away becomes a scapegoat."

My first concerts in America were set for the middle of November. Due to the war, concerts in Europe were scarce. My only engagements for the beginning of October were two concerts in Amsterdam. I accepted them readily, planning to sail from Holland to America. I even secured reservations for the family on the lovely Dutch steamer *Nieuw Amsterdam*, feeling certain that it would not be attacked by submarines.

When the time came to leave, Nela suddenly became terribly nervous. "Even if a submarine doesn't sink the boat, they might get on board to take us with them as Polish citizens. The United States has sent a rescue boat for their citizens in France. I feel sure that Ambassador Bullitt will help us in every way." At first I was very much against it. It was not in my nature to run away. Giving the concerts in Amsterdam and leaving in a normal way on a regular steamship was more to my liking. Of course, I was due in America five weeks later, but I owed it to my family to take them away from a country at war, living in blackouts. But Nela insisted on leaving immediately; the American steamer *Washington* was already in Bordeaux; I had to give in.

We went to the American Embassy, where our friend Ambassador Bullitt received us very cordially, and after Nela had given him a long explanation of our case, he consented to provide us with the necessary visas on our now rather sad Polish passports and he gave orders for our passage to be arranged in the best possible way.

We were told to take little with us, a rather frustrating order; I had planned to take on the *Nieuw Amsterdam* our big wardrobe trunks with all I hated to leave behind. We packed a few suitcases with only the things we strictly needed but I felt a slight heartbreak leaving my beloved books, my precious volumes of music, and my lovely Picasso.

The night before leaving, Germaine came to say goodbye and, as before, offered us her large car to take us to the station; she even took care of ours during our absence.

We left for Bordeaux on a rainy day with the children and Mademoiselle Yvonne. Sophie Kochanska, who was going with us, joined us on the train. Bordeaux, which I admired for its beautiful opera and splendid restaurants, looked like a refugee camp. One heard nothing but exclamations of joy or surprise: "Where do *you* come from?" "I didn't know you were American!"

We too heard shouts: "Arturo, Nela!" Mrs. Estrella Boissevain was taking her mother to the ship. We had become friendly in Paris one night after going to some cabarets with her and Germaine Tailleferre. Toward four in the morning we had tried in vain to remember an aria from *Prince Igor*. Back home in Montmartre, I couldn't sleep, I had to find the aria. Finally at eight in the morning I cried, "I got it!" I was so enraged after the sleepless night that I got dressed, went to a flower shop, wrote on a card the first few bars of this wretched aria, and signed inelegantly: "Here is the aria, damn you!" After that, we became friends.

The other unexpected person in Bordeaux was my old friend Jeanne Blanchard, in whose house Ravel, Thibaud, and I used to dine, sup, and make music.

All this made up a rather picturesque departure. Of course, none of us took this *"drôle de guerre"* seriously, although the boat was inhumanly crammed, filled to three times its normal capacity. Some people were apprehensive about its weight. "We will sink in the open sea," they said.

Poor Nela was assigned a very large cabin which she had to share with Yvonne and our children, Sophie Kochanska, and another woman with a child.

As for myself, I was treated like a king, with an apartment-de-luxe consisting of two cabins and a bathroom between them. I was alone in mine but the other was occupied by three Catholic priests. It turned out to be a funny combination: Whether it was that I was a Jew and they didn't want to be contaminated by my presence, or that I was physically repellent to them, I don't know, but all through the journey they gave me no chance to lay eyes on them. They disappeared in the morning before I woke up and they were locked in before I went to sleep. The bathroom was never touched by them, so I used it regally all by myself.

The worst part of this trip was the mealtimes. Three services were necessary at breakfast, lunch, and dinner. My family and Sophie Kochanska were given the first service, probably thanks to Mr. Bullitt, but this privilege made us the most hated diners, thanks to our little Eva. Since she was three, she refused to swallow her food. She would settle a big piece of meat or fish or anything else in one cheek or the other and nothing would induce her to swallow it. This was torture for poor Yvonne, who had to sit with her all through the second service and sometimes well into the third. Even the commissary complained about this nuisance. Tomatoes were the only food which saved Eva's life; she simply adored them but they were not always available.

This ordeal lasted for a few more years. I remember once in Mexico that in desperation I screamed at the poor child, "Don't tell me you can't swallow it. One can swallow anything." With that, I tore a big piece off a newspaper and munched it painfully, succeeding in swallowing it in front of the flabbergasted, terrified girl.

102

Mr. Hurok received us at the dock very helpfully. He had reserved a very comfortable apartment at the Buckingham Hotel, which was unpretentious but splendidly situated. The Steinway building was next door to us and Carnegie Hall was practically opposite; Hurok's offices were within five minutes' walk.

We reached the hotel at teatime; I signed the register for all of us and we were shown our nice three-room apartment. Miss Yvonne and the children made themselves at home right away, when I suddenly realized that Nela had not come up with us. As she didn't appear for quite a while, I went down to the lobby to find her but neither the porter nor the receptionist had seen her anywhere. It was a mystery because she had clearly come in with us.

We lived a whole hour in a nervous state; it came to the point where I wanted to call the police, when there was finally a knock at the door. I rushed to open it and Nela entered escorted by two tall black men, each one carrying a huge crate. She was rather flushed and addressed me without any explanation: "Have you got your checkbook on you? I have to pay these men."

While I was filling out the check and signing it, the two men piled the table, chairs, and the floor with a full array of kitchen equipment—even an oven made its appearance—crockery and cutlery, a tablecloth and napkins. When they finished unloading, Nela took one man to the small kitchenette off the drawing room, where he finally emptied his crate, filling the icebox and the cupboards with food. When all was done, I handed them the check and they left.

Now came the climax: Nela announced: "Dinner will be ready in half an hour." The children and I were really speechless. Unbelievable as it sounds, the five of us were sitting happily around the dinner table within half an hour. The children had everything they liked best. There was a large tomato salad and ice cream, and I could enjoy my cigar with a good cup of coffee. This became the pattern of our longish stay at this hotel.

I had more than a month before I started my actual tour, which gave me ample time to attend concerts, theaters, and movies.

Jan Kiepura, a famous Polish tenor, wanted to give a concert for the Polish refugees. I immediately wanted to join him. Hurok obtained the Metropolitan Opera House for it and Kiepura and I each performed two parts of the program; he arranged it so that before intermission he was the last to sing with his accompanist and in the second part the end was for me. I played, of course, nothing but Chopin. The Opera House was filled and seats were at high prices. There was great enthusiasm for both of us but mainly for the cause.

One morning, I had a call from Philadelphia. A gentleman introducing himself as Mr. Fred Mann told me a long story about a dinner he was going to give for the benefit of the newborn Israeli Orchestra. "Professor Einstein, the famous scientist, will be present at my table of honor. I have three hundred guests at fifty dollars a head. I know you are a friend of Hubermann, so I feel sure you will play one or two pieces after my dinner." He was very shrewd, that Mann, I thought. He knew that bringing in the names of Professor Einstein, Hubermann, and the Israeli Orchestra would make it impossible for me to refuse to do something which I have never done before or since. After a friend from Philadelphia had confirmed that the dinner would actually take place as he said, I accepted.

We arrived in Philadelphia an hour before the dinner. At the Warwick Hotel, where we had to change, a young man in his early thirties was expecting us in an apartment-de-luxe which he had reserved for the few hours of our stay. "I am pleased to meet you, I am sure," he said, giving me a little trinket which turned out to be a lovely little pocket watch of a modern Swiss make. "You will be glad to see my party. I got all the rich people of Philadelphia and you will sit next to my wife with Professor Einstein and myself at the table of honor. I hired Leonard Liebling, the editor of *Musical America*, to make a big speech on the Israeli Orchestra." I became quite pale; with my famous elephant's memory I had never forgotten his dishonest card game and the IOU's he had kept. I told Mr. Mann that I couldn't tolerate this man appearing at his dinner.

After hearing my story he used some nasty adjectives and left right away to get rid of Liebling. I liked this quick action, and when we were ready, Nela and I followed Mr. Mann cheerfully into the ballroom, where the many tables were already occupied.

At ours we found Mrs. Mann talking to Professor Einstein. When we were introduced to the great man, a photographer asked the professor if he would pose with me. "Of course," he said with a charming smile. I have kept this photograph up to this late day and the fun of the picture is that my serious deferential face has the air of a deep-thinking philosopher and his long hair and broad smile make him resemble a German café fiddler.

The Professor was seated next to my wife, and the beautiful Mrs. Mann had me on her right. Mann himself as the host was constantly busy and slightly nervous before his introductory speech, which he had to improvise.

The Manns were both of a very expansive nature and made us feel as though they were our best friends by the end of the dinner. Professor Einstein declared he was too shy to make a speech but was very interested in hearing me play. Knowing that he was a passionate amateur violinist, I played for his benefit the Chaconne of Bach arranged by Busoni, which apparently pleased him very much, and afterward I couldn't do less than play the Polonaise for the benefit of the rich diners. Fred Mann was delighted with the success of his dinner and we returned that same night to New York.

It was interesting to hear recitals by Rachmaninoff and Hofmann again. These two great pianists were reaching the end of their careers and their lives. I had heard them at the peak of their celebrity. Hofmann used to amaze me with his concentrated power and his iron-clad dynamics and he easily gave the impression of a great performance. Therefore it was contradictory to hear him speak of music with utter indifference and lack of interest in its progress. Now at this concert late in his career, when he had lost his aforementioned powers due to his unfortunate addiction to alcohol, his playing was devoid of any sincere musical feeling.

Rachmaninoff's performance gave me quite the opposite impression. In his earlier concerts I was always under the spell of his glorious and inimitable tone, which could make me forget my uneasiness about his too rapidly fleeting fingers and his exaggerated rubatos. There was always the irresistible sensuous charm, not unlike Kreisler's. Both were at their best in their own compositions, which were often too dependent on their sensuality. In this last concert I heard a more pure approach to music. It was evident that one was breathing a fresh musical air. The tempi were right and there was the due respect for the intentions of the composers. I remember particularly a nocturne and two études of Chopin. It was fascinating to realize that when their race for careers and their fear of rivals came to an end, they showed their basic personality.

The Tchaikovsky concerto played by Horowitz and conducted by Toscanini was issued. When I bought a copy, I was amazed that not only were conductor and soloist not in accord, but the record as such was technically defective. My opinion was shared by everybody I met and I was glad to hear that they also stated their great preference for my own record with Barbirolli. But the whole matter became a subject of great annoyance to me. I heard from many different quarters that people were told in record shops that my record had been withdrawn and the Horowitz version was the only one on the market. Highly alarmed, I went to the RCA office and protested rather angrily. The head of the classical record department said with a false smile, "Your master recording is broken."

This was too much for me. "You must have broken it yourself," I shouted. "I shall complain about it."

David Sarnoff, the famous creator of the RCA complex, felt very friendly toward us; he and his wife had dined with us at the Pavillon. So I was prepared to ask him directly to relieve me of the contract I had with the Victor Company, which was owned by RCA. My decision was prompted by the offer of a splendid contract from Goddard Lieberson, the president of Columbia Records.

Samuel Chotzinoff, who was Heifetz's brother-in-law and the right hand of David Sarnoff, was the man I approached about a meeting with his boss. When I told him what it was about, he gave me a strong warning: "Mr. Sarnoff hates to hear complaints about any of his staff."

"Never mind," I answered. "Please make an appointment anyway." Two or three days later, I received a message to be at Mr. Sarnoff's office at 11 a.m. on such and such day.

At 30 Rockefeller Center an express elevator took me to the fifty-second floor, where I was shown to the private office of this very powerful person. I entered with the friendly smile of a good acquaintance, and he received me very politely but with a set expression. "Be seated," he said. It amused me to realize that he seemed afraid I was going to ask him to lend me a large sum of money. "What can I do for you?" he asked sternly from behind his desk.

I made a humble face. "I came to ask you a very great favor," I said timidly. His face became somber. He probably thought that I wanted twice as much as he had assumed. "Well," he said, "I can't promise you anything."

"It really is a great favor, Mr. Sarnoff, but you are the only man who can grant it." Now he became impatient. I felt he was prepared to refuse me any impossible amount.

"Could you please relieve me of my contract with your Victor Record Company?"

He seemed not to understand what I was saying. "Why? Why?" He suddenly became excited.

"That is unimportant," I replied calmly. "I only ask you to free me from my contract."

"You mean you would go to Columbia?"

"Of course," I said.

He became a little nervous. "If I allowed all my artists to go, I would be out of business."

"Now, now, Mr. Sarnoff," I said soothingly, "this is a small matter for you, but for me, one of the utmost importance."

The friendly smile of a dinner party came back to his face. "You must have very good reasons for wanting to leave my company, which is better than Columbia, so tell me what they are."

I did not give in. "I hate to complain," I said, "and all I want is to leave your company."

Now he asked me with urgency, "Arthur, write me in a letter anything you have against my company—I must know it—and give me all the details. Then I shall decide whether to grant your request."

"I shall certainly do as you wish," I said. That was the end of our interview.

Returning to the hotel, I wrote in less than ten minutes all I had to say about the way Mr. O'Connor made records and the whole case of the Tchaikovsky concerto, including the suppression of my most successful record. I sent it immediately.

After the dinner in Philadelphia for the Israeli Orchestra, Fred Mann became a frequent visitor at our hotel room. He would bring toys for our children and sit down for long talks about his life. "I am a businessman," he said, "but my heart is in music. I was on my way to becoming a concert pianist when something happened to my hand which shattered my hopes, but I still practice and play whenever I have the time to."

The beautiful Mrs. Mann was his second wife. "I used to work for my ex-father-in-law in his cardboard-box factory. As I made no headway there, I decided to set up on my own. I found a partner and began to do very well."

While listening to his stories, I sized him up as a dynamic businessman and what I liked best about him was his deep attachment to his Jewishness. His parents were Russian immigrants. He had three younger sisters and a brother and he himself was the father of three daughters and it became evident that he had them all in his care. With all this, he was passionately interested in affairs of music, especially in the pianistic world with its concert and managerial problems.

My difficulties with the RCA Victor Company irritated him beyond measure. He went so far as to give poor O'Connor a sharp talking to and intervened in the whole matter. Being of an impetuous nature, he would have talks with Lieberson about obtaining me for Columbia at a high price. At another moment, he would threaten RCA with their losing me to Columbia if they did not give me full satisfaction. In spite of him, great things began to happen at RCA. Mr. Sarnoff gave orders to dismiss a few important men in the classical record department, among them O'Connor, and there was a threat that other dismissals would follow.

Apropos, there is a funny scene to relate: One afternoon, I was sitting at the piano in our hotel room while Nela remained in the adjoining bedroom. The telephone rang and announced the visit of a vice-president of RCA Victor. After I asked him to come up, a little man came in with open arms and a broad smile. "Arthur, it is good to see you again [I had never met him before]. I am so happy," he continued, "to have gotten rid of that dreadful O'Connor for you. Now I have a wonderful colleague who will be happy to make records again. Can I ask her up?"

"Of course," I said curtly.

A minute or so later, a voluptuous young woman, with an unexpected décolleté for the time of day, entered the room. "She is an excellent musician too," the man said, introducing her with a slight wink. We were just about to sit down when my wife came in. After giving the lady a look fit to kill, she said, "My husband is accustomed to being assisted by men when making his records."

"My wife is right," I added. "Recording is exhausting work, not fit for delicate ladies." They took the hint and departed hastily.

The dismissals at the RCA office soon included that man too, and a brand-new team was set up, chosen personally by Mr. Sarnoff. My Tchaikovsky concerto with John Barbirolli reappeared gloriously in the shops.

Fred Mann would not stop at that. If RCA promised to give my records the right attention and respect, he would persuade me not to leave them for Columbia. As a matter of fact, as soon as the new team was set up, I wouldn't have dreamed of changing. Incidentally, RCA began to use Fred Mann's cardboard boxes.

Mr. John Pfeiffer, my new record producer, telephoned one morning: "My company has decided to compensate you for the moral and financial damage it caused with your Tchaikovsky concerto and offers to make a record of the Grieg concerto with Ormandy and the Philadelphia Orchestra. You can be sure that the sale of such a combination will by far surpass everything else." I listened to this rather coldly; this concerto had been rather disdained by the musical circle of my early Berlin days and I was greatly influenced by that, so my answer was negative. They persisted stubbornly with their idea and went as far as to ask my wife to persuade me. Nela responded by buying the piano score and putting it open on my music stand. By sheer curiosity, seeing it for the first time in print, I ran through the whole work and found, to my surprise, that it was easy and lovable.

The RCA people were delighted. The date for the recording was set for three days hence. "We have no other date, but you can read it from the score," they said. However, I learned it rapidly and played it by heart. They were right; the Grieg recording had a sensational sale. Years later, I made a stereo recording of it with Alfred Wallenstein which was for a long time a favorite among collectors. The immense popularity of the Grieg concerto never lessened in the United States.

My tour in North America during the season 1939–40 was much more extensive than the previous ones and I was kept constantly on the road. It is intentional that I do not give details of my tours; I shall, as I have promised, write about music and musicians and my feelings and convictions about them, but in my opinion, writing about each individual concert has no place here. They are an intimate exchange between interpreter and public.

At Christmas time, Mr. Theodore Steinway, head of the famous piano firm and a warmhearted gentleman, honored me with an invitation to be the guest of honor at the yearly luncheon he was giving for his main employees and craftsmen. "Paderewski has been our only guest before you," he said to me.

It was a large affair. One table was occupied by ten or twelve old men who wore golden badges—the men who had worked for the firm for fifty years. During drinks, Mr. Steinway introduced me to his most important workers. "This man is in charge of the pedals and this man here is master of the keyboards." Another supervised the strings; the quality of the woods was in the hands of three men, the metallic soundboard had its own specialist, and then came the men from the office, publicity, the cashiers, the correspondence clerks, and others.

At the end of the meal, when champagne was served, Mr. Steinway proposed a toast to me, praising in high terms my pianistic merits, attributing other gifts to me, and ending with a flourish. The moment came for my reply. I began by saying that all through Mr. Steinway's speech, I wanted to hide under the table with shame. Then I pointed at the different individuals I had met earlier. "Here is the great master of the keyboard, these gentlemen choose the perfect woods, and we owe the finest soundboards to that gentleman over there." After expressing my gratitude and my admiration for these builders of the wonderful Steinway pianos, I wrung my hands in despair and exclaimed, "And what do I do? Ruin them!"

103

In April, still on tour, I read about Hitler's shocking occupation of Denmark and a few days later we learned that this provided him with a springboard to Norway. There, however, he met strong opposition from English troops and their navy as well as some French forces. The whole of the United States followed with awe the progress of this long battle for supremacy. The Norwegians themselves fought bravely in defense of their land but were shamefully betrayed by their leader, Quisling, who, like Judas, will always remain the symbol of treason.

One morning at Hurok's office I learned that the Ballet de Monte Carlo would tour South America during the summer of 1940. "Mrs. Hurok and I are sailing with them," he said, "and I could arrange a tour for you, too."

"Uh-uh. South America is my own domain and my managers in these countries still live on small percentages." But then and there, I decided I would go too. Attracted by this trip, Ruth Draper also arranged a tour for herself.

We all were looking forward to it when some more dangerous news came from Europe. Hitler had attacked Holland, Germany's quiet, neutral neighbor, with a savagery never heard of before. At the same time, he overpowered half of Belgium including Brussels. We were suddenly horribly terrified by this man who was blindly obeyed and worshipped by all the Germans and whose powerful and efficient army and air force had not yet encountered any serious resistance. But we still had high hopes that the French, the English, and the rest of the Belgian Army would counterattack.

Imagine our dismay when the Belgian Army surrendered, leaving the French and English in a tragic situation, fighting back heroically near the last port which remained free. I shall not attempt to describe what the brave and fantastic retreat from Dunkirk represented, but I know that it will remain unforgotten by many generations to come. Comfortably embarked with the children and their French governess on a pleasant American steamer, we lived day and night in suspense, having the news blared out daily over a loudspeaker.

Besides the Ballet de Monte Carlo with its conductor, Efrem Kurtz, Hurok and his wife, Ruth Draper, and other interesting persons, we had a famous French professor of art, Henri Focillon. He was a strangely misshapen man; a slight hunchback made him bow his head to the right and he had thinning white hair. My description of him does not sound engaging but I must assure my readers that there was no greater charmer to be found; as soon as one came in contact with this fascinating man, one fell in love with him. He, like the rest of us, found the latest news from the front terribly disquieting.

After the first few days at sea, the news became highly alarming. The bulk of the German Army had crossed the Belgian frontier into France and was progressing rapidly toward Sedan in exactly the same way as General von Kluck had in 1914. This time it found a weak defense because the French had expected the enemy to attack them on the eastern front, counting mostly on the Maginot Line. Day after day we followed the relentless advance of the Germans with deep despair. Poor Professor Focillon, who followed the events completely frustrated, allowed himself a few short moments of relief when the loudspeaker would announce some line of French defense here and there.

All through these tragic days, life on board was as gay as on any other sea voyage because the Ballet de Monte Carlo, which had succeeded the Diaghilev Ballet, was international and was more preoccupied with its own little problems than with the European battlefields. Even Hurok and his wife kept aloof from the events and so nightly the dinner dancing was attended by the exuberant ballet dancers enjoying their free time to the fullest.

We arrived in Rio on the ominous date of June 10; Paris was taken by the Nazis. Poor Focillon was in turn brooding and crying. He was deeply affected by the rapid defeat of the victorious French Army of 1918. For me it was the end of the world. I immediately imagined the Nazis in my house, the Jews pursued and treated as in Germany and all of Europe in Hitler's hands. An additional little shock was the so well-timed attack by the treacherous Mussolini on Nice.

All our companions continued toward Buenos Aires, but we had to stay in Brazil for some concerts before joining them.

It was a touching surprise to find in Rio some of our best friends from Warsaw. We had them all for dinner—Tuwim and his wife, Lechon, Casimir Wierzynski, a romantic poet, and a Prince Czartoryski. We had a bitter laugh sitting around the table, as though in Warsaw on a happy day in the recent past. Our friends gave us terrifying details of the invasion of Poland and of the dangers and difficulties they had to endure before arriving in Rio. The hot Brazilian climate disagreed with them and they were determined to go to New York in spite of having to face great difficulties over immigration. We promised to do our best to help them.

The concerts went well because the only relief from my gloom was practice. I had many concerts in the provinces, north, west, and south of Rio and São Paulo, happy to be alone in the midst of my moral despondency.

On one of my returns to Rio, a young man, whom I knew quite well from previous visits, insisted on taking me to a painter whom he considered the greatest Brazilian artist, one of the greatest in the world, he thought, urging me to see his paintings. Giving little credit to either his intelligence or his taste in art, I resisted for some time, but one day he simply forced us to accompany him to see the artist, whose name was Candido Portinari.

In the entrance hall of a small villa, a lame little man was telephoning and did not interrupt his talk. Our companion took us silently upstairs. In the first room some engravings which were scattered on a table caught our eye and they certainly proved, as we looked at them one by one, to be works of a master.

"His paintings are in the next room," said our friend, and there hung a most original collection of large paintings showing scenes and aspects of the life of Brazilian Negroes. They all reflected a most original treatment of their subjects and seemed to be imbued with the hot sun of their country; blues were prominent and beautiful.

Both Nela and I fell under the spell of this Portinari, the little lame man, who now came into the room. He broke into a broad smile seeing the expression on our faces. "Ah," he exclaimed, "I have always wanted to meet you. I love your playing and, you know, I was born in a little town called Brodowski, the name of the man who discovered it." He bubbled over like that for quite a while.

"How I would love to paint you," he said. "Would you sit for me?" We agreed after he had shown us some excellent portraits of two well-known poets and we soon became close friends. He attended my next concerts and we spent several evenings with him.

When he saw my children, he insisted on painting them right away and made two very original sketches of them which became quite well known and provided him with not a few commissions by people who wanted similar portraits of their children. Before we left, he painted Nela and me too.

In Argentina, life asserted itself again. Ruiz rented a charming ground-floor apartment for us in Buenos Aires, which was let for the season by a wealthy bachelor. Here we often had the Huroks, Ruth Draper, and the Focillons for lunch, and we even gave a large party for the ballet.

A surprising telegram arrived from Nelson Rockefeller, who was then secretary for Latin American affairs, asking me to give a concert at the Museum of Modern Art in New York to honor Portinari at his one-man exhibition there. He asked me to give a program with works of Villa-Lobos. I was more than pleased to be of use to two great artists who happened to be dear friends of mine, but it meant also working solidly at the *Rudepoêma* of Villa-Lobos, which I hadn't played for quite a while.

We attended some beautiful performances of the Ballet de Monte Carlo, saw the famous flamenco dancer Carmen Amaya, and were present at the debut of a young couple called "Los Chavalillos." This Antonio and his cousin Rosario, both in their teens, were by far the best Spanish dancers I had ever seen. Antonio later became world-famous. Carmen Amaya was a woman with a wild temperament who invariably made the combs fall out of her hair. Actually Hurok made one of the big mistakes of his life when he engaged Amaya, proclaiming that she would become a sensation in the United States. He then produced her with much publicity and a big show but without great success. He ended up placing her in various nightclubs. Antonio, as I write this, is still a star.

My first concert at the Colón, which was a matinee, was a most moving occasion. During the intermission, dozens of familiar faces from Warsaw, Lodz, and other Polish cities, all of them fleeing Hitler's occupation, came as usual to greet me, but a heartbreaking scene ensued. Many of the people in the audience had not known of one another's presence in Buenos Aires. Suddenly there was a lot of calling out, crying, hugging, and some found relatives they had given up for lost and others discovered their best friends. I suppose none of them returned to their seats after intermission, but I was gratified that it was my concert which brought them together. By my next visit, some of them had become prominent in their fields and were highly respected, well-to-do citizens of their new country.

The music lovers in both Brazil and Argentina were very excited by the visit of Toscanini and his NBC Orchestra and Stokowski with his youth orchestra. Both these men impressed more by their great personalities than by the merits of their orchestras. My general impression during these nerve-racking times was that Argentina, in spite of her German-trained army, was on the side of France, whereas Brazil made me unhappy by a certain indifference toward the European tragedy.

About a week before returning to New York, Eva contracted chicken pox. It was a slight case, but when we embarked she still had some pockmarks and got on the boat hiding behind the large bulk of our friend Nena Salamanca. Everything went well until the second day on board, when Paul showed the same symptoms. Dealing with his case we made a big mistake: Our French governess, Yvonne, who feared a possible quarantine, did not report his case to the ship's doctor but instead got friendly with the nurse and persuaded her to leave the doctor out of it. Paul was kept in the cabin during the whole trip and we closed our eyes to this rather illicit procedure. As a matter of fact, Paul did better than Eva, and when we reached New York, he was on his feet again. Unfortunately, however, he too was left with some rather visible pockmarks.

Now a little drama ensued. Before passengers were allowed to disembark, doctors came to examine them and after that one had to face passport control. While waiting for our turn, a man approached Nela and asked her to follow him. I felt right away something was wrong. Poor Nela had to face both the ship's doctor and the local health inspector. Apparently a passenger had denounced us for hiding a case of smallpox, noticing the constant absence of our boy, whom he had seen embarking with us.

Nela's excuse for not notifying the ship's doctor was that it was quite evident Paul had only a slight case of chicken pox, but the doctors announced sternly that they would keep both children for a prolonged quarantine on Ellis Island. They had some harsh words of criticism for Nela.

We went through passport control and, instead of being allowed to collect our luggage the other side, we were taken to Ellis Island under the pretext of showing us where the children would spend their quarantine. Little Paul had hysterics and clung to his mother, crying desperately, but my Eva became very maternal. "Don't worry. I will look after him," she said. When we were about to leave, a policeman told us to follow him and led us into a large room where immigrants who did not have permission to land were detained until they were cleared or refused entry. We heard the big door bolted after us and we were actually imprisoned.

This hall was a dreadful place. Miserable, unclean, and unhealthy people were constantly wandering around. A telephone booth was besieged and I had a hard time getting hold of Hurok, who was very disturbed but promised to get our release from Washington.

In my unhappy mood, I suddenly saw an upright piano in a corner of the huge room. I made a dash for it, opened the lid, took hold of the piano stool, and started working at the *Rudepoêma* of Villa-Lobos. Nobody paid any attention; they all talked and rushed around as before. While completely oblivious to my surroundings I practiced hard at the difficult passages of this long work.

Toward evening we were led to a prison dining room with the usual long tables and benches and offered a shamefully disgusting meal, which we refused to touch. Back in the big hall, women and men were rudely separated. I saw Nela and Yvonne disappear without being allowed to say good night to them and I found myself in a little room with four bunks and three rather repulsive roommates. I tried to sleep with my clothes on but could close my eyes only toward morning.

They offered us for breakfast some foul eggs which I could not swallow, after which two armed policemen led us to a courtyard where men and women were asked separately to walk around in pairs. At noon, out of nowhere, I saw Richard Ordynski of all people. "You poor fellow, you are in prison too," I shouted.

"No," he answered calmly. "Hurok entrusted me with your release papers but before we leave you must promise me something. I need help and would like to become your secretary." Of course I promised; I would have promised anything to get out of there. He obtained permission for us to visit our children and we were terribly afraid of finding them in a state of deep depression, but when we entered their corridor, we heard happy screams and laughter, easily recognizable as theirs. They had the whole hospital in their pockets and seemed to be greatly enjoying their stay.

The Ellis Island incident left me with bitter feelings for the American immigration department. I resented the fact that unhappy human beings who risked prison or death in their old countries and tried to enter one which boasted of its liberty, were subjected to a most degrading treatment for the only reason that they were not in possession of the right papers. Our own case was a silly mistake. The doctors thought our son had smallpox, whereas he had simple chicken pox, which had run its course before we reached port.

104

Finally back at the Buckingham Hotel, we decided to rent a little house on East Forty-eighth Street which belonged to a complex called Turtle Bay. It was pleasant for the children, who had a charming garden for a playground.

Refugees from the European continent, which was now almost completely occupied by the Germans, arrived in ever-increasing numbers. It was pathetic to learn that Edouard and Germaine had been forced to leave Paris precipitately, leaving everything behind; this first flight of their lives was the still much-feared stretch from Lisbon to New York. They stayed at the Gladstone Hotel, as they were unable to bring much money with them. We had dinner with them at this dreary hotel, at which the Baron Edouard showed what a grand seigneur he was. All through the meal, he behaved as if we were sitting at his royal palace in the rue St. Florentin, but his wife confided what a hard time he had dressing and shaving without the help of his valet.

Nela invited them to her box for my next concert at Carnegie Hall and a charming incident took place: At a party given by the Rothschilds in Paris, Nela had much admired Germaine's dress. "It would give me great pleasure to offer it to you, as I feel that it is too young for me," said the baroness. Nela accepted delightedly but had no occasion to wear it. Now in New York, Germaine said, "Unfortunately I cannot accept your invitation, chérie, as I have nothing to put on."

Nela suddenly remembered. "But yes, you have a beautiful dress—your own!" A nice story of a good deed compensated.

Here is another picturesque aspect of this family: My friend the cellist Gregor Piatigorsky, who had married Edouard and Germaine de Rothschild's daughter Jacqueline, had left Europe for New York before us; we went to visit them at the Hotel Pierre, where they had a beautiful apartment. Great was my astonishment when Jacqueline entered their drawing room with a bassoon in her hand and, after greeting us, began to play a tune on it. "In case the Rothschilds lose all their fortunes, I decided to make my living playing the bassoon. I found out that this is the instrument most in demand in America." We laughed but had to admit that she already played it rather well.

Hurok compiled an exceptionally large number of concerts for this season. "Europe cannot send us pianists anymore," he said with a malicious smile, "so we have the whole country to ourselves." I did not like his sally because it touched a tragedy of which I became more and more aware. The arrival of refugees from Europe came practically to a standstill. All possible exits were sealed off and I was terribly worried about my family.

Hitler's cruel treatment of the Jews in all the countries which he occupied became known, so it was rather surprising to see my niece Marila Landau and her brother Jan in New York. My niece, who had been twice married and twice divorced, had been living in Brussels until the war broke out. She fled to Lisbon, like so many others, to find a visa for any of the countries across the ocean. She found her way to Bogotá, Colombia, where she ran a successful millinery shop. The war had surprised her brother in Lodz, where he owned a textile factory. He escaped in his big car to Sweden, where he picked up his wife and his child and managed in Lisbon to join his sister on the flight to Colombia. He, too, did quite well in Bogotá, establishing a textile factory there.

Both brother and sister felt unhappy to be away from the great centers and craved New York. Crafty as they were, they soon succeeded in getting there and were happy to find me financially well established. From that moment on, I could be of great use to them. Marila was able to find a job in the millinery department of Saks Fifth Avenue, where she stayed for quite a few years.

Another arrival in New York made us very happy. Thanks to Fred Mann's connection with a Jewish immigration committee, we succeeded in obtaining visas for Juljan Tuwim (the great Polish poet) and for his wife and cousin. The night they disembarked, we gave a lovely party of welcome for them. Jan Lechon, the poet, our other friend whom we had seen in Brazil, also found his way to New York, thanks to some Poles. Their presence, together with Anatole Mühlstein, enriched my life considerably; I found wonderful men to talk to again.

The concert at the Museum of Modern Art was a great success. Both Portinari and Villa-Lobos became names in the United States. The

Rudepoêma impressed the public with its savage impact, its content, and its length. At the same concert, another work was performed which pleased and astonished the listeners; it was a *choros* (a kind of serenade) for twenty cellos.

My concert tour of that year was the most successful one yet, in terms of both the reception by my public and the sold-out houses. It was the beginning of a great career which continued without hindrance until my last concert at Carnegie Hall in March 1976 at the age of eighty-nine. My tour covered practically all the United States and Canada from Montreal to Vancouver. My wife accompanied me for the first concerts but had to give it up when Yvonne declared that she must return to her country. The South of France was still under the Pétain regime, so she could return safely.

The war against Hitler was waged now by England alone. Hitler did not dare to attack the British island in force, but his air force made a terrifying onslaught with day and night attacks, bombing and destroying large parts of London and many other great cities. The Royal Air Force counterattacked ferociously and the whole British population stood up grimly and bravely in defense of their country.

We exiles in America were greatly in awe of and full of admiration for the brave British people and felt acutely that the United States should come to the rescue. President Franklin Roosevelt stated often, in clear terms, his disapproval of Hitler and deep sympathy for England. He allowed American citizens to join the Canadian Army and Air Force but he feared a strong opposition to an actual declaration of war. A powerful body of Americans joined in protest against any American interference in the war, calling their organization America First. Their ranks were augmented daily by important men in politics—not the least, Charles Lindbergh, the hero of the first solo transatlantic flight. They showed pro-German sympathy and naturally made anti-Semitic declarations. Many Americans of German descent were obviously impressed by and even exultant about Hitler's victories. When Hitler attacked Russia, Roosevelt came to her aid by giving orders to send arms of all kinds. Every day, ships unloaded this precious cargo at the northern port of Archangelsk.

For the spring, Hurok proposed a concert in Hawaii after Los Angeles and San Francisco. I liked the idea, the names Hawaii and Honolulu having always attracted me. Our stay in Honolulu was very charming, but I could not help feeling the whole time as though playing a role in a movie. The exaggerated welcome at the port where native girls in their grass skirts forced around your neck the beautiful leis (the local garlands imposed on every passenger upon arrival); the constant shouts of "aloha," their word for welcome, sounding slightly shrill to our ears—but all in all, it was a good show. We had a nice hotel in the local style, right on the beach. We were introduced to the real taste of pineapples, the fruit this island is very proud of. We were also offered dances by some native girls who would certainly not have been used by any serious American producer. It was good to know that this important job was still in the hands of the pretty American girls.

The show for our departure was even greater than for our arrival. The leis which we dutifully threw into the sea with large gestures promised our return to these fairy islands. The steamer brought us back to San Francisco early in the morning. Our plan was to go to Los Angeles to rent a house there for the summer on our way back to New York. The whole day had to be spent in San Francisco because our train, *The Lark*, was leaving at midnight.

It was a strange day, all right. After a nice breakfast at the St. Francis Hotel, and having nothing else to do, we decided to go to a cinema where they were showing two full-length films. The three-hour show whetted our appetites for more. We had a rapid bite at a coffee shop and hurried to be on time for the next long session at a large cinema. The show, which lasted almost four hours, did not satisfy us; on the way out we saw a new successful picture announced and we rushed to see it. It became late dinnertime. We were not hungry, a quick bite was sufficient, and we dashed to see a movie we had read about in the paper. This picture was the longest of them all; it was a fantastic thriller. A tragic moment arrived: we had to leave before the end or we would miss our train. A terrible inner fight ensued: should we see the end of the story and stay for another twenty-four hours in San Francisco, or take the train? In despair, we chose the latter and spent the gloomy night in a sleeper speculating "who dunnit." I venture to think that we beat the record for one day's movie attendance.

We found a nice house in Brentwood, a residential area of Greater Los Angeles; it had a swimming pool, a large terrace overlooking the garden, and a big playroom with a billiard table in the basement. We rented it for the summer and left for New York to bring the good news to the children.

A new world opened to me at a dinner given by Alfred and Blanche Knopf. During that evening, I was in my most talkative mood and never stopped telling anecdotes and adventures of my life. The Knopfs seemed to be thrilled. "Arthur," Alfred exclaimed, "you must write it all down. You could make a brilliant book of it."

I laughed. "I am too lazy to write letters and you expect me to write a book!" They both suddenly became quite serious. "Don't take it lightly," said Blanche. "We feel that you can do it. If you write down the stories you have told tonight, it would make interesting reading."

"Do come tomorrow to my office," said Alfred persuasively, "and we can sign a contract." His offer did something to me. My passion for books often gave me a burning impulse to write. I shall not try the patience of my readers any longer—I accepted. The next day, when we signed up, Alfred handed me two hundred and fifty dollars. "This is your retainer, it makes our contract legal." With this document and the money in my pocket, I could hardly wait to begin writing.

Ernesto de Quesada invited me to Mexico City for a few concerts. Ordinarily, I would have refused the offer, but somehow I felt that I could begin writing undisturbed in this faraway capital and, as a matter of fact, I spent the first night there feverishly scribbling the opening pages. My concerts on that visit took second place; I was writing in every spare moment.

One night, after a concert, a Polish refugee gave me some important information. "We Poles now have a chance to enter the United States as immigrants. As the emigration from Poland has stopped completely due to the war, the American authorities have opened a new list for the Polish refugees. This is a great chance for us because normally we would have had to wait five years."

I was very impressed by this news and decided to act straightaway. I learned the next day at the American consulate that my Polish informant was right. The only condition was that I had to enter the United States accompanied by my family. I sent a telegram to Nela, telling her to come right away with the children. She arrived with Mrs. Fred Mann, who was pregnant but insisted on accompanying my family. In spite of some difficulties on the Mexican frontier, as they had no visas, with my help they finally landed safely in Mexico City. These were busy days for me with concerts, writing the book, and filling in endless forms for the American consulate. Fred Mann appeared in person two days after his wife, so on top of my other activities I had to act as guide and interpreter for them.

Finally the day came when we passed the American frontier with papers showing our intention to become American citizens, which was to happen five years later.

Soon after, we settled in the house, called Carmelina, in Brentwood, California. We loved it. Basil and Ouida Rathbone gave a lavish party in our honor, Ouida proving to be the most extravagant hostess I had ever known. At the entrance of their beautiful house in Bel Air, a butler would receive one with a large dish of caviar with the accompanying drinks. All the famous actors and producers of Hollywood were their guests. Two photographers were busy taking snapshots of different groups of us. In the dining room, the center table, seating about forty people, was covered with the most elaborate flower decorations and there were smaller tables for the rest of the guests. Two huge silver candelabra, each with twenty candles, illuminated the room. That was the evening we met Charlie Chaplin, Charles Laughton, Bette Davis, Leslie Howard, Rex Harrison, Ethel Barrymore, Nigel Bruce, Merle Oberon, Hitchcock, Errol Flynn, and Marlene Dietrich. I also was delighted to find Charles Boyer, my old friend from Paris, who had married a charming Scottish actress.

Later at a small dinner in Charles Boyer's house, I met Ronald Colman, whose beautiful cello voice and splendid acting had fascinated Paul Kochanski and me. "Whenever you appeared in a movie we would rush to see you," I told him. He was delighted to hear it. "This is quite a coincidence, because my wife, Benita Hume, who met and heard you in London, promised to introduce me to you one day." Nela and I wholeheartedly joined this brilliant English group.

At the same time, Charles Boyer introduced us to the French Hollywood colony. We found at his house Jean Renoir, eldest son of the famous painter and a fine film director, René Clair, one of the greats of the cinema, the actors Jean-Pierre Aumont and Marcel Dalio, and the brilliant author Jacques Deval.

After being so warmly introduced to all these people by the Rathbones and the Boyers, we decided to give a party in our new home, which lent itself to entertaining comfortably. Lola Kaper, whom we asked for information about caterers, wine merchants, and rental of tables and chairs, answered simply, "I shall send you someone who can do all that for you."

A dark-haired, fattish woman wearing glasses and of German extraction came to help us with the party. She looked slightly forbidding, but it took less than ten minutes to discover how efficient she was. In no time, all the essentials for the party were arranged. Thanks to her, we could make it a formal dinner party. Kathryn Cardwell became indispensable to us. She found for us an excellent Japanese cook named Kamiko, and made our life easy in every way. The dinner was one of Nela's greatest accomplishments. With the help of Kamiko she cooked the whole dinner. I chose the wine and, remembering the party I had given at Montmartre when I used floodlights in the trees, I decided to repeat it here. An electrician with the engaging name of Nightingale proved to be an artist. Nela's food and Nightingale's floodlights were the triumph of the evening.

Our guests were a strange mixture. We had Charlie Chaplin; the top male dancers and prima ballerinas of the Ballet de Monte Carlo; Erich Maria Remarque, the famous author of *All Quiet on the Western Front,* who escorted Greer Garson; the Boyers, the Colmans, Ernst Lubitsch, and Anatole Litvak; Gottfried Reinhardt, son of the famous Max; the Basil Rathbones; Salka Viertel, the authoress of Greta Garbo's screenplays; Alfred Wallenstein, the conductor, and his wife; Harry Kaufman, a fine pianist and accompanist; and, of course, Bronek and Lola Kaper. Charlie Chaplin told me, "My son has all your records and is a great admirer of yours, so when I told him you had invited me he said, 'Rubinstein invited *you?* Impossible.'" We had a good laugh.

After dinner we offered an unusual entertainment. Chaplin performed for us the funny little tricks of his latest movies. Nela danced beautifully a Mazur with Frederic Franklin, star of the Ballet de Monte Carlo, and later large parts of *Petrushka* were danced by Danilova and the other stars to my accompaniment. The party lasted until three in the morning.

The next day I was relieved to hear that Remarque had managed miraculously to drive Greer Garson safely home after drinking over a quart of brandy.

One day we learned with relish that Hitler had attacked Russia and had thrown all the might of his army into the battle. We hoped that he would meet his nemesis here but were soon bitterly disappointed to hear that he advanced victoriously on the whole line and occupied all of the Ukraine, encountering only weak defense. Stalin and his aides left Moscow precipitately to a safe refuge in the far interior of the country. Only Leningrad resisted the siege.

Carmelina grew on us. The children adored the playroom—one couldn't get them out of there. One day, on an impulse, we felt like staying in California and buying our own house. We heard from friends that Pat O'Brien, the film star, was building a new house for himself in Brentwood and was ready to sell his old one next door. We loved it at first sight, especially the garden, which had silver birches so typical of Poland and so rare in California. The swimming pool had an outbuilding with showers for changing.

Pat O'Brien was a lovable and generous man. He let us have his large home and everything included, in perfect condition, for only fifteen thousand dollars. "If you had agreed to give lessons to my daughter Mavourneen, I would have given you my house for nothing," he said later.

Great bargain as it was, it did give me some trouble. Some weeks later, when I was in full possession of the house, I received a letter from the Sacramento Income Tax Authority asking in sharp terms how my bank had processed my check, as it was against the law. Poles in America had their money blocked and banks were held responsible for any breach. I was petrified. "I feel sure that the bank didn't know that I am a Pole," I said to Nela, "and they will be held responsible."

I left for New York before the concert season began and went right away to see my bank manager, who told me smilingly, "We knew very well that you are a Polish citizen but I decided not to let you down on your great opportunity to buy that house. Don't worry about the bank, we can take it."

I was not satisfied, so I went to Washington to see the Secretary of the Treasury, Henry Morgenthau, Jr., who received me most graciously. "In your case, we would have forgotten the whole thing, but I will give orders to the bank to allow you to draw twenty thousand dollars a month if you need it. I hope it is sufficient." This was a nice end to the story.

We spent seven happy years in that house. I remember the arrival of my friend Moïse Kisling, who stayed with us a few weeks. After heroic efforts on our part we got my mother-in-law out of Lithuania via Sweden, where my manager Enwall helped her onto a plane for New York. Her son Bronislaw, after terrible hardships, reached the United States via a Russian concentration camp, Iran, Cairo, and London, and then after his arrival in Hollywood acted as my secretary. When they finally appeared safely at Los Angeles Airport, there was great joy in the family.

The high points of the Brentwood days were, of course, the births of our daughter Alina, who was born ten years after Paul, and our son Johnny, who came two years later.

105

My concert tours forced me to leave California with its intense and amusing life for long periods of time. As my appearances were overwhelmingly more numerous in the eastern states, New York obviously became the center of my activities; Hurok and his organization and the RCA Victor recording company were in constant touch with me. I gave three to four concerts a week in those times. I took a nice little apartment consisting of a drawing room and a bedroom at the Madison Hotel, situated on Madison Avenue and Fifty-eighth Street. Whenever possible, I returned to New York after my concerts in neighboring towns and the Madison Hotel became like a second home.

At the end of 1941 my tour was particularly interesting; I played with all the orchestras as soloist and could compare the different conductors. I played in Minneapolis with the Greek Dimitri Mitropoulos, for instance, a strange ascetic personality and a wonderful conductor endowed with an uncanny memory. And then there was the charming, much-beloved Koussevitzky of the Boston Symphony, who was good with Russian music; he was rather conceited—an ecstatic lady admirer told him after a concert, "You are a god." "Yes," answered Koussevitzky promptly, "but what a responsibility!"

Ormandy and his Philadelphians were always reliable. Pittsburgh with the fine but too irascible Fritz Reiner; Cleveland, now in the hands of George Szell, whom I admired, and New York, where my friend John Barbirolli was replaced by Artur Rodzinski. It was with the latter that I performed the B-flat major Concerto of Brahms on the ominous Sunday afternoon of December 7. The orchestra had finished the symphony and after a lengthy intermission I was about to take the steps leading to the platform when I heard an outcry of horror from several stagehands and from Rodzinski himself, who arrived gesticulating dramatically. "Japan has attacked the United States in Honolulu. They bombed the harbor and destroyed the American fleet anchored there. The radio just gave terrible accounts of the many dead and the great destruction."

We were all thunderstruck but the concert had to go on. Rodzinski was charged with announcing the dreadful news to the public. On my way to the piano he said to me, "You must first play 'The Star-Spangled Banner.'" We found the audience in a great state of agitation but "The Star-Spangled Banner" restored order; everyone stood at stiff attention but then settled down quietly to listen to the Brahms concerto, which we played with special fervor. With the last note, the audience ran to the doors, and the orchestra, Artur, and I went to listen to the radio, hoping to hear new developments but instead enduring the constant repetition of the disaster.

Back at the hotel, Nela called to tell me that the whole West Coast was panic-stricken, fearing grave danger. From then on, it was history: Roosevelt declared war on Japan and at the same time on Hitler, who became Japan's ally. Overnight we were engaged in the world conflict. The conditions of daily life changed considerably; everything was subordinated to the war effort. The whole of young America was called to arms, women formed auxiliary armies, and the rest of the nation forgot partisan quarrels, standing to a man behind its President. Everyone was buying war bonds and soon the first troops were landing in Ireland and England. Travel by airplane was reserved for the Army and civilians were rarely allowed to fly, so I was again forced to use trains for my concerts. It took four days to go home to Los Angeles.

At that time, the New York press was beginning to publish horror stories about Hitler's plans to annihilate the Jewish race. Reports stated that the Gestapo chief, Heinrich Himmler, was collecting Jewish men, women, and children in all the conquered countries and taking them to unknown destinations. As nobody knew their whereabouts or what happened to them, the most terrible stories were rumored. At that time, no one could imagine the abominable, unimaginable holocaust perpetrated by the Nazis. Of course, everybody who had family left in Europe was living in deep anguish about the fate of their relatives, as no communication of any sort was possible.

At home in Brentwood, the war had also brought changes. Nela joined a small group of women—Pat Boyer, Verree Mangoo, and Heather Angel —who were brought by bus three times a week to the military camp, where they worked in the canteen serving coffee, sandwiches, and cakes to the boys. My wife was also assigned to spend an hour daily in a special booth watching for alarms of enemy planes and she also passed her first-aid examination.

As for myself, I felt pretty useless; too old for fighting, with a son too young to serve. All I could do was buy war bonds, and I was eager to give concerts with my fellow musicians in aid of the different needs of the war effort. A particularly colorful one took place at the swimming pool of the Beverly Wilshire Hotel. A round building containing a large number of dressing rooms for the swimmers was converted into elegant boxes and the seats were sold at exorbitant prices. A platform was erected at one end of the swimming pool and the program consisted of Beethoven's *Kreutzer* Sonata played by Jascha Heifetz and me, two cycles of lieder sung by Lotte Lehmann and accompanied by Bruno Walter, and, in between, solo pieces by Heifetz with his own accompanist and by me. A combination of this kind would be a coup for any concert manager and on this occasion it indeed yielded a large sum of money. We, the performers, were delighted that the open pool lent an unexpected fullness to the sound of the music.

Samuel Goldwyn then asked me to organize a concert for his own charity. "I feel sure that Jascha Heifetz will be glad to play sonatas with you. I made a film with him which lost me a lot of money." Heifetz refused to play, but Joseph Szigeti, that fine violinist, readily agreed. We filled the Philharmonic auditorium, playing two sonatas and solo pieces.

Soon after, my concert work started again, but not without many hardships. It took thirty-six hours by train from Los Angeles to Seattle. From there, one reached Vancouver and its neighboring Victoria in a few hours, but following up toward the east, I had to play in Calgary and Edmonton in the province of Alberta, which had become wealthy overnight due to its precious mines. Both these cities increased their population month by month and both were still far behind in amenities. In Calgary, the local manager made me play on a skating rink covered with wooden planks, with a tent erected over it—all this at a temperature of ten below zero.

Upon my arrival in Edmonton next morning, the concert organizer met me at the station. After introductions I said, full of rancor, "You wouldn't believe where your charming colleague in Calgary made me play last night." He made a sad face, which I thought was in commiseration. After a short silence he said timidly, lowering his voice, "I'm terribly sorry, but you will also have to play on our skating rink here." This was too much! However, my inborn sense of humor came back to me and I laughed heartily. "From now on, I want to play everywhere on skating rinks." Both these wealthy cities now have the finest concert halls imaginable.

The war turned New York into a medley of European cities. A luncheon in the best Parisian tradition given by the Robert de Rothschilds in their beautiful apartment on Fifth Avenue would be followed by a reception at teatime by Hulda Lashanska, the well-known lieder singer, where one would meet quite a few people one used to see in Vienna, Prague, or Budapest. After dinner, on my free days, I would join Tuwim, Lechon, and some friends from Poland and we would talk late into the night as though we were in Warsaw. At all these various reunions the war took on a different aspect. The Rothschilds and their friends would discuss all the political and economical probabilities for any turn the war might take. At the tea parties we felt as though sitting in Vienna surrounded by loud and gesticulating members of the operatic world. Later on, Tuwim and Lechon would bring back to me many a fascinating hour spent together in Warsaw.

Two new arrivals from Europe gave me a much-needed moral lift— Jan Masaryk, son of the first President of Czechoslovakia, of the good London days, and Moïse Kisling, the Polish painter, whom I admired and loved. As in the First World War, he volunteered for the French Army but was rejected this time because of his age. The clever fellow not only managed to escape miraculously from the South of France but succeeded in bringing over the bulk of his pictures. We spent a whole day making plans for him; he badly needed help. "Come and live with us in Brentwood. It would be an honor and a joy for us and I think the climate of California is very much like that of the Riviera. You will paint happily there." My invitation appealed to him. He arrived in the spring and stayed for a few lovely weeks. One or two days after his arrival, we drank champagne to the victory of the English at El Alamein. It was a considerable relief to feel that the formidable Rommel was beaten. The English of Hollywood were exultant.

Kisling made a precious portrait of little Eva, aged nine, and then of the four of us as a gift for our tenth wedding anniversary. We feted it in grand style, with fifty people for a sit-down dinner. Our standard guests were the Charles Boyers, the Ronald Colmans, the Basil Rathbones, the Adolphe Menjous, the Bronislav Kapers, and the Edwin Knopfs. Among the newcomers were Barbara Hutton with her third husband, Cary Grant, the Samuel Goldwyns, the David Selznicks, and many others. As a Hollywoodian touch, we rented synthetic grass to put over our own lawn, which was covered with evening dew. After dinner, there was a charming interlude; my little Eva in her tutu and ballet shoes, her blond hair falling to her waist, danced the Death of the Swan modeled after Anna Pavlova's famous performance. She danced on point the whole lovely melody of Saint-Saëns and died so movingly that she brought tears to the eyes of many guests. She had begun serious training as a ballet dancer, and Madame Maria Bekeffi, one of the best of the Diaghilev troupe, gave her daily lessons and she received her schooling at home.

The party was a great success. But Kisling was not happy with the whole affair, for he had still too recently arrived to be able to forget, even during this heartwarming celebration, the European tragedy he had left behind. The two of us finished the feast by talking about our absent friends and families, for whom we feared the most dreadful fate.

One morning, I was agreeably surprised by a telephone call. It was Rachmaninoff himself. He had taken a house in Beverly Hills and invited us for tea in unusually polite and friendly terms. We were the only visitors. He settled down with me for a nice chat in a most urbane mood. "You must be glad to have Hofmann as a close neighbor," I ventured. Hofmann was his lifelong friend but had lately become an alcoholic. "He has even lost his technique" was all Rachmaninoff answered, with a shrug.

A few days later, we had a small dinner in his honor. The other guests were the Ronald Colmans and the Charles Boyers. At the table, the Russian master declared emphatically: "The Grieg is the greatest piano concerto for me." A rather astonishing opinion. When I announced that I had made a recording of it with Ormandy, he insisted on hearing it right away. We were served coffee around the gramophone and I put on the proofs, which I had just received. He listened attentively with his eyes closed while my other guests watched him intently. As for myself, I sat like a conservatory pupil being examined. Not a word was uttered until the end of the concerto. His eyelids rose lazily. "Piano out of tune" was all he said. But at a Carnegie Hall concert where I played this very concerto with the Philadelphia Orchestra, Rachmaninoff came up to the platform during the ovation and, visible to everyone, he applauded with his hands in the air.

On another occasion, Rachmaninoff called again. "We would like you and your wife to come for dinner tomorrow night. There will only be the Stravinskys."

"What? The Stravinskys?" I couldn't believe it.

"Ah, my wife and Mrs. Stravinsky became very friendly at the Farmer's Market." Ah-ha, that is more like it. The two men had spoken with such disgust of each other's works that it was inconceivable to imagine them dining together.

We arrived a little late and here was the picture: Rachmaninoff, sitting on a low chair, complained about a stomachache, holding his hand on his tummy. Stravinsky walked around the room looking at the books on the shelves with apparent great interest.

"A-a-h, you read Hemingway, do you?" he asked the host.

"We rented this house, books and all," our host grunted. The two ladies chattered happily in a corner.

After a while, we were called to the dining room. When we were seated, Rachmaninoff, in his best Russian manner, poured out vodka from a carafe. He raised his little glass and, nodding toward us, drank. We reciprocated with a few "*zakouski*'s"; he repeated the gesture and we all drank. After a little while, a third small glass was emptied by us. It was only at that moment that the conversation became alive and our voices rose. Swallowing a morsel of pressed caviar, Rachmaninoff addressed Stravinsky with a sardonic laugh. "Ha-ha-ha, your *Petrushka*, your *Firebird*, ha-ha, never gave you a cent of royalties—eh?" Stravinsky's face was flushed and suddenly turned gray with anger. "What about your C sharp Prelude and all those concertos of yours, all you published in Russia, eh? You had to play concerts to make a living, uh?"

The ladies and I were terrified that it might lead to a nasty scene between the two composers but, lo and behold, quite the contrary happened. Both great masters began to count out the sums they could have earned and became so involved in this important matter that when we got up they retired to a small table and continued happily daydreaming of the immense fortunes they might have earned. When we were leaving, they exchanged a hearty handshake at the door and promised each other to find more sums to think of.

With all the comfort and pleasure we derived from our house in Brentwood, I was not wholly satisfied; I badly needed a driver's license. Our house was in a secluded part of Brentwood and a considerable distance from shops and cinemas. Sometimes I had bitter thoughts about being my wife's prisoner. "Could you drive me to the barber?" I would ask her. "Can't you go there tomorrow?" Nela would say. "I am very busy."

After a few of these "postponements," I decided to act. Bronek Kaper recommended a driving instructor to me. He was a German American who took his job seriously; he made me repeat every maneuver ten to twenty times. After two weeks of lessons, I was ready to face the most difficult test on my driving and knowledge of the highway code. I passed my exam brilliantly and clutched with emotion the precious driver's license which finally gave me the freedom of the land. But this was not enough for me; I wanted to give the family the surprise of their lives.

At that time, the outskirts of the city were full of secondhand-car dealers, and we noticed many places advertising fabulous reductions on cars only two or three years old. My instructor took me to one of these places, where we found a dazzling white convertible Cadillac looking as fresh as if it had just left the factory.

I bought this beautiful instrument of power on the spot, took my seat at the wheel, and drove proudly home. Turning slowly into the entrance of the garage, I gave a few strident hoots and my whole family, plus the servants, came running out of the house and gaped speechless while I drove majestically into the second space of the garage. My driver's license changed my life considerably; the friendly coffee shop at the Beverly Wilshire Hotel, faraway cinemas, shopping centers, and visits to friends were now wide open to me.

That summer, I played for the first time in the famous Hollywood Bowl, where a natural chasm had formed an amphitheater, which gave a committee of citizens the idea of converting it into an open-air concert hall. At the bottom of this bowl a building was erected with a large platform in the form of a shell and artist's rooms and accommodations around it. The boxes and row after row of benches rose steeply around the bowl. The place could hold up to twenty-eight thousand people.

I played the Tchaikovsky concerto with Leopold Stokowski conducting. To my amazement I could play without loudspeakers and be heard clearly on the last bench. The semitropical Los Angeles had no rain and mild evenings during the whole summer, which contributed much to the popularity of the Hollywood Bowl. I always hated to play in the open air because the piano needs solid walls to transmit a vibrating tone, which becomes defenseless in the open air. In the Hollywood Bowl alone, the shell was sufficient to make the piano sound beautifully.

New York also had summer concerts at the Lewisohn Stadium, where Hurok induced me to play the Tchaikovsky concerto with Pierre Monteux. It was a windy night. A wind makes me panic-stricken when I have to face it without my hat on, so there I was helplessly exposed to the growing hurricane while striking the mighty chords of the beginning. I tried to hide my head from the mortal enemy. The wind did not give in and it began cruelly to dishevel my hair, so—as far as I remember, and you wouldn't believe it—I played with my head buried under the keyboard.

On another occasion, at the Robin Hood Dell in Philadelphia, another open-air calamity occurred. I had just started, in high spirits, the Brahms Concerto No. 2 in beautiful collaboration with George Szell when a terrific rainstorm burst forth from the skies and made the audience and all of us run in terror for shelter. There was no concert that night. Next morning there was nothing but sneezing all over Philadelphia.

With Hollywood living in perfect euphoria and I accomplishing a long and most successful tour, the war news became most alarming. After the Japanese surprise attack on Pearl Harbor, the United States had to endure a stinging defeat in the Philippine Islands, compelling General MacArthur to take refuge with the rest of his army in Australia. He swore, however, to come back and he kept his word.

Litvinov, the Soviet ambassador to the United States, implored Washington to come to the rescue of his hard-pressed country. The brave English stood stubbornly in defense of the whole world. Winston Churchill, now the right man at the right moment, promised his countrymen nothing but blood and sweat.

Now it began to be known that Hitler was perpetrating the most abject and unpardonable crime ever committed in the history of mankind—that he had erected special concentration camps where millions perished in gas chambers. I cannot write explicitly about it because it breaks my heart; the vision of practically my entire family, who with the six million Jews were part of this inhuman holocaust, is constantly before my eyes.

The ghetto uprising in Warsaw showed for the first time the indomitable courage of the Jews, who fought to the last man, the courage which led them later to their old homeland—Israel.

In the meantime, life in California became more exciting than ever. Due to the war, the wealth and promise of Hollywood attracted the cream of the artistic and intellectual world which remained free. Music was represented by the world-famous composers Stravinsky, Schönberg, Rachmaninoff, and others. The conductors Stokowski, Bruno Walter, and Alfred Wallenstein lived there, but others came from all parts of the United States and turned the Hollywood Bowl seasons into the most attractive of all open-air festivals. Pianists, violinists, cellists, and singers galore were there. Literature was richly represented by great writers like Thomas Mann, Aldous Huxley, Franz Werfel, and Lion Feuchtwanger, and of course the best producers, actors, and actresses were active in the great cinema studios of Hollywood. Film stars became millionaires overnight but, more often than not, couldn't stand the strain, so the gossip papers never had enough space to report all the divorces, drunken parties, gambling, and other sensational news.

It was common knowledge that Thomas Mann was working on a great novel and that Aldous Huxley lived in a faraway suburb so he could write in peace. Max Reinhardt came to town to make a film of his famous production of *Midsummer Night's Dream*; Stravinsky and Schönberg never stopped composing.

The latter gave us musicians quite a lot of trouble. He was left without money after his dismissal from the University of California, simply because of his age. I joined a group of musicians who decided to help him. The best way was to obtain a commission for him to compose music for films. We were lucky to persuade one of the moguls of the cinema to receive the great composer and offer him a contract. Schönberg was not only willing to do it but became interested in the project. It became common knowledge how the interview ran: The mogul says: "Professor, I have a film right up your alley. You will write the best music of your life for it."

Schönberg says quietly: "I would like to settle the financial question first. I need fifty thousand dollars for my music."

The mogul raises both hands in the air. "But, Professor, we've never paid more than ten thousand to our composers."

Schönberg protests: "It takes me a year to compose my music and this is the least I can ask for it."

"But, Professor," laughs the mogul, "why a year? You can write a few tunes and my boys will arrange it for the orchestras and they will do whatever you want."

"Your sons?" asks Schönberg.

"No. We have, at the studio, fellows who finish up the music overnight, arrange it for orchestra or other things. They know what they're doing."

The two men separated without understanding each other. His worried friends were of the opinion that he should have accepted the ten thousand, but the master made this sublime reply: "I cannot commit suicide by making a living on ten thousand dollars."

Stravinsky was a man of a different caliber. When, on my advice, he discovered the easy way of making money by appearing in public, whether as pianist or conductor without any real talent for either, but relying entirely on his great name as a composer, he never stopped making concert tours and amassed a considerable fortune.

I was happy to have been able to arrange for my friend Alexander Tansman to write the music for a film which starred Charles Boyer, who had graciously helped me in this project.

The presence of Jascha Heifetz, Emanuel Feuermann, and myself in the same city did not escape the attention of the RCA Victor Company. It didn't take much persuasion to get us to record the great *Archduke* Trio of Beethoven, the wonderful Schubert B flat, and the Brahms Trio in B major. To play with Heifetz was always an experience; nobody could touch his perfection. There was always the beautiful tone, the impeccable technique, and the pure intonation, but when it came to the interpretation proper there was often a fundamental discord between us.

Emanuel Feuermann was an artist after my heart. A supreme master of his instrument, he was a source of inspiration throughout our recordings. In the Schubert and the Beethoven, I had constant arguments with Heifetz, never with Feuermann. But we ended up making fine recordings of both these trios which still remain collector's items. The Brahms Trio did not quite satisfy any of us but I was happy to make a very decent one as recently as 1972 with Henryk Szeryng and Pierre Fournier.

After those recordings with Heifetz and Feuermann the three of us, joined by other musicians, spent glorious days and nights playing chamber music. Once in Heifetz's house on a neighboring beach, I begged my colleagues to play for me my beloved string quintet with two cellos by Schubert. I implored Heifetz and Feuermann to give faintly heard accompaniment to the long-held-out chords played by the others in the second movement. It was Schubert's last work and this music has always sounded to me like a serene and resigned entrance to death. I have always wished to hear this movement, even on a record, in my own last hour. On that night at Heifetz's house, I seemed to have inspired them. The host, the wonderful violist William Primrose, Feuermann, and two other excellent musicians gave a most memorable performance which brought back to me the times at the Drapers' with Thibaud, Tertis, and Casals.

Thomas Mann, who was a great music lover and never missed my concerts, came to our house as an avid listener. When he heard that I had been a fervent reader of his great novel *Buddenbrooks* in my early Berlin days, he was so pleased that he honored me with long conversations about the novel he was currently working on, *Doctor Faustus*, in which music was the main theme. There was an interesting dinner in his house at which the only guests were Stravinsky and Vera Sudeikin (whom he married after his wife's death) and us. Intellectually it was a highly interesting evening.

Kisling found a wonderful studio in Beverly Hills and left us, to my great regret. "I don't have enough light in your house," he excused himself, "but you must come to see me any time of the day or night and I promise you a good time." We helped him put on an exhibition which was much admired. The newly rich of the film colony discovered a sudden love of art and bought quite a few pictures at a good price. We celebrated his success with a little feast in his honor.

That autumn I had the good luck to be able to play for the first time the Symphony Concertante by Karol Szymanowski, which he had dedicated to me. Eugene Ormandy agreed to include it in his usual tour of six concerts with his Philadelphia Orchestra. We rehearsed this beautiful work thoroughly in three rehearsals. These concerts remain in my memory in a quite particular way. The work grew with me with every performance and at the last one, which happened to be in New York, I played it with so much freedom that I felt as though improvising a work of my own.

At that time, a little tiff between me and Steinway comes to my mind. Their publicity department had irritated me for a long time with their monotonous advertisement of their pianos. It always read: "The piano of the immortals. The piano of Paderewski, Hofmann, Rachmaninoff, and others." Even if this famous trio were much greater artists than the rest of us, it was not up to Steinway to decide that. I complained about this to Alexander Greiner in sharp terms. You can imagine my astonishment when he sent me a page of their publicity in *Time* magazine where I found four or five lines of names of pianists, accompanists, and chamber musicians. My own name appeared in alphabetical order and was underlined in red by Mr. Greiner. That did it! I wrote to him:

"Dear Alexander Greiner. Thanks from the bottom of the heart for the wonderful publicity. But as a matter of fact, I want you to know whenever we talk about Bechstein, Blüthner, Bösendorfer, Erard, Pleyel, Mason and Hamlin, Knabe, and Baldwin I never omit to mention Steinway pianos."

Next day, I received a short telephone call. "When can I come to see you?" asked Greiner curtly. Ah-ha, here comes another break with Steinway, I thought. I received him that afternoon. He began: "I showed your letter to Theodore Steinway."

"You did very well," I said. "It was no secret."

"You know what he said?" he continued. " 'Greiner, he is absolutely right. Our publicity men are damn fools.' " We laughed heartily.

From then on, they gave all of us our due.

The Brahms B-flat Concerto seemed to have a mysterious connection with the war. Artur Rodzinski asked me to play it again with him. "Last year, the Pearl Harbor attack disrupted your performance. Let us give them a chance to hear it undisturbed." But then a strange thing happened. Just before the concert, the great victory at Stalingrad was announced. It seemed that Europe began to breathe again and Hitler's doom was in sight. My long and tiring tour that winter, all by train, was given with a hope and enthusiasm visibly shared by my audiences.

I had a bit of fun one day at the Madison Hotel. A journalist, who worked at night, took a room next to mine. His morning sleep was rudely disturbed by my practicing the Tchaikovsky concerto. In a fit of fury he violently complained to the management. "That fellow next door bangs his piano in the morning when I need my sleep most. Can't you make him stop that damn noise?" The manager asked him politely, "Which is your room again?" and when he was told the number: "Oh, you have the one next to Arthur Rubinstein. We will have to charge you five dollars more."

Back home, I received letters from Blanche and Alfred Knopf inquiring about the book. I had sent them the eighty-odd pages which I had started to write in Mexico City for approval without having added a single word since. It had been easy and pleasant to write about the little child who played the piano, who amused his family and was the toast of the city of his birth at the ripe age of four. Now it was another story at ten, when my short manuscript stopped; I remembered myself as a dreadful boy with revolutionary ideas, left in Berlin in the care of complete strangers, and the thought of writing about it paralyzed me. I asked the Knopfs to release me from my contract and take back the retainer, but they wouldn't hear of it. "You will finish it one day," they insisted. It was more than a quarter of a century later on a rainy day in Deauville that my family persuaded me to write again. "Your cover stories and interviews are so full of false statements and mistakes," they said, "that you owe it to us to write the whole truth about your life."

106

A strong current of hope took hold of us. One felt the promise of victory everywhere. Italy was invaded by the American troops. It was slow going, but after many battles fought and won, they reached Rome, where King Vittorio Emanuele was forced to dismiss Mussolini. Everybody knows the shameful end of this colorful personality who paid a terrible price for playing the wrong card.

The rest of the Polish Army under General Anders, after marching through half of Russia, Asia, and Africa, succeeded in joining the American troops in Italy and after many bloody attacks won the battle of Monte Cassino.

We in Hollywood continued our rich and happy lives, but now with heads held high. We made ourselves believe that our galas, feasts, concerts, hundred-dollar-a-head dinners for the war effort were making the victory possible, but the lavish and costly movies and the stars' earning millions never ceased.

My own life consisted of giving more and more concerts. Hurok increased the number from year to year and I was delighted to face new audiences. I became more and more popular, not only as a pianist but as one who never cancels a concert. My time was divided between East and West with my headquarters at the Madison Hotel. I spent winters mostly in the East and Midwest and summers and vacations at home.

My love of life, which had never changed, helped me to enjoy the strenuous concert tours with their hardships of travel, changes of climate and food. Contrary to so many of my colleagues who hated it, I loved every bit of it. Up until the last concert I gave in the year 1976, every train, plane, hotel meant adventure and I was always looking forward to every change with tremendous anticipation. On the other hand, staying in the same place for more than a month would make me feel restless.

Musical life in the United States was not very stimulating during the war. True enough, every city had an orchestra, many of them fully professional, but the musical menus remained the same. The public was fed Beethoven and Tchaikovsky to fill the halls. There were a few years of imposed Sibelius which finally caused a touch of indigestion. The country had only two operas to live on: the Metropolitan of New York for the East and the San Francisco for the West. Chicago had ups and downs but was not able to keep a foothold in the Midwest.

The only constant progress intimately linked with music was the ballet. Sol Hurok, whose managerial talent was stimulated by Anna Pavlova's ballet, which he had the chance to bring to America, steadily developed a love for this art which bordered on a craze. One can frankly declare that ballet became the most popular form of art in the United States. After the war, Hurok was mainly active in bringing all the great ballet companies from Europe to America.

Soloists during the war were scarce. Those of us who came to America before the country entered the war remained and in many cases eventually became American citizens; but the many who stayed in Europe were cut off for the duration of the war, and so for some years America had to put up with the few of us. The great Kreisler discontinued his concert activities due to his age. Emanuel Feuermann tragically died prematurely during an operation.

Heifetz and Horowitz remained most in demand, but their difficult characters created constant obstacles to their real popularity. Heifetz and Horowitz were demanding fees which the managers were reluctant to meet and Horowitz drove them to distraction by his constant last-minute cancellations. Hurok exploited this by keeping his demands for his artists within the reach of the concert promoters. There were also excellent artists who stimulated concert life: Milstein, Szigeti, Rudolf Serkin, Robert Casadesus, and Marian Anderson. The repertoire of all of us was more or less the same. It ran from Bach to the romantics with a sprinkling of Debussy, Ravel, and Prokofiev.

The violinists lived mainly as soloists playing the well-known concertos. Their recitals had changed considerably since my early years, when the giants Sarasate, Ysaye, Kreisler, and Thibaud, as well as Kochanski, Mischa Elman, and their contemporaries, played music written for the violin with an accompanist or gave recitals of piano and violin sonatas with a pianist of equal standing. Now their programs consisted of the same sonatas presented as violin pieces with an accompaniment, ignoring the fact that the piano part is always the more difficult, and to show their independence even more, they liked to add to the sonatas a long partita of Bach for solo violin. The audiences were impressed by the stark severity of these works. I, for one, did not enjoy this great change. For me, the violin playing concertos with orchestra is in its element. Left to itself, it charmed me and sometimes brought tears to my eyes when Ysaye or Kreisler played music of a lighter kind, so true to the character of the violin. On the other hand, I feel the deepest respect for this instrument when it plays chamber music, including the sonatas, and when it imposes its presence in an orchestral body. Bach, in my opinion, wrote his important solo violin and cello works in the form of dances as superior studies, never dreaming that they could be performed to great audiences in a concert hall.

During the war, there were not many chamber concerts. There were ensembles which played appropriately in smaller halls; its accepted title in all languages being "music for the chamber." The Budapest Quartet had a great following and their permanent seat was the Library of Congress.

After all this has been said, I must express my admiration for the music-loving Americans. The two opera houses I mentioned and the orchestras were entirely supported by the American people, who endured many vexing discomforts during the war but never weakened in their great need for music. I, for one, owe a great debt to these years. Rid of so many distractions, which had been fatal to my work in my younger years, and stimulated by the growing contact with my audiences, I began to enlarge my repertoire with a greater interest than before and to prepare my recordings with more care. At the same time, I became aware of the importance of the interpreters. We are the ones who give life to the science written down by the great creators of music.

This, of course, was the purely professional side; my life with music was of a sort which I will try to explain: From my early childhood, music has always lived in me as naturally as my heartbeat and my breathing; whatever I heard, I absorbed. I was and am able to play any music I know in my head exactly as I wish to hear it; whole operas, long symphonies, songs, chamber music, and, thank goodness, all the music written for piano. Besides being born with music, which I could call a sixth sense, I was endowed with a gift of memory which allowed me to play after two or three readings any of the piano pieces by heart. Although I did not take the time to work out difficult passages, I felt clearly the intentions of the composers of all styles and nations, even in the popular field.

My playing in concerts and my attitude toward my audiences have been distinctly different from that of all other pianists I can think of. When I loved a piece, and I never played anything in public which I did not love, I was impatient to offer to my listeners the first impact I felt of the great line of the work and, more often than not, it was readily understood and loved. I venture to say with great conviction that every concert was for me a lesson for the next concert. Right there in front of the public, I discovered things which I applied on the spur of the moment.

During the war years, I learned in my way many new works which I tried out at concerts; I retained the ones which continued to live with me and abandoned those which wore out my interest. For instance, I began by liking the piano concerto by the Armenian composer Aram Khachaturian. Its Oriental flavor charmed me, and in spite of its technical difficulties, I somehow mastered it and performed it in a few concerts; but at the last one the inherent banality of the work left me devoid of any emotion and I abandoned it. The Grieg, on the contrary, which I had called "cheap stuff" in my impudent young years, later became more endearing with every performance for its simply expressed Nordic tenderness. I played with pleasure the diabolic rhapsody of Rachmaninoff on the good old worn-out theme of Paganini. There was, as in the rest of his work, a lack of nobility, which is the attribute of great music, but there is a sexual impact which tickles your musical senses.

I played also for the first time the Symphony Concertante of Szymanowski. It is dear to my heart, but difficult to convey to my audience; his emotional essence is hidden by a mass of changing harmonies, modulations, and a heavy orchestration and can only be discovered by frequent and loving study of its beautiful nature. The concertos of Saint-Saëns and Tchaikovsky were old friends upon whom I could rely and I made several recordings of each, every time trying to play them better. But the first versions remained the best.

I was always, and still am, a deep admirer of Prokofiev and am proud to have had his friendship, but I performed in public only a small trickle of his works. In my early career I played his *Suggestion diabolique* and other short pieces with great success. Much later, I took up the lovely *Visions fugitives* but left aside his wonderful sonatas and concertos, whose difficulties demand long and hard work. I was too lazy to learn them sufficiently for a public performance but I read them at home, played them often in my head with great perfection, and remained satisfied with that. I often heard them performed by my colleagues and shall never forget the Sixth Sonata played by Sviatoslav Richter and the first world performance of the wonderful Third Concerto by the composer himself at Carnegie Hall in New York.

The nucleus of composers whom I played in public all through my life consisted of Beethoven, Mozart, Schubert, Schumann, Brahms, Chopin, and Liszt. With time, I added new works by these composers to my repertoire, made many records, and ended up recording practically all of Chopin except the études. I played many of them in concerts but left out those to which I felt I couldn't do justice.

107

Eisenhower's victorious attack in Normandy and his slow but successful advance toward Paris lifted our hearts. The horrible nightmare of the past years was slowly fading. Hollywood was simply bursting with vitality. Parties were given to celebrate the good news and film makers were already anxiously preparing their victorious war films.

The great Philadelphia Symphony Orchestra with Ormandy came for a guest performance in which I was the soloist with the Brahms B-flat Concerto. I remember particularly the presence of Thomas Mann and Aldous Huxley at this concert. Both loved music and the latter could be called a music scholar.

The Hollywood Bowl concerts became more and more popular. All the available conductors showed their diverse interpretations, and as I played there each of the thirteen years I lived in California, I had the opportunity to be soloist with all the following: Stokowski, Ormandy, Szell, Steinberg, Rodzinski, Beecham, Klemperer, Wallenstein, Barbirolli, and Bruno Wal-

ter; I think I played twice with some. Koussevitzky was the last, but there is
a story attached to that which I will tell in due time.

In spite of my dislike for playing in the open air, I enjoyed these
summer concerts. It was interesting to have to establish a musical contact
with so many distinct temperaments; I often learned something from it. At
other times I had to impose my own conception.

There were also some incidents which later became good stories. For
instance, I remember a rehearsal of the Beethoven G-major Concerto with
Sir Thomas Beecham one hot morning. He was in a bad mood, so was I.
The piano was at the edge of the shell and after playing my opening phrase
I settled down for the long tutti. Sir Thomas was extremely impatient with
the orchestra that morning. He stopped them every second bar, addressed
this or that player with sharp criticisms, and repeated endlessly the same
passage; all this without the slightest apology for making me sit there in my
short-sleeved shirt with the hot sun beating down on me. When I was finally
allowed to put my fingers on the keyboard, I was pretty boiled up in every
way. Through the rest of the rehearsal, Beecham and I exchanged only
short words about the tempi and finished in undisguised hostility.

At the parking lot, as I settled into my brand-new Fleetwood Cadillac,
Sir Thomas emerged from nowhere. "I say, my dear fellow," he said most
politely, "I am staying with a friend of mine, Brownlee, from the Metropolitan Opera House, and he lives in your neighborhood. Would you be kind
enough to give me a lift?"

With my arms still burning from the sun, I said coolly, "Certainly, Sir
Thomas, get in." Out on the road, my bad temper got the upper hand. "It is
indeed a great honor, Sir Thomas, to have you as my passenger today." He
smiled contentedly. "Not at all, not at all, my dear fellow."

"Oh yes," I said with venom boiling in me, "this is a great occasion. It
is the first time that I am driving alone. I only got my driver's license this
morning, so you can imagine . . ."

On hearing that, Sir Thomas shrank in his seat. His face became pale
with terror. "I shouldn't have come with you, I shouldn't have come with
you," he murmured. Now I thoroughly enjoyed the situation. Having become, after two years, an expert driver, I pretended to be very nervous at
the wheel. Poor Sir Thomas was sweating with anxiety. "Look out, look
out, there is a red light!"

"Thank you, Sir Thomas, I didn't see it." This little game went on for
the whole of the three quarters of an hour it took me to reach his destination. When I stopped, he tottered out unsteadily, gave me a murderous
look, and whispered, "Thank you."

On another occasion, I was about to play the Schumann concerto with

George Szell conducting. Just before going out on the platform, somebody told me, "Stravinsky is sitting in a box." This upset me. Igor, as we know, hated the piano, hated romantic music being written for it, and hated to go to concerts with soloists. My performance, due to his presence, was especially careful, I did not miss one single note. Next morning at breakfast, the telephone rang. "It is Mr. Stravinsky for you," Eva said. I picked up the receiver, ready for a good fight. "Artur," Igor said in Russian, "I was at the concert last night."

"Yes, I know. Why did you come?" I said drily.

"I wanted to hear this concerto of Schumann which I never heard before," he said. "You know, this concerto is well composed and it sounds good and is quite beautiful."

Ha-ha, I thought; this is a great victory over a believer in music without emotion!

Another Hollywood Bowl story comes back to my mind. It happened when I played there for the last time with Serge Koussevitzky. He had just retired after twenty-five years as conductor of the Boston Symphony and the Tanglewood summer festival. It was therefore the first time that he would be giving concerts as a guest conductor. The Bowl offered him two appearances, the first without a soloist and the second with one of his choice. Koussevitzky insisted on having me, to my great regret because I knew from my own experience—and it was well known among others—that he was the worst accompanist. However, remembering his great help in the old days in Russia, I did not want to hurt him by refusing.

The concerto was to be Rachmaninoff No. 2. He arrived on the eve of his first rehearsal. We sent flowers to his hotel and invited him for dinner the night before our performance and I offered to fetch him in my car. As usual, without soloists the attendance at his first concert did not reach more than four thousand and this upset him greatly. After the packed houses he was used to in Boston, he had become very spoiled and conceited.

When I arrived at his hotel on the night of our dinner, he made me wait quite a while in his drawing room, came out very elegantly dressed, kissed me three times in the Russian way, took my arm, and we walked toward the elevator. In the middle of the corridor, he stopped and said in a solemn way, "Artur, I want you to promise me something."

"Certainly," I answered, "what is it?"

"You must promise without asking me."

I laughed. "Why can't you tell me?"

"We are old friends, Artur. I think I have the right to ask you to give me your word blindly." I was a little perplexed.

"Well, if it is not to commit a murder, I think I can promise anything," I answered.

After that, he took both my arms and said, "I want you to promise not to give any encores tomorrow after your concerto."

"Serge, this is impossible, they always expect encores." Now he became very serious: "Art*ur*, you promised."

I said, "Yes, I did."

"So you must keep your word," he added. I was not happy with my promise but was determined to keep it.

When we reached my home, I complained to Nela about his strange demand. She took it lightly. "I will tell him during dinner that you can't do it because it would offend your public, which is so fond of you." When she brought up the subject, he became stern. "Please don't speak about it. Artur gave me his word."

The next morning, before the rehearsal, she complained to the manager about it and he became quite furious. "We would be out of business if we accepted such stupid talk." But he was rebuffed severely by Koussevitzky when he tried to change his mind.

The rehearsal was the worst I ever had. In the first movement, we had a hard time finishing together; I could only hope that it would go better in the evening. But in the second movement, I flared up; his tempo was so slow that it was impossible for me to sing out the long melody, due to the open-air acoustics. When I demanded a quicker pace, he became adamant. "Art*ur*," he cried, "this is so beautiful, so beautiful, it would be ruined quicker." At that point, I had had enough of everything. I played the concerto until the bitter end with complete indifference and left without saying a word. The rest of the day I spent in anger and apprehension until the hour of the concert.

That evening, I entered my artist's room brooding. Koussevitzky, of course, assigned my concerto before intermission. He was going to close the concert with the Fourth Symphony of Tchaikovsky, which never failed him. An attendant entered and said, "The Maestro asks that you to come to his room. He would like to talk to you."

I found him lying comfortably on a couch. "My dear friend," he said, "don't be angry with me anymore. I know you were not satisfied with me but I promise to take your tempo in the second movement. For the rest, we will make a beautiful performance, and," he added, "remember, no encores."

"Of course," I said, "but I have a good idea. If the public insists, as I fear, I simply will tell them over the mike: I am sorry, but Mr. Koussevitzky does not tolerate encores and I am sorry to disappoint you."

He answered hotly, "Why mention my name? It would be quite enough to say that you do not like to give encores."

"This is out of the question. They know me too well for that." He stood still for a while, sweat shining on his forehead. "Well . . . Well . . . Give them one little encore."

I will shorten the rest of the story, which is long enough. I played the A-flat Polonaise, which produced a hurricane of applause, after which I had to add two more encores. Many left before the symphony.

108

When the Allies retook Paris, the little French colony of Hollywood was deeply moved. I attended a reunion with them at which they toasted the victory with tears in their eyes. All of America rejoiced; Paris seemed to be the real symbol of victory.

From that moment on, we began to hear the horrifying stories about the German concentration camps, where all the prisoners had been subjected to abominable tortures and experiments and finally burned alive. When, some time later, the American Army confirmed the facts and added all the dreadful details, I became aware that my whole family which remained in Lodz and Warsaw had been put to death in this inhuman way. I must admit that now, in my late years, my mind cannot grasp the idea that a civilized people, highly respected for its contribution to music and art, could commit this unspeakable, unpardonable crime against humanity.

There was still no way of getting direct news. It was a year or so later that I heard from a niece who had fled to Rumania that she and her husband, her two brothers with their wives, were the only survivors from the whole large family. I would have fallen into the depths of depression if it had not been for the news that we were going to have another child. It was a soothing thought that a new life would appear after the holocaust of my whole family.

Back in New York, I received a wholly unexpected and pleasant invitation. The famous Arturo Toscanini at the head of the NBC Orchestra announced a series of Beethoven concerts including the five piano concertos by different pianists. He asked me to play the Third Concerto with him. His invitation delighted me for many reasons: In the first place, I was thrilled to have the chance to make music with the great conductor and I was also fascinated to meet him at last. A little puzzle was involved; Toscanini was the father-in-law of Vladimir Horowitz, with whom I had not been on speaking terms for eight years. I wondered if he meant to bring us together again. All I needed for this was Horowitz's apology for his discourteous behavior toward my wife and me. Whatever the issue, I accepted his invitation enthusiastically.

I ran with the news to Hurok, who received it phlegmatically. "They phoned, but the date is wrong. That night you play a Chopin recital at Carnegie Hall."

This upset me. "Can't you change the date, can't they change the date?"

He said, "No, it's impossible. You know what dates are." Then he laughed. "His concert begins at five-thirty and your recital at eight-thirty, so if you want to make both, I have nothing against it. I shall make more money."

"Of course I shall take both dates the same day."

Hurok dropped his ironical tone and became enthusiastic. "A sensation!" he exclaimed. "Nobody would dare to play with Toscanini in the afternoon and two hours later give a recital at Carnegie Hall."

Chotzinoff arranged a private rehearsal for the Maestro and me at one of the NBC studios. I brought my music with me, prepared to play the whole work for the Maestro, with him following from my score. While we waited for him, Chotzinoff said, "You know, the Maestro has never conducted this concerto before and is pretty nervous about it." I knew that as a rule Toscanini hated to have soloists at his concerts, but I was rather astonished that I would be the first to play it with him.

Toscanini entered the room. He was an elegant, well-proportioned man of small stature. His head was handsome and, as he was extremely shortsighted, his very dark eyes had an unusual range of expressions from sad softness to wild fury. His outbursts of rage at rehearsals were well known and this made me a little apprehensive, but he shook my hand warmly and greeted me with a few polite words in Italian. "They think that I am so disagreeable but I am nothing of the kind. I suffered so much as a young man." And then he told me with a wealth of gesticulations, exclamations, and assorted grimaces what he suffered when he was a young assistant to an old conductor with a difficult character at La Scala. "Oh, what I suffered, I suffered," he said. "He made me conduct a new work one morning and I implored him, 'Commendatore, non venire a la prova,' but he did, the terrible man. After only a few minutes, I heard a shout: 'Toscanini! Toscanini! Tromboni, tromboni.' I thought I would die but I continued," he almost cried. "After twenty bars, I heard again: 'Toscanini, corni, corni.' This was too much for me. I thought I was going to lose my mind, but then

I turned around and screamed with my fists in the air: 'Commendatore, you son of a bitch. I will kill you.' Ah, Rubinstein, you don't know how I suffered."

I walked toward the piano but he stopped me. "What tempo do you take for the first movement?"

I smiled, "I would call it 'tempo giusto.' "

He pretended not to hear me but said irritably, "The other night, I heard a pianist on the radio and he played it like this . . ." and he sang out the first bars of the concerto exaggeratedly fast.

"But this is impossible. One can't play it like that," I said impatiently.

"Ah-h," he said with satisfaction, "you play it slower." This is the super-smart way the Maestro learned the real tempo of the concerto he didn't know so well. When I offered to play the whole concerto for him as I did for many conductors, he said proudly, "No, not at all necessary. Just play the end of the cadenza." He made me repeat these few bars several times. Then, quite satisfied, he said, "Molte grazie," shook my hand cordially, and left the room.

On the morning of the famous "two-concert day" I took a taxi for the only rehearsal of the concerto. At Fifth Avenue, my chauffeur made a brutal stop and I banged my forehead against the back of the front seat. Being nervous and in a hurry, I did not pay much attention to it, but when I entered the artist's room, Mrs. Toscanini screamed, "Dio mio, lei e pieno di sangue." The Maestro gaped, but before I could open my mouth, his wife went to work on my forehead. In a few minutes I had a lovely pink bandage on my proud brow.

This little incident mellowed the Maestro considerably. He took me by the hand to the piano, introduced me to the orchestra in nice Italo-English words, and gave the signal to begin the concerto. The tempo was a little too fast, but he played the whole tutti with extraordinary energy and rhythm. He never stopped the orchestra as conductors usually do. I began the solo entrance in my own tempo but I soon felt that he was not going along with me and at many important moments we simply were not together. The Maestro didn't pay any attention to it and continued the movement as though everything were in order. When we reached the cadenza, I was pretty discouraged, I must admit. I played the cadenza through and it was like the previous day as the Maestro made me repeat the end of it two or three times for the re-entrance of the orchestra. When we finished the movement, he smiled at me. "Would you please kindly repeat the movement?" I thought with dismay: What is the good of it? He did not take the trouble to work it out with me or the orchestra and showed an indifferent complacency, but I smiled back, of course, and he started the movement from the beginning. Now, a real miracle happened; the tempo was right this time and the tutti sounded with all the nuances required. I made my entrance with fresh hopes, and lo and behold, Toscanini did not miss one tiny detail. He was right there and we finished every phrase beautifully together. He respected all my dynamics, held up the orchestra when I made the tiniest rubato, came in after the cadenza on the dot, and we finished the movement with a flourish. During the performance he gave me little winks at dangerous moments. The second movement went smoothly and beautifully because its music is a wonderful dialogue between the piano and the orchestra. The third movement was worked out very professionally and with bravura by the Maestro. "I very much look forward to the concert," he said to me afterward. His son-in-law's name was never mentioned.

The Victor Company, which was recording all the concerts of Toscanini, was so enchanted with our rehearsal that they decided to make a live recording of the performance. I must say, quite honestly, that we were both inspired. To my great satisfaction, the whole country heard it on radio and the record was a great success.

Back at my hotel, my Dionysian euphoria about the Beethoven changed suddenly into a nervous fear: What will happen to Chopin tonight? I just had time to change, drink a cup of coffee, and go to Carnegie Hall. My first piece was the *Polonaise Fantaisie*, difficult to play and to recompose because of its intricate form, but it seemed that the inspiration of my previous concert was still alive for this one. I never played Chopin with more enthusiasm; it certainly was a memorable day in my career.

Toscanini sent me a lovely picture with the inscription: "To Arthur Rubinstein in remembrance of the unforgettable date (October 29, 1944) of our first artistic meeting. Arturo Toscanini."

That autumn I had more concerts in the East than ever, but I planned to be home the last weeks in December and stay for the first days of January, when our child was expected. Hurok promised to end my tour on December 15, so one can imagine my astonishment when during an intermission at the Metropolitan Opera House a man ran up to me. "We need your program for December 19, Mr. Rubinstein."

"You must be mistaken," I answered.

"No no no, you play with the RCA Orchestra."

"This is absurd."

Next morning, I went to see Hurok. "Last night a fellow wanted a program for a concert on the nineteenth and he insisted. What do you know about it?"

Hurok put on his slyest smile. "Well," he said, "as you have a recital that night at Carnegie Hall, I thought you would like to play in the afternoon with the RCA Orchestra."

I was speechless and then became furious. "You broke your word," I shouted. "I don't know about either of these concerts."

Of course, he won; both concerts were duly announced and there was no way out of it.

"Don't be angry," said Hurok in a fatherly manner, "it isn't as bad as you think. I got a priority flight for you, so you will lose only one day." This news soothed me immediately. "How did you do it?" I asked.

"Oh, you see, I promised that on the way to Los Angeles you would stop in El Paso and just play the Tchaikovsky for the war bond drive. I knew you would like to do it." The devilish old fox; I was ready to murder him.

The El Paso business turned out to be a frightful ordeal. The concert was postponed until the following day because of fog. I arrived in Los Angeles half dead at Christmas. First thing, I sent a nasty telegram to Hurok with my decision to postpone all my solo concerts until after my tour with the Philadelphia Symphony Orchestra beginning on January 16. The wily fellow knew when to give in. "Everything arranged," he wired. "Do not worry about anything."

I had a lovely rest at home while waiting excitedly for the baby. But the baby was late. Day after day it postponed its arrival until I had to leave for Philadelphia rather frustrated.

At my rehearsal with Ormandy on January 17, a man interrupted us with a telegram: "Our little daughter was born this morning." I gave a joyful shout: "I have a little daughter!"

Instead of the expected good wishes, I heard the voice of a violinist: "Where are the cigars?" Seeing my astonished face, Ormandy explained: "In America after the birth of a child, the father is expected to offer cigars to his friends." During the break I ran to a cigar shop at the corner of the street. The choice of cigars put me into a dilemma. Everybody knows, I thought, that I smoke nothing but the best cigars. Can I give them inferior ones? No. I bought two boxes of my brand, rushed back, opened the first one, and, when the orchestra assembled again, I held out the open box to the concert master. "My baby daughter offers you a cigar." He took three. His example was followed with great zeal by the other violinists. Before I reached the third row of them, it was empty. The other box had an even shorter life and the whole bulk of the orchestra still remained cigarless. I promised to bring a new supply for the concert. To shorten this long tale about tobacco: It took fifteen boxes to satisfy these cigar addicts. I was not stingy. The birth of my little baby deserved all of it and much more, but I became rather vexed when after the sixth concert with this orchestra, a double-bass player came up to me with a reproachful expression on his face. "I did not get any," he said. He went without.

This time my concerts in the East made me impatient; I longed to see my new baby. When I finally returned to California, I saw her as a lovely baby and no longer the crying bundle. A happy father faced a new world after a victory which cost humanity the massacre of millions of innocent people, as well as millions who fell on battlefields and the brave people of England who fought to the glorious end. Of course, the Yalta Peace Conference of Roosevelt, Churchill, and Stalin with its weak surrender to practically all of Stalin's demands infuriated us. We, born Poles, felt that the two Western leaders had sold out our country.

109

My season was ending with a few concerts on the Pacific Coast —among them, the Hollywood Bowl and a recital in San Francisco. The latter caused me great irritation. After my appearance the year before in that city, two prominent critics had censured me for playing classic and romantic music without including some of the new, unknown composers.

My San Francisco impresario, a woman, sent me these reviews, advising me to introduce a new work this year. I remember my answer. "I shall compare my programs with paintings. I do not like to open an exhibition of an unknown painter unless I am enthusiastic about him, but prefer to invite my public to see again the great works of the immortals, forever admired in the museums."

I thought the woman would understand it, but imagine my anger when I received a letter from her: "The critics, Mr. Frankenstein and Mr. Fried, were good enough to send me, at my request, two or three sample programs for you. I hope you will use one of them." I wired: "Cancel my concert. Your impudence calls for it."

The woman did not expect that. She was desperate. Endless telephone calls ensued. "The Opera House is practically sold out even though the concert is two months away." I stuck to my stubborn refusal to play, but in the meantime the United Nations chose the San Francisco Opera House for its solemn inauguration at the end of April. Living in a euphoric state following the glorious end of the war in Europe and Hitler's suicide, I hoped that my concert could not take place, but there was a Sunday when the Opera House would be free. This fact, I must admit, weakened my decision, but I made a condition: there would be no printed program; instead, the usual booklet would contain my explanation:

"A concert without a printed program demands a few words of explanation.

"This is not my first recital with an improvised program. I have given concerts of this kind in Paris, Madrid, Barcelona, Buenos Aires, and Sydney, cities where I felt sure I would not be suspected of seeking novelty or publicity, and I have the same certainty as to the music-loving, cultured public of San Francisco. The chief reason for this departure from the accepted rule is my discovery from long experience of the fact that a prearranged and published program tends to become a heavy obstacle to the mature and free artist for the best expression of his art.

"Facing an audience from the stage, we interpreters possess a sense of fine perception of the 'climate' of the hall, of its acoustics, of the always different qualities of the piano placed at our disposal, and last, but not least, of our own state of inspiration—and yet, to be aware of all this becomes of no avail if we are compelled to play compositions which are unsuitable for the occasion, merely because they were announced in print long before!

"While composing our programs ahead of time, we have to overcome still other difficulties; for instance, the legitimate desire of our managers for pieces attractive to the box office or the suggestions given us by critics to play unusual, unpopular, rarely heard compositions, advisers who seem to forget that they form but a small part of an audience of quite different tastes and that we are artists with individual temperaments and not living catalogues of music.

"The absolute conviction that audiences all over the world enjoy and understand best the kind of pieces which awaken our inspiration of the moment has prompted me to appear at this afternoon's concert without a printed program—announcing personally each item from the stage."

I wondered maliciously how the critics would react to that. Nela, anxious about it, accompanied me this time. It was an impressive sight for me when I entered the stage of the Opera House on that Sunday morning. A long range of multicolored flags represented the nations which had convened for the historic act of signing the charter. I tried to find the Polish flag but there was no sign of it. A long table with a green cloth and microphones stood in the center where I usually found my piano, which on this occasion was placed on the covered orchestra pit. Several boxes were taken up with television cameras and other equipment.

The appearance of the hall made it difficult to concentrate on an adequate program. For a time, I thought of nothing but marches and hymns. A tall loudspeaker was put up next to my piano for the announcements of the pieces I had chosen. Dorothy Granville, the manageress, told me triumphantly, "Most of these ambassadors asked me for tickets, as they don't speak English; they can take a concert. I had to put in extra seats." Needless to say, I fell into a state of fear mixed with anticipation—what of the battle with the critics and this solemn occasion?

It was only one hour before the concert that I decided what to play. All I remember was the Funeral March Sonata of Chopin and pieces by Brahms and Schumann with *Petrushka* at the end. Nela decided to watch me from the wings; she was too nervous to sit in a box. A Polish friend, the painter Juliusz Kanarek, who was without a ticket, accompanied her. He told me casually, "Isn't that funny, there is no Polish flag because no one is sure which kind of government will take over in Poland." I was dismayed at that news.

I walked on the stage, quite composed but with my heart beating, ready to play "The Star-Spangled Banner," which had to precede all the concerts in the United States during the war. The audience duly rose to their feet and listened with great respect to my solemn performance, inspired by the occasion.

When I finished, I stood up to announce my first piece and something strange happened; a blind fury took hold of me. I addressed the audience in a loud, angry voice: "In this hall where the great nations gather to make a better world, I miss the flag of Poland, for which this cruel war was fought." And now I shouted, "I shall play the Polish anthem."

I sat down at the piano and played the hymn created by the Polish army which fought for Napoleon. It begins with the words: "Poland is not lost as long as we live." I played it with a tremendous impact and very slowly and repeated the last phrase with a big resounding forte. The audience stood up as one man when I finished and gave me a great ovation.

It took some time for me to calm down, and then, in a quiet voice, I announced the Funeral March Sonata of Chopin. This concert was memorable for both the audience and myself. When I left the stage, I found Nela and Kanarek very moved. "Why didn't you tell me you were going to do that?" she asked. "It just came over me," I murmured. I did not know then that the Polish army would never forget this spontaneous gesture. They thanked me for having restored at that historic moment the flag of Poland to its rightful place.

The next morning, I opened the papers, sure to find a venomous attack by my two critics for my open challenge in giving them a lesson for their arrogant advice, but to my astonishment each wrote a glorious account of my patriotic outburst.

Hollywood was following with breathtaking interest the victorious campaign of the Japanese war by Douglas MacArthur. "He kept his promise to come back," people were saying; and now the victory was in sight. It was thrilling to watch General Doolittle's brilliant retaliation for Pearl Harbor when he bombed Tokyo.

During this postwar time, Quesada arranged a tour in South America beginning in Mexico and Cuba. My wife, Eva, and Paul accompanied me. Concerts in Mexico felt like home, its musical public never failed me. I gave two concerts in the Teatro de Bellas Artes, the famous opera house built of marble.

During the first concert, something disagreeable happened, but, as usual, it turned out to be a good story. It was a great national holiday. The city was lavishly illuminated. My concert was announced for 9 p.m., immediately following a patriotic drama. It was a drizzly evening, and we noticed a huge crowd standing in front of the theater; when questioned, a man said, "We are waiting for Rubinstein's concert. The play is not over yet." We stayed in the car until the play's audience left the theater and then I went through the stage door straight to my artist's room. We were late and I was waiting impatiently when suddenly the light went out and came on again after a few minutes. The same thing happened three times. Becoming very nervous, I went out for information. A stagehand told me, "The elevator which has to bring your piano up to the stage fails every time we push the button and the whole house is in darkness. The illuminations in the street are using all the electricity," he added, laughing.

We were over an hour late, and they continued to work on the elevator but without results. The minute they would try to bring the piano up, we were drowned in darkness. The public was half amused but mostly angry. The gallery burst into noisy protests. They tried everything and even wanted to bring out a baby grand piano from the director's office.

At 11:30 p.m. someone was brave enough to tell the public that the concert couldn't take place and that the tickets would remain valid for two days later. I have never heard such protests, booing, and shouting. Early next morning, my piano was on the stage and remained there for two days, indifferent to the dramatic productions played in its presence.

Quesada planned to continue my tour of South America through Cuba, Venezuela, and Brazil to Argentina, but when we reached Havana we were brutally stuck; neither ship nor plane was available. All transportation had been taken over by the military forces of the United States.

For two long weeks we had to endure heat and humidity which were almost unbearable. I tried to practice on an upright piano in my sitting room but the keys became stuck and after striking them I would have to lift them again. Sometimes I got up with the stool clinging to me. Nela and the children could hardly stand it, but I found a bar which boasted air conditioning and had to drink two gin and tonics before feeling its cooling effect.

After some two weeks of this nightmare, a small plane was available to take us to Mexico. A difficulty with the re-entry visas kept us for a few days in the Mexican capital, which fortunately was cool, thanks to the altitude. What a relief to be home!

On December 8, 1946, our son John was born and a week or so later, Mrs. Emil Mlynarska, Nela's mother, arrived. After all her hardships this was a happy reunion indeed.

At that time, a letter arrived which made me cry; it was from my brother Ignacy, with whom I had lost all contact before my departure, and I was left with little hope for his fate in occupied France. His was one of those tragic cases of constant hiding in terror. When Paris was liberated, he was admitted to the Rothschild Hospital completely exhausted, having endured three heart attacks. This hospital treated him, hoping that they would eventually be remunerated by me.

Very moved by his survival against such odds, I asked Hurok, who was leaving for Europe to search for new attractions and talent, to visit him and offer on my behalf all the money which he might need to reimburse the hospital and doctors. Hurok, on his return, told me about the deplorable sight my poor brother presented—all skin and bones but still with his usual charm and sharp mind. "I gave him one thousand five hundred dollars in French money and that covers all he owes. He told me with a little smile, 'Well, my brother didn't send this money any too soon.' "

110

A new era opened up in my life. The complete victory of the Allies when Hitler finally committed suicide in his bunker, the self-inflicted punishment for his unspeakable crimes, did something to my character. All during the hard-won war, music and my family had kept my love of life

intact. But my morale had been paralyzed living for years with the knowledge of what was happening to my people and the poor boys fighting on
battlefields, and so I never let myself quite enjoy my growing success and all
the good fortune which had befallen me. Now I felt fresh strength. There
was a promise for the future.

Quesada offered a tour in Argentina, Uruguay, and Chile. "A new
regime under General Perón," he wrote, "has made the great Colón Opera
available for six recitals." He assured me that if I allowed him to open a
subscription it would be sold out in no time. "These people have not heard
you for seven years and on account of the war they have had practically no
visiting artists. Now they long to hear and see you again."

I was delighted to go back to my dear Argentina, to which I owed so
much, and this time I could offer them a much richer repertoire. Nela was
thrilled to go and we could leave the children in the care of their grandmother and Kathryn Cardwell.

The winter season began successfully with New York and a number of
concerts in the southern states. In Columbus, Georgia, the day after my
concert, I had a quiet dinner with the president of the local music society.
During the meal there was a telephone call for me from Brentwood. My
mother-in-law informed me in a calm voice, "Nela just underwent an operation on her gall bladder. It was very satisfactory and I give you the surgeon." The latter assured me about the success of the operation. "There is
nothing to worry about," he added.

The news angered me. I felt that I should have been consulted. Nela
did mention that she wanted to have it over and done with before leaving
with me for Argentina, but I didn't think that she would do it in my absence
and without my consent.

Back in New York, two days later, I had a call from Nela herself. Her
voice sounded weak, she complained about pains, and she was bitter about
some checks which had not been honored and were returned. "You forgot
to put funds in," she said. This infuriated me because before leaving home I
left a biggish sum in the Bank of America in our joint account. When Nela
heard me shouting threats to sue the bank, she began to cry and put down
the receiver. The bank, of course, apologized and acknowledged its mistake.

The next morning, Hurok woke me up at seven, telling me that my
brother-in-law had not succeeded in reaching me to tell me that my poor
Nela was having an emergency operation to remove a clot which had
formed and was endangering her life. He advised me to fly home right
away.

In panic I begged Hurok to help me get a ticket for the next plane to
California. He showed a big heart, full of concern and friendship on this

occasion. He fetched me in the morning, drove me to the airport, and worked on getting me onto a full plane by persuading a passenger to give up his seat for me.

I shall never, never forget this endless flight with many stops in the full knowledge that my wife was on an operating table in mortal danger. I did not eat or change my position until we arrived at Los Angeles Airport. My brother-in-law came to take me to the hospital and I saw from his face that Nela was still alive but with little hope of survival. I found her so exhausted after this last operation that she had no strength left. I heard her mumur, "I want to die, I can't anymore." The whole long night I tried to give her back the will to live. Toward morning, she finally fell asleep and the battle was won. She recovered very slowly and a good nurse was with her night and day for weeks, but thank heavens she was on the way to regaining her strength.

I left for Argentina alone, stopping for a concert in Puerto Rico, where Quesada joined me for Buenos Aires. I had sent a good Steinway concert grand by boat straight to Buenos Aires two months beforehand. Upon arrival, we were pleased to hear that the six concerts at the Teatro Colón were sold out.

The next day, Ernesto came with bad news: "The new President, Juan Perón, is quite a dictator. He is on the way to ruining the country—you will not recognize it—and one of his latest decrees is that every performance given at the Colón has to be broadcast under the pretext of bringing culture to the people." I could not take that and I answered, "I hate the radio, as you know, and as these concerts are at my own risk, I have the right to refuse it."

"No, no, there is no exception."

"And they don't pay for it?" I asked angrily.

"No," said Quesada.

This was too much. "I simply will not play at the Colón," I said. "You can take any big hall—a theater or a cinema—we will give the money back to the ticket holders, and tell them we will open up the same subscription elsewhere."

Quesada was very efficient. The very same day he arranged my appearances on a percentage basis in a cinema which had a greater capacity than the Colón and where I would not have to dish out whole boxes gratis to government officials.

At the first announcement, my faithful public of Buenos Aires rushed to the box office and to my great pleasure I felt sure I would play to sold-out houses.

I sent Quesada to the port to make arrangements for the delivery of the piano, which had probably been there quite a while. He came back with an incredible story: "The boat with your piano is there," he said, "but the Port Authority said that it would be at least three weeks before the ship is allowed to unload it. They said there is congestion in the port and many ships are ahead of ours."

Without saying a word, I asked for a taxi and left with Ernesto for the port. When I told the man in charge that he must help me get my piano out of the wretched boat, that I needed it desperately, he smiled politely. "It is utterly impossible before three weeks or more." At that, I asked furiously, "Would you refuse if I were giving my concert at the Colón?"

He smiled again. "We might have to make an effort." Then I understood—it was an order from Mr. Perón.

My brain worked fast. I returned to the hotel and dashed to the telephone and after a few minutes got through to Theodore Steinway. After telling him my predicament and asking for his advice, he answered me cheerfully, "Arthur, if you are willing to bear the heavy expense, I can send you a beautiful concert grand by plane right away." I was amazed—it sounded like a fairy tale. But he reassured me very calmly, "We have special cargo planes now."

"Ho-ho!" I said. "Send it right away, please, please."

A splendid instrument landed in less than twenty-four hours at the Buenos Aires airport and there was no congestion—ha-ha. A few hours later it stood triumphantly backstage in our cinema and I could try it out, enchanted with its wonderful tone.

The newspapers naturally reveled in the story and it reached the New York magazines. Malicious tongues thought it was a publicity stunt but I think Mr. Perón knew better.

In retaliation, I received a few vexatious visits from some officials about my passport, length of my stay, etc., which had never happened to me before. I took it with Olympian smiles but in my little way I had one on him too. I told my friends an amusing story concerning Perón's wife, Eva, who before her marriage to the dictator was known to have been a member of the oldest profession. At an official reception, she took aside the American ambassador, a retired admiral. "Some of your magazines," she told him angrily, "call me a prostitute. Even as a joke, I strongly object to that."

"Madam," answered the ambassador, "I have been retired for twenty years, but they still call me Admiral." My friends liked this story and made good use of it.

That season in Buenos Aires remains in my memory as the best. Thanks to the very exacting audiences in the United States, my programs had many new works to offer, much better prepared, and I must say I was not a little helped by the seven years which had elapsed since my last tour.

It was fun also to see a lovely gray-haired lady who at a closer look turned out to be my old friend of the flower-pot signals at the Plaza Hotel. We had a charming séance of reminiscing.

After three additional concerts in Buenos Aires and four in Montevideo, where my old pals were happy to see my progress and where I enjoyed happy reunions, I left for Chile, where after the first concert my dear Juanita gathered all my friends in her house, giving me a magnificent welcome. Renato Salvati, director of the Opera, was delighted with the four completely sold-out concerts.

After a short and happy stay in Santiago, the capital of Chile, a small and slow plane took me to Lima, Peru, where on the day after my arrival, I had to perform the Beethoven G major, the Chopin F minor, and the B-flat Tchaikovsky on the same evening with the orchestra under an unknown conductor.

After seven long hours of a wicked flight, I arrived half dead in Lima. "I just want a bite to eat and then to bed," I told the local manager, who came to fetch me. "But . . . they are waiting for you," he said timidly.

"Who?" I asked impatiently.

"The orchestra, they have been waiting for you for half an hour for the only rehearsal, but tomorrow you are free until the concert."

"I shall probably collapse in the middle of the rehearsal," I said to him. But I was resigned, as usual.

When I came out on the stage of the Opera House, I found the orchestra and the conductor in their places but also a few hundred people who came to watch the rehearsal. This I could not tolerate. "They must leave, or I won't play," I said with authority. After some difficulty in getting them out, I began, half dazed, the G major Beethoven, and by some miracle we finished together. "An intermission?" the conductor asked. "No," I said. "If there is a pause now, I will fall asleep and nobody could wake me, so please let us play the Chopin right away."

The orchestra started the tutti, but there I jumped to my feet; they were playing the E minor Concerto and not the F minor, which was announced.

"This is the wrong concerto," I yelled to the conductor. But this strange fellow continued waving his baton and answered quietly without stopping the music: "We do not have the score for the F minor, so we play this one."

I dropped helplessly down on my seat and listened open-mouthed to the whole long tutti, but when my entrance arrived I began, like an automaton, and believe it or not, I played the whole damn concerto to the bitter end.

After this unusual exploit, the big heavy Tchaikovsky became child's play. After the rehearsal they practically had to carry me to the car and up to my room, where I went to bed with nothing to eat and slept twelve hours. At the concert I played and felt fresh as a daisy.

After this enjoyable South American tour, I flew home via Panama and Mexico. To my joy, I found my wife well on the road to recovery.

The end of that summer remains in my memory as one of the most delightful vacations I ever spent at home with my family. With my wife daily gaining her strength, the great victory of the war won after five years of horror and dread, and my own success growing, I loved life more than ever. In the mornings after breakfast, my greatest pleasure was to play with my little Alina in our sunny playroom. We called her Lali and she was the cleverest little baby you can imagine. At two, she could build a castle out of cards better than I could myself. Eva made good progress with her dancing and showed a promising future as a ballerina. There was a golf course five minutes' drive from the house where after a few lessons Nela and I were brave enough to play this difficult but so healthy sport.

Hurok settled down in Los Angeles in a house with a nice garden not far from ours. One day he came up with a funny proposition. "Republic Studios are making a film about a pianist and a conductor. They want you to play the music for it. The girl, the pianist, will be seen playing it on the screen."

"How is it possible?" I asked.

"They call that dubbing. The head of the music department at Republic will explain it to you." Then he laughed. "You know the fee I obtained for your work? Sixty thousand dollars."

"Wh-a-a-t? This is simply unbelievable and they refused to give Schönberg more than ten thousand dollars for a year of work?"

"Yes, I know," Hurok said shrewdly, "but your contract would run for two months." Then both of us had a good laugh. Still, I had my little apprehensions. "Look here," I said, "in spite of all this money, I still want to see the script. I must know what kind of a movie I am mixed up in."

Hurok was quick. That same afternoon, I had the script in my hand. The story proved to be absolutely idiotic. It gave a ridiculous picture of the life of a professional pianist and the approach to the serious matters of music. I telephoned Hurok right away. "I will have nothing to do with such rubbish." He objected with strong arguments, mainly concerning the money, but I received a visit from the powerful president of Republic Studios and the director of the film, Frank Borzage. Both of them were very agitated but immediately betrayed their ignorance of musical matters. I thanked the president for his generous contract but explained in strong terms that I couldn't have my music used in such an undignified way. The president was put out by my words. "Mr. Rubinstein," he said, "my studio has a good name and I do not agree with your hard criticism of this screenplay." Borzage nodded with great conviction. "But," he continued, "I will ask Mr. Borzage and his scriptwriters to come over tomorrow for a consultation with you. I shall order them to eliminate or change all the objectionable items you find in the script." This indeed was a generous offer. "In that case," I answered, "I am more than willing and delighted to collaborate."

On the afternoon of the next day, Mr. Borzage, accompanied by six or seven men, entered my music room. "We came to work it out with you," said the chief writer. We settled on my large sofa and the chairs around and I offered coffee or a drink. "I could do with a drop of whiskey on the rocks," one of them said. The others seconded that with conviction. I brought up a bottle of my favorite whiskey, ice, and soda. They all helped themselves, each in his own way, smacking their lips. "This is mighty good whiskey." After two or three libations, they opened their scripts and a loud discussion began. They fought hard for their text but were not able to satisfy me with a better one. I brought up my points, which they wrote down reluctantly at the boss's orders, but they drowned their disgust during a hot hours-long discussion with three bottles of my best whiskey. After they left, I triumphantly announced my victory to my family. "They had to accept all my changes."

A few days later, work began at the studio. Mr. Scharf, who was in charge of the music, gave me all the necessary instructions for my work. All this was new to me but proved to be useful for my future activity in the cinema. My main job was to play the Rachmaninoff Concerto No. 2, first as a whole and then in separate fragments, strictly conforming to the action. Now and then I had to play as though studying parts of it. I am ashamed to admit it, but that is all I had to do. I asked Mr. Scharf what the word "dubbing" meant and he told me, "You record it and the girl on the screen will pretend to play while listening to your recording, which will be preceded by three or four beats to allow her to begin at the right time."

I finished my part in three days to the full satisfaction of Mr. Scharf. "Is there any additional work to do during the two months of my contract?" I asked him. "Only if there is a mechanical fault," he said. "But I doubt it, everything sounded perfectly fine."

I met the charming actress who played the pianist and the Dutch actor who was to be the conductor. I gave them both some demonstrations of my stage manners, the right position at the piano, bowing to the public, and the way one walks on and off the stage.

Out in the street, I banged my head in disbelief—all this money for so little work!

111

One day Hurok telephoned from New York: "I have a very interesting offer for you. Mr. Harold Holt, the most important impresario in London, wants you to give three recitals at Albert Hall, as Queen's Hall was bombed. You will get a high percentage with a minimum guarantee. Holt told me that your name is now very well known in England, thanks to your success in America and the great sale of your records." I was thrilled. It was a big jump from little Wigmore Hall to three recitals in the huge Albert Hall. Nela was enchanted. "I've been dreaming of going back to Europe," she exclaimed. "And we can take Eva and Paul."

I flew off to New York to make all the arrangements. The excitement about returning to Europe made my head swim with all sorts of ideas. Of course, to go to Paris after London—see what had happened to our house —our notary had rented it to some family, but I wanted to get it right back. Suddenly I felt a wish to give a concert for the brave French Resistance, whom I admired. I asked Charles Munch, the conductor, about conditions in Paris. He was enchanted. "If you like, you could play three concertos and I would contribute the services of my orchestra with me conducting. We could call it a gala." I loved the idea and we fixed a date at the Théâtre des Champs-Elysées.

I lived a few days in joyous expectation and then the big blow came. The papers were full of dreadful tales from Palestine. For quite some time, I had heard sad stories about the despairing homeless Jews who had miraculously escaped the holocaust. No wonder that they had lost faith in all those countries which had allowed it to happen, so it is obviously why they saw a future for themselves and their children in their own ancient beloved land, the land of their forefathers, where they could live and die. The survivors from Germany, Poland, Russia, and Rumania flocked into Tel Aviv and Jerusalem by all possible means, only to find another kind of persecution beginning. The English, to whom the League of Nations had given the mandate over Palestine and Transjordania after the First World War, remained, after the peace conference, in charge of a small part of old Palestine proper. The new kingdom called Jordan was created, which included both banks of the Jordan River and the old city of Jerusalem, with King Abdullah on the throne and a strong army built up by the English Glubb Pasha. The remaining territory in Palestine included the newly built modern city of Jerusalem and fast-growing Tel Aviv and Haifa. These three cities were the goal of the newcomers and wherever they could they bought the land from the Arabs, even if it was sheer desert.

At that point, the new state of Jordan and the remaining Arabs, afraid of the rapid influx of Jews, urged the British authorities to put a halt to the immigration. I think it unnecessary to go on writing about this. The whole world knows what followed and what led to the cruel fights of the exasperated Jewish underground against the British, who enforced new laws against them. Shiploads of desperate refugees were turned back from the shores of Palestine to camps in Cyprus and even Hamburg. The Hitlerian tragedy, the brave fight of the Warsaw ghetto brought back to the harassed Jews the heroic courage of their biblical forefathers. It began with the underground Irgun and the rapidly formed Jewish army, the Haganah. Even a third armed force appeared but its violent terrorizing attacks on the British were disapproved by the other armed forces.

The climax came when I was preparing my programs for the three Albert Hall concerts in London. The extreme violence on both sides, the Irgun and the English soldiers, with killings of hostages, resulted finally in the hanging of a British sergeant for his cruelty. In retaliation, Jewish shops were burned and ransacked in Manchester and Liverpool. Like all the Jews in America, I was horrified by this post-Hitler tragedy, but when it reached England itself, I decided not to appear in London.

Hurok wouldn't accept my decision. He said quite grimly, "I held you in high respect for never canceling a concert and now you want to act like Horowitz and all those other cancelers. Holt will have a heart attack if he hears about such a thing." He shouted and gesticulated but I kept calm.

I said to him, "Nothing will induce me to play in a country which so heroically defended her own existence but has no heart for my people."

Hurok was right; Holt was infuriated by my decision and conveyed his indignation to my friends in England. I received a long telegram from Lady Reading, the widow of the Viceroy of India, Sir Rufus Isaacs. She expressed in many words her regret about my decision. "Instead of appeasing the enraged British, it will only make matters worse." She finished by inviting me to a meeting of important members of the Jewish community to discuss the matter. Hurok wired from London: "Beseech you to come to London and promise you to fix the whole matter."

We sailed with Eva and Paul and arrived safely at Southampton, where we took the train to London. It was late in the evening. Hurok was waiting for us at Waterloo Station. "The Savoy Hotel is full," he said. "I could only find rooms in some little hotel you won't like, but in a day or two the Savoy can take you."

Our return to Europe started out on the wrong foot. Paul was carrying a box of fine Havana cigars which I had opened on the train. Walking toward the customs, Paul carelessly let the box slip out of his hands and the cigars were all over the dirty platform. I could save only a few and I must say I was pretty put out. At that time, there were no Havanas available in England.

The hotel proved to be worse than we feared. There were no private bathrooms and it had no restaurant, but the next morning a bright sunny day welcomed us to the old English capital. However, it was a sad sight to see the proud old city partly in ruins. All of Holborn was destroyed, which to my surprise allowed an eerie view of the previously invisible beautiful St. Paul's Cathedral. The dear old Queen's Hall was no more; it gave me a pang in spite of my never being able to fill it. Severe rationing in food and commodities was still imposed and on top of that the whole population was mercilessly taxed. But the brave British never complained, the love for their country was just as great in peace as in war. The Churchill coalition government appointed my friend William Jowitt as Lord Chancellor.

A day later we settled in the Savoy Hotel and on the same afternoon I attended the meeting at Lady Reading's home. She received me with a cool and haughty air and the twenty-odd members of the Jewish community stolidly accepted her propositions. "Mr. Rubinstein," Lady Reading addressed me, "I fully understand your anger about recent events, so I have prepared a perfect solution for you. I preside over an organization in aid of Jewish children in our colonies, and I think it would be a noble gesture on your part if you would donate the proceeds of one of your concerts to my charity."

I interrupted her hotly: "If I *do* give these concerts," I said rather sharply, "I would give the money from all three of them for the poor victims of your cruel Palestine administration which sent them back to Hamburg, where they were kept behind barbed wire waiting to be sent into new exile." These words produced a heated exchange between Lady Reading and me and I left with a cool handshake. When I faced Holt and Hurok, they both smiled, expecting a favorable solution to all the trouble, but they were greatly mistaken. I stuck stubbornly to my decision, which had come to me on the spur of the moment. They found it unacceptable; Holt said, "It might anger a lot of people when they learn what you will do with the money they paid for their tickets."

I refused even to listen to them. "Gentlemen, I will give these three concerts only under the following condition: the posters advertising my concerts must state clearly: 'For the Jewish victims in Hamburg.'"

My decision terrified the two impresarios but the sale of tickets was so promising that their managerial blood couldn't resist, especially when they learned that the London head of the Rothschild bank was heading a committee for the very same purpose and would take charge of the matter.

These concerts in Albert Hall remain memorable for me. They were sold out and the lovely Marina, Duchess of Kent, who as a young girl had shown a friendly interest in my music, appeared in the royal box at all three of them. During intermissions, I was invited by Her Highness for a cup of tea and she graciously praised me for my firm stand. To the overwhelming relief of both of my managers, the whole affair passed without incident. The Rothschild bank gave a lunch in my honor and Lesley Jowitt invited us proudly for dinner in the chancellor's residence at Parliament.

Some of my London friends did criticize my attitude: "Arthur, you must understand that Palestine belongs to the Arabs."

"You are quite right," I retorted. "I must have heard somewhere that it was called the Promised Land of the Jews and that Jerusalem was built by them. Perhaps I was misinformed. Of course, everybody knows that India, Gibraltar, Malta, and Singapore are purely English."

They were not amused—neither was I, but now, as I write this book, I am happy to say that they changed their point of view. We departed in a happy mood for Paris.

112

The French capital was a complete contrast to London. This city, which survived the war without damage, continued the blackout three years after the Nazis had left. Here some of my best friends, especially Misia Sert, were full of praise for the Nazis' "good manners" during the occupation, but were incensed about the American "invasion," as they called it,

and their "vulgar" familiarity. Unlike the English, the French bitterly resented their own shortages, especially of white bread, *baguettes*. Of course,
all this put me out terribly, but soon enough I discovered that Misia and her
like were made up of the most concentrated kind of egoism, incapable of
realizing the real tragedy of the war. But there are no words to express my
admiration for the thousands who fought with the Resistance. These brave
Frenchmen who daily risked torture, the concentration camp, or death
throughout the occupation showed the utmost heroism. I am proud to say
that some of them later became my closest friends.

Our concert for the benefit of these heroes was to take place three days
later; there was only one rehearsal with the Beethoven No. 4, the Chopin E
minor, and the *Rhapsody on a Theme of Paganini* by Rachmaninoff. The
day after our arrival, I had to face two disagreeable surprises: The first one
happened at the Rothschild Hospital, where the four of us went to visit my
brother Ignacy; he was standing in the hall in his dressing gown waiting for
us, looking like a living skeleton, but his mind was as alert as ever. He
impressed us, and especially Eva and Paul, with tales about his life during
the occupation.

During our visit, I was invited to see the director; I was pleased to be
able to thank him for the kindness he had shown to my brother, but before I
could open my mouth, he asked me very urgently if I was prepared to pay
for the three years my brother had spent in the hospital. I thought at first
that it was a not very funny joke after the large sum I had entrusted to
Hurok for the payment; but when the director repeated quite seriously that
nothing had been paid, I returned quite dismayed to my brother to find out
what had happened. Ignacy put up his well-known grand manner of the
past. "You should have known," he said with bitterness, "that I had to give
presents to the doctors and nurses, and help some young painters who were
starving and came to me for artistic advice." I understood and went back to
the director to pay him in full.

Our visit to our house at the Square du Bois de Boulogne was certainly
the second very disagreeable surprise. After the war, the notary who had
legalized our acquisition of the house had written that he had had to let it to
a French family because of a new law that uninhabited houses would
automatically be confiscated.

We found, to our astonishment, that the prewar concierge, who had all
the keys to the houses on the square, was still at his post in his lodge. He
and his wife received us with friendly demonstrations, but informed us that
throughout the occupation all the houses, including ours, had been taken
over by the Gestapo. "Yours," he added smilingly, "was the residence of
doctors and dentists." In reply to our timid question whether they had left

any of our belongings in the house, he broke into a broad grin. "They emptied it thoroughly like all the other houses." His wife came out with a dirty rolled-up picture which turned out to be my portrait by Roman Kramsztyk done during the First World War in Paris. She said with great satisfaction, "We found it in the gutter and saved it for you." At that moment, a great suspicion came over me that this all too friendly couple had stolen all the valuables out of my house at the very approach of the German Army. It was also significant that they were allowed to remain at their post, obviously as willing collaborators.

We rang the bell of our house in apprehension. A young woman opened the gate and we could see two small children playing in the little front garden. She said, "The notary told us you were coming and we are delighted to meet you. Let me add," she said with an engaging smile, "that we enjoy very much living in your lovely house."

So far, so good, I thought, but when we entered the house, the shock made my heart stop. The inside was in a terrible state. The floors in all the rooms were undulating with humidity. They had installed a primitive stove by the staircase with a cheap blackened tin chimney which went up through the roof and served to heat the whole house. The dirt of the rooms was indescribable.

In this dreadful state of things I found an amusing touch: In the bathroom, the lady's washbasin was clean and the shelf above it was filled with a large and orderly assortment of cosmetics. The bathtub looked as though it had never been used. Hurt and disgusted, we left the Augean stable, escorted to the door by the smiling couple, who seemed to have decided to stay forever.

The notary, who was straight out of a Balzac novel, had bad news for us. "You are lucky," he said, "that I found this family to occupy your house, but of course they are too poor to pay any rent. They paid me a small sum for the first year, but nothing since."

"When will our house be free for us?"

The man smiled nastily. "By the latest decree, one cannot turn anybody out without finding them an equivalent home." I learned later from reliable sources that he gave them my house in exchange for their apartment, which he needed for his son.

Very depressed, we returned to our hotel, the Raphael, which was opposite the good old Majestic of happy memories. The rehearsal next morning at the Théâtre des Champs-Elysées went very smoothly. Munch accompanied the Beethoven and the Chopin with care and love, but the Rachmaninoff cost him much work. He said to me with disgust, "A horrible piece of music, this. I don't mind conducting it for you but I am afraid the

Parisian public might hate it." Not only the *Rhapsody*, but the whole concert seemed to be in danger. On that very morning a transport strike was called and so we were sure we would face an empty hall in spite of its being sold out.

Toward evening, Nela sent Paul in a hired car to deliver to my brother in the hospital food and warm clothing which she had brought for him. When he returned, it was time to go to the concert.

A small crowd waited outside the theater hoping for returned tickets because of the strike, but somehow everybody found their way to the hall. Munch and I were received very warmly and, settling down to the Beethoven, I saw many of my old friends in the stalls. It turned out to be one of my best concerts in Paris. They loved the Beethoven, they adored the Chopin, but the greatest ovation was given to the Rachmaninoff, as I had secretly guessed. Mr. Munch, who had to bow with me many times, declared, "This piece is not as bad as all that."

Since that evening, every concert in Paris until my last one in 1976 was always sold out by a devoted public. Afterward in the wings, there was a long procession of friends with many hugs, kisses, and tears. It was a lovely reunion with the Achards, the Benouvilles, Marie Blanche de Polignac, who had become a widow, and of course Misia Sert, in spite of her silly remarks, Poulenc, Auric, Jacques Février, and many others.

After the death of Dr. Schiff in America, his old partner, Mr. Friedrich Horowitz, inherited me; the poor man had remained in France and had had a terrible time hiding from the Gestapo, but now, apparently fully recovered, he picked up his prewar partnership with Marcel de Valmalète. When I informed him of my return to Europe, he immediately got busy arranging a concert tour, and now with my American success in my pocket, I enjoyed wholeheartedly the echo in the form of sold-out houses.

The four of us traveled to Brussels, to Ghent and Ostend. After two recitals in Paris at the Théâtre des Champs-Elysées, the tour continued in Switzerland, after which I had the immense satisfaction of playing in Rome for the same Santa Cecilia that, after my telegram to Mussolini returning my decoration, threatened never to let me play in Rome again. Clara Camus, my Italian impresario and faithful friend, showed me with pride the letter imploring her to persuade me to play in Rome again, written by the same secretary who had sent me the rude letter in 1938.

Rome was followed up by Bologna and Milan. In all these towns I was received like an old friend after a long absence. The tour ended gloriously and I could bask in the beauty of my beloved Venice. We returned happily to California for a lovely reunion with the babies and the household.

At that time, Nela again felt the urge to find a better house for the family and as usual I acquiesced. Luck was with us again. An Italian actress offered us a good price for our house and after a short search we found a dream house, really a small estate I would say, on Tower Road, Beverly Hills. The price was right and we moved in, proud of our new possession. We had five acres of land with a rich English lawn, a lovely formal garden surrounded by cypresses and with a goldfish pond in the center, a tournament-size tennis court, an orchard, a large playground for the children. There was an oval drive with a large front lawn in the middle, surrounded by eucalyptus trees. A place of this sort needed four gardeners at least, but we were lucky even there. We inherited a Japanese gardener from the previous owner, a man with an incredible capacity for work who was not only able to keep everything in order but every week created new flower beds with great taste. There were the rarest specimens of flowers which grew easily in the semitropical climate; we had amaryllis, gardenias, and many other kinds which my poor knowledge of botany does not permit me to name.

The house itself was built of stone and was designed by its architect for his own family. It had many rooms and all the comforts one could think of. There were even two pleasant surprises: a huge cellar ideal for storage and a real, small theater in the attic with a stage and wings, which the children took charge of immediately.

This place automatically put us in the class of the "well-to-do." Hollywood lived according to a system of different strata; the top would not consider inviting people who earned less than $100,000 a year, the same treatment was applied to those in the $50,000 bracket, and below that nobody cared who was who. Of course, all this does not apply to what I call real people; fortunately, they were in the great majority.

We lived seven years of a beautiful life in this house. There was the declaration of the free State of Israel by the great statesman Ben-Gurion. My heart swelled with joy at this news. Soon after, the young army of Israel showed its courage and brilliant intrepidity by winning its first fight for survival against the overwhelming mass of Arabs which surrounded it. After obtaining an armistice they were constantly harassed by guerrillas and snipers. But nothing prevented them from turning the desert they found into a beautiful country, thriving in agriculture and industries, with the great Weizmann Institute, which achieved wonders in technology, including turning salt water into the fresh water they needed for irrigation. Meier Dizengoff, the great mayor of Tel Aviv, made that city what it is today. The country became, with Italy and Spain, the great attraction for tourists. In spite of living in constant danger of attacks by its neighbors, it pursues its destiny in perfect serenity. Anti-Semitism, ever latent in the whole world, cannot silence the admiration which this brave little country inspires.

There was music at home on Tower Road. I remember a lovely concert which took place on the lawn in front of the house. The Los Angeles Chamber Orchestra, which had good players and a good conductor, fell into financial difficulties, and so with the help of the University of California, which lent me its big shell, which we settled at the end of the lawn, we put down the famous synthetic grass and a few hundred rented chairs and gave a concert devoted to Mozart. The orchestra played a symphony and *Eine Kleine Nachtmusik*, and I played a concerto. A large audience gathered at ten dollars a seat and we had as guests Stravinsky, Thomas Mann, and some music-loving film stars. So the orchestra was saved for a season!

Other, more important musical events took place there. The records of the trios of Tchaikovsky, Ravel, and Mendelssohn which I made with Heifetz and Piatigorsky were often rehearsed there. I had two beautiful Steinways, one a gift of my friend Theodore Steinway, which were used for the accompaniment of concertos or simply for the performance of some original works for two pianos.

At that time, I was in great demand by the film makers, who were convinced that only popular music was wanted. Classical music was derided in favor of jazz in many films. I fought energetically against this prejudice and refused stubbornly to be involved in any story which belittled the noble art of music.

I shall give here a little example of my contact with them: One day, Jack Warner of Warner Brothers called me: "Arthur, I have a lovely movie for you. Please come to my office and I will tell you all about it." When I was seated comfortably, facing him at his desk, he told me the story in vivid colors: "It is very moving, Arthur, and we need the best music for it. You can play whatever you choose. Any piano stuff you like—even Beethoven."

I was quite impressed. "Is it a drama about serious musicians?" I asked.

"Oh no, we wouldn't go that far, but it is pretty sad."

"Well, I have to play to console somebody or what?"

"W-e-e-ll, well, you see, Arthur, you sit down, play one of these sad pieces, when behind you a door opens and Jack Benny comes in with his fiddle and, seeing him, you immediately play his famous tune for him and you both roar with laughter. Isn't that wonderful?"

"Goodbye, Jack," I said, "be seeing you," and I walked out.

Later at a dinner party, Jack Warner said to me ironically, "You musicians have no sense of humor."

"How wrong can you be, Jack? Your comics live on gags written for them, but we musicians are famous for our repartee, good stories, and quick wit, but *we* don't do it for money."

Another time, I actually fell into the trap. Boris Morros, a Russian-born musician and head of the music department of Columbia Pictures, made a picture called *Carnegie Hall*, the historical story of this famous site. He engaged all the known names to contribute to it. I remember there were the conductors Bruno Walter, Stokowski, and Rodzinski, as well as Jascha Heifetz, Piatigorsky, and Lily Pons, and so, of course, I accepted. There was an absurd detail connected with it; we all had to fly from the Mecca of films, where we lived, to the infernal summer heat of New York to appear on the authentic stage of Carnegie Hall.

Mr. Morros welcomed me at the New York airport and drove me in his Rolls-Royce limousine to my hotel. During the long drive the verbose Mr. Morros treated me to a big avalanche of names he had obtained for his film, even resorting to a good deal of lying. "I'll get Toscanini, Kreisler, the whole bunch of them," he shouted. At that point, I lost my patience. "Boris," I said severely, "I can bet that before your film is over, Harry James will play the trumpet and win the day."

"Only for three minutes," Boris said. I was only guessing at random but fell on the right name! The film was about a charwoman at Carnegie Hall whose son showed talent for music, so of course she called on all of us to help him in his career. But secretly the boy loved only jazz, only jazz! Terrible drama between mother and son, who got married and then produced a composition (vide Gershwin) in the idiom of popular jazz, with the trumpet trumpeting the triumphant end.

A somewhat more interesting picture was offered me by Columbia Studios. It was a story about a blind pianist-composer whose concerto I had to play in person with Ormandy conducting. The composer had written a pleasant melody and we made a recording of it with full orchestra, but it was killingly funny during the actual filming to see Ormandy conducting with passion, using many gestures as though conducting a full orchestra, while the ten musicians needed by the camera pretended to play with fervor. Still funnier was when we had to bow and smile to an empty hall with a huge faked ovation while only a handful of people applauded for the camera.

A film which gave me real pleasure was the one which MGM made of the life of Robert Schumann. This time I had to contribute all the music which had to be performed later on the screen by the actors who played Robert Schumann, Clara Schumann, his wife, Johannes Brahms, and Franz Liszt.

It was a moving experience for me to try to imagine how these great artists performed and once I had to play the same piece in different ways. Robert Schumann presented to Clara, his young bride, the lovely and touching song called "Widmung" (dedication) and played it for her rather imperfectly but with the right feeling. At a great party, at which the Schumanns and Brahms were present, Liszt, who performed his own *Mephisto Waltz*,

gave as an encore his brilliant and showy concert version of that same song.
Clara Schumann, displeased with his showy performance, gave the great
pianist a lesson by playing it to him in its original form, simply and beautifully. I had the hard task of making all this sound authentic. Katharine
Hepburn did wonders impersonating Clara Schumann, playing the concertos
of Liszt and Schumann, and other works, as if she were a born pianist. The
whole film was made with love and respect for the subject.

A Mr. Rudolf Polk, a friend of ours and a fine musician, formed a
company to make short television films, with Marian Anderson, Heifetz,
Piatigorsky, Jan Peerce, and me as investors and artistic contributors.
Heifetz and I each made a half-hour film of our lives at home with much
music and another one in which we were joined by Piatigorsky for trios.
The company broke up after two years because films became too costly to
make but they are still shown in colleges and universities.

Alina and Johnny showed a talent for music very early. Alina
became a fine pianist but did not want to appear in public and Johnny
revealed a talent for composition. Once on my return from a tour, Alina,
almost six, played for me a little piece with one or two daring modulations;
little Johnny, barely four, jealous of his sister, banged on the other piano
and was ordered out of the room. After a while, I fetched the crying little
boy and sat down at the piano, taking him on my lap. "Now you can play
all you want, my darling," I said, expecting some more banging, but to my
astonishment, the little chap played his sister's piece without a mistake and
in another tonality. I could not believe my ears. "Who taught you that,
Johnny?" I asked suspiciously. "Oh, Daddy," he said, "I can start it from
any key." Well, he proved it and much more. He composes brilliantly in the
modern American idiom and, to boot, has become a well-known actor.

113

European audiences, as I discovered, felt an inveterate snobbism
toward a much-publicized success in the United States, especially when
large sums of money were involved. In several capitals like London, Paris,
Amsterdam, and Stockholm, where before the war I could not fill the large

halls, the mere announcement of dates would now automatically sell out before the programs and other details were revealed. Even the provinces offered large fees in order to present me to their usually lazy audiences. Playing in all these cities gave me the joy of getting acquainted with the beauty of these countries. My concerts in Montpellier, Narbonne, and Toulouse allowed me to visit the old town of Carcassonne, where the old fortress town has been preserved intact since the Middle Ages.

It was fun to take part (only once!) in the newly created Edinburgh Festival. Here the organizer choked the audiences with so many events that the poor public was forced to make difficult choices; for instance, in the morning you could watch the graceful kilted Scotch soldiers dancing their famous reels, but you might miss a Mass by Bach performed by a visiting orchestra with a great conductor. In the early afternoon there would be a recital by a pianist or a famous violinist—mind you, there was probably another pianist or violinist of the same caliber waiting for his date—and you could miss a matinee by the Comédie Française or a fine concert of chamber music. But this is not all. Of course, everybody in the whole town of Edinburgh never missed their tea—that was sacred. The evening provided new trouble; there would be a great opera performance, a premiere of a play, and a smash-hit film to be seen at the same time. And I forget great performances by the best English and foreign orchestras. I hope I didn't leave out too many other events. Needless to say, I never played there again.

Italy went through the most amazing change. This country had been completely dominated for more than a century by opera; the ancient Società del Quartetto of Milan kept its series at the Conservatorio Verdi, and Rome, thanks to the Count San Martino, had the concerts and the orchestra of the Santa Cecilia, but there was practically no concert or symphonic music in the provinces.

I shall never forget my astonishment when I went to Milan for the first time after the war with Nela, Eva, and Paul. We traveled full of excited expectation at the thought of seeing an opera at the great Scala. When we arrived, we rushed to the porter to inquire about which opera was to be given that night. He answered condescendingly, "The great concert season has already started and will last for another six weeks." We were flabbergasted. It was the same thing in Rome and the other important cities—no opera but the great symphonic and concert season. To my great joy, the Italians had rediscovered the very essence of music. Donizetti, Rossini, Bellini, and Verdi, with their beautiful arias, cavatinas, the high C's of the tenors, and the star coloraturas and dramatic sopranos began to fade into the background. They now proudly remembered that the great art of music was born in their country. Beautiful ensembles sprang up like mushrooms which revealed the greatness of Vivaldi, of Monteverdi and Pergolesi. I Musici, I Virtuosi di Roma, the Quartetto Italiano, the Trio di Trieste, the Scarlatti Chamber Orchestra of Naples revealed to the world the great Italian art. Operas, of course, continued all over Italy, but as in Germany, France, and England, they were only a part of the musical life now.

I was happy to be able to fill the great Scala of Milan, the San Carlos Opera of Naples, the Opera of Genoa, the Fenice in Venice, the Opera in Florence and Bologna, and the great auditorium of the Vatican in Rome, with one or two recitals and sometimes as soloist with their excellent orchestras. In the lovely mountain city of Perugia, Mrs. Alba Buitoni generously offered to her fellow citizens the most beautiful season of concerts.

In Siena, Count Guido Chigi, a nobleman like the art-loving dukes of the Cinquecento, built a modern concert hall in his famous old palazzo. He engaged his artists for their usual fee but used the proceeds for the embellishment of the city. I had played for him twice before the war and had been his guest in the palazzo. Now I offered to play for him without remuneration; but after the concert, this grand seigneur came on the platform holding in both hands a picture by an Old Master as a present for me. At my next concert in Siena he repeated the same gesture. Those pictures certainly represented much more than any fee.

The two Brahms concertos, which I love so much, became firm favorites and anything I played was heard now with great interest and understanding.

France, too, discovered a sudden love for Brahms, perhaps due to the long occupation by the Germans. The wonderful Dietrich Fischer-Dieskau and the lieder singer Elisabeth Schwarzkopf sang Schubert to sold-out houses and even the difficult works of Mahler became much in demand.

England, once regarded as having little interest in music, dedicated only to sport, became after the war the country most deeply devoted to the masters of chamber music in all its forms, with many first-class chamber music ensembles and orchestras. London alone has five first-rate symphony orchestras with the best conductors available.

After the disappearance of Queen's Hall, a large modern hall called the Royal Festival Hall was built on the other side of the Thames just across the bridge from the famous Savoy Hotel. The Festival Hall was adopted immediately by all the great music events. After the war, London succeeded Berlin as the most important musical center. A novel operatic venture was created by a man of vision, Mr. John Christie. He built a small opera house on his estate about seventy kilometers from London, Glyndebourne, which was devoted mainly to fine performances of Mozart operas. Rudolf Bing, late director of the Metropolitan Opera House, and the conductor Fritz Busch helped him to achieve an ideal atmosphere for enjoying the finest in opera.

While I was playing in Zurich, Mr. Horowitz wired me that my brother Ignacy had died at the Rothschild Hospital in Paris. He gave me more details by telephone and offered to help arrange the funeral because I could not interrupt my Swiss tour. The funeral was attended by many of his friends and I was touched to learn that Germaine was also present.

On our return to Paris, we were still forced to live in hotels, unable to dislodge my unwanted tenants. Life in France after the war had changed considerably. The war, which had caused so much loss of life and destruction to Great Britain, which fought for three years all alone, and to the United States, which finally helped to obtain the victory, deploying all its might in the last year, left France practically untouched. True enough, a few cities and some villages in Normandy had suffered in the Allied attack, but the rest of the country remained intact. Of course, the French Jewish population was murdered as in all the countries occupied by the Nazis, and the brave Resistance, which behaved heroically, suffered losses. The French Army in Africa helped England to fight General Rommel and were allowed by Eisenhower and Montgomery to be the first to enter Paris led by General de Gaulle, who initiated the Resistance and directed it from London.

Although the picture of France remained the same, the people themselves had changed. As in the time of Zola and the Dreyfus affair, the country was divided in two. There were the Vichy collaborators on one side and the Resistance and non-collaborators on the other.

As for myself, I found with bitter sadness that many of my best prewar friends had been too friendly with the Nazi occupiers. Melchior de Polignac, Sacha Guitry, and a few others were among them and I never saw them again. My new friends included Pierre Brisson, the prewar drama critic of *Le Temps*, who courageously revived *Le Figaro*, the famous daily, with a flock of the best writers and reporters. He resisted all attempts of the shareholders to turn it into a more commercial newspaper and directed it gloriously until his death. I owe it to his faithful friendship to have found a great support for my Paris career. It was he who introduced me at one of his dinners, where he had gathered many interesting people, to Professor Louis Pasteur Vallery Radot, the only grandson of the great Pasteur and in his own right a great medical figure. As in the case of Pierre Benouville, we became close friends from that evening on. He was a man of the highest intellect, an admirable doctor endowed with an enthusiasm for the arts and, thank God, with a magnificent sense of humor. His friendship embellished my life and his death left behind a great void. A brave Resistance fighter, he worshipped De Gaulle, who, in appreciation, bestowed all possible honors on the professor. A member of the Académie Française, he became president of the Conseil d'Etat and was awarded the Grand Cross of the Légion d'Honneur. After De Gaulle arrested General Salan and a few other generals for their revolt against him in Algiers, he appointed a special court of ten judges, including Vallery Radot; when the Attorney General demanded a unanimous death sentence for Salan, the only negative vote was that of Vallery Radot. De Gaulle never forgave him. When I asked my friend why he went against De Gaulle's wishes, he answered simply, "I try to save lives and not to kill."

It was De Gaulle's attitude which broke his heart. He never recovered from his disillusion and died a few years later. It was a terrible loss to all of us, his friends. He was the kindest, most understanding and generous man I have ever known.

My readers might be interested to know about what happened to the many people with whom they have become acquainted through my writings. Poor Pola died in Warsaw after suffering from cancer for a long time. When she had heard of my marriage, her sad comment was: "He begins his life when I finish mine."

Gabriella Besanzoni, who gave up her career after marrying the multimillionaire Brazilian ship owner, soon became a widow and led the lonely life of the rich. Later she came to her native Rome, where I often saw her at my concerts; she died prematurely, disappointed with her life.

Armand de Gontaut-Biron, whom I remember with much gratitude, fought in the First World War and married a wealthy Brazilian lady. To my regret, I did not see him and lost contact with him. When I arrived in Paris I learned the news of his death.

Joseph Jaroszynski and Antek Moszkowski, my pals of old times, miraculously survived not only the Nazi occupation but also the tragic Polish uprising. They absolutely flabbergasted me when shortly after the Allied victory they both wrote to me, not complaining or asking for help, but recommending a young pianist to me named Wladislav Kedra, who, as a matter of fact, made a career but died very young. Jaroszynski himself, poor fellow, died in Cracow in an old men's home and Antek was dead before I returned to Warsaw.

Paderewski as a widower left his home in Morges for the United States to do some patriotic work for Poland and give some concerts, mainly to be able to pay his taxes to the American treasury. His last concert in New York drew a huge crowd in Madison Square Garden, but the poor old master, then eighty, felt such a moral prostration that he thought he had finished the concert when he hadn't even begun it. It was one of the saddest evenings I can think of. His last records, which he was probably induced to make against his better judgment, unfortunately leave a bad testimony to the real artist he was. He died during the most tragic days of the war at the Buckingham Hotel in New York, a lonely, broken man. He was honored by the American government with burial at Arlington Cemetery.

Rachmaninoff, who kept his artistic powers until the end, died two years after Paderewski. With the death of Richard Strauss, the world of music turned now to Stravinsky, Schönberg, and Ravel.

Prokofiev triumphantly entered the international scene with his symphonies, piano and violin concertos, and piano sonatas, his beautiful ballets and his music for the famous films of Eisenstein. Bartók, who had been recognized by musicians from his earliest works, became overnight the most widely played composer after his sad, lonely death in New York.

114

The first few years at Tower Road were a dream as long as the whole family lived together. Nela's mother had a lovely sunny room with a bay window and a gay bird singing in his cage. Eva graduated brilliantly from the Westlake School, continued her dancing lessons with Madame Bekeffi, but entered the University of California at Los Angeles and took classes in acting, for which she showed quite a talent. Paul was graduated *cum laude* from the Cate School near Santa Barbara and was accepted at Yale University.

Alina and Johnny were a pair of darlings whom we simply adored. They had a happy life, constantly at play with the children of actors who lived in our neighborhood. Their nurses saw to it that no birthday party could be given without having them all invited and so at the big children's parties in our house there was Juliette Colman, Geraldine Chaplin, Liza Minnelli, Candice Bergen, Rebecca Wells. Little Johnny at the ripe age of three fell in love with the beautiful little Candy. After every party he would shout, "I want Candy, I want Candy."

I had the open veranda, which served to store the wood for the fireplace, turned into a lovely closed one with large windows overlooking the lawn and we had happy family meals there. Our friend Kanarek painted a large triptych, which hung in the veranda.

It was also at Tower Road that I found in myself the courage to build up a new library and to begin a new collection of pictures. The postwar years brought to America many Europeans who came with all they had been able to save from the Nazis. Los Angeles and New York were the best markets for them and I had the good fortune to be able to acquire books of the greatest value and some Impressionist pictures which I could never have dreamed of finding in Paris. The widow of a French antiquarian book dealer brought from Paris a unique first edition of La Fontaine's fables published in Amsterdam by the Fermiers Généraux. From other sources I found a limited edition on Japanese paper of the work of Renoir by the famous art dealer Vollard. A *Ulysses* by Joyce illustrated by Matisse. Heine's first edition of the *Buch der Lieder* with his autographed dedication to a friend. The complete collection of the *Yellow Book* with the contributions of the greatest English writers of its time, all illustrated by Aubrey Beardsley and beautifully bound.

I cannot go into detail about the few hundred books of great interest which I managed to acquire. One particular collection, however, I must describe: On a visit to play in Kansas City, I went into the hotel book shop to buy some magazines and a paperback novel. A long row of magnificently bound books caught my eye, an unusual sight in such a place. When I questioned him, the man answered animatedly, "This is the most complete collection of the first editions of Charles Dickens. It even includes his speeches and first magazine pieces. A man who lived here, a fanatical lover of Dickens, bought up these precious books wherever he could in the world and I was lucky to acquire them after his recent death."

I became pale with emotion, but put on my poker face. "If it is not too expensive, I would be glad to buy it," I said casually. "Oh," he said, "the collection is practically sold. The University of Kansas wants to buy it but I have to wait until a quorum decides about spending the money."

"Ha-ha," I said, "these universities are always very slow with their decisions, but if the price is not too high, I have a check ready for you."

The price was not too high and the university was still undecided, so the good man grabbed my check and this marvelous collection became the pride of my library in Paris and the great envy of my English friends.

It was in Los Angeles that I met Reuven Rubin, the Israeli painter. Edward G. Robinson, the film star, who had one of the finest art collections in the world, advised me to visit an exhibition of Rubin's. I fell in love with his pictures and bought four of them. My enthusiasm for his work and his appreciation of my playing developed with time into a very close friendship. I later visited him often in the beautiful house which he designed and built in Caesarea in Israel. He, his lovely wife, Esther, and his son and daughter formed one of the happiest families I have ever known. The last time I saw him, shortly before he died, he drew a portrait of me at the piano with some stars and dedicated it to me with a trembling hand; I played for him his most beloved nocturne of Chopin. In my humble opinion he was the greatest painter of flowers of his time.

One summer the organizers of the Ravinia Park concerts near Chicago invited Heifetz, Piatigorsky, and me to give four concerts of trios and sonatas in one week. This novel form of playing in public appealed to us. We made up four interesting programs which contained among others the trios of Mendelssohn, Tchaikovsky, and Ravel and the well-known sonatas we had often played together. Our ensemble created quite a sensation. Our concerts drew the largest audiences and a critic had the bad taste to call us the Million-Dollar Trio. This title was picked up all over the country and as a result I immediately discontinued appearances of this kind.

These concerts remind me of a funny little quarrel with Heifetz. He bitterly resented that all the publicity bore the names Rubinstein, Heifetz, Piatigorsky—always in the same order. "Why can't we change it and give each one of us a chance to be the first-named?" said Jascha.

"I couldn't care less," I answered indifferently, "but as far as I know, all trios are published for piano, violin, and violoncello, and it is the tradition to publicize the players in this order."

Jascha didn't want to give in so soon. "I have seen some trios printed for violin and violoncello, accompanied by the piano," he said.

"They must have been printed by yourself, Jascha."

"What do you mean?" he said indignantly. "I've really seen them."

I began to see red. "Jascha," I shouted, "if God played the violin, it would still be printed Rubinstein, God, and Piatigorsky." No reply from Jascha. But we did make records of those three trios and put much work and love into them.

I also made some solo records in Hollywood in the RCA studio, where it was pleasant to work. My concerts became more numerous and more successful in the United States. Alfred Wallenstein, conductor of the Los Angeles Philharmonic, invited me to play with his orchestra the five Beethoven concertos, for which I had to learn the first two, and the *Emperor* which I had never performed in public before. I worked happily at them and gave a loving performance at the concert. The warm reception they received encouraged me to prepare for future concerts five Mozart concertos which I had always dreamed of playing in public but was never allowed to do because the American orchestras insisted on the showpieces, the Tchaikovsky, Saint-Saëns, and Liszt.

It was at Tower Road that I added to my repertoire of recordings the

Franck *Variations symphoniques* and the difficult *Paganini Variations* by Rachmaninoff, which I had never dared to play while the composer was alive. I keep a most grateful memory of our big salon with the two marvelous pianos which inspired me to enlarge my repertoire with many much-loved solo pieces by Chopin, Schumann, Schubert, and Brahms—music to which I had been too lazy to give the much-needed technical work for proper concert performances. Some evenings of beautiful chamber music with my friends also enriched my life in California. For our evenings of chamber music, we had the Thomas Manns and a few real music lovers. We had the Stravinskys a few times for dinner and went to their house for cocktails, but the long distances from house to house made frequent gatherings of friends very difficult.

I must even shamefully boast about winning in two consecutive years a silver cup for the largest attendance—with Menuhin, Heifetz, Horowitz, and Serkin as runners-up. In connection with this, I received a pleasant letter from the Hollywood Bowl committee; they notified me that they had to pay Horowitz and Heifetz six thousand dollars each for their appearances. As I was always satisfied with my fee of three thousand dollars, they felt a moral obligation to send me a check for an additional three thousand dollars.

For our twentieth wedding anniversary, we gave a dinner and dance in the best Hollywood tradition. More than one hundred guests attended. Drinks were served at two large bars for more than two hours. A large dance floor was erected on the great space surrounded by the eucalyptus trees and tables were laid for six or eight around the dance floor. We were lucky in securing one of the finest bands in town for the evening.

There was also a charming interlude. A colleague of Eva's at the university wrote a one-act playlet which was performed in the small theater in our attic in our honor by Eva and a few of her classmates. As it was rather short, the performance took place during cocktail hours. At one point, Nela clapped her hands for silence and said, explaining the occasion, "Whoever wants to see it is welcome but you are by no means obliged." To our great pleasure, our most important guests, such as the Samuel Goldwyns, the David Selznicks, Charles Laughton, Deborah Kerr, Greer Garson, Cary Grant, and twenty or thirty others, climbed the stairs to the attic, where they sat in comfortable chairs and listened politely to the unpretentious little one-act play. We all applauded it heartily and the Goldwyns were even enthusiastic about Eva.

When we all joined the others at the bars, Charles Laughton, reaching for a large whiskey on the rocks, said to me, "My dear fellow, the next time I invite you for dinner, you will have to listen to six Beethoven sonatas before you get anything to eat." The dinner, splendidly prepared by Nela and served by a lot of hired help, was a great success. French champagne was served throughout. The dancing went on until late hours.

The house lent itself to large receptions. I remember a particular one on the other side of the house where the guests enjoyed the view of the whole garden, beautifully illuminated by my old friend Mr. Nightingale. It was given in honor of Germaine de Rothschild, who had come to visit the Piatigorskys. Our guests were mainly the musical world and many friends from Europe and French and English actors.

Nela's brother, Bronislaw Mlynarski, married Doris Kenyon, the beautiful film star of the silent movies, and started a small mail-order antiquarian book business. As he was in touch with antiquarian book shops, he was well informed about auctions. Thanks to him, I was able to acquire Chopin's only passport at a sale in London. On another occasion he sent us in Paris the catalogue of an important sale of autographed letters in Geneva. One can well imagine my astonishment when I found in this catalogue a few letters by myself, the most reluctant letter writer in the world. As I didn't want to be seen at that sale, Nela went to Geneva to buy them. Real collectors always know what is rare, so there was quite a demand for them and Nela had to pay an unusually high price for letters by a still-living correspondent. She bought on the same occasion a large number of letters by Saint-Saëns and Jacques Thibaud for a lower price because there were so many in existence. All these letters were addressed to Gabriel Astruc, who had been the manager of all three of us. Of my letters, some were the ones sent from America in 1906 with my horrible, urgent demands for money, while the others were the result of a few years of accepting or refusing contracts for programs and other items. They are all now fortunately safe in my hands.

On my frequent returns to Paris, I now found a great market for pictures and books at accessible prices. I became one of the passionate buyers and still live happily with my acquisitions.

At that time, I would give tours in Europe in the autumn and in America after New Year, with the summer spent at home in Beverly Hills. Nela always accompanied me to Paris, where we settled at the Royale Monceau, avenue Hoche. I would open my tour with two or three concerts at the Salle du Trocadero or at the Théâtre des Champs-Elysées, followed by London, the Scandinavian countries, and Italy.

On one of the early tours, Eva came, and it was the year when I had agreed to go to Israel with Eva for the whole month of December and give twenty concerts there. It was a difficult tour. I was obliged to repeat the

Concerto in B flat of Brahms eight times in eight days in Tel Aviv, as the hall was small and the subscription was large enough to fill it eight times over.

After a few days' rest, I had to play the concerto a few times in Jerusalem and in Haifa; the remaining performances were recitals with some free days in between. To my dismay, the airline was on strike and we had to wait six days in Rome before taking off for Tel Aviv. When I suggested shortening the tour, the Israel Philharmonic implored me not to do so, and thus I had to play all twenty concerts in twenty days. We stayed in a little house provided for visiting artists, managed by a nice Bulgarian lady and her husband. After the last performance of the Brahms, when the audience refused to leave without some encores, a small crowd of enthusiasts broke into the hall.

It was for me an unforgettable experience to be for the first time in the newborn State of Israel. Yigael Yadin, the commander in chief of the Israeli forces in the 1948 war and a great music lover, became my friend. At a small dinner in our artists' house, he told us the amazing story of how the victory was won. As he was really by profession an archaeologist, he told us, he discovered the ancient Biblical road to Egypt, from which he took the Egyptian army by surprise, captured many prisoners, among them a young Lieutenant Nasser, and routed the rest of them.

"Our fight against the Syrians was rather a funny affair. As we were extremely poor in cannons, I used a little stratagem of my own." Here he smiled broadly. "You know the terrific noise American war films can produce. Well, I placed some of them at strategic points using huge megaphones. The effect was fantastic," he laughed, "the Syrians fled, panic-stricken."

Eva behaved beautifully and was a great help to me. During the day, she would visit the hospital to talk to the wounded soldiers and cheer them up with her charm and vitality. The evenings she spent at all my concerts, either in the hall or reading in the artists' room. On our return to California, she gave lectures about Israel at several private gatherings.

When Eva was eighteen, we decided to give her a grand coming-out party. Beverly Hills was not the appropriate place and in New York we did not know any young people. Our great friend Mrs. Robert Low Bacon from Washington gave us the right advice. Virginia Bacon was one of the three great hostesses of the capital; the others were Mrs. Robert Bliss of Dumbarton Oaks and Alice Longworth, daughter of Theodore Roosevelt and widow of Nicholas Longworth, the Speaker of the House. I met these ladies at all the important parties in Washington. Alice Longworth, at Virginia's suggestion, made it possible for me to give Eva's ball at the Sulgrave Club, the finest, most suitable place for our party. Eva stayed with Mrs. Bacon for two weeks and was invited to all the other coming-out parties, where she became acquainted with all the other young people. We invited over a hundred of them, plus the elite of Washington society. Over three hundred guests attended. I had a Steinway grand placed on the platform with the wonderful dance band specially selected for us by Jules Stein, the all-powerful president of these bands in America. The flower decorations, the buffet, the champagne were supervised by Nela, who knew how to find the best caterers and florists. It was quite a sight when Nela, Eva, and I received our guests. The *grande toilettes* of the ladies and the obligatory white ties and tails of the men reminded me nostalgically of the old days of Edwardian London. After "The Star-Spangled Banner," played by the band, I sat down at the piano and announced, "I shall play for you the Grand Polonaise of Chopin to introduce my dear daughter to society." Needless to say, I never played it better. After which I had the privilege of dancing the first waltz with my Eva. This party went on until the early hours and was not forgotten by those present.

Back at Tower Road, I became busy recording and driving my Cadillac proudly to the RCA studios—quite a few records were born there. I remember especially a not too bad version of the *Carnaval* of Schumann and the *Fantasiestücke* and a record devoted to Grieg. I chose from the *Lyric Pieces,* my favorites. It had always annoyed me that little children were given sonatas of Mozart and the Grieg pieces as "easy" to play when the poor darlings didn't know what to do with them.

It was in the fifties that I recorded the violin sonatas of Brahms and three of my favorite Beethovens with Henryk Szeryng, a young Polish violinist whom we met and heard in Mexico after the last war; he, like so many others, was an exile. We invited him to our home in Beverly Hills and introduced him to our musical friends. As he was completely unknown in the United States, Hurok showed no interest in him, but finally RCA agreed to make the sonata records. They had always wanted me to do them with Heifetz but I refused because he treated these sonatas as solo pieces with accompaniment. These records with Szeryng came off beautifully. Upon his return to Europe after the war, Szeryng appeared everywhere with growing success and is now one of the foremost violinists.

Around 1953 our life at our home in Tower Road began to deteriorate. Poor Nela went through a very difficult operation, but thank heaven soon recovered her strength. Our Japanese gardener, who kept the whole place so beautiful, left us because of illness and proved to be irreplaceable. We had to hire two, then three men, who were unable to keep it in order.

We were seriously thinking of selling the place, but were advised against it. "Nobody can run a place like that," our friends would tell us. "It is too expensive and the rich film colony are satisfied with their own houses, so you would sell it at a great loss." After this pessimistic talk, we did not make any decisions, especially as I had previously had a disagreeable experience. I had acquired three lots in the most promising neighborhood of Beverly Hills. I felt proud of being a happy speculator when the unexpected blow came. One morning, I received a severe letter from the municipality with the order to hire a watchman night and day because the whole neighborhood deposited their rubbish on my lots. The next day, I sold my lots with only a tiny weeny gain.

I left for my tour, which opened with some concerts in eastern Canada and took me in rapid succession through Boston, New York, and Washington down to the tropical Florida, to which I added Havana as usual. In this cigar paradise I played with particular pleasure at the lovely auditorium built by a committee of wealthy ladies. The subscription series there was always sold out, but a strange thing usually occurred. The artist who was engaged always played to an empty hall because the subscribers, who formed the elite of Havana society, used to spend their winters in New York or in Europe and were not allowed to give their tickets to outsiders, only to their household. So it happened that the few members of the audience were maids and butlers of rich houses, unless the owners had forgotten to leave them. I, for my part, could not complain because they insisted on having me for a date before their departure!

After Cuba, my concerts covered the Midwest. The day after my performance in Detroit, I could not get a taxi to the airport and at the last minute I had to take the airport bus. I was just running down the steps to the street when a bellboy screamed, "Mr. Rubinstein, there is a call from Los Angeles for you." Calls from home always frightened me—something might have happened, so I begged the unwilling bus driver to wait a minute for me, ran to the telephone booth, and picked up the receiver. It was Nela: "There is a buyer for our house. He offers fifty percent more than we paid for it. Shall I sell?" Without taking a breath, I said, "Sell it." And this is how we left California.

115

A new page of our life began in New York. Nela found an apartment in a very nice house on Park Avenue and Sixty-sixth Street. We moved in with Nela's mother, the two younger children, and Kathryn. Eva found a studio nearby with a roommate and Paul was finishing at the Wharton School of Finance at the University of Pennsylvania. It was rather small, but big events took place there. Alina entered Nightingale School, where she was happy; she was a brilliant pupil, loved by everybody. Johnny took over his school right from the beginning. He always played the main roles in the school plays, and I remember him with pride as Peter Pan. As for myself, I took a much greater part in the concert life in the East.

I must write here about a little girl who came after a recital at Carnegie Hall with a little flower in her hand and murmured a few nice words. From then on, year after year, she repeated this gesture. When we moved to New York—she was by then about fifteen—she continued her little ritual. One evening my wife stopped her and asked, "What do you do in life?"

"I am a pianist," she said, "and study at Juilliard."

"Why didn't you say so before?" said Nela, and I added, "Come tomorrow for a cup of tea and play me something."

She was better than good, she was very talented. She was from Yugoslavia, and her name was Dubravka Tomsic. Later, whenever she learned a new piece, she would come to play it for me.

One day, she burst into tears and told us that she had to go back to Yugoslavia. "The government has stopped its grant because dollars became too expensive, but if I leave New York before finishing school," she said, "there is no hope for a career for me."

I felt terribly sorry and had to do something about it. I called up the ambassador of Yugoslavia and asked if he could receive me on an important matter. We found a convenient day and I left for Washington. Fortunately, he turned out to be a man of culture and understood the poor girl's plight. "I shall inform the government about your intervention and shall give you the answer as soon as possible." The ambassador was also a man of good manners. He announced his wish to come to New York to give me the government's answer. "There is a proposal from our President Tito for you. He has consented to continue to pay for Miss Tomsic's studies in America out of his own pocket if you would give her lessons." It was a startling condition indeed! But remembering Dubravka's talent, I agreed, and for two years, on and off, I gave her lessons until she finished brilliantly high school and Juilliard at the same time.

On one of my frequent returns to New York, I saw with astonishment a poster in front of Carnegie Hall announcing a recital by Dubravka Tomsic at the odd hour of five in the afternoon, sandwiched between an afternoon and an evening concert. She sent me tickets for a box without further explanation. My whole family accompanied me to the concert, greatly puzzled about the affair. The house was quite well filled, mainly with young people. Dubravka, who had grown to be a tall strong young lady with dark hair, appeared in a long dress to our great amazement. I remember perfectly a few items of her program. A brilliant performance of the *Appassionata* by Beethoven and the *Mephisto Waltz* by Liszt, played in a tremendous tempo which brought the house down. Many large bouquets of flowers were brought on the stage. She had to give two or three encores and was allowed to stop only when the manager reminded the audience that the hall had to be evacuated for the next concert. We dashed to the artist's room to embrace her and to find out how it had all happened.

"I did it by myself," she said, "because my friends from my school and Juilliard promised me to fill the house and I made a little money. I was lucky but I had decided to go to jail if I couldn't pay."

Soon after, this brave girl returned triumphantly to her country, where President Tito invited her to his summer residence. She is now the most prominent pianist of Yugoslavia and is very successful in Germany, Italy, Spain, and many other countries. We always remain in touch with her.

During these years Horowitz, who was constantly canceling his appearances, gave up giving concerts altogether, due to some illness which he said was colitis. It made me sad to see this magnificent pianist stop his career at the height of his success. So my rivals remained Rudolf Serkin and Robert Casadesus.

My young protégé William Kapell, who rose so rapidly in his career and promised to become the best American-born pianist, met his death in a tragic accident when the plane bringing him back from a tour in Australia crashed before landing in San Francisco.

Walter Gieseking, the self-declared Nazi follower, had the bad taste to fly to America for some fresh dollars but was refused entrance by the authorities.

Emil Gilels, the great Russian pianist and a dear friend of mine, was brought to America by Hurok after his enormous success in England and France. He has remained a great favorite in all the countries where he has appeared and still is now as I write this book.

As for violinists, Heifetz was the only one who filled houses after Kreisler's death. Thibaud came to New York to give a single concert at Carnegie Hall, played beautifully the Havanaise by Saint-Saëns and all the rest to perfection, but was criticized for his small tone. Dear Jacques was then killed two years later in an airplane on his way to Japan. Isaac Stern, a young violinist from San Francisco, came to the fore and has progressed ever since.

The New York Philharmonic had a new conductor, Dimitri Mitropoulos, a Greek idealist and a fine musician endowed with an uncanny memory. Among many fantastic performances, I remember particularly the opera *Wozzeck* of Alban Berg conducted entirely from memory. He never used a score for the accompaniment of soloists in any concertos. Himself a fine pianist, a pupil of Busoni, he liked to play from time to time the difficult Third Concerto of Prokofiev or a Bartók or Křenek, conducting from the keyboard, and for once the New York Philharmonic loved their conductor.

It was at that time that the young Leonard Bernstein made a sensation replacing Rodzinski at the last minute. Immediately he became assistant to Charles Munch in Boston, from where he was often engaged in many other cities.

Our first meeting took place in Montreal, where I was to play the Grieg concerto and the *Nights in the Gardens of Spain* of de Falla. The conductor for this concert was to have been my old friend Désiré Defauw, who became ill, so was replaced by young Bernstein, with whom I was delighted to play. At the morning rehearsal on the day of the concert, after the exchange of usual compliments (I: "I've heard so much about you." He: "I've always loved your concerts"), we set to work on the Grieg. After the octave introduction by the piano, he took the rather melancholic theme in a quick gay mood. I stopped playing, went up to him, and whispered, "I play the theme slower; it is rather sad, you know."

To which he answered quite rudely, "This music is not even worth talking about, and as for the de Falla piece, it's not much better."

That did it. "Why did you agree to play these pieces in the first place? You could have asked for some concertos for which you feel a little more respect, but as you dislike my program so much, I shall not play with you at all. I'll play some piano music after intermission and you can begin the concert with your own stuff," and I walked away.

Music, art, culture, and living are divided in Montreal between the native French and the English. I had played until then strictly for the French Canadians. My decision not to play with Bernstein provoked a hysterical outcry from the temperamental French organizers which made poor Bernstein regret his youthful impulse. He ran to a shop, bought me a beautiful cashmere scarf, and came to my hotel room with loud apologies.

"All right," I said, "but how shall we play tonight without a rehearsal?"

The answer was one of a real musician: "Oh," he smiled, "I could conduct both these works by heart. No problem." And he did conduct them beautifully. After a huge success and our taking five or six bows, he conceded, "I'm beginning to like both works."

We became great friends, played many times together, and up to this late hour he still dominates the musical life of New York both as a conductor and as a composer. The Philharmonic Orchestra, which he led for years, adored him for his inventive ways of making money for them—television, recordings, children's concerts, etc., etc.

George Szell, whom I admired from the first moment when I heard him conduct a new opera in Prague, became musical director and conductor of the Cleveland Orchestra, which reached, after a few years, such a perfection that it put in the shade the Philadelphia and Boston orchestras, which had previously reigned for decades. Unfortunately he died too young, but his glorious records of the symphonies of Beethoven, Brahms, Schumann, and many others fill my last years with indescribable joy.

The programs played all over America still relied mostly on the so-called classics and the old romantics, but the genius of a Stravinsky, Bartók, and, above all, Mahler was beginning to be discovered. A trickle of Schönberg and his disciples, Berg and Webern, was heard here and there, but the audiences listen to this music reluctantly, showing respect only for the names.

Pianists began to treat their audiences to one or a few evenings of the same composer and it became quite common to hear all the Beethoven sonatas and especially all-Chopin recitals because both these composers, so different musically, manage to attract the largest audiences.

My own programs had changed considerably since my European and South American days. I discovered that Albéniz inspired endless ovations not only in Spain and South America but even in France, Italy, and Poland. In London *Navarra* had to be one of my encores and the *Ritual Fire Dance* of de Falla was an eternal winner.

In 1955, suddenly I felt the urge to do something out of the ordinary. My plan was to play all the concertos which I had accumulated over the years and perform them in five concerts to be given in Paris, London, and

New York. Fortunately, the best orchestra of Paris, the Conservatoire, and one of London's finest accepted my idea of giving these concerts in collaboration with me. New York was more difficult, but to Hurok's great disappointment, I decided to hire an orchestra with Wallentsein conducting, which diminished considerably my own profit and Hurok's percentage.

My program consisted of seventeen works, but to give it a form, I began each concert with a Beethoven concerto. The others were by Brahms, Chopin, Schumann, Mozart, Liszt, Saint-Saëns, and the Rachmaninoff *Paganini Variations*, the Franck *Variations symphoniques*, and *Nights in the Gardens of Spain* of de Falla. In London, I played the Grieg instead of the Saint-Saëns. My conductor in Paris was Jean Fournet and in London, Sir Adrian Boult.

It was a great undertaking which I simply adored. I played in London and Paris on alternate days with one rehearsal for each concert and flew back and forth, until one day there was an air strike and, alas, I was obliged to take the old trains and the nasty boat between Calais and Dover.

At one of the rehearsals of a London concert, a young man appeared. "I came to replace Sir Adrian, who is not feeling well." We had to rehearse for five hours because he didn't know the works well enough. But my enthusiasm remained undaunted. The public in both cities received my concerts with clamorous ovations, but the critic of *The Times*, who never liked my playing, went so far as to declare after the first concert: "His performance of the Beethoven had no depth and does not bode well for the next concerts." After the second concert, however, he must have realized that I could have sued him for trying to discourage my public from attending; he expressed admiration for the Beethoven I played that evening but added that the English pianists have a different conception!

In New York these concerts not only were a great success but were considered a remarkable feat, although my own private feeling was rather that it was an easy task because all these concertos were part of my current repertoire and so it was sheer pleasure to be able to play them all in only five concerts.

After two of them, I spent the whole night recording some of the concertos with Wallenstein.

Eight

Home Again in Paris,
More Concert Tours
and Recordings

116

During this time, I finally regained possession of my house in Paris. Various circumstances, both agreeable and disagreeable, helped me. The agreeable one was that the couple who were living in my house were getting divorced and both were without money. The disagreeable one was that, on the advice of my lawyer, I had to dish out to them one million francs (about three thousand dollars) to leave the premises of my very own home, instead of sending them to prison for occupying it for so many years without paying rent.

We immediately engaged an architect, highly recommended by Germaine, who practically rebuilt the house. It took him ten months to finish his work but it was then that Alina and Johnny came with us for their first visit. These two exceptionally gifted children took to the beauties of Paris in no time.

We finally entered a beautiful home with an enlarged ground floor, topped by a large balcony. The entrance was transformed into a veranda with three steps leading up to it; two charming flower beds embellished the little front garden. We gained five rooms on the second floor and, thanks to Nela, a large modern kitchen next to the dining room replaced the old dirty one in the cellar. Large oak shelves covered a wall in the salon and one in the dining room. We brought in some furniture from storage in New York, which with some of our best paintings and some new acquisitions made the interior into a warm and elegant house.

From now on, my life was evenly divided between Europe and the United States; I must include also Israel, where I was giving concerts every year in aid of the orchestra and a chair of musicology at the Hebrew University of Jerusalem.

On my return to New York, Hurok told me with great satisfaction that he had finally succeeded in bringing over to America the famous Russian pianist of German extraction, Sviatoslav Richter, who until then had not been allowed to travel abroad. This fact made the American and European public anxious to hear this legendary absent figure. Hurok announced three concerts at Carnegie Hall, which were sold out even before his arrival, so he promptly added three more, repeating the same programs.

We heard the first of the new series and I must admit that I was very excited to hear him, especially after reading in the program that he was the pupil of my old friend Harry Neuhaus. I waited expectantly to hear the Liszt sonata and was rather disappointed when somebody announced that he would play the C major Fantasia of Schumann instead.

He walked quickly up to the piano, sat down with a short nervous gesture, and began to play immediately. The interpretation of the Fantasia of Schumann is a very controversial one, every pianist feels it differently, but Richter's conception was rather strange. He produced a beautiful tone but showed a tendency to exaggerate the tempi. His allegros were too fast and andantes too slow, and so his Schumann puzzled me.

After the Fantasia, he hurriedly left the stage for a few moments and came back to play three pieces by Ravel. These I had never heard played so beautifully; his *Oiseaux tristes* still remains with me. But then came a complete revelation. The Fifth Sonata by Scriabin, of which, God knows, I had given the first performance in London years ago, and now I heard a brand-new piece miraculously played. Here Richter emerged as the great pianist we had all heard so much about.

There was no opportunity for me to meet him or hear him again, as I had to leave immediately for my tour, but the following season I heard him in an all-Beethoven recital at which he played four early sonatas, finishing with the *Appassionata*. This time, extremes of his tempi upset me in no small measure.

A few days later, Hurok gave a small supper in his honor, to which he invited us. As I came through the front door, before I could take off my coat, Hurok, holding a bottle of vodka, came out with Richter, filled small glasses for the three of us, and that was the formal introduction. We drank each other's health in turn and entered the room with less than clear heads.

There were a dozen guests standing around a rich buffet filled with Russian goodies such as caviar, Kiev cutlets, and herrings, but Hurok planned better things for Richter and me. He took us into his study, had a table set up with two chairs, brought a magnum of champagne, and served us all the best tidbits himself. And there we sat, Richter and I, until the early hours of the morning, becoming more and more talkative with every new glass of champagne. I learned on that occasion that he had come to my recital in Odessa the same time I met and heard Gilels. "I was studying architecture at that time and had no intention of becoming a concert pianist but on that night your playing inspired me and I left for Moscow to study with Neuhaus." After another sip I was not sure if I should really be happy at having inspired him, but after the next sip, I decided yes.

At one point, I danced a little ballet for him—we were quarreling about tempi: "You played the allegretto so slowly," I said, and quoted a minuetto of Beethoven which he had played.

"But allegretto *is* slow," he said with tremendous conviction, emptying another glass.

At that, I jumped to my feet and danced for him my kind of adagio, andante, allegretto, allegro, and getting to presto, I fell heavily on the chair and luckily not on the floor. I remember that night as a lovely meeting of two pianists with much to say to each other.

The next day I had one of the worst hangovers of my whole life, feeling badly enough to call a doctor. After he gave me some soothing pills, I saw him to the door, where he stopped for a moment and said smilingly, "What a curious coincidence. I was called to see another pianist this morning—his name is Richter."

In 1960, when Hurok asked me about my next season in New York, I answered bluntly, "I do not want to play with orchestra, but I shall give ten piano recitals instead."

He laughed. "You are joking," he said, "but it would be good to give three recitals," he added.

"Not three, but ten," I retorted emphatically.

Now he saw that I meant it. "Arthur, six will be good enough—and it is a lot."

"I shall give ten recitals or nothing," I said with stern decision.

Hurok tried hard to dissuade me. "It will look bad," he said. "People will say that you want all the money you can get in New York."

"That's right," I said. "I want to make as much as I can because I intend to give all these concerts for ten charities as a gesture of gratitude for the love and support given me all these years."

Hurok was dumbfounded. "Nobody has done that before."

"That's just it. I want to show for once that an artist can also be grateful and not always demand more."

Now he had to give in. I selected the charities carefully; they should be as I wished but also dear to New York. As far as I remember, they included the Musicians' Emergency Fund, The United Jewish Appeal, one for colored people, a charity called Big Brother concerned with children, and the two schools of Alina and Johnny.

My public covered practically all the concerts as soon as they were announced; I insisted on giving ten different programs. Here I would like to confess a not too nice side of my character. With all my admiration for

Richter, I was not a little vexed by Hurok's too great enthusiasm for his six concerts with some repeated programs and the readiness of the New Yorkers to adopt him at his first appearance.

It was quite a considerable undertaking. It meant twenty hours of different music to be performed. I had to gather all the repertoire I had accumulated over the years. There were sonatas of Beethoven I had not played for thirty years. Schumann's *Symphonic Études* and *Fantasia*, added to the *Carnaval* and *Kreisleriana*, which I had recently performed. The great sonatas of Brahms and Liszt, the heavenly B flat by Schubert, and all the shorter pieces I could think of by Mozart, Schumann, Brahms, Schubert, and Liszt, and the whole topped off by the avalanche of Chopin, including his two sonatas, scherzos, ballades, impromptus, mazurkas, waltzes, polonaises, preludes, and the few études I was able to play properly. Besides the Stravinsky, Szymanowski, some Prokofiev, Villa-Lobos, Ravel, and Debussy, I played a few of the best pieces from *Iberia* of Albéniz; de Falla's *Fire Dance* and *Navarra* were the steady standbys among the encores. The whole series was given in twenty-four days. The sold-out houses with the stage crammed with people provided very large sums for the different charities, which, in turn, added to the proceeds by selling blocks of tickets to their supporters at very high prices.

I remember a funny little incident. At the first three or four concerts a young boy of about eleven in a blazing red pullover sat on the stage quite close to me and after every movement of a sonata, while my educated public waited silently, he would jump to his feet, applaud furiously, and shout "Bravo, bravo," to my great annoyance. The joke of it was that he was stealing my show. After my concerts I heard nothing but "Did you notice this darling little boy shouting?" I think it was during the intermission of the fourth concert that Hurok caught him roughly by the arm and screamed at him, "If you don't take that goddamn red sweater off, I will throw you out." The boy, terrified, obeyed immediately and at the next concerts, peace reigned during all the sonatas. By the way, he later developed into a very fine pianist named Joe Alfidi.

RCA carefully recorded all the concerts, but I allowed them to issue only the four mazurkas of Szymanowski, the *Visions fugitives* by Prokofiev, and *O Prole do Bebe* of Villa-Lobos because I was afraid that in the rest of the programs there were too many wrong notes; I had played freely, as in the old days, giving out all my heart and not caring much for these little incidents. This time, even the severe American critic-detectives didn't take any notice of it.

During these years many changes took place in my life. We moved to a larger apartment, a duplex on Park Avenue, which was much nearer to the schools of Alina and Johnny, where I was able to hang my pictures and place my books.

Eva, on the advice of Agnes de Mille, the well-known dancer and choreographer, was sent by the State Department to Europe to dance with three others in a fine production of *Oklahoma!*, a musical by Rodgers and Hammerstein. After the successful tour, she gave up dancing for acting and played successfully in several dramas, such as *The Dybbuk*, Off-Broadway. Garson Kanin, the celebrated playwright, offered her an important role in his first production of *The Diary of Anne Frank*, which had an overwhelming success. Garson and his wife, Ruth Gordon, the famous actress, became our intimate friends. On my future visits to Los Angeles they gave some lovely parties for us.

Eva played for a whole year in *The Diary of Anne Frank*, but suddenly decided to marry William Sloane Coffin, a Presbyterian minister. The marriage took place a year later in a church in New York and I gave her away with great sadness. On that day, I lost the daughter who had responded so much to my dreams, who was my ideal companion all through her young years at home. Her husband taught first at a prep school, then at Williams College, where my first granddaughter was born, and in quick succession they had two sons before he finally became chaplain of Yale University.

Paul, who worked first in New York and then in California, was taken for national service by the Army.

As for myself, all through these times I was giving at least one hundred concerts every year.

My appearances in Washington were very special. It is the only place in the world where I welcomed the hospitality of a private home. Virginia Bacon was the kind of hostess who had the gift of making you feel really free in her home. It is true that her house was considered a historic mansion with a lovely garden and was quite near Constitution Hall, where I used to play. She lived alone, in the luxury of the good old days. Over the years she considered us family. She loved to travel with us and had accompanied me with Nela, Eva, and Paul on a tour to South America which took us to Brazil, Argentina, Chile, and Peru. She came with us to Greece, to Poland and Paris. In Washington itself she gave parties after every concert of mine. A woman of extraordinary vigor, she would never miss any social gathering; lunch, dinner, supper, or ball, one could always count on her presence and she keeps it up until this hour as I write.

117

In 1958 the Warsaw Philharmonic Orchestra invited me to give a few concerts with them and solo. I was burning to see Warsaw again; although the thought of seeing it still in ruins and the people living as I had seen them in Moscow frightened me, I couldn't resist the temptation that I might find some surviving members of my family or friends. Nela, for her part, had had news of a large number of her family who settled in Warsaw after the tragedy of the war.

We took with us Alina and Johnny, aged about eleven and nine. I described to them the life they were going to see based on my experiences in Russia, but an immense surprise awaited us. We took a plane in Paris and landed at the Warsaw airport, where a big crowd welcomed us. Nela's large family, my two nephews and a niece, and many members of the musical world surrounded us. We drove in to the city straight to the old Hotel Bristol on a good road. It was a Sunday; when we were finally shown into our rooms, we heard some strange sounds in the street and, to our great astonishment, we saw from our windows an enormous Catholic procession followed by a huge crowd. My children laughed. "Daddy, you told us that there is no religion in Poland." And I must admit I was amazed.

I gave three concerts in the splendidly rebuilt Filharmonja and an additional one for the old Chopin Society, whose seat was now in one of the famous palaces of Warsaw, just reconstructed after the very precise paintings of Canaletto, the Venetian artist who lived many years in the Polish capital. I was received more enthusiastically than ever before; I remember having addressed my audience after the last concert: "I was always afraid of you, but I always loved you."

The Poles are a proud and stubborn people. Hitler had given orders to dynamite the city, house by house, declaring that there would never be a Warsaw again. After the Allied victory, the Poles not only rebuilt the whole city but made it much more beautiful than it was before. After a wonderful concert in Cracow, where my children could admire the untouched beautiful old city, we returned to Warsaw, where I played another matinee in the so-called House of Culture, a very high tower which dominates the whole city, given by Stalin as a present to the Polish Communists. The Warsaw citizens would love to raze it to the ground, as they did to the Orthodox Russian Cerkiew (temple), a gift from a Tsar. When you ask a man in the street where one has the best view of Warsaw, he invariably answers, "From the top of the Russian tower, the only point where this nasty building is not seen."

The town of my birth, Lodz, begged me to come and play there, but I refused. I couldn't bear the idea of seeing the destroyed cemetery where my parents were buried and the streets where every house reminded me of someone dear to me, wantonly murdered.

I returned to Poland the next season for a larger tour and this time something unusual happened: The mayor of Lodz, accompanied by the secretary of the Communist Party, came one morning to Warsaw by car to invite me to return with them and receive an honorary citizenship of the town of my birth. This very great honor bestowed upon an anti-Communist Jew, who even changed his nationality, was impossible to refuse. So I drove with them, followed by my family and many friends, straight to the old concert hall where I had played so often. Seated on the stage with the city officials, I heard the mayor read the proclamation and this was followed by a procession of committees of the orchestra, the conservatory, the university, and even some factories. They brought flowers, and books with great dedications with words of so much love and admiration that I had tears in my eyes. I suddenly felt humbly how happy my parents would have been at such a great event. I could do no less than walk to the piano and play some of the pieces which had been most loved by my public in this hall.

It was a proud day for music in Tel Aviv when the beautiful modern hall which would be used only for concerts was ready. It was Fred Mann of Philadelphia who had taken the initiative by contributing a large sum and obtaining much larger sums from other American music lovers, and these gifts encouraged the city of Tel Aviv and the government of Israel to give the final sums for the construction. The Israel Philharmonic Orchestra found, at last, a worthy and steady home. For the inauguration, a great gala took place; Leonard Bernstein conducted, Isaac Stern played a concerto, Piatigorsky should have played but couldn't come, so he was replaced by the fine French cellist Paul Tortelier, and I played the *Emperor* Concerto by Beethoven. The hall was named after Frederick Mann, who had made the first contribution. Bernstein opened the concert with the Israeli national anthem, which is very moving. Then Ben-Gurion gave a long inaugural speech in Hebrew, which neither Bernstein, Stern nor I could understand. To our great shame and surprise, Tortelier, the Christian, was the one who translated it for us. He had fallen in love with Israel and lived a whole year with his family in a kibbutz.

Fred Mann expected to be introduced to the public by Ben-Gurion after the speech, but he was not called. The whole program was performed with a long intermission and I had just finished the concert when I noticed that Fred Mann was still waiting in the wings. I felt that something had to be done and, instead of giving an encore, I made him come up with me on the stage and introduced him in my best English as the man who had initiated the construction of the hall. After due applause, the gala was over.

Ben-Gurion gave a party after the concert, at which I introduced Fred Mann to him. He gave him an angry look. "Why did you think of a hall for Tel Aviv and not Jerusalem?" Poor Fred had no answer.

Music became an ever greater need both in Europe and in America. Even the countries in the Far East showed not only interest in but talent for this great art. Their monotonous folkloric chants gave way now to excellent conservatories and orchestras where our European music was performed with growing understanding.

Competitions for the performing arts were springing up everywhere. At the first one in Moscow, named after Tchaikovsky, the first prize was given to a young American pianist, Van Cliburn, who upon his return to New York was received like a hero with a downtown paper shower. Marguerite Long and Jacques Thibaud created a *concours* in France which became a rival of the Queen Elizabeth one in Brussels; Geneva, Rio de Janeiro, Lisbon, and Leeds followed suit. Warsaw's Chopin Competition opened fine careers for its winners. Even in faraway Fort Worth, Texas, a rich Texan honored his fellow citizen and created a Van Cliburn prize, giving the unusual sum of ten thousand dollars to the winner. Violinists, cellists, and singers had their own events. Masses of pianists invaded all these competitions, preparing their programs for years, working eight hours a day. In my modest opinion, they degenerated into a mass production, far from the original noble idea of Queen Elizabeth of Belgium.

Now it reached such a point that when a young winner of a first prize in a small city returned triumphantly to his professor with the good news, the teacher asked, "Were the others as bad as all that?" Hurok promptly engaged the winners in the big cities but he was not able to book engagements for them for a second season.

In my eyes another important factor contributed to the unfairness of the juries' choices. The Soviets, who were determined to grab the first prizes in all international competitions like the Olympic Games, chose their pianists after a whole year of local trials all over their country and then picked their candidate for the international. The poor boy knew, of course, that if he failed, his career was over. The result of this maneuver was clear. Their candidates were easily the winners against their colleagues from free countries where no authority could force their best artists to compete, and the Russians did not risk much as they were facing young students who mostly had never played in public. This state of things reminds me of horse races where there is a handicap. The winning horse has to carry more weight for the next race. All I can say is that my heart bleeds for the losers.

I remember a case in Warsaw when I was invited to be the honorary chairman of the Chopin Competition. The jury was very numerous, including names like Nadia Boulanger, Marguerite Long, Magda Tagliaferro on the French side, and my old friend Neuhaus and five or six other prominent Russian musicians, and representatives of many other countries. There were also many international competitors. Right from the beginning, Maurizio Pollini showed a complete supremacy over the others. Another young pianist, Michel Block, had plenty of personality with a perfect technical equipment. The ten others admitted to the finals played their programs but showed no particular talent.

When the votes were counted, Pollini won by an overwhelming majority, but to my astonishment, the second prize went to a Russian girl who banged through her program, the third to a pretty Iranian whose looks must have pleased too many of the jurors, the fourth to a nice-looking Russian without talent, the fifth and sixth to Poles who shouldn't have been admitted, the eighth to a Japanese who played Chopin in Japanese, the tenth to a Chinese who played Chopin in Chinese, and finally the eleventh to Michel Block.

I am a person who cannot stand obvious injustice. During the deliberations of the jury I noticed a hostile attitude toward Block, who had no supporters behind him like the others. When the result of the votes was announced by the acting president, Zbigniew Drzewiecki, it was my duty to thank the jury for their work and for electing me as their honorary president. Instead of sitting down, however, I addressed the jury in a raised voice: "As the dean among you, I decided to add to the prizes a special one, which you might call the Arthur Rubinstein Prize, which would carry with it the money corresponding to the second prize, and I bestow it upon Mr. Michel Block." I think the readers will have fun imagining the faces of the jurors. As for myself, I could not have cared less about their indignation. Many of them, however, congratulated me hypocritically on my gesture and the general opinion in Poland was entirely on my side.

118

After the Second World War, Stravinsky was universally regarded as the foremost composer of his time.

Richard Strauss, his prewar rival, lost many of his admirers partly because it became clear in time that a certain vulgarity was apparent in his music and also because of the sympathy he showed for the Nazi regime. When he reappeared in London, the public and the press received him with all the respect due to a great composer. All he had to say in an interview was: "I came to London only to collect my long-overdue royalties."

Bartók became suddenly famous upon his death after a life of struggle and poverty. Schönberg and his two disciples, Anton von Webern and Alban Berg, became more and more prominent; the musical world was listening to them with greater interest and understanding. As to Stravinsky, I have a sad confession to make: The exaltation and enthusiasm which I felt on hearing his first ballets, *The Firebird* and *Petrushka*, and the conviction that his *Le Sacre du printemps* opened up new ways to music, have faded with the years. I discovered that something of an essential importance was lacking in his musical production; I mean an original melodic invention. It was a great shock to discover when I was first in Russia that practically the whole melodic material of *The Firebird* and *Petrushka* was taken from some well-known folklore, and as everybody knows, he used a waltz by Josef Lanner and a French popular tune to illustrate the Easter fair in St. Petersburg. Later on, I was not a little astonished when he agreed to write a ballet made up entirely of Tchaikovsky's music for Ida Rubinstein's company and another for Diaghilev with the music of Pergolese. It is not farfetched to think that his dismissal of the piano as nothing but a percussion instrument has something to do with his inability to make the piano sing and thus contribute anything of value to the rich pianistic literature.

A remarkable thing was the way he changed his style, not unlike Picasso, from one work to another. After the colossal orchestral drama of *Le Sacre du printemps*, he sat down to the charming lyrical *L'Histoire du soldat* and later to *Les Noces*, still very Russian but set in a completely original way; four pianos replaced the usual orchestra. From then on, his basically Russian music became more and more international. He was involved with ancient classical legends and dramas. His ballet *Apollon Musagète* was very successful. For his oratorio *Oedipus Rex* he used, strangely enough, a text written in Latin by Jean Cocteau. I, for one, could never derive any great impression from this work. It sounded artificial to me and too cerebral. He did write, among other instrumental work, a beautiful Symphony of Psalms. His full-fledged opera, *The Rake's Progress*, with a libretto built around the famous series of painting by Hogarth, was described by Stravinsky himself as Mozartian. The arias and ensembles were written in Mozart's style all right, but the music itself, in spite of being brilliantly written, would have exasperated poor Mozart to distraction.

Toward the end of his life, he devoted his time to religious music, for which he chose the latest idiom of the ultra-moderns. I heard the cantata commissioned by the Patriarch of Venice, and dedicated by Stravinsky in elaborate Latin to the glory of San Marco. The Patriarch, the future Pope John XXIII, dreamed of a Mass to replace the well-known ones, but the cantata turned out to be so short that at its first performance it had to be preceded by a work by Monteverdi conducted by Robert Craft and repeated after intermission. I must sadly report that the cantata, even after the repetition, failed to convey any religious feeling to the audience and myself.

After my very personal appraisal of this great musician, this past master of his métier, to which all his works bear testimony, I must state that he had one of the most interesting personalities, endowed with a considerable charm and wit. I am proud to say that our vastly divergent points of view about musical matters never marred our warm friendship.

In the last years, I had hardly an occasion to see him. He was constantly on tour conducting his own works; as a matter of fact, only a small part of them, because most were taken over by Robert Craft, who lived and traveled with him. The latter also published a few volumes of his conversations with Igor, quoting here and there his sayings, opinions, and paradoxes, written in a very fine but unauthentic English. Igor spoke French beautifully, but his English was far from Craft's interpretation of it. Stravinsky's need for and love of money made him continue his tours even when he was in very poor physical condition. Earlier in his life he did not disdain writing a march for the elephants for the opening of the Barnum & Bailey Circus and making a contribution to Herman's jazz band.

He died in New York but left the wish to be buried in Venice, next to the grave of Diaghilev. It was a touching posthumous sign of his friendship and gratitude for the man who discovered his musical genius.

In time, Arnold Schönberg's music became more agreeable to my ears. His new system and complete atonality remained incomprehensible to me, but I began to discern unusual but charming and sometimes beautiful sounds. Later on, his opera *Moses and Aaron* impressed me very much because, with the libretto in hand and voices expressing clearly the different moods, I could easily follow the action and even admire musically some dramatic moments like the orgy and Moses' wrath.

With Berg's opera *Wozzeck*, I was more at home. In spite of Schönberg's great influence, his music sounded somewhat familiar and the action was more moving with every hearing. Anton von Webern, Schönberg's main disciple, was generally accepted, but for myself, I can only say that after listening to a performance of his work, I always wished to hear it again.

My deep unhappiness with the latest development of music began when I heard some of the works of the major exponents: Boulez, Stockhausen, Cage, Nono, and many imitators. I can do no less than blame Stravinsky's paradoxical manifesto that music has no need of emotion and should be produced as simple utility, like shoes, made in a workshop. Knowing Igor well, I have taken it for one of his quips which he liked to use. Once, when I called a ballet by a friend of ours heavy-handed, Stravinsky right away clapped his hands and said, "That's it, that's what I like best, the heavy-handedness." But unfortunately, as I could judge from their published literature, the emotionless music became the credo of the whole ultramodern musical movement.

I never allowed myself to emit judgments upon works of art which I do not understand, and I am strongly opposed to people who dismiss them through sheer conceit. I protest, however, the way the ultra-modern composers use our noble and much-beloved instruments, which enriched the world with the heavenly music of Mozart and Beethoven, Schubert and Schumann, and that genius of the piano, Chopin. The arbitrary treatment of the pianos, banging them with fists, knocking rhythmically on the pedals, I call simple misdemeanor.

The tragedy of it all is that this new trend, which denies emotion in music and all the other arts, is born, in my opinion, out of the world in which we have been living since the last war. The deep mistrust among nations, accompanied by greed for power and a constant fear of tomorrow, has now developed to such a state of complete hypocrisy that emotion and moral ethics have no place. I shall go more deeply into these matters when I come to the Six-Day War, won by Israel.

119

For more than two decades the advantages of a concert pianist's profession seem to have attracted thousands of young people. I have received hundreds of letters from students of other professions asking me for advice, and my answer is that only those born with talent can have any hope of succeeding. Far from being discouraged, many of them went ahead and pursued a life of hard work at the piano. The result of it all is that almost every young pianist reaches a complete technical mastery of the instrument. I know of conservatories where the best pupils compete for the fastest performance of a difficult work, especially in staccato octaves, in études for thirds, and thus equipped they can earn great acclaim from the public, but the very essence of what music means and represents is absent.

In my opinion, music began with the voice, which expressed emotional sounds of pleasure and love and of fear and rage. I have the feeling that the whole animal world always has had some means of expressing their emotions. Ancient history cites music at emotional events like battles, weddings, and funerals. Our planet is inhabited by different human beings who have developed their individual folklores. And finally, Italian monks put order into the use of these traditional sounds and thus began what I like to call the art of music. All this is simple general knowledge but it is worth reviewing as a protest against the notion so prevalent today that art should be devoid of emotion.

It makes me laugh when I am sometimes asked by an innocent interviewer, "Mr. Rubinstein, do you prefer our Western music or Oriental music?" Nowadays, the answer is given by the Orient itself in the way in which it has adopted so enthusiastically our glorious art of music.

After this long pessimistic digression, I must affirm that my unconditional love of life remains untouched. My great hope is that a new renaissance will take place before I die, and that future artists will add to the great heritage left by the masters who have filled us with the noblest emotions and gratitude. In the meantime I continue to hear and learn more and more of the heavenly music of Bach, Mozart, Haydn, and Schubert, which I never had the time to know throughout my long life as a concert pianist. I also learn better to evaluate by contrast the paintings and sculptures of the great ones.

120

In the mid-1950's, my love for Venice and the memories of the summers in the Palazzo Polignac made me long to return there for the summer. I was trying to find an apartment in one of the palazzi when the Countess Volpi generously offered her beautiful villa in the Giudecca. It had two gardens on either side, one with lovely flower beds and white turtledoves, and the other with a fruit and vegetable garden. I put a piano in and worked in the mornings, and I left it for the rest of the day to Alina and Johnny, who showed a gift for playing four-hands and played quite a repertoire by memory. I shall never forget one large cocktail party when our guests included musicians like Stravinsky, Nadia Boulanger, Marguerite Long, Nikita Magaloff, and three or four well-known music critics. When Alina and Johnny, completely unaware of those present, played in their jolly way the whole *Dolly* Suite by Fauré and *Ma Mère l'oye* by Ravel, I must state here with some legitimate pride that the group of musicians who listened under the windows in the garden or in the other room were quite overcome. Even Stravinsky exclaimed, "Ils ne jouent pas mal du tout."

We spent two unforgettable summers in Venice. Later we were invited by René Clair, who was then president of the jury for the film festival, and we stayed at the Excelsior Hotel on the Lido. It was quite exciting to live with all the famous film stars and producers in the same place; to lunch with a Vittorio de Sica, whom we so greatly admired, and many others. There were big receptions at the Palazzo Ducale and great parties in other palazzi after the films. However, the heat and humidity of Venice made it not the best place for a rest after the season, so the next year, 1957, Nela rented a charming farm belonging to Jean-Louis Barrault and Madeleine Renaud situated near Deauville. The children adored their first experience on a farm and were happy to continue their piano lessons with their teacher, Mlle. Herard, whom we invited to spend the summer with us.

As for myself, I preferred to join the family on one or two weekends, being not much of a farmer. But Nela and I gave a memorable party at the casino in Deauville for our twenty-fifth anniversary. It was a great dinner for twenty-five friends, who came from Paris and London—a gala and we danced late into the night.

All this was pleasurable but at the end of every summer the approach of the concert season hung over me like the sword of Damocles. A long vacation always made me doubt whether I could persuade any public to listen to me with pleasure. I needed desperately the applause and approval of the first concert of the season, and from then on I began to enjoy my tour.

One of my European tours was interrupted by an invitation to the Cannes Film Festival from Marcel Achard, who was president of the jury. We sat every evening behind the jury and, duly dressed in evening clothes, would watch the films. One night, leaving the hall after a Spanish film, I noticed a man in a dinner jacket and mentioned to Nela, "If it were not for the dinner jacket, I could swear that is Picasso." As at our first meeting in Madrid, he stopped me and said, "Arturo?" We embraced and he said, laughing, "I'm wearing the same dinner jacket which you made me order in London twenty-five years ago." He invited us for the next afternoon to his studio in Cannes, where he showed us not only his recent paintings but many sculptures and some large ones in the garden. As an innocent but passionate lover of art, I was struck by his genius as a sculptor even more than by his latest paintings. They were completely original but by no means abstract and, of course, there was not the distortion in his sculptures that there was in some of his paintings.

He saw with pleasure the deep impression they made on me and said with a shy smile, "And I *still* don't understand music, eh . . . ?" I was suddenly happy, I felt a current of a new strong friendship between us, and it came from him, because the night before, I addressed him formally with the French "vous." "What is the matter with you?" he answered. "We always called each other 'tu.' "

When I told him that I had lost everything in my house during the war, including my lovely "Blue" Picasso and his drawing of me, he said, "I don't do these things anymore, but if you have a free moment, come to Cannes and I will draw you again." I felt suddenly very Jewish—"I should not find a free moment yet"! I simply felt that I had nothing but free moments for him.

At the end of the same month, I called him and announced that I had three free days. He answered, "Do come, I am free too." I took the earliest plane for Nice and on the way to the Carlton Hotel in Cannes, I ordered a bouillabaisse for two at a famous restaurant specializing in it in Golfe-

Juan and upon arrival I called him: "Pablo, I ordered the best bouillabaisse in the world for us at one o'clock or whenever you want to come."

He answered sadly, "I can't possibly lunch with you but come at four o'clock and we will make plans."

I am ashamed to say that after my own portion of the delicious bouillabaisse I could not resist and finished the other one as well. Feeling doubly happy, I arrived at Picasso's villa in high spirits, ready for a sitting. Both he and Jacqueline received me excitedly: "Arturo, you must come with us tonight to St. Tropez. There are some friends I want to see and we can dine there."

We left at about eight o'clock. It is a long drive from Cannes to St. Tropez but it seemed short that night because of our excellent mood. The car stopped in the very center of the city, in the large square surrounded by cafés and restaurants presided over by a huge monument to some French hero.

Picasso, without losing a moment, entered an art gallery which was still open and began studying all the pictures on view. He suddenly asked the owner, "Have you any by Juan Gris?" (a Spanish painter who died young). He seemed annoyed that they hadn't. "There is another one," he said, pointing to another gallery, and there again, after examining every picture, he received the same answer. It was getting on toward midnight when he asked us with an innocent expression on his face, "Are you hungry?" and without waiting for an answer, he took us on a longish walk to his restaurant and said, "It is a good place. I have ordered our dinner."

We were joined by some friends and sat down in a charming private room. The dinner Pablo had ordered arrived after quite a long wait; it was a huge bouillabaisse! That did it; this was a great red-letter day of three bouillabaisses in twelve hours! But no sitting for a picture. He asked me to come the following day in the late afternoon. "I shall show you my latest engravings of bullfights; it might amuse you." Still no mention of anything else. He showed me at least a hundred of them, a magnificent collection. All that time, he was mainly occupied in selecting his works for exhibitions; each city asked him for a personal touch—a little signed sketch for their publicity, a terrible task. The demand for my programs seemed a small matter to me after that.

They invited me for the next day for lunch at their villa—I call it a villa, but it was rather a large house with palatial pretenses, where the grand salon was turned into a typical studio, filled with pictures, photographs, sculptures as well as big crates, and there were two tables filled with brushes, crayons, and all sorts of instruments needed for his work. In a small entrance hall, among all sorts of discarded objects, he showed me a little old upright piano standing crookedly in a corner. "You see, I have a piano too," he said with pride.

I began to feel a little disappointed. The next day was my last day in Cannes; he never referred to his promise and I did not dare to remind him of it. The luncheon the next day was a grand affair deluxe—lobster *à l'Armoricaine*, a special dish *à la Provençale*, and a splendid dessert, accompanied by a Dom Pérignon of the best vintage. Everything was beautifully served in the dining room.

Some visitors arrived for coffee, which was served in the salon-atelier. The time has come, I thought, to say goodbye. My plane was leaving from Nice in a few hours and I had to pack. With great thanks and a hand kiss for Jacqueline, I turned to Picasso to say goodbye. He looked at me very severely. "You can't go," he said. "Don't you remember? We have work to do."

Without waiting for an answer, he led me back to the dining room, locked the door with a key, and sat me in a chair facing the window. He pushed, with all the length of his arm, everything left on the table from lunch to one side, picked up a large block, put a little table next to his seat; he opened the block to the first page, disposing of his utensils on the little table. When all this was done, he looked at me with his famous Picasso eyes and asked me with a touch of irony: "You want, of course, full resemblance."

My answer was prompt. "Not at all," I said, "I am not interested in my face, only in what you can see in it." He liked that and began quickly to draw. After a short while, he turned the page, glanced at me, and started again. He turned another page and after three or four more pages I became slightly nervous. "If you are not disposed today, Pablo, why not try it another time?"

"Are you tired?" he asked.

"No, not at all."

"Then sit still, and I give you a cigar."

I lit a Montecristo and posed happily as he turned page after page for about three hours until he found that there were no pages left. "There are only twenty-four pages in these blocks," he said with regret. Then he showed me.

There were twenty-four finished drawings, each completely different from the other and in each I was another character. An amazing accomplishment. "Take the one you like the best," he said. A terrible thing to say. I looked with a hungry eye at every one of them. He finally gave me four of them and signed them with a dedication and the date. A generous gift indeed.

On another visit, he took me to Vallauris to show me the exhibition of his ceramics—another aspect of his genius. I fell in love with a tall vase; he had decorated it with beautiful nudes in the noble classical style and used its curves to expose the different aspects of their behinds. When I offered to buy it, I was told that it was limited to twenty examples and they were all sold. The sad expression on my face had the old effect of Bayreuth; Picasso promised to have an additional one made for me and send it to Paris. I thought it was a lighthearted gesture to console me, but what a surprise when I received this beautiful vase duly signed by him a few weeks later.

One day in the middle of the summer, we received the sad news about the death of my mother-in-law in Kansas City, where she was living with her eldest daughter. Nela left immediately and arranged to take her mother's body to Warsaw and bury her next to her father, who lay in the resting place for men of merit. As I did not want to leave Alina and Johnny alone in Paris, I took them with me for my concerts in Monte Carlo and Aix-en-Provence.

121

In the early 1960's, and to my great amazement, several important universities bestowed upon me the title of Doctor Honoris Causa.

The president of Yale University, Mr. Alfred Griswold, invited us to spend the night before commencement, as they call the graduation ceremony, at his official home. There was the usual dinner for the honored guests. Our host informed us confidentially that the President of the United States, John Kennedy, would join us in receiving the honor. "So do not be astonished," he said, "if you see a great number of policemen and photographers. The President will come at the last moment."

The next morning, there was a great ado. We tried on our gowns and mortarboards. After a long parade, two by two, we took our seats in the tribune around Griswold facing a huge crowd on the square below.

John Kennedy appeared just at the beginning of the ceremony. Mr. Griswold called him to receive his citation, and after the applause of the crowd, Kennedy gave a speech of about half an hour on a controversial political issue, which the students of Yale received rather coolly, as President Kennedy was a Harvard man.

When my turn came, and my name was heard, the crowd outside

seemed to consist of my usual concert public. I imagined I was hearing "Encore, encore!" It was fortunate that I was neither a Harvard nor a Yale man. It was quite a memorable occasion and hundreds of photos were taken due to the presence of President Kennedy. This commencement was certainly the most interesting one of the eight others at which I was subsequently honored.

What a terrible shock to the whole world when this young courageous President, so full of promise for a better world, was assassinated in so cowardly a way. John Kennedy will never be forgotten.

Then there was the tragic aftermath when his much-liked and very capable brother Robert was killed by an Arab in Los Angeles for expressing support for Israel when seeking nomination for the presidency.

It was at this time that I made several important records which I still love to hear. The Brahms B-flat Concerto and my beloved C minor of Mozart with the Austrian conductor Josef Kripps, who was not a great conductor, but a fanatic lover of music, which showed in his accompaniment of these masterpieces. During a playback, he would scream in ecstasy, "This is metaphysic!"

A little later, Alfred Wallenstein, after Barbirolli the most perfect accompanist as far as rhythm and ensemble go, made a series of brilliant recordings with me. The Grieg, the Liszt E flat, the *Variations symphoniques* of Franck, the Saint-Saëns G minor, the Szymanowski, and most important of all, four of my preferred Mozart concertos. These recordings, which I made intermittently while on a long tour in the United States, kept me busy for the whole season.

My daughter Alina, who had brilliantly graduated from her high school, was now a lovely young girl of eighteen. On my next visit to Washington, I became busy with the preparations for her coming-out ball. We were determined to make it as brilliant as the one we had given for Eva twelve years earlier. Again Alice Longworth made it possible for us to give the ball in the Sulgrave Club, and Virgina Bacon, generous as ever, invited Alina to stay with her for the preceding balls. This time, Nela and I were masters of the situation. We remembered the caterers, florists, vintners, and all the rest of it. We had kept the list of Washington society. The dance band was the best at the moment and my concert grand was at its post. Alina had a lovely dress and looked ravishing. The affair was an enormous success and both these balls of my two daughters remain proudly in my memory.

My yearly tours in the United States and Europe were vastly extended by a return to Australia. On that occasion, I was accompanied by my wife and Alina and Johnny. An enterprising impresario offered a good contract to include New Zealand and promise for concerts in Hong Kong and India on the way back. I remember this tour with particular pleasure. For one who had never traveled as a tourist, this time it was a super-touristic adventure because in addition to the tremendous lot of sightseeing, I had the chance, thanks to my concerts, to be received and welcomed as a friend.

We started out from New York to San Francisco, where we changed planes for Honolulu, and had a lovely week's stay there. Having been there before, we were excellent guides for the children, who enjoyed this en-chanted island to the fullest—swimming, surfing, and eating the delicious pineapples.

A long, long flight took us to Sydney, Australia, with a stop at the Fiji Islands for a night. It amused me upon arrival to find out that it was still "yesterday."

Harry Miller turned out to be not only an excellent manager but an exceptionally nice fellow. Thanks to him, we enjoyed every bit of our visit.

It was a pleasant surprise for Nela and me to find many distinguished Poles. The Australian government, after their terrible scare with the Jap-anese after the war, abandoned their proud "Keeping up the high standard of living" (as Mr. Menzies had told me on my previous visit) and opened their doors to white immigration and welcomed one hundred thousand Poles coming from England and offered them excellent occupations. We found in Melbourne a Polish aristocratic club and in Sydney a club of poets, painters, and musicians who gave us receptions as if we were in Warsaw or Cracow.

This time, our visit to the famous zoo was very different from my first visit with poor Schneevoigt. The director of the zoo gave us a royal tour in a motorcar, stopping at every interesting cage, allowing the children to caress and cuddle the little koala bears. He took us to the maternity quarters of the kangaroos, where some mamas sat quietly with their children in their pouches. Even the naughty laughing birds did not dare to disobey the director and scared us with their nasty cynical outbursts.

That day, on our return to the hotel, we were greatly amused by a colorful scene. The famous English group the Beatles, who were at the height of their fame, had arrived and were staying at the Sheraton Hotel right opposite our hotel. Our side of the street was crowded with young hippies acclaiming their idols. On that morning, we had a hard time pushing our way through to our car. On our return from the zoo at lunchtime, our car was not able to approach the entrance; the Sheraton side of the street was jammed by another crowd holding several placards which read: "We love Arthur." This meant nothing to me, I thought it referred to one of the Beatles, but my son Johnny, an expert, said quietly, "They came for you, Daddy." He was right. When they caught sight of me, a few of them grabbed my arms and presented me to my followers, who began shouting, "Long live Arthur, we love Arthur," and such. I had to shake hands with many of them. The hippies on the other side did not like it. They shrieked at the tops of their voices the names of the Beatles and it looked as if a battle between the Beatleites and the Arthurites would ensue. We somehow managed to get into the hotel and the dining room, hungry and exhausted.

My tour began in Brisbane with two concerts, after which we returned to Sydney, where I played only once. Harry Miller flew with us to Melbourne and later to Adelaide. I played several concerts in each city. Miller got along beautifully with all four of us, pleased as he was with my success and the packed houses. Alina and Johnny became quite friendly with him, delighted to be taken to shows and good restaurants. The Poles were showering hospitality on us wherever we went and it was quite touching to be welcomed at the airports by their small children dressed in beautiful Polish costumes.

Our Australian tour was interrupted in Adelaide; it was time to fly to New Zealand. The flight to Wellington was long and dangerous—we almost landed in the sea. Wellington and Auckland seemed to us as English as Manchester or Birmingham; Great Britain had the genius to leave its stamp on all the dominions and colonies.

We found, however, an exotic touch in Wellington—a genuine French restaurant! Needless to say, we took all our meals there! My debut was very promising. The two first recitals were received with an exceptional warmth and musical understanding.

The next two concerts on consecutive days took place in Auckland but there I met with a severe obstacle. On trying the Steinway, which they told me had arrived from London, reconditioned for my concerts, I discovered to my horror that two keys had perniciously decided to get stuck every time I touched them. An old tuner, reeking of beer, reassured me with a smile, "Don't worry, I'll fix them." I had no choice but to leave it in his hands. At the concert, which I started with the Moonlight Sonata, the two disobedient keys caused a revolution, the whole keyboard became insecure. I played the entire sonata, and the rest of the program, busy lifting the stubborn keys. I still don't understand how I could finish this concert without giving up, but, of course, I refused to play the next night, as there was no other instrument. Harry Miller begged me to give him a chance. "I know of an excellent tuner who works at the radio station and I feel sure that he can repair it." I promised.

The next morning, the young expert was brought in, with no smell of beer on him. He went straight to the piano, took the lid off, and suddenly exclaimed, "The keyboard is not in place!" He gave one push to it, put on the lid, and asked me to try it. The rebels of the night before proved to be the most obedient keys, producing a lovely sound on the piano.

That night I never played better. When the enthusiastic audience shouted for encores, I stopped them with my raised hand and said, "If you are not too tired, I would love to play for you the program of last night again." Without waiting for their acceptance, I repeated the Moonlight Sonata.

We toured the island thoroughly: the Maoris, their dances, and the hot springs in which the natives boiled their eggs. After playing in beautiful Christchurch, we returned to Sydney to finish the tour with two more concerts and after my last appearance in Perth, we left with Harry Miller for Hong Kong.

This time it was not the hot roof of 1935 but a beautiful modern hall. I played with particular pleasure on this Chinese island where the English had communicated their love for music. We had dinner in the house of the all-powerful producer of Chinese films, a charming and most intelligent man.

Another highlight of this visit was a Chinese dinner offered by the concert organizers consisting of thirteen courses served in delicate small quantities. And the marvel was that the aftereffect was lighter than a three-course dinner in a French restaurant.

Hong Kong has another irresistible attraction: the clothing, cameras, radios, and jewelry you can get at bargain prices. You can buy Swiss and Japanese precision instruments at cheaper prices than in their countries of origin. I remember having ordered twenty-four shirts of the finest cotton and a silk robe, silk day pajamas, twelve shirts for Johnny, and six blouses for Alina; the whole finished in forty-eight hours at one fifth the price in Europe.

We left this fairy island with a deep wish to return. From now on it was a simple touristic visit to wonderful places. After a stop in Singapore, we spent a few happy days in Bangkok with its beautiful temples and its life on the river Me Nam, the very pulse of the city.

The next place was New Delhi, capital of India. Thanks to Harry Miller, we met some distinguished Sikh family who showed us all the beauties of this fascinating city and, of course, we decided to see the Taj Mahal.

There was only one morning plane, at seven, to Agra, which returned to New Delhi in the late afternoon, but it was worth making any effort to see this unique temple. We spent a happy day in this old capital of the moguls, one of which built this white wonder called Taj Mahal in memory of the young wife, whom he loved so deeply.

Back in New Delhi, Miller surprised me with the news that he had obtained a concert in the largest hall of Bombay. We had to leave for there the next day, and that evening there were two surprises in store for me. My daughter Eva, who was accompanying her husband, William Coffin, on an official mission to India, would be joining us for my concert in Bombay. The other surprise was Johnny, who was so enchanted with the Taj Mahal that he drove out to Agra in a taxi, which took three hours there and back, to film the beautiful temple. He returned that same evening in a terrible state, just in time for the plane to Bombay, but his film of this day was one of the most beautiful I have ever seen and would easily deserve an Oscar. The concert in Bombay, the only one I have given in India, was the crown of the whole tour. Nowhere was I received with more enthusiasm by the public and in a more gracious and hospitable way by the local organizer. Harry Miller left us there, to our regret.

After two days in Teheran, where we admired the fabulous collection of crown jewels kept in a special vault at the National Bank, we arrived happily in Istanbul, a city of many memories. Being a good guide, I showed Alina and Johnny everything worth seeing and they stayed behind to see more of the Byzantine past and the palaces of the sultans.

122

Hurok was intent upon making me accept a short tour in Russia but he encountered great reluctance on my part. "I am very much against it," I said, "because you pay the Russian artists you bring over to America great amounts of dollars, while they offer our artists, in exchange, loads of papers they call rubles which can't be used anywhere in the world—only in Russia, where there is nothing worth buying."

"Don't worry about it," Hurok answered, "they will pay you two thousand dollars a concert, just like the other Communist countries."

I laughed. "The rich, powerful Soviet Russia pays a fee which I would not accept in the poorest country of the West, but I know that you need them, dear Sol," I added, "so for you I will do it."

Deep in my heart, I was pleased to play again for the wonderful Russian public. We set off for Moscow and Hurok came with us. Many musicians welcomed us at the airport. Among them, my dear Emil Gilels, who had to leave the same day but published a lovely article about me.

My debut was with orchestra under Kyril Kondrashin with the B-flat Brahms, F minor Chopin, and the Tchaikovsky. It was received with one of the greatest ovations of my life. When I learned that the tickets for the sold-out house were much more expensive and therefore prohibitive for music students and professors, I persuaded Kondrashin to repeat the program next morning at eleven with free tickets and strictly for musicians. I even had to add the *Emperor* Concerto of Beethoven.

The Hotel National, where we stayed again, had deteriorated more than ever. We were given the two best rooms in the place, but the furniture was simply shameful. The food in the restaurant was inedible, but Hurok had his ways and means, so thanks to him, we had some fresh chicken brought to our room by a woman who cheated the Soviet regime by taking money for it, which she hid furtively.

Leningrad was a revelation. The city was clean. The churches, which on our first visit had been turned into dirty anti-Christian museums, were now gloriously cleaned up and guides showed with pride the beautiful mosaics of Christ and the saints.

My two concerts at the hall of the old club of the aristocrats were unforgettable evenings. The Leningrad Orchestra stood up on the stage and joined the audience in a long ovation. After the first concert, supper was served at the restaurant in the hotel, where the noisiest jazz band I ever heard made it impossible to remain there. When I asked to be served in an adjoining smaller room, the headwaiter answered, "Impossible. There is Artur."

This sounded too silly. "I would like to speak to him," I said. Entering the room, we found a large table with American diners, among whom were many good friends of mine who rushed up to greet us. "We are in Russia on an art tour," they said. The evening finished in a jolly mood.

My last concert in Moscow was a Chopin recital. Madame Elena Furtzeva, the Minister of Culture, sat in the audience and the official box was occupied by a lonely lady, the wife of the Communist Party chief, Nikita Khrushchev. The next day, her famous husband was ousted by his colleagues.

After my last encore, Madame Furtzeva appeared in the door of the artist's room, then advanced slowly toward me and put her arms around me, making me very conscious of her huge soft bosom.

On our return to Paris, we decided to sell the very expensive apartment in New York, because Alina was studying at the university and had her own apartment and Johnny, after his graduation from the Collegiate School, left for Los Angeles to study acting at the University of California there.

In 1965 there was a great tour in Europe and we managed to go to Warsaw to see Szymanowski's *King Roger* at the beautiful new Opera House. It sounded rather like an oratorio, the action was somewhat static, but the music was, throughout, noble and moving. The chorus had a prominent role and sang to perfection.

For the summer, we found a lovely place in Marbella in Spain. I built a studio there, separated from the main house, and brought my Steinway from Paris. Nela found some charming rustic furniture and a large fireplace gave it a warm cozy feeling. It turned out to be ideal for working. It was in this studio that I wrote *My Young Years* during six summers of vacation and I began this second volume of my life in the same studio.

In 1966, I returned for a tour in Japan accompanied by my wife and by my daughter Alina. Japan, not unlike Germany, had recovered rapidly after the lost war, thanks to its incredible capacity for work, and reached the peak of prosperity. An important Tokyo newspaper sponsored a large symphony orchestra which played a great part in the musical life of Tokyo. I was engaged by them for fifteen concerts.

What a change since poor Strok's time. The cities were swarming with music students, many of them prizewinners in international competitions, always showing respectable aptitudes and understanding for our Western music. A few small cities which I visited in 1935 had now become huge industrial centers. Osaka, at the other end of the island, had its own newspaper, which also subsidized an orchestra. The whole country had become passionately interested in music. I enjoyed this tour immensely and shall never forget the last concert, which took place in the sporting hall which they had built for the Olympics. I played the Tchaikovsky concerto with Iwaki conducting. There was an audience of fourteen thousand; the hall was so crowded that they had to bring a chair from the artist's room for Alina. The whole imperial family was there, save the Emperor himself.

After the concert, Alina and I had difficulty reaching the car. Once we were seated inside it, a huge crowd of a few thousand people surrounded us and clamored for autographs. Our car could advance only after an hour, when a detachment of police made way for us. I would like to say here that the crowd behaved in a friendly way, smiling at me all the time, but was too large to allow the car to move.

Nela had left Japan earlier, flying over the North Pole to Paris, and Alina and I decided to go back to Paris via Hong Kong and Bangkok, etc.

On the way to Hong Kong, I gave a concert in Seoul, the capital of Korea. There I spent an agitated day indeed. We landed on the rainiest day of my life, but were not allowed to take refuge in our hotel before receiving the key to the city from the mayor at the municipal building. A bad piano awaited me at the concert hall of the university.

After Hong Kong, that wonderful place where you could buy things so cheaply, Alina said shyly to me, "Daddy, we arrive in Rome at seven in the morning. Couldn't we stay there for the day? I would love to see Rome again."

I never refused anything to my children, and this time I agreed whole-heartedly. A visit to the travel agency and a call to the Excelsior Hotel in Rome, which reserved rooms, settled it.

We flew off in the happiest mood. The long stops in Singapore, Bang-kok, and New Delhi were familiar to us, but the one in Teheran at three in the morning was awaited with excitement. "We must get some caviar."

We both hopped out of the plane, dashed to the shop, and bought four half-kilo boxes, which we took triumphantly back to the plane. At the next stop, in Tel Aviv, we just had two Jewish cups of coffee and then dozed peacefully until Rome. It was six o'clock in the morning. We grabbed a taxi quickly, as we were in great need of a hot bath and a fine breakfast.

At the reception desk, a polite gentleman said with a smile, "The Excelsior is full, but we arranged for you to have rooms at the Savoy across the street."

A little discouraged, we crossed over. At the Savoy, the receptionist smiled at us. "Your rooms will be ready by eleven o'clock when the other guests are gone."

This was a terrible blow. We felt very sweaty and dirty. "Well," I said, "we will have a long breakfast and wait."

"Breakfast is served at eight." The sight of us sitting in the lobby could have made anybody cry with pity. We were only allowed into the dining room at eight-thirty to have finally a rich breakfast of prosciutto, eggs, endless cups of coffee, as we read all the newspapers of Europe while looking constantly at the clock, which seemed to dislike reaching the hour of eleven.

When the great moment arrived, we dashed to the desk, where a non-smiling gentleman announced drily that our rooms would be ready in the early afternoon. Now I became angry and shouted at him some indignant words of protest: "Do you want us running around Rome tired and dirty the whole day long? I will complain about you and inform the papers how the Savoy treats its guests."

"Oh, signore, I have a little room where you can wash up."

I screamed, "Take me to that room." There we found running water but no bathroom; however, we did our best to wash up, one after another. A little refreshed, we found ourselves in the street. I said to Alina, "We have plenty of time and I think you've already seen most of Rome worth seeing, but I doubt if you know the Villa Farnesina with its beautiful frescoes by Raphael. What about going to visit them?"

We hailed a taxi and I ordered the driver: "Andiamo alla Villa Farnesina."

He asked where it was. "Our luck," I said to Alina, "to take probably the only taxi in Rome that doesn't know the Villa Farnesina."

"Ask another chauffeur," I told him sharply in my best Italian. He did, but the other fellow had no idea about the Villa Farnesina. I knew only that it was on the bank of the Tiber. We asked drivers, people in the street, but nobody had ever heard of the Villa Farnesina.

I am stubborn, and so is Alina; we did not give up. We drove alongside the river and our driver stopped at a palazzo and asked the porter without much hope, but this porter pointed with his finger at the palazzo across the street and said, "Eccolo la," and I suddenly recognized it. We entered timidly and I asked the typical museum guard, "Is this the Villa Farnesina?" "No, this is the Academy of Italy." It had not changed at all and we were led into the beautiful room where Raphael's frescoes shone in the sun.

In a corner there was a bust of Guglielmo Marconi; the guard explained: "Il primo presidente dell'Accademia." I suddenly remembered Mussolini had endowed Italy with an Academy along the lines of the French one, but accessible to all the arts.

After this visit, I took Alina for a late lunch to Passetto. After two strong *caffè espressos*, we felt like visiting the Villa Borghese again with the beautiful Pauline Bonaparte in the nude, "Sacred and Profane Love" by Titian, and the lovely "Eve" by Lucas Cranach.

Only then did we return to the Savoy. The hotel man announced, "Your rooms will be ready in half an hour." This time it was Alina who became enraged. "This horrible man," she screamed. "Daddy, why do we stay here at all? We might find a plane for Paris tonight."

She was quite right. There was a nearby travel agency, which arranged for a flight at six o'clock. We just had time to go to the airport. We gathered our luggage at the Savoy, had it packed into a taxi, and I said to the receptionist, "I hope you will have your rooms free forever, but for other people, not for us." We reached the Leonardo da Vinci Airport just in time, landed safely in Paris, and fortunately found a car to take us home.

My wife was in America and my Polish valet, Adam, had retired for the night. "What about dinner?" I asked Alina. Suddenly we felt very hungry.

We kept the car, I left the luggage in the hall and the caviar in the refrigerator, and drove off happily to Fouquet's in the Champs-Elysées for a good old French meal.

After coffee and a fine cigar, I asked Alina a little bit shyly, "The movies are just beginning their last show—how do you feel about it?" An enthusiastic look in her eyes gave me the answer. We watched a long picture with great interest but I forgot what it was, and we finally consented at one o'clock to go to bed.

I could call it with reason the longest but most enchanting twenty-four-hour day of my life.

That same year, I played in Budapest, in Yugoslavia, and in Istanbul.

On my next tour in America, I had the joy of making records of chamber music with the young and brilliant Guarneri Quartet. We finished, in a short time, the three piano quartets of Brahms, his quintet, and the quintet of Schumann. They came out exceptionally well and I still listen to them with great pleasure. Encouraged by our success, we later gave a good account of Dvořák's piano quintet and quite exceptional ones of the E-flat quartet and the piano quartet in C minor by Fauré.

During those two or three years, I was extremely busy recording my solo repertoire. In New York I played my final version of all the mazurkas of Chopin, the *Kreisleriana* of Schumann, both Chopin sonatas. The same year, I made in Rome, where the RCA Italiana had built a perfect studio on the outskirts of Rome, the Liszt sonata, the *Wanderer Fantasia* of Schubert, the Schubert Sonata in B flat, and all the waltzes of Chopin. Of course during previous years I had also recorded the preludes, scherzos, ballades, polonaises, and impromptus of Chopin. Having been so busy recording all my orchestral repertoire, my solo pieces, and much of the chamber music, I derived many conclusions from the experience.

The first one, as I noted before, was that chamber music, as it is called in all languages, should be heard in intimate surroundings. The great Italians, Haydn, Mozart, Beethoven, and later Schubert, Schumann, and Brahms poured out their genius in this intimate medium. The private rehearsals of the Joachim Quartet, which I was allowed to attend in my early youth, remain most vividly in my memory; while all through my life I suffered from the insufficient sound, even by the best chamber ensembles, in the modern concert halls.

In my late years, after so long a contact with the public, I realized that the delicate short pieces by Schubert, Schumann, or Brahms and even Ravel, Debussy, Prokofiev, or Szymanowski, and pieces which end softly, could not establish an immediate contact with the public. The same chamber music, the same solo pieces have an immediate enthusiastic impact on the listener when played by the latest perfected records in the intimacy of a room at home. For that very reason, there are quite a few pieces, most beloved by me, which I did not play in public but never stopped playing in private.

123

The year 1967 started with great news! My first Rubinstein grandson, named Jason, was born to Paul and his second wife.

In June of that year, while resting quietly in Paris after concerts and travels, terrible news appeared in the papers. President Nasser of Egypt ordered the United Nations to recall the peace-keeping force from the border with Israel. He was immediately obeyed with the tacit consent of the whole world. After the buffer zone was cleared, he advanced at the head of his troops the whole length of Sinai and announced that Egypt, Jordan, and Syria had decided to reoccupy Israel, which he accused of having stolen the land of the Arabs and threatened to throw their citizens into the sea. Jews, wherever they lived, were panic-stricken, but no objection was heard from any foreign government.

During this time, we were invited by the Israeli ambassador to a dinner at which the other guests, to our astonishment, were the chiefs of the military and naval staffs and our old friend Hervé Alphand, the General Secretary of the Foreign Office. We were sure then that France intended to intervene. But General de Gaulle declared pompously that he would condemn that sort of aggression, although the population of Paris showed their sympathy with Israel by a strong demonstration. Pierre Benouville, whom I saw only too rarely but who always proved to be the "friend in need," took us through all the police lines and crowds to the Israeli consulate, where he gathered popular figures of France, like the heroic General Koenig, the famous film actor Michel Simon, Alain Delon, and a few others, and asked us to speak to the immense crowd outside about the tragic danger once again facing our race. Many brave Jews flew immediately to Israel, among them my young colleague Daniel Barenboim and his fiancée,

Jacqueline du Pré, the great cellist; she married him upon arrival and adopted his faith.

As to ourselves, we lived from hour to hour in a state of terrible anxiety. Suddenly, on June 5 in the early morning, the radio announced that Israeli aircraft had smashed before dawn the air bases of its three adversaries, Egypt, Syria, and Jordan, following it up with an attack by its ground forces.

A cry of admiration and triumph was heard everywhere. We lived one of the greatest moments of our lives. The story of the Six-Day Victory is well known, I do not need to go into detail. What I retain for my readers is the astonishing attitude of De Gaulle, who condemned the Israelis, in sharp words, as "aggressors." He refused later on to deliver forty fighter planes already paid for by Israel and together with England refused to sell them the spare parts for arms.

Nasser's army fled home in panic, leaving thousands and thousands of slippers in the desert, but Jordan and Syria offered serious resistance and had to be overpowered after heavy fighting.

Jerusalem, the capital of the Jews, was united again after two thousand years, and the Old City, shamelessly desecrated by the Jordanian occupation, was cleared up and shines in glory thanks to its admirable mayor, Teddy Kollek.

In every country of the Western world, the people in the street acclaimed the courage and intelligence of the Israeli Army, while their governments were apprehensive of the political results. As for myself, I was exuberantly happy on my first visit to Israel a few months later to see the Old City of Jerusalem back with its legitimate owners and to kiss the hands of Golda Meir in deep gratitude and to express my admiration to Dayan and Rabin, the heroes of the victory.

But I was deeply ashamed of our world. After Hitler's attempt to exterminate our race, after the heroic conquest of their own land by the poor survivors of the holocaust, justice demanded that the civilized world should feel relieved to see the Jews back in the country of their forefathers who gave to the world the great religion of the creator they called the only God, doing away with the golden calf. Later, the whole civilized world adopted their dogma, whether Christians or Moslems. Even the intelligent Greeks parted from their lovely family of gods with whom they had lived in familiar intimacy.

During the two-thousand-year-old diaspora, the intelligence and inborn gifts of the Jews proved to be of great use to the countries where they found a new home. The response was calumny, jealousy, and hatred, which developed into an anti-Semitism which still persists.

Fortunately, Israel found the right men and a great woman to stand up in her defense. Ben-Gurion, Yigael Yadin, Moshe Dayan, Yitzhak Rabin, Ariel Sharon, and the brave Golda Meir gave the world a lesson, and now as I write these words, that great statesman Menachem Begin makes ready for peace with Egypt, which I hope will open the way to forcing the others to leave Israel alone.

I remember two important sessions organized by a French panel presided over by Professor André Lwoff, the first French Nobel Prize winner for medicine. One hundred and fifty prominent people were invited to protest the expulsion of Israel from UNESCO on a fatuous accusation concerning their excavations on "occupied" land—meaning the Old City of Jerusalem. In two articles, in *The New York Times* and *Le Monde* of Paris, I had previously criticized the Jew with the Hebrew name, Yehudi Menuhin, president of the music department of UNESCO, for not resigning, but voting with them against Israel.

During the whole day of the first session, the panel expressed a polite criticism of UNESCO for its stand against Israel on purely political grounds. UNESCO, as everybody knows, is an institution for nothing but cultural affairs of the world.

In my speech to the assembly, I demanded a strongly worded vote proclaiming Jerusalem as the undeniable capital of Israel for five thousand years and affirming the Israelis' right not only to clean it up after the Jordanian desecration but to carry out the excavations for the benefit of mankind and with the help of many Christians.

My argument was rejected by the panel as too "political." I left the assembly with harsh words of indignation: "A protest by this great assembly of important men would impress the world but your soft reproach will create nothing but indifference," I said, and left.

A year later, I was invited to a second session of exactly the same kind, but with a smaller attendance. I went, strictly as an observer, hoping for a stronger attitude toward UNESCO; but I heard nothing but weak denunciation, not one strong word. When Professor Lwoff invited me to express my views, I said sternly and curtly, "Stop being sorry for Israel. Israel does not need UNESCO but UNESCO is the poorer without Israel," and I left without waiting for their indifferent votes.

124

One afternoon in Paris the well-known critic of *Le Figaro*, Bernard Gavoty, came to see me. "I would like you to meet a young friend of mine who makes films and is very talented. He would like to make one with you for French television," he began. "May I bring him to see you sometime?"

I had been asked in the United States by several well-known producers to do this sort of thing, my wife had urged my doing it, but I had seen too many unfortunate pictures of that kind with Stravinsky and Casals and I, as another octogenarian, did not want to join them in such an unhappy venture.

So now, in Paris, I was rather skeptical, but I was willing to meet the man. "Can you both lunch with me and we shall see?" I said. The lunch was very enjoyable; François Reichenbach appealed to me. He had original ideas and personal charm. Gavoty himself was an inveterate talker and I wasn't far behind. This being France and not America, it took quite some time before we mentioned the matter on hand. They proposed to let me talk about anything I had on my mind—my life, my music, my family, and all I could think of. With our coffee and my cigar, I became very interested in the project. "I'm leaving for Marbella to spend a good part of the summer, but later I have concerts in Iran and Israel, so make up a scenario and send it to Marbella as soon as possible. I shall read it with great attention." They departed in good cheer.

When I arrived at our pleasant place above the little town of Marbella, which I loved for its modest simplicity and comfort, I gave my wife the good news. "I wonder what they will concoct for me," I said with a smile.

Ten days passed and no scenario. Ah-ha, they abandoned the whole idea, I said to myself; but the next day, our house was invaded by six or seven men, including Mr. Reichenbach and Gavoty. "We came to start work," said Reichenbach casually.

"But the scenario did not arrive!" I cried, quite alarmed.

"With you, we have no need of any scenario," he said. "Let's go into the garden and Gavoty will make you talk."

And thus started the film which earned me an Oscar. We explored Marbella, they accompanied me to Iran with my wife and Alina, where I played in Persepolis in front of the magnificent ruins of Darius and Xerxes. The beauty of Ispahan was captured by the talent of Reichenbach. But to show the entirely improvised filming: It was after a luncheon where the main course was a heavenly dish of Iranian caviar, in the garden of the palace of a caliph right out of the *Thousand and One Nights*, that Gavoty asked me if I had known the Finnish conductor Schneevoigt. This prompted me to tell the ridiculous story of some laughing birds in the zoo in Sydney, Australia. And of course, as the absurd so often triumphs, this story made many audiences laugh.

We also lived some dramatic moments in Iran. In Shiraz one morning, my wife had an attack of a mysterious illness. She could not move and was absolutely incapable of traveling. It was a hard dilemma for me. My schedule obliged me to go with the team to Teheran with a stop in Ispahan. That same night, we had to take a plane for Israel, where the next morning there was to be the filming of my rehearsal with orchestra.

Alina stayed with her mother to take care of her and they were to join us in Tel Aviv as soon as possible. Arriving in Teheran, I phoned the hotel in Shiraz for news. The answer was: "Both ladies have left." That terrified me. I imagined them being taken by ambulance to some hospital for an emergency operation. I rushed to the airport to inform my companions that I must return to Shiraz. Can one imagine my surprise when, reaching the waiting room at the airport, I saw Nela and Alina sitting quietly at a table with my companions. We left happily for Israel, where, however, my poor wife had to stay in bed for a few days.

In Israel we made the most moving sequence of the film. After having gone to New York, we returned finally to Paris and from then on I started my season of concerts. I did not think much about our film—it was too hectic, too improvised; I had to speak and play without warning—all in all, I found everything incomplete.

But during my absence, Reichenbach was showing the finished product to friends, who wrote me how much they loved it and were moved by it. Voices must have reached America, for after a concert in Monte Carlo, Bernard Gavoty shouted from the door, "NBC is offering an enormous amount of money for one showing if you will consent to speak with their man in English in as many instances as possible." This was really great news and we drank champagne to it.

With this money in hand, Reichenbach was able to make a full-length film out of the hour-long television program we already had.

I saw it for the first time at the festival in Cannes when this documentary film was shown during the regular afternoon session. The house was crowded and the whole jury present in spite of its not being in the competition. During the show, I wanted to run away—I saw myself talking nonsense and playing everything badly. My wife and Eva, who were with me, had a hard time keeping me in my seat. By the end, I was prepared to hear some booing and a strong protest, but instead I received a standing ovation.

For the rest of the day and night, I was actually beleaguered by interviewers and had to make long statements on television to many countries and in many languages.

Our film had a gala opening in a Paris cinema on the Champs-Elysées and the famous *tout Paris* was present. It was shown for months in five cinemas in Paris alone; I am ashamed to admit that I gloated over the queues in the street outside the cinema from a café opposite. The French film board sent our film, together with a "real" film, as the only representative of France to Hollywood to compete for the Oscar. My wife and Reichenbach were in Los Angeles at the great annual presentation.

I was scared to death and remained in New York for a concert and could not even watch the proceedings on television. When Fred Astaire opened the ominous envelope and proclaimed our film the winner, he handed the Oscar to Reichenbach and Nela, who thanked him in my name, but . . . the Oscar really went to a man named Bernard Chevrey, simply because he happened to be the producer. The trophy had to go to the producer because I couldn't be chosen as the best actor of the year, nor Reichenbach as the best director, but the whole long affair finished like a fairy tale. The thousand members of the Academy of Cinematographic Art voted unanimously a special Oscar for me, which its president, Gregory Peck, brought to my house in Paris, holding it in his hands. Now on a round table in my drawing room stands the glorious golden figure, and opposite him, the feminine Emmy which I received for the best television film of the year in the States.

125

On my next visit to Israel, our film was shown there for charities and Golda Meir was present at the opening. The government and Teddy Kollek, the mayor of Jerusalem, honored me in the most touching way. A forest was to be planted on the outskirts of Jerusalem and named after me.

The forest committee appealed to my friends all over the world to contribute to the trees. The inaugural ceremony moved me to tears. My wife and I planted the first tree, Mr. Rosen, the Minister of Justice, and Teddy Kollek himself were the speakers, and a large stone with an inscription bore testimony. Many friends from Tel Aviv attended, among them the painter Rubin and his lovely wife. I shall never forget that day.

The last decade brought me much sorrow and many honors. In my eighties, I lost all my dear, close friends. I felt the death of the brave and noble Louis Vallery Radot, Sioul to his friends, very deeply. My friend and close neighbor Marcel Pagnol and Marcel Achard, my old pal, died soon after. The charming Vladimir Golschmann had a fatal heart attack while writing his memoirs.

All the conductors with whom I had been so happy to play for many years died one after another and left the field to young men who changed considerably the picture of orchestral life in the United States.

Fortunately, some splendid records are available which allow me to hear in the intimacy of my room symphonies by Schumann, Brahms, and Beethoven conducted by the great, one and only George Szell.

It was my good fortune to make some records with the brilliant Daniel Barenboim and Zubin Mehta, not to speak of the much older Eugene Ormandy with his Philadelphia Orchestra and Eric Leinsdorf and the Boston Symphony. I was lucky enough to have the chance to make new records of the same compositions in the hope of improving them.

With the years, I lived more and more in Paris, where I could enjoy my books, my pictures, and my piano.

The year 1971 remains in my memory as a time of unexpected honors. The French Republic promoted me to the grade of Grand Officer of the Légion d'Honneur. I received notification of it from President Pompidou and Prime Minister Chaban Delmas. Two months later, Italy bestowed upon me the equivalent of the same decoration.

In Amsterdam, after a concert at the wonderful Concertgebouw, I was quite overcome by the signs of friendship from the Dutch. Right after my last piece a huge bouquet of about a hundred roses was presented to me with a letter from Queen Juliana. At the same time, the Minister of Culture appointed me a Commander of the high order of Orange-Nassau. The president of the orchestra nominated me an honorary member of this splendid body; but that was not all. I was taken to a special hall where representatives of the flower industry of Holland announced the creation of a new tulip called the Arthur Rubinstein tulip. This lovely gift touched me very specially.

Of course, I felt that all these honors were given more because of my exalted age than because of any artistic merit of mine.

On my return to Paris, that same month and right out of the clear blue sky, there was a telephone call. It was my friend Gaston Palewski, the president of the French Conseil d'Etat. "Arthur, you have just been elected a member of the Académie des Beaux Arts, come right away to the Brasserie Lipp, where tradition demands that you dish out champagne to your fellow academicians." I fell on the floor and fainted—I mean, I should have—it was that kind of a surprise. Me an academician! I had never graduated from an academy, a university, a conservatory, or even, let me say it, a school, and here I am going to function as a full-fledged member of the Institut de France, dressed up in the glorious uniform with hand-embroidered green and gold leaves!

Let me tell you right away, I accepted and Nela and I rushed to the Lipp. Right at the entrance, I was congratulated by some members of the five academies which form the Institut de France. "Let's go up," they said, "many members await you upstairs."

At the bottom of the staircase, a very old man was sitting on a chair, apparently waiting to greet me. "It is Maître Marcel Dupré. He cannot climb the stairs at ninety-five but insisted on congratulating you." I was very touched; Maître Dupré was a famous organist and composer and for some years director of the National Conservatory. When I thanked him for being gracious enough to come, he whispered, "Do you remember when you took me on your lap in Rouen when I was five years old?"! This was rather preposterous and for a moment I couldn't make out what he meant, but then I guessed it. It was my famous namesake Anton Rubinstein who made little Dupré hop on his lap. The story went around and produced a good laugh.

Upstairs many academicians were waiting for me, among them some good friends, and now began the champagne orgy. They seemed to be thirsty for at least three hours; bottle after bottle was emptied. It was a happy day.

I inherited the chair at the Academy from a Swiss sculptor, Edouard Marcel Sandoz, but he himself was the heir of Paderewski, to my great surprise and pleasure. Ten foreign members who in some way helped the arts are admitted, less for their artistic achievement than for their personalities, and so I found among my future colleagues Queen Elizabeth of Belgium, Field Marshal Montgomery of Alamein, Count Cini from Venice—even King Alfonso of Spain was a member. One can see that I couldn't exactly call them my chums or pals.

The official reception of a new academician is a solemn affair. The great hall is filled with guests, and the members of the Academy, in full attire with swords and all, are assembled to accompany the newly elected one to a table at the foot of the dais. The actual president, the permanent secretary, and an aide at his side receive the future academician with a very long speech, with biographical details and other items of merit. At the end, the new *élu*, after thanking the president, has to deliver a long eulogy of his predecessor and, worse still, to read it because the academy prints these speeches, which are kept in the archives.

This last obligation scared me to death, but there was no way out of it. The eulogy for Mr. Sandoz gave me lots of homework. It included a visit to Lausanne, where the sculptures of Sandoz could be seen in a museum of his works and in a park filled with quite beautiful animal sculptures which he had donated to the city. His daughter helped me most graciously with many biographical notes and necrologies.

In our small apartment in Geneva, I settled down at my desk and began to work on this formidable assignment. Please, dear readers, don't have too much pity on me, it went easier than I thought. I finished it in three hours. I must admit that Paderewski, my sort of grandfather at the Academy, came to my rescue because I could include him with much facility.

At my reception, things went smoothly. Everybody seemed to be grateful that my eulogy was rather short but they enjoyed much more my improvised speech which followed. It goes without saying that I was proud to wear my beautiful uniform, in spite of the ruinous price I had to pay Cardin!

126

Darius Milhaud was going to be eighty years old. He, like myself, hated official birthdays with friends, cakes, presents, telegrams, and all that goes with it, but he graciously accepted my invitation for a small dinner *à quatre*. We drove out to a charming place near Geneva, where we settled down on the terrace of a good restaurant.

It was a happy celebration full of memories of Brazil, Claudel, his opera *Bolivar*, and the great evenings of his music. Unfortunately it was the last time that I saw him, which makes this evening poignantly memorable.

As for myself, I complained during dinner about a little spot on my right cheek which worried me. The next day, the whole right cheek had a rash. A doctor at the American Hospital in Paris declared it was shingles. An abominable indescribable pain ensued but there was nothing one could do about it. It was heartbreaking to ask Hurok to postpone eleven concerts in America; I was sitting in a daze for long hours, not daring to move my head, but by some phenomenon I was able to sleep twelve hours flat on my back each day—a rest which helped my resistance.

I decided, however, pain or no pain, to be present at the great party given by the Baron Alain de Rothschild and his lovely wife, Mary, in the palace, avenue Marigny, for the presentation of the sword of honor which by custom is given to a newly elected academician by his friends; in my case, friends from many countries who were invited to the ceremony by the hosts. The sword is, by itself, a work of art and could be used in a battle or for duels. It is designed by an artist and made by specialists.

This time, the gods were against me; the eve of the feast, a strong rash developed on my other cheek. My urgently called doctor was rather alarmed: "Shingles never attacks both sides," but at a better look he exclaimed delightedly, "You have chicken pox, my dear fellow. Quite natural, you never had it and that gave you the little present in the form of shingles." This time, I didn't share his hilarity because without asking me for my agreement he took me straight to hospital. The next day, I no longer had a temperature, but I was not allowed to leave the hospital. There was nothing else to do but stay in bed and hate myself. At the reception my wife represented me and replied to the speeches.

At that time, the premiere was announced on Broadway of a musical comedy called *Pippin*, in which my son Johnny played the star role. We all were thrilled by the news and Nela announced that she would leave for the premiere. I could not stand it; shingles or not, I had to go too.

Before the show, I had been nervous and had my misgivings. The summer before, Johnny had read to me the libretto, and I found it absurd. The story was supposed to be about the great King Charlemagne and his son Pippin le Bref, Pippin for the play.

I do not object to fun being made about anything and the play, at the cost of millions, turned out to be one of the greatest successes on Broadway for several seasons, but I for one resented, in this crazy take-off of these historic personalities, the fact that the role of Pippin himself was a straight part. This Pippin might have been any American boy in Michigan or Nebraska.

John was brilliant; he had to play serious comedy, sing many songs, and dance with gusto. He held stardom on Broadway for two full years. At the opening of *Pippin*, I made a curious and pleasant discovery. All through the performance, I was so intensely involved in the show that, as at my concerts, I was completely oblivious of my shingles.

The next day, I asked Mr. Hurok to reinstate all my concerts. As I thought, the shingles did not interfere with my playing, but continued their hold on me before and after.

127

After having postponed writing for twenty years and then taking it up again every summer, with agonies about the style and grammar—and very often being tempted to give it up—the momentous day finally arrived when I wrote the last word of my book *My Young Years*.

To my great surprise, a noted literary agent offered me his services. Loyal by nature, I thought to deliver my manuscript to my old friend Alfred Knopf, who had waited so patiently for over thirty years. Poor Blanche, his wife, who prodded me for all those years, died before seeing it finished. But my agent saw it with other eyes. When I told him that the Knopf publishing house was willing to give me a small guarantee before printing, he laughed out loud. "We'll get good money for your little book," he said with a vengeance and, by Jove, he succeeded.

He received the same large guarantee from the French and the German publishers. It was the first time that I was offered a large sum of money, not for the pianist I was, but for the writer I wasn't. So, in order to remain honest with myself, I donated the proceeds of the book to my wife and children.

I saw it in print first in French in a translation which was not quite to my taste, but it had an excellent press. It was on my return to America that the original version came to life. All through the editing, the house of Knopf was rather apprehensive, wondering if the "American reader" might be uninterested in the many descriptions and other items, but I shall never forget the triumphant telephone call from Knopf: "The Book-of-the-Month Club has chosen your book! Come right away, the champagne is on the table." My much-suffered effort in literature turned out to be a great success. Alfred Knopf gave a memorable party on the very stage of Carnegie Hall, the whole literary and artistic elite was invited. Speeches by

Knopf and men of letters and music feted the event in front of a huge reproduction of a photo of me. Many bottles of champagne were emptied. *My Young Years* was on the best-seller list for three full months, and reviews of the book appeared all over the United States. Only some music critics reproached me for not devoting my book to music, forgetting that I was writing about my full and rich life. I was born with music, it was my sixth sense. I always became angry when interviewers asked me, "What are your other hobbies besides music?"

"I have no hobbies," I would answer, "but passions for books, paintings, and travel, and I felt always a deep love for life in all its aspects. But music had nothing to do with all this, it was always in me."

When my book came out in Germany, Japan, Israel, Finland, Yugoslavia, and even Poland, I was beseeched to write the continuation of my memoirs, but I had no intention of evoking present times with all it involved.

My concert life became richer than ever. My film, the Oscar, the television programs, and finally the book made people everywhere aware of me as a person and not only as a concert pianist. My heart was warmed by many letters from people who had never heard me play but expressed friendship and understanding and by many persons who simply felt the need to talk to me about the book or the film. Apropos, a little example: In some town on a rainy morning, I was hurrying to be on time for my rehearsal when I was stopped in the street at the entrance to the concert hall by an elderly man. "Could I speak to you, Mr. Rubinstein?" he said with great urgency.

"It is utterly impossible," I replied. "I have a rehearsal which will last two hours," and I left him there. The rehearsal lasted longer than I thought. When I left the hall, it was still raining and the man was standing there waiting for me. I felt sorry for him, thinking that he was in great need of money. "What can I do for you?" I asked, a little concerned.

He flushed. "I read your book," he said timidly, "and I wanted to ask you, what happened to Pola?" The man walked away happily when his curiosity was satisfied.

One morning in Paris, I read an exuberantly enthusiastic account about a recital of a young French pianist by the name of François Duchable. I am rarely impressed by French critics—our opinions diverged too often—but on that occasion, an instinct told me that I should meet the young man.

My friend Diane Benvenuti informed me that he had studied with her husband and arranged for him to come and see me. A charming young boy, simple and not conceited, went to the piano, sat for a moment with his head bowed as in prayer, and thundered out, in an unbelievable tempo, the octave étude in B minor of Chopin as if it were child's play, but in the trio of this same étude, he showed a fine musical sensibility.

For once, I was in full agreement with the critic. I took this young man to my heart and was happy to become a little useful in obtaining concerts for him. His great success in Spain followed almost immediately. Now, François Duchable is one of the finest young pianists of whom France can be proud.

The State of Israel was about to celebrate its twenty-fifth anniversary. The gifted organizer of the Chopin competitions in Warsaw, Jacob Bistritzky, left Poland for the new state, where he planned a piano competition in my name as the high point of the festivities. I laughed it off. "Another competition? You are completely crazy. We must wait for a new flock of pianists to be born, the living ones have played in enough competitions already." He stubbornly persisted. The Israeli ambassador in Paris, the Minister of Tourism, and the Prime Minister, Mrs. Golda Meir herself, beseeched me to accept it. Bistritzky convinced even my wife of the importance of it. This was too much for me, I had to give in.

But then something dreadful happened. The Egyptians and the Syrians attacked Israel on the very morning of the most sacred Jewish holiday, Yom Kippur (the Day of Atonement). I shall not describe in detail this cruel war. This time, the Israelis endured many losses, but won again through their incredible courage and intelligence and gave a lesson to the world by allowing the trapped Egyptian army to return home instead of starving it to death. The festivities were postponed until the following year.

Sad news reached me. My good old friend Sol Hurok, to whom I owed so much, died in New York. He had not been well for quite a long time, but continued his activities right up until the last moment. It was a consoling thought that, a few months before, he was offered a tribute rarely given to men of merit. It was a gala at the Metropolitan Opera House, where many artists performed for him. His grateful admirers from all over the world were there; unfortunately, I was absent because of my concerts in Europe but my wife represented me.

The Hurok management remained in the hands of three faithful ones, Walter Prude, Sheldon Gold, and George Perper—but not for long. A Boston businessman bought the concern, but went bankrupt a year later. The three Hurok men set up their own management.

To my great pleasure and relief, Bistritzky showed his unique talent in organizing the piano competition. Young master pianists from everywhere came to Jerusalem to compete in spite of the distance and certain danger involved. A jury of fine musicians was present; one of them, Arturo Michelangeli, gave a concert and offered the proceeds toward the expenses of the competition. The four first prizes went to young pianists well on the way to making a fine career: Emanuel Ax, Eugene Indjic, Janina Fialkowska, and Seta Tanyel. The President of Israel and the government headed by Mrs. Golda Meir took an active part in the proceedings. Bistritzky had a series of special gold, silver, and bronze medals minted to commemorate the competition, showing a reproduction of one of Picasso's portraits of me.

Later in Paris, New York, and Marbella, I saw much of Miss Fialkowska when she proudly played for me her greatly enriched repertoire. Mr. Bistritzky deserved high praise, for everything; on top of it all and in order to soften my resistance and give me special pleasure, he rather indiscreetly asked twelve prominent composers to write and dedicate to me piano pieces in any form they chose. Jordi Cervello, Carlos Chavez, Henri Dutilleux, Henri Gagnebin, Camargo Guarnieri, Rodolfo Halffter, Marlos Nobre, Marcel Poot, Alexander Tansman, Haim Alexander, Menahem Avidom, and Josef Tal responded generously and sent their manuscripts to be given to me during the competition. This friendly homage touched me very much.

After the competition, I had a lovely tour in Spain which warmed my heart. The end of this year and New Year were spent in Paris in a cheerful and happy mood.

128

The year 1975, and my eighty-eighth, began as one of the most promising, interesting, and active of my life, starting with a large tour in America which included California. In Los Angeles I played with Zubin Mehta, whose wonderful accompaniment always inspired me, and gave a recital, and another one in San Diego.

A strange invitation arrived from a Dr. Joseph Rubenstein of Stanford University for a symposium called "The Majesty of Man." The panel included the famous Linus Pauling, twice a Nobel Prize winner, another Nobel Prize winner, and some important professors of physics and medicine. I was, of course, highly flattered at being invited to join such an important group of learned men, but on second thought, it occurred to me that I might be used as a guinea pig. "When you get up in the morning, do you remember who you are, Mr. Rubinstein?" This was the sort of question I expected, but I was mistaken.

In the big aula of the university, with a large audience in attendance, we heard a long lecture by Professor John Nicholls about the genius of the human brain, its millions of branches and its dominating power.

After this lecture, I was invited to take a seat with the panel on the stage. To my relief, I was not asked any silly questions but was asked about matters which I explored in my book. When they wanted to know what I meant by my "unconditional" happiness, I tried my best to explain it to them by mentioning my great belief in contrast. "Loving life as I do, I came to the conclusion that bad times are needed in order to realize the wonder and interest of life. I cannot accept the teachings of all the religions that treat life as a sinful preliminary to a better one after death. I have listened with great attention and respect to the lecture of Professor Nicholls but I must admit that I am not convinced by it. In my own case, my brain worked rather as a calculator. My mental decisions always found an alternative—I had to make a choice. But in my life, I mostly followed an urge." I asked the learned gentlemen if the brain is connected with the soul, a word used in every language, the meaning of which was never clear. Of course they had no answer. "At most of my concerts, the brain, which helps me to prepare my work, is at peace. It is the inspiration, the urge to transmit the music to my listeners which I like to call soul." I stopped, I felt I had gone too far, but to my great satisfaction, my words were not lost—especially on Professor Linus Pauling, who at a luncheon the next day at Dr. Rubenstein's engaged me at length on the subject. All in all, it was a great experience for me.

A few days later I had a concert in New York with Daniel Barenboim playing the D minor Brahms. On the eve of this concert, my wife called from Los Angeles to tell me that she had to undergo a serious operation on the very day of the concert. I was prepared to cancel it and fly back but both she and her surgeon urged me not to do so because my presence might upset her.

After a rehearsal at which I could hardly think of the music, I hurried back to the hotel and settled down by the telephone to wait for Johnny's call about the result of the operation. It was six in the evening when the telephone rang and I heard Johnny's voice saying that my wife was completely out of danger. He was followed by the surgeon, who assured me that there was nothing to worry about.

I played that evening in a glorious mood and later had my good friends for supper in my hotel room, where we drank a whole case of champagne until the very late hours.

That same morning, I flew to Los Angeles, where I rushed to the hospital and saw my wife in a deep sleep. The surgeon assured me that she was in the best state, and two days later I found her up having her breakfast at a small table and looking her best. Unfortunately, I had to leave right away for my many commitments in Europe.

The first one was the recording of the five Beethoven concertos with Daniel Barenboim and the London Philharmonic Orchestra in London. We both did good work and it was moving to have the presence of Daniel's wife, Jacqueline du Pré, that great artist who had been so cruelly struck by multiple sclerosis. Fortunately her records are testimony to her sublime art.

After the recording, I had a large tour in Europe including England, Holland, Switzerland, and a glorious tour in Spain. During the Easter break, there was an interesting interlude. Young Herbert Kloiber, the producer of my video cassettes, invited me to fly with him in his private plane to Salzburg, Mozart's birthplace, which I had always dreamed of seeing. My first visit was to Mozart's house, where to my joy I found his parents had lived quite comfortably. When I saw the clavichord of this beloved master, I could not resist and played the beginning of the second movement of the A major Concerto, which brought a tear to my eye. The tourists who filled the room felt, as I did, the presence of this genius and were wiping their eyes.

I heard there Herbert von Karajan conducting *La Bohème*, which I never liked because its book lends itself rather to a Delibes or Messager with French elegance of style rather than the heavy-handed Italian Puccini.

I was compensated the next day by an unforgettable performance of my dear *Meistersinger*, where Karajan showed his mettle. After four wonderful days, my charming cicerone flew me back to Paris. I was to work for him a few weeks later on a new series of video cassettes, this time with André Previn and the London Symphony in London. It was good work, Previn proved to be a fine musician, but I suffered abominably facing the many spotlights, which my poor eyes resented for weeks.

My next step was a rapid visit of three days to Jerusalem, where its mayor, my friend Teddy Kollek, invited me for the anniversary of Israel's independence and to give a concert as part of the celebrations.

After my return to Paris and concerts in Madrid, I took a plane for New York to receive a Doctor Honoris Causa on commencement day at Columbia University, where, to my great pride, my daughter Alina was admitted to the very exclusive medical school of this university.

It was a trying, hot day and I had to sit for hours with the sun in my eyes and in front of students and other people. There were five of us receiving the honor; three professors from other universities, unknown to the crowd, received a tepid applause, but after a wonderful ovation for me, a young man received his citation with shrieks of enthusiasm from all the women in the crowd. When I asked my neighbor why he deserved this sort of reception, he answered quietly, "He invented the Pill."

Back in Europe after only six days and six concerts in England, I accepted the invitation of Lodz, the city of my birth, to play for the anniversary of its Philharmonic Orchestra. After many years of absence from Poland because of my being persona non grata to the government of Gomulka, who called me a demagogue, this invitation gave me much pleasure. The short visit moved me very much. At the Warsaw airport, many friends welcomed me: my niece and nephew and my old friend Roman Jasinski and Henryk Czyz, the conductor of the Lodz Philharmonic, who came in his car to take me to Lodz.

Before leaving Warsaw, I wanted to see the reconstructed Royal Palace, which had been entirely demolished by the Nazis. At this beautiful sight, which I always admired, standing there proudly as if nothing had happened, I loved the Poles for their courage in risking criticism from their meddling neighbors. When I asked if it would become a museum, university, or other public building, the answer was: "No, the interior will be the same as the exterior, exactly as it was before."

We drove to Lodz in less than two hours. I found my city entirely untouched. Every street, every house stood in its place as in my childhood. In the courtyard of the house where I was born, I was able to point to our apartment and describe the exact disposition of the rooms to some newspapermen who accompanied me. One of them, after I left, was curious enough to find out if I could really remember so exactly a place I hadn't seen since I was four. He told me that he had rung the bell and a middle-aged woman let him in and he mentioned my name. She and a young daughter of hers who studied piano became quite excited and allowed him to visit the whole apartment. "I was flabbergasted," he added. "It is exactly as you described it."

During my concert with Czyz, in which I played the Chopin F minor and the Fifth Concerto of Beethoven, I was given a reception which was very moving for both my public and me, as we felt it would be the last time I would play for them.

I was paid in zlotys a large sum for the concert, an equal amount for the radio broadcast, and a still larger one for the televising of the concert. They even paid a big sum for the filming of my whole stay there. Altogether, it was an exhausting but unforgettable experience. I was happy to distribute the fortune which I accumulated in zlotys toward the expenses of the Palace in Warsaw, the orchestra in Lodz, and the Association of Polish Composers, and I left a sum with the Lodz Philharmonic for a prize to be given yearly to a young musician.

After my return from Poland and a few nice concerts in Spain, I played the so-called *Emperor* Concerto, with Daniel Barenboim conducting the Orchestra of Paris, twice on the same evening at Congress Hall—first at seven o'clock and then at nine, both to sold-out houses. The next concert took place in Zurich in June; I considered it my best performance of the year. But the last concert of the season was given in Monte Carlo for the Weizmann Institute. It was a Chopin recital patronized by the charming Princess Grace of Monaco. I was not too happy with my playing and charity concerts are seldom attended by a musical audience, so I was disagreeably surprised to find that Sviatoslav Richter, the great Russian pianist, came especially to hear me play.

The summer in Marbella was the busiest of my life, reading. Some instinct made me finish all the books I either had not finished or had neglected to read. I took the trouble to take in all of *Ulysses* by Joyce, understanding it perfectly and very impressed by it. I had bought in Paris all of Proust, including his biography by Painter and even the volume written by his old maid, swallowing it all up without stopping. After which, I again read *Buddenbrooks* by Thomas Mann, which I first read in Berlin when it appeared, and also *The Magic Mountain*, which I never had the time to absorb earlier; it moved me very much.

In September, Roman Jasinski came to stay with us and I began to read some of my German books, among them the *Memoirs* of Clara Schumann, which impressed me by its revelation of her difficult character. She was certainly a very possessive woman who must have caused much trouble to her great husband and also to Brahms, who remained, in spite of his rather rude character, her lifelong devoted friend. Roman was a delightful companion in our discussion of these matters.

My concerts began again in Edinburgh and Glasgow, followed by Paris with Lorin Maazel and the Cleveland Orchestra, then back to England for the Windsor Festival, Birmingham, and Aldershot. In this last city, there was an unusual end to the concert. I was pleased to learn that Juanita Gandarillas' family, who lived nearby, were present and I played with particular pleasure a lovely program. My encores were planned to remind them of old times, but when I finished my program, the manager rushed up to me and said, "Mr. Rubinstein, I will take you right down to the street." I protested while the audience clamored for encores, but he took my arm and led me almost by force to the exit. "We had a call about a time bomb placed in the building," he said. That was enough for me; we left the building in a hurry. There I observed the courage of the English. Informed about the danger, they departed placidly and went quietly home. Fortunately, it was a hoax.

My next concert took place at my dear Concertgebouw of Amsterdam, where my faithful and so musical Dutch audience always inspired me to give them my best.

On the following day, we had a charming intimate dinner at the palace of the Crown Princess Beatrix with no other guests but ourselves. She and her husband gave one of the best dinners of my life. A strange group this Dutch royal family—all of them utterly unmusical, they always showed me a particular friendship. On a previous occasion, Queen Juliana offered a state dinner in our honor. I remember how amused she was when I told her that, as a young boy, I played a concert in honor of her grandmother's birthday in Mecklenburg in the presence of her recently married mother. She then read all the details in *My Young Years*.

After a fine performance of the D-minor Concerto of Brahms with Barenboim in London, I had a tour in Switzerland in the company of Roman. We went to Bern, Lausanne, Geneva, and Basel. After that, at the end of October, I left for Los Angeles to give the first eight concerts on the Pacific Coast which were part of twenty which I had promised to give on condition that concerts in the same cities would be offered to Janina Fialkowska and François Duchable for the next season.

We arrived happily in California, pleased to see our friends and my son Johnny, his wife and adorable little children, Jessica and Mike, again. The first recital was in the beautiful new music center and I felt as though playing for my friends and family at home. I played with all my heart and finished with six études of Chopin with much bravura, but in the last one, a few bars did not come off. My audience ignored it and gave me the usual ovation, but returning to the stage, I declared to them, "Before I give you any encores, I shall repeat the last étude, which I fouled up before." And I sat down and played it with all the right notes, and only then followed with three encores. The San Diego audiences were like an echo of Los Angeles.

The last concert in Los Angeles was with the orchestra conducted by Mehta and I played the Chopin F minor and the Beethoven *Emperor*. This concert was memorable for many reasons, but still mainly for the inspiration of our performance. As before with George Szell, to play with Mehta was always a feast.

The next morning, at breakfast in our sitting room at the Beverly Wilshire Hotel, Nela shouted, "You must read the criticism in the Los

Angeles *Times*. It is the best I ever read." I reached for the paper, and easily found the right page, but when I looked at the printed lines, I was unable to distinguish the words. This was the fatal morning when the center of both my eyes refused to see what I tried to read. I was suddenly desperately aware that my mail had to be read to me and I found myself incapable of dialing the telephone, but still, I took it lightly.

Nela took me to Jules Stein's eye clinic, where I was examined by the best doctor and he told me I had a degeneration of the cells of the macula and there was no cure for it—especially at my age. This was the last straw. Two years before, the same thing had happened to my left eye alone and I was not too distressed about it because for ten years I had been annoyed by seeing double at a certain distance, and with the loss of the one eye, the remaining one again saw everything single and allowed me to see quite normally.

If my readers feel sorry for me, I would like to console them by stating that right up to my eightieth year, I enjoyed the best pair of eyes, and so my motto, "Nie dam sie" (I shall never give in), was stronger in me than ever. With a bright light on the keyboard, I was still able to play and decided to continue my tour. I took off for San Francisco with my Sancho Panza, the faithful Louis Bender. It was reassuring that the concert went well, I must admit quite frankly. Portland was even better, but in Seattle, at the beginning of the D minor Mozart Concerto with Milton Katims, something dreadful happened: At one point, I looked carelessly away from the keyboard, and suddenly could not see the following sequence. My deep love and respect for Mozart did not allow me to continue as though nothing had happened. I stopped dead and asked Katims to start again from the beginning and we finished beautifully together. The last concert was at Salt Lake City, with my good friend Maurice Abravanel. The only difficulty I had there was the steps on the platform of the Tabernacle. I had to study them carefully so as not to fall on my nose.

In New York, I went to see my old eye specialist, Dr. Milton Berliner, who after a careful examination confirmed the verdict of the previous ones, but he added: "Arthur, don't be too sad, because you will never be blind." This was the first optimistic phrase I had heard since the loss of my direct vision and it gave my morale a tremendous lift. All was not lost, I felt. I still could see around, I could still be independent in many ways, and I could still walk alone in the street.

I returned hopefully to Paris, where I dared to give a solo recital at the new huge Congress Hall and offered all the proceeds to the American Hospital.

My last concert in Paris took place at the Champs-Elysées, where I played for the first time with the Radio Orchestra in spite of my dislike of having my concerts broadcast. The few times I was forced to accept the radio I played with the vision of a man who was shaving and shouting, "Stop that damn music."

My partial blindness gave me a lot of trouble but I was stubbornly determined not to give up any of my engagements, and so in the beginning of 1976 I performed my last three concerts in Spain: one in Palma de Mallorca and two in Barcelona; then there were two concerts in Strasbourg and a recital in Milan at the Società del Quartetto—a fine concert after which I had supper with Pollini and other musicians.

After one day in Paris, we took a plane for America, where I owed the twelve remaining concerts with the duplicate contracts. This time, they took place in the East. This last tour, I shall remember as my best in many ways. My faithful audiences felt it was the last time and I responded by expressing my gratitude and love, which was all I could give.

My recitals in Boston and New York stand out; the others were in Chicago, two in Philadelphia, Washington, Cleveland, Houston, Columbus, Montreal. The last concert took place in Cincinnati, from where early next morning the Presidential plane took me to Washington. There President Ford bestowed on me the Medal of Freedom at the White House in the presence of the whole diplomatic corps and three hundred guests. The President read a long complimentary speech on a specially erected dais, which I answered with a spontaneous improvised one after a sleepless night.

Following the ceremony and greeting the guests, Mr. Ford and the First Lady gave a small luncheon at which, besides my family, Virginia Bacon, our friend Bill Cook, and Mr. Kissinger were present. The Presidential plane took us back to New York, where one hour later we watched the whole reception on television.

I returned to Paris in a mellow mood. I was now due for my last public appearances and recordings. I had promised to make a record with Zubin Mehta and the Israel Philharmonic. We flew to Tel Aviv to keep my promise and we made the record of the D minor Concerto of Brahms in two full days; it turned out to be by far the most satisfactory of all my previous attempts. We finished by giving a public performance of it in Tel Aviv and Jerusalem.

A week later, I made in London my last solo recording with Max Wilcox: Schumann's *Fantasiestücke* and the E-flat Sonata Op. 31 No. 3 of Beethoven. I would have liked to record a few other pieces but did not dare to do it because of my inability to read the music.

My last concert in France took place in Toulouse, where I played the Schumann concerto with a newly created orchestra under an excellent conductor, Michel Plasson. Roman Jasinski came with us. A strange incident occurred at the rehearsal. At the end of the second movement, I suddenly could not see the top notes but fortunately this did not happen again at the evening performance.

The last concert of my career was the one I gave at Wigmore Hall in London for the benefit of the hall, which was in danger of being demolished. My concert was to give an example to other artists in order to save this old endearing place. As for myself, it was a symbolic gesture; it was in this hall that I had given my first recital in London and playing there for the last time in my life made me think of my whole career in the form of a sonata. The first movement represented the struggles of my youth, the following andante for the beginning of a more serious aspect of my talent, a scherzo represented well the unexpected great success, and the finale turned out to be a wonderful moving end.

129

I suddenly found myself with a wealth of time on my hands. The long, long hours I had spent reading—mornings, afternoons, and late in bed, all through my life and often to the detriment of my pianistic activities —had to be filled up now with a new way of living. My wife taught me to listen to the radio, which I had always refused to do; she put an apparatus on my night table and made me become a reluctant novice, but by and by, I became like the rest of my family, an obedient servant of this diabolical intruder into our privacy. But still, I was trying desperately to find other possible occupations.

Since the success of *My Young Years,* my publishers had urged me to continue my memoirs. After the hard work my first volume had given me, I did not look forward with pleasure to undertaking a much more important and more voluminous opus. I was also frightened of the responsibility to write the truth and nothing but truth without hurting many people I had known who were still alive or had descendants. But now, there was no other alternative. I felt my memory continued to be clear and sharp; I was able to tell every detail of my whole life in one session.

A young friend of ours from Marbella, Tony Madigan, accepted the difficult task of writing down what I had to dictate and we progressed quite nicely. We made a good and swift beginning.

My old Ernesto de Quesada, who died in 1973, brought to his office in Madrid a young English woman, Annabelle Whitestone, who proved to be remarkably efficient in her work. Thanks to her I had better conditions and better concerts in Spain and, accompanying me on my tours, she obtained promptly my fees and good accommodations. She was the one who responded warmly to my recommendation of the young French pianist François Duchable, who, thanks to her, conquered Spain at his very first appearances. Later, she did wonderfully well for Janina Fialkowska, the brilliant winner of my competition in Jerusalem. Miss Whitestone arrived in Marbella for Janina's concert there, became interested in my project with the book, and accepted my proposal to type it page by page. The three of us did so well that Tony Madigan gave up his theatrical work in Barcelona and Miss Whitestone her post in Madrid with Quesada and both joined me in Paris to continue my book.

The first hundred pages proved so satisfactory that, after reading them, Alfred Knopf bought the rights to publish it. When, toward Christmas, Tony Madigan decided to return to his theatrical work, this time in Madrid, Annabelle agreed to both write down and type my book and has remained faithfully with me while I am dictating these last lines of my memoirs.

My ninetieth birthday was feasted unexpectedly in the most moving way while I visited New York to see my children and pay my taxes. The telephone rang all throughout the day with calls from all over the world. Flowers filled all the rooms and I remember particularly ninety beautiful roses from my young colleague Van Cliburn, who never missed an opportunity to shower them on me. Interviewers besieged me the whole day. In the late afternoon, my family gathered many of my friends for cocktails. Since my fourth birthday in Lodz, I had never been feted so lavishly and so generally; only then, it was the whole town of Lodz, and now, the whole world.

Since then I have been living the happiest time of my life. My excellent gramophone, my wealth of records, allow me to hear the most divine music from morning until night, while previously my constant concert tours hardly let me hear a sprinkling of recitals and here and there a good orchestral performance. Now, suddenly, Miss Whitestone has revealed to me all the glorious chamber music of Mozart, Haydn, and Beethoven with all sorts of combinations of string and wind instruments of which I never even heard of. The great songs which I enjoyed sight-reading in my early days in Berlin, I hear now beautifully sung by Kathleen Ferrier, Dietrich Fischer-Dieskau, Elisabeth Schwarzkopf. The whole of Mahler's genius is revealed to me. I can hear the music of my never forgotten Karol Szymanowski and George Szell's great performances of the Beethoven, Brahms, and Schumann symphonies. The *Sinfonia Concertante* of Mozart played by Arthur Grumiaux and Arrigo Pelliccia brings tears to my eyes. Jacqueline du Pré's and Daniel Barenboim's performances of all the cello sonatas are unequaled. They put even the great Pablo Casals in the shade. Please don't laugh, my readers, but I have four complete recordings of *Die Meistersinger* of Wagner and *Aida* of Verdi and heard them with Annabelle, without losing a note, two or three times.

Through all these auditions, I have made a few interesting discoveries —in the first place about England, for so long judged as completely addicted to sport to the detriment of music; well, I found, by careful comparison, that the English players of chamber music, which as one knows is its highest expression, are by far the most satisfactory. Their respect and devotion to the beauty of the most intricate combinations by the masters make me feel deeply grateful.

Of course, I have as many records as possible of the work of my colleagues up until the last hour. Here my feelings are obviously very personal. It is difficult for me to remain completely objective. I do get annoyed when familiar pieces are played off rapidly, the common habit of the youngest ones, or much too slowly, as some super-intellectuals insist on playing. But there is loads to admire from a Richter, Gilels, Pollini, Brendel, Barenboim, and others. Horowitz returned to the concert life as the great virtuoso he always was, but in my view does not contribute anything to the art of music.

Thanks to the great devotion of Miss Whitestone, although severely handicapped by my partial blindness, I have been able to visit again my beloved Venice and Rome and even Israel—this time, not for concerts, but to breathe the air of the sacred place of my ancestors. I did affirm to my readers in *My Young Years* that I was the happiest man I had ever met and I can proudly reaffirm it at the age of ninety-two.

Even my deus ex machina has remained devoted to me. There were moments, I must admit, when I was slightly discouraged by enjoying life and music so fully, receiving so much, without giving out anything. One day François Reichenbach introduced me to a friend from Mexico, who was at the head of the Mexican Television Company Televisia and also owned some stations in North America. After getting better acquainted in Paris, this gentleman, Mr. Emilio Azcarraga, proposed that I make a series of half-hour television programs. When I reminded him with many regrets that I don't play anymore, he exclaimed, "I want your personality, not your playing." His offer proved to be most tempting. He simply allowed me to choose the places, the people, and the subject of my talks. "I want to bring to my television audiences the great music in your conception, words, and choice of performers," he said. I could do no less than accept such terms. Reichenbach was to be the director; he would travel with a special team. Annabelle was charged with supervising the details, my statements, and the different music to be used for illustration.

All of a sudden, we became furiously busy. After one or two takes in Paris with the wonderful cellist Paul Tortelier, our team set off for Venice, Padua, Vicenza, and Verona, where I had much to talk about and Reichenbach to show. After a short stay in Deauville, where I had a nice musical rendezvous with a fine pianist, Bruno Leonardo Gelber, we went to Lucerne for the festival and to Israel, where a few very talented young students played for me at the music center in Jerusalem and where we heard a wonderful concert conducted by Leonard Bernstein.

Now this long tale is finished, but before I close my book, I must say a few words about the world which I must soon leave.

The world in which we live is at its lowest point—morally and artistically. *My Young Years* received some praise because of the good account it gave of the so-called "Belle Epoque." I, for one, think the term is misused. My own life, which I have now described in detail in both books, has been, since my earliest years up until now as I write, an affair of an unconditional love of life, but what I have seen, heard, and observed is the very opposite of a "belle époque."

From my first years, I remember with horror the Dreyfus affair in France—an ugly spot which I have never been able to quite erase from my memory. Then I remember an avalanche of wars: the Spanish-American (resulting in many occupied lands which were never dis-occupied); the Russo-Japanese; several violent Balkan wars; and the year-long threat of war because of the German Emperor William II's political activities. But with all that I could call those years the "civilized époque." After peace, both sides would pursue good relations with Old World good manners and the cruel days of hostilities would be forgotten.

But both world wars put an end to the "civilized époque." Now we live in a constant state of cold war, hypocrisy, and the fear of being wiped out by the dangerous inventions of scientific geniuses: atom bombs and missiles which can destroy whole countries without difficulty.

And the saddest thing of all is that the whole world, represented by the automatic majority of the United Nations, always takes the side of the strong against the weak in deadly fear of the unwanted Communists and the price of oil going up higher (because of the good old scapegoat, of course— the Jews). The faith in God, which was deeply needed because of the fear of death by the human race in general, is distorted as people fight and kill each other in the name of the same God—a God who simply speaks another language and to whom another name may be given. Look at the noble Irish who forget that the Protestant and Catholic God is their same patron. They behave as if God were a pretty woman for whose favors they fight. Consider the hundreds and millions of Arabs who cannot conceive that Allah and his Mohammed cannot persuade their brethren of race, refusing to admit that Moses established his God five thousand years earlier and that Allah and Mohammed are not the Jews' "cup of tea." It is tragic that the war of religions is becoming more intensified every day, involving a general economic chaos. I myself have always felt a high respect for individual men and women who have a deep faith and who thus create a God for themselves.

But who am I to judge? In my view, I do have the right to come to some conclusions about the state of things which I have tried to describe. In Europe, family life and morals have sunk to the lowest level in its history— pornography out in the open, drugs consumed by masses of demoralized youth. And what about the wealth of beautiful literature of the last century and, alas, the arts? The proclamations of the new composers of music, painters, and sculptors that no emotion need be expressed belies the very reason for the artist's existence. I observe with sadness that the young who approve and applaud indiscriminately these recent artistic creations are neither moved nor convinced by them, but use them as a revolutionary gesture against their elders. The lovely elegance of the old days has given way to sloppy, ugly attitudes in complete disharmony with the historically preserved beauty of the cities.

The state of the world, however, cannot and does not interfere with my deep love of life. Not unlike a historian, I believe strongly in a future new renaissance—and that this pessimistic view of the present will fill but a few pages of history as a necessary contrast to the full appreciation of better times.

Epilogue

Before closing this book, I want to express my deep, deep gratitude for the warm signs of friendship given me by people from all over the world and so I want to reassure them that I am still the happiest man I have ever known.

My partial blindness has deepened my love of life. My feeling for music, my thoughts and ideas have become clearer and my dear deus ex machina has provided me with the most beautiful last years of my life.

As I write this, we plan to make some interesting film in New York, Spain, and Poland. During these five months of intense travel and filming, Annabelle and I have never abandoned the book; the result is that I can come, thank God, to the end of it.

Index

Throughout the index the name of Arthur Rubinstein has been abbreviated to AR.

Abdul-Hamid (Turkish sultan), 183
Abetz, Heinrich (German diplomat), 438
Abravanel, Maurice (American
    conductor), 598
Achard, Marcel (French playwright),
    164, 177, 178, 192, 207, 287, 304, 308,
    319, 356, 407, 526, 565, 585
Achard, Madame Marcel (Juliette), 164,
    178, 192, 207, 287, 304, 319, 356, 526
Adam (Polish valet), 577
Aherne, Brian, 436
Alan, Maude (English dancer), 96
Alba, Duke of, 117–18, 119
Albéniz, Isaac, 32, 54, 82, 407, 415, 434,
    546
    Albaicin, 122
    Iberia, 9, 56, 64, 554
    Navarra, 6, 26, 79, 90, 122, 148, 162,
        189, 200, 208, 236, 297, 546, 554
    Triana, 41, 48, 54, 122, 297
Albert (King of the Belgians), 238
Alexander, Haim (composer), 592
Alfidi, Joe (American pianist), 554
Alfonso XIII (King of Spain), 38, 69, 117,
    253, 296, 298, 586
Alpar, Gitta (German singer), 347
Alphand, Hervé (French diplomat), 579
Altmann, Dr. Theodor (AR's teacher),
    350
Alvear family, 7
Amaya, Carmen (gypsy dancer), 475
Anderson, Marian, 399–400, 406, 436–7,
    498, 530
André, Grand Duke, 404
André, Madame Dominique, 246
Angel, Heather, 487
Ansermet, Ernest (Swiss conductor), 11,
    12, 32, 150
Antonio (Spanish dancer), 475
Arbos, Enrique (Spanish violinist and
    composer), 197–8, 226, 227
Arditi (concert manager), 177, 181–6
    passim, 189, 214, 215, 264, 308, 309
Arrau, Claudio, 242

Arthur, Frank (estate agent), 441, 442
Asquith, Anthony, 81, 82
Asquith, Herbert Henry Asquith, Lord,
    81
Asquith, Lady Margot, 81–3, 322
Astaire, Adele, 60
Astaire, Fred, 60, 280, 404, 584
Astor family, 127
Astruc, Gabriel (impresario), 103–4, 121,
    122, 539
Aumont, Jean-Pierre (French actor), 483
Auric, Georges (French composer), 100,
    105, 131, 133, 173, 192, 267, 526
    Fâcheux, Les, 179
Avidom, Menahem (composer), 592
Avila, Juan, 20–6 *passim*, 30–4 *passim*, 78,
    92–3, 101, 109, 121, 122, 125, 126–7,
    150, 162–3, 165–7, 175, 184, 196, 227,
    299, 345–7
Ax, Emanuel (pianist), 592
Azcarraga, Emilio (Mexican television
    executive), 602–3

Bach, Johann Sebastian, 5, 6, 56, 112, 182,
    492, 563
    chaconne: transcribed by Busoni, 195,
        467; transcribed by Tertis, 144
    concerto for two violins, 232
    Italian Concerto, 442
    Partita in C minor, 442
    toccatas: C major, transcribed by
        Busoni, 152, 163, 311, 447; F major,
        122, 389, 390
Bachauer, Gina (pianist), 189, 190–1
Bacon, Mrs. Robert Low (Virginia),
    447, 540–1, 555, 569, 599
Badet, Regina (French actress), 3, 4
Bagby (concert manager), 57
Baliev, Nikita (Russian director), 106
Balletta (dancer), 178
Balsan, Mrs. Jacques (Consuelo
    Vanderbilt), 129
Balzac, Honoré de, 211, 329

Bankhead, Tallulah, 165
Baratz (Polish pianist), 188, 191, 215
Barbara (cook), 445
Barbirolli, Sir John (English conductor), 281–2, 319, 320, 424–9 *passim*, 450, 471, 486, 500, 569
Barenboim, Daniel (Israeli pianist and conductor), 579–80, 585, 593, 594, 596, 597, 602
Barrault, Jean-Louis (French actor), 564
Barrientos, Maria (Spanish singer), 42, 46
Barrymore, Ethel, 483
Barrymore, John, 449
Barrymore family, 60
Barth, Heinrich (German pianist and teacher), 8, 10, 200, 225, 236, 350, 442
Bartók, Béla, 53, 251, 429, 545, 546, 560
Baudelaire, Charles-Pierre, 294
Bauer, Harold (English pianist), 8, 58
Baur, Harry (French actor), 177, 279
Bax, Sir Arnold (English composer), 144
Beardsley, Aubrey, 536
Beatles, 570–1
Beatrice, Infanta, 298
Beatrix, Crown Princess, 597
Bechstein (company and piano), 76, 80, 212–13, 232, 233, 242, 296, 410
Beecham, Sir Thomas, 500, 501
Beethoven, Ludwig von, 5, 6, 8, 48, 50, 64, 102, 109, 132, 138, 155, 159, 182, 228, 236, 354, 430, 497, 500, 562
  Archduke Trio, 320, 494
  chamber music, 578, 601
  concertos, 537, 594; Third (C minor), 225, 504, 506–7; Fourth (G major), 55–6, 146, 240, 247, 249, 263, 313, 409, 432, 448, 501, 517, 524, 525, 526; Fifth (*Emperor*), 206, 537, 557, 574, 595, 596, 597
  Leonore overture, 247
  sonatas (piano), 159, 546, 552, 554; D minor, 159; E flat, 389, 390, 416, 599; *Les Adieux*, 152, 159; *Appassionata*, 159, 163, 221, 240, 254, 329, 544, 552; *Hammerklavier*, 159; Moonlight, 571, 572; *Waldstein*, 48, 122
  sonatas (violin and piano), 541; C minor, 99, 298; *Kreutzer*, 8, 56, 298, 487; Spring, 78
  symphonies, 546, 585, 602; *Eroica*, 409; Fifth, 247
Bekeffi, Madame Maria (ballet teacher), 489, 535
Bellini, Vincenzo, 218, 531
Belmont, Mrs., 128, 130
Belmonte (Spanish matador), 117, 299
Bender, Louis, 598
Ben-Gurion, David, 527, 557, 558, 581

Benouville, Pierre, 526, 533, 579
Benvenuti, Diane, 590
Bérard, Jean, 287
Berenson, Bernard, 145
Berg, Alban, 546, 560
  Wozzeck, 545, 562
Bergen, Candice, 535
Bergheim, John, 73, 74
Bergheim, Mrs. John, 69, 73, 74, 80–1, 99
Berliner, Dr. Milton, 598
Bernard, Tristan (French author and playwright), 253
Berners, Lord (English composer and author), 175, 176, 258
Bernstein, Henri (French dramatist), 253, 287, 288, 407
Bernstein, Leon, 209, 236
Bernstein, Leonard, 545, 546, 557, 603
Berri, Jules (French actor), 279
Bertrand, Eusebio, 315
Bertrand, Mercedes, 315
Besanzoni, Adriana, 106, 107, 108, 269
Besanzoni, Gabriella (Mrs. Enrique Lage; Italian singer), 20–1, 23, 32, 35–42 *passim*, 45, 48–52 *passim*, 60–8 *passim*, 83–4, 106–7, 108, 269, 534
Biancamano (concert agent), 34, 35, 36, 37, 40
Bibesco, Prince Antoine, 112
Bibesco, Princess Elizabeth (Asquith), 111–12, 322
Bibesco, Prince George, 257, 261, 262
Bibesco, Princess Marthe, 257, 261, 262
Bieliankin, 138–41
Billington, Miss (English nanny), 341–2
Bing, Sir Rudolf (opera director), 533
Bistritzky, Jacob (Polish concert manager), 591–2
Bizet, Georges: *Carmen*, 20, 32, 51, 65, 66, 195; transcription of dance from, 246, 255
Björnson, Björnstjerne (Norwegian author), 400
Blac-Belair, Mimi, 254, 318
Blanchard, Emile, 232, 299
Blanchard, Mrs. Emile (Jeanne), 232, 299, 464
Blanck, de (Dutch musician), 41
Bliss, Sir Arthur (English composer), 144
Bliss, Mrs. Robert, 540
Bloch, André (French engineer), 235
Bloch, Ernest, 145
Block, Michel (pianist), 559
Blum, Léon (French politician), 452
Blumenfeld, Felix (piano teacher), 255
Blüthner piano, 281
Böcklin, Arnold (Swiss painter), 205
Bodanzky, Artur (conductor), 57–8, 112, 114

Boissevain, Mrs. Estrella, 464
Bok, Mrs. Mary, 430
Bolm, Adolf (Russian dancer and choreographer), 47
Borden, Mrs. Ellan, 373
Borodin, Alexander: *Prince Igor*, 12, 47
Borzage, Frank (film director), 518–19
Bösendorfer piano, 410, 495
Boskoff, George (Rumanian pianist), 89, 90
Boucher, Victor (French actor), 177–8, 238, 279
Boulanger, Nadia (French music teacher), 192, 559, 564
Boulez, Pierre, 53, 562
Boult, Sir Adrian (English conductor), 547
Bourdelle, Emile (French sculptor), 104
Bourdet, Edouard (French playwright), 238, 239, 284, 287, 304, 305, 308, 407
Bourdet, Madame Edouard (Denise), 284, 286, 287, 304, 305, 308
Bowman (concert manager), 57, 84
Boyer, Charles, 448, 483, 484, 489, 493
Boyer, Mrs. Charles (Pat), 483, 484, 487, 489
Boy-Zelenski (Tadeusz Zelenski; Polish writer and translator), 211
Braccale, Antonio (opera director), 40–1, 42, 279
Braga, Francisco (Brazilian composer and teacher), 27
Brahms, Johannes, 58, 64, 163, 236, 500, 511, 529, 532, 538, 554, 578, 596
chamber music, 578
concerto (violin), 99, 113
concertos (piano), 58, 532; No. 1 (D minor), 85, 593, 599; No. 2 (B flat), 85, 223, 240, 250, 281, 282, 296–7, 409, 425, 431, 448, 486, 492, 495, 500, 539–40, 547, 569, 574, 597
Paganini *Variations*, 122, 439, 440
quartets for piano and strings, 320, 578
quintet for piano and strings, 578
sonatas (piano), 554
sonatas (violin and piano), 541; D minor, 8, 56, 99, 288, 298, 299
symphonies, 585, 602
Trio in B major, 494
Brailowski, Alexander (Russian pianist), 197, 230
Branca, Count, 204
Brendel, Alfred (pianist), 602
Brisson, Pierre (French critic), 254, 287, 533
Britten, Sir Benjamin (English composer), 81
Bruce, Nigel, 483
Buchanan, Jack (English actor), 167

Budapest Quartet, 498
Buitoni, Mrs. Alba (music patron), 224, 532
Bullitt, William C. (American diplomat), 464, 465
Bülow, Hans von (German pianist and conductor), 223, 335 *n.*
Busch, Adolf, 176
Busch, Fritz (conductor), 176, 241, 533
Busoni, Ferruccio (Italian pianist and composer), 31, 54, 88, 122, 195, 263, 350, 545
Bach transcriptions, 152, 163, 195, 311, 447, 467

Cadaval, Marquesa Olga (Robillant) de, 203, 233
Cage, John, 562
Caillavet, Gaston de (French playwright), 178
Callas, Maria, 129
Calvé, Emma (French singer), 74, 78–9
Camus, Clara (Italian concert manager), 213, 215, 223, 224, 526
Cardin, Pierre, 587
Cardwell, Kathryn, 483, 514, 543
Carpenter, John Alden (American composer), 373, 374, 375, 431
Carpenter, Mrs. John Alden (Helen), 373, 374, 431, 432
Carranza, Venustiano (Mexican politician), 65
Carreras (Argentine concert manager), 32, 46
Carreras, Maria (Italian pianist), 32
Caruso, Enrico, 4, 8, 41–2, 51, 57, 61, 68, 84
Casadesus, Robert (French pianist and composer), 446, 498, 544
Casals, Pablo, 8, 78, 132, 195, 303, 494, 582, 602
Castelnuovo-Tedesco, Mario (Italian composer), 194
Castro, Juan José (Argentine conductor), 272
Cendrars, Blaise (French poet), 99, 131, 149, 207
Cervantes, 273
Cervello, Jordi (composer), 592
Chabrier, Emmanuel: *Bourrée fantasque*, 442
España, 160, 256
Valse romantique, 134
Chadwick, Mrs. Dorothy, 425, 426, 429
Chaliapin, Feodor (Fedja), 143–4, 146–7, 405
Chamberlain, Neville, 443

Chanel, Coco, 124, 125, 151, 192, 246, 254, 285, 339, 403-4
Chanler, Robert (American painter), 59
Chaplin, Charlie, 60, 279-80, 448, 483, 484
Chaplin, Geraldine, 535
Charlottavotte (French demimondaine), 22, 25
Chavez, Carlos (Mexican composer), 592
Chekhov, Anton, 294, 331
Chevrey, Bernard, 584
Chigi, Count Guido (music patron), 532
Childs, Calvin (recording executive), 51-2
Chlapowski, Alfred (Polish diplomat), 290
Cholmondeley, Marchioness of (Sybil), 163, 223, 276-7, 299, 320, 321, 322
Cholmondeley, Marquis of (Rocksavage), 276, 277, 299, 320, 321
Chopin, Frédéric, 6, 26, 32, 41, 48, 64, 76, 82, 88, 102, 123, 154, 182, 192, 199, 200, 207, 208, 212, 221, 228, 229, 236, 248, 254, 255, 276, 315, 322, 326, 327, 354, 389, 409, 411, 416, 426, 427, 428, 430, 434, 442, 444-5, 451, 466, 468, 500, 538, 546, 547, 554, 562, 578, 596
  ballades, 554, 578; F major, 229; F minor, 242
  Barcarolle, 47, 122, 131, 255, 281, 409
  concertos: E minor, 202, 524, 525, 526; F minor, 144, 228, 230, 517, 574, 595, 597
  études, 122, 308, 442, 500, 554, 597
  impromptus, 554, 578
  mazurkas, 424, 554, 578
  nocturnes, 122-3, 298, 344
  Polonaise Fantaisie, 255, 507
  polonaises, 356, 357-8, 554, 578; A flat, 26, 41, 123, 228, 229, 317, 357, 427, 428, 467, 504; A major, 460; F sharp minor, 357-8; Grand Polonaise, 541
  preludes, 554, 578
  scherzos, 554, 578; Fourth, 152, 204, 233
  sonatas, 554, 578; B flat (with Funeral March), 93-4, 382, 511; B minor, 56, 122, 308
  Sylphides, Les, 12
  waltzes, 554, 578
Chotzinoff, Samuel (Russian-American pianist and critic), 468-9, 505
Christie, John (music patron), 532-3
Churchill, Sir Winston, 408, 492, 509
Ciechanowski, Jan (Polish diplomat), 447
Cini, Count, 586
Citroën (French auto manufacturer), 350
Clair, René (French film director), 483, 564
Claudel, Paul (French diplomat and poet), 27-9, 29-30, 100, 587

Clemenceau, Georges (French statesman), 75
Cliburn, Van, 558, 601
Coates, Albert (British conductor), 296-7
Coats, Audrey, 219, 220, 221
Cocteau, Jean, 100, 101, 105, 125, 126, 133, 149, 150, 192, 207, 267, 287, 561
Coffin, Rev. William Sloane, 555, 573
Coffin, Mrs. William Sloane (Eva Rubinstein; AR's daughter), 340-4 *passim*, 350, 352, 353, 356-7, 387, 388, 392, 397, 398, 403, 404-5, 412, 416, 424, 438, 442, 446, 451, 459, 460, 464, 465, 466, 476, 477, 478, 481, 482, 484, 488, 502, 512, 513, 520, 522, 524, 531, 535, 538-43 *passim*, 555, 569, 573, 584
  dancing and acting, 342, 404, 489, 518, 535, 538, 555
Colefax, Lady Sybil, 408
Colman, Juliette, 535
Colman, Ronald, 448, 483, 484, 489
Colman, Mrs. Ronald (Benita Hume), 483, 484, 489
Conrad, Joseph, 229
Consolo, Ernesto (Italian pianist), 194
Cook, Bill, 599
Cooper, Alfred Duff (English political figure), 408
Cooper, Lady Diana, 79, 80-1, 144, 164, 408
Cooper, Gary, 448
Cooper, Gladys (English actress), 143
Copernicus, Nicolaus, 229
Coppicus (American concert manager), 404, 405-6
Cortot, Alfred (French pianist), 109, 123, 132, 195, 197, 241, 242, 243, 317, 446
Courteline, Georges (French humorist), 294
Cousiño, Arturo, 162-3, 165, 166
Coward, Noël, 167, 222, 375, 376, 379
Craft, Robert, 561
Curie, Eve (French musician and playwright), 230-1, 287, 288
Curie, Hélène, 230, 231
Curie, Madame Marie (Marja Sklodowska), 229, 230, 231
Curie, Pierre, 229, 230
Czartoryski, Prince, 474
Czerny, Karl (Austrian pianist and teacher), 283
Czyz, Henryk (Polish conductor), 595

D'Albert, Eugen (Scottish pianist and composer), 56, 122, 247
Dalio, Marcel (French actor), 483

Damrosch, Walter (musical director), 52, 58, 113, 114, 165, 428–9
Damrosch family, 165, 426
Danilova, Alexandra, 484
D'Annunzio, Gabriele, 194, 205
Darrieux, Danielle (French actress), 436
Daudet, Alphonse, 294
Davis, Bette, 483
Davydov, Denis, 124
Davydov, Madame Nathalie, 124–5
Davydov family, 98, 124, 329
Dayan, Moshe, 580, 581
Dearly, Max (French actor), 279
Debussy, Claude Achille, 18, 32, 48, 53, 54, 58, 90, 104, 123, 194, 254, 378, 427, 442, 498, 554, 578
  Après-midi d'un faune, L', 12
  En Blanc et noir, 256
  performed by Gieseking, 195, 197, 430
  Nocturnes, "Fêtes," 256
  "Ondine," 123, 132
  Pelléas et Mélisande, 32, 133
Debussy, Madame Claude Achille, 132
Defauw, Désiré (Belgian violinist and conductor), 545
de Gaulle, Charles, 532, 534, 579, 580
Delalande, François (AR's valet), 237, 238, 243, 244, 245, 251, 253, 282, 286, 287, 288, 290, 291, 305, 314, 318, 355, 359
Delius, Frederick, 144
Delon, Alain (French actor), 579
Demidov, Prince (Russian diplomat), 184, 187, 188, 189
de Mille, Agnes, 555
Denis, Maurice (French painter), 104
Derain, André (French painter), 150, 179
Dernbourg, Ilona (Eibenschutz), 163
Destinn, Emmy (Bohemian singer), 51, 310
Devonshire, Duchess of, 453
Devonshire, Duke of, 453, 454
Diaghilev, Sergei (and ballet company), 11, 12, 25, 59, 101, 104–5, 107, 109, 131, 133–4, 150, 151, 164, 173, 178–9, 280, 293, 436, 561
Dickens, Charles, 536
Diederichs, André (Bechstein agent), 327
Dietrich, Marlene, 279, 483
Dizengoff, Meier (Israeli mayor), 527
Dluski, Dr., and Mrs. Josef, 231
Dohnányi, Ernö (Hungarian conductor and composer), 250–1
Donizetti, Gaetano, 531
Dostoevski, Feodor, 177, 294
Downes, Olin (American music critic), 427
Drangosh, Ernesto (music teacher), 8, 9, 200

Draper, George, 60
Draper, Muriel, 45, 46, 50, 60, 320, 326
Draper, Paul, 46, 50, 60, 69, 85, 165, 277
Draper, Ruth, 60, 89, 320–1, 473, 475
Draper family, 69, 85, 89, 494
Dreyfus (French music student), 242
Dreyfus case, Alfred, 431, 533, 603
Drzewiecki, Zbigniew (Polish musician), 559
Dubman, Laura (American music student), 452, 458, 459
Duchable, François (French pianist), 590–1, 597, 601
Dukas, Paul (French composer), 452
Duke, Doris, 379, 384
Dukelsky, Wladimir (composer), 114
du Maurier, Sir Gerald (English actor-manager), 143
Duncan, Isadora, 134
Duparc, Marie Eugène (French composer), 18
du Pré, Jacqueline (Mrs. Daniel Barenboim; English cellist), 579–80, 594, 602
Dupré, Marcel (French organist), 586
Dushkin, Samuel (violinist), 151, 283
Dutilleux, Henri (composer), 592
Dvořák, Anton, 320, 578

Edward VII (King of England), 104, 121
Einstein, Alfred (German music scholar), 466, 467
Eisenhower, Dwight D., 500, 532
Elena (Queen of Italy), 171, 410
Elgar, Sir Edward: Cello Concerto, 144
Elizabeth (Queen of the Belgians), 344, 439, 558, 586
Elizalde, Germán, 272, 416
Elman, Mischa, 57, 58, 84, 127, 498
Enesco, Georges, 89
Engels, George (American concert manager), 99, 113, 114, 148, 164, 169
Enright, Thomas (police official), 86
Enrique (AR's valet), 33, 35–9 *passim*, 45, 61, 62, 73, 90, 96, 97, 98, 100, 109, 110, 113, 115, 117, 135, 136, 157–8
Enwall, Helmer (Swedish concert manager), 399, 400, 485
Erard piano, 76, 125, 130, 216
Erlanger, Baroness d', 82
Errazuriz, Mrs. Eugenia, 17, 33, 73, 95, 130, 149, 207, 235
Eschig, Max (music publisher), 195
Evans, Warwick, 74, 222

Fabini, Eduardo (composer), 10, 157
Fairbanks, Douglas, 60, 127

Fall, Leo (Austrian composer), 251
Falla, Manuel de, 4, 18, 19, 32, 41, 77, 134,
    176, 232, 407, 414, 415, 434
  Amor brujo, El, 111, 176
  Andaluza, 19
  Atlántida, 414
  Fantasía Bética, 111, 200, 228–9
  Fire Dance, 18, 41, 79, 122, 148, 200,
    208, 228, 229, 236, 297, 445, 546, 554
  Nights in the Gardens of Spain, 240,
    241, 545, 547
  Three-Cornered Hat, The, 214
Fargue, Léon-Paul, 126, 150, 192, 233, 267,
    398
Farouk (King of Egypt), 184
Farrar, Geraldine, 51, 84, 129
Fauré, Gabriel, 18
  Dolly Suite, 564
  quartets, 320; C minor, 578; E flat, 578
  sonata for violin and piano, 56, 99
Faussigny-Lucinge, 287
Fellows, Daisy, 253
Ferrier, Kathleen, 601
Feuchtwanger, Lion (German author),
    492
Feuermann, Emanuel (cellist), 493–4, 497
Février, Jacques (French pianist), 131–2,
    246, 256, 526
Fialkowska, Janina (Polish pianist), 592,
    597, 601
Fischer-Dieskau, Dietrich, 532, 601
Fiszer, Franc, 211
Fitelberg, Gregor (Polish conductor
    and composer), 202, 207, 228, 230,
    272, 273, 317, 318, 460
Flers, Marquis de (French playwright),
    178
Flier, Jacob (Russian pianist), 440
Flynn, Errol, 483
Focillon, Henri (French art historian),
    473–4, 475
Follman, Nathan (AR's uncle), 115
Follman, Mrs. Nathan (AR's aunt), 115
Fontaine, Joan, 448–9
Ford, Gerald, 599
Fournet, Jean (French conductor), 547
Fournier, Pierre (French cellist), 494
Franck, César, 7, 18
  Prelude, Chorale, and Fugue, 82, 427,
    428, 447
  sonata for violin and piano, 99, 344–5
  Variations symphoniques, 198, 261, 538,
    547, 569
François (AR's valet), *see* Delalande,
    François
Franklin, Frederic (English dancer), 484
Frescobaldi, Girolamo, 176
Fresnay, Pierre (French actor), 177, 234,
    235, 344
Frías, Brigidita, 18

Frías, José (Argentine critic), 8, 18
Friedman, Ignaz (Polish pianist), 96, 160,
    439–40
Frieman (Polish pianist and teacher),
    187–91 *passim,* 308
Frohman, Mrs. Mae, 436
Furtwängler, Wilhelm (German
    conductor), 398
Furtzeva, Madame Elena (Russian
    minister), 574

Gable, Clark, 279, 448
Gabrilówitsch, Ossip (Russian pianist
    and conductor), 58, 86, 88
Gagnebin, Henri (composer), 592
Gainza-Paz family, 7, 157
Gaisberg, Fred (English recording
    executive), 280–1, 288–9, 296, 297,
    298–9, 319–20
Galafres, Elsa, 251
Gallito (Spanish matador), 117, 299
Gandarillas, Carmen, 414
Gandarillas, José Antonio, 73, 79, 81, 100,
    143
Gandarillas, Juanita, 17, 73, 81, 98, 99,
    143, 163, 343, 414, 415, 416, 517, 596
Gandhi, Mahatma, 457
Garbat, Dr., 450
Garbo, Greta, 279, 484
Garden, Mary, 57, 84, 127, 129, 168
Gardner, Mrs. Isabella Stewart, 145
Garson, Greer, 484, 539
Gatti-Casazza, Giulio (opera manager),
    51, 58, 84, 127
Gaveau piano, 125
Gavoty, Bernard, 582, 583, 584
Gelber, Bruno Leonardo (pianist), 603
George (King of Greece), 283
Gershwin, George, 230
Gieseking, Walter (German pianist),
    195, 197, 430, 439, 440, 544
Gilels, Emil (Russian pianist), 328, 329,
    439, 545, 552, 574, 602
Ginastera, Alberto (Argentine
    composer), 18
Gluck, Alma (Russian-American singer),
    117–20
Godebski, Cipa, 151, 251, 287
Godebski, Mrs. Cipa (Ida), 151, 287
Godebski, Jean, 151
Godebski, Mimi, 151
Godowsky, Dagmar, 45, 46, 47, 49, 52, 69
Godowsky, Leopold (Russian-American
    pianist, teacher, and composer), 52,
    54, 58, 276, 427, 428
Gold, Sheldon (concert agent), 591
Goldflam, Dr., 209, 236
Goldwyn, Samuel, 448, 487, 489, 538
Goldwyn, Mrs. Samuel, 489, 538

Golschmann, Vladimir (French conductor), 449, 585
Gomulka, Wladyslaw, 595
Gontaut-Biron, Count Armand de, 534
González, Rafael (Argentine pianist and teacher), 272, 338, 416
González, Mrs. Rafael (Victoria), 272, 337, 338, 340–1, 414, 416
Goossens, Eugene (English conductor and composer), 424
Gordon, Ruth, 555
Gore, Lord, 421–2
Gottlieb, 126
Gould family, 57, 127
Gounod, Charles: *Faust*, 195
Grace (Princess of Monaco), 596
Gradstein, Alfred (Polish composer), 317
Gramont, Duke and Duchess of, 128
Granier, Jeanne (French singer and actress), 178
Grant, Cary, 279, 448, 489, 538
Granville, Dorothy, 511
Grassi (concert agent), 92
Greiner, Alexander (Steinway agent), 426, 495
Grew, Joseph (American diplomat), 373
Grieg, Edvard, 58, 400
Concerto (piano), 471, 489, 499, 545, 547, 569
Lyric Pieces, 541
Griffes, Charles Tomlinson (American composer), 58
Gris, Juan, 234, 566
Griswold, Alfred (American educator), 568
Gromadzski, Jan, 444, 445
Grumiaux, Arthur (violinist), 602
Guanabarino, Oscar (critic), 29
Guarneri Quartet, 578
Guarnieri, Camargo (composer), 592
Guinle, Carlos, 154, 155, 172, 173, 199, 269, 337
Guinle, Mrs. Carlos (Gilda), 154, 155, 172, 269, 337
Guinness, Benjamin (Irish brewer), 167
Guitry, Lucien (French actor), 178
Guitry, Sacha (French actor and dramatist), 152, 178, 279, 344, 533
Guller, Youra (pianist), 131

Hahn, Reynaldo (composer), 222–3, 279
Halffter, Rodolfo (composer), 592
Harman, Frederic, 207
Harman, Pola, *see* Pola (Harman)
Harrison, Rex, 483
Harty, Sir Hamilton (English conductor), 98–9
Havilland, Olivia de, 448

Hawtrey, Lady, 120–1
Hawtrey, Sir Charles (English actor), 121, 143
Hay, Clarence, 113
Hay, Mrs. Clarence (Alice), 113
Haydn, Franz Joseph, 563, 578, 601
Hebertot (French theater director), 121, 122, 123
Heifetz, Jascha, 52, 58, 68, 86, 145, 289–90, 290–91, 292, 487, 493–4, 497–8, 528, 529, 530, 537, 538, 541, 545
Heine, Heinrich, 536
Hemar, Marian, 249
Hemingway, Ernest, 409
Hempel, Frieda (German singer), 341
Hepburn, Katharine, 530
Herard, Mlle. (French music teacher), 564
Hermant, Abel (French writer), 246
Hertz, Alfred (German conductor), 85, 113, 145
Himmler, Heinrich, 487
Hindenburg, Paul von, 336
Hitchcock, Alfred, 483
Hitler, Adolf, 324, 336, 337, 347, 357, 398, 411, 414, 438, 439, 440, 443, 452, 459, 460, 463, 472, 473, 474, 476, 480, 484, 486, 487, 492, 510, 513, 556, 580
Hochman, George (piano tuner), 54
Hofmann, Josef (Polish pianist), 50, 58, 84, 86, 88, 206, 289, 426, 430, 446, 468, 489, 495
Hofmann, Mrs. Josef, 206
Hofmannsthal, Raimund von, 292–3
Holt, Harold (English impresario), 520, 521, 522, 523
Honegger, Arthur, 100, 105, 206
King David, 133
Pacific 231, 133
Hoover, Herbert, 75
Hoppenot, Henri (French diplomat), 29, 30, 374
Hoppenot, Madame Henri, 374, 375
Horowitz (father of Vladimir), 331
Horowitz, Friedrich (concert manager), 335–6, 526, 533
Horowitz, Vladimir (Volodya), 246–7, 251, 254–8 *passim*, 289–90, 303, 331, 334, 335, 336, 446, 451, 468, 497–8, 505, 538, 544, 602
Horowitz, Mrs. Vladimir (Wanda Toscanini), 334, 335, 446
Howard, Leslie, 483
Hryncewicz, Henryk, 445
Hubermann, Bronislaw (Polish violinist), 251, 398, 418, 421, 455, 466–7
Hugo, Jean, 105
Hull, Mrs. Helen (formerly Mrs. Vincent Astor), 426, 428, 429

Huneker, James (American critic), 50, 58
Hurok, Sol (impresario), 68, 147, 148, 404, 405–6, 424, 425, 427, 428, 433, 435, 436, 437, 446, 447, 465, 466, 473, 474, 475, 477, 479, 480, 485, 491, 497, 498, 505, 507–8, 513, 514–15, 518, 520–4 *passim*, 541, 545, 547, 551, 552, 553, 554, 558, 573, 574, 588, 589, 590
Hurok, Mrs. Sol, 473, 474, 475
Hutton, Barbara, 489
Huxley, Aldous, 492, 493, 500

Ibsen, Henrik, 400
Imperio, Pastora (gypsy singer and dancer), 4–5, 6
Indjic, Eugene (pianist), 592
Ireland, John (English composer), 144, 280
Irion (Steinway associate), 428
Isabel, Infanta, 298
Iturbi, José, 197, 257
Iwaki (Japanese conductor), 575
Iwaszkiewicz, Jaroslaw (Polish writer), 211

Jackowski, Tadeusz (Polish diplomat), 238–9
Jackowski, Mrs. Tadeusz, 238–9
Jacob, Max (French writer), 234
James, Harry, 529
Janocopoulos, Vera (Greco-Brazilian singer), 47
Jaroszynski, Joseph, 98, 209, 329, 534
Jasinski, Roman (Polish pianist), 304, 595, 596, 597, 600
Jeanne (Polish maid), 354, 355, 359
Jeanson, Henri, 164
Joachim, Joseph (Hungarian violinist and composer), 115
Joachim Quartet, 578
John, Augustus, 222
Johnson, R. E. (American concert manager), 32, 42, 45–50 *passim*, 54, 55, 57, 58, 69, 84, 85, 86, 112, 113, 114, 115, 144, 145, 147, 148, 164
Jouvet, Louis (French actor and director), 164
Jowitt, William (English political figure), 79, 81, 82, 143, 408, 522
Jowitt, Mrs. William (Lesley), 79, 81, 82, 129, 143, 163, 174, 184, 222, 320, 321, 408, 523
Joyce, James, 536, 596
Judith (concierge), 235, 237
Judson, Arthur (American concert manager), 404, 405
Juliana (Queen of the Netherlands), 585, 597

Kahn, Otto (banker and music patron), 127
Kalbeck, Max (music biographer), 163
Kamiko (Japanese cook), 483
Kanarek, 511, 536
Kanin, Garson, 555
Kapell, William, 429–30, 544
Kaper, Bronislaw (Bronek), 448, 449, 484, 489, 490–1
Kaper, Mrs. Bronislaw (Lola), 448, 483, 484, 489
Kapurthala, Maharajah of, 104
Karajan, Herbert von, 594
Karl (Emperor of Poland), 142
Karlowicz, Mieczyslaw (Polish composer), 229
Karola (Polish nurse), 343, 344, 347, 350, 352, 353, 356, 359, 397, 398, 412, 413, 414, 424, 438
Karsavina, Tamara (Russian dancer), 12
Katims, Milton (American conductor), 598
Kaufman, Harry (pianist), 484
Kedra, Wladislav (Polish pianist), 534
Kemal Pasha, 182, 183
Kennedy, John, 568, 569
Kennedy, Robert, 569
Kent, Duchess of (Princess Marina of Greece), 57, 523
Kerenski, Alexander, 142
Kerr, Deborah, 538
Khachaturian, Aram: piano concerto, 499
Khrushchev, Madame Nikita, 544
Kiepura, Jan (Polish tenor), 466
Kierkegaard, Sören, 280
Kirov, Sergei (Soviet leader), 363
Kisch, Col. Aaron, 454–5, 455–6
Kisling, Moïse (Polish painter), 126, 232, 287, 407, 485, 488–9, 494
Kissinger, Henry, 599
Klemperer, Otto (German conductor), 431, 432, 500
Kloiber, Herbert, 594
Knabe (company and piano), 54, 168
Kneisel, Franz (Rumanian violinist), 61
Knepler, Hugo (Austrian concert manager), 240, 251
Knopf, Alfred, 425, 448, 481–2, 496, 589
Knopf, Mrs. Alfred (Blanche), 425, 481, 496, 589
Knopf, Edwin, 448, 489
Knopf, Mrs. Edwin (Mildred), 448, 489
Kochanski, Paul (Polish violinist), 8, 10, 45, 60, 97, 98–9, 103, 109, 112, 113, 114, 121, 134–5, 141, 143, 144, 145, 148–9, 151–2, 153, 157, 159, 161, 164, 165, 169, 173, 174, 197, 226, 229, 232, 257, 258, 274–5, 277, 285, 287, 292–3, 295, 296, 298–9, 317, 318, 319, 322, 323, 333, 342–3, 356, 358, 426, 445, 483, 498

Kochanski, Mrs. Paul (Sophie [Zosia]),
97, 98, 99, 109, 112, 113, 114, 134–5,
141, 144, 148, 151, 153, 157, 161, 164,
173, 174, 197, 232, 257, 258, 260, 267,
274, 285–6, 287, 288, 292, 319, 322,
342, 356, 426, 435, 442, 446, 464, 465
Kochanski family, 59, 75, 285
Kochlova, Olga (Russian dancer; later
Mrs. Igor Stravinsky), 150
Koczalski, Raoul (Polish pianist), 439
Kodály, Zoltán, 251
Kolischer, Wilhelm (Polish pianist), 10,
160
Kollek, Teddy, 580, 584, 585, 594
Kondracki, Michel (Polish composer),
350
Kondrashin, Kyril (Russian conductor),
574
Konoye, Viscount (Japanese conductor),
367
Kosciuszko, Tadeusz, 418, 422
Koussevitzky, Serge, 173–4, 330, 448, 486,
502–4
Kramaztyk, Roman (Polish painter), 525
Kranz, Kazimir, 411
Krehbiel, Henry Edward (American
critic), 50, 58
Kreisler, Fritz (Austrian-American
violinist), 52, 58, 61, 86, 164, 195, 468,
497, 498, 545
Kreisler, Mrs. Fritz, 164
Křenek, Ernst (Austrian-American
composer), 545
Kripps, Josef (Austrian conductor), 569
Krzesinska, Mathilde (Polish dancer), 404
Kurtz, Efrem (conductor), 473
Kwapiczewski (Polish diplomat), 70

Labunski, Wiktor (Polish pianist), 248,
407
Labunski, Mrs. Wiktor (Wanda
Mlynarska; AR's sister-in-law), 248,
343
Lacretelle, Jacques de (French writer),
246
Lafita, Juan, 82–3, 295, 316–17
La Fontaine, Jean de, 536
Lage, Enrique (Brazilian shipowner),
108, 269
Laguardia (Argentine critic), 6, 31
Lamond, Frederic (Scottish pianist), 132
Landau, Mrs. Adolf (Helena [Hela];
AR's sister), 75, 109, 116, 212
Landau, Jan (AR's nephew), 479
Landau, Marila (AR's niece), 98, 479
Landau, Maurycy (AR's brother-in-law),
98, 116
Landau, Mrs. Maurycy (Jadwiga
[Jadzia]; AR's sister), 59, 75, 98, 109,
115, 116, 211

Landowska, Wanda, 317, 318
Lanier, Charles, 59–60
Lanier, Mrs. Charles (music patron), 57,
59–60, 85, 113, 117
Lanvin, Madame Jeanne (French
couturier), 131, 339
La Rochefoucauld, 287
Lashanska, Hulda (singer), 488
Laughton, Charles, 483, 538–9
Laurencin, Marie (French painter), 179
Lawrence, Gertrude, 167, 168, 322
Lechon, Jan (Polish writer and
diplomat), 211, 249, 407, 411, 474, 479,
488
Lehmann, Lotte (German singer), 487
Leinsdorf, Eric, 585
Lenin, Nikolai, 142, 404
Leoncavallo, Ruggiero: "Mattinata, La,"
67
Leschetizky, Theodor (Polish teacher
and composer), 350
Levi, Giorgio, 293
Levitzki, Mischa (Russian pianist), 54,
58, 86, 88–9
Lewis, Sir George (English solicitor), 79
Lhévinne, Joseph (Russian pianist), 50,
58, 427, 428, 429–30
Lhévinne, Madame Joseph (Rosina;
Russian-American pianist and
teacher), 58, 427
Lieberson, Goddard (American
recording executive), 468
Liebling, Leonard (American magazine
editor), 61, 62, 70, 467
Lifar, Serge, 247, 287, 403
Likiernik, Jadwiga, 116
Likiernik, Leo (AR's brother-in-law),
116, 307
Likiernik, Mrs. Leo (Frania; AR's
sister), 75, 109, 116, 307
Likiernik family, 116
Lillie, Beatrice, 167, 168
Lilpop, Halina, see Rodzinski, Mrs.
Artur
Lindbergh, Charles, 480
Lipton, Sir Thomas, 81
Lipatti, Dinu (Rumanian pianist), 262
Liszt, Franz, 53, 64, 112, 123, 198, 236,
308, 329, 356, 430, 500, 529, 554
concertos, 537, 547; E flat, 333, 569
Mephisto Waltz, 56, 123, 529, 544
Paganini études, 255
sonata for piano, 122, 554, 578
Twelfth Rhapsody, 6, 180, 389, 390
Wagner's *Tristan*, transcription of, 64
Litvak, Anatole, 484
Litvinov, Maksim (Russian statesman),
326, 327
Long, Marguerite (French pianist and
teacher), 123, 310, 311, 442, 558, 559,
564

Longo, Alessandro (Italian musicologist), 194
Longworth, Mrs. Alice Roosevelt, 447, 540, 569
López, Juanito, 384, 385, 387–8
López Buchardo, Carlos (Argentine composer), 18, 109, 338
Lopoukhova, Lydia (Russian dancer), 11
Lorraine, Sir Percy (English diplomat), 184, 263, 264
Loti, Pierre, 182
Lubitsch, Ernst, 484
Lubomirski, Prince, 98
Luboschutz, Pierre (pianist), 146, 152, 292
Ludendorff, Gen. Erich, 324
Lukasiewicz (Polish diplomat), 452
Lulu, 46, 49, 50, 69, 86, 148
Luro, Señora Amelia, 272
Lwoff, André (French microbiologist), 581
Lyon (Pleyel agent), 107
Lyon, Mrs., 373–4

Maazel, Lorin, 596
MacArthur, Gen. Douglas, 512
MacDowell, Edward, 58
Madigan, Tony, 600–1
Magaloff, Nikita, 564
Mahler, Gustav, 532, 546, 601–2
Malraux, André, 157, 409
Mangoo, Verree, 487
Mann, Frederick, 466–7, 470, 471, 479, 482, 557, 558
Mann, Mrs. Frederick, 467, 470, 482
Mann, Thomas, 492, 493, 494, 500, 528, 596
Mann, Mrs. Thomas, 538
Marcello, Benedetto, 176
Marconi, Guglielmo, 120, 121, 577
Marfá, Isabel, 315
Maria, Princess, 171
Marie José, Princess (later Queen of Italy), 344, 410, 439
Marie Pavlovna, Grand Duchess, 178
Marjerie, Madame Jeanne de, 234, 235, 237, 246, 343
Martínez de Hoz, Señora Elena de, 158, 200
Martínez de Hoz, Miguel, 7, 11, 33, 200, 270–1
Masaryk, Jan (Polish diplomat), 163, 357, 488
Massenet, Jules: *Manon*, 195
Massine, Léonide (Russian dancer and choreographer), 11, 104, 133
Mastrogianni, Miguel (Argentine newsman), 6, 8, 338
Matisse, Henri, 536

Matzenauer, Margarete (Hungarian singer), 83–4
Maugham, Somerset, 222
Maugham, Syrie, 222
Maxwell, Elsa, 127–30, 134, 286–7
McClaren, Cristabel, 81, 184, 222, 322
Medtner, Nikolai (Russian composer), 9, 18
Mehta, Zubin, 585, 592, 597, 599
Meir, Mrs. Golda, 580, 581, 584, 591, 592
Melba, Nellie, 421
Mendelssohn, Felix, 64, 528, 537
Mengelberg, Willem (Dutch conductor), 85, 334–5, 409
Menjou, Mr., and Mrs. Adolphe, 489
Menocal, Señora, 166
Menuhin, Yehudi, 538, 581
Mercé, Antonia ("Argentina"; dancer), 342
Mérito, Marqués del, 409
Mero, Yolanda (Hungarian pianist), 428
Merry del Val, Domingo, 291–2
Meyer, Stanislaw (Staś), 236, 248
Meyer, Mrs. Stanislaw (Sophie Bernstein [Zosia]), 209, 236, 247, 248
Michelangeli, Arturo (Italian pianist) 439, 592
Mickiewicz, Adam (Polish poet), 294
Milhaud, Darius, 27, 28, 29, 30, 100, 101, 108, 109, 123, 133, 155
  Boeuf sur le toit, 133–4
  Bolivar, 587
  Saudades do Brazil, 246
  Suite Provençal, 133
Miller, Harry (American concert manager), 570, 571, 572, 573
Milstein, Nathan, 255, 303, 498
Minnelli, Liza, 535
Mitchell (English concert manager), 74, 79, 83, 97, 99, 115, 163, 219, 267, 298, 350, 357
Mitre, Luis, 4, 5, 6, 10
Mitre family, 157
Mitropoulos, Dimitri (Greek conductor), 263, 264, 349–50, 486, 545
Mlynarska, Alina, *see* Raue, Mrs. Jan
Mlynarska, Mrs. Emil (AR's mother-in-law), 304, 310, 333, 343, 347, 355, 359, 396, 397, 424, 444, 445, 446, 451, 458, 485, 513, 514, 535, 543, 568
Mlynarska, Hela, 247, 248
Mlynarska, Nina, 459, 460
Mlynarska, Wanda, *see* Labunski, Mrs. Wiktor
Mlynarski, Bronislaw (Bronek; AR's brother-in-law), 248, 257, 260, 320, 321, 333, 396, 397, 485, 539
Mlynarski, Mrs. Bronislaw (Doris Kenyon), 539

Mlynarski, Emil (Polish conductor; AR's
father-in-law), 212, 228, 229, 230,
247, 249, 259, 288, 304, 308, 310, 333,
348, 350, 355–6, 359, 369
Mlynarski, Felix, 230, 248
Mlynarski family, 98, 324, 556
Mocchi, Walter (music director), 24–5,
26, 29, 78
Mocenigo family, 203
Modigliani, Amedeo, 126
Moiseiwitsch, Benno (pianist), 58, 86,
88–9, 425, 453
Molière, 179, 211
Molinari, Bernardino (Italian conductor),
192–3, 225
Monaco, Baron del, 314
Monteux, Pierre, 47, 69, 113, 114, 144, 409,
424, 432–3, 491
Monteverdi, Claudio, 176, 536, 561
Montgomery, Field Marshal Bernard,
532, 586
Moore, Mrs. 129
Mora, Joaquín, 10, 157, 160
Moreno (Argentine diplomat), 7
Morgan (American diplomat), 156
Morgenthau, Henry, Jr., 485
Morosini, Contessa Annina, 175, 293
Morros, Boris (Russian-American
musician), 528–9
Moszkowski, Antek, 207, 209, 534
Moszkowski, Moritz (Polish pianist and
composer), 207, 223
Mounet-Sully (French actor), 105
Moussorgsky, Modest: *Boris Godunov*,
143, 144
Mozart, Wolfgang Amadeus, 102, 179,
320, 500, 528, 554, 561, 562, 563, 594
chamber music, 578, 601
concertos (piano), 537, 547, 569;
A major, 594; C minor, 569;
D minor, 598
Eine Kleine Nachtmusik, 528
operas, 533
Sinfonia Concertante, 602
sonatas, 541; D major, 160
Mühlstein, Anatole (Polish diplomat),
287, 288, 459, 460, 463, 479
Mühlstein, Mrs. Anatole (Diana de
Rothschild), 459, 460
Müller, Fritz (German-Australian
pianist and composer), 421
Muller, Max (English diplomat), 259, 261
Muller, Mrs. Max, 259, 261
Munch, Charles, 520, 525–6, 545
Munch, Edvard (Norwegian painter),
400
Munz, Mieczyslaw (Polish pianist),
260–1, 268, 272, 288, 304, 316, 317,
318, 321

Murphy, Frank (American diplomat),
384
Musset, Alfred de, 294
Mussolini, Benito, 171–2, 193, 313–14, 439,
443, 457, 474, 496, 526, 577

Napoleão, Arturo (Brazilian pianist and
music publisher), 92
Narros, Marqués Marcelino, 196
Nasser, Gamal Abdel, 540, 579, 580
Negri, Pola, 60
Nemirovitch-Dantchenko, Vladimir
(Russian director), 331
Nepomuceno, Alberto (Brazilian
composer and teacher), 27, 91
Neuhaus, Harry (German music teacher
and administrator), 326, 329, 333,
552–3, 559
Newton, Ivor (English pianist), 99
Nicholas II (Tsar of Russia), 142
Nicholls, John (American educator), 593
Nicolson, Harold (English writer and
biographer), 408
Nightingale (electrician), 483, 539
Nijinsky, Vaslav, 11–16 *passim*, 25
Nijinsky, Madame Vaslav, 11, 12
Nikisch, Arthur (Hungarian conductor),
159
Nin, Joaquín (Spanish pianist and
composer), 152, 153
Niven, David, 436
Noailles, Vicomtesse Marie-Laure de, 284
Nobre, Marlos (composer), 592
Nono, Luigi (Italian composer), 53, 562
Novaës, Guiomar, 31, 79

Oberon, Merle, 483
Obolensky, Prince, 57
O'Brien, Pat, 484
Ocampo, Victoria (Argentine author), 12
Ochs, Adolph, 59
O'Connor, Charles (recording engineer),
447, 470
Ojeda, José (Argentine music critic),
5, 6
Olivier (French maître d'hôtel), 238, 239
Oppenheim, Irving (American concert
manager), 145–6
Oppenheim, Mrs. Irving (Blanche), 145
Oppenheimer, Sir Ernest (South African
industrialist), 453, 454, 456
Oppenheimer, Lady, 454, 456
Oppenheimer, Arthur (American
concert manager), 145
Oppenheimer, Mrs. Arthur, 145

Opperman, Anne, 436
Ordynski, Richard (Polish film director),
    47, 75, 109, 207, 212, 236, 243–4, 245,
    247, 248, 249, 250, 259, 303, 304, 477
Orloff, Nicholas (pianist), 439–40
Ormandy, Eugene, 424, 471, 486, 495,
    500, 508, 529
Ornstein, Leo (Russian-American
    pianist), 54
Oswaldo (Brazilian music director), 26,
    91

Pachmann, Vladimir de (Russian
    pianist), 276–7
Paderewski, Ignacy Jan, 6, 9, 51, 58, 74,
    75, ⁴23, 317–18, 426, 453, 472, 495,
    534–5, 586, 587
Paganini, Nicolo: Brahms *Variations*,
    122, 439, 440
    Liszt études, 255
Paggi, Ada (Italian singer), 63, 65, 67
Pagnol, Marcel (French actor), 177, 585
Palewski, Gaston (French statesman),
    586
Palladini, Princess Carla, 176, 181–2,
    192–3, 193–4, 198–9, 200, 201, 204–5,
    223, 224–5, 256–68 *passim*, 271
Pallenberg, Max (actor), 251
Papaioannou, Marika, 188, 190, 191, 215,
    263, 308
Parr, Audrey, 311, 312
Patek, Stanislaw (Polish diplomat), 326,
    347
Patou, Jean, 253
Pauling, Linus, 592, 593
Pavlova, Anna, 25, 489, 497
Pecci-Blunt, Countess Mimi, 193, 194,
    225, 245, 246
Peck, Gregory, 584
Peerce, Jan, 530
Pekmezian, 182, 183, 214, 308
Pekmezian, Sappho, 182, 183, 214, 308
Pellas (concert manager), 149, 153, 156,
    199, 268, 269, 295, 336, 337
Pelliccia, Arrigo, 602
Pembauer (German music teacher), 241,
    242
Peña, Joaquín (Spanish concert
    manager), 21, 76, 78
Pergile (singer), 65
Pergolesi, Giovanni Battista, 178–9, 532,
    560
Perper, George (concert manager), 591
Perón, Eva, 516
Perón, Juan, 514, 515, 516
Pétain, Maréchal Henri, 206
Pfeiffer, John (American recording
    executive), 471
Pfitzner, Hans (German composer), 312

Philippe, Isidor (French music teacher),
    123
Piatigorsky, Gregor (Russian cellist),
    255, 303, 478–9, 528, 529, 530, 537,
    539, 557
Piatigorsky, Mrs. Gregor (Jacqueline de
    Rothschild), 323, 479, 539
Picasso, Pablo, 126, 130, 149–50, 162, 234,
    287, 464, 560, 565–8, 592
Picasso, Mrs. Pablo (Jacqueline), 566,
    567
Pickford, Mary, 60, 127
Pilsudski, Josef (Polish statesman), 98,
    115, 142, 207, 460
Pizzetti, Ildebrando (Italian composer),
    194
Planté, Francis (French pianist), 195–6
Plasson, Michel (French conductor),
    599–600
Pleyel (company and piano), 76, 101,
    107, 112, 125, 131, 162
Pola (Harman), 35, 45, 207, 213–14, 248,
    534
Polacco, Giorgio (Italian-American
    conductor), 41
Polignac, Princess Edmond de
    (Winnaretta Singer), 105, 134, 174–5,
    176, 177, 191, 202, 203, 204, 212, 213,
    214, 232, 233, 253, 282–3, 287, 293,
    322, 323, 441
Polignac, Count Jean de, 131, 176, 434
Polignac, Countess Jean de (Marie
    Blanche), 131, 176, 434, 526
Polignac, Marquis Melchior de, 131, 133,
    206, 284, 533
Polignac, Marquise Melchior de (Nina),
    133, 206
Polk, Rudolf, 530
Pollini, Maurizio (Italian pianist), 559,
    599, 602
Pompidou, Georges, 585
Ponce, Manuel (Mexican pianist and
    composer), 64, 67–8, 278
Poniatowski, Prince, 287
Pons, Lily (French singer), 529
Ponsonby, Sheila (later Duchess of
    Westminster), 293
Poot, Marcel (composer), 592
Porter, Cole, 100, 280
Portinari, Candido (Brazilian painter),
    474, 475, 479
Potocka, Countess Joseph, 307
Potocki, Count, 266
Potocki, Count (of Lancut), 356
Poulenc, Francis, 100, 105, 109, 131, 133,
    134, 173, 192, 206, 233, 526
    Biches, Les, 179
    Promenades, Les, 105, 246
    sonata for two pianos, 131
Poznanski family, 207

Previn, André, 594
Primo de Rivera, José, 296
Primrose, William (American violist), 494
Printemps, Yvonne, 152, 178, 279, 344
Prokofiev, Serge, 9, 18, 31, 47–8, 49, 50, 60, 82, 114, 122, 127, 134, 172, 192, 327, 333, 498, 500, 535, 554, 578
  concertos (piano): First, 47; Second, 47; Third, 47, 114, 191, 192, 226, 500, 545
  concertos (violin): First, 226; Second, 226–7
  Love for Three Oranges, The, 168–9
  Prodigal Son, The, 240
  Sixth Sonata, 500
  Suggestion diabolique, 500
  Visions fugitives, 47–8, 500, 554
Proust, Marcel, 112, 596
Prude, Walter (concert manager), 591
Prunières, Henry (French publisher), 403
Puccini, Giacomo: *Bohème, La,* 594

Queensberry, Lord, 96
Quesada, Ernesto de (Spanish concert manager), 3, 4, 9–13 *passim,* 16, 17, 19–20, 76, 78, 89, 90, 96, 148, 159, 197, 267, 275, 278, 295, 433, 434, 435, 482, 512, 514, 515–16, 601
Quezon, Manuel (Philippine statesman), 384
Quintana, Señora Susana, 7–11 *passim,* 19, 33, 200, 270
Quintana family, 92
Quisling, Vidkun, 472

Rabaud, Henri (French music director), 242, 243
Rabin, Yitzhak, 580
Rachmaninoff, Sergei, 87, 88, 112–13, 398–9, 427, 428, 468, 489–90, 492, 495, 499, 535
  concertos: First, 331; Second, 331, 432, 502, 519; Third, 251
  Isle of the Dead, 205
  as pianist, 46, 58, 84, 86, 87–8, 446
  Prelude in C-sharp minor, 18
  Rhapsody on a Theme of Paganini, 499, 524, 525–6, 538, 547
Raczynski, Count, 357
Radot, Louis Pasteur Vallery (Sioul), 533–4, 585
Radziwill, Prince, 356
Radziwill, Dolly, 287
Raimu (French actor), 177
Raisa, Rosa (singer), 65
Ramuz, Charles (Swiss writer), 102
Raphael, 179, 254

Rasputin, Gregori Efimovitch, 164
Rathbone, Basil, 482–3, 484, 489
Rathbone, Mrs. Basil (Ouida), 482–3, 484, 489
Rathenau, Walther (German industrialist and statesman), 296
Raue, Jan, 459, 460
Raue, Mrs. Jan (Alina Mlynarska; AR's sister-in-law), 247, 248, 249, 305, 307, 312, 313, 314, 315, 442, 459
Ravel, Maurice, 9, 18, 31, 47, 54, 100, 172, 181, 230, 232, 299, 310–11, 378, 398, 442, 498, 535, 554, 578
  Bolero, 18
  Concerto in G for Piano and Orchestra, 310
  Gaspard de la nuit, 32; "Ondine," 6
  Jeux d'eau, 329
  Ma Mère l'Oye, 151, 564
  Oiseaux tristes, 552
  Trio, 528, 537
  Valse, La, 151
  Valses nobles et sentimentales, 180, 181
Reading, Lady, 521–2
Reger, Max (German composer), 334
Régnier, Henri de (French writer), 246
Reichenbach, François (French television producer), 582, 583, 602, 603
Reiner, Fritz (conductor), 486
Reinhardt, Gottfried, 484
Reinhardt, Max, 47, 164, 484, 493
Remarque, Erich Maria, 483–4
Rembrandt van Rijn, 179
Renaud, Madeleine (French actress), 564
Renoir, Jean (French film director), 483
Renoir, Pierre Auguste, 536
Respighi, Ottorino, 225
  Boutique fantasque, La, 179
Respighi, Mrs. Ottorino, 225
Richter, Sviatoslav, 329, 500, 551–3, 553–4, 596, 602
Rimini, Giacomo, 65
Rimsky-Korsakov, Nikolai: *Capriccio Espagnol,* 255
  Coq d'or, transcribed by AR, 64
  Schéhérazade, 12
Risler, Edouard (French pianist), 132, 159–60, 160–1, 200
Rivera, José (Mexican impresario), 61, 62, 63
Robillant, Count, 203, 233, 293
Robillant, Countess Clémentine, 203, 233, 293
Robinson, Edward G., 536
Roca, Julio (Argentine statesman), 339
Rockefeller, Nelson, 475
Rockefeller family, 57, 127
Rocksavage, *see* Cholmondeley, Marquis of

Rodzinski, Artur (American conductor), 348, 424, 431, 486, 495, 500, 529

Rodzinski, Mrs. Artur (Halina Lilpop), 303, 348, 424, 431

Rogers, Ginger, 280, 404

Roosevelt, Franklin, 480, 486, 509

Roosevelt, Mrs. Franklin, 437

Rosa, Faustino da (Argentine impresario), 3, 4, 5, 6, 19, 21, 22, 23, 24, 26, 32, 34, 78

Rosario (Spanish dancer), 475

Rossini, Giacomo, 531
  Soirées musicales, 179

Rothschild, Baron Alain de, 588

Rothschild, Baroness Alain de (Mary), 588

Rothschild, Baron Edouard de, 123–4, 206, 244, 245, 403, 478

Rothschild, Baroness Edouard de (Germaine), 123, 124, 206, 244, 245, 287, 317, 322, 323, 412–13, 441, 445, 452, 458, 464, 478, 533, 539, 551

Rothschild, Baron Gustave de, 163, 277

Rothschild, Maurice de, 291

Rothschild, Baron Robert de, 318, 322, 403, 459, 488

Rothschild, Baroness Robert de (Nelly), 459, 488

Rouché (French opera director), 254, 403

Rubenstein, Dr. Joseph (educator), 592, 593

Rubin, Reuven (Israeli painter), 536–7, 585

Rubin, Mrs. Reuven (Esther), 537, 585

Rubinstein, Alina (AR's daughter), 485, 504, 507, 508, 509, 518, 526, 530, 535, 543, 551, 555, 556, 564, 568–77 *passim*, 582, 594

Rubinstein, Anton (Russian pianist and composer), 88, 122, 146, 332, 586

Rubinstein, Mrs. Arthur (Aniela [Nela] Mlynarska), 108, 129
  and AR: first meeting and courtship, 247–51 *passim*, 253–4, 256–61 *passim*, 267–8; gifts from, 67, 322, 348, 350, 434, 438, 453, 456, 457, 458; her marriage to Munz, 272–3, 274; second meeting and courtship, 303–21 *passim*; wedding and honeymoon, 321–2, 323
  childhood, 324, 445
  children: Alina, 485, 507, 508, 509; Eva, 333–41 *passim*; John, 485, 513; Paul, 350, 355, 357, 358
  dancing, 249, 307, 452, 484
  driving, enjoyment of, 351, 352–3
  in France and Italy, 312–15, 322, 323, 458–60, 531, 564, 565; Paris, 318–19, 333, 334, 335–6, 342, 343, 350, 351,

352, 355, 356, 398, 403–8 *passim*, 424, 438–46 *passim*, 452, 463–4, 526, 539, 551, 586, 588
  health, 376, 377, 438, 514–15, 518, 541, 583, 593, 594
  as hostess, 407, 445, 483, 538–9, 541, 565, 569
  in Japan and the Far East, 355, 365–95 *passim*, 569–70, 575
  languages, gift for, 339
  in Latin America, 336–42 *passim*, 411, 413–16, 473–6, 512, 513, 555
  in London, 319, 320, 344, 408, 520, 522
  marriage to Mieczyslaw Munz, 272–3, 274; divorce, 304, 316, 317, 318, 321
  in the Middle East, 347, 583, 585
  in Poland, 350, 352–9 *passim*, 396–7, 411, 556
  in Russia, 324–33 *passim*, 363–5, 394, 395, 396
  in Spain, 315–17, 575, 582
  in the U.S., 124, 406, 424–6, 429–33, 446–51, 465–7, 470, 471, 477–91 *passim*, 503, 510, 511, 526–7, 538–9, 542, 543, 577, 584, 588, 591, 597

Rubinstein, Eva (AR's daughter), *see* Coffin, Mrs. William Sloane

Rubinstein, Frania (AR's sister), *see* Likiernik, Mrs. Leo

Rubinstein, Hela (AR's sister), *see* Landau, Mrs. Adolf

Rubinstein, Ida (dancer), 560

Rubinstein, Ignacy (AR's brother), 75, 109, 115, 513, 524, 526, 533

Rubinstein, Isaak (AR's father), 75, 109, 115, 208, 557

Rubinstein, Mrs. Isaak (AR's mother), 75, 109, 115, 208, 557

Rubinstein, Jadwiga (AR's sister), *see* Landau, Mrs. Maurycy

Rubinstein, Jason (AR's grandchild), 579

Rubinstein, Jessica (AR's grandchild), 597

Rubinstein, John (AR's son), 485, 513, 526, 535, 551, 555, 556, 564, 568–74 *passim*, 593, 597
  acting, 530, 543, 574, 588

Rubinstein, Karol (Polish concert manager), 208, 212

Rubinstein, Mike (AR's grandchild), 597

Rubinstein, Nicholas (Russian music teacher), 335 and *n.*

Rubinstein, Paul (AR's son), 358, 397, 411–13, 416, 438, 446, 451, 458, 459, 460, 464, 465, 466, 476, 477, 478, 481, 482, 484, 512, 513, 520, 522, 524, 526, 531, 535, 543, 555, 579

Rubinstein, Stanislav (Staś; AR's brother), 115, 116, 208

Rubinstein, Tadeus (AR's brother),
115–16
Rubinstein family, 208
Rublev, 329–30
Rudge, Antonietta (pianist), 31
Ruffo, Titta (Italian singer), 61, 63,
147–8, 405
Ruiz, Francisco (concert manager), 92,
149, 159, 200, 268, 271–2, 295, 336,
338, 340, 413
Rutland, Duchess of, 79, 164
Rytel, Piotr (Polish music teacher), 208

Saint-Saëns, Camille, 192, 195–6, 241, 539
Concerto for Piano and Orchestra in
G minor, 85, 499, 537, 547, 569
Havanaise, 545
Variations on a Theme by Beethoven,
160
Salamanca, Marqués Luís de, 7, 22, 271
Salamanca, Marquesa Nena de, 7, 9, 22,
92, 152, 153, 157, 158, 271, 337, 340–1,
476
Salmond, Felix (cellist), 80, 320
Salvati, Renato (Chilean opera director),
10, 415, 517
Salverte, Countess, 253
Samaroff, Olga (pianist), 439
Sammons, Albert, 74, 80, 222
Sánchez, Rafael (Mexican lawyer), 63,
64, 68
Sánchez-Elia, Anchorena, 7
Sandoz, Edouard Marcel (Swiss
sculptor), 586, 587
San Martino, Count (Italian concert
manager), 169, 193–4, 213, 313, 531
Santo Mauro, Duke of, 296
Sapieha, Prince and Princess, 74, 75
Sarasate, Pablo de (Spanish violinist and
composer), 498
Sargent, John Singer, 144–5
Sarnoff, David, 468–70
Satie, Eric, 104, 133
Sauer, Emil (German pianist and
composer), 240, 439
Sauguet, Henri (French composer), 131
Scarlatti, Domenico, 194
Scharf, 519
Schelling, Ernest (American pianist and
composer), 241, 242
Schiafarelli, Luigi (music teacher), 31,
199, 337
Schiedmeier piano, 373
Schiff, Dr. Paul (German concert
manager), 335–6, 356, 357, 398, 399,
404, 405, 406, 417, 444, 445, 526
Schindler, Kurt (German-American
conductor and editor), 58
Schmitt, Florent (French composer), 172

Schnabel, Artur (Austrian pianist), 109,
159, 263
Schneevoigt, George (Finnish
conductor), 421, 422–3, 583
Schönberg, Arnold, 492, 493, 518, 535,
546, 560, 561–2
Moses and Aaron, 562
Pierrot Lunaire, 133
Schrammel, Ernst (German concert
manager), 159
Schubert, Franz, 67, 102, 320, 494, 500,
532, 538, 554, 562, 563, 578
chamber music, 578
Sonata in B flat, 554, 578
symphonies, 58
Tausig *Marche militaire*, 48
Trio in B flat, 494
Wanderer Fantasia, 578
Schuch, von (conductor), 309
Schumann, Elisabeth (German singer),
83, 95–6, 99
Schumann, Robert, 18, 64, 67, 88, 102,
228, 236, 276, 354, 500, 511, 529–30,
538, 554, 562, 578, 596
Carnaval, 26, 122, 541, 554
chamber music, 578
concerto (piano), 501–2, 547, 599
Fantasia, 552, 554
Fantasiestücke, 541, 599; "In der
Nacht," 53
Kreisleriana, 554, 578
quintet for piano and strings, 578
Symphonic Études, 122, 156, 554
symphonies, 58, 585, 602
Variations, 160
Schumann, Mrs. Robert (Clara;
German pianist and teacher), 225,
529, 530, 596
Schuschnigg, Kurt von (Austrian
statesman), 439
Schwarzkopf, Elisabeth, 532, 601
Scriabin, Alexander, 9, 18, 122
Fifth Sonata, 552
Segovia, Andrés, 67
Segurola, Andrés de (Spanish singer), 61
Selznick, Mr. and Mrs. David, 489, 538
Sem (French caricaturist), 104
Serkin, Rudolf, 438, 446, 498, 538, 544
Sert, José Maria (Spanish painter), 134,
151, 164, 287
Sert, Madame José Maria (Misia), 104,
107, 109, 124, 133, 151, 164, 192, 246,
251, 254, 274, 285, 287, 318, 342, 356,
403–4, 409, 440, 523–4, 526
Sharon, Ariel, 581
Shaw, George Bernard, 294
Shearer, Norma, 449
Shostakovich, Dimitri: First Symphony,
348
Lady Macbeth of Mzensk, 348

Shröder, Raúl von, 35
Sibelius, Jean, 497
Sica, Vittorio de, 564
Sienkiewicz-Lafont, Basia, 411, 412
Siloti, Alexander (pianist and conductor), 112–13
Simon, Sir John (English diplomat), 357
Simon, Michel (French actor), 164, 579
Singer, Paris, 134
Singer, Fred, 441
Singer, Mrs. Fred, 441, 442
Singer, Washington, 134
Sitwell, Osbert, 81, 222
Sitwell, Sacheverell, 81, 222
Skirmunt, Constanty (Polish diplomat), 320
Skrzynski, Count Alexander (Polish statesman), 211–12
Slonimski, Antoni (Polish writer), 211
Smetona, Antanas (Lithuanian statesman), 444, 445
Smith, 379–80
Sokolnicki, Henryk (Polish diplomat), 326, 363
Sokolow, Dr. Nahum (Zionist), 357
Solomon (pianist), 293
Sonnerschein, 310, 311–12
Soutine, Chaim (Lithuanian painter), 126
Sparrow, Sylvia (English violinist), 73, 74, 174, 222, 320
Stalin, Joseph, 363, 395, 459–60, 484, 509, 557
Stanislas Leszczynski (King of Poland), 161
Stanislavski (Russian actor and director), 331
Stefanides (Greek banker), 189, 190, 191, 263, 264, 265, 308
Stein, Jules, 541, 598
Steinberg, William (American conductor), 500
Steinert, Alexander (American composer and conductor), 114, 251, 255
Steinert, Mrs. Alexander, 114
Steinway (company and piano), 19, 21, 26, 40, 41, 47, 76, 125, 168, 370, 376, 382, 425, 426, 429, 433, 459, 465, 472, 495, 515, 528, 571, 575
Steinway, Theodore (American piano manufacturer), 472, 495, 516, 528
Steinway, William (American piano manufacturer), 425, 426
Stern, Isaac (American violinist), 545, 557
Stinnes, 116
Stock, Frederick (German-American conductor), 46, 168
Stockhausen, Karlheinz (composer), 53, 562

Stokowski, Leopold, 69, 85, 476, 491, 492, 500, 529
Storrs, Sir Ronald, 184–5, 186
Stransky, Joseph (Austrian-American conductor), 52, 113
Strauss, Mrs. Minka, 441
Strauss, Richard, 176, 208, 309, 535, 560
  Arabella, 399, 400
  Heldenleben, 272
  Salome, 95; dance transcribed by AR, 64
Stravinsky, Igor, 12, 47, 48, 59–60, 101–2, 105–9 *passim*, 123, 134, 136, 138, 139, 141, 150–1, 163, 192, 233, 283, 287, 293, 490, 492, 493, 502, 528, 535, 538, 546, 554, 560–1, 562, 564
  Apollon Musagète, 561
  Capriccio for Piano and Orchestra, 283
  Concerto for Piano and Wind Instruments, 151, 173, 283
  Coq et le renard, 105
  Histoire du soldat, L', 102, 560
  Mavra, 109, 131, 135, 138, 141
  Noces, Les, 102, 105, 560
  octet for wind and brass, 173–4
  Oedipus Rex, 561
  Oiseau de feu, 560; transcribed by AR, 64
  Petrushka, 12, 159, 560; sonata transcribed by Stravinsky, 102, 134, 135, 138, 147, 148, 154, 176, 182, 189, 254, 308, 326–7, 328, 329, 389, 390, 405, 416, 427, 428, 430, 484, 511
  Piano Rag Music, 60, 85, 101–2, 133
  Pulcinella, 151, 178–9, 232, 560
  Rake's Progress, The, 561
  Sacre du printemps, Le, 29, 102, 133, 252, 560
  Symphony of Psalms, 561
  television film of, 582
Stravinsky, Mrs. Igor, *see* Kochlova, Olga; Sudeikin, Vera
Strok (impresario), 355, 365–9 *passim*, 372, 375, 379, 381, 575
Styczynski, 209
Sudeikin, Vera (later Mrs. Igor Stravinsky), 106, 163, 293, 494, 538
Supervielle, Mrs., 153
Szell, George (Czech conductor), 312, 409, 421, 486, 492, 500, 501–2, 546, 585, 597, 602
Szer, Mania, 210–11
Szeryng, Henryk (Polish violinist), 494, 541
Szigeti, Joseph (Hungarian-American violinist), 487, 499
Szymanowska, Mrs. Anna, 212
Szymanowska, Nula, 212
Szymanowska, Sophie (Zioka), 212

Szymanowska, Stanislava (Stasia), 212, 411

Szymanowski, Alexander, 207

Szymanowski, Felix, 212

Szymanowski, Karol (Polish composer), 9, 18, 27, 31, 45, 47, 60, 98–109 *passim*, 112, 113, 114, 122, 157, 207, 211, 212, 214, 216, 248, 255, 297, 318, 326, 399, 403, 410–11, 426, 554, 569, 578, 602

concertos (violin): First, 229; Second, 274, 317, 342

études, 56

Fontaine d'Aréthuse, 157

Hagith, 112, 114, 212

Harnasie, 403, 410

King Roger, 212, 575

"Masques," 103

mazurkas, four, 229, 236, 246, 442, 554

Symphony-Concertante, 268, 403, 495, 499

symphonies: Second, 114; Third, 230

Szymanowski family, 59, 75, 98, 103, 212, 445

Tagliaferro, Magda (pianist), 559

Tailleferre, Germaine (French composer), 100, 131, 133, 206, 464

Tal, Josef (composer), 592

Tansman, Alexander (Polish composer), 315, 316, 493, 592

Tanyel, Seta (pianist), 592

Tauber (hotel owner), 122, 149

Tchaikovsky, Peter Ilyitch, 497, 528, 560

Eugene Onegin, 331

Fourth Symphony, 503

piano concerto in B flat, 202, 312, 319–20, 334–5, 359, 367, 420, 421, 426, 427, 431, 436, 447, 451, 468, 470, 471, 491, 499, 517, 537, 574, 575

Tebaldi, Renata, 129

Tertis, Lionel (violist), 73, 74, 80, 144, 222, 320, 494

Tessier, Valentine (French actress), 164

Thibaud, Jacques (French violinist), 50, 74, 78, 79, 80, 132, 195, 232, 320, 442, 443–4, 494, 498, 539, 545, 558

Titian, 179

Tito, Marshal, 544

Tokugawa, Marquis, 370–1

Tolstoy, Leo, 294

Tomsic, Dubravka (Yugoslav pianist), 543–4

Tortelier, Paul (French cellist), 557–8, 603

Toscanini, Arturo, 171, 176, 431, 451, 468, 476, 504–7

Tree, Iris, 222

Trefusis, Violet, 232–3

Trotsky, Leon, 142, 230

Trzcinski, Teofil (Polish concert manager), 212, 307

Turczynski, Josef (Zozio), 249

Tuwim, Juljan (Polish poet), 211, 249, 474, 479, 488

Tuwim, Mrs. Juljan, 474, 479

Unzue family, 7

Urchs, Ernst (Steinway agent), 47, 168

Valéry, Paul (French poet), 129

Vallin, Ninon (French singer), 32

Valmalète, Marcel de (concert agent), 125, 148, 161, 169, 170, 171, 222, 228, 240, 241, 246, 267, 282, 283, 293, 322, 323, 333, 335, 336, 526

Vanderbilt, Mr. and Mrs. Cornelius, 113, 164

Vanderbilt, William K., 130

Vanderbilt family, 57, 127

Vandervelde, Emile (Belgian statesman), 268–9

Van Wyck, Wilfred, 451

Varèse, Edgard (American composer), 53

Velázquez, Diego, 179

Vendôme, Duke of, 253

Verdi, Giuseppe, 176, 531

Aida, 41–2, 84, 602

Verdura, Duke of (Fulco), 204

Verlaine, Paul, 294

Victoria (Queen of England), 221, 375

Victoria Eugenia (Queen of Spain), 117, 119, 137, 180, 181, 296, 298, 321

Viertel, Salka (screenwriter), 484

Villa-Lobos, Heitor, 90, 91–2, 94, 154–5, 172–3, 195, 199, 214, 251–2, 269–70, 479, 480, 554

"Amazon, The," 91

"Choros," 91

Prole do Bebe, O, 92, 123, 554

Rudepoêma, 252, 475, 477, 479–80

Villa-Lobos, Mrs. Heitor (Lucille), 92

Vilmorin, Louise de (French writer), 156–7

Vittorio Emanuele (King of Italy), 496

Vivaldi, Antonio, 176, 532

Vix, Geneviève, 95

Vladimir, Grand Duke, 104, 178

Vollard, Amboise (French art dealer), 536

Volpi, Countess, 564

Volpi, Giuseppe, 233–4

Vuillard, Jean Edouard (French painter), 104

Wagner, Richard, 58, 85, 218, 223, 255–6
  Meistersinger, Die, 341, 594, 602
  Parsifal, 247, 249, 309
  "Preislied," 55
  "Ride of the Valkyries, The,"
    transcribed by AR, 64, 236
  Tristan and Isolde, 64, 218
Walden, Lady Howard de, 144
Wales, Prince of, *see* Windsor, Duke of
Wallenstein, Alfred (conductor), 448,
    449, 471, 484, 492, 500, 537, 547, 569
Wallenstein, Mrs. Alfred, 484
Walter, Bruno, 487, 492, 500–1, 529
Walton, Sir William (English composer),
    81
Ward, Mrs. Dudley, 219, 220, 221
Warden, Mrs. Irene (Madame
    Cittadini), 356, 357, 358
Warner, Jack, 528
Weber, Karl Maria von: *Spectre de la
    Rose, Le,* 12
Webern, Anton von, 546, 560, 562
Weingartner, Felix von (Swiss
    composer and conductor), 160
Wells, H. G., 222, 446
Wells, Rebecca, 535
Wendell, Mrs. Ruth, 113
Werfel, Franz, 492
Wesendonk, Mathilde, 218
Westminster, Duke of, 280
Whitestone, Annabelle, 601, 602, 603, 605
Wiborg, Hoyty, 113–14, 298, 426
Wiéner, Jean (French pianist), 100, 133
Wierzynski, Kazimierz (Polish writer),
    211, 474

Wigman, Mary (American dancer), 307
Wilcox, Max (conductor), 599
Wilde, Oscar, 105
Willard, Joseph E. (American diplomat),
    39
Williams, Alberto (Argentine
    composer), 6, 7–8, 18
Wilson, Hilary (later Lady Munster),
    293
Wilson, Woodrow, 74–5, 143
Windsor, Duchess of, 408, 409
Windsor, Duke of, 127, 129, 219–22,
    408–9
Wolfson, 51, 84
Wood, Sir Henry (English conductor
    and composer), 83, 144, 280

Yadin, Yigael, 540, 580
Ysaye, Eugène (Belgian violinist), 32, 46,
    55–6, 69, 84, 85, 113, 344–5, 498
Yussupoff, Prince, 164
Yvonne, Mlle. (French governess), 458,
    459, 464, 465, 466, 476, 477, 480

Zamoyski, Count August, 139, 452, 459
Zatajevitch, Alexander, 331
Zimbalist, Efrem (Russian-American
    violinist), 58, 61, 117, 144
Zola, Emile, 431, 533
Zukertort, Johannes (Polish chess
    master), 81

Photograph Credits

All photographs appear as a courtesy of the author excluding the following:

Clive Barda   21st page, Rubinstein with Daniel Barenboim

Franklin Brouszak   17th page, with Myrna Loy and Hedda Hopper; and with
     Benita and Ronald Colman

City News Bureau, Washington, D.C.   23rd page, with Indira Gandhi

Loomis Dean, Life Magazine, © *1948, Time Inc. and* © *1958, Time Inc.*   9th page,
     Rubinstein family, 1948; and 11th page, a family outing

Courtesy of Duc Decazes   4th page, portrait of the Princess de Polignac

B.J. Dorys   6th page, Nela in 1928

Courtesy of Bill Fitz-Patrick, White House Photo   24th page, with President Carter

Herbert Gehr, Life Magazine, © *Time Inc.*   19th page, Toscanini

© *Israel Sun*   23rd page, with Golda Meir

Dmitri Kissel, Life Magazine, © *1959 Time Inc.*   14th page, playing at Symphony Hall,
     Boston

Patrice Picot, Jours de France   17th page, receiving an Oscar

Courtesy of RCA Records   10th page, accompanying Eva dancing; and 15th page,
     recording in the RCA studio with Ormandy

Courtesy of Eva Rubinstein   22nd page, with Sol Hurok

© *1978 Peter Schaaf*   16th page, Rubinstein at 92

J. Siegelman   18th page, with Wallenstein

Courtesy of Mrs. Vera Stravinsky   5th page, Stravinsky and the Princess de Polignac

Alton Taube   19th page, with Andrés Segovia

© *1976 Avraham Toren*   14th page, rehearsing with the Jerusalem Symphony
     Orchestra; and 16th page, Rubinstein at 90

Twentieth Century-Fox Productions   9th page, with family in Beverly Hills

Courtesy of the White House   24th page, with President Ford

A Note on the Type

This book was set on the Linotype in Janson, a recutting made direct from type cast from matrices long thought to have been made by the Dutchman Anton Janson, who was a practicing type founder in Leipzig during the years 1668–87. However, it has been conclusively demonstrated that these types are actually the work of Nicholas Kis (1650–1702), a Hungarian, who most probably learned his trade from the master Dutch type founder Dirk Voskens. The type is an excellent example of the influential and sturdy Dutch types that prevailed in England up to the time William Caslon developed his own incomparable designs from them.

Composed by Maryland Linotype Composition Co., Baltimore, Maryland. Printed and bound by The Haddon Craftsmen, Inc., Scranton, Pennsylvania.
Designed by Anthea Lingeman.